Philosophical Methodology: The Armchair or the Laboratory?

What methodology should philosophers follow? Should they rely on methods that can be conducted from the armchair? Or should they leave the armchair and turn to the methods of the natural sciences, such as experiments in the laboratory? Or is this opposition itself a false one? Arguments about philosophical methodology are raging in the wake of a number of often conflicting currents, such as the growth of experimental philosophy, the resurgence of interest in metaphysical questions, and the use of formal methods.

This outstanding collection of specially commissioned chapters by leading international philosophers discusses these questions and many more. It provides a comprehensive survey of methodology in the most important philosophical subjects: metaphysics, epistemology, philosophy of language, philosophy of mind, phenomenology, ethics, and aesthetics.

A key feature of the collection is that philosophers discuss and evaluate contrasting approaches in each subject, offering a superb overview of the variety of methodological approaches – both naturalistic and non-naturalistic – in each of these areas. They examine important topics at the heart of methodological debates, including the role of intuitions and conceptual analysis, thought experiments, introspection, and the place that results from the natural sciences should have in philosophical theorizing.

The collection begins with a fascinating exchange about philosophical naturalism between Timothy Williamson and Alex Rosenberg, and also includes contributions from the following philosophers: Lynne Rudder Baker, Matt Bedke, Gregory Currie, Michael Devitt, Matthew C. Haug, Jenann Ismael, Hilary Kornblith, Neil Levy, E. J. Lowe, Kirk Ludwig, Marie McGinn, David Papineau, Matthew Ratcliffe, Georges Rey, Jeffrey W. Roland, Barry C. Smith, David Woodruff Smith, Amie L. Thomasson, Valerie Tiberius, and Jessica Wilson.

Matthew C. Haug is Associate Professor of Philosophy at the College of William & Mary, USA.

D1714431

Philosophical Methodology: The Armchair or the Laboratory?

Edited by
Matthew C. Haug

 Routledge
Taylor & Francis Group

LONDON AND NEW YORK

First published 2014
by Routledge
2 Park Square, Milton Park, Abingdon, Oxon OX14 4RN

Simultaneously published in the USA and Canada
by Routledge
711 Third Avenue, New York, NY 10017

Routledge is an imprint of the Taylor & Francis Group, an informa business

British Library Cataloguing in Publication Data
A catalogue record for this book is available from the British Library

Library of Congress Cataloging in Publication Data
Philosophical methodology : the armchair or the
laboratory? / edited by Matthew C. Haug. -- 1 [edition].
pages cm
Includes bibliographical references and index.
1. Methodology. I. Haug, Matthew C., editor of compilation.
BD241.P435 2013
101--dc23
2013004443

ISBN: 978-0-415-53131-3 (hbk)
ISBN: 978-0-415-53132-0 (pbk)
ISBN: 978-0-203-79899-7 (ebk)

Typeset in Garamond
by Taylor & Francis Books

MIX
Paper from
responsible sources
FSC® C013604

Printed and bound by CPI Group (UK) Ltd, Croydon, CR0 4YY

Contents

Contributors

Lynne Rudder Baker is Distinguished Professor of Philosophy at the University of Massachusetts, Amherst

Matt Bedke is Assistant Professor of Philosophy at the University of British Columbia

Gregory Currie is Professor of Philosophy at the University of Nottingham

Michael Devitt is Distinguished Professor of Philosophy at the Graduate Center, City University of New York

Matthew C. Haug is Associate Professor of Philosophy at the College of William & Mary

Jenann Ismael is Associate Professor of Philosophy at the University of Arizona

Hilary Kornblith is Professor of Philosophy at the University of Massachusetts, Amherst

Neil Levy is Head of Neuroethics at the Florey Institute of Neuroscience and Mental Health, University of Melbourne

E.J. Lowe is Professor of Philosophy at Durham University

Kirk Ludwig is Professor of Philosophy at Indiana University, Bloomington

Marie McGinn is Emeritus Professor of Philosophy at the University of York

David Papineau is Professor of Philosophy of Science at King's College London

Matthew Ratcliffe is Professor of Philosophy at Durham University

Georges Rey is Professor of Philosophy at the University of Maryland, College Park

Jeffrey W. Roland is Associate Professor of Philosophy at Louisiana State University

Alex Rosenberg is the R. Taylor Cole Professor of Philosophy at Duke University

Barry C. Smith is Professor of Philosophy and Director of the Institute of Philosophy at the School of Advanced Study, University of London

David Woodruff Smith is Professor of Philosophy at the University of California, Irvine

Amie L. Thomasson is Professor of Philosophy and Parodi Senior Scholar in Aesthetics at the University of Miami

Valerie Tiberius is Professor of Philosophy at the University of Minnesota, Twin Cities

Timothy Williamson is Wykeham Professor of Logic at the University of Oxford

Jessica Wilson is Associate Professor of Philosophy at the University of Toronto

Acknowledgments

I would like to thank the students in my Fall 2009 seminar on naturalism and philosophical methodology for their helpful discussion of methodological issues in epistemology, metaphysics, and ethics, especially in relation to the challenges posed by some versions of experimental philosophy. I am grateful to the College of William & Mary for QEP/Mellon funding that improved that seminar. I would also like to acknowledge financial support from a National Science Foundation Scholar's Award, Grant No. SES-0957221, which funded a research leave during academic year 2010/11, and from the William & Mary Philosophy Department, which provided a pre-tenure research leave during Fall 2011. This support facilitated my initial work on this volume, and some material in the introduction is based on work supported by the NSF grant. Any opinions, findings and conclusions or recommendations expressed in this material are those of the author and do not necessarily reflect the views of the National Science Foundation. Thanks to Paul S. Davies and Jeffrey W. Roland for discussions on some issues covered in the introduction.

Thanks to Tony Bruce, at Routledge, for suggesting that I edit a volume on philosophical methods and for sage advice and encouragement as the project progressed. (And thanks to my colleague Neal Tognazzini for putting me on Tony's radar in the first place.) Thanks also to Adam Johnson and Ruth Berry for their gracious assistance during the various stages of production and to Jim Thomas for his expert copy-editing.

Finally, thanks to Laurelin, for her patience and good humor as I worked on the volume, and to Bennett, whose presence puts that work in perspective.

Introduction

Debates about methods: from linguistic philosophy to philosophical naturalism

MATTHEW C. HAUG

Two dimensions of methodological debates: methodological naturalism and the fate of armchair methods

The last few years have seen a surge of interest in philosophical methodology. If there is a single question that unifies the disparate currents of this surge it is whether philosophical questions can successfully be answered "from the armchair." However, the unity produced by viewing debates about methodology in terms of this question is superficial, for it conceals widespread disagreement about what the implications of an answer to this question (whether affirmative or negative) would be. This is because philosophers disagree about whether "armchair" methods share philosophically important features (e.g. delivering a priori justification) that are not possessed by other methods (say, the methods of the natural sciences). Thus, any particular position on the viability of doing philosophy "from the armchair" does not by itself settle debates about the integrity and viability of the methods, if any, which have those features.

So, for example, even those who agree that philosophers should not remain in their armchairs are still divided about whether or not this also undermines a priori knowledge, or conceptual analysis, or appealing to "intuitions" about possible cases, or relying on introspection. Some philosophers who raise concerns about the reliability of armchair methods see this as part of an argument for abandoning some or all of these methods. (Think of the burning armchair, the unofficial logo of some experimental philosophers.) Others, though, intend their call to leave the armchair merely as a suggested *improvement* to the very practices that their fellow reformers would consign to the flames. Such philosophers see cooperation and mutual reinforcement, rather than conflict, between empirical methods and armchair reflection. On their view, performing, or substantively engaging with, empirical work is merely a healthy corrective to the nearsightedness that they think results from remaining in the armchair too long. For them, appealing to the methods and results of empirical science will not itself solve (or dissolve) philosophical problems. Rather, these methods and results are merely a distinct kind of epistemic tool, which they believe will lead to deeper insights when philosophers inevitably (and rightly) return to their armchairs.

There is similar disagreement among philosophers who think that philosophers should remain in their armchairs without substantively engaging with empirical science. Some see this as supporting the autonomy and authority of a priori reflection, introspection, or the use of intuitions. Others, however, think that armchair methods are viable, not because they are fundamentally different from those used by the natural sciences, but because they are *no different in kind* from empirical methods. From this perspective, all of the above positions are misguided because they are based on a misconception about the nature of the methods that can be carried out from the armchair. On this view, armchair methods are not, at bottom, epistemically distinct from scientific methods, so it makes no sense to say that the former are independent sources of epistemic authority or input that could be either undermined by, supported by, or autonomous from the latter.[1]

The above discussion is rough and incomplete, but it reveals another dimension against which to chart different positions in debates about methodology—namely, with respect to different views about how to understand "naturalism" and whether naturalism should be adopted as a methodological program within philosophy, however it is understood.[2]

The essays in this volume cover a broad swath of the conceptual terrain of current debates about philosophical methods when measured on both of the above dimensions. That is, together they both provide a range of views on the prospects of various "armchair methods," and situate these discussions about methods within the context of those about naturalism, addressing whether naturalism is a substantive, coherent approach to philosophy, and, if it is, how it should be understood, and which methods are compatible with (different versions of) it.

In the third section of this introduction, "The Prospects for Armchair Methods," I provide a brief overview of how issues along the first dimension—the prospects for different "armchair methods"—are treated by particular contributions to the volume. However, the bulk of the introduction concerns the second dimension—how different versions of, and attitudes toward, naturalism figure in debates about methodology. One of the main goals of this volume is to help move debates about methodology beyond a simplistic opposition between naturalism and non-naturalism. By facilitating dialogue between competing methodological viewpoints within and across different subdisciplines, the volume illustrates not only that debates between naturalists and non-naturalists are complex and multifaceted but also that each of these positions is far from monolithic.

In the second section, "The Evolution of Debates about Methods," I begin to explore these issues in the course of situating current discussions of methods in their recent historical context. In particular, I compare some of the motivations for contemporary interest in philosophical methodology to those that dominated twentieth-century discussions. Since we are still in the middle of the current resurgence of interest in philosophical methodology, it is difficult to impose a single, coherent storyline on what is in fact a heterogeneous collection of different (often competing) motivations and research programs, much less to connect that narrative to past discussions of methodology. The issues are complex, and I do not attempt to provide a full account here. What follows is simply one tentative attempt at making sense of current debates and at charting some of the most prominent continuities and discontinuities between these debates and those of the recent past. No doubt there are important aspects that I have left out, and, even if I have identified central features of these debates, I have only done so in the barest outline. Much more deserves to be said. Future philosophers will have the advantage of hindsight and will be better able to undertake this task.

I shall use the introduction and retrospective essays that Richard Rorty wrote for his influential anthology, *The Linguistic Turn* (1967b/1992), to structure my discussion. As we'll see, although some issues have been transformed since Rorty wrote these documents, a number of common concerns remain.[3]

The evolution of debates about methods

Rorty's anthology, first published in 1967 and then reissued in 1992, did a lot to popularize the idea that philosophy had taken a "linguistic turn" during the twentieth century.[4] As the essays collected in Rorty's volume illustrate, the role of language in philosophy was the fulcrum around which debates about methodology revolved. For over fifty years, the dominant methodological views held that all philosophical questions could be solved (or dissolved) either by simply investigating what we actually say, by uncovering the logical form of what we actually say, or by constructing new languages in which traditional philosophical questions would either have definitive answers or simply not arise at all. According to this view of philosophy, all epistemological, ontological, and moral questions should be answered (or dismissed) through linguistic investigation. Although some philosophers still hold this view today (at least when restricted to some issues[5]), it does not command the allegiance that it once did. Questions about language are still part of recent methodological discussions, but they are no longer dominant, nor do they serve to

unify and structure current debates. Instead, as noted above, contemporary work on methodology tends to center on the prospects for, and
possible limitations of, various forms of naturalism, i.e. on the relation
between the methods of philosophy and those of the sciences.

As I discuss in the next three subsections, we can use Rorty's introduction and two retrospective essays to help understand (1) the relation
between metaphilosophical or methodological debates, on one hand, and
debates about particular philosophical issues, on the other, (2) how
naturalism supplanted linguistic philosophy as a organizing theme for
discussions of methodology, and (3) how different   conceptions of
naturalism call for different methodological recommendations.

The relation between philosophy and metaphilosophy

Rorty claims that every would-be methodological revolution in the past
has attempted to be "presuppositionless," to be "dependent upon no
substantive philosophical theses," but that none has succeeded (1967a/
1992, 1–2, 4). Rorty suggests that this failure is inevitable, since "it
would indeed be hard to know what methods a philosopher ought to
follow without knowing something about the nature of the philosopher's
subject matter, and about the nature of human knowledge" (ibid., 1).[6]

If Rorty is right that methodological programs always involve commitment to some substantive philosophical theses, then proponents of *any*
methodological program face a dilemma. On one hand, if the epistemological and ontological theses that are required to support a given method
can, in turn, be defended only by employing that method, then they are
open to the charge of circularity. On the other hand, if these theses are
left undefended but are still (at least implicitly) used to support their
favored method, then they are left open to the charge of begging the
question.

This dilemma is often pressed against methodological naturalism.[7] If
Rorty is right, then this is not a potential problem that is unique to
naturalism. Naturalists may not be alone in thinking that it is ill-advised
to always demand that the reliability of a method be established without
using that method (see Sosa 1994, 290 n. 37; Ludwig this volume, n.
13). However, as Jeffrey W. Roland's contribution to this volume indicates, naturalists in the Quinean tradition have a distinctive reason to
endorse this claim. Namely, it follows from what Roland calls the principle of "inclusion," which holds, roughly, that the organizational and
methodological rules associated with a system of belief are themselves
integral parts of that system. Thus, anyone who endorses *inclusion* will
eschew searching for "theory-neutral methods or standpoints to use in
philosophizing" (Roland, this volume, p. 56).

Of course, even if a kind of circularity with respect to the validation of certain methods is inevitable, this does not show that it is benign or unproblematic.[8] In any case, I think that Rorty is right that there is often important "interplay between the adoption of a metaphilosophical outlook and the adoption of substantive philosophical theses" (1967a/1992, 38–39). Several of the essays in this volume clearly display this kind of interplay. I mention just two. First, Matt Bedke argues that the use of intuitional methods in ethics supports a quasi-realist or expressivist view in metaethics. Second, in the other direction, Jenann Ismael explores, among other things, the methodological consequences of giving up the idea that representation consists in thought or language mirroring the world.

The latter example is one which Rorty would have found particularly interesting since it is closely related to the pragmatist version of naturalism that he endorses and that emerges in his discussion of whether linguistic philosophy was successful, to which I now turn.

The fall of linguistic philosophy

In his original introduction, Rorty praises linguistic philosophy for "putting the entire philosophical tradition … on the defensive," but he also claims that "linguistic philosophers' attempts to turn philosophy into a 'strict science' must fail" (1967a/1992, 33). He predicts that future metaphilosophical debates will center on the struggle between positions which see philosophy as, at most, making proposals about how we should talk and think about the world in order to achieve certain practical ends and those that see philosophy as chiefly in the business of making discoveries about the world.[9] According to Rorty, this contrast between "philosophy-as-proposal" and "philosophy-as-discovery" is linked to a long-standing "tension produced by the pull of the arts on one side and the pull of the sciences on the other" (1967a/1992, 38). He claims that the chief value of linguistic philosophy has been to make philosophers more self-conscious about this tension, rather than to lessen it (ibid.). I will return to this contrast and tension in the following subsection, "Constructive Naturalism and Deflationary Naturalism."

Rorty concludes his introduction by shifting gears somewhat and taking up a theme that becomes more prominent in the two retrospective essays. Namely, he urges the overthrow of what he calls the traditional "spectatorial" account of knowledge (ibid., 39), which he suggests will lead to a reformulation of metaphilosophical debates. Specifically, the contrast between science and philosophy—which Rorty notes, is presupposed by all six of his possible paths for philosophy—will "come to seem artificial and pointless" (ibid., 39). This, in turn, will lead to a reframing of future debates between philosophy-as-discovery and philosophy-as-proposal.

However, one might wonder why such debates will continue at all if the contrast between science and philosophy is abandoned. Instead, one might see this move—one form of naturalism—as simply a way of *resolving* the tension produced by the opposition of the arts and sciences. The tension will no longer be felt if philosophy is simply assimilated into, or seen as continuous with, science.[10]

Indeed, this is the conclusion that Rorty draws in his retrospective essays. "Ten Years After" concludes with the thought that the "death of meaning" (or, more broadly, the abandonment of the linguistic turn) brings with it "the death of philosophy as a discipline with a method of its own. If there are no meanings to analyze, ... then perhaps there are *no* central or foundational questions in philosophy" (1977, 370). In the conclusion of "Twenty-Five Years After," Rorty returns to this theme and suggests that we would be wise to abandon "the idea that philosophy is a special field of inquiry distinguished by a special method" (1992, 374). If philosophy becomes continuous with science, on one hand (and, perhaps, poetry, on the other), then "our descendants will be less concerned with questions about 'the method of philosophy' or about 'the nature of philosophical problems.' The fifty-year history of linguistic philosophy, a history which is now behind us, suggests that such questions are likely to prove unprofitable" (ibid., 374).

Thus, in the end, Rorty suggests that the "distinctive contribution" of the linguistic turn was not "metaphilosophical" or methodological at all (ibid., 373). Rather, he claims that it introduced a new research program with a new set of questions, focused on how language allows us to achieve certain goals, such as solving social-coordination problems. This new agenda made it easier, Rorty claims, for philosophers to discard the idea of representation and develop a new pragmatist understanding of knowledge and inquiry.

How can we use Rorty's discussion to understand current debates about methodology? Overall, I think that Rorty had mixed success in assessing the long-term impact of linguistic philosophy and in predicting the future of philosophy. On the positive side, several of the contributions to the present volume follow more or less directly in the tradition of one of the six possible paths for philosophy from Rorty's original introduction. (Take, for instance, David Woodruff Smith's and Matthew Ratcliffe's discussions of phenomenological methods, or Marie McGinn's defense of a liberal, Wittgensteinian naturalism.) So, parts of the current volume can be thought of as picking up where Rorty's discussion left off. A second virtue of Rorty's discussion of linguistic philosophy is that it identifies a number of questions, broadly connected with the viability of naturalism, which still structure debates about methodology today. I return to the relation between linguistic philosophy and naturalism and discuss more specific naturalistic themes in the remaining subsections, "Constructive Naturalism and Deflationary Naturalism" and "Varieties of Naturalism and Their Viability."

However, there are several limitations of Rorty's treatment of methodological issues, which imply that it would at best be an oversimplification to see this volume simply as a descendent of his. For one thing, the approaches of many of the contributors do not fit nicely into Rorty's taxonomy. For another, he was clearly wrong to predict that we would be less concerned with questions about the methods of philosophy and the nature of philosophical problems. Instead, in the last decade or so, interest in philosophical methodology has grown significantly.

Both of these failures can be explained by the simple fact that Rorty's discussion in *The Linguistic Turn* overlooks, or fails to anticipate, important developments in philosophy.[11] I mention two that are important for the present volume. First, some important versions of naturalism in the last few decades are not represented in Rorty's original taxonomy, nor are they in his subsequent discussion of the end of linguistic philosophy. That is, many naturalists think of philosophy as discovering truths about the world but are not doing philosophy in the style of J.L. Austin or P.F. Strawson (see note 9). They downplay the language-centered component of Rorty's methodological nominalism and instead focus on the "empirical inquiry concerning ... particulars" that it sanctions, coupled with an appeal to global criteria (such as simplicity and explanatory fecundity) that they think govern the rational selection of any theory.[12]

There are of course many variants of this broad kind of naturalism, and delineating them and tracing their historical development is a complicated task. Here I mention two influences that are particularly relevant to one naturalistic approach to metaphysics. (1) Such naturalists take Quine to have identified the tools to provide substantive, factual answers to some traditional metaphysical questions.[13] This idea is captured in part by the following passage from Ted Sider:

> Today's ontologists are not conceptual analysts; few attend to ordinary usage of sentences like "chairs exist." ... Their methodology is rather quasi-scientific. They treat competing positions as tentative hypotheses about the world, and assess them with a loose battery of criteria for theory choice. ... Theoretical insight, considerations of simplicity, integration with other domains (for instance science, logic, and philosophy of language), and so on, play important roles.
>
> (2009, 385)

(2) Many of these naturalists take Saul Kripke to have shown that there are modal truths that can be known only through empirical investigation.

These truths are grounded in the nature of things and cannot be discovered through conceptual or linguistic analysis alone.[14]

A second important development that Rorty failed to anticipate is the growth of interest in various forms of rationalism from roughly the 1990s on. Again, the terrain is complicated, but these forms of rationalism are all united, at least, in rejecting Quine's attack on a priori knowledge. Many also share the goal of re-establishing the connection between a priori conceivability and metaphysical possibility that Kripke's work seemed to call into doubt.

Some of these varieties of rationalism attempt to show that all modal knowledge can be factored into two components: one that is knowable a priori through logic and conceptual analysis and one that is knowable only a posteriori through the methods of natural science. However, other versions of rationalism claim that there are some philosophical truths that can be discovered only through rational insight into the structure of the world. Roughly, such views defend the autonomy and priority of philosophical reflection, and they reject the factoring procedure just mentioned, claiming rather that some metaphysical knowledge can only be acquired through the distinct discipline of metaphysics. (See Lowe's contribution to this volume.)

The collision between these two developments animates many current debates about methodology.[15] They also intersect with a further, more recent strand within contemporary naturalism: namely, work that has been carried out under the banner of "experimental philosophy." This work has in part prompted intense discussion about the nature of intuitions and their proper role, if any, in philosophy. Some inspiration for (some approaches to) experimental philosophy comes from outside of philosophy, such as research in social psychology which seems to call into question the reliability of our introspective and intuitive judgments (e.g. Nisbett and Wilson 1977) or which suggests that patterns of thought vary systematically across cultures (e.g. Nisbett *et al.* 2001).

To sum up, although Rorty's introduction to *The Linguistic Turn* correctly predicts some current methodological trends, it overlooks (a) naturalistic approaches to philosophy that have not grown out of the remnants of linguistic philosophy in the way he anticipated, and (b) non-naturalistic approaches that survive the decline of linguistic philosophy. Both (a) and (b) offer the prospect of solving (rather than deflating) some traditional philosophical problems by non-linguistic means.

A case can be made that Rorty's retrospective essays do a better job of accommodating the first of these developments, since in those essays he adverts to the idea that philosophy may have no distinctive "method of its own," along with the "Neurath–Quine picture of knowledge" (1977, 369), and the Quinean idea that there is no fundamental difference between a change in theory and a change in language (Rorty 1992, 373). However, even so, the main thrust of his discussion there is aimed at sketching a *specific* form of naturalism, one that takes a more deflationary attitude toward philosophical questions than neo-Quinean versions do. I turn to the contrast between these two forms of naturalism in the next subsection.

Constructive naturalism and deflationary naturalism

Above, I praised Rorty for identifying naturalistic aspects of linguistic philosophy, since these are one of the main foci of current debates about methodology. Rorty's contrast between "philosophy-as-discovery" and "philosophy-as-proposal" corresponds to a distinction between two main tendencies, or approaches, within contemporary naturalist thought. The first approach claims that many philosophical questions deserve substantive answers, but insists that they can be provided by the methods of science. Call this the "constructive approach." The second approach claims that philosophical questions either have trivial answers or are misguided and should be replaced by questions that can be addressed by the sciences. Call this the "deflationary approach."

Penelope Maddy provides a nice description of the constructive approach:

> [The naturalist] will ask traditionally philosophical questions about what there is and how we know it, but she will take perception as a mostly reliable guide to the existence of medium-sized physical objects, ... and she will treat questions of knowledge as involving the relation between the world—as she understands it in her physics, chemistry, optics, geology, and so on,—and human beings—as she understands them in her physiology, cognitive science, neuroscience, linguistics, and so on. ... [The naturalist] proceeds scientifically and attempts to answer even philosophical questions by appeal to its resources.
>
> (2007, 18–19)

On Maddy's view, "there are important questions (typically classified as philosophical) that don't fit within a single scientific discipline," and the reliability of perception, the scientific study of the methods of science itself, and the ground of logical and mathematical truth are among these (ibid., 115).

By contrast, Rorty adopts a deflationary approach when he suggests that we turn our attention from philosophical questions to, for example, "biological or sociological questions about how we managed to make the particular language we have made, or how we teach it to our young"

(1977, 370). This quotation follows a passage where Rorty suggests that skeptical worries become trivial once we focus on language rather than experience (or "ideas"). For, he claims, it is unproblematic that language represents reality—we *made* it do so (ibid.). In his second retrospective essay, Rorty says that even to grant this much to the skeptic was a mistake: he now claims that the notion of representation is completely unnecessary (1992, 372 n. 2). Rorty seems to suggest that, as a result, skeptical problems no longer have even a trivial solution; they simply fail to arise at all.

There is vigorous debate among naturalists about which of these approaches should be adopted. I do not intend to engage in that complicated dispute here. Instead, I want merely to note that it reveals a difference in opinion about the proper starting points of a naturalistic approach to philosophy.

Since "constructive naturalists" take the sciences to be trying to discover facts about the world and take philosophy to also be involved in this endeavor, they tend to take what Huw Price (2004) has called a "material conception" of placement problems. Faced with the task of placing prima facie non-natural phenomena—such as mentality, mathematics, or morality—in the natural world, these naturalists think that we should start with our best understanding of these phenomena themselves and determine if (and if so, how) this understanding finds a coherent place within a scientific conception of the world. On this view, philosophy is in the business of making straightforward factual claims, only one of which can be true regarding any given issue or phenomenon.

By contrast, "deflationary naturalists" tend to begin with a "linguistic conception" of placement problems. Instead of starting with our best understanding of, say, the mind, they start with our best understanding of "human linguistic practices" regarding the mind (Price 2004, 76). Further, by abandoning the assumption that descriptive language has the core function of representing reality, they claim that we need not think of the task as one of trying to locate some apparently non-naturalistic entities in the natural world. Rejecting representationalism relieves deflationary naturalists of the burden of having to reconcile apparently disparate ontological domains. From their perspective, philosophy is not directly involved in the project of discovering the way the world is. Rather, it either clarifies our existing conceptual frameworks or proposes new ones—frameworks outside of which the factual/non-factual distinction fails even to make sense. This view contrasts with constructive naturalism not merely in that proposals are not the sort of thing that could be true or false but also in that there is no assumption that any one proposed framework is better than others for a given purpose.[16]

This difference in starting points reveals that the relation between contemporary naturalism and linguistic philosophy is complex. On the one hand, many deflationary naturalists will follow Rorty in thinking that constructive naturalism and linguistic philosophy are both "deeply implicated in a *non*-naturalistic picture of human knowledge and inquiry" (1992, 374, italics in original) insofar as they both incorporate the idea that language is "a structured medium of representation, capable of standing in determinate relations to a distinct entity called 'the world'" (ibid., 373–74). On the other hand, constructive naturalists will not see a commitment to "representationalism" as what was wrong with linguistic philosophy. Instead, many will allege that linguistic philosophy went astray in assuming that a focus on human language use is the best way to begin answering philosophical questions. And they will think that deflationary naturalists are misguided in continuing this practice.

This debate may seem to amount to one form of naturalism accusing the other of not being fully naturalistic. I think that Timothy Williamson is right that dismissing an idea as inconsistent with naturalism is, in itself, "little better than dismissing it as 'inconsistent with Christianity'" (this volume, p. 30). This kind of critique is no more powerful than the underlying doctrine or methodological program that is invoked. And, I think that in this case the debate at least in part bottoms out in empirical questions about the function and structure of human language use, including whether the kind of "linguistic pluralism" endorsed by some deflationary naturalists turns out to be true (cf. Price 2009, 334–35).[17]

Varieties of naturalism and their viability

The seven essays in Part I of this volume discuss both constructive and deflationary versions of naturalism and address whether naturalism is even viable at all. The opening exchange between Timothy Williamson and Alex Rosenberg focuses on the latter issue. Williamson claims that a dilemma faces would-be naturalists. If they are too inclusive in defining what counts as science, then naturalism "loses its bite." On the other hand, if they are too exclusive in defining science, then naturalism distorts or fails to accommodate certain areas of knowledge.[18] (Williamson emphasizes mathematics, but also mentions logic, linguistics, history, and literary theory.)

Williamson also outlines a second line of criticism, which, in its strongest form, alleges that naturalism is self-undermining—that naturalists must rely on methods that are non-naturalistic in order to defend their position.[19] For instance, Williamson claims that natural science alone cannot establish the "extreme naturalist claim" that all truths are discoverable by hard science (this volume, p. 37).

Instead of endorsing naturalism, Williamson lauds the "aspiration to think in a scientific spirit," but notes that this aspiration is applicable outside of natural science (this volume, pp. 30–31). He claims that "[n]aturalism tries to condense the scientific spirit into a philosophical theory" but that this cannot be done because "any theory can be applied in an unscientific spirit, as a polemical device to reinforce prejudice" (ibid.).[20]

In response to the second line of critique, Rosenberg emphasizes the inductive character of naturalists' argument against non-scientific methods of knowledge acquisition—the "track record" of science (this volume, p. 39). In his view, a "demonstration in a 'first philosophy'" that naturalism is true may require non-naturalistic methods or assumptions, but, fortunately, naturalists desire no such thing (this volume, ibid.).

With respect to Williamson's first critique, Rosenberg in effect claims that, with respect to any purported domain of knowledge that is prima facie non-naturalistic, naturalism will be able to either (i) accommodate it or (ii) provide good reasons why such accommodation is neither available nor needed. Rosenberg claims that naturalists should continue to strive for (i) regarding mathematics. And, against the charge that they have had little success in this project, Rosenberg offers a *tu quoque*: non-naturalists do not have very good accounts of mathematical knowledge either (this volume, p. 34).[21] With respect to other putative knowledge domains, such as history and literary theory, Rosenberg is more open to (ii), that is, relegating these disciplines to providing "fun" rather than knowledge (this volume, pp. 35, 42).

The next three contributions discuss different versions of naturalism. Jeffrey W. Roland identifies twelve principles that he claims are essential to any Quinean version of naturalism – arguably the most influential "constructive" form of naturalism. He then discusses two areas of disagreement among views that endorse (versions of) these principles: first, whether any knowledge is a priori, and second, whether a reductive account of causation is possible.

Marie McGinn's contribution defends a more deflationary, Wittgensteinian form of "liberal naturalism." On this approach, the goal of the naturalistic philosopher is neither discovery nor explanation, nor is it to propose new conceptual frameworks (or "language games"). Rather, it is to clarify the content and structure of our existing conceptual frameworks so that our philosophical perplexities fade away. McGinn focuses on our concepts of understanding, meaning, and intention, and she diagnoses the shortcomings she finds with John McDowell's treatment of these issues as resulting from his failure to fully embrace the liberal naturalist principles that he claims to share with Wittgenstein. McGinn interprets Wittgenstein as urging us to abandon "the mysterious idea of a logical fit between a state of mind and what fulfils it" (this volume, p. 77). Once we see that the meaning of a sign is its use, we will see that our ordinary practice with respect to the concepts of understanding and intending something "is in perfectly good order just as it stands" (ibid., p. 65). Among other things, we do not need to ground intentionality in non-intentional, non-normative facts.

Jenann Ismael outlines a third kind of naturalist approach that is, at least in the version she endorses, arguably intermediate between Quinean and Wittgensteinian approaches. Ismael calls the kind of pragmatist naturalism she endorses the "Sydney Plan," both as a nod to the intellectual home of its "father ... sponsor and primary benefactor," Huw Price (this volume, p. 86) and in contrast to the influential "Canberra Plan," adopted by David Lewis and Frank Jackson, among many others. Like those who take the Wittgensteinian approach, Sydney Planners reject the idea that representation amounts to a kind of mirroring of the world by our language and thought. Instead of asking "'what do x beliefs represent?' the Sydney Plan raises the question 'what facts about ourselves and the world jointly support the formation of x beliefs and the role they play in our lives?'" (ibid.).[22] As a result, Sydney Planners have a similarly "liberal," non-metaphysical, and non-reductive conception of what is required to place phenomena like moral properties, modality, causes, and chances in the natural world.

However, unlike the Wittgensteinian approach, the Sydney Plan does not assume that the facts about our linguistic usage that are relevant to these projects are "open to view." In this respect, Sydney Planners are closer to those who accept the Quinean idea that philosophy is continuous with the sciences. In assuming that the materials latent in ordinary practice are sufficient to dissolve philosophical problems, Sydney Planners may claim that Wittgensteinian naturalists overlook the fact that language is a tool that "we have inherited without an engineer's insight into why [it] work[s]" (Ismael, this volume, p. 89). Thus, they may claim that gaining such insight requires empirical research and not merely conceptual clarification.

The prospects for armchair methods

Parts II–IV of the book are divided along subdisciplinary lines, and I provide introductory summaries of the chapters in the order in which they appear, grouped into subsections concerning (1) conceptual analysis; (2) intuitions, thought experiments and reflective equilibrium; and (3) introspection and the first-person perspective. I depart from this order as needed, e.g. briefly returning to a chapter when it covers more than one method.

Methods in metaphysics and epistemology

Conceptual analysis

The first three essays in Part II discuss methodological issues in metaphysics, and two of them hold that conceptual analysis plays an important role in metaphysical inquiry.

Amie Thomasson defends what she calls the "easy approach" to ontology, in which analytic truths and conceptual analysis play a key role. According to the easy approach, debates about whether certain entities exist can be resolved by making trivial inferences from uncontroversial premises. In some cases, these premises are (alleged) analytic truths; in others, they are empirical claims. However, in all cases, the inference from the premise to an ontological conclusion proceeds via conceptual truths. Thomasson rebuts Ted Sider's charge that the easy approach is "just more metaphysics"—that it is committed to the world *lacking* any quantificational structure—by calling into question the very idea of joint-carving quantification and claiming that logical terms, including quantifiers, are merely formal.[23]

E.J. Lowe argues that metaphysics is a universal discipline concerned with "the fundamental structure of reality as a whole," whose "primary concern" is to "chart the *possibilities* of real existence," and whose claims are not (primarily) supported or confirmed by empirical evidence (pp. 128, 136). Conceptual analysis also plays an important role in metaphysics, according to Lowe, since using metaphysical concepts like *object, event, causation, space*, and *time* to articulate the fundamental structure of reality requires that we have a clear understanding of these concepts. However, he does not endorse a "semantic conception of metaphysics," according to which all metaphysical possibilities are grounded in the meanings of words. Nor does he accept a two-stage model for acquiring modal knowledge, as for example the Canberra Plan does, in which reflection on our concepts together with empirical inquiry is sufficient to acquire knowledge of metaphysical modality. For he argues that claims that on this model are supposedly established by purely empirical means together with conceptual analysis in fact require metaphysical principles concerning e.g. the identity conditions for different kinds of objects.

Jessica Wilson does not offer a positive methodological program for metaphysics. Rather, she suggests that the widespread disagreement in contemporary metaphysics is best explained by the current lack of consensus regarding methodology. Wilson thinks that some methodological progress has been made. (For example, she approvingly cites those, such as Mark Wilson and Andrew Melnyk, who raise concerns about "whether conceiving alone can provide a suitable basis for a priori deliberation"

(Wilson, this volume, p. 149), which calls into question views that rely on conceptual analysis.) However, much of her essay diagnoses three "dogmas" that she sees as impediments to progress in metaphysics. Discarding one of these dogmas—the assumption that metametaphysical debates are best approached through semantics—would undermine the metaphysical significance of the entire debate between Thomasson and Sider over such issues as whether there are "joint-carving" quantifiers and whether logical terms are "contentful" or merely "formal."

In contrast to Thomasson and Lowe, David Papineau denies that conceptual analysis, understood as delivering analytic truths, plays any significant role in the "theoretical" branches of philosophy. He argues that claims in metaphysics, epistemology, philosophy of mind, and philosophy of language are like scientific claims in being synthetic, a posteriori, and primarily concerned with how the world actually is, not how it metaphysically could be. However, he does not take his view to call for philosophers to get out of their armchairs and engage more substantively with scientific research. Rather, he claims that the philosophy as it is, with its use of "abstract theorizing, argument, and reflection on possible cases" is *already* like science (p. 167).

The next two essays focus on methods in epistemology. Hilary Kornblith agrees with Papineau that the methods of epistemology are not different in kind from those of science. However, he is less sanguine about the prospects for inquiry from the armchair that is conducted without significant input from the empirical sciences. Kornblith claims that it is hard to see how the project of conceptual analysis can be insulated from the results of experimental investigation, given their broad agreement on the causal-explanatory roles that concepts play. Indeed, he claims that philosophers and psychologists who work on concepts likely have identical objects of study and that "[t]he traditional methods of conceptual analysis amount to little more than social psychology done badly" (p. 207). However, Kornblith claims that, even if it were done well, conceptual analysis would still have the wrong object of inquiry. For, he argues, epistemologists should study states and processes like knowledge, justification, reasoning, and memory, themselves, rather than our concepts of those states and processes.

Kirk Ludwig defends the role of conceptual analysis in epistemology within the context of a broadly Fregean account of concepts and concept possession that supports the existence of conceptual truths. On this account, when we engage in successful conceptual analysis we come to know a proposition solely by exercising competence with the concepts deployed in it. Ludwig argues that Kornblith's claim that epistemologists should aim to study knowledge itself, rather than our concept of knowledge, is based on a false dilemma, since, Ludwig claims, the *analysans* of a given conceptual analysis of knowledge "both *expresses* the application conditions of the concept of knowledge and *states* what it is for someone to have knowledge" (p. 221, italics in original). He discusses a number of possible sources of this alleged error, including, in some detail, the idea that epistemic terms are natural kind terms.

Intuitions, thought experiments, and reflective equilibrium

Developing and evaluating an analysis of a given concept typically involves performing thought experiments—testing the analysis against intuitions elicited by hypothetical cases. Many of the contributors discuss the use of intuitions and thought experiments in philosophy.

For example, Papineau suggests that intuitions are "general principles informing our counterfactual reasoning" (p. 179). Even if philosophical intuitions are not directly falsifiable by observation, he claims that they are still indirectly beholden to experience (through global theoretical constraints like simplicity), and he believes that philosophical intuitions should not be trusted unless they have been subject to "serious a posteriori investigation" (p. 186).

By contrast, Ludwig defends the use of thought experiments as a first-person endeavor, as a method that relies solely on an individual's own conceptual competence. He points out that the use of thought experiments in the program of conceptual analysis assumes that most of our judgments made in optimal conditions will be correct, and briefly outlines how facts about conceptual competence support this assumption.[24]

Some philosophers, like Kornblith, deny this assumption and claim that intuitions should play no substantive role in philosophical inquiry. Others claim that intuitions about possible cases can play roles other than justifying conceptual analyses, some of which roles can be played even if the intuitions involved are not reliable. For example, Papineau claims that thought experiments serve to "unearth hidden assumptions" that lead to conflicting judgments (p. 188). Similarly, in Part IV Valerie Tiberius holds that thought experiments "sharpen our views about what matters and what is at stake in choosing between different theories" (pp. 400–401). And, Neil Levy notes that intuitions can serve as heuristics, illustrate arguments, and "may function as evidence ... by drawing our attention to features of cases we might otherwise have overlooked" (p. 385). Further, Levy claims that even if some intuitions are "contaminated," by e.g. order effects, they may still facilitate communal progress by prompting more thorough scrutiny of competing views (p. 390).[25]

Should intuitions play a more central role in philosophy? Should they be used as evidence for philosophical claims? And if so, what weight should we put on them relative to agreement with general, theoretical principles and integration into well-supported empirical theories? Are intuitions reliable guides to the nature of reality, and what, if anything, could explain such reliability? The essays in Part III and IV suggest that the answers to such questions may vary across philosophical domains.

Methods in philosophy of language and philosophy of mind

Intuitions in philosophy of language and linguistics

Georges Rey, Michael Devitt, and Barry C. Smith discuss the role of intuitions in linguistics and the philosophy of language. Rey and Devitt debate whether it is empirically plausible to take our competence with a language to provide the informational content of our intuitions about that language (e.g. intuitions about grammaticality and ambiguity).

Rey argues that it is "scientifically respectable" to take humans to have a language faculty that outputs "structural descriptions," i.e. representations of the syntactic and semantic properties of the expressions being processed. He suggests that linguistic intuitions are reliable when they are caused by these representations, just as reports of perceptual experiences are reliable when they are caused by the outputs of a visual module. This is part of his overall project of defending a modest form of Cartesianism, which accords a special role to reflection on *some* of the products of introspection and intuition. However, Rey denies that achieving reflective equilibrium is sufficient for an adequate philosophical theory. Instead, we should aim to *explain* the results of introspection and intuition, in order to distinguish those that are reliable from those that are not. Further, this is not a task that can be conducted a priori.

By contrast, Devitt argues that linguistic intuitions, like intuitions in general, "are empirical theory-laden central-processor responses to phenomena, differing from many other such responses only in being fairly immediate and unreflective" (p. 269). He claims that the analogy to vision does not support Rey's view, for the visual system supplies only a representation of what is seen and not *a description of* that representation. Further, he argues that there is no good reason to suppose that the language faculty provides structural descriptions to the central processor, and, even if it did, no reason to think that these descriptions would cause the relevant linguistic intuitions. Devitt also points out that his account has important methodological implications for both linguists and philosophers of language: they should rely more heavily on evidence from actual usage—both sentences from the corpus and those elicited in controlled experiments—and when they do appeal to intuitions, they should give preference to those of experts.

Barry C. Smith suggests that reflection on the nature of linguistic phenomena motivates an "internal" conception of language, according to which the subject matter of linguistics is a cognitive phenomenon, primarily the phonological and grammatical structures that "people impose on ... sounds and signs as a result of their internal states" (p. 300). Smith diagnoses dissent from this conception as arising, in part, from the assumption, shared by Quine and Wittgenstein, that language is a public phenomenon. (He claims that there are vestiges of this idea in Devitt's work.) Further, he argues that Devitt misunderstands the nature of structural descriptions and linguistic intuitions. According to Smith, the latter are not beliefs about an "external reality" but rather conscious presentations, or "seemings," of a "reality constituted by the underlying states of the language faculty that, in part, gives rise to them" (p. 313). He concludes by claiming that the biggest challenge for those with an "external" conception of language, like Devitt, is "how to motivate an account of the syntactic structure of sentences and their recombinable parts – needed to explain the potential for a discrete infinity of sentences – without making any mention of speakers' psychology" (p. 314).

Introspection and the first-person perspective

Introspection plays an important role in much of contemporary philosophy. For example, as Kornblith points out, introspection is commonly taken to provide information about the content, sources, and justification of our beliefs. Further, some philosophers hold that fundamental questions in philosophy must be addressed from the first-person perspective: What should *I* believe? How should *I* act? For instance, Ludwig claims that the most fundamental reason that work in experimental philosophy cannot replace the first-person approach to conceptual analysis is that we "need to have insight ourselves into the correct answer" (p. 229).[26]

Recently, a number of philosophers have drawn on work in social and cognitive psychology to call into question the reliability of introspection and the indispensability of the first-person perspective. For example, in this volume, Kornblith suggests that the deliverances of introspection often amount merely to confabulation and post hoc rationalization. Because of this, he claims that work in empirical psychology must figure in any profitable approach to epistemological debates. Further, Kornblith suggests that the belief that the first-person perspective is a "neutral and unproblematic starting point for epistemological inquiry" is the product of false Cartesian views about the power of reflection and the fact that introspection delivers a psychologically compelling, but misleading, view of our mental life (p. 212f.).

Lynne Rudder Baker argues that the first-person perspective cannot be adequately treated by the natural sciences: it can neither be eliminated nor reduced to non-first-personal phenomena. In particular, she claims that the first-person perspective includes the ability to refer to oneself as oneself in the first person, and that the distinction ("distinction (D)") between this ability and the mere ability to think of someone who is in fact oneself cannot be captured by the methods of natural science. According to Baker, there are empirical and theoretical reasons to accept distinction (D). In response to the kind of empirical studies that Kornblith draws on to question the reliability of introspection and the primacy of the first-person perspective, she claims that cognitive science does not even have the resources to make distinction (D), much less provide an account of it in third-personal terms. Baker takes her argument to show that the methods of natural science are not sufficient to exhaustively describe reality; armchair methods are also required. However, she does not claim that armchair methods are "extra-empirical," and notes that such methods will typically not be independent of experience.

Baker closes by illustrating her *"bricolage"* approach to philosophy—using whatever materials are at hand—by discussing introspection. Like Rey, she holds that introspection is a reliable, empirically defeasible, source of evidence about some of our mental states, but she does not attempt to explain this reliability. Rey, by contrast, offers a model of introspection analogous to his account of linguistic intuitions, and he suggests that this model could explain cases that others have used against introspection as instances of selective inattention. More generally, Rey claims that such cases provide no evidence of *across the board* failures in introspective competence.[27]

David Woodruff Smith presents one way of articulating what is allegedly left out by the third-personal methods of natural science. He outlines the main elements of a phenomenological approach to the intrinsically subjective, i.e. phenomenal, character of conscious experience. Smith suggests that a kind of awareness—inner awareness—is built into conscious experiences themselves, and he claims that this awareness is the ground of phenomenological reflection. Although introspection may suggest that conscious experience is transparent—that when one has a conscious experience, one is not conscious of the experience itself—Smith argues that phenomenological reflection on the structures of different forms of experience results in a more nuanced view of consciousness. Smith also discusses Husserl's technique of "epoché," or bracketing, and suggests that it involves two levels, both of which are "transcendental" in that they concern either the epistemological or logical/semantic conditions on the possibility of experience.

Matthew Ratcliffe suggests that the phenomenological tradition, especially some of Husserl's later work, can be used to question common assumptions in debates in analytic philosophy of mind about "cognitive phenomenology," i.e. about whether the phenomenal content of perception includes conceptual, or other cognitive, aspects and whether non-sensory cognitive states and processes have phenomenal content. He argues that experience is much richer than most participants in these debates have supposed. In particular, a complete phenomenological bracketing reveals that experience incorporates a "sense of being situated in a shared world," i.e. "world-experience," which Ratcliffe claims can be analyzed in terms of a space of possibilities that determines the kinds of experience that are accessible to us. World-experience is neither an attitude nor the content of an attitude but rather a structure common to both perception and cognition. He suggests that this framework is supported by, and can also illuminate, first-person reports of those with psychiatric disorders such as depression and schizophrenia.

Intuitional methods in ethics and aesthetics

The chapters in Part IV address questions about the proper role of intuitions and thought experiments in ethics and aesthetics. Neil Levy notes that the worry that our intuitions are not good guides to the nature of our concepts, or of the supposed referents of those concepts, lies behind some recent challenges from experimental philosophy. Levy focuses on one of these, the "arbitrariness critique," which claims that the apparent diversity of intuitions among groups of people raises the prospect that intuitions reveal idiosyncratic features of those groups rather than the nature of reality (or some universally shared concept). He argues that the use of intuitions—understood as intellectual seemings produced by "fast, automatic, perhaps encapsulated processes triggered by relevant stimuli" (p. 382)—can be vindicated in the face of the arbitrariness critique.

According to Levy, some intuitions may serve as non-redundant evidence in that they are required "for appreciation of the force of an argument" (p. 387). However, Levy does not take himself to be defending the autonomy of armchair methods. Rather, he argues that if philosophy is to justifiably rely on intuitions, then it must (a) become more responsive to empirical evidence and (b) restructure its institutions. Further, Levy claims that it is largely an empirical question whether our intuitions in a particular domain are reliable or not. For example, he suggests that there are reasons to think that our collective moral intuitions cannot systemically be wrong, reasons that do not extend to intuitions about the mind.[28]

Valerie Tiberius discusses accounts of well-being, or "prudential value in the most general sense" (p. 398). She suggests that an acceptable theory of well-being must capture at least some of our pretheoretic intuitions about what it is to live well. (Otherwise, it would just be changing the subject.) However, she argues that the method of reflective equilibrium as commonly practiced puts too much emphasis on intuitions about possible cases and not enough on broader theoretical criteria. She then argues that correcting our methods in this way lends support to her "value fulfillment theory" of well-being. In particular, she focuses on what she claims is an overlooked normative criterion: a theory should explain why claims about well-being are reason-giving. She also claims that meeting empirical adequacy constraints will require normative philosophy to engage with social science.

Matthew Bedke's contribution concerns the use of intuitions in ethical theory in general.[29] When the subject is "procedural justification"—"how one ought to go about making up one's mind about what to believe, given the information available" (p. 421)—he claims that there can be no method other than trying to get one's intuition-based judgments about ethical cases and principles into reflective equilibrium. However, he thinks that in ethics this method is independent of the project of conceptual analysis, and thus any worries about the latter can be avoided. Worries about disagreement and "cosmic coincidence" lead Bedke to doubt that intuitive methods in ethics are part of "a justified way of discovering [stance-independent] facts" (p. 425). In his view, the further fact that our first-order ethical views (as a type) are not disposed to change in the face of such worries motivates an expressivist or quasi-realist position in metaethics, rather than the abandonment of intuitional methods.

Gregory Currie argues that certain cases in aesthetics (such as the issue of whether aesthetic qualities supervene on the intrinsic, non-aesthetic properties of objects) are insulated from skeptical worries about the reliability of intuition. For one thing, he argues that our ability to form intuitive-based judgments about certain hypothetical cases draws on the same capacity that operates when we make aesthetic judgments about actual artworks. Further, aesthetic judgment has a "peculiar status," in that we have to rely on the judgments of "the least biased, the best prepared, [and] the most sensitive and attentive among us," if we are to say anything worthwhile about aesthetic value at all (p. 442). (Cf. Tiberius's broadly similar claim about well-being, mentioned above.) However, Currie argues that with respect to other issues in aesthetics—such as the connection between aesthetic and educative value and whether narrative fiction improves those who read or watch it—philosophers ignore empirical work at their peril.

Concluding remarks

As the contributions to this volume indicate, current work on philosophical methodology is rich and varied.[30] Will this work lead, in the long run, to philosophical progress and insight? As we've seen, Rorty moved from bold optimism to profound pessimism about the importance and utility of debates about methods—from claiming that the era of linguistic philosophy, with its focus on method, was "among the great ages of the history of philosophy" (1967a/1992, 33), to predicting that questions about philosophical methods will, in general, "prove unprofitable" (1992, 374). I suspect that neither of these extreme views is correct. Contemporary work on philosophical methods will likely lead to many advances, but this will not warrant calling this period a "great age of philosophy," if only because those very advances may render moot the presuppositions of such a claim.

Notes

1 The practical upshot of this view may be similar to the "collaborative" view mentioned in the previous paragraph—both could allow for important contributions from, and interaction between, armchair reflection and empirical work. However, these views understand the relation between these inputs differently. The collaborative view sees them as epistemically distinct kinds of method (perhaps mapping onto the a priori/a posteriori distinction), which, in principle, could either support or conflict with one another. By contrast, the view currently under discussion will claim either that the a priori/a posteriori distinction is itself confused or that armchair methods are themselves a posteriori. If philosophical methods are compared to tools one might use to move a vehicle up a hill, then the "collaborative" view sees empirical and armchair methods as connected to two distinct sources of force – say, an internal motor and an external winch. The latter view sees empirical and armchair methods as more akin to overlapping strands of a single rope connected to one source of force.

2 In this introduction, I use the term "naturalism" to refer to a methodological program rather than an ontological position.

3 When I was planning the present volume I did not have Rorty's anthology in mind. However, when I started to draft this introduction, I revisited his collection and noted that his essays could serve as a productive foil for current debates about methods.

4 Rorty cites Gustav Bergmann as coining the phrase "the linguistic turn" in his paper "Strawson's Ontology," first published in 1960 and reprinted in Bergmann's 1964 collection *Logic and Reality* (Rorty 1967a, 9 n. 10). The phrase certainly caught on. Cf. Michael Dummett's claim that "analytical philosophy was born when the 'linguistic turn' was taken" (1993, 5).

5 See, for example, neo-Carnapian views of meta-ontology according to which apparent ontological disputes are "merely verbal." Perhaps a larger number of philosophers take a more modest view that appealing to linguistic data is an important part of answering many philosophical questions but that it is not the *only* (or even always the best) way to answer such questions.

6 See D.W. Smith (this volume, p. 338) and Matthew Ratcliffe (this volume, p. 354) on the relation between subject matter and methods in the context of phenomenology. According to Rorty, linguistic philosophy presupposes what he calls "methodological nominalism," the thesis that the only way to answer philosophical questions about "concepts, subsistent universals or 'nature's'" is through empirical investigation of either (a) the particulars that are subsumed under them or (b) our use of linguistic expressions concerning them (1967a, 11).

7 For some discussion relevant to whether naturalism is problematically circular, see Hylton 1994, 272; Fumerton 1995, 177, 180; Rea 2002; Maddy 2007, 235. Rosenberg identifies this critique in Williamson's contributions to this volume (p. 39).

8 This issue is related to work in epistemology on basic methods, epistemic circularity, and the problem of "easy knowledge." See, for example, Alston 1986, Vogel 2000, and Cohen 2002.

9 Rorty lists six possible paths for philosophy after its traditional problems have been dissolved, along with at least one major adherent of each (1967a, 34–35). (The numbering that follows is also Rorty's.) Three of these—(1) phenomenology, as practiced by Edmund Husserl, (5) philosophy-as-descriptive-linguistics, or the analysis of ordinary language, as practiced by J.L. Austin, and (6) philosophy-as-transcendental-linguistics, or as discovering necessary conditions on the possibility of any language, as suggested by P.F. Strawson—fall on the side of philosophy-as-discovery. The other three—(2) philosophy-as-poetry, as suggested by Martin Heidegger, (3) philosophy-as-linguistic-proposal, as promoted by Friedrich Waismann and Rudolf Carnap, and (4) the kind of quietism offered by the later Wittgenstein—take philosophy to be (at most) offering proposals for how to talk about the world.

10 This could be done in two different ways. First, we could simply absorb philosophy into an independently understood category of science and discard any parts of philosophy that do not fit into the scientific mold. Second, we could question whether the contrast between science and philosophy even makes sense in the first place.

11 I am not claiming that Rorty was unaware of all of these developments. For example, he published a review of Kripke's *Naming and Necessity* in the *London Review of Books* (Rorty 1980). Rather, I am merely suggesting that Rorty's retrospective essays do not reveal a full appreciation of how these developments complicate his assessment of linguistic philosophy and the consequences of its decline. In the review just mentioned, he touches on some of these complications (1980, 5). However, even there, Rorty tends to dismiss the essentialist metaphysics ushered in by Kripke as "merely technical" and as irrelevant to settling larger disputes, say, between pragmatism and realism. Thus, he seems to fail to see how work inspired by Kripke could provide an alternative path for philosophy after the decline of linguistic philosophy.

12 One might think that appealing to these criteria implies that such naturalists do not in fact accept methodological nominalism. I think that this is plausible only if one reads "empirical inquiry" in an overly narrow way, since, if these naturalists are correct the use of such criteria is an integral part of theorizing in empirical science. See Papineau (this volume, under "A Priori Provenance, A Posteriori Justification," n. 4).

13 Whether or not this is an accurate interpretation of Quine is controversial, as some philosophers argue that the Quinean position on metaphysics is much more deflationary, and much closer to Carnap's, than is commonly assumed. See e.g. Alspector-Kelly 2001 and Price 2009.

14 I set aside the dispute about the origins of the causal theory of reference and associated ideas. For a discussion of this controversy, see Humphreys and Fetzer (1998). In any case, Kripke's work is mainly responsible for popularizing these ideas.

15 This is not to say, however, that these developments, broadly characterized as above, are mutually exclusive.

16 Jessica Wilson (this volume) draws a distinction between "vertical progress" within a framework, typical of the natural sciences, and "horizontal progress" in cultivating different frameworks, typical of the arts and mathematics. This nicely spells out the connection between philosophy-as-discovery vs philosophy-as-proposal, on the one hand, and the tension in philosophy produced by taking either the sciences or the arts as a model for philosophy, on the other. Crudely put, constructive naturalists will favor vertical progress as a model for philosophy, while deflationary naturalists will be attracted to horizontal progress.

17 In this connection, Rorty claims that bits of language are "strings of marks or noises used by human beings in the development and pursuit of social practices—practices which enabled people to achieve their ends, ends which do not include 'representing reality as it is in itself'" (1992, 373). One might ask how Rorty knows that this is not an end that humans (whether past or present) have had.

18 Barry Stroud (1996) and Lawrence Sklar (2010) have made similar claims.

19 This charge has also been made often in the past. For example, in the introduction to their edited volume, Steven Wagner and Richard Warner note that "[s]everal of our contributors argue that the naturalist's strictures are outright self-refuting, since naturalism itself is no scientific view" (1993, 4). See also Stroud 1996, 43, 48, Moser and Yandell 2000, and Lowe, this volume.

20 This recalls Bas van Fraassen's (2002) claim that empiricism can only be consistently formulated as a "stance" and not a philosophical theory.

21 See e.g. Roland (this volume, Section 1.5, nn. 22 and 23, and Section 3) on the relation between mathematics and naturalism.

22 In this, they seem to agree with the "dynamic" picture of thought that McGinn finds in Wittgenstein (this volume, p. 77). As Ismael writes: "In place of the static, two-term relation 'reference', [Sydney Planners] have a rich plurality of relations mediated by, or passing through, embedded agents, and tailored to perform practical, epistemic, or social functions that cannot be understood in static, disembodied, or unembedded terms" (Ismael, this volume, p. 94).

23 Thomasson notes that the formal/material distinction fits nicely with a functional pluralist view of language, such as that adopted by Huw Price. Ismael counts Thomasson among followers of the Sydney Plan (this volume, n. 20).

24 Rey criticizes a similar proposal by George Bealer as "superficialism," asking how he knows that intuitions "in even the best cognitive conditions and the richest conceptual repertoires don't depend on all manner of background empirical assumptions about the nature of the world and the context in which the intuitive verdict is being elicited?" (p. 259).

25 Even Kornblith grants that some investigation of our epistemic concepts may be necessary as a starting point for epistemological inquiry, "if only to fix its subject matter," although he claims that this investigation is "utterly trivial" and is not unique to philosophy (2006, 12–13).

26 Bedke endorses a similar view, at least with respect to first-order ethical theorizing (p. 420ff.).

27 Cf. Baker's claim that "Global distrust of introspection is self-defeating: the more emphasis on the unreliability of what you think that you* [i.e., you thinking of yourself as yourself] are thinking, the more unreliable is your view of unreliability" (p. 330).

28 Among these is the metaethical view he favors, according to which "the moral facts are partially constituted by the responses, including the linguistic responses, of suitably placed observers" (Levy, this volume, p. 392). Although I include Levy's article in Part IV since its last section focuses on moral intuitions, clearly his claims about the relation between experimental philosophy, intuitions, and thought experiments apply more generally. Papineau makes similar claims about the prospects for experimental philosophy improving armchair methods (p. 189). On the other hand, Kornblith discounts experimental philosophy; in his view, even if its methods are reliable, it shares the same misguided target of inquiry with conceptual analysis. Bedke, Currie, Devitt, Ludwig, Rey, and Barry C. Smith also discuss experimental philosophy (sometimes very briefly).

29 Bedke uses the term "intuition" to pick out "a kind of initial reaction" to possible cases and principles (p. 421). Since, on his view, intuitions are "appropriately called seemings" (ibid.), he, like Levy, seems to adopt something like George Bealer's account of intuitions. However, unlike Levy, Bedke does not take intuitions to be "conclusions from rapid half-conscious processing" (ibid.:, cf. Levy, p. 382).

30 Space and other limitations prevented discussion of other interesting methodological issues, such as the way in which the history of philosophy bears on methodological debates, the use of modeling and other formal methods in philosophy, and the relation between applied and theoretical areas of philosophy. (For a provocative take on the last issue see Kitcher 2011.)

References

Alspector-Kelly, Marc (2001) "On Quine on Carnap on Ontology," *Philosophical Studies* 102: 93–122.

Alston, William P. (1986) "Epistemic Circularity," *Philosophy and Phenomenological Research* 47: 1–30.

Cohen, Stewart (2002) "Basic Knowledge and the Problem of Easy Knowledge," *Philosophy and Phenomenological Research* 65: 309–29.

Dummett, Michael (1993) *Origins of Analytical Philosophy*, London: Duckworth.

Fumerton, Richard (1995) *Metaepistemology and Skepticism*, Lanham, MD: Rowman & Littlefield.

Humphreys, Paul W. and James H. Fetzer (eds) (1998) *The New Theory of Reference: Kripke, Marcus, and Its Origins*, Dordrecht: Kluwer.

Hylton, Peter (1994) "Quine's Naturalism," *Midwest Studies in Philosophy* 19: 261–82.

Kitcher, Philip (2011) "Philosophy Inside Out," *Metaphilosophy* 42: 248–60.

Kornblith, Hilary (2006) "Appeals to Intuition and the Ambitions of Epistemology," in Stephen Hetherington (ed.), *Epistemology Futures*, New York: Oxford University Press, 10–25.

Maddy, Penelope (2007) *Second Philosophy*, Oxford: Oxford University Press.

Moser, Paul K. and David Yandell (2000) "Farewell to Philosophical Naturalism," in William Lane Craig and J.P. Moreland (eds), *Naturalism: A Critical Analysis*, London: Routledge, 3–23.

Nisbett, Richard E., Kaiping Peng, Incheol Choi, and Ara Norenzayan (2001) "Culture and Systems of Thought: Holistic versus Analytic Cognition," *Psychological Review* 108: 291–310.

Nisbett, Richard E. and Timothy DeCamp Wilson (1977) "Telling More than We Can Know: Verbal Reports on Mental Processes," *Psychological Review* 84: 231–59.

Price, Huw (2004) "Naturalism Without Representationalism," in Mario De Caro and David MacArthur (eds), *Naturalism in Question*, New York: Columbia University Press, 71–88.

——(2009) "Metaphysics after Carnap: The Ghost Who Walks?," in David J. Chalmers, David Manley, and Ryan Wasserman (eds), *Metametaphysics: New Essays in the Foundations of Ontology*, Oxford: Oxford University Press, 320–46.

Rea, Michael (2002) *World Without Design: The Ontological Consequences of Naturalism*, New York: Oxford University Press.

Rorty, Richard (1967a/1992) "Introduction: Metaphilosophical Difficulties of Linguistic Philosophy," in Rorty 1967b/1992, 1–39.

——(ed.) (1967b/1992) *The Linguistic Turn*, Chicago: University of Chicago Press.

——(1977/1992) "Ten Years After," in Rorty 1967b/1992, 361–70. (Originally published in *Journal of Philosophy* 74: 416–32.)

——(1980) "Kripke vs Kant," *London Review of Books* 2(17): 4–5.

——(1992) "Twenty-Five Years After," in Rorty 1967b/1992, 371–74.

Sider, Theodore (2009) "Ontological Realism," in David J. Chalmers, David Manley, and Ryan Wasserman (eds), *Metametaphysics: New Essays in the Foundations of Ontology*, Oxford: Oxford University Press, 384–423.

Sklar, Lawrence (2010) "I'd Love to Be a Naturalist – If Only I Knew What Naturalism Was," *Philosophy of Science* 77: 1121–37.

Sosa, Ernest (1994) "Philosophical Scepticism and Epistemic Circularity," *Proceedings of the Aristotelian Society, Supplementary Volume* 68: 263–90.

Stroud, Barry (1996) "The Charm of Naturalism," *Proceedings and Addresses of the American Philosophical Association* 70: 43–55.

van Fraassen, Bas (2002) *The Empirical Stance*, New Haven, CT: Yale University Press.

Vogel, Jonathan (2000) "Reliabilism Leveled," *Journal of Philosophy* 97: 602–23.

Wagner, Steven J. and Richard Warner (1993) "Introduction," in Steven J. Wagner and Richard Warner (eds), *Naturalism: A Critical Appraisal*, Notre Dame, IN: University of Notre Dame Press, 1–21.

Part I

NATURALISM: VARIETIES AND VIABILITY

1 What is naturalism?

TIMOTHY WILLIAMSON

In *The Philosophy of Philosophy*,[1] I defended a view of philosophy as much less different in aims and methods from other forms of intellectual inquiry than its self-images usually suggest. Some commentators treated this anti-exceptionalism about philosophy as a form of *naturalism*, and wondered why I did not characterize it explicitly as such. I will explain why not.

Many contemporary philosophers describe themselves as naturalists. They mean that they believe something like this: there is only the natural world, and the best way to find out about it is by the scientific method. So why do I resist being described as a naturalist? Not for any religious scruple: I am an atheist of the most straightforward kind. But to accept the naturalist slogan without looking beneath the slick packaging is an unscientific way to form one's beliefs about the world, so not something that even naturalists should recommend.

What, for a start, is the natural world? If we define it as the world of matter, or the world of atoms, we are left behind by modern physics, which characterizes the world in far more abstract terms. Anyway, the best current scientific theories will probably be superseded by future scientific developments in various respects. Naturalism is not intended to be hostage to the details of scientific progress. We might therefore define the natural world as whatever the scientific method eventually discovers. Thus naturalism becomes the belief that there is only whatever the scientific method eventually discovers, and (not surprisingly) the best way to find out about it is by the scientific method. That is no tautology. It is not self-evident that there cannot be things only discoverable by nonscientific means, or not discoverable at all.

Still, naturalism is less restrictive than one might think. For example, some of its hard-nosed advocates undertake to postulate a soul or a god, if doing so turns out to be part of the best explanation of our experience, for that would be an application of scientific method. Naturalism is not incompatible in principle with all forms of religion. In practice, however, most naturalists doubt that belief in souls or gods withstands scientific scrutiny.

What is meant by 'the scientific method'? Why assume that science only has one method? For naturalists, although natural sciences like physics and biology differ from each other in specific ways, at a sufficiently abstract level they all count as using a single general method. It involves formulating theoretical hypotheses and testing their predictions against systematic observation and controlled experiment. This is the hypothetico-deductive method.

One challenge to naturalism is to find a place for mathematics. Natural sciences rely on it, but should we count it a science in its own right? If we do, then the description of scientific method just given is wrong, for it does not fit the science of mathematics, which proves its results by pure reasoning, rather than the hypothetico-deductive method. Although a few naturalists, such as Quine, argue that the real evidence in favour of mathematics comes from its applications in the natural sciences, so indirectly from observation and experiment, that view does not fit the way the subject actually develops. When mathematicians assess a proposed new axiom, they look at its consequences within mathematics, not outside. On the other hand, if we do not count pure mathematics as science, we thereby exclude mathematical proof by itself from the scientific method, and so discredit naturalism. For naturalism privileges the scientific method over all others, and mathematics is one of the most spectacular success stories in the history of human knowledge.

Which other disciplines count as science? Logic? Linguistics? History? Literary theory? How should we decide? The dilemma for naturalists is this. If they are too inclusive in what they count as science, naturalism loses its bite. Naturalists typically criticize some traditional forms of philosophy as insufficiently scientific, because they ignore experimental tests. How can they maintain such objections unless they restrict scientific method to hypothetico-deductivism? But if they are too exclusive in what they count as science, naturalism loses its credibility, by imposing a method appropriate to natural science on areas where it is inappropriate. Unfortunately, rather than clarify the issue, many naturalists oscillate. When on the attack, they assume an exclusive understanding of science as hypothetico-deductive. When under attack themselves, they fall back on a more inclusive understanding of science that drastically waters down naturalism. Such manoeuvring makes naturalism an obscure article of faith. I don't call myself a naturalist because I don't want to be implicated in equivocal dogma. Dismissing an idea as 'inconsistent with naturalism' is little better than dismissing it as 'inconsistent with Christianity'.

Still, I sympathize with one motive behind naturalism, the aspiration to think in a scientific spirit. It's a vague phrase, but one might start to explain it by emphasizing values like curiosity, honesty, accuracy, precision, and rigour. What matters isn't paying lip-service to those qualities – that's easy – but actually exemplifying them in practice – the hard part. To speak of the scientific spirit is not to make the naive (and unscientific) claim that scientists' motives are always pure. They are human. Science doesn't depend on indifference to fame, professional advancement, money, or comparisons with rivals. Rather, truth is best pursued in social environments, intellectual communities, that minimize conflict between such baser motives and the scientific spirit, by rewarding work that embodies the scientific virtues. Such traditions exist, and not just in natural science.

The scientific spirit is as relevant in mathematics, history, philosophy, and elsewhere as in natural science. Where experimentation is the likeliest way to answer a question correctly, the scientific spirit calls for the experiments to be done; where other methods – mathematical proof, archival research, philosophical reasoning – are more relevant it calls for them instead. Although the methods of natural science could beneficially be applied more widely than they have been so far, the default assumption must be that the practitioners of a well-established discipline know what they are doing, and use the available methods most appropriate for answering its questions. Exceptions may result from a conservative tradition, or one that does not value the scientific spirit. Still, impatience with all methods except those of natural science is a poor basis on which to identify those exceptions.

Naturalism tries to condense the scientific spirit into a philosophical theory. But no theory can replace that spirit, for any theory can be applied in an unscientific spirit, as a polemical device to reinforce prejudice. Naturalism as dogma is one more enemy of the scientific spirit.

Philosophy should be done in a scientific spirit. Therefore we should not do it by invoking slogans about naturalism, or dismissing philosophical theories or methods on the basis of results in natural science whose relevance to them is unclear, or engaging in any of the other forms of lazy-mindedness that the word 'naturalism' has so striking a capacity to encourage.

Note

1 Timothy Williamson, *The Philosophy of Philosophy*, Oxford: Blackwell, 2007.

2   Why I am a naturalist
ALEX ROSENBERG

Naturalism is the philosophical theory that treats science as our most reliable source of knowledge and scientific method as the most effective route to knowledge. In his introductory essay, Timothy Williamson correctly reports that naturalism is popular in philosophy. In fact it is now a dominant approach in several areas of philosophy: ethics, epistemology, the philosophy of mind, philosophy of science and, most of all, in metaphysics, the study of the basic constituents of reality. Metaphysics is important: if it turns out that reality contains only the kinds of things that hard science recognizes, the implications will be grave for what we value in human experience.

Naturalism is itself a theory with a research agenda of unsolved problems. But naturalists' confidence that it can solve them shouldn't be mistaken for "dogmatism," nor can its successes be written off as "slick packaging," two terms Williamson used in his essay to describe why he rejects naturalism.

Before taking up Williamson's challenges to naturalism, it's worth identifying some of this success in applying science to the solution of philosophical problems, some of which even have pay-offs for science. Perhaps the most notable thing about naturalism is the way its philosophers have employed Darwin's theory of natural selection to tame purpose. In 1784 Kant wrote, "There will never be a Newton for the blade of grass." What he meant was that physical science could never explain anything with a purpose, whether it be human thought or a flower's bending toward the sun. That would have made everything special about living things – and especially us – safe from a purely scientific under-standing. It would have kept questions about humanity the preserve of religion, mythmaking and the humanities.

Only twenty years or so later the Newton of the blade of grass was born to the Darwin family in Shropshire, England. *On the Origin of Species* revealed how physical processes alone produce the illusion of design. Random variation and natural selection are the purely physical source of the beautiful means/ends economy of nature that fools us into seeking its designer. Naturalists have applied this insight to reveal the biological nature of human emotion, perception and cognition, language, moral value, social bonds and political institutions. Naturalistic philosophy has returned the favor, helping psychology, evolutionary anthropology and biology solve their problems by greater conceptual clarity about function, adaptation, Darwinian fitness and individual versus group selection.

While dealing with puzzles that vexed philosophy as far back as Plato, naturalism has also come to grips with the very challenges Williamson lays out: physics may be our best take on the nature of reality, but important parts of physics are not just "abstract," as he says. Quantum mechanics is more than abstract. It's weird. Since naturalistic philosophers take science seriously as the best description of reality, they accept the responsibility of making sense of quantum physics. Until we succeed, naturalists won't be any more satisfied than Williamson that we know what the natural world is. But 400 years of scientific success in prediction, control and technology shows that physics has made a good start. We should be confident that it will do better than any other approach at getting things right.

Naturalists recognize that science is fallible. Its self-correction, its continual increase in breadth and accuracy, give naturalists confidence in the resources they borrow from physics, chemistry and biology. The second law of thermodynamics, the periodic table and the principles of natural selection are unlikely to be threatened by future science. Philosophy can therefore rely on them to answer many of its questions without fear of being overtaken by events.

Williamson writes, "It is not self-evident that there cannot be things only discoverable by non-scientific means, or not discoverable at all" (this volume, p. 29). Naturalism doesn't claim self-evidence for much of anything, and certainly not for its denial that there are non-scientific routes to knowledge. This denial is inductive: nothing that revelation, inspiration or other non-scientific means ever claimed to discover has yet to withstand the test of knowledge that scientific findings attain. What are those tests of knowledge? They are the experimental/observational methods all the natural sciences share, the social sciences increasingly adopt, and that naturalists devote themselves to making explicit. Are there facts about reality "not discoverable" by scientific means "at all"? About the only way to go about answering this question is to use the methods of science.

As Williamson notes, naturalism's greatest challenge "is to find a place for mathematics" (p. 30). The way it faces the challenge reveals just how undogmatic naturalism really is. It would be easy to turn one's back on the problems mathematics presents. There is the metaphysical problem of whether there are numbers in addition to our mental concepts of numbers, which like the numerals, "2," "II" or " $=$ " (the Chinese for the number two), should not be mistaken for the number two that they seem to refer to. There are the epistemic problems of how if they are abstract objects, we can have any knowledge about numbers, let alone the certainty about them that math reveals. One excuse naturalists might give to turn our backs on these problems is that mathematicians and scientists don't care much about them. Another is that no one has ever provided a satisfactory answer to these questions since they were raised by Plato. So, no other philosophy can be preferred to naturalism on this basis. In fact, as all philosophers recognize, naturalism has invested a huge amount of ingenuity, even genius, seeking scientifically responsible answers to these hardest of questions. Not with much success as yet by our own standards, one must admit. But that is the nature of science. Naturalists acknowledge that mathematics presents them (and all philosophers) with serious unfinished business. That is why Williamson is wrong to accuse them of "manoeuvring" or treating their theory as "an obscure article of faith." Not yet having the solution to all its problems doesn't make naturalism into an "equivocal dogma" (p. 30).

Naturalism takes the problem of mathematics seriously, since science cannot do without it. So naturalism can't either. But what about other items on Williamson's list of disciplines he thinks it would be hard to count as science: logic, linguistics, history, literary theory? Naturalists won't have any trouble counting logic and linguistics as knowledge, though logic raises all the same problems for epistemology and metaphysics that mathematics does. History is a harder problem. As a chronicle of the human past, history is no more problematical for naturalism than natural history. But the explanations it provides can't satisfy the tests the natural sciences impose on their own explanations. This raises another problem on naturalism's research agenda: in some ways it's a problem like the one mathematics raises for naturalism, how to certify historical explanations as real knowledge without adopting a double standard for what counts as knowledge. That would "water down" naturalism into the equivocal dogma Williamson charges it with being. When it comes to history, naturalists have an option we won't help ourselves to in trying to figure out mathematical knowledge. We might well come to see that historical explanations are not contributions to knowledge at all. Instead they should be treated as works of literature. Historical narratives have never gained the predictive power of scientific explanations, but the best of them have stirred our emotions, shaped our values, and affected human affairs decisively. (Think of *The Gulag Archipelago*.) They could do all of these things, and be prized for them, without however ever providing predictively useful knowledge. The question of whether history should count as science remains an open one for naturalism. (More on this in my rejoinder to Williamson's reply to this essay; Chapter 4, this volume.)

What about literary theory? Can science, and naturalistic philosophy, do without it? This is a different question from whether people, as consumers of literature, can do without it. The question naturalism faces is whether a discipline like literary theory provides real knowledge. (Naturalism can't dodge these questions because it won't uncritically buy into Williamson's "default assumption … that the practitioners of a well-established discipline know what they are doing, and use the available methods most appropriate for answering its questions"; p. 31.) If semiotics, existentialism, hermeneutics, formalism, structuralism, post-structuralism, deconstruction and postmodernism transparently flout science's standards of objectivity, or if they seek arbitrarily to limit the reach of scientific methods, then naturalism can't take them seriously as knowledge. That doesn't mean anyone should stop doing literary criticism, any more than they should be foregoing fiction. Naturalism treats both as fun, but neither as knowledge.

What naturalists really fear is not becoming dogmatic or giving up the scientific spirit. It's the threat that the science will end up showing that much of what we cherish as meaningful in human life is illusory.

3 The unclarity of naturalism

TIMOTHY WILLIAMSON

In response to my question 'What is naturalism?', Alex Rosenberg defines it as 'the philosophical theory that treats science as our most reliable source of knowledge and scientific method as the most effective route to knowledge' (p. 32). In 'Why I Am a Naturalist' (Chapter 2, this volume), he nicely exemplifies one of my main complaints, by leaving it unclear what he means by 'science' or 'scientific method', even though it is crucial for what he is committing himself to as a 'naturalist'. Still, there are clues. He describes 'the test of knowledge that scientific findings attain' as 'experimental/observational methods', which suggests that theorems of mathematics would not count as scientific findings. The impression is confirmed by Rosenberg's phrase 'mathematicians and scientists', as though he doesn't see mathematicians as scientists (p. 34). That's bad news for his naturalism, for mathematical proof is just as effective a route to knowledge as experimental/observational methods. Of course, since the natural sciences depend on mathematics, Rosenberg is desperate to find a place for it – but admits that he doesn't know how.

In just the way I noted, Rosenberg's defence of naturalism trades on ambiguities between boring truths and obvious falsehoods. Rightly noting the successes of physics, he says 'We should be confident that it will do better than any other approach at getting things right' (p. 33). Which things? If he means questions of physics, what reasonable person denies that physics will do better than any other approach at answering those questions? But if he means all questions, why on earth should we be confident that physics will do better than history at getting right what happened at Gettysburg?

I raised history and literary theory as test cases. According to Rosenberg, naturalism treats literary criticism as fun, but not as knowledge. Does he really not know whether Mr Collins is the hero of *Pride and Prejudice*? Every normal reader has that sort of elementary literary critical knowledge. Those who know far more about the historical context in which literary works were produced, read them many times with unusual attention, carefully analyse their structure, and so on, naturally have far more knowledge of those works than casual readers do, whatever the excesses of postmodernism.

As for history, Rosenberg leaves the question of whether it should count as science open. He doubts that it can provide 'predictively useful knowledge' (p. 34). Scientific predictions about complex systems with initial conditions of which we have only approximate knowledge are probabilistic. Historical knowledge enables us to make probabilistic predictions too: for example, that if a US president publicly describes his policy on the Middle East as a 'crusade', it is more likely to inflame than to calm the situation. Does Rosenberg really think that historical knowledge of the past records of politicians is of zero value in making probabilistic predictions about their future behaviour? It isn't even clear how natural science could manage without historical knowledge, as Collingwood long ago pointed out, since knowledge of the results of past experiments and observations is itself historical.

Rosenberg apparently expects it to turn out that 'reality contains only the kinds of things that hard science recognizes' (p. 32). By 'hard science' he presumably means something like physics. He doesn't explain how that could turn out. How could physics show that reality contains only the kinds of things that physics recognizes? It sounds embarrassingly like physics acting as judge and jury in its own case. That physics does not show that there is such a thing as a debt crisis does not mean that physics shows that there is no such thing as a debt crisis: physics simply does not address the question. That is no criticism of physics; it has other work to do. For it to turn out that reality contains only the kinds of things that hard science recognizes, where they exclude things like debt crises, it would have to turn out that a radically reductionist metaphysical theory is true. That in turn would require industrial-scale argument at a characteristically philosophical level of reasoning. Does Rosenberg count philosophy as hard science?

We can formulate the underlying worry as a sharp argument against the extreme naturalist claim that all truths are discoverable by hard science. If it is true that all truths are discoverable by hard science, then it is discoverable by hard science that all truths are discoverable by hard science. But it is not discoverable by hard science that all truths are discoverable by hard science. Therefore the extreme naturalist claim is not true. 'Are all truths discoverable by hard science?' is not itself a question of hard science. Truth is a logical or semantic property, discoverability an epistemic one, and hard science a social process. Although truths discoverable by hard science may be relevant to whether *all* truths are discoverable by hard science, by themselves they do not answer the question, since they are framed in the wrong terms – for example, those of physics.

Such problems pose far less threat to more moderate forms of naturalism, based on a broader conception of science that includes mathematics, history, much of philosophy, and the sensible parts of literary criticism, as well as the natural and social sciences. But we should not take for granted that reality contains only the kinds of things that science even in the broad sense recognizes. My caution comes not from any sympathy for mysterious kinds of cognition alien to science in the broad sense, but simply from the difficulty of establishing in any remotely scientific way that reality contains only the kinds of thing that we are capable of recognizing at all. In any case, Rosenberg does not rest content with some moderate form of naturalism. He goes for something far more extreme, in the process lapsing into hard scientism.

Rosenberg concludes: 'What naturalists really fear is not becoming dogmatic or giving up the scientific spirit. It's the threat that the science will end up showing that much of what we cherish as meaningful in human life is illusory' (p. 35). But what people really fear is not always what most endangers them. Those most confident of being undogmatic and possessing the scientific spirit may thereby become all the less able to detect dogmatism and failures of the scientific spirit in themselves. If one tries to assess naturalism in a scientific spirit, one will want to get more precise than most self-labelled naturalists (and anti-naturalists) do about what hypothesis is under test. Nor will one dogmatically assume that, once a clear hypothesis is on the table, testing it will be just a matter for hard science. The evidence so far suggests otherwise.

4 Can naturalism save the humanities?

ALEX ROSENBERG

Timothy Williamson challenges not just the adequacy but the very coherence of naturalism's claim – that science is our most reliable source of knowledge (Chapter 3, this volume). He is confident that it cannot meet these challenges: First the only resource naturalism can consistently appeal to is science itself, which would be circular. Second, Williamson claims naturalism cannot do justice to the kind of understanding conferred by history, literature, and the "sensible parts of literary criticism" (p. 38).

Williamson writes: "If it is true that all truths are discoverable by hard science, then [that] is discoverable by hard science. But it is not discoverable by hard science that all truths are discoverable by hard science" (p. 37) QED. This clever argument ignores the inductive character of naturalism's confidence. Science proceeds by induction, not demonstration, and naturalism is a scientific theory. It has no use for demonstration in a "first philosophy," prior to and more secure than inductive knowledge.

The "industrial-scale" inductive argument for naturalism is the track record of science. Science began with everyday experience, recursively reconstructing and replacing common beliefs that turned out to be wrong by standards of everyday experience. The result, rendered unrecognizable to common belief after 400 years or so, is contemporary physics, chemistry and biology (plus the theorems of mathematics). Why date science only to the 1600s? After all, mathematics dates back to Euclid, and Archimedes made empirical discoveries in the third century BC. But 1638 was when Galileo first showed that a little thought is all we need to undermine the mistaken belief that neither Archimedes nor Aristotle had seen through, but which stood in the way of science.

Galileo offered a thought experiment that showed, contrary to common beliefs, that objects can move without any forces pushing them along at all. It sounds trivial and yet this was the breakthrough that made physics and the rest of modern science possible. Galileo's reasoning was undeniable: roll a ball down an incline, and it speeds up; roll it up an incline, it slows down. So, if you roll it onto a frictionless horizontal surface, it will have to go forever. Stands to reason, by common sense. But that simple bit of reasoning destroyed the Aristotelian world picture and ushered in science. Four hundred years of everyday experience continually remodeling itself has produced a description of reality radically at variance with common sense; that reality includes quantum mechanics, general relativity and Darwinian natural selection.

Science should be confident that its powers to know are not limited owing to its track record of starting at a point no one can question, and going on successfully to unify an incredibly diverse range of phenomena under one explanatory "roof." That success has had a never-ending pay-off in technological application. It's possible that there are limits to science. But it would be foolish to bet there are. Maybe science will even solve the problems that mathematical knowledge poses.

The ever-mounting evidence for science as our best way to acquire knowledge raises Williamson's second challenge. Four hundred years ago, when science got started, Descartes, Leibniz and other philosophers almost immediately realized that science would be hard to reconcile with the kind of claims made in history, the human "sciences," the humanities, theology and in our own interior psychological narrations. These claims trade on a universal, culturally inherited "understanding" that interprets human affairs via narratives that "make sense" of what we do. Interpretation is supposed to uncover the significance of actual (and fictional) events, usually in motivations that participants themselves recognize, and sometimes by uncovering meanings the participants don't themselves appreciate. History has to do more than just "get it right about what happened at Gettysburg" (p. 36) – the task Williamson sets. It has to make sense of what happened: "Whatever could Lee have been thinking when he ordered Longstreet to have Pickett's division charge the Union center?"

Natural science deals only in momentum and force, elements and compounds, genes and fitness, neurotransmitters and synapses. These things are not enough to give us what introspection tells us we have: meaningful thoughts about ourselves and about the world that together bring about our actions. Non-naturalistic philosophers since Descartes have agreed with introspection, and they have provided fiendishly clever arguments for the same conclusion. These arguments ruled science out of the business of explaining our actions because, they argued, it cannot take thoughts seriously as causes of anything.

Descartes and Leibniz claimed to show that thinking about one's self, or for that matter anything else, is something no purely physical thing, no matter how big or how complicated, can do. What is most obvious to introspection is that thoughts are about something. When I think of

Paris, there is a place 3,000 miles away from my brain, and my thoughts are about it. The trouble is, as Leibniz famously argued, no chunk of physical matter could be "about" anything. The size, shape, composition or any other physical fact about neural circuits is not enough to make them be about anything. Therefore, thought can't be physical, and that goes for emotions and sensations too. Some influential opponents of naturalism still argue that way.

We naturalists have to figure out what is wrong with this and similar arguments. Or we will have to conclude that interpretation, the stock-in-trade of history and the humanities, does not after all really explain much of anything at all. What science can't accept is some "off-limits" sign at the boundary of the interpretative disciplines.

It's not enough merely to show that there is no logical conflict between the hard sciences and the interpretive disciplines. The reason is simple: natural science requires unification. It cannot accept that the right explanations of human activities must be logically incompatible with the rest of science, or even just independent of it. If science were prepared to settle for less than unification, the difficulty of reconciling quantum mechanics and general relativity wouldn't be the biggest problem in physics. For the same reason biology would never fully accept the gene as real until it was shown to have a physical structure – DNA – that could do the work geneticists assigned to the gene. For exactly the same reason science can't accept interpretation as providing knowledge of human affairs if it can't at least in principle be absorbed into, perhaps even reduced to, neuroscience.

Scientists have shown how physical processes bring about chemical processes, and through them biological ones. Nowadays neuroscientists are learning how chemical and biological events bring about psychological processes. That makes it a good bet that science will show, at least in principle, how all the rest of human affairs are also complex physical processes. Showing this won't make clouds and clocks, cabinets and kings, or for that matter "social constructions" like "debt crises" (Williamson's example) disappear. It will explain them. But if science ends up explaining and predicting human affairs in ways that bypass interpretative understanding, the consequences for history and the humanities will be grave.

Few people are prepared to treat history, (auto-)biography and the human sciences as so much folklore. On the other hand, betting against science has long proved to be a mug's game. This is where naturalism comes in. It's why defenders of human interpretive understanding should in fact hope naturalism succeeds, instead of denying its chances of doing so.

Naturalism's agenda is to show how interpretative understanding could really turn out to be causal explanation of the sort hard science seeks. These explanations may have to be "reductionistic." If they succeed we won't have to give up historical narratives for scientific theories when it comes to figuring out our past, nor substitute causation for interpretation when it comes to plotting our future.

The narratives of history, the humanities and literature provide us with the feeling that we understand what they seek to explain. At their best they also trigger emotions we prize as marks of great art. But that feeling of understanding, that psychological relief from the itch of curiosity, is not the same thing as knowledge. It is not even a mark of it, as children's bedtime stories reveal. If the humanities and history provide only feeling and fun, in the provocative terms of my original article, that will not be enough to defend their claims to knowledge. The humanities, history, literature need naturalism to show how interpretation is grounded in science.

The real threat to interpretative understanding as a source of knowledge arises if naturalism's reconciling project fails. For in a forced choice between science and the humanities, we all know which recipe for knowledge will win.

5 On naturalism in the Quinean tradition

JEFFREY W. ROLAND

I take as uncontroversial that philosophical naturalism occupies a position of prominence in contemporary philosophy and that the position of prominence occupied by naturalism is occupied by naturalism in the tradition of Quine, i.e. naturalism rooted in Quine (1953) and developed in a long list of publications, chief among them Quine (1960, 1969a, 1969b). Despite this lack of controversy, there is disagreement both (i) among views all of which have a legitimate claim to being considered naturalistic in the tradition of Quine and (ii) among philosophers concerning what it takes for a view to qualify as naturalistic in the Quinean tradition.[1]

In this chapter, I identify principles commitment to some versions of which is arguably essential to being legitimately considered naturalistic in the Quinean tradition and then discuss divergent versions of Quinean naturalism against the backdrop of these principles. The former addresses (ii) while the latter addresses (i), though admittedly neither issue is fully resolved here. In Section 1, I draw a number of candidate essential principles of naturalism from Quine's work. I then (Section 2) identify an independent subset of these principles which is reasonably taken to form the core of Quine's naturalism. I follow this with a discussion of two major fault lines that have formed in the development of Quinean naturalism from its beginnings in Quine's naturalism (Sections 3 and 4). I finish (Section 5) with brief concluding remarks.

I The principles

1.1 Two holisms and inclusion

Quine advanced naturalism in response to perceived attempts by logical empiricists, most notably Carnap, to give science a priori foundations. Carnap's efforts were modeled on *Principia Mathematica*, with which he was much impressed. Quine notes the parallel between *Principia* and the *Aufbau*:

> Just as mathematics is to be reduced to logic, or logic and set theory, so natural knowledge is to be based somehow on sense experience. This means explaining the notion of body in sensory terms ... . And it means justifying our knowledge of truths of nature in sensory terms.
>
> (Quine 1969a, 71)

And shortly thereafter: "To account for the external world as a logical construct of sense data – such, in Russell's terms, was the program. It was Carnap, in his *Der logische Aufbau der Welt* of 1928, who came nearest to executing it" (Quine 1969a, 74).

According to this received view of Carnap's project, empirical justification has a foundational structure. We're immediately justified in holding *sense-data beliefs*, beliefs the content of which reports an immediate sensation,[2] and we're justified in holding other beliefs concerning matters of fact since statements capturing the contents of such beliefs can be reduced via translation to statements involving only the contents of immediately justified sense-data beliefs plus the machinery of logic and mathematics.

Quine famously takes aim at this type of reductionism in (1953), where he associates reduction to sense data with the verification theory of meaning and offers a now well-known response: "My countersuggestion ... is that our statements about the external world face the tribunal of experience not individually but only as a corporate body" (Quine 1953, 41).[3] Why? Because

> in a scientific theory even a whole sentence is ordinarily too short a text to serve as an independent vehicle of empirical meaning. It will not have its separable bundle of observable or testable consequences. A reasonably inclusive body of scientific theory, taken as a whole, will indeed have such consequences.
>
> (Quine 1981b, 70)

According to Quine, reductionism is correct only if individual statements have observable consequences. They generally don't, so reductionism is incorrect. Quine here relies on his view of empirical content, which in turn relies on his view of what it takes for a collection of statements to achieve *critical semantic mass*.[4]

A collection of statements reaches critical semantic mass when it (deductively) implies some observation categorical, a conditional saying that when such-and-such observable conditions obtain then so does observable phenomenon such-and-so.[5] The observation categoricals implied by a collection of statements having critical semantic mass constitute the *empirical content* of that collection. In other words, the empirical content of a collection of statements is the class consisting of its observational consequences. Thus, Quine endorses

> *Principle 1 (semantic holism)* Typically only sufficiently rich collections of statements, as opposed to individual statements, have empirical content.[6]

Since on Quine's view only collections of statements that have empirical content admit of confirmation (or disconfirmation), this principle underwrites[7]

> *Principle 2 (moderate confirmation holism)* Confirmation (or disconfirmation) accrues to a body of statements having empirical content as a whole.

The idea behind moderate confirmation holism is that in order for a body of statements to be linked to observation in such way that experience can bolster or undermine our confidence in it, the body must have observational consequences (achieved critical semantic mass). But since testing of such consequences is not fine-grained enough to confirmationally distinguish between statements in the body, the body is confirmed (or disconfirmed) in its entirety. According to Quine, it's a pragmatic matter which state-ment(s) we reject in response to recalcitrant observation. This is a mod-erate holism because, in contrast to a natural reading of Quine's early writings on holism, this view doesn't require a body of statements to encompass all of science in order to have empirical content.[8]

Hard on the heels of Quine's rejection of Carnap's reductionism and embrace of moderate confirmation holism comes a series of metaphors used to illustrate the resulting structure of belief systems.[9]

> The totality of our so-called knowledge or beliefs, from the most casual matters of geography and history to the profoundest laws of atomic physics or even pure mathematics and logic, is *a man-made fabric which impinges on experience only along the edges.* Or, to change the figure, total science is like a *field of force whose boundary conditions are experience.* A conflict with experience at the periphery occasions readjustments in the interior of the field. Truth values have to be redistributed over some of our statements. ... No particular experiences are linked with any particular statements in the interior of the field, except indirectly through considerations of equilibrium affecting the field as a whole.[10]
>
> (Quine 1953, 42–43, emphasis added)

A man-made fabric, a field of force, and finally, a metaphor which is not included in this passage but which is most often associated with this picture of belief systems: a web of belief.

This view of belief systems radically departs from the foundationalist epistemology embraced by the received Carnap. One might think of a traditional foundationalist system of beliefs as comprising both mundane and scientific beliefs along with a structure induced on those beliefs by certain rules of transformation and (deductive) inference. In the *Aufbau*, these rules of transformation are *construction rules*, and they have the form of definitions.[11] Such rules appear devoid of empirical content. Moreover, Carnap argues for the claim that *"science deals only with the description of structural properties of objects"* (Carnap 1928/1967, §10, original emphasis), and structural properties are purely formal, i.e topic neutral.[12] What we have on this view, then, are structure-inducing rules of derivation – definitional and logico-mathematico – which are topic neutral and lacking empirical content. Furthermore, since they lack empirical content these rules are apparently irrevisable in light of experience, no empirical data could rationally lead us to abandon them. We can think of such rules as riding in the background, inducing an arrangement on the system of empirical beliefs without being among those beliefs – similar to a formal axiomatic theory in mathematics, where the axioms are given explicitly with the understanding that a certain (perhaps specified) logic is in use even though its rules and axioms are not stated as part of the theory. When Quine introduces the web of belief, he rejects the claim that the organizing rules associated with a system of beliefs are topic neutral and devoid of empirical content, bringing them out of the background and into the system of beliefs itself. Hence, we have

> *Principle 3 (inclusion)* Any system of beliefs that has empirical content includes beliefs whose content reflects the organizational rules which give structure to the system.

1.2 Diffusion and methodological monism

The next two principles of naturalism can be found in the following remark of Quine's on his so-called fourth milestone of empiricism, *methodological monism*:

> Holism blurs the supposed contrast between the synthetic sentence, with its empirical content, and the analytic sentence, with its null content. The organizing role that was supposedly the role of analytic sentences is now seen as shared by sentences generally, and the empirical content that was supposedly peculiar to synthetic sentences is now seen as diffused through the [belief] system.
>
> (Quine 1981b, 71–72)

The first principle is reasonably close to the surface:

> *Principle 4 (diffusion)* Any statement that ineliminably figures in a body of statements achieving critical semantic mass shares in the empirical content of that body, and hence also in any confirmation (disconfirmation) that accrues to the body.

The idea here is that the empirical content a body of statements gains by achieving critical semantic mass spreads among the statements of the body responsible for that achievement; it's not reserved for any special class of statements. Drawing out the second principle requires more work, since as is often the case with Quine the brevity of the remark somewhat masks the point. It helps to bear in mind the dialectic between Quine and the logical empiricists, Carnap in particular.

Logical empiricists advanced a foundationalist picture of belief systems according to which beliefs are related (with respect to justification) unidirectionally and analytically: beliefs "higher up" depend on beliefs below them, and the dependence is analytic. Analytic relations are a priori accessible. So for foundationalists there are two types of method in play in one's doxastic system: empirical (for obtaining particular beliefs about the world) and a priori (for accessing the evidential structure of the system constituted in large part by those beliefs). Quine rejects this duality of methods. Inclusion brings the dependence relations (or corresponding beliefs) into the web of belief and the principle of diffusion undermines their claim to irrevisability and so also their (alleged) a priori status (provided one thinks that a priori beliefs are empirically irrevisable, as Quine does).[13]

In denying the duality of methods, Quine denies that there are methods of theorizing distinctive of epistemology, and of philosophy more generally. He advocates one type of methodology, namely, empirical methodology. So we have

Principle 5 (methodological monism) Scientific theorizing is entirely empirical.[14]

Steeped as contemporary philosophy is in naturalism, this principle might strike many as an empty truism. However, given Quine's broad construal of science and the dominance of foundationalism when Quine advanced his position it's anything but a truism.

To Quine's thinking, "nearly any body of knowledge that is sufficiently organized to exhibit appropriate evidential relationships among its constituent claims has at least some call to be seen as scientific. What makes for science is system, whatever the subject" (Quine and Ullian 1978, 3). So for Quine just about any systematization of beliefs counts as part of science, just about any belief that is integrated into a web of belief counts as scientific. Thus, despite appearances methodological monism applies quite broadly. Importantly, it applies to philosophy, mathematics, and logic.

1.3 *Continuity, anti-apriority, and anti-foundationalism*

Consider the following passage:

> (I) [M]y position is a naturalistic one; I see philosophy not as an *a priori* propaedeutic or groundwork for science, but as continuous with science. I see philosophy and science as in the same boat – a boat which, to revert to Neurath's figure as I so often do, we can rebuild only at sea while staying afloat in it.
>
> (Quine 1969b, 126–27)[15]

We can straightforwardly see here one of the best known slogans of naturalism: Philosophy is continuous with science.

It's reasonable to interpret this slogan as asserting that philosophy and science are under the same kinds of pressure vis-à-vis experience and confirmation. Science and philosophy may differ in their deliverances, but both involve systematic theorizing and so the results of each have a home in our web of belief. So they both must meet the "tribunal of experience." The importance of this lies in its implicit rejection of the traditional understanding of philosophical methods as a priori and, hence, epistemically prior to (in the sense of having epistemic priority over) scientific methods. This also allows us to reject the idea that we must solve certain philosophical problems, in particular that we must have a well-worked out epistemology, before we can be reasonably secure in our scientific knowledge. Given this, we have

> *Principle 6 (continuity)* Philosophy is continuous with science, in the sense that both are subject to experiential checks.

For Quine, who holds that irrevisability is necessary for apriority, and that confirmation comes via verification of empirical content, a corollary of continuity explicit in (I) above is

> *Principle 7 (anti-apriorism)* There are no a priori scientific (including logical, mathematical, and philosophical) statements or beliefs.

According to the principle of continuity, philosophy is subject to the same sorts of experiential checks as science is. Being subject to such checks is taken by Quine to show that no scientific statement is irrevisable. The same reasoning shows that no philosophical statement is irrevisable. So all philosophical statements are revisable, and hence (by Quine's lights) no philosophical statement is a priori. This principle also has a corollary.

Quine opposes naturalism to foundationalism. He does not accept any priority of philosophy over science. This is clear in passages such as:

> Unlike the old epistemologists [foundationalists], we [naturalists] seek no firmer basis for science than science itself; so we are free to use the very fruits of science in investigating its roots.
>
> (Quine 1995, 16)

Judging by this contrast between naturalists and foundationalists, it appears that Quine's general target in his remarks about "prior" and "first" philosophy is foundationalism. But since Quine (e.g. in (I) above) appears to understand foundationalism in such a way that it depends on there being a priori philosophy,[16] for naturalists the principle of anti-apriorism is sufficient to undermine foundationalism. So we have

> *Principle 8 (anti-foundationalism)* Justification does not have a foundationalist structure, i.e. there are no a priori or a priori specifiable beliefs in which the rest of our beliefs are deductively grounded.

1.4 Inheritance

So far we have principles (a) collapsing the distinction between the empirical parts of a belief system and the deductive structure of the system, (b) asserting the empirical nature of all systematic theorizing and the continuity of philosophy with science, and (c) denying a priori philosophical statements and foundationalism. Now consider:

> (II) The naturalistic philosopher begins his reasoning within the inherited world theory as a going concern. He tentatively believes all of it, but believes also that some unidentified portions are wrong. He tries to improve, clarify, and understand the system from within. He is the busy sailor adrift on Neurath's boat.
>
> (Quine 1981b, 72)

In this passage, Quine illuminates a bit the metaphor of Neurath's sailor of which he is so fond. He gives one of the clearer indications of his understanding of that metaphor in (1950):

> We can change [the conceptual scheme with which we grew up] bit by bit,
> plank by plank, though meanwhile there is nothing to carry us along but
> the evolving conceptual scheme itself. The philosopher's task was well
> compared by Neurath to that of a mariner who must rebuild his ship on the
> open sea.
>
> (78–79)

So the boat is our conceptual scheme, codified in and taken as virtually
identical to our best scientific theory of the world.[17] The idea is that we
must deploy our theory to revise our theory; we cannot change our conceptual scheme without at the same time utilizing its resources. There is
no theory-neutral point of view from which to examine and revise our
theory, no port to put into while we make repairs to the ship. Passage (II)
makes it plain that we have *never* been in port – the naturalist "*begins* his
reasoning within the inherited world theory." We start our voyage
already at sea. This gives us

> *Principle 9 (inheritance)* Theorizing is theory dependent. There is no
> theory-neutral vantage point from which a theory can be assessed or revised.
> We begin theorizing in the middle of an ongoing process of theorizing,
> taking from our intellectual predecessors and giving to our intellectual
> heirs.

This principle codifies the *in medias res* character of Quinean naturalism.

1.5 *Two types of deference to science and anti-supranaturalism*

Naturalism is often loosely characterized as having a science-based
worldview: what there is is what our best science says that there is and
what we know about what there is we know by the methods of our best
science. It's not too hard to locate these sentiments in Quine's work. For
example, consider:

> What reality is like is the business of scientists, in the broadest sense,
> painstakingly to surmise; and what there is, what is real, is part of that
> question. The question how we know what there is is simply part of the
> question ... of the evidence for truth about the world. The last arbiter is
> so-called scientific method, however amorphous.
>
> (Quine 1960, 22–23)

> Naturalism looks only to natural science, however fallible, for an account of
> what there is and what what there is does.
>
> (Quine 1992, 9)

Two types of deference to science can be identified in these quotations. On one hand, we have the position that science constrains the metaphysics that philosophy may endorse. If an entity[18] is not recognized as one of or cannot be reduced to – in some sense of 'reduced', including but not limited to supervenience – entities countenanced by science, then it cannot legitimately be taken to exist, and so cannot legitimately be employed in philosophical theorizing.[19] The upshot is that the metaphysics countenanced by philosophy cannot outstrip that countenanced by science. Thus, we get a complete picture of metaphysics as a whole that is ultimately emergent from and grounded in our best science. In this case, the *findings* of science are doing the work. The furniture of the world and its arrangement are the stuff of scientific propositions, i.e. scientific findings. So we have

> *Principle 10 (deference to science_{findings})* Philosophy should defer to science, in that the theories it advances should be consonant with those of the sciences. In cases of conflict between philosophical and scientific theories, the latter prima facie trumps the former.[20]

On the other hand, there is more to science than its findings. In particular, there are the methods used to obtain those findings. Precisely what the methods of science are isn't as clear or determinate as we might like, but nonetheless we see Quine invoking those methods in the above quotations – explicitly in the first and implicitly in the second.[21] But our present inability to completely characterize (or even specify) the methods of science is beside the point to naturalism. Naturalism recommends that we defer to the methods of science because those methods, *whatever they actually are*, are by all accounts successful: contemporary science has proven an excellent explanatory and predictive instrument, measured in terms of our ability to intervene in the world to induce desirable events and prevent undesirable ones. The apparent success science has enjoyed over time and the conviction that emulating the methods employed by science will result in a similar level of success in prima facie non-scientific domains, philosophy, in particular, gives rise to a commitment to the methods of science. This commitment is codified in

> *Principle 11 (deference to science_{methods})* Philosophy should defer to science, in that the methods it employs should be or be analogous to those of the sciences.[22]

The last principle of Quinean naturalism falls out of the above quotations plus the recognition that the methods and findings of science are restricted to natural entities (not to be identified with physical entities).

It is a principle of denying what goes beyond the natural, i.e. the supranatural.

> *Principle 12 (anti-supranaturalism)* Supranatural entities and faculties should be eschewed by philosophical theories.

Such a principle raises the question of distinguishing supranatural entities from natural entities; we have at least a serviceable answer to this question. Supernatural entities, deities, say, in the Judeo-Christian-Islamic tradition or the Hindu pantheon, are supranatural. So are Cartesian minds – non-corporeal substances the existence of which doesn't depend on material substance – and Platonic forms. On some conceptions of mathematical ontology, conceptions according to which the subject matter of mathematics consists of acausal, eternal, necessarily existing entities, much (perhaps all) of the stock-in-trade of mathematics (numbers, functions, sets, etc.) are supranatural. What makes these sorts of entities supranatural is that science, on Quine's view, is the arbiter on matters of naturalness. The operative intuition is that natural entities are dependent on or otherwise governed by the causal network. Since science is charged with telling us about this network, anything that transcends science also transcends the causal network and hence goes beyond the natural, i.e. is supranatural.[23]

2 Independence of the principles

In the previous section we identified twelve principles deployed by Quine in his naturalism. By considering entailments between principles, this list can be reduced to seven: deference to science$_{findings}$ yields anti-supranaturalism; and methodological monism yields continuity, anti-apriorism, anti-foundationalism, and deference to science$_{methods}$ – leaving (1) semantic holism, (2) moderate confirmation holism, (3) inclusion, (4) diffusion, (5) methodological monism, (6) inheritance, and (7) deference to science$_{findings}$.[24] (Due to space constraints, I leave it to the interested reader to work out the details.) These *surviving principles* form the core of Quine's naturalism. In the remainder of the chapter, I briefly explore what I take to be the most significant points of disagreement between different versions of Quinean naturalism. There seem to me to be two major fault lines: one focused on apriority, and the other on causation.[25]

3 Fault line: apriority

Many self-identified Quinean naturalists subscribe to anti-apriorism, some going so far as to suggest that rejecting apriority is constitutive of Quinean naturalism. For instance: Richard Boyd holds that the "epistemology, semantics, and metaphysics of scientific (and everyday) inquiry are matters of *a posteriori* empirical inquiry continuous with the (other) sciences, just as Quine suggested" (Boyd 2010, 231); Philip Kitcher includes among the commitments of his (Quinean) naturalism the thesis that "[v]irtually nothing is knowable a priori, and, in particular, no epistemological principle is knowable a priori" (Kitcher 1992, 76); Penelope Maddy holds that "naturalism ... doom[s] the time-honoured notion of a priori knowledge" (Maddy 2000, 114); and Michael Devitt identifies naturalism with the view that "there is only one way of knowing, the empirical way that is the basis of science (whatever that may be)" and concluding from this, "I reject *a priori* knowledge" (Devitt 1996, 2). Other Quinean naturalists reject anti-apriorism. For example, Louise Antony (2004) and C.S. Jenkins (2008) both attempt to reconcile naturalism and apriority. Some philosophers who are either not clearly Quinean naturalists, such as Alvin Goldman (1999), or not clearly naturalists at all, such as Georges Rey (1998), similarly attempt to reconcile naturalism and apriority.[26]

The major stake in this largely in-house disagreement is the status of logico-mathematical statements (beliefs). Anti-apriorism has it that logico-mathematical statements (beliefs) are not a priori. Just this rejection of the apriority of logic and mathematics is one of the most striking features of Quine's naturalism, as it flies in the face of traditional thinking on the nature of logic and mathematics. Jenkins and Rey are explicitly motivated by a desire to preserve the apriority of logic and mathematics.[27] I share this desire. Here's a (very) brief sketch of how it might be satisfied.

Quine's conception of epistemology as the project of explaining "the flow of evidence from the triggering of the senses to the pronouncements of science" (Quine 1990, 41), of answering "the question how we human animals can have managed to arrive at science from such limited information [as the irritations of our surfaces]" (Quine 1981b, 72), is well known. Likewise his view that this is a project to be pursued within science itself. This is in some sense the essence of Quine's naturalized epistemology. Boyd has advanced a slogan to capture this essence – "the epistemology of empirical science is an empirical science" (1990, 366) – and building on Goodman (1955) and Quine (1969b) he has argued for this at length on the basis that theory-dependent projectibility judgments are both an integral part of scientific methods and critical to the reliability of those methods.[28] The crucial point in these arguments is that, since projectibility judgments are judgments of theoretical plausibility and theories in light of which such plausibility judgments are made are empirical, projectibility judgments themselves are empirical.

I contend that the relevant sorts of projectibility judgments, and Boyd's arguments from those judgments to the empirical nature of the epistemology of science, only require a much weaker version of anti-priorism, namely,

> *Modest anti-apriorism* Rationally acceptable principles of inductive inference are irreducible to a priori principles of inference.[29]

Replacing anti-apriorism with modest anti-apriorism preserves the empirical status of projectibility judgments while allowing logic and mathematics to be a priori. After all, the apriority of logic and mathematics isn't enough to make theories that deploy logic and mathematics *in addition to various empirical claims* a priori, and just such theories are used in making the projectibility judgments at issue.

One might object that what I'm proposing either (a) violates moderate confirmation holism or (b) violates inclusion. The idea behind both (a) and (b) is the same, to wit, that the view of scientific theories underlying Quinean naturalism is that of a methodologically homogeneous web of beliefs, each node of which is justified or not according to the confirmatory fortunes of the web, and empirically so. However, on the view I'm entertaining logic and mathematics are either in the web but not subject to empirical confirmation (violates moderate confirmation holism) or are not in the web at all (violates inclusion). So goes the objection. It seems to me that something like the following provides a plausible response.

Start with a web of beliefs, including those parts of mathematics and logic relevant to the subject matter of the web. Inclusion is satisfied. Now suppose that we have a satisfactory a priori epistemology for logic and mathematics (or at least the logic and mathematics included in this web). In this case, we have a heterogeneous epistemology, the mathematics and logic in the web subject to one justificatory story and the non-mathematical parts of the web subject to a different such story. This doesn't violate moderate confirmation holism, since it may well be that the logic and mathematics included in the web share in whatever confirmation accrues to the web as a whole. Indeed, I see no reason to deny this confirmation-sharing. I do deny, however, that this confirmation is the *only* source of justification for the logic and mathematics included in the web.

On this view, logico-mathematical beliefs have both empirical and a priori sources of justification. Their justification is, in a sense, over-determined.[30] But this is compatible with moderate confirmation holism. Moreover, this view provides an alternate explanation of the Quinean observation that in practice we almost unfailingly resist revising our logico-mathematical beliefs: those beliefs have independent sources of justification that are very difficult to undermine. Note that I don't intend to be arguing that this position is correct – only that it's plausible, which is sufficient to defuse the worries in (a) and (b).

Adding modest anti-apriorism to the surviving principles precipitates modifying some of those principles. First, methodological monism can no longer be taken to apply to *all* systematic theorizing. Its scope becomes restricted to those areas where inferential practices are inductive. But this is unproblematic as its reach still extends far enough to deny an a priori epistemology to empirical science. Restricting the scope of methodological monism leads to a similar restriction in scope of continuity. The philosophy subject to experiential checks will now be philosophy concerning those areas where inferential practices are inductive. But again, this is a long enough reach for continuity to do the work Quine required of it. Lastly, the scope of anti-foundationalism is also restricted. In particular, logic and mathematics still might admit a foundationalist epistemology. I see this as a feature, not a bug.

4 Fault line: causation

Quine's own view of causation is reductive. He's not uniform about what the notion of cause is to be reduced to – e.g. in some places[31] it's natural kinds and in others[32] it's microphysical forces – but he's consistent in suggesting reductions of it. Other Quinean naturalists similarly endorse a reductivist conception of causation. Kitcher, for instance, defends a view of science that "proposes to ground causal claims in claims about explanatory dependency" (1989, 436).[33] But some Quinean naturalists firmly reject reductivist conceptions of causation. Boyd and Hilary Kornblith are prime examples.

Boyd holds that an "essential feature of naturalism in epistemology is the unreduced appeal to causal notions in the analysis of knowledge" (1980, 625). Causation can be investigated in such a way as to deepen our understanding of it, but we are free to use causal concepts, including the concept of causation itself, without offering any sort of reductive or eliminative analysis of it, without offering even a promissory note for such an analysis. The idea is that causal powers and processes exist "out there" in the world, independently of us, and needn't be explained away via some reductive analysis in order to be appealed to in doing epistemology. Moreover, such appeals are necessary if we are to make sense of the reliability of scientific methods in a scientifically acceptable way. For both Boyd and Kornblith, the epistemology of science, indeed epistemology generally, turns on a homeostatic property cluster conception of natural kinds and a sophisticated account of reference for theoretical terms. Each of these makes critical use of unreduced causal notions.[34]

This disagreement suggests putting an additional principle of naturalism in play:

> *Principle 13 (non-reductive causal realism)* Causal powers and processes (i) exist in the world independently of us and our theorizing and (ii) may legitimately be appealed to in our philosophical theorizing independent of any reductive analysis.[35]

Boyd and Kornblith are committed to this principle, and they take it to be a commitment of contemporary science. So they will take it to be a consequence of deference to science$_{findings}$, and deference to science$_{methods}$. If it is a consequence of these principles (and it prima facie appears to be), then it's a consequence of the surviving principles and Quinean naturalists are already committed to it whether they realize it or not. Of course, it might not be a consequence of deference to science$_{findings}$, and deference to science$_{methods}$, appearances notwithstanding. Even so, it's pretty clearly consistent with the surviving principles. So there's no problem with adding it to the surviving principles plus modest anti-apriorism. Either way, non-reductive causal realism is available to Quinean naturalists. Should a Quinean naturalist accept this principle?

Quine and Kitcher would resist accepting non-reductive causal realism. The latter has Humean worries concerning access to causal truths[36] while the former considers causal idioms disreputable and wayward, though useful,[37] and the notion of causation dim.[38] These misgivings about causation give rise to the reductivist inclinations of both Quine and Kitcher. However, embracing non-reductive causal realism enables Boyd and Kornblith to cogently take on the prime epistemological project identified by both Quine and Kitcher: to explain the reliability of the methods of science. For Quine this means giving a theory of projectibility, which in turn means giving a theory of natural kinds.[39] For Kitcher this means understanding how to identify and improve belief-regulating cognitive processes.[40] Boyd and Kornblith arguably accomplish both by deploying an unreduced notion of causation. This recommends accepting non-reductive causal realism.

5 Concluding remarks

I realize that for a chapter of a volume on philosophical methods, precious little has been said here about methods. Methodological lessons, however, can be extracted from the foregoing. From the surviving principles we learn: that we should avoid reductionism in meaning and confirmation; that we should not look for theory-neutral methods or standpoints to use in philosophizing; that we should ground systematic theorizing, philosophical and traditionally scientific, in experience; and that we should conduct our philosophical business in accordance with the methods and findings of our best science. From the modifications set out in Sections 3 and 4 we learn that we should not overreach in applying the surviving principles and that we should avoid reductivist conceptions of causation. By restricting the scope of methodological monism, continuity, and anti-foundationalism, and adding modest anti-apriorism, the Quinean epistemological project can be fulfilled without incurring the counter-intuitive and prima facie undesirable commitment to logic and mathematics being a posteriori; moreover, endorsing a non-reductivist conception of causation is arguably necessary to making good on the Quinean epistemological project. Thus Quinean naturalists don't get what they (might) want, but they get what they need. Who can ask for more?[41]

Notes

1 I'll use 'naturalism in the tradition of Quine', 'naturalism in the Quinean tradition', and simply 'Quinean naturalism' interchangeably. Unmodified uses of 'naturalism' through Section 2 (but not after), should be understood as 'Quinean naturalism'.

2 Here and elsewhere, I gloss over the distinction between beliefs and statements and their (propositional) contents.

3 Quine cites Duhem and Lowinger as having argued for a similar position.

4 See Quine 1991, 268–70, and 1981a for more on this and the next paragraph. For brevity, I don't give Quine's account of empirical content in full detail.

5 Interesting cases are collections that imply observation categoricals they don't contain.

6 Quine does recognize some individual sentences as having empirical content, namely so-called *observation sentences*, sentences such as 'It's raining' and 'That's a ball'. See e.g. Quine and Ullian 1978, 22.

7 On my view, moderate confirmation holism is based on semantic holism. Other philosophers read the situation as reversed, i.e. that semantic holism is based on moderate confirmation holism. See e.g. DeRosa and LePore 2004, §1. Which view is correct is immaterial for present purposes.

8 Cf. e.g. Quine 1953, 40. Quine later explicitly endorses moderate confirmation holism (see Quine 1991).

9 I hesitate to say 'structure of empirical justification' because it's unclear that a full account of justification is encoded in the structure of a system. I think that for Quine, being favorably situated in the right kind of structure makes a belief rational to hold, but rationality of belief is to be distinguished from justification. The latter requires an appropriate connection to (approximate) truth, and, as will come out in Section 2, it's not obvious that Quine's view fully incorporates this.

10 Note that the holism expounded here is not moderate. It's not difficult to see, though, how to appropriately weaken it.

11 See Carnap 1928/1967, §2.

12 See Carnap 1928/1967, §11. It's worth noting that Carnap understands 'object' to apply to "anything about which a statement can be made" (ibid., §1).

13 Quine took his no-irrevisability argument in his 1953 as an argument against analyticity. But as Hilary Putnam points out (1976), it's really an argument against the a priori. The idea is that since an a priori statement does not depend on sensory experience for its justification, such a statement is immune to revision. (It's important to note that Quine takes revision to be undertaken in response to recalcitrant experience.) So if every statement is revisable, then no

statement is a priori. But if this is correct, it just provides a more direct means of rejecting the duality of method: no a priori statements, no a priori methods.

14 This principle might more appropriately be called 'methodological empiricism' or simply 'empiricism'. But as Quine calls it 'methodological monism', I'll call it that as well.

15 Cf. "I admit to naturalism, even glory in it. This means banishing the dream of a first philosophy and pursuing philosophy rather as part of one's system of the world, continuous with the rest of science" (Quine 1998, 430).

16 Certainly prominent Quinean naturalists understand foundationalism in this way. See e.g. Boyd 1989, Kitcher 1992, and Kornblith 1993.

17 Indeed, Quine writes of "the conceptual scheme of science" (1953, 44). It should be noted, however, that conceptual schemes for Quine are linguistic. See Quine 1981c, 41. Thus, his use of 'conceptual scheme' is compatible with his well-known antipathy toward intensional entities.

18 I use the term 'entity' generically to cover objects in the Fregean sense as well as properties, relations, events, states of affairs, facts, etc.

19 At least not at present. Science is dynamic, and if it changes in such a way that it becomes possible to naturalize the entity in question at a later time, then at that time philosophy will be welcome to use that entity in its theorizing.

20 Not all sciences are equal in the eyes of this principle. The strength of our confidence in privileging a science over philosophy will vary with our assessment of the profundity of the science in question. By this I mean that sciences which seem to be onto the deep structure of the world will inspire greater confidence than those which appear to be concerned with artifacts of human social arrangements. For instance, if philosophical theory conflicts with physics, chemistry, or biology, our confidence that something is amiss with the philosophy will be much higher than if the theory conflicts with economics. In light of the way he often seems to privilege physics, I think Quine would agree with this. The general thought here, however, is simply that the objects of social science are much less stable and entrenched than the objects of natural science, and with greater stability and entrenchment comes greater confidence in our theoretical findings.

21 Note that much of what Quine writes in his 1969a can be construed as an appeal to defer to the methods of science, specifically psychology, in doing philosophy, specifically epistemology.

22 Notice that while some mathematical methods (e.g. those of analysis, group theory, and non-standard geometries) are included in the methods deferred to, not all obviously are. I strongly suspect that the methods of higher set theory ultimately involve a commitment to realism about mathematics strong enough to violate anti-supranaturalism (see below). Given this, including the methods of higher set theory here would be building an inconsistency into naturalism. See my 2009.

23 Quine–Putnam-style indispensability arguments (Quine 1981d; Putnam 1971) work (if at all) by bringing at least some mathematical entities indirectly into the causal network by way of their role in securing empirical content for our best science. This is why at least some mathematical entities are, for some naturalists, not supranatural. But see my 2007, 2008, and 2009.

24 One might think that these don't exhaust the entailments between the principles I've identified. In particular, one might think that the dependence of moderate confirmation holism on semantic holism indicated earlier means that the former follows from the latter. Given the controversy over the direction of dependence between these two principles noted in n. 7, I'm not confident the dependence I advocate rises to entailment. That said, whether one of these holisms entails the other is of little significance to the main thrust of the paper.

25 Other points of disagreement worthy of consideration focus on normativity, truth, and the role of evolutionary theory in naturalism. Space precludes discussion of these.

26 Questioning Rey's credentials as a naturalist might seem odd in light of his contribution to this volume. I'm uncertain regarding said credentials owing to the sense I get reading Rey 1998 and Rey's other papers on similar topics that his commitment to apriority, analyticity, and the like are stronger than his commitment to confirmation holism and other arguably "bedrock" components of naturalism. It's one thing to say, "I'm a naturalist and my view can accommodate such-and-such notions traditionally thought to be at odds with naturalism." It's another to say, "Such-and-such notions are traditionally thought to be at odds with naturalism, but naturalists can stop worrying

about them because I have a way of reconciling them with naturalism." The philosopher who says the latter sort of thing isn't clearly a naturalist (though of course she may be). Rey often seems to me to be saying the latter sort of thing in his papers, such as his 1998, that explicitly address naturalism. I hope it's clear that nothing substantive in this chapter rides on my classification of Rey as a potential non-naturalist. And I hope he'll forgive me if I've misread him!

27 On the success of the former, see my 2010.
28 See e.g. Boyd 1973, 1979, 1980, 1985a, 1985b, 1989, 1990, and 2000.
29 Cf. Boyd's *inference foundationalism* (1989, 12).
30 Cf. Casullo 2005.
31 See Quine 1969b, 132.
32 See Quine 1974, §2.
33 See also Kitcher 1985, 1986.
34 For details on all this see the references in n. 28 and Kornblith 1993.
35 (Neo-)Kantian conceptions of causation don't satisfy (i). Humean conceptions of causation may or may not satisfy (i), but don't satisfy (ii).
36 See e.g. Kitcher 1993, 170.
37 See Quine 1974, §2.
38 See Quine 1969b, 131.
39 See Quine 1969b.
40 See e.g. Kitcher 1992, 1993. For more on this, see my 2008.
41 Thanks to Richard Boyd, Jon Cogburn, Matthew Haug, Aaron Lercher, and Ted Poston for helpful discussion and comments. Ancestors of parts of this chapter also benefited from discussion with Harold Hodes, Zoltán Gendler Szabó, and Richard Shore.

References

Antony, L. (2004) "A Naturalized Approach to the *A Priori*," *Philosophical Issues* 14: 1–17.

Boyd, R. (1973) "Realism, Underdetermination, and a Causal Theory of Evidence," *Noûs* 7: 1–12.

——(1979) "Metaphor and Theory Change," in A. Ortony (ed.), *Metaphor and Thought*, Cambridge: Cambridge University Press, 481–532.

——(1980) "Scientific Realism and Naturalistic Epistemology," *Proceedings of the Philosophy of Science Association*, vol. 2, Seattle, WA: Philosophy of Science Association, 613–62.

——(1985a) "Lex Orandi est Lex Credendi," in P. Churchland and C. Hooker (eds), *Images of Science: Scientific Realism versus Constructive Empiricism*, Chicago: University of Chicago Press, 3–34.

——(1985b) "Observations, Explanatory Power, and Simplicity: Toward a Non-Humean Account," in P. Achinstein and O. Hannaway (eds), *Observation, Experiment, and Hypothesis in Modern Physical Science*, Cambridge, MA: MIT Press, 47–94.

——(1989) "What Realism Implies and What It Does Not," *Dialectica* 43: 5–29.

——(1990) "Realism, Conventionality, and 'Realism About,'" in G. Boolos (ed.), *Meaning and Method: Essays in Honor of Hilary Putnam*, Cambridge: Cambridge University Press, 171–95.

——(2000) "Kinds as the 'Workmanship of Men': Realism, Constructivism, and Natural Kinds," in J. Nida-Rümelin (ed.), *Rationality, Realism, Revision: Proceedings of the Third International Congress*, Society for Analytical Philosophy, Berlin: Walter de Gruyter, 52–89.

——(2010) "Realism, Natural Kinds, and Philosophical Methods," in H. Beebee and N. Sabbarton-Leary (eds), *The Semantics and Metaphysics of Natural Kinds*, London: Routledge, 212–34.

Carnap, R. (1928/1967) *Der logische Aufbau der Welt*, Berlin-Schlachtensee: Weltkreis-Verlag; trans. by R.A. George as *The Logical Structure of the World* (Berkeley: University of California Press).

Casullo, A. (2005) "Epistemic Overdetermination and A Priori Justification," *Philosophical Perspectives* 19: 41–58.

DeRosa, R. and LePore, E. (2004) "Quine's Meaning Holisms," in R.F. Gibson (ed.), *The Cambridge Companion to Quine*, Cambridge: Cambridge University Press, 65–90.

Devitt, M. (1996) *Coming to Our Senses: A Naturalistic Program for Semantic Localism*, Cambridge: Cambridge University Press.

Goldman, A. (1999) "A Priori Warrant and Naturalistic Epistemology," in J.E. Tomberlin (ed.), *Philosophical Perspectives*, vol. 13, Malden, MA: Blackwell, 1–28.

Goodman, N. (1955) *Fact, Fiction, and Forecast*, Cambridge, MA: Harvard University Press.

Jenkins, C.S. (2008) *Grounding Concepts: An Empirical Basis for Arithmetic Knowledge*, Oxford: Oxford University Press.

Kitcher, P. (1985) "Two Approaches to Explanation," *Journal of Philosophy* 82: 632–39.

——(1986) "Projecting the Order of Nature," in R.E. Butts (ed.), *Kant's Philosophy of Physical Science*, Dordrecht: D. Reidel, 201–35.

——(1989) "Explanatory Unification and the Causal Structure of the World," in P. Kitcher and W. Salmon (eds), *Studies in Explanation*, vol. 33 of *Minnesota Studies in the Philosophy of Science*, Minneapolis: University of Minnesota Press, 410–505.

——(1992) "The Naturalist's Return," *Philosophical Review* 101: 53–114.

——(1993) *The Advancement of Science*, Oxford: Oxford University Press.

Kornblith, H. (1993) *Inductive Inference and Its Natural Ground*, Cambridge, MA: MIT Press.

Maddy, P.J. (2000) "Naturalism and the A Priori," in P. Boghossian and C. Peacocke (eds), *New Essays on the A Priori*, Oxford: Oxford University Press, 92–116.

Putnam, H. (1971) "Philosophy of Logic," in *Mathematics, Matter, and Method*, 2nd edn, Cambridge: Cambridge University Press, 323–57.

——(1976) "'Two Dogmas' Revisited," *Realism and Reason: Philosophical Papers*, vol. 3, Cambridge: Cambridge University Press, 87–97.

Quine, W.V. (1950) "Identity, Ostension, and Hypostasis," *From a Logical Point of View*, 2nd edn, New York: Harper & Row, 65–79.

——(1953) "Two Dogmas of Empiricism," *From a Logical Point of View*, 2nd edn, New York: Harper & Row, pp. 20–46.

——(1960) *Word and Object*, Cambridge, MA: MIT Press.

——(1969a) "Epistemology Naturalized," *Ontological Relativity and Other Essays*, New York: Columbia University Press, 69–90.

——(1969b) "Natural Kinds," *Ontological Relativity and Other Essays*, New York: Columbia University Press, 114–38.

——(1974) *The Roots of Reference*, LaSalle, IL: Open Court.

——(1981a) "Empirical Content," *Theories and Things*, Cambridge, MA: Harvard University Press, 24–30.

——(1981b) "Five Milestones of Empiricism," *Theories and Things*, Cambridge, MA: Harvard University Press, 67–72.

——(1981c) "On the Very Idea of a Third Dogma," *Theories and Things*, Cambridge, MA: Harvard University Press, 38–42.

——(1981d) "Success and Limits of Mathematization," *Theories and Things*, Cambridge, MA: Harvard University Press, 148–55.

——(1990) *Pursuit of Truth*, Cambridge, MA: Harvard University Press.

——(1991) "Two Dogmas in Retrospect," *Canadian Journal of Philosophy* 21 (3): 265–74.

——(1992) "Structure and Nature," *Journal of Philosophy* 89: 5–9.

——(1995) *From Stimulus to Science*, Cambridge, MA: Harvard University Press.

——(1998) "Reply to Hilary Putnam," in L.E. Hahn and P.A. Schilpp (eds), *The Philosophy of W.V. Quine*, expanded and revised edn, vol. 18 of Library of Living Philosophers, LaSalle, IL: Open Court, 427–31.

Quine, W.V. and Ullian, J. (1978) *The Web of Belief*, 2nd edn, New York: Random House.

Rey, G. (1998) "A Naturalistic A Priori," *Philosophical Studies* 92: 25–43.

Roland, J.W. (2007) "Maddy and Mathematics: Naturalism or Not," *British Journal for the Philosophy of Science* 58: 423–50.

——(2008) "Kitcher, Mathematics, and Naturalism," *Australasian Journal of Philosophy* 86: 481–97.

——(2009) "On Naturalizing the Epistemology of Mathematics," *Pacific Philosophical Quarterly* 90: 63–97.

——(2010) "Concept Grounding and Knowledge of Set Theory," *Philosophia* 38: 179–93.

6   Liberal naturalism: Wittgenstein and McDowell

MARIE MCGINN

Wittgenstein's choice of the quotation from Nestroy as the motto for the *Philosophical Investigations* signals his work's critical relation to contemporary Western thought, which he suggests is characterized by the word 'progress' (*CV*, 9).[1] One reading of the motto – 'It is in the nature of all progress that it looks much greater than it really is' – is that it is intended to alert us to the danger of our almost exclusive concern with progress, which, Wittgenstein remarks, '[t]ypically … constructs' (*CV*, 9). The spirit of progress, which is characteristic of our age, expresses itself in, among other things, our attitude to science. The method of science 'elbows all others aside' (*CV*, 69), and we 'are irresistibly tempted to ask and answer questions in the way science does' (*BB*, 18). Thus, we have the idea in philosophy that we need to arrive at 'new, unheard of elucidations' (*BT*, 309). The clear implication of the motto is that this is not the spirit in which the *Philosophical Investigations* itself is written; the kind of enquiry Wittgenstein is concerned with is undertaken in a quite different spirit from the one which finds expression in the novel, constructive, explanatory goals of science.

Wittgenstein's repudiation of the methods and aims of science as a model for his philosophy is not, however, a rejection of the central importance of the concept of nature for his philosophical enquiry. Appeals to nature, and an emphasis on describing what is there before our eyes, are a recurring theme of Wittgenstein's remarks from 1930 onwards. The concept of nature which Wittgenstein has in mind is clearly not the one associated with what is described using the conceptual resources of the special sciences. It is implicitly a more open conception of nature as something that we encounter: 'Just let nature speak' (*CV*, 3); 'Things are right *before our eyes*, not covered by any veil' (*CV*, 8), remarks from 1929 and 1930, respectively. This conception of nature is one that Wittgenstein finds in the works of Goethe, and it is no doubt significant that he considered taking a quotation from a Goethe poem as his motto for the *Philosophical Investigations*: 'Nature has neither core nor husk.' The connection between Wittgenstein's conception of the role of the concept of nature in his investigations and the ideas of Goethe is also made explicit in the following remark from 1931:

> 'What a sensible man knows is hard to know.' Does Goethe's contempt for the laboratory experiment and his exhortation to go out into uncontrolled nature & learn from that, does this have some connection with the idea that a hypothesis (wrongly conceived) is already a falsification of the truth? And with the beginning I am now thinking of for my book which might consist of a description of nature.
>
> (*CV*, 20)

The idea of nature as something we encounter, as something that is sensuously present and which can be investigated by means of the intelligent use of our ordinary perceptual capacities, is clearly distinct from the idea of nature as it is represented in the scientific image. However, Wittgenstein's emphasis is less on these contrasting conceptions of nature, or with defending one over the other, than on the contrasting approaches to the task of understanding natural phenomena: one that is concerned with investigating nature in the controlled and artificial conditions of the laboratory experiment, with a view to constructing explanatory hypotheses; and one that aims to achieve a clarified view of complex, natural phenomena in their natural setting, with a view to describing patterns and connections that are there in plain view.

Furthermore, he shows no interest in defending Goethe's conception of scientific method, but only in observing an affinity between Goethe's morphological enquiries and his new conception of his philosophical method. The important difference here, clearly, is that Wittgenstein's investigation is not concerned with the discovery of scientific truth, but with achieving conceptual clarification. The connection he sees with Goethe's approach to understanding living forms, their genesis and transformation, is that it might be taken as a model for how he now intends to undertake his primary task of conceptual investigation. The central idea is that conceptual enquiry should not look at language in abstraction from its natural embedding in human life, but look at it when it is functioning, and where everything lies open to view.

One of the principal aims of the *Philosophical Investigations* is to attain 'greater clarity about the concepts of understanding, meaning something, and thinking' (*PI* §81). As we've just seen, although Wittgenstein sees himself as taking a naturalistic approach to this task, his method contrasts sharply with the reductive, explanatory approach of scientific naturalism: 'I want to say here that it can never be our job to reduce anything to anything, or to explain anything' (*BB*, 18). However, perhaps more significantly, this new approach of looking at language when it is functioning also contrasts sharply with the dogmatic, psychologistic approach of the *Tractatus*. The spur to Wittgenstein's development of his later, naturalistic approach to the task of clarifying how the concepts of meaning, understanding and thinking function is not merely his conviction that science cannot solve the conceptual problems that interest him, but his sense that his naturalistic approach is what is needed to resolve what he now sees as fundamental flaws in his early conception of the nature of a proposition.

In the *Tractatus*, Wittgenstein conceives of a proposition as a propositional sign which is projected onto reality; to mean something by the words one utters is to project a propositional sign onto reality in such a way that it becomes the correlate of the state of affairs it represents. Implicit in this conception is the idea that a thought achieves something which no mere sign can achieve, and that meaning involves an essential, mental act of projecting a sign onto reality:

> We use the perceptible sign of a proposition (spoken or written, etc.) as a projection of a possible situation. The method of projection is to think of the sense of the proposition.
>
> (*TLP* 3.11)

In *PI* §95, Wittgenstein expresses this idea of meaning as follows:

> "Thinking must be something unique". When we say, *mean*, that such-and-such is the case, then, with what we mean, we do not stop anywhere short of the fact, but mean: *such-and-such – is – thus-and-so*.

He now sees this conception of meaning as arising out of a temptation 'to purify, to sublimate, the sign itself' (*PI* §94), that is, to transform it from a mere sign into something higher: something which now *represents* that '*such-and-such – is – thus-and-so*'. Wittgenstein calls the sublimated sign, the representation as such, 'a pure intermediary between the propositional *sign* and the fact' (*PI* §94), 'a shadow of the fact' (*BB*, 32), 'a shadowy being' (*BB*, 36), 'a picture which we don't interpret in order to understand it, but which we understand without interpreting' (*BB*, 36). It is this idea of the proposition or thought as a shadow – as a 'sublimated' sign – which he now recognizes as problematic.

Instead of sublimating a sign into a representation as such, the idea is that we should clarify how the concepts of meaning, understanding and thinking function, by viewing '[g]iving orders, asking questions, telling stories, having a chat' 'as part of our natural history' (*PI* §25). We need to concern ourselves with 'the spatial and temporal phenomenon of language' (*PI* §108), with 'the whole, consisting of language and the activities into which it is woven' (*PI* §7), if we are to arrive at a non-mythological picture of the workings of our language. Wittgenstein's later, naturalistic method aims to show, on the one hand, that the proposition conceived as a shadow is a mere 'chimera' (*PI* §94), and on the other, 'that nothing extraordinary is involved' (*PI* §94). His aim is to bring meaning down to earth and to rid us of the idea that understanding is a mental state that gives life to a sign, or that a proposition is 'a remarkable thing' (*PI* §94).

***

John McDowell has also developed a conception of naturalism which contrasts with the restrictive conception of scientific naturalism, and which aims to reveal meaning, understanding and thinking as natural powers of human beings who have undergone a certain sort of ordinary education. There is a clear parallel between the view that McDowell develops and the sort of naturalism that is central to the *Philosophical Investigations*. In particular, there is a shared commitment to avoid both a reductive approach to meaning and what McDowell calls 'supernaturalism', that is, the idea that meaning and thinking are 'strange' processes that are fundamentally alien to ordinary nature. In rejecting both reductionism and supernaturalism, both Wittgenstein and McDowell are committed to holding that our ordinary practice of describing ourselves and others as understanding, or meaning, or intending such-and-such is in perfectly good order just as it stands; our ordinary employment of these concepts in descriptions of human behaviour is not in need of an analysis which grounds them in descriptions which do not themselves employ these concepts; they are to be accepted without further ado in characterizations of human behaviour.

However, it is also the case that while Wittgenstein is principally preoccupied with what he sees as the dangers of supernaturalism, McDowell is concerned as much with defending the anti-scientistic conception of nature which they both share. Thus, much of McDowell's attention is taken up with defending the claim that there is no good reason to identify nature with what the scientific image comprehends, or to hold that in order for normative phenomena, such as meaning and intending, to qualify as aspects of the natural world, they must be explicated using the conceptual resources of the special sciences. McDowell defends the idea of a 'liberal naturalism': a form of naturalism that can accept meaning, thinking, intending, and so on as aspects of our natural lives, without attempting to ground them in non-normative facts. Once we have in this way expanded our idea of what the concept of the natural can embrace, then, he argues, we will no longer feel a pressure to provide a constructive account of what meaning and thinking consist in, which integrates these phenomena into nature as it is conceived within the scientific image. Rather, we will be able to accept that meaning, thinking, intending, and so on 'are concepts of occurrences and states in our lives' (McDowell 2009b, 262), and thus an irreducible aspect of the natural world.

This difference between McDowell and Wittgenstein may not, at first sight, appear to be anything more than a matter of emphasis. It is certainly the case that their shared, anti-reductionist conception of nature, and of the normative phenomena of ordinary human life, makes for a fundamental harmony between them. However, I want to argue that this difference in emphasis also leads to a significant contrast in how each conceives the philosophical project of clarifying the nature of meaning and understanding. By casting the issue as one of what our concept of the natural should be allowed to comprehend, McDowell is thereby led to conceive the central question about meaning as one that relates, above all, to the *factual* status of descriptions of an individual as meaning, or thinking, or intending something. For McDowell, accepting that descriptions of what someone means, or thinks, or intends are in perfectly good order just as they stand is equivalent to thinking 'of grasp of a rule or meaning as a *fact* about the person who grasps it' (McDowell 1998b, 267), which is to say that there is something which 'constitutes [their] understanding something in a determinate way' (McDowell 1998b, 268).

Conceiving matters this way, McDowell sees himself as defending a realist conception of meaning, thinking and intending against, on the one hand, a reductive form of anti-realism, and on the other, against an unacceptable version of Platonism. McDowell describes the view he defends as a form of 'naturalized Platonism', which still holds onto the idea that 'meaning, understanding, and so forth [are] definite states of mind' (McDowell 2009a, 88). McDowell's version of liberal naturalism amounts to the claim that statements about what someone means or intends should, just as they stand, be accepted as factual statements, which, when they are true, are true in virtue of the particular mental state that the subject of the description is in at the time. Once we have taken the step of recognizing that the capacity to mean or intend such-and-such belongs to our nature as rational animals, then, McDowell argues, we are in a position to recognize that 'there is no need to be suspicious of including intentionality among the occurrent phenomena of consciousness' (McDowell 1998c, 303).

McDowell recognizes that there is a threat of falling into Platonism in holding that meaning or intending such-and-such can be an occurrent state of consciousness. However, he believes that we *must* succeed in making sense of this idea, if we are not to lose our grip on the phenomenon of intentionality. If we deny that meaning something by an expression could be a matter of 'a meaning com[ing] to mind' (McDowell 1998c, 304), then we are left with the idea that everything introspectably present to the mind is 'a brute chunk of the "in itself" [which] could not have the internal links to performance that a grasped meaning would have to have' (McDowell 1998c, 308). It is this idea, McDowell argues, that leads to the fatal regress of interpretations, that is, to the idea that what comes to mind is something that just 'stands there', and which can have the required links to performance only under an interpretation.

Thus, for McDowell, rejecting reductionism does not mean merely accepting that we do indeed speak, say, of grasping the meaning of a word at a stroke, or that, in certain circumstances this description of what we do is correct, but also that we show that our speaking this way is not 'merely notional' (McDowell 1998b, 269), by making sense of the idea that 'a person's understanding could be her having something in mind' (McDowell 1998b, 270). This means that we *must* make room for the idea that what comes to mind is something 'to whose very identity [a] normative link to the objective world is essential' (McDowell 1998b, 270). We must see that it 'is innocuous – indeed compulsory, on pain of losing our grip on the purported topic – to take it that intentions contain within themselves the distinction between conformity and non-conformity' (McDowell 1998c, 315). The question is whether the idea that meanings 'come to mind', which McDowell's liberal naturalism sets out to preserve, amounts to a commitment to the 'shadowy beings' which Wittgenstein's naturalism aims to overcome.

***

McDowell's liberal naturalism aims to defend a form of realism which conceives of meaning and intending as inner states which have an intrinsic, determinate content, which in itself settles what counts as conformity or non-conformity with them. His conception of a liberal naturalism is precisely that it can embrace these intrinsically normative states as part of the furniture of the natural world. It is clear that in taking this view, McDowell implicitly commits himself to a particular conception of how the concepts of meaning and intending function, namely that the word 'intention' stands for 'something that can be, in some sense, all there in one's mind before one acts on it' (McDowell 1998c, 315); a state which 'once identified, determines of itself, and in particular independently of its author's subsequent judgements, what counts as conformity with it' (McDowell 1998c, 316); a state which is to be conceived in such a way that we do not 'lose our entitlement to the idea that a grasped meaning imposes demands on a person's behaviour' (McDowell 1998b, 272).

The idea of normative constraint appears problematic, McDowell claims, only if we imagine that what determines the content of an intentional state is an act of mind in which the subject hits on an interpretation that settles future applications. It is this idea, McDowell suggests, that is the object of Wittgenstein's critique in the remarks on private language. However, the idea becomes innocuous and common-sensical, McDowell believes, once we recognize that a speaker's capacity to be in an intentional state which 'determines of itself ... what counts as conformity with it' depends upon 'a context of human life and initiation into it' (McDowell 1998c, 317). However, we should not go so far as to suppose that we can locate what gives content to the idea of conformity and non-conformity entirely in facts about social practice and unsolicited agreement in the employment of expressions. This would be to run the risk of 'under-mentalizing the behaviour', so that there is no longer any 'question of *acting on an understanding*' (McDowell 1998b, 276). The claim is that anyone who has been initiated into the relevant practice is in a position to perceive, and act in the light of, the meaning of the expressions of his language, as it were, 'directly'.

As McDowell sees it, the key element of his liberal naturalism is that it makes room for the idea that the internal states of a rational subject, who has acquired a second nature, have *normative* force, that is to say, normative links with subsequent behaviour. McDowell believes that to try to place all sources of normativity in the outer realm of public practice and human agreement in how we operate with signs would be to adopt a reductive form of anti-realism and destroy the very idea that the life of a human being is 'normatively shaped'. Our common-sense conception of ourselves as beings who engage in essentially normative practices *requires*, McDowell believes, that our actions are guided by norms that fully rationalize our action. For McDowell, this just amounts to the idea that internal intentional states have a normative force, such that they in-themselves determine what counts as conformity or non-conformity with them. It is no doubt a contingent matter that there are natural beings who can acquire the status of rational animals, but given that this is the case we *must*, McDowell argues, have a conception of nature that can accommodate the existence of inner states with normative force, for without that the whole idea that there are rational animals, whose actions are describable in normative terms, is undermined.

***

The idea of inner states with normative force is the idea that mental states have an intrinsic representational content which an external state of affairs can either fit or fail to fit. At first sight, this appears to be the very idea of representational content that Wittgenstein means to capture when he remarks that '[w]hen we say, *mean*, that such-and-such is the case, then, with what we mean, we do not stop anywhere short of the fact, but mean: *such-and-such – is – thus-and-so*' (PI §95). If that is so, then clearly

Wittgenstein takes the idea of such internal representational states to be an instance of our tendency to sublimate the sign, which he now regards as problematic, and which his new naturalistic approach is intended to counter.

Insofar as McDowell takes liberal naturalism to give expression to ideas he finds in later Wittgenstein, he is clearly committed to denying that it is the idea of inner states with normative force that is the object of censure in *PI* §95, and more generally, to claiming that this idea is not the target of Wittgenstein's attack in the discussion of rule-following. McDowell believes that to suppose either of these things would be to convict Wittgenstein of falling into an incoherent form of reductive anti-realism, which renders our ordinary conception of ourselves as meaning something by our words untenable. Whether the latter claim is true is something I will consider later. First of all, I want to look at whether there is anything in McDowell's claim that the idea that, when a speaker hears and understands a word, something comes before his mind 'to whose very identity [a] normative link to the objective world is essential' (McDowell 1998b, 270) is not a target of Wittgenstein's critique.

As McDowell sees it, rejection of a reductive form of anti-realism is essentially equivalent to a rejection of the idea that meaning is founded upon ongoing agreement in the use of expressions, or of the idea that sources of normativity lie exclusively in the outer realm. Although he accepts that agreement in the use of expressions is essential if there is to be any such thing as meaning, McDowell believes that the concept of meaning is altogether destroyed if we cannot make sense of the idea that 'a linguistic community is conceived as bound together, not by a match in mere externals (facts accessible to just anyone), but by a capacity for a meeting of minds' (McDowell 1998a, 253). Thus, he holds that it is essential to a satisfactory reading of Wittgenstein that we do not see him as 'deny[ing] that a person's understanding could be [a matter of] her having something in mind' (McDowell 1998b, 270). We have to be able to hold onto the idea that 'a thought, just as such, is something with which only certain states of affairs would accord' (McDowell 1998b, 270), to 'the conception of understanding as an inner state from which correct performances flow' (McDowell 1998c, 314), and to the idea 'that a mind can fully encompass something that contains within itself a determination of what counts as conformity with it' (McDowell 1998c, 320).

Thus, on McDowell's view, we must preserve what he calls 'the contractual conception of meaning'. Everyone's agreeing, say, in developing the series 'Add 2' beyond 1,000 must be *explained* by the fact that they all have the meaning of the expression 'Add 2' 'in mind', and are now simply acting in the light of what that meaning requires of them. The use of the word 'explanation' here is crucial, for it is only if we can make sense of the idea that grasp of the meaning of 'Add 2' *explains*, or *grounds*, the consensus in extending the series in new cases that we have what McDowell thinks is a *genuine* case of normativity. On this view, to grasp a rule, or to understand a word, is to be in a state which in itself determines what is normatively required at each new stage, so that what one goes on to say is explained by one's moving 'along paths marked out by meaning' (McDowell 1998a, 259). Thus, the response of each individual speaker at each new stage is to be understood as 'made in the light of' the normative requirements of the meaning that comes to mind when he hears and understands the command 'Add 2', and this is what *explains* our all agreeing when we go on and extend the series beyond 1,000.

This falls short of a problematic form of Platonism, McDowell argues, because there is no suggestion that the normative force of the rule 'Add 2' is apparent to anyone who sees it written or hears it spoken; a process of initiation into a custom is required in order for anyone to perceive what the rule requires. However, for anyone who has successfully undergone that process, it is correct to say that the expression 'Add 2' has a normative power, which shapes his future behaviour. It is hard not to see this as an instance of the idea that, if subsequent behaviour is to count as a case of following a rule, there must be something between the sign and the speaker's response to it, namely, the speaker's perception of the meaning, or normative power, of the sign, which settles what counts as a correct application of it. The idea is that a meaning comes to mind *prior* to the speaker's going on to use a sign, so that his future use may *fit*, or *fail to fit*, it.

If it is merely the sign 'Add 2' that comes before a speaker's mind, then clearly this could not constrain the application of it. For McDowell, it is the assumption that only a sign comes before the mind which leads inexorably to the idea that what comes before the mind requires an act of interpretation, and hence to the infinite regress that generates the sceptical paradox. If we are not to be forced by this reflection into accepting the idea that normativity can be made sense of only in the public realm – an idea which McDowell believes destroys the phenomenon of meaning altogether – then it must be more than a mere sign that comes before the mind; it must be the meaning of the sign, at least for those who have been initiated.

Thus, McDowell's naturalized Platonism depends upon the idea that there is an innocuous sense in which 'the meaning of an expression can be present in an instant' (McDowell 1998a, 258), a sense in which it is not the target of Wittgenstein's deliberations on rule-following. According to McDowell, we can avoid the fatal regress of interpretations *only* if we conceive of what is present to the mind neither as a mere sign ('a brute chunk of the "in-itself"'), nor as a sign *plus* an interpretation of it. Thus, we need, not merely the sign and the application which, in the course of time, is made of it, but a *third* thing: the thing which normatively connects the sign to its application, which comes before a speaker's mind and makes the application he goes on to make the one which is *correct*. However, this does not yet tell us how we are to conceive of this third thing, which is neither the sign nor the application of the sign. McDowell believes that anti-reductionism comes to his aid here: we can only tell someone what comes before a speaker's mind when he hears and understands the words 'Add 2', if our informant understands the language we are using. In that case, we can say that what comes before the speaker's mind is *that he is to add 2*.

It is not only that this looks very close to the idea that Wittgenstein intends to lampoon in *PI* §95, but it also suggests that what Wittgenstein regards as the central issue is not really addressed by McDowell. For Wittgenstein, the central issue is how does the concept of meaning function: does the word 'mean', for example, in the sentence *I mean you are to add 2*, stand for a state 'that occurs in a moment' (*PI* §151)? McDowell takes the issue to be our right to use the expression 'mean' in the way that we do, and his transcendental argument is meant to show that our right to use it as we do depends upon the word's standing for a state in which the meaning of 'Add 2' 'comes to mind' and has 'normative links to the objective world'. We have not, so far at least, been able to see how it *is* the case, but McDowell believes there is a philosophical argument which shows that '*this* is how it *has to be*' (*PI* §112). This suggests that McDowell's conception of understanding, as a mental state which grounds, or makes true, the assertion, *I mean addition by 'plus'*, is committed to a view about how the concepts of meaning and understanding *must* function, if they are not to be empty. To this extent, his liberal naturalism incorporates an a priori element which is, prima facie at least, at odds with the naturalistic approach to conceptual clarification which is distinctive of Wittgenstein's later philosophy.

According to McDowell, we *must* leave room for the idea that 'understanding is grasping patterns that extend to new cases independently of our ratification'; this is required 'for meaning to be other than an illusion' (McDowell 1998a, 256). The constraint on future applications of an expression must have autonomy, but it cannot be 'the platonistic autonomy with which they are credited in the picture of the super-rigid machinery' (McDowell 1998a, 256). If we reject the possibility of a constructive account of meaning, then, McDowell suggests, all we can say is that we, as a community of speakers, go right in calling a newly encountered object 'yellow' 'according to whether the object in question is, or is not, *yellow*; and nothing can make a thing yellow, or not, dependent on our ratification of the judgement that that is how things are' (McDowell 1998a, 256). The question is: how are we to understand this idea of a *fit* between the world and what we *mean*? McDowell suggests that the crucial idea of meanings coming to mind and determining what counts as correct or incorrect must 'be carefully understood in the light of the thesis that there is a way of grasping a rule that is not an interpretation' (McDowell 1998a, 258), but he gives no further explication of how exactly this 'thesis' enables us to avoid what Wittgenstein clearly regards as the 'strange' idea that 'this *meaning the order* ['Add 2'] had in its own way already taken all [the] steps' (*PI* §188).

McDowell accepts that when I follow a signpost, 'I simply act as I have been trained to' (McDowell 1998a, 239). However, the question arises what makes my immediate response to the signpost an instance of following a rule. 'The reply,' McDowell suggests, 'is that the training in question is initiation into a custom' (McDowell 1998a, 239). It is the fact that there is a custom of using signposts, into which I have been initiated, that 'entitles us to speak of following (going by) a sign-post' (McDowell 1998a, 239). This is clearly an echo of *PI* §198, but so far it appears to amount to a thought that McDowell rejects, namely that '[o]rdinary cases of following a sign-post involve simply acting in the way which comes naturally to one in such circumstances, in consequence of some training one underwent in one's upbringing', on the grounds that it 'under-mentaliz[es] the behaviour' (McDowell 1998b, 276). There is nothing in what has been said so far that corresponds to McDowell's talk of 'acting on an understanding', of 'meanings coming to mind', or of mental states which 'contain within themselves the distinction between conformity and non-conformity'.

So far, there is only talk of the natural responses of those who have undergone a certain training, which occur in the context of an established usage of signposts, that is, in a context in which there is something that is called 'going by a signpost' and something that is called 'failing to go by the signpost'. McDowell has argued that if we are restricted to these resources, then we shall not be able to accommodate meaning at all, for we have not succeeded in showing that 'a person's understanding could be her having something in mind' (McDowell 1998b, 270). McDowell recognizes the danger in this appeal to natural responses and the existence of a custom, but all he says in response to it is to repeat the point that, if we allow norms to leach out of our conception of the immediate response in this way, then we 'cannot prevent meaning from coming to seem an illusion' (McDowell 1998a, 242). He adds, once again, the suggestion that 'the key to finding the indispensable middle course [between the infinite regress and a reductive anti-realism] is the idea of a custom or practice' (McDowell 1998a, 242), but he does not show how, once we have this idea in place, we can make sense of the idea that 'the meaning of an expression can be present in an instant'. Given his commitment to the idea of internal states with normative force, it seems clear that appeal to natural responses and existing customs cannot be the end of the story; there is a sense that something further needs to be said. Thus, McDowell concedes that '[u]ntil more is said about how exactly the appeal to communal practice makes the middle course available, this is only a programme for a solution to Wittgenstein's problem' (McDowell 1998a, 242).

McDowell's implicit assumption is that it is not enough to accept that we employ normative notions in the description of what we and others say and do, in an ongoing stable practice in which our use of these normative notions is woven in with a host of non-linguistic responses and activities. Rather, we must show that our employment of these notions has the status of sound currency, by showing that our use of them is *backed* by states of affairs which can be conceived as 'meanings coming to mind', and which in themselves determine how expressions are to be applied in the future. As I remarked earlier, this appears to be a commitment to how normative concepts *must* function, if there is to be any genuine normativity. McDowell's trans-cendental argument has the effect of imposing a standard which any concepts must meet, if they are to qualify as concepts of *meaning* and *understanding* at all.

From McDowell's perspective, to take Wittgenstein's remarks on rule-following to show that our ordinary concepts of meaning and understanding do not function in the way his transcendental argument requires, is to 'destroy meaning altogether'. I want to suggest that, for Wittgenstein by contrast, the aim is to see how our concepts of meaning and under-standing *actually* function. The legitimacy of our ordinary language game is not in question, but it is possible that we will come to see that our concepts do not function in the way we initially supposed they *must*, namely as standing, respectively, for 'shadowy beings' which are distinct from the sign, or for states of mind which somehow anticipate the future. In the context of Wittgenstein's approach to conceptual clarification, coming to see this does not represent either a threat to our ordinary ways of speaking and acting, or a claim that 'all we really mean' by these nor-mative expressions is something that can be expressed in non-normative terms.

***

The suggestion is that in holding that we need to preserve the idea that 'meanings come to mind', McDowell is committed to the very idea of shadows that Wittgenstein's naturalism is intended to liberate us from. Wittgenstein describes the temptation to picture meaning and understanding as processes involving shadows in *The Big Typescript*:

> *Being able* to do something has a shadowy quality, i.e. it seems like a shadow of actually doing, just as the sense of a proposition seems like the shadow of its verification; or the understanding of a command the shadow of its being carried out.
>
> (*BT*, 112)

He sees the temptation to create shadows as springing from a difficulty in reconciling two things: (1) that the meaning of a word is the *use* that we make of it; (2) that we speak of grasping the meaning of a word 'at a stroke' (*PI* §138), or of knowing what a word means *when* someone says it to me. The question this prompts is: 'can the *use* of a word come before my mind when I *understand* it in this way?' (*PI* §139). As he remarks in *The Big Typescript*, '[t]he most difficult problem seems to be the contrast, the relationship, between carrying out linguistic operations over time and instantaneous grasping of a sentence' (*BT*, 113).

In *PI* §139, Wittgenstein asks us to consider the example of hearing and understanding the word 'cube' when someone says it to me. He asks us to imagine that what comes before my mind when I hear and understand it in this way is a drawing of a cube. McDowell's thought is that, considered in itself, the drawing does not introduce a unique constraint on its application, but is interpretable, and thus applicable, in indefinitely many ways. However, for someone who has been trained in the practice of employing it, the picture which comes before his mind has a normative power, so that what comes before his mind in itself determines what counts as a correct, and what as an incorrect, application of it. But isn't this just the problematic idea that 'understanding [is] an instantaneous grasping of something, and all one had to do was then draw out its consequences; so that these consequences already existed in an ideal sense before they were drawn' (*BT*, 127)?

Wittgenstein's own response to the example contrasts sharply with McDowell's:

> The picture of the cube did indeed *suggest* a certain use to us, but it was also possible for me to use it differently.
>
> (*PI* §139)

The idea that the picture *'suggests'* a use amounts to the observation that I *respond* to the picture in a particular way, so that, if I were asked to apply it, then immediately and without reflection, I would apply it in one particular way. This is a fact that 'lies open to view', the kind of fact which Wittgenstein's naturalism sets out to describe. In describing the facts this way, the possibility is clearly left open that someone else may respond to the picture differently, so that, if he were asked, he would make a quite different application of it. And the clear implication is that the very idea that what comes before my mind is something which 'forces' a particular application – that is, imposes a normative constraint – on me is an illusion:

> What is essential now is to see that the same thing may be in our minds when we hear the word and yet the application still be different. Has it the *same* meaning both times? I think we would deny that.
>
> (*PI* §140)

The implication of this, clearly, is that the meaning is *not* something which 'comes to mind'. It is true that in *PI* §141, Wittgenstein goes on to respond to the interlocutor's question, 'but can't an *application come before my mind?*', by saying, 'It can'. And this may be taken to indicate that he does, after all, accept McDowell's view that meanings, and not merely signs, can come to mind. However, it is crucial that Wittgenstein follows the response, 'It can', by observing 'only we need to become clearer about our application of *this* expression' (*PI* §141). McDowell takes it that in responding, 'It can', Wittgenstein is accepting that there is a determinate mental state of understanding a sign, which already determines what counts as conformity or non-conformity with it. However, this is just to make the very assumption about 'our application of *this* expression', which Wittgenstein's reflections put in question.

The only idea of 'constraint' that Wittgenstein mentions, in connection with the picture that comes before my mind, is this one: 'that only the one case and no other occurred to [me]' (*PI* §140). Asked whether there can be a collision between the picture and an application that is made of it, Wittgenstein responds:

> Well, they can clash in so far as the picture makes us expect a different use; because people in general apply *this* picture like *this*. I want to say: we have here a *normal* case and abnormal cases.
>
> (*PI* §141)

Again, these are facts that are 'open to view'. There is a practice, or regular use, of the drawing that comes before my mind, and a particular application of the drawing may conflict with the practice of using it. Someone who applies the picture to a triangular prism, say, does not agree with us in how he *acts* with the picture, in how he responds to it. He is similar to the person for whom 'it comes naturally ... to react to the gesture of pointing with the hand by looking in the direction from fingertip to wrist, rather than from wrist to fingertip' (*PI* §186).

There is clearly no sense that in speaking of 'normal' and 'abnormal' cases, or of the way someone 'naturally ... react[s]', Wittgenstein intends to preserve the idea that understanding is a 'definite state that we come to be in when we come to understand, [say], the principle of a series' (McDowell 2009a, 95), so that 'in the light of [it] it is completely settled what numbers it is correct to write when one reaches a certain point in extending the series' (McDowell 2009a, 95). The sense is that we are making a fundamental mistake as long as we are tempted to ground the idea of a clash between a sign and its application in the psychological realm, or in what comes before my mind when I understand it. What comes before my mind is a sign which, as a result of my training and my own natural ways of going on, I have an established way of *operating* with. Not only that, but the way in which I operate with the sign is in agreement with an established practice of using it. The rule 'already settles' the future applications for me, in the sense that I make these applications 'as *a matter of course*' (*PI* §238). In the context of the practice in which I have been trained, I not only respond to the sign in a particular way, but my particular way of operating with the sign is in agreement with a practice of using it. It is in these circumstances, Wittgenstein suggests, that we can speak of a sign's having a use, and thus of a *clash* between the practice of using it and an (abnormal) application that is made of it.

All of this suggests that Wittgenstein believes that the concept of meaning doesn't function in the way McDowell describes. The meaning of the sign is not something which 'comes to mind' and fixes what counts as a correct application of it; rather, we can speak of a sign's having a meaning when there is an established practice of using it. The meaning of a sign *is* its use in the practice of operating with it, in which all of us agree, and which is woven in, in countless ways, with other things we say and do. All of this is open to view; it is part of 'the natural history of human beings' that they do, independently and without guidance, agree in how they operate with signs. It's by such observations as these that Wittgenstein hopes gradually to persuade us that we have no need of the mysterious idea of a third thing – the meaning of the sign which comes before the mind in an instant – which mediates between a sign and its application. Grasping a rule is not a matter of something's 'coming to mind' – is not, in this sense, an 'internal state' – but is what 'from case to case of application, is *exhibited in what we call* "following the rule" and "going against it"' (*PI* §201, my italics). Wittgenstein expresses these thoughts clearly in *The Big Typescript* as follows:

> I want to say that signs have their meaning neither by virtue of what accompanies them, nor because of what evokes them – but by virtue of a system to which they belong – one, however, in which when a word is uttered nothing need be present other than that word.
>
> (*BT*, 155)

> But let's not talk about "meaning something" as an indefinite process, that we don't know very well, but about the (actual) "practical" use of the word, about the actions that we carry out with it.
>
> (*BT*, 157)

> I would like to say: A sign only works dynamically, not statically. Thought is dynamic.
>
> (*BT*, 126)

The picture of thought as 'dynamic', I want to argue, is central to Wittgenstein's naturalism. It is central to his new conception of philosophical method, which aims to make the way concepts function clear by looking at how the relevant expressions are used in our life with language: at how we are taught to operate with an expression, at the circumstances in which we learn its use, at the criteria by which we judge that someone has understood an expression we are trying to teach him, at the way its use is woven in with other activities, and so on. More particularly, it is also central to Wittgenstein's attempt to liberate us from the idea of meanings as 'shadowy beings', and from the picture of understanding as a process which flies ahead and takes all the steps before we physically arrive at this or that one. The idea is that we should forget the mysterious idea of a logical fit between a state of mind and what fulfils it, and look instead at the way in which it is against the background of an ongoing practice of using signs, which is woven in with countless human activities, that what counts as accord and failure to accord is settled. In these circumstances, there are clear criteria by which we judge that someone asserted so-and-so, or thought such-and-such, and criteria by which we judge whether what he said or thought is correct, but none of this involves the idea of an inner state which anticipates the future.

By holding that we have to preserve the idea that understanding is a mental state which makes its appearance at a moment, in its entirety, McDowell's view is prima facie at odds with this dynamic element in Wittgenstein's naturalistic vision. The idea of thought as dynamic is, in part at least, what is expressed in the idea that 'everything lies open to view' and 'there is nothing to explain' (*PI* §126), which is fundamentally opposed to McDowell's central claim, namely, that our ordinary language game, with the words 'mean', 'understand', and so on, must be backed by mental states which *normatively* explain our all agreeing in the application of words, in so far as the latter *must* be understood as our all 'keeping faith' with the meaning that comes to mind, or with what is anticipated in our earlier state of understanding. The whole point of Wittgenstein's naturalistic approach is that the concepts of meaning and understanding do not stand for internal states which in themselves impose a normative constraint on what we do, but function within an agreed way of operating with expressions which is the *natural*, that is to say, *normal* outcome of the training we receive. Normative notions come in insofar as what we say and do is part of a practice in which saying and doing *that*, in this context and in these circumstances, is what *we call* 'following the rule' and 'going against it'; the idea of what *must* or *ought* to be done is given content by there being something that, in the particular circumstances, *we call* 'following the rule' or 'obeying the order' and 'going against it'.

Earlier, I suggested that McDowell doesn't acknowledge a clear distinction between, on the one hand, the idea that we must reject the anti-realist assumption that what counts as correct is constituted by community agreement; and on the other, the claim that we must make sense of the idea that 'meaning comes to mind'. What is now becoming clear is that Wittgenstein is committed to rejecting a reductive account of what constitutes correctness, but does not accept that this requires us to make sense of the idea that 'meaning comes to mind'. The latter idea is nothing but an expression of a tempting picture, one which we find very compelling, but which makes no connection with how the concepts of meaning and understanding actually function. The picture gives rise to the mythological idea that 'in a *strange* way, the use itself is in some sense present' (*PI* §195). This idea of 'a superlative link' between, say, a formula that we grasp and an application we go on to make of it arises, he suggests, '[a]s a result of the crossing of different pictures' (*PI* §191). The 'must' in 'You must say 1,002 after 1,000' points to our practice of mathematics; it is not an anthropological statement. There is, however, no psychological analogue of this 'must', that is to say, no idea of a logical fit between what comes before someone's mind and what they go on to do.

***

At *PI* §195, Wittgenstein responds to the interlocutor's insistence 'that, in a *strange* way, the use itself is in some sense present', as follows:

> But of course it is, 'in *some* sense'! Really, the only thing wrong with what you say is the expression "in an odd way". The rest is right, and the sentence

seems odd only when one imagines it to belong to a different language-game from the one in which we actually use it.

The idea that the use is present 'in an odd way' arises, Wittgenstein suggests, when we misunderstand the use of the word, and take 'it to signify an odd *process*' (PI §196). He goes on:

> "It's as if we could grasp the whole use of a word at a stroke." – Well, that is just what we say we do. That is, we sometimes describe what we do in these words. But there is nothing astonishing, nothing strange about what happens. It becomes strange when we are led to think that the future development must in some way already be present in the act of grasping the use and yet isn't present. For we say that there isn't any doubt that we understand the word, and on the other hand that its meaning lies in its use.
>
> (PI §197)

Wittgenstein clearly does not want to deny the words 'I grasped the meaning at a stroke', 'I suddenly understood', and so on are used, that is, that they are *correctly* used, on certain occasions. The question, however, is *how* are they used. That, he believes, is something which calls for clarification, by reflecting on how we operate with these sentences. The move that he now makes asks us to compare the use of these sentences with the use of the words 'Let's play a game of chess.' He tries to get us to see that it isn't anything which happens 'at the time', or which is intrinsic to my mental state, which makes it *chess* that I intend to play, but the human context – the particular circumstances, which include facts about my own history – in which I say the words, 'Let's play chess.' Thus, *PI* §197 continues:

> There is no doubt that I now want to play chess, but chess is the game it is in virtue of all its rules (and so on). Don't I know, then, which game I want to play until I *have* played it? Or is it, rather, that all the rules are contained in my act of intending? Is it experience that tells me that this sort of game usually follows such an act of intending? So can't I actually be sure what I intended to do? And if that is nonsense – what kind of super-rigid connection obtains between the act of intending and the thing intended? – Where is the connection effected between the sense of the words "Let's play a game of chess" and all the rules of the game? – Well, in the list of rules of the game, in the teaching of it, in the everyday practice of playing.

In these circumstances, my saying, 'Let's play a game of chess', is a criterion of my having the intention to play chess. And what is chess? Well, it is *this*, and here we point to the list of rules, the everyday practice, and so on. Nothing extraordinary is involved. I fulfil my intention only if I go on to do what *we call* 'playing chess'. Everything we need to understand the use of the words 'Let's play a game of chess' is in the public domain and no idea of an internal state which anticipates the future, or of logical fit between what comes before my mind and what I go on to do, comes into it. Similarly, in certain circumstances, my saying, 'Now I understand', or a certain formula's coming to mind, is a criterion of my grasping the principle of a series. And if we want to know where the connection between the words, 'Now I understand' – or the formula that comes to mind – and a particular mathematical series is made, then it is in the rules of mathematics, in the everyday practice of applying those rules in calculation, and in my having undergone a training in that practice. In these circumstances we say that I understood the principle of the series, when the formula 'came to mind', but there is nothing mysterious in that. Nothing need be present in my mind *other than* the formula.

Thus, the idea is that everything we need to understand what distinguishes a case of following a rule (understanding a sign) from a mere regularity is 'there before our eyes'. It is not only that the former is connected with an idea of teaching, and of correcting a pupil's responses until he performs 'to our satisfaction' (*PI* §145), 'that is, as we do it' (*PI* §145). There are also distinctive ways of behaving that make it apt to speak of someone's seeking confirmation from others, of his acknowledging a mistake, of what he says and does having a point within the context of a wider activity, and so on. The idea that everything we need to understand is in the public domain, or manifest in the ongoing practice of our life with signs, is meant to counter the 'disastrous effect [of] the preoccupation with the "sense" of a proposition, with the "thought" that it expresses' (*BT*, 210), but it is not intended to revise, reconstruct or provide a philosophically novel explication of our ordinary notions. It is intended merely to describe the criteria on the basis of which we describe someone as having meant such-and-such, or as grasping the meaning of a word, and to get us to see that they relate to what the speakers *do* with words, and to the context in which they do them, and not to what goes on in their heads when they hear or say them. Given that there is a practice of operating with words, the words someone says have a meaning and are thus a criterion of his having said, or thought, such-and-such; and that means that we can predict a great deal, both about the world and the other things that someone will say and do, from what he says, and generally nothing occurs to worry us.

All this may still leave a sense of puzzlement about the first-person present indicative use of the word 'understand'. The first-person expression of sudden understanding may once again tempt us to picture understanding as a state which makes its appearance 'in a moment', and which explains our ability to go on correctly. If this were not the case, then how could I know that I am justified in saying 'Now I understand', when, for example, the formula which gives the principle of a mathematical series comes to mind. We have agreed that, in certain circumstances, the formula's coming to mind is a criterion of understanding. If the formula's occurring to me does not *on its own* justify my saying 'Now I can go on', then how can I know that I use these words correctly? Do I have to rely on my knowing that a connection has been established between the formula's coming to my mind in this way and my actually continuing the series correctly? And do I have to be claiming that such an empirical connection exists when I say, in particular circumstances, 'Now I can go on', on the basis of a formula's occurring to me? All this, Wittgenstein points out, gives a wrong picture of the way in which our having been trained in the practice of mathematics 'set[s] the stage for our language-game' (*PI* §179). Wittgenstein writes:

> The words "Now I know how to go on" were correctly used when the formula occurred to [me]: namely, under certain circumstances. For example, if [I] had learnt algebra, had used such formulae before. – But that does not mean that [my] statement is only short for a description of all the circumstances which set the stage for our language-game.

My mastery of the practice of mathematics is not something that occurs *while* I think of the formula, but it is the background which gives my thinking of the formula the significance it has. My words do not implicitly *refer* to this background, my training in the practice of mathematics forms the horizon within which my use of the words 'Now I understand' functions. The formula's occurring to me is not, of course, the only criterion of my grasping the principle of the series; there are different criteria, including, in certain circumstances, my simply going on working out the series without thinking of a formula. Moreover, it is clear in the latter case that '[i]t would be quite misleading … to call the words ["Now I know how to go on"] a "description of a mental state"' (*PI* §180). We would, Wittgenstein suggests, be better off (less likely to misunderstand) if we think of these words as a 'signal' (*PI* §180), or as 'an instinctive sound, a glad start' (*PI* 323). Whether they are rightly employed is not determined by anything occurring in my mind at the time I say them; rather 'we judge whether [they were] rightly applied by what [I] go on to do' (*PI* §180).

Wittgenstein also considers the first-person, past-tense use of the verb to mean. In *PI* §666, Wittgenstein asks us to imagine a case in which someone is in pain and simultaneously hearing a nearby piano being tuned. He says 'It'll soon stop'. It clearly makes a difference whether he means the pain or the piano-tuning, but what does this difference consist in? In *PI* §678, Wittgenstein takes up the question: 'What does this meaning (the pain, or the piano-tuning) consist in?' Hasn't he shown that whatever comes before a person's mind does not have its significance 'written into it'? So it seems that '[n]o answer comes – for the answers which at first sight suggest themselves are of no use' (*PI* §678). Doesn't it follow, then, that we cannot say that he meant one thing rather than the other when he said the words 'It'll soon stop'? Wittgenstein's interlocutor clearly feels that it does follow, for he objects: '"And yet at the time I *meant* the one thing and not the other."' (*PI* §678). Wittgenstein responds:

> Yes – now you have only repeated with emphasis something which no one has contradicted anyway.
>
> (*PI* §678)

This dialogue echoes the exchange at the opening of *PI* §187:

> "But I already knew, at the time when I gave the order, that he should write 1002 after 1000" – Certainly; and you may even say you *meant* it then; only you shouldn't let yourself be misled by the grammar of the words "know" and "mean".

In both cases, we are inclined to picture the knowing or meaning as a mental state in which the mind, in some unique way, flies beyond itself. The problem is that nothing corresponds to this idea. It is not, however, that Wittgenstein is asserting that it is incorrect, or makes no sense, to say 'I knew at the time I gave the order that he should write 1,002 after 1,000', or 'I meant the piano-tuning, not the pain.' Rather, as he observes in *PI* §187, '[y]our "I already knew at the time ... " amounts to something like: "If I had then been asked what number he should write after 1000, I would have replied '1002'."' In certain circumstances – for example, ones in which the speaker has learned arithmetic and is familiar with the technique of expanding series in response to the order 'Add *n*' – his saying *now*, 'If I had been asked ... , I would have answered ... ', is a criterion of his knowing, at the time he gave the order 'Add 2', that the pupil should write '1,002' after '1,000'.

Analogously, 'I meant the piano-tuning at the time I said the words "It'll soon stop"' amounts to something like: 'If I had been asked at the time I said those words what I meant, I would have answered "the piano-tuning".' In certain circumstances – for example, ones in which the speaker has learned English – this is a criterion of his having meant the piano tuning, and not the pain. In response to the question, '"But can you doubt that you mean *this*?"' (*PI* §679), Wittgenstein responds: 'No; but neither can I be certain of it, know it' (*PI* §679). The suggestion is, that it belongs to the grammar of the word 'mean' that we learn to give spontaneous and confident expression, not only to what we mean, but also to what we *meant*; there is no question of knowledge of a process, and thus no question of *how* we know it occurred. This is a description of how the word 'mean' is used.

It is clear that it would be fundamentally contrary to the spirit of Wittgenstein's conception of his philosophical aims to take the above observations in the reductive spirit of anti-realism. The forms of activity that are part of human natural history – '[g]iving orders, asking questions, telling stories, having a chat' (*PI* §25) – are ones which are intrinsically normative, that is to say, are ones in which it is settled, not by agreement but by what, in our practice is called ' ... ', whether what someone does counts, in the circumstances, as obeying an order, giving a correct description, carrying out a calculation, and so on. Taking part in these characteristic forms of activity is something that is manifest over time in what we say and do. In the context of these human practices, it makes sense to speak of someone's being struck by a thought, under-standing an order, forming an intention, expecting something, imagining something, and so on. The essential thing to see, Wittgenstein believes, is that our ways of describing what we do do not depend upon there being mental states which make their appearance in a moment, and which contain within themselves conditions of conformity or non-conformity. Rather, these descriptions get their point, not from something which happens at the time, but from the context of a form of life which we naturally come to share through the kind of training and education we receive. The focus on the form of our life with language is how Wittgenstein works to persuade us that, in these characteristically normative practices, 'nothing extraordinary is involved', our participation in them is a refinement of natural human responses, and everything we need to understand their normative nature is there before our eyes in the form of the practices them-selves; the picture of mental states which mysteriously anticipate the future, and which subsequent performances fit or fail to fit, does not come into it.

***

I've argued that there is a clear divergence between Wittgenstein and McDowell in respect of both their approach to the philosophical problem of the nature of meaning and understanding, and, more importantly, in respect of their critical relation to the idea that 'meanings come to mind'. It is not clear, however, what the philosophical significance of this alleged divergence is. From a Wittgensteinian perspective, perhaps the most appropriate question is whether either approach succeeds in achieving the aim of 'giv[ing] philosophy peace' (*PI* §133). From that perspective, it could be argued that the problem with McDowell's position is that it does not put an end to the problems Wittgenstein raises, in the remarks on rule-following, for the idea 'that in meaning ... , your mind, as it were, flew ahead and took all the steps before you physically arrived at this or that one' (*PI* §188).

If Wittgenstein's naturalism gets us out of this bind, then clearly, by his own account, it is not in virtue of any sort of discovery. It is, rather, that the problems that he believes will torment us as long as we try to make good the idea of a state which in itself determines what counts as conformity or non-conformity with it, disappear when we are reminded of the aspects of our use of expressions that Wittgenstein's naturalistic approach to conceptual clarification focuses on. If he is right in claiming that this approach 'leaves everything as it is' (*PI* §124), then it might be argued that McDowell's conception of a liberal version of naturalism loses nothing in giving up the idea which, according to Wittgenstein, is the source of philosophical paradox.

It remains the case that it is often correct to say that someone understands such-and-such by so-and-so, means such-and-such, thought such-and-such, and so on. What being correct amounts to is something which is manifest over time, but there is no reductive account of what these things being true consists in. If we are tempted to suppose that its being correct to say these things depends on the subject's being in a mental state which mysteriously anticipates the future, then Wittgenstein's descriptions of what goes on in particular cases – of the criteria by which we judge these things, of the context in which we learn to use the relevant expressions, of the contexts in which we apply them, and so on – can enable us to see that no such idea comes into it. There is no need to make this strange idea intelligible; it rests entirely on a misunderstanding of how we use these words. Nothing is lost in abandoning it and, by abandoning it, we can see practices such as giving and obeying orders, calculating, describing, inferring, and so on as part of our natural history.

Note

1   Abbreviations of works by Wittgenstein in this chapter are as follows; references are to pages of these translations (unless otherwise specified):

BB   *The Blue and Brown Books*, Oxford: Wiley Blackwell, 1958
BT   *The Big Typescript: TS 213*, ed. and trans. C.G. Luckhardt and M.A.E. Aue, Oxford: Wiley Blackwell, 2005
CV   *Culture and Value*, rev. edn, ed. G.H. von Wright, Oxford: Wiley Blackwell, 1998
PI   *Philosophical Investigations*, rev. 4th edn, ed. P.M.S. Hacker and J. Schulte, trans. G.E.M. Anscombe, P.M.S. Hacker and J. Schulte, Oxford: Wiley Blackwell, 2009
TLP   *Tractatus Logico Philosophicus*, trans. D.F. Pears and B.F. McGuinness, London: Routledge, 1961.

References

McDowell, J.H. (1998a) 'Wittgenstein on Rule-Following', in *Mind, Value and Reality*, Cambridge, MA: Harvard University Press, 221–62.

——(1998b) 'Meaning and Intentionality in Wittgenstein's Later Philosophy', in *Mind, Value and Reality*, Cambridge, MA: Harvard University Press, 263–78.

——(1998c) 'Intentionality and Interiority in Wittgenstein', in *Mind, Value and Reality*, Cambridge, MA: Harvard University Press, 297–324.

——(2009a) 'Are Meaning, Understanding, etc., Definite States?', in *The Engaged Intellect: Philosophical Essays*, Cambridge, MA: Harvard University Press, 79–95.

——(2009b) 'Naturalism in the Philosophy of Mind', in *The Engaged Intellect: Philosophical Essays*, Cambridge, MA: Harvard University Press, 257–78.

7   Naturalism on the Sydney Plan
JENANN ISMAEL

The most influential self-proclaimed naturalistic approach in the contemporary philosophical literature in metaphysics is the Canberra Plan.[1] On the Canberra Plan, questions of what the world is like are left to physics. It falls to metaphysics to say what features of the world described by physics various classes of everyday belief represent. I will contrast this with naturalistic metaphysics on the Sydney Plan. The Sydney Plan is a style of naturalism that has been advocated and practised over the years by Huw Price, who is not only the father, but the sponsor and primary benefactor of the Sydney Plan, actively bringing together different strands of pragmatism in the philosophical community under its auspices.[2] Neither the Sydney nor the Canberra Plan are presented here as the view of any one person. They rather collect some unifying commitments and a common approach to metaphysical questions. Sydney Planners are united by opposition to the view of representation as a kind of mirroring which still shapes traditional approaches in metaphysics and epistemology, and by a commitment to naturalism. Their work in various ways makes contributions to a positive, anti-representationalist understanding of linguistic and mental phenomena. Where the Canberra Plan asks 'what do x beliefs represent?' the Sydney Plan raises the question 'what facts about ourselves and the world jointly support the formation of x beliefs and the role they play in our lives?' Where the Canberra Plan conceives of the relationship between everyday concepts and the Absolute structures described by a fundamental theory in terms of semantic notions (reference, truth, and satisfaction), the Sydney Plan substitutes a fully detailed side-on account of use that may or may not take the form of a traditional theory of reference.[3] There will be a story about agents and their relation to the world and how concepts facilitate their interaction, but there won't always be something that looks like reference to an independently well-defined feature of the landscape. As I see it, the Sydney Plan as a generalization of the Canberra Plan, that is conservative of much of the work done under the auspices of the Canberra Plan but comes with a somewhat more permissive understanding of what it is for some everyday concept to 'find a place' in a scientific vision of reality.[4]

In the first section, I'll introduce the Canberra Plan. I'll spend the rest of the chapter contrasting it with the Sydney Plan and saying how the attempt to fit everything into its mould leads to certain kinds of recognizable errors.

The search for truthmakers: naturalism on the Canberra Plan

The body of everyday belief is a motley collection of partially overlapping loosely integrated representations. There are words, images, maps, sounds, symbols, and sensory impressions organized around concepts connected in a Quinean web of inferential relations.[5]

There was a time when philosophy was all about conceptual analysis. We were interested in norms that govern relations among concepts and their relations to perception and action. The methods were a priori, and for some who thought that the structure of our concepts was authoritative about the structure of Being, this was a way of exploring the structure of Being. When naturalistic philosophers began to look to science for an understanding of what the world is like, the project turned from one of describing relations among concepts to one of relating concepts to the world. The Canberra Plan introduced a division of labour. The job of science, according to The Canberra Plan, is to give us an account of what the world is like, and the task of the metaphysician is to find something in the scientifically given world that can serve as reference for objects and properties we quantify over in everyday discourse. David Lewis generalized and perfected the method introduced by Ramsey and developed further by Horwich. First we collect everyday platitudes using the concept to be interpreted. We pull these together in the form of an implicit theory, and then we Ramsify. Whatever comes closest to satisfying the Ramsified theory is then presented as an explicit physical characterization of the concept's extension. This is a picture of representation born of experience with the maps and models. Concepts are interpreted by extensional mapping that assign referents from the target domain. It is built on the paradigm of what Price calls 'matching games'.

> Imagine a child's puzzle book, designed like this. On the right side of each page there's a picture of a complex scene, on the left side a column of peel-off stickers. For each sticker – the Opera House, the Harbour Bridge, the koala, and so on – the child needs to find the corresponding object in the picture. The game is successfully completed when every sticker has been placed in its correct location.

Now think of the right-hand side as the world, and the column of stickers as the set of statements we take to be true of the world. For each statement, it seems natural to ask what makes it true – what fact in the world has precisely the 'shape' required to do the job. Matching true statements to the world seems a lot like matching stickers to the picture ... [6]

That is a very natural and compelling picture of how the terms in a natural language (or the concepts that furnish components of everyday belief) relate to the world. Beliefs encode information about identifiable configurations of elements in the landscape, and the direction of fit is from belief to world. If there is a mismatch, something is wrong with the belief. But it doesn't fit very well with a naturalistic view of representational practices. It builds in from the get-go a quite restricted view of the function of belief that fails in a way that is readily apparent when we take a side-on view of our own representational practices.[7]

Representational practices: facade construction

Representations of all kinds (from the mental models generated by the brain to the everyday maps and artefacts that we steer by, to the specialized products of professional science) have the status of user interfaces designed to facilitate interaction between an active system and an open environment. In practice, representation isn't about constructing scaled models or copies of the world. It is about constructing facades. Facades capture the stable structures in restricted domains, at a certain scale, and against the background of unrepresented, and often unknown, scaffolding.[8] They are idealized, simplified, sometimes distorted. They filter, transform, and embellish with auxiliary structures designed to facilitate specialized uses.[9]

Most of us, in our day-to-day lives, steer by a collection of partially overlapping, and loosely integrated, facades. Whether we are talking about the everyday maps that we steer by or the norms governing the use of concepts that we internalize with our languages, these are not hatched fully formed, but grown over generations. They are evolved, and structured, to provide a user interface between a situated agent and her environment. We represent with concepts we inherit and steer by maps that were selected, not as best copies, but because they fared best in a competition judged on practical grounds. They typically reduce high-variable spaces to low-dimensional spaces that highlight strategically important structures for solving epistemic and practical problems.[10] Mark Wilson's *Wandering Significance* is an immensely rich exploration of the complexity of the relationship between concepts, and is summarized here by Brandom:

When things work well, when the concepts we deploy succeed in making the phenomena they address tractable, the result is the fabrication of a conceptual platform: a kind of workbench-with-tools that is the context in which things become available to us to observe, work on, manipulate, reason about, and investigate theoretically.

(Brandom 2011, 189)

Wilson introduces the very apt term 'facade' to describe these conceptual platforms.[11] Facades are tools, natural and human-made, designed to help us navigate a complex and changing world, and the structures defined on them earn their place in our lives because they work in the tasks for which they are appointed. We use the tools that we have inherited without an engineer's insight into why they work. Just as the cook learns to use the implements of his trade without needing to understand the physical principles that make them work, the gambler who knows how to use probabilities need have no understanding of the facts about the world that make the practices embodied in the norms that govern probabilistic reasoning work well (or well enough) as a guide to betting behaviour. Our belief-forming practices often have a quite complex behind-the-scenes rationale that is not explicitly represented at the level of content. We learn to use concepts by internalizing the norms that govern their use without needing to worry about that rationale. The side-on view makes the behind-the-scenes 'rationale' explicit, exhibiting the facts about Nature on the one hand, and ourselves on the other, that make them useful, giving us an engineer's insight into why those practices were selected and what they do for the creatures that use them.

Towards a conception of Being qua Being

Metaphysics means different things to different people, but there is a good tradition stemming from Aristotle according to which metaphysics is inquiry directed at the study of Being qua Being, which is to say, the study of what there is in the most general sense, not from a particular perspective in space and time, or as it appears to a particular class of creatures, but as it is *in itself*.[12] Physics aims for such a conception, but it doesn't stand on its own. It is part of an integrated science that has its own internal account of the relationship between the structures described by physics and everyday belief. And the part of science that describes that relationship is not separable from the physics. They are joint products of a form of analysis that gradually decouples our conception of the properties of things from the appearances and affordances they present to the likes of us. The result of this analysis is an articulated vision of the world presented as an object to be viewed through different kinds of sensory lenses and presenting affordances to beings with different capacities and ends.

The process of articulation is slow, laborious, and unavoidably empirical. It finds its most sophisticated expression in science and does not preserve the kinds of reference relationships between pre-articulated beliefs and elements of the post-articulated world that the Canberra Plan demands. Consider the complexity of the physical analysis of sound. A knocker hits the side of a bell, setting up sound waves that traverse the space between that vibrate the hairs on the inner ear, that in turn vibrate the eardrum, which then sends signals to the brain, producing the impression of a chime. Where, or what, in all of this is the sound? Is it at the source where the ringer hits the metal? Is it in the airwaves between the bell and the ear? Is it in the hairs on the ear, in the eardrum, in the brain or mind of the perceiver? I think there is not a clear answer. The everyday conception of sound locates sounds at their source more or less, for many purposes, because it is useful to do so. But it is easy to sway people's intuitions. If you aren't moved by trees falling in the forest with no one around to hear, think of a vacuum in which there are lots of clangers hitting bells, but no sound waves, or think of a world in which bell-clangings produce sound waves, but things are arranged differently between skin and skull so that sound waves produce olfactory rather than auditory experiences. The everyday notion of sound doesn't distinguish between the event that produces the sound, the sound waves themselves, and the qualitative state produced in the hearer if these things are co-present, partly because everyday practice doesn't demand this distinction for practical purposes. Concepts tend to become articulated in response to practical needs, as Dennett remarks here:[13]

> Mother Nature is a stingy, opportunistic engineer who takes advantage of rough correspondences whenever they are good enough for the organism's purposes, given its budget.
>
> (Dennett 1998, 69)

If the goal is to arrive at a conception of Being qua Being, reflecting on the character of our experience won't do us any good in the hard cases, i.e. cases in which we are trying to determine whether some shared feature of experience is part of the mind-independent fabric of the world. We have to take the complex physical interaction between a situated agent and her environment, and try to sort out the various contributions of brain and environment, all the way from the irritations of sensory surfaces out to the distal sources. That's why the side-on view afforded by the study of the situated agent in her environment is indispensable to forming a conception of the way the world is in and of itself. Adopting a side-on view is part and parcel of separating *how things seem* from *how they are*, i.e. how they appear from our perspective in space and time, and in relation to our particular sensibility. There is nothing a priori about that process. It is all part of the ongoing project in which physics partners with the cognitive and human sciences in forming an articulate conception of the natural world and our place in it. The account of Being is not the starting point, but the end point of an inquiry that takes its departure from the familiar world of everyday sense. It is, as I understand it, what the whole of natural science is up to. For these reasons, it is hard to see how there can be a separable enterprise of pure ontology.

The normal progression of physics is in the direction of increasing depth, precision, generality, and objectivity.[14] And it is part of the logic of that progression that the structures to which we have the most immediate phenomenological access are recovered as emergent, scaffolded, approximate, and implicitly relativized to a frame defined by our own situation in the world. Because it is a product of this hermeneutics of experience, the scientific conception of the world implicitly contains an understanding of how the objects of everyday experience relate to the structures described by physics. The familiar world of everyday sense is not reduced, but recovered, from a deeper and more general description as an emergent, approximate order that characterizes elements of Being in terms that implicitly relate it to our own modes of sensory access and interventional capabilities.

Although we have gained a good deal more sophistication about the complexity of the subpersonal preparation that generates the perceived world, it is still correct to think of perception as broadly in the business of feature detecting, carrying information about the landscape to the agent. But if we turn our attention away from concepts that have immediate connections to perception, to moral properties, normativity, modality, causes, and chances, the story is much more complex. The full body of everyday belief is full of concepts that don't simply have the function of describing in the sense of 'reflecting features of the world as it is anyway'. So consider the practice of probabilizing (forming beliefs about probabilities). This grew up as a way of overcoming epistemic deficits, guiding expectation in the face of ignorance. The practice comes with norms embodied in the probability calculus, for forming beliefs about probabilities, reasoning with them, and using them to guide expectation. Or consider the practice of causal modelling, which grew up as a way of guiding action for creatures with limited practical input to the world. The practice comes with its own tacit norms, which we all learn in the course of forming beliefs about causes, reasoning with them, and using them to guide practical inference.

Forming an articulate understanding of what our practices are for and why they work calls for a kind of self-directed hermeneutics that takes a side-on view of the coupling between agent and environment in which those practices have their role. Probabilities and causes have a use for creatures with our particular mix of capacities and limitations. They were developed to help us navigate and guide our contributions to a complex and changing world. They are recovered from the account of Being not as labels for features of the landscape, but as partially prepared solutions to frequently encountered problems.[15] There are all sorts of distinctions we draw at the level of belief that don't reflect structure that is there anyway, but reflect distinctions in our practical and epistemic relations to events. The whole battery of concepts organized around helping us overcome our limitations. The natural function of cognition is to extend our epistemic and practical powers, not by making them stronger, but by making them more effective.

Closing the circle: in retrospect, the relationship between everyday belief and fundamental ontology

Earlier I remarked that the Canberra Plan assumes a division of labour; the job of science is to give us the ontology, and the task of the meta-physician is to interpret our beliefs by an extensional mapping into the ontology provided by physics. The problem is that the overall account of Being embodied in a fully articulated scientific vision of the world, itself contains an account of the relationship between everyday concepts and the fundamental structures. That account goes something like this: it starts with fundamental ontology and talks about how macroscopic structures stabilize out of microinteractions in a way that produces a macroscopic world with a thermodynamic gradient and a good number of open systems that maintain their internal regularity well enough to be predictable. And it chronicles the emergence of creatures (information gathering and utilizing systems) that exploit that regularity by developing the practice of mod-elling. Once there is a fully developed practice of modelling up and running, with creatures utilizing concepts that have evolved through a process of natural and cultural selection to help them cope with a complex and changing environment, it will provide a side-on view of the relationship between the concepts these creatures employ and the Absolute structure of the world as it appears in our fundamental theory. And that side-on view will not support the extensional mappings expected by the match-ing game. The side-on view of the relationship will be in general more complex.

A naturalistic perspective on representational activity views representa-tions of all kinds – from everyday concepts to the specialized products of professional science – as part of a user interface designed to act as an epistemic and practical intermediary with a partly known and locally controllable world, fashioned by an evolutionary design process that balances costs and rewards. There are concepts that reflect the way things are with the world, and concepts that reflect the way things are with us, and then the great, grey area in-between of structures that are simultaneously self- and world-involving in a mix that can't be described in terms that are in general any more compact than the account of their role in the coupling described above. If you want an account from the perspective of physics itself of how our concepts relate to the fundamental structures that it describes, put some scaffolding in place, add some epistemic and practical asymmetries together with a set of cognitive needs and resources, let it evolve until structures have stabilized. The product of this process is not a mirror-like reproduction of the manifold it represents, but something restructured to serve as a user interface for an agent with our native perceptual equipment and all of the acquired tools we have picked up along the way to help us navigate and transform our environment. Representation is something that agents do with all kinds of structured internal images and external artefacts. Because those tools are the product of a combination of biological and cultural engineering that took place outside our field of explicit awareness, for everyday purposes we don't need to have any explicit understanding of the physics behind the facade. That is something that will emerge (if at all) from an inquiry that takes a side-on view of our practices.

Our concepts and the representational practices in which they are embedded have this status. We inherit them with our languages and learn to use them with little explicit awareness of *why* they work. Just as the user of a toaster needs to know how to feed bread in, and the sequence of operations he needs to perform to achieve results, the gambler who uses probabilities needs to know what conditions license an assignment of probability, the inferential calculus that governs the formal operations in probabilistic reasoning, and how to use such assignments to guide his betting behaviour. He needs, in short, to know the norms that guide the practice of probabilizing, but he need not possess an articulate understanding of why the practices work.

Viewed through a naturalist's eyes, all of our practices of applying and using concepts are ways of *coping*, a peculiarly human way of mediating interaction with the world. The Sydney Planner sees the relationship between concepts and Being (from the perspective of Being) as itself an object of investigation whose product will describe how a class of beliefs function, what they do, and what facts about ourselves and the world cooperate to support their use. Where Canberra Planners insist that the relationship between belief about Xs and Being should take the form of an account of what at the level of Being beliefs about Xs 'refer to' or (in the material mode) what Xs are, Sydney Planners viewing the relations from the side-on standpoint see a differentiation of roles. They distinguish concepts that track features of the environment from those that guide expectation and choice. And then there are products of culture, answering to much more complex needs, many of them social in character. In place of the static, two-term relation 'reference', they have a rich plurality of relations mediated by, or passing through, embedded agents, and tailored to perform practical, epistemic, or social functions that cannot be understood in static, disembodied, or unembedded terms. Methodologically, this style of explanation opens up separate (but complementary) explanatory spaces for phenomenology, cognitive science, and the physical sciences, treating them as partners in a fully developed naturalistic worldview.[16]

Naturalism on the Canberra Plan was conceived as addressing placement problems. For any familiar everyday concept, the 'placement problem' vis-à-vis that property is to say how and why the property does or does not 'get ... a place in the scientific account of our world' (Jackson 1998, 3). The Sydney Planner can agree with this. Her disagreement with the Canberra Planner was not with his conception of the problem but his idea of what a solution would look like and the methods that were to be employed to achieve it. The Canberra Planner expects the placement problem to be solved by an account of reference. He collects platitudes about *X*s in a theory that is used to pick out the best satisfier. The role of empirical investigation is limited to providing the ontology. The Sydney Planner has a more liberal conception of what it is to place something. She doesn't look for truthmakers for an implicit theory. She tells a non-reductive story about why creatures like us would develop those beliefs, and what they do for us. And it is an entirely scientific matter, not in any sense transparent to the users of a vocabulary, what facts about the world and ourselves viewed from the perspective of Being jointly support the fixation and use of *X*-beliefs.[17] The Sydney Planner sees the process of relating concepts to Being as a wholly empirical matter of investigating the physical underpinnings of our representational practices: the physics behind the facade.[18]

The characteristic errors of the Canberra Plan: reification and over-articulation

The side-on view is that part of our account of Being that relates the Absolute structures that are part of a fundamental theory to the structures at the user interface. Although in some special cases, it takes the form of reference, it does not do so in general. And the attempt to force everything into the mould of reference is behind two characteristic errors to which Canberra Planners are prone. First, there is no need to find a referent for every structure on the user interface. The side-on view will explain why our concepts aren't articulated enough, where they are not, to make the discriminations needed to deliver a referent. So in the case of interpreting sound vocabulary mentioned above, it will resist the temptation to say that there is an answer to the question 'what (or where) are the sounds?' Any extensional mapping of sounds into the more articulated physical framework will over-articulate the concept, i.e. attribute to it more articulation than it possesses.[19] And there is a general point to be made here. The point of the Dennett remark I quoted earlier about Mother Nature being a stingy engineer is that user interfaces are *selected* in part because they don't represent what they don't need to. They provide reduced variable spaces that register only those differences that need to be discriminated for practical purposes.

Second, there is no need either to reduce or to reify where the side-on story doesn't take the form of an account of what the terms in question refer to.[20] Causes and chances provide especially good examples of the tendency to reify.[21] Here is what the Sydney Planner says about chance. Chances play a certain epistemic role for creatures with our mix of knowledge and ignorance. They guide expectation about the future, in a manner that Lewis formalized (more or less) in his Principal Principle.[22] The Sydney Planner's account of chance has several parts. He details the facts about why creatures like us have a use for beliefs about chance, he describes the norms embodied in the probability calculus that tell us how to use them in reasoning. And he tells us how we form beliefs about chance. And he ends there. The part of the story that tells us how we form beliefs about chance is effectively his account of scientific theorizing. Chance and laws are doxastic outputs of scientific theories, the products of a very complicated, holistic induction that uses observed regularities to generate quantities designed to aid us in the kinds of practical and epistemic inferences that creatures like us face.

The Canberra Planner wants to find a referent for chance beliefs. He sees two choices:[23] either he finds something in the pattern of fact that could be assigned as truthmaker to beliefs about chance, or he reifies chances by adding to his account of the mind-independent fabric of the world. Lewis famously attempted the first, and the difficulties with his views are instructive about the difficulties that the Canberra Planner faces. He began by looking at how beliefs about chances are formed as part of a package that systematizes information about the overall pattern of fact. He then presented the account of how beliefs about laws and chances are formed (his best-systems analysis) as an account of the *truthmakers* for those beliefs. Because all chance beliefs are joint products of the same holistic induction, if this is taken seriously as an account of truthmakers, it turns out that particular chance claims and every statement of law have the same truthmaker, namely the overall pattern of actual fact. What makes it true on Lewis's account that the chance at t that a particular radium atom decays within an hour is x is that that it is a theorem of the best systematization of the overall pattern of fact. And likewise for the chance that a particular spin measurement at t^* is y. Likewise for the laws of diffraction and the fundamental equations of motion.

The Sydney Planner's diagnosis of where Lewis went wrong is not that he had the wrong ontology, but that when he just looked for an unmediated extensional interpretation of beliefs about laws and chances, he lost all of the important differences that appear from a side-on view when we take into account their role in the practical and epistemic lives of users. They are all outputs of the same holistic induction, based on restricted information about the way things generally hang together. They differ not in which *part* of Being different concepts represent, but in what those concepts *do*.[24] They are differences in function, not differences in extension. The Sydney Planner's diagnosis of where Lewis and his proponents went wrong is that they succumb to the allure of reification. And succumbing to the allure of reification is succumbing to the temptation to think that all belief takes the form: there are ways the world is and we form beliefs that are intended to reflect the way the world is and those beliefs are made true or false by the way the world is. Neither reduction nor reification is the right story here. We get full insight into concepts like chance by looking at the human contingencies that explain why those concepts play the role they do in our cognitive and epistemic lives, i.e. the contingencies that give rise to the cognitive and epistemic practices in which they are embedded, and for which they are − so to speak − designed. Concepts have a role in the context of a specifically human combination of human capacities and limitations in which they are used to modify an evolving body of knowledge which is brought to bear on a history in progress. The side-on account of that role takes the form of an account of the relationship between agent and environment, viewing that as the nexus of a coupled interaction in which information flows in both directions. There is no natural way to paraphrase it as an account of reference.

If you feel yourself pulled by the idea that there must be something in the world that these beliefs represent that is not captured by the side-on account of use, consider the following. Once when I borrowed an apartment from a friend in Paris, I brought with me a store-bought map of the city, but found that she had left a personalized map to help me get around. The store-bought map was a perfectly generic map that had everything that you'd expect such generic maps to have on it. It represented all of the parts of the city and their relations to one another. It was carefully labelled and complete up to the same level of resolution as the personalized map, but the personalized map had a whole battery of secondary structures that had been written overtop in coloured pencil: stars marking favourite spots, Xs marking spots to be avoided, yellow highlighting marking busy streets, purple marking hills too steep to make on bike, green for safe neighbourhoods and grey for parts of the city that aren't well known. Now imagine the two maps side by side. Even though they represent the same terrain at the same level of resolution, one will find no extensional mapping of the secondary structures on the personalized map into the structures on the generic map. There is no metaphysical mystery about what these secondary structures represent. They are there to facilitate the user's interaction with the landscape. They are part of a user interface that she has constructed to navigate the space represented in Absolute terms in the generic map. Once you understand what those structures are for and the role they play in the lives of the users of the map, the expectation of an extensional correspondence to anything represented in Absolute terms on the generic map is deflated. There isn't an extensional mapping, because the structures on the user interface are relational. They relate the structures on a generic map to the situation, location, purposes, etc., of the user. They are built around distinctions that have significance for her, but that are not part of the intrinsic structure of the landscape.

One might try to resurrect correspondences by pointing out that the structures on the user interface don't correspond to structures represented on the generic map, because in the example, the user isn't herself represented on the map.[25] That would be correct. In our overall theories of the world, we are included in the description, and the structures that populate our everyday world are related to the Absolute structures of the fundamental ontology in a way that is mediated by the side-on account of use. The side-on view *is* that part of the scientific account of Being that relates everyday concepts to the Absolute structures described in a fundamental theory. That's the whole story. The Canberra Planner supposes that concept-level structure can be related to Being by a two-term relation that takes the form of a static mapping into Absolute structures. The Sydney Planner says that is a truncated attempt to substitute a static, two-place relation of reference for a complex interaction mediated by the agent in which there are differences in direction of fit and use. We need to unpack that side-on view before we know whether and when to expect correspondences between concepts of things and things as they are in themselves. Our understanding of what there is fundamentally – in the Absolute mind-independent fabric of reality – is itself a product of a self-directed hermeneutics.

Not instrumentalism, not expressivism, not anti-realism

One reaction to this example is to view the structures on the embellished map instrumentally, or expressively, or in some other sense as not genuinely representational. Here, I refer to Price's work on why those distinctions don't do the work that proponents want them to do: separating structures that have extensional correspondents in the sense of the matching game and those that have a more complex relationship to the Absolute structure of the world.[26] But even if we put that aside, there is a question here about how to use the vocabulary of representation. Do we hang onto the conception of representation built on the model of the matching game at the cost of regarding a good deal of everyday belief as not genuinely representational, or do we generalize 'representation' to allow the full range of roles that beliefs can play? The Sydney Planner generalizes the notion of representation and finds a use for a special class of representations that have the function of labelling or standing for independently well-defined features of the world.

Here is what a side-on view reveals about how the contents of everyday belief relate to the world described by physics: first, imagination often assumes that the microscopic world is a scaled down version of the macroscopic, but as we've learned in recent years, there is a great deal of non-trivial physics between the macroscopic and microscopic. We anchor words to stable macroscopic targets in the landscape that make good landmarks to steer by, but macroscopic targets of reference do not typically correspond to collections of microscopic particulars and the macroscopic regularities that describe how things hang together in the everyday world are stabilized out of low-level laws in a manner that is often too complex to compute. Second, pretheoretic reflection assumes that perception is a transparent channel for conveying information about the macroscopic environment to the mind; the cognitive sciences and neuropsychology have revealed how much restructuring is effected below the level of consciousness. Third, not all of our concepts have the function of referring to what is there (or, as it is sometimes put, what is 'there anyway'). If we want to bridge the gap between everyday concepts and physics, we have to tell every part of this story. No part of that story is a priori, and it can't be bypassed in general by using everyday intuitions to formulate an implicit theory of a concept, and then Ramsifying. To understand why our concepts have the shape they do, we need to understand the environment in which they are born and used and the forces that shape their growth. They find applicability and practical purpose in a context. Epistemic practices like prediction and inference make sense for example only under conditions characterized by epistemic asymmetries, and the specific character of those practices requires understanding the epistemic context in which they are deployed, the problems that they are introduced to solve, and the tasks that they are introduced to perform. Concepts like disgust or shame have a complex setting and an anatomy that can't be understood in isolation from it. All of this is part of a naturalistic ecology that casts light on the networks of concepts and auxiliary representational tools that mediate our interaction with the environment.

One might worry at this stage that I have been criticizing a straw man by saddling the Canberra Planner with a conception of reference that imputed a direction of fit and ruled out the more complex relationships described in the side-on view. The conception of representation that I have been criticizing is more insidious than a consciously held view. It can be seen in the complaint that the side-on account of use which explains how and why we form beliefs about employing a target vocabulary leaves the metaphysical questions unanswered. And it needs to be openly displayed, explicitly criticized, and actively disavowed, so that we don't fall into the traps it holds. Consider, for example, this remark in the introduction to a book developing the new insights into the content and role of causal thinking that have come out of the work on causal modelling in the past thirty years:

> This book isn't about metaphysics. It's about representation. It's about how people represent the world and how we should represent the world to do the best job of guiding action. ... the logic of causality is the best guide to prediction, explanation, and action. And not only is it the best guide around; it is the guide that people use. People are designed to learn and to reason with causal models.
>
> (Sloman 2005, 20)

Most discussion of the 'metaphysics of causation' proceeds on the assumption there is a question here that is left untouched by those developments. The thought seems to be that once we have clarified the logic of causal claims,[27] their connection to other beliefs, and their role in epistemic and practical inferences, we merely have an account of the *epistemology* of causal belief and the function of causal thinking. This – the thought is – is the place where metaphysics begins; there remains a question about what causal relations *are*, or what causal models *represent*. This thought is mistaken. Understanding what causal modelling is *for*, how to build and use a model, the role models play in the natural history of embedded agents, the practical role the distinction between fixed and variable structure plays ... that's all there is to understand. There's nothing more that God could add to this story to answer the question of what causes are.

Or consider how different the discussion of modal metaphysics would be if people stopped looking for truthmakers and began doing what Boris Kment is suggesting here:

> A comprehensive philosophical account of modality should not only tell us what metaphysical necessity is, but should also tell us which ordinary-life

practices give rise to modal notions, and what role modal concepts play in them. It should thereby elucidate what the purpose of these notions is, why creatures with our interests and concerns have developed them.

(Kment 2006, 237–38)

Kment is one of the good guys, someone doing exactly the kind of work that the Sydney Planner thinks should replace metaphysics on the Canberra Plan, but even he pays lip service in this remark to the need to say 'what metaphysical necessity is'. The Sydney Planner denies that there is a *separate* question about what metaphysical necessity is. The whole story is given by the story of how modal beliefs arise and the role they play in ordinary-life practices. The Sydney Plan as I am presenting it is not quietist.[28] It has a lot to say about how different classes of concepts find their place in a scientific vision of the world, but it refuses to paraphrase what it says in the form of an account of truthmaking.

Conclusion

Because we ourselves and our representational practices fall within the scope of our physical theories, they come with a side-on view that relates them to the world. In some cases, the side-on view will go like this: there are these things in the world and people come by and gather information about those things, and they form beliefs that are intended to reflect the way things are with the world, and (if all goes well) the way things are with the world makes their beliefs true. But in other cases, the story will not look like that at all. In the case of beliefs about chance, and cause, and disgust and democracy, the side-on story doesn't involve facts that are well-defined independently of our representational practices and that act (in that sense) as truthmakers for our beliefs. It is a much more complex story that recognizes that not all terms in a mature language have the job of reflecting features of the domain of fact. There has been a slow shift of practice in response to the demands of the subject matter, but the vocabulary of truthmaking has remained.

Bridging the gap between physics and the familiar world of everyday sense involves two movements, one vertical and one horizontal. The vertical movement requires understanding how high-level structures are stabilized out of low-level interactions. The horizontal movement requires understanding how an active mind coupled to a changing environment generates personal-level experience. There have been huge changes and advances in scientific thinking on both fronts, and on both fronts the developments have been unanticipated and transformative. Research on complexity has undermined entrenched philosophical assumptions about the relationship between the microscopic and macroscopic. Scientific study of the mind has forced us to acknowledge that the objects and structures disclosed in experience are not a transparent reflection of the mind-independent structure of reality, but distilled out of coupled interaction between mind and environment as part of a user interface honed over generations to produce adaptive behaviour. Culturally incubated practices of concept application add a further layer of complexity. To think that we could bypass all of these processes with a simple two-term relation of truth to truthmaker is a mistake that leads to some clearly identifiable diseases of contemporary analytic metaphysics: (i) the tendency to over-articulate, (ii) the tendency to reify, and (iii) the tendency to over-appreciate the role of a priori methods. The Canberra Plan had a good run. The advances that were made under its auspices have been deep, but it is time to fly a new banner.

Notes

1 The origin of the expression 'Canberra Plan' was in drafts of O'Leary-Hawthorne and Price 1996. As O'Leary-Hawthorne and Price say, 'Canberra's detractors often charge that as a planned city, and a government town, it lacks the rich diversity of "real" cities. Our thought was that in missing the functional diversity of ordinary linguistic usage, the Canberra Plan makes the same kind of mistake about language' (O'Leary-Hawthorne and Price 1996, 291, n. 23). The label was adopted by Canberra Planners themselves (see, for example, Lewis 2004, 76 and 104, n. 3), who talk about the 'Canberra Plan' for causation, referring to the theories proposed in Tooley 1987 and Menzies 1996, and is now widely used without prejudice. For an excellent new volume of essays from Canberra Planners and their critics, see David Braddon-Mitchell and Robert Nola 2008. There are a number of people that call themselves Canberra Planners whom my narrow characterization would not fit. Here and throughout the term is used to describe my character-ization, and self-modelled Canberra Planners are free to escape criticism by demurring from my characterization.

2 Price has moved to Cambridge, but the Sydney plan grew up in Sydney, and that is properly its hometown. The Sydney Plan has deep roots in Deweyan pragmatism, with connections to Sellars, Rorty, and Wittgenstein. Sydney Planners, aside from Price, include Blackburn, Michael Williams, Mathew Chrisman, Brandom, Lionel Shapiro, and in some respects, Mark Wilson, Allan Gibbard, and Jamie Dreier. It can be seen from the range of interests and positive views represented here that Sydney Planners are a disparate lot. My version of the Sydney Plan is not in every respect Price's. See, for example, n. 28.

3 I use semantic notions (truth, reference) in a non-deflationary way, unless otherwise indicated, for ease of exposition. The Sydney Planner characteristically holds a deflationary theory of reference, preserving semantic notions to play a formal role, but qualifying to allow the possibility of deflationary readings makes the exposition tortured. I also speak throughout in naively realistic terms about physics, but everything I say is compatible with treating physics as just one more representation, with its own internal standard of what the Absolute structure of the world is like. In that case, my naive realism will be a kind of internal realism.

4 The phrase is Jackson's. For Jackson, the naturalistic metaphysician's job is to say how the things we quantify over in everyday discourse 'get ... a place in the scientific account of our world' (Jackson, 1998, 3).

5 Concepts are components of thought and thought is distinguished from these other forms of representation in several ways that won't matter for our purposes. There are individual and communal versions of the body of everyday belief. I'll give the communal version priority, though nothing hinges on it.

6　Huw Price, 'Expressivism, Pluralism and Representationalism – A New Bifurcation Thesis', University of Sydney, 27 August 2007. <http://sydney.edu.au/time/conferences/epr/price.pdf>.

7　And we can see why the procedure would be useful: for the same reason it is useful to give the coordinates of a collection of familiar and well-loved places known by common names (Sam's restaurant, mom's house, the old police station) in a systematic vocabulary. The result will be an explicit, non-redundant catalogue of what there is that characterizes all objects in Absolute terms and locates them relative to one another.

8　Scaffolding (in its use here) is structure in the environment that supports connections that are used, but not represented. So, for example, the connection between visual impressions of red-ness and the reflectance properties of surfaces that allows us to use the former to track the latter depends on things being set up correctly in the ambient environment.

9　What gets included and left out, which idealizations and simplifications are allowed, and what auxiliary structures get onto one's map, depends on their use. The map I use to navigate the dinner party at a conference will be highlighted with labels that identify what institution the people in attendance work at and what their field is. The map I use to navigate a purely social situation will be quite different. The map a biker uses to cross a city is different from the one a driver or walker uses. And those are different from the one that someone using a wheelchair deploys. The same context- and task-dependent criteria are at work in choice of models in science. The biologist and physicist modelling signalling pathways may deploy different descriptive coordinates and different equations.

10　The design process is natural and cultural selection. The user of a facade needs to know how to carry out content-level manipulations that provide effective procedures for achieving ends. Things are arranged by the designer so that a simplified set of content-level manipulations produce the desired effect, but a side-on view reveals the complex underpinnings.

11　I adapt his term here for my purposes.

12　This is not to rule out other perfectly legitimate inquiries, equally deserving the name metaphysics.

13　See Ismael (2007), in particular the discussion of Sellars and the Myth of Jones for an account of the process of articulation.

14　'Depth' is measured in terms of resolution; 'generality' is measured in terms of the range of applicability of its laws (do they hold only under special conditions or universally); and 'objectivity' is measured in terms of the independence of relations from our sensory states or interventional capabilities.

15　See Ismael, unpublished, for development of the idea of models as partially prepared solutions to frequently encountered problems.

16　Naturalism is not necessarily physicalism, on my view, because it doesn't come with the reduc-tionist aspirations of many physicalists. But that is a long and separate story. On consciousness, here and throughout, my position will be that I take it for granted that our mental lives are conscious, that they have both a quality and content, and that quality and content are both introspectively available. I take it for granted that the conscious mind is well enough for our purposes coincident with the introspectively available mind. I take no position on whether consciousness is reducible, but consciousness does not figure anywhere as an explanatory primitive. For my purposes, consciousness can be treated as either epiphenomenal or reducible.

17　Realism/anti-realism, objectivity/subjectivity, we let all of the important distinctions get drawn in the hermeneutic story, which makes explicit what different kinds of belief (e.g. beliefs about laws, causes, counterfactuals, morals, beauty, etc.) commit us to from the perspective of Being. All of the distinctions we want to draw between what different classes of belief commit you to (about the world, about the self, about the relationship and interaction between them) will get drawn in a more nuanced and articulated form.

　　It is important that these distinctions get drawn from the side-on and not the top-down. The Sydney Planner denies simple division into representational and non-representational (or sub-jective and objective). Most of our beliefs are both world- and self-involving and teasing apart what realism about Xs commits us to is a matter of developing an articulated, side-on view of the practices in which they arise.

18 It retains a role for a priori methods establishing the norms that govern the use of concepts, but even there, a priori methods aren't authoritative. Those norms are partially internalized by the users of concepts to the extent needed to guide their behaviour, but they have their source externally, in the give and take of reasons. Because the practices are widely distributed (they have to be culled from the social interactions among no small number of interacting individuals), it is no trivial matter to discern the norms that govern them.

19 The tendency of the Canberra Planner is to elicit intuitions about counterfactuals to strengthen the implicit theory enough to discriminate the various candidates. The counterfactuals will characteristically describe situations that don't arise in practice. In many cases this has the feel of introducing articulation rather than manifesting articulation that was already in place, somehow implicit in the practice. The counterfactuals transform the concept. And although there may be more or less natural ways of extending use to these sorts of cases, if the goal was to elucidate the everyday concept, there may not be an answer.

20 This has to be put quite delicately. The Sydney Planner wants to reserve the right to use the vocabulary of truth and reference, so this is where the distinction is between inflationary and deflationary conceptions of semantic notions (truth, reference, satisfaction) matter. For a fuller discussion of the distinction and generally illuminating discussion of metaphysics from a Sydney Planner, see Thomasson, unpublished.

21 I have discussed both examples in more detail in Ismael, forthcoming.

22 There has been controversy about the precise formulation. See Lewis 1980 for the original formulation, and see Lewis 1994, Hall 1994, and Thau 1994 for some of the controversy.

23 Or, two choices if he wants to hold that chance beliefs express truths. There are non-cognitivist alternatives.

24 See Ismael, forthcoming, where I argue that no beliefs about what merely is the case could play the role that beliefs about laws or chances do in practical and epistemic reasoning. The Sydney Planner recognizes connections to perception and to action in the guise of roles in epistemic and practical reasoning, and connections to other concepts in the guise of roles in inference. And he thinks that all of these are essential to a full understanding of how beliefs relate to the Absolute structure of the world. Differences among beliefs can arise along any one of these dimensions.

25 The operative distinction here is the distinction between a relation between the content of the map and its user, which is external to the map, and a relation internal to the content of the map between a representation of the user and a representation of the map.

26 Price 2011.

27 By this I mean nothing more than the sorts of inferences that beliefs about causes support, and the sorts of beliefs from which they can be inferred.

28 That contrasts it with Cambridge pragmatism and with some of the things that Price himself can be found saying.

References

Braddon-Mitchell, David and Nola Robert (eds) (2008) *Conceptual Analysis and Philosophical Naturalism*, Cambridge, MA: MIT Press.

Brandom, Robert (2011) 'Platforms, Patchworks, and Parking Garages: Wilson's Account of Conceptual Fine-Structure in *Wandering Significance*', *Philosophy and Phenomenological Research* 82: 183–201.

Dennett, Daniel (1998) *Brainchildren*, Cambridge, MA: MIT Press.

Hall, Ned (1994) 'Correcting the Guide to Objective Chance', *Mind* 103: 505–18.

Ismael, Jenann (2007) *The Situated Self*, Oxford: Oxford University Press.

——(forthcoming) 'How to Be Humean', in Barry Loewer and Jonathan Schaffer (eds), *Companion to Lewis*, Oxford: Oxford University Press.

——(unpublished) 'Modelling and Modality'.

Jackson, Frank (1998) *From Metaphysics to Ethics*, Oxford: Oxford University Press.

Kment, Boris (2006) 'Counterfactuals and the Analysis of Necessity', *Philosophical Perspectives* 20: 237–302.

Lewis, David (1980) 'A Subjectivist's Guide to Objective Chance', in R.C. Jeffrey (ed.), *Studies in Inductive Logic and Probability,* vol. 2, Berkeley: University of California Press.

——(1994) 'Humean Supervenience Debugged', *Mind* 103: 473–90.

——(2004) 'Causation as Influence', in J. Collins, N. Hall and L. Paul (eds), *Causation and Counterfactuals*, Cambridge, MA: MIT Press, 75–106.

Menzies, Peter (1996) 'Probabilistic Causation and the Pre-emption Problem', *Mind* 105: 85–117.

O'Leary-Hawthorne, John and Huw Price (1996) 'How to Stand Up for Non-cognitivists', *Australasian Journal of Philosophy* 74: 275–92.

Price, Huw (2011) *Naturalism without Mirrors*, Oxford: Oxford University Press.

Sloman, Steven (2005) *Causal Models*, Oxford: Oxford University Press.

Thau, Michael (1994) 'Undermining and Admissibility', *Mind* 103: 491–504.

Thomasson, Amie (unpublished) *The Descent of Metaphysics*.

Tooley, Michael (1987) *Causation: A Realist Approach*, Oxford: Clarendon Press.

Part II

METHODS IN METAPHYSICS AND EPISTEMOLOGY

8 The easy approach to ontology: a defense

AMIE L. THOMASSON

Over the past sixty years or more—ever since Quine was seen as reviving metaphysics in the wake of the positivist attacks—metaphysics has been dominated by neo-Quinean methodology, so much so that some simply refer to neo-Quinean metaphysics as "mainstream metaphysics" (Manley 2009, 4). On the neo-Quinean conception, metaphysics is "of a piece with" scientific inquiries, and they are jointly devoted to finding the best "total theory." Yet the neo-Quinean approach is also thought to give metaphysicians serious and difficult work to do in determining what really exists.[1] The metaphysician has work to do, first, in helping determine what our best theories are (weighing up the theoretic virtues of competing theories), and second, in determining what (when best expressed in canonical first-order logic) those theories commit us to. We are then to believe the ontology required by our best theories.[2] The work is neither empirical nor conceptual (indeed those two cannot be separated, according to the neo-Quinean view); instead, it involves a kind of weighing up of theories on grounds of criteria such as simplicity, explanatory power, unity with other theories, etc. As Sider writes: "Admittedly, those criteria give less clear guidance in metaphysics than elsewhere; but there's no harm in following this argument where it leads: metaphysical inquiry is by its nature comparatively speculative and uncertain" (2011, 12). The work indeed has proven so difficult and uncertain that during the reign of neo-Quinean metaphysics we have seen a great proliferation of metaphysical views rather than anything like convergence.

But an alternative methodological undercurrent has survived despite the dominance of neo-Quinean metaphysics. This is an approach we may call the "easy" approach to answering existence questions. It has its roots in Carnap's (1950) treatment of internal existence questions (the only existence questions he saw as meaningful) as answerable straightforwardly by empirical and/or conceptual methods.[3] Questions such as "is there a piece of paper on my desk?," Carnap suggests, may be resolved by empirical methods like looking, while questions like "is there a prime number between one and five?" we may answer by mathematical methods of reasoning and proof. In either case, we may use the answer to the specific question (obtained by empirical or conceptual methods) to easily answer more general questions: from the first we may infer that if there is a piece of paper, there is at least one material object; and from "there is a prime number between one and five" we may infer that there are numbers (1950, 209).

In more recent metaphysics, the approach has occasionally resurfaced in work on particular topics, though the different cases have seldom been identified as part of a unified movement, the methodology of which we can clarify and assess. One can find a version of the easy approach in the work of neo-Fregeans such as Bob Hale and Crispin Wright about mathematical entities (2001, 2009, and Wright 1983), in Stephen Schiffer's work on propositions, properties, and events (among other things) (1996, 2003), and in my (2007) defense of ordinary objects.

The basic idea that unifies these approaches, and gives them title to being called "easy," is that certain disputed existence questions can be answered by starting from uncontroversial premises and making trivial inferences that take us to ontological conclusions. As a result, these existence questions are not the subjects for prolonged metaphysical debate, nor do they require difficult and uncertain speculative work.

Although it remains a minority approach, interest in and sympathy for the idea that existence questions may be answered easily has slowly been growing. In addition to those who (like Hale, Wright, Schiffer and myself) defend it as an approach to at least some debates, it has become increasingly common even for serious metaphysicians to accept that existence questions, asked in ordinary English, may be answered easily in much the way that the easy approach suggests, and as a result to suggest that serious metaphysics must move to other territory.[4]

The view is attractive at least in part because it greatly clarifies and demystifies the methodology and epistemology of metaphysics. For it gives us ways to resolve debates about existence on the basis of nothing more mysterious than straightforward empirical and conceptual work. As a result, it leaves no distinctively metaphysical project of figuring out what exists—except to the extent that some of the conceptual work may be profitably undertaken by philosophers. Moreover, it eases many of the Platonist's traditional epistemic worries about how we could come to know facts about mathematical entities, properties, etc., given their causal disconnection from us. For on the easy approach, we can come to know mathematical truths, property-truths and the like again by way of trivial inferences from uncontroversial premises.

In this chapter I aim to clarify what the easy approach is and what follows from it for first-order metaphysical debates. I also aim to provide a partial defense of the approach—positioning it as a viable and appealing alternative to neo-Quinean mainstream metaphysics.

The easy methodology and its results

The core idea shared by those who accept an "easy" approach to some debate or other is this: that we may begin from an undisputed claim, and by way of apparently trivial reasoning (making use of what Hale and Wright call a conceptual truth, or what Schiffer calls a transformation rule) derive from it an ontological conclusion. In the philosophy of mathematics, for example, neo-Fregeans such as Bob Hale and Crispin Wright (2009) have argued that the existence of numbers can be inferred as follows:

Undisputed claim: The cups and the saucers are equinumerous.

From there, we may make use of Hume's principle, which they take to be a

Conceptual truth: The number of *n*s = the number of *m*s iff the *n*s and the *m*s are equinumerous,

to move from the right to the left and conclude:

Derived claim: The number of cups = the number of saucers.

But since the derived claim is a true identity claim, they hold, we are entitled to conclude that the terms in it ("the number of cups" and "the number of saucers") refer, and so get the

Ontological claim: There are numbers.

Thus we get a resolution to an ancient ontological problem by starting from an undisputed truth that does not make use of the disputed concept (*number*) or make reference to the disputed entities (numbers) at all. There is on this view simply no need for determining whether our best theories include reference to numbers, or whether (if they do) we can find some way of paraphrasing them to relieve us of the apparent commitment.

Schiffer (1994, 1996, 2003) develops similar easy arguments for the existence of such entities as propositions, properties, events, states, and fictional characters. In Schiffer's terms, an undisputed claim in which there is no mention of an entity of type *J* (and no use of the concept *J* or any supposed to be coreferential with *J*) may be combined with a conceptual truth (what he calls a "transformation rule"), to give us a derived claim that is, intuitively, redundant with respect to the undisputed claim. Yet the derived claim apparently entails the existence of *J*s (numbers, propositions, events, possible worlds …)—thus settling what seemed like serious disputed ontological questions easily, by way of undisputed basic claims and their trivial entailments.

So, for example (making the intervening steps somewhat more explicit than Schiffer (2003) does), we can move from

> Undisputed claim: Snow is white,

and

> Conceptual truth: If P then that P is true,

to infer the

> Derived claim: That snow is white is true,

and get the

> Ontological claim: There is a proposition (namely that snow is white).

Or from

> Undisputed claim: Jane was born on a Tuesday,

and

> Conceptual truth: If P was born on D, then P's birth occurred on D,

to the

> Derived claim: Jane's birth occurred on a Tuesday,

and get the

> Ontological claim: There is an event (namely of Jane's birth).

Given the rules of use that introduce such new terms, existence questions formulated *using* those terms are easy to answer, for the rules of use for the terms enable us to make easy inferences from the undisputed claim to the existence of the entities in question.[5]

There is one important variation to point out here: while, in the above cases, the undisputed claim is an empirical truth, in other cases one may make the relevant transformations from a conceptual truth. So, for example, we may move from "Janice is tall or it's not the case that Janice is tall" to *"That Janice is tall* is or is not true" to infer the existence of the proposition that Janice is tall—relying on no empirical truth, though we do begin from an uncontroversial true claim—a conceptual truth. These are genuinely something-from-nothing transformations, for they require nothing of the empirical world for them to be guaranteed to be true.[6]

I have argued elsewhere (2007) that even disputed existence questions about concreta may be answered by easy methods. For example the question "Are there tables?," I have argued, may be straightforwardly answered by beginning from a claim that is not a point of controversy between realists and eliminativists:

Undisputed claim: There are particles arranged tablewise.

We can move from there to introduce the noun term "tablewise arrangement" as follows:

Conceptual truth: If there are particles arranged tablewise, there is a tablewise arrangement of particles.

And yet there being a tablewise arrangement of particles seems to guarantee that the conditions are met for the ordinary application conditions of the term "table" to apply. (Or we could, if there weren't one in our language, introduce the new noun term "table" as short for "tablewise arrangement of particles.") Thus we can, by trivial inferences, move to the

Derived claim: There is a tablewise arrangement of particles.

And so to the

Ontological claim: There is a table.

In this way, ontological debates about the existence of concrete objects may be settled just as easily as debates about disputed abstracta, events, etc.

Defenders of the easy approach sometimes speak as if there is an important difference between the "shallowness" of "pleonastic" entities to which we may become committed via trivial transformations, and the "depth" of "more robust" natural entities like trees (e.g. Schiffer 1996). Indeed Hofweber paraphrases Schiffer's view as holding that these are "second-class entities, whose existence is guaranteed merely by talking a certain way" (Hofweber 2007, 5), and those who defend an easy approach to resolving certain existence questions are often dubbed "deflationists."

But we must be cautious about the sense in which the view is and is not "deflationary," and should be hesitant to embrace anything like the view that the entities to which we become committed via trivial transformations are "shallow," "deflated" or "second-class."[7] For, as I have argued, we may answer questions about the existence of tables or trees no less easily than questions about the existence of events or properties. The only significant contrast is between entities the existence of which is guaranteed *given the truth of an undisputed empirical claim*, and entities the existence of which we may infer from a conceptual truth. For in the first case, it does require some empirical work to discover their existence: we must know that some uncontroversial empirical claim that can be fed into the transformation rule is *true* to know that the entities exist. In the latter case, by contrast, no empirical work is required.[8]

But in each case we end up being realists about the questioned entities by affirming that there are properties, propositions, numbers, tables, etc., *in the only sense these terms have.* This is a straightforward, out and out, realism about the entities in question. The proper conclusion to draw is not that the *entities* are deflated or have some "second-class" status. What is deflated instead is the *ontological debates* about the entities: for it is silly to engage in prolonged theoretic disputes about questions that can be answered so easily. Thus, to be clear, I call the first-order position that results from the easy approach "simple realism," and the metaontological position that results "deflationism."

Objections to the easy approach

But despite its appeal, a great many objections have been raised against the easy approach to ontology. Perhaps most notorious is the "bad company" objection raised against neo-Fregean views. The easy approach relies on what it takes to be conceptual truths to take us from uncontroversial premises to ontological conclusions. But the "bad company" objection arises from noticing that certain purported conceptual truths (which look quite similar to those the easy ontologist endorses) may lead us to palpable trouble: to contradictions or conflicts with obvious empirical truths. Thus the defender of the easy approach is apparently left with the challenge of saying why what she takes to be conceptual truths are acceptable while the problematic ones are not.[9] Another line of objection is to ask what guarantees that there are the relevant entities to ensure that the conclusion of the easy argument holds true—with the insinuation being that it would take some kind of "magic" to guarantee this.[10] Others have objected that the easy arguments don't give us ontological conclusions, either because the conclusion should be read as employing a use of the quantifier without ontological import (Hofweber 2005a, 2005b, 2007), or because the conclusion should be read as implicitly in the context of a pretense (Yablo 2001, 2005).[11] Still others have denied that there are any conceptual or analytic truths at all, and so *ipso facto* denied that there are the conceptual truths needed to ground the inferences from the undisputed truth to the ontological claim.[12]

Since they have been much discussed elsewhere, I will leave those objections to the side here. Instead, I want to focus on a recent line of objection that hasn't yet been given sufficient attention: Sider's (2011) arguments that the easy ontologist may accept the idea that there are the needed analytic claims only if she also commits herself to claims that would undercut her claim to have epistemic and methodological advantages over serious metaphysics.

Just more metaphysics?

Sider (2011) argues that deflationists (including easy ontologists) are committed to claims that are *epistemically metaphysical* in the sense that they may be answered neither by empirical nor conceptual methods (nor by a combination of these) (187). As a result, he argues, the deflationist cannot legitimately claim any epistemic or methodological advantages for her view over that of the serious metaphysician. To see why he thinks this, requires a brief detour to describe his alternative metametaphysical position.

On Sider's view, there is a distinctive language, Ontologese, in terms of which metaphysical debates can be phrased, assuring them of being non-trivial and substantive. Lewis (1983) argued that certain natural features of the world (with natural joints between them) serve as "reference magnets" to attract the reference of many of our predicates, and help avoid the indeterminacy of reference. On this view, we can allow that the structure of the world (e.g. into natural kinds) contributes to what these terms refer to. Sider's innovation is to expand that idea beyond predicates, holding that as well as a natural kind structure, the world has a logical structure—so that we can ask, "of expressions in any grammatical category, whether they carve at the joints" (2011, 8). The Ontologese language in which ontological debates can safely be couched is then supposed to be one that stipulates that its quantifier is to have a meaning that carves the world at its logical joints. I will not endeavor here to discuss further what sense we can make of the idea of "logical joints" of reality or of the meanings of Ontologese expressions. Instead, I will focus here just on whether Sider's arguments against easy ontology hold sway.

Sider argues that those who favor easy ontology turn out to be committed to the thesis that *there are no quantificational joints of reality:* "any such metametaphysics is committed to at least this much substantive metaphysics: reality *lacks* a certain structure" (2011, vii). This, however, he takes to be a substantive metaphysical thesis about the structure of reality: that that structure does not include quantificational structure—a thesis that cannot be simply established through empirical or conceptual inquiry. But that would undercut the central epistemic and methodological advantages of the easy approach.

Sider gives two separate arguments for the conclusion that the friend of easy ontology must reject the idea that there is a joint-carving quantifier available in which ontological disputes are, or may be, couched. The first is that she must do so to preserve her easy arguments. For those arguments rely on the idea that there are conceptual truths to take us from the undisputed claim to the ontological conclusion. These are supposed to be definitional, in a sense (they introduce the noun term "property," "event," etc.), and to entitle us to reason from, for example, "this shirt is red" to conclude that there are properties. But Sider argues that we should call a sentence "analytic" only if it is both definitional and true (2011, 193). Once we stipulate that our terms—particularly the quantifier or "there is"—are to be joint-carvers, however, we can no longer know, just by mastering the use of the terms, whether a definitional claim is also true: "linguistic reflection can deliver at best the conclusion that [a given claim] (T) is definitional. And being definitional is insufficient for truth: (T)'s definitional status might be trumped by some other factor" (196): there might be a more natural joint-carving candidate to be meant by "there is" that does not make (T) true. Thus if we are making use of a joint-carving Ontologese meaning for the quantifier, easy arguments can no longer settle ontological disputes, for any linking principle we may think of as analytic could turn out not to be so. "Easy ontologists cannot, therefore, claim merely that (T) is definitional. They must also reject joint-carving quantification" (196).

To this, Sider adds a second argument: Even if the deflationist is right, and *ordinary English* quantifiers do not (and do not aim to) carve at the joints, this will not render ontological disputes pointless. For the serious ontologist can say to the easy ontologist,

> when applied to *English* quantification, [your] picture might well be correct, even if ontological realism [taken as the thesis that there are ontological questions that are epistemically metaphysical] is true. But in that case, the appropriate language for conducting ontology would be Ontologese, in which the quantifiers are stipulated to carve at the joints ... Ontology in Ontologese remains hard—and better.
>
> (2011, 197)

That is, even if the easy ontologist is right about how our standard English quantifier works (and right about the easy inferences we can make using our English terms), serious metaphysics may be retained—and relocated to the metaphysics room—as long as we can shift to Ontologese and make use of a quantifier that does carve the world at its logical joints:

> we could discard [the ordinary, natural language expression] *E*, and enter the metaphysics room, so to speak. We could replace the ordinary expression *E* with an improved expression *E** that we stipulate is to stand for the joint-carving meaning in the vicinity ... This is plan B.
>
> (74)

Thus if the easy ontologist wants to render *all* existence disputes pointless, she must reject the idea that we can introduce a joint-carving use of the quantifier.

In each case, the key point Sider wants to press is that the easy ontologist—along with all metaontological deflationists—must reject the idea that there is, or could be defined, a joint-carving quantifier. But, he assumes, the only way to reject joint-carving quantification is to deny that there is any structure of the right sort to attract the reference of the quantifier, so that the attempted introduction of the Ontologese quantifier must fail: "Of course, ontological deflationists will think that the attempted introduction of Ontologese misfires, since the world lacks the necessary structure" (2011, 172). But this in itself, he holds, is a metaphysical claim about the world, "this rejection of joint-carving is just more metaphysics" (83)—for it involves a claim about what does and does not belong to the structure of the world. Moreover, it is metaphysics in precisely the sense the deflationist claims to be suspicious of: "the assertion that quantifiers do *not* carve at the joints ... seems to be epistemically metaphysical" in the sense that they "resist direct empirical methods but are nevertheless not answerable by conceptual analysis" (187).

This, Sider holds, prevents the deflationist from holding the "epistemic high ground." That is, the deflationist wants to insist that an attraction of her view is that she can put to rest the old debates, and needn't rely on the idea that there are ontological questions that cannot be straightforwardly answered by conceptual and/or empirical means. But if the deflationist, too, relies on claims that are epistemically metaphysical—claims about what is and is not part of the structure of the world—she cedes the metaphysical high ground and can claim no such advantage for her view.

Rejecting joint-carving quantifiers

Is the easy ontologist just relying on more metaphysics—of an epistemically metaphysical sort she herself should find objectionable? I will argue that the easy ontologist does *not* need to make the metaphysical claim that reality's structure does not include logical joints in order to reject the idea that there is a meaningful joint-carving quantifier.

It is true, as Sider says, that those who endorse easy ontological arguments had better not *accept* the idea that the world has quantificational structure tracked by our (actual or Ontologese) quantifier. Sider's main motivation for broadening the notion of structure beyond the predicate is because it can then be used to help distinguish which metaphysical disputes are and are not substantive (2011, 86) and to enable us to better evaluate trades of ideology for ontology (87). But the latter is only motivating for those who share the neo-Quinean methodology; the former only for those looking for a way to draw the line between substantive and non-substantive debates in metaphysics. (This is not a task I have undertaken: I have little interest in the terminology of "substantiveness," and I think that ontological debates can be answered, but that the answers come as the straightforward result of conceptual and/or empirical inquiry. Does that make them non-substantive or substantive? I suppose that makes them substantive, but nonetheless not distinctively metaphysical.) So the deflationist will not be moved by these motives to accept the notion of quantificational structure.

The deflationist also can easily refrain from accepting what Sider calls the "best argument" for the view that quantifiers carve at the joints. For that "best argument" is squarely based on (neo-)Quinean methodology: that we should accept that quantificational structure is part of the "objective structure of the world" given its indispensability in our theories (2011, 188). But of course the easy ontologist in any case rejects this neo-Quinean methodology and so has no reason to be moved by an argument like this one. So she has no reason to endorse the view that follows from this neo-Quinean argument either.

So: the defender of easy ontology can (and should) refrain from *endorsing* the idea that there is quantificational structure. This is precisely where Sider's argument comes in, as he claims that the deflationist must reject it—but is thereby making a(n epistemically) metaphysical claim herself: the claim that reality lacks the structure needed to ground the reference of a joint-carving quantifier.

There is, however, more than one way to refrain from endorsing a statement. To refrain from endorsing *P* is not to endorse its negation; there are other attitudes one can take. Even if the easy ontologist wishes to *reject* the claim that reality has quantificational structure, she need not do so by *endorsing* the metaphysical claim that the structure of reality is such as to lack quantificational structure. One need only look at the history of philosophical debates to see that that is not the only move available in rejecting a position. Consider Ryle's (1949) way of rejecting the claim that the mind is immaterial: it was not by embracing the contrary position that the mind is material, but rather by showing that the whole way in which the debate was set up was based on a faulty set of categories: thinking of talk of mental states as aiming to describe some special features in a substance of a particular kind (a mind) rather than thinking of it as licensing inferences. Or think of Husserl's rejection of serious forms of metaphysical realism (1960/1977, 84–88): he does not reject the realist's claim that there is a real world outside of experience by making the opposing idealist assertion (or even embracing a Kantian transcendental idealism). Instead he argues that all it can *mean* to say that something is real is given in terms of actual or possible experiences—so that both the traditional positions of metaphysical realism and idealism are without sense. I don't mean to endorse either of those positions, but merely to issue a reminder that one classical way of rejecting a philosophical position is not to embrace its negation, but rather to show that something is wrong with the way the position (and thus perhaps its negation too) is put: that the terms involved lack sense, employ the wrong set of categories, involve a mistake about the role of the terms involved, or something along those lines.

To choose an ordinary life example, imagine that you are taking a two-year-old to the zoo, and approaching the giraffes. The child says, "Can we go see the elephant now?"; you reply, "We'll see that after." "The after! I want to see that after! Pick me up now so I can see the after!" Now you need to correct the child's misunderstanding—"No, I didn't mean to say we could see an after … " you begin. "What!" the (curiously precocious) child responds. "Are you saying that of all the creatures in the world none are afters? Why, you're making a substantive biological claim about the kinds of creatures there are and aren't—but how do you know that, of all the kinds of animal in the world, none are afters!" But of course to correct the child's mistake you needn't be making a substantive claim about the kinds of creature there are (and are not). You need only be pointing out that a mistake has been made about the role of a term like "after": that it is to mark an ordering of events (we'll go see the elephant *after* we see the giraffes), not a term attempting to name a sort of creature.

In Charlotte Zolotow's classic story *The Bunny Who Found Easter*, a lonesome rabbit heads off to the east in search of Easter, after being told that "There are always rabbits at Easter." The owl, of course (had he not dozed off), could have corrected the bunny without making substantive geographical commitments about what places did and did not lie to the east.

Problematizing the joint-carving quantifier

The deflationist about ontology may employ a similar strategy: not saying that the structure of the world is such as to lack quantificational structure, but rather problematizing the very idea of joint-carving quantification that plays the central role in both the statement that there is quantificational structure and its negation. The idea of terms that carve at the joints of course (as Sider fully acknowledges) was introduced to characterize natural kind terms—predicates of a particular kind. And in that context it may be well motivated. But whether it generalizes to logical terms such as the quantifier is another question.

Against the idea that some predicates may carve at the joints, although quantifiers do not, Sider says that is "hard to square with purity" (2011, 186)—the idea that fundamental truths involve only fundamental notions. But why accept purity? The only motivation Sider gives for it is the idea that "When God was creating the world, she was not required to think in terms of nonfundamental notions like city, smile, or candy" (106). But however compelling that may seem, it does nothing to argue for full-blown purity, in which *every notion in a fundamental truth must be fundamental*, over a restricted sort of purity of the form that every *predicate* in a fundamental truth must be fundamental. Both theses would handle the motivating examples equally well, acknowledging that God would not have to think in terms of notions like city, smile or candy to create the world. The examples only speak to the need to state fundamental truths using fundamental *predicates,* and don't motivate thinking that the quantifier must be fundamental (joint-carving) in order for there to be fundamental truths expressed using the quantifier.

Do we have any grounds to resist broadening the notion of structure in this way? I think we do. It is roughly the fourth source of resistance Sider notes to treating logical notions as joint-carving:

> It is the thought that it is appropriate to evaluate expressions for carving at the joints only when they are "contentful." *Predicates* are paradigmatically contentful. But logical expressions, on the other hand, are purely "formal," so the thought goes. They do not describe features of the world ... Since logical expressions are not "worldly," it is inappropriate to speak of the world as containing structure corresponding to those expressions.
>
> (2011, 97)

To overcome this source of resistance, Sider suggests that it arises from a covert attachment to conventionalism, and proceeds to critique "the very idea of something's being 'true by convention'" (2011, 100–4). His criticisms center on the idea that we cannot, merely by legislation, make logical truths true: "the world must also cooperate; the world must really be as the sentence says" (101); we cannot make sense of the idea that adopting conventions makes the claims true (101). His criticisms are aimed at the following target understanding of conventionalism: as the view that "We can *legislate-true* the truths of logic" (103).[13]

But the idea that logical notions are merely *formal* by far predates logical conventionalism. Early versions of the idea appear already in Aristotle, and arise again among medieval philosophers such as Duns Scotus. In its modern form, the view can be traced back at the very least to Kant (who was certainly no conventionalist).[14] In Kant's memorable summary at the start of the *Groundwork*:

> All philosophy insofar as it is founded on experience may be called empirical, while that which sets forth its doctrines as founded entirely on a priori

principles may be called pure. The latter, when merely formal, is called logic; but when limited to determinate objects of the understanding, it is called metaphysics.

(1785/1981, 1)

The idea that logic is—in some sense—formal or topic-neutral is, as John MacFarlane (2000) makes clear, historically *central,* indeed perhaps *the* historically dominant conception of logic—and one endorsed by such diverse philosophers as Kant, Lotze, Husserl, Frege and de Morgan. It is not to be quickly tossed aside by associations with the conventionalism of logical positivists. The basic idea has nothing to do with logical truths being "made true" by our adoption of certain conventions, or with the idea that we may "legislate" certain sentences to be logically true. Sider's arguments against conventionalism (however successful they may or may not be against the views of the positivists[15]) leave this view untouched.

So how else, apart from by embracing conventionalism, can we develop the idea that logical terms (including quantifiers) are not "contentful," are purely "formal," or "do not describe features of the world"—to justify saying that, even if it may be appropriate to think of (many) predicates as attempting to carve the world at its joints, it is inappropriate to think of logical terms as even attempting to map structure?

We can again look to the history of treatments of logic as formal for some ideas along these lines. The basic idea behind the classical treatment of logic as formal is the idea that logic is topic-neutral, or independent of subject matter (MacFarlane 2000, 51). But if logic is topic-neutral, then its topic is not the structure of the world; unlike the terminology of biology, political science or physics, it is not attempting to map the structure of a particular part of reality. Once we have a formal/material distinction to hand, we can suggest a picture like this: material predicates may (often) be designed to carve the world at (certain of) its joints, to map a certain structure—e.g. a structure of the world into biological or physical natural kinds.

But the distinctive feature of logical terms is that they may apply to material terms of any kind, indifferent to the distinctions among the objects and properties described, or the domains discussed (MacFarlane 2000, 57). This provides at least one way of articulating the idea that logical terms such as the quantifier are content-neutral: they may govern terms with any particular material content, many of which may aim to map different structural features of the world, while logical terms are neutral between them.

What of the idea that logical terms do not aim to describe the world, or tell us anything about the world? Kant employs a slightly different conception of formality that may express a version of this idea: that logical terms abstract entirely from semantic content:

> For example, general logic treats "all horses are mammals" simply as the unification of two concepts in a universal, affirmative, categorical, and assertoric judgment. It abstracts entirely from the content of the concepts. The way in which the concepts are united in thought is not, for Kant, a further constituent of the thought (a "binding" concept), but a feature of the thought's *form*.
>
> (MacFarlane 2000, 61)

To the extent that we think of semantic content as what connects our words to the world, we can then also see a way of making sense of the idea that logical terms are not "about the world," and even that pure logical truths do not aim to describe features of the world.

I don't mean to endorse either of these conceptions of formality. They are not equivalent, and adopting either (even without the other) might take us a good way towards making good on the idea that logical terms do not have a structure-mapping function. Other conceptions of formality are also available that might do the job—I have simply focused on two that most nearly match Sider's initial description.[16] Certainly I have not argued for them, but have merely sketched them. But all that is crucial here is to point out at least two ways—both of which are intuitively plausible and have played a central role in the history of philosophical thought about logic—in which we can develop the idea that logical terms are merely formal without embracing anything like the conventionalism Sider argues against, an idea that may enable us to raise suspicions against the idea that the quantifier is intended to carve at joints of any kind.

The idea that there is a distinction between the formal and material terms of our language may be adopted as part of a functional pluralist view about language.[17] The mistake of thinking that a structure-tracking Ontologese quantifier may be defined can be thought of as arising from an implicit functional monism. Ryle warned against this long ago (1957) in accusing Mill of assimilating far too much of language to names (thinking that their role is to name entities in the world). Thinking of the quantifier as a would-be joint-carving term seems to arise from the attempt to assimilate all parts of speech to the structure-tracking function of (some) predicates.

But if the role of logical terms such as the quantifier and connectives is not to carve the world at the joints of its "logical" structure, what roles do such terms serve? We can gain some ideas from the above discussion. Even if some terms (certain predicates) aim to describe features of the world (perhaps even natural features distinguished by natural joints), other terms may serve other roles: they may, for example, instead enable us to make *use* of these predicates in *making judgments* and *reasoning with* those judgments. Terms like "is" enable us to combine names and predicates into a judgment, as when we say "Lucky Feet *is* a horse." Other terms enable us to reason with judgments, as the quantifier enables us to reason from "Lucky Feet is a horse" to "∃x(Hx)," and "or" enables us to infer "Lucky Feet is a horse or Lucky Feet is a cow." There is no need to think of these terms as aiming to map a special kind of logical structure to account for their role and importance in our thought and language: not a role in tracking structure but enabling us to reason with concepts that do involve material (sometimes perhaps structure-tracking) content.

It is also important to note that taking our logical terms to have a function other than tracking a "logical" structure of the world does not commit us to the idea that our choice of certain logical terms and concepts (with certain rules of use rather than others) is merely arbitrary, conventional, or unconstrained. On the contrary, it is entirely compatible with the idea that what logical language we use is subject to constraints that are transcendentally grounded, and/or pragmatic, and/or based on what it takes for these terms to fulfill their characteristic functions. We are only barred from appealing to constraints to match some "logical structure" of the world.

If our logical terms, including the quantifier, are not aiming to map structure—if they are not terms with that function at all—then we can reject the Ontologese quantifier without pronouncing on what the actual structure of the world does or does not include. This is fundamentally a thesis about the role of logical terms in our discourse, not about what sort of metaphysical structure the world has or lacks. We can even deny that any term with such a material content as to be joint-carving could be a good candidate meaning for anything deserving the name "quantifier" (just as we may reject the idea that any kind of creature could be a good candidate for the meaning of "after"). And so we can reject the claim that the quantifier is joint-carving (or that there is a joint-carving quantifier to retreat to on plan B) without making a new and substantive metaphysical commitment.

Sider admits that "all I have to offer in support of Russellian realism about logic is a critique of conventionalism; discussion of intermediate positions remains a lacuna" (2011, 98). If I am right it is an important lacuna. For the view that logical terms are formal (so far only broadly sketched, but widely held throughout the history of modern and contemporary philosophy), while associated by some with conventionalism, is merely *associated* with it in the minds of some, not tied to it, and not defeated by the standard arguments Sider invokes against the idea that we can legislate-true the truths of logic. There are many ways—indeed the most dominant ways in the history of philosophy of thinking about logical terms—of resisting the move to Ontologese without embracing conventionalism or any substantive metaphysical position about what sorts of structure the world has and lacks. While I have not fully developed and defended any particular conception of logic as purely formal, I hope to have shown that Sider's arguments have not *defeated* that conception. Moreover, given the prominence of the idea of formality in thought about logic throughout the history of philosophy, the burden of proof would seem to fall on those who reject that idea and propose a different, structure-mapping, function for our logical notions. But if we can retain the idea that logical terms are merely formal—not contentful—easy ontologists may have grounds for rejecting the idea that the quantifier carves at the joints without making a metaphysical claim about the structure of the world, and thus without being committed to any epistemically metaphysical claim.

Conclusion

I hope to have made clear that, despite the dominance of neo-Quinean approaches to metaphysics, there is a competing alternative method available. The easy approach, descended from Carnap's treatment of internal questions, has often been overlooked, and even those who employ it have seldom presented it as part of a unified methodology for addressing ontological questions. I have aimed to show that there is a unified approach available, which in many ways presents an appealing alternative. For it enables us to clarify the epistemology of metaphysics, to put an end to seemingly endless ontological debates, and to answer existence questions using nothing more mysterious than straightforward empirical and conceptual work.

Many objections have been raised to the easy approach (or versions of it)—particularly by those who dedicate their careers to pursuing existence questions they regard as deep and difficult. Much work remains to be done to respond to each of those objections, only one of which has been discussed here. Nonetheless, I hope at least to have shown what the approach is, why it would be attractive, and how it can resist accusations that it relies on claims about the world's structure that are themselves epistemically metaphysical.

Notes

1 Though see Price 2009 for doubts that this conception of metaphysics is truly *Quinean*.
2 Sider (2011, 12) argues that one should not only accept the ontology of our best theory, but also regard the ideology of our best theory as carving at the joints, revealing the structure of reality.
3 Carnap of course considered external questions—existence questions asked outside of a linguistic framework—as pseudo-questions if construed as factual, and as better treated as pragmatic questions about which framework to adopt. For an interpretation and discussion of Carnap's distinction, see my forthcoming.

4 Fine 2009; Cameron 2010; Schaffer 2009.

5 This seems to correspond to Carnap's talk of introducing new noun terms with new rules of use, as parts of new (or expanded) linguistic frameworks (1947/1956, 211–12).

6 While the pleonastic and neo-Fregean views have much in common, there are also some notable differences between them. First, the neo-Fregeans employ an equivalence principle, Hume's Principle, in reaching their ontological conclusions, whereas Schiffer's pleonastic inferences take the form of $S \rightarrow \exists x(Fx)$, only requiring one-way entailments from the uncontroversial premise to the transformed claim. Secondly, the transformed claim of the neo-Fregean has the form of an identity statement, and it is because it has the structure of an identity statement that Hale and Wright insist that the terms in it must refer, and thus that we are licensed to say that numbers exist. By contrast, Schiffer's transformed claims do not have to take the form of an identity statement, and he makes no use of that idea in reaching the ontological conclusion that there are the disputed entities. I will leave those differences to the side for the present. For discussion, see my unpublished, ch. 3.

7 See also my 2001 for criticism of Schiffer's claims that pleonastic entities are lightweight entities that are in some sense creations of our linguistic and conceptual practices.

8 There may also be a difference in the discoverability of their modal properties: In the first case, although the most basic modal features of the entities to be referred to are fixed by way of the rules of use for the relevant terms, talk of their natures may also be deferential to the world in ways that enable us to fill in the details via empirical investigation. So, for example, it may be knowable simply to anyone competent in the use of the term "tree" that a tree cannot survive being burned to the ground, but we may go on to discover exactly what temperatures lead a tree to burn to the ground, and thus lead to its destruction—thereby learning more about the "natures" of trees. There doesn't seem to be any comparable empirical role of learning about the natures of those entities whose existence we may infer from a conceptual truth. I will, however, leave issues about modal properties to the side here, to focus on existence questions.

9 For discussions of the bad company objection see Matti Eklund 2009, Oystein Linnebo 2009, Stephen Yablo 2000, Hale and Wright 2009 and 2001, 132–37, and Schiffer 2003, 53–61.

10 See Yablo 2000, 197–99; Bennett 2009, 50–57. For replies see my 2009a and Hale and Wright 2009.

11 Replies to both of these objections appear in Thomasson, unpublished, chs 6 and 7.

12 See Quine's 1953 for the original objection, along with replies in Strawson and Grice 1956 and my 2007. For more recent objections to the idea that any claims are epistemically analytic, see Williamson 2007, 73–133. For replies see my unpublished, ch. 5.

13 I have argued elsewhere (2009b) that this interpretation also misrepresents classical conventionalism—the point of which was not to hold that logical truths are made true by our legislating or adopting certain conventions, but rather to deny that logical truths should be taken as attempted descriptions (in need of truthmakers) at all. But I will leave that to one side here.

14 For an excellent discussion of the history of formal conceptions of logic, see MacFarlane 2000.

15 For discussion of this, see my 2009b.

16 MacFarlane (2000) identifies three separate conceptions of logic as formal, and argues that they are not equivalent.

17 Along the lines of the functional pluralism advocated (for different terms) by Price 2009, 334–35, and 2011, 136–37.

References

Bennett, Karen (2009) "Composition, Colocation, and Metaontology," in Chalmers *et al.* 2009, 38–76.

Cameron, Ross (2010) "Quantification, Naturalness and Ontology," in Allan Hazlett (ed.), *New Waves in Metaphysics*, New York: Palgrave-Macmillan, 8–26.

Carnap, Rudolf (1947/1956) *Meaning and Necessity: A Study in Semantics and Modal Logic*, Chicago: University of Chicago Press.

——(1950/1956) "Empiricism, Semantics, and Ontology," repr. in *Meaning and Necessity*, 2nd edn, Chicago: University of Chicago Press.

Chalmers, David, David Manley and Ryan Wasserman (eds) (2009) *Metametaphysics*, Oxford: Oxford University Press.

Eklund, Matti (2009) "Bad Company and Neo-Fregean Philosophy," *Synthese* 170(3): 393–414.

Fine, Kit (2009) "The Question of Ontology," in Chalmers *et al.* 2009, 157–77.

Hale, Bob and Crispin Wright (2001) *The Reason's Proper Study: Essays towards a Neo-Fregean Philosophy of Mathematics*, Oxford: Clarendon.

——(2009) "The Metaontology of Abstraction," in Chalmers *et al.* 2009, 178–212.

Hofweber, Thomas (2005a) "A Puzzle about Ontology," *Noûs* 39(2): 256–83.

——(2005b) "Number Determiners, Numbers, and Arithmetic," *Philosophical Review* 114(2): 179–225.

——(2007) "Innocent Statements and Their Metaphysically Loaded Counterparts," *Philosophers' Imprint* 7: 1–33.

Husserl, Edmund (1960/1977) *Cartesian Meditations*, trans. Dorian Cairns, The Hague: Kluwer.

Kant, Immanuel (1785/1981) *Grounding for the Metaphysics of Morals*, trans. James Ellington, Indianapolis, IN: Hackett.

Lewis, David (1983) "New Work for a Theory of Universals," *Australasian Journal of Philosophy* 61: 343–77.

Linnebo, Oystein (2009) "Bad Company Tamed," *Synthese* 170(3): 371–91.

MacFarlane, John (2000) "What Does It Mean to Say That Logic Is Formal?," PhD diss., University of Pittsburgh.

Manley, David (2009) Introduction to Chalmers *et al.* 2009, 1–37.

Price, Huw (2009) "Metaphysics after Carnap: The Ghost Who Walks?," in Chalmers *et al.* 2009, 320–46.

Quine, W.V.O. (1953/2001) "Two Dogmas of Empiricism," in *From a Logical Point of View*, Cambridge, MA: Harvard University Press.

Ryle, Gilbert (1949) *The Concept of Mind*, London: Hutchinson.

——(1957/1971) "The Theory of Meaning," in *Collected Papers,* vol. 2, London: Hutchison.

Schaffer, Jonathan (2009) "On What Grounds What," in Chalmers *et al.* 2009, 347–83.

Schiffer, Stephen (1994) "A Paradox of Meaning," *Noûs* 28: 279–324.

——(1996) "Language-Created Language-Independent Entities," *Philosophical Topics* 24: 149–67.

——(2003) *The Things We Mean*, Oxford: Oxford University Press.

Sider, Theodore (2011) *Writing the Book of the World*, Oxford: Oxford University Press.

Strawson, P.F. and H.P. Grice (1956) "In Defense of a Dogma," *Philosophical Review* 65(2): 141–58.

Thomasson, Amie L. (2001) "Ontological Minimalism," *American Philosophical Quarterly* 38(4): 319–31.

——(2007) *Ordinary Objects*, New York: Oxford University Press.

——(2009a) "The Easy Approach to Ontology," *Axiomathes* 19(1): 1–15.

——(2009b) "Non-descriptivism about Modality: A Brief History and Revival," in Center for Cognitive Sciences and Semantics (ed.), *Baltic International Yearbook of Cognition, Logic and Communication*, vol. 4: *200 Years of Analytical Philosophy*, Riga: Center for Cognitive Sciences and Semantics, University of Latvia, 1–26.

——(forthcoming) "Carnap and the Prospects for Easy Ontology," in Sandra LaPointe and Stephan Blatti (eds), *Ontology after Carnap*, Oxford: Oxford University Press.

——(unpublished) *Deflating Existence*.

Williamson, Timothy (2007) *The Philosophy of Philosophy*, Oxford: Blackwell.

Wright, Crispin (1983) *Frege's Conception of Numbers as Objects*, Aberdeen: Aberdeen University Press.

Yablo, Stephen (2000) "A Paradox of Existence," in Anthony Everett and Thomas Hofweber (eds), *Empty Names, Fiction, and the Puzzles of Non-existence*, Palo Alto: CSLI Publications, 275–312.

——(2001) "Go Figure: A Path through Fictionalism," *Midwest Studies in Philosophy* 25: 72–102.

——(2005) "The Myth of the Seven," in Mark Eli Kalderon (ed.), *Fictionalism in Metaphysics*, Oxford: Oxford University Press.

9 Metaphysical knowledge

E.J. LOWE

My topic in this chapter is metaphysical knowledge, by which I mean knowledge of metaphysical truths. And my principal questions are whether, and if so how, such knowledge is attainable by creatures like ourselves. I shall argue that we can and do possess metaphysical knowledge. But, of course, how controversial this claim is deemed to be will depend on what one takes to be distinctive of metaphysical truths. Consequently, I must first offer some account of what I take to be the nature of metaphysics as an intellectual discipline. It will soon be seen that on my account of the nature of metaphysics, the claim that we can and do possess metaphysical knowledge is indeed a controversial one and consequently one whose defence may prove interesting. But in offering this account and defending this claim, I have a deeper motive. This is to promote a certain conception of the methodology of metaphysics which is regrettably still very much in abeyance, largely on account of the dominance of, first, epistemology, and then the philosophy of language, in the Western philosophical tradition of the last 300 years.[1]

The slogan for my preferred conception of metaphysical method might well be this: *metaphysics must be done directly*. What I am opposing is the view – so widespread that it often goes unspoken – that metaphysics, to the extent that it can be done at all, has to be done through the medium of some other branch of philosophy, such as epistemology, logic, philo-sophical semantics, or the philosophy of mind. What is particularly absurd about this view is that each of these branches of philosophy has, inevi-tably, certain distinctively metaphysical commitments which cannot pos-sibly be warranted by doing metaphysics in the way that the view recommends. All that sustains the view in the face of this absurdity, as far as I can see, is the unspoken conviction of so many philosophers that metaphysics *cannot* be done, as I put it, 'directly'. I think we owe this pernicious conviction in large measure to the 'modernist' legacy of Descartes, Hume, and Kant – great philosophers all of them, but all philosophers whose work contributed to the demotion of metaphysics from its central role in philosophy. It has been encouraging to see evidence of a revival in the fortunes of metaphysics in recent years, but contemporary metaphysics is still a tender plant that needs much nurturing and one that is constantly in danger of reverting to the degenerate type propagated by the modernist legacy.

The nature of metaphysics

People who are not familiar with metaphysics are apt to have a false, or at least a somewhat distorted, conception of what it involves. Sometimes they think that it has something to do with mysticism and magic, for reasons which might be interesting to pursue if one were engaged in a sociological or historical study, but which have little bearing on the true character of metaphysics as a branch of philosophy. Sometimes they think that metaphysics has something to do with *physics*, which is a little nearer to the truth. However, it would be quite wrong to suppose that metaphysics is to physics as metalogic is to logic, or as metaethics is to ethics – that it is a type of second-order inquiry into the conceptual foundations and methods of a first-order discipline. Metaphysics does include some features of such an inquiry, but even in that respect its focus is not exclusively upon the concerns of physics. Indeed, it is largely just an historical accident that metaphysics is called what it is, an outcome of the fact that Aristotle's *Metaphysics* was so named simply because it was placed in the canonical order of his works *after* another treatise of his, the *Physics* (the Greek prefix *meta* signifying this relation).[2] Even so, this was perhaps a happy accident, inasmuch as physics and metaphysics do overlap in many of their fundamental concerns.

What is it, then, that metaphysics and physics have in common? Well, physics – and here I speak of modern physics – is an empirical science concerned to explain certain basic and ubiquitous phenomena in the natural world, that is, in the realm of things existing in space and time. Physics appeals to putative causal laws to explain such phenomena – for example, the laws of electromagnetism and of gravitation, which causally explain the motions of electrically charged and massive objects respectively. Metaphysics also is concerned, although not exclusively, with the nature of things existing in space and time, with the nature of space and time themselves, and with the nature of causation. But metaphysics is not at heart an empirical science – it does not typically appeal to experimental or observational data in support of its claims. Nor are metaphysicians solely concerned with the nature of the physical world – unless they happen to espouse the doctrine of physicalism, which maintains that the only things that exist are physical entities in space and time. They are also concerned with the nature of abstract entities, such as the objects of mathematics and logic – numbers, sets, propositions, and so forth. Such entities plausibly do not exist in space and time, but need not be deemed any the less part of reality on that account. Moreover, there are, very arguably, entities which do exist in space and time but which are, even so, not the proper subject matter of the empirical science of physics – entities such as people and their mental states of thought and feeling, and entities such as social and political groups. According to many philosophers and scientists, the behaviour of these entities can never be explained solely by appeal to the laws of physics, not least because their behaviour is, in large measure, subject to *rational* rather than merely to *causal* explanation. Of course, physicalist philosophers may want to challenge this view; but then they are engaging precisely in a *metaphysical* debate, not one which belongs to the province of physics itself.

What begins to emerge from these observations is that one of the roles of metaphysics, as an intellectual discipline, is to provide a forum in which boundary disputes between other disciplines can be conducted – for instance, the dispute as to whether the subject matter of a special science, such as biology or psychology or economics, can properly be said to be subsumed under that of another allegedly more 'fundamental' science, such as physics. According to a once-dominant traditional conception of metaphysics – which is basically the conception of metaphysics that I wish to defend – metaphysics can occupy the interdisciplinary role just described because its central concern is with *the fundamental structure of reality as a whole*. No special science – not even physics – can have that concern, because the subject matter of every special science is identified more narrowly than this. For instance, biology is the science of living things, psychology is the science of mental states, and physics – as has already been indicated – is the science of those states and processes (energetic states and dynamic processes, for example) that are apparently common to all things existing in space and time. Even if it could be successfully argued, as the physicalist maintains it can, that the whole of reality is confined to things existing in space and time, it wouldn't follow that metaphysics reduces to physics – because the very argument that reality *is* thus confined, which is a metaphysical argument, is not an argument that physics can provide.

Metaphysics, as traditionally conceived, is very arguably ineliminable and conceptually necessary as the intellectual backdrop for every other discipline. Why? Ultimately, this is because truth is single and indivisible or, to put it another way, because the world or reality as a whole is unitary and necessarily self-consistent.[3] The various special sciences, and other intellectual disciplines whose practitioners would probably not care to call themselves 'scientists' – such as historians and literary theorists – are all concerned, at least in part, with the pursuit of truth, but pursue it according to their own methods of inquiry and within their own prescribed domain. But the indivisibility of truth means that all of these forms of inquiry must, if they are to succeed in their aim, acknowledge the need to be consistent with each other. Nor can any one of them presume to adjudicate such questions of mutual consistency, because none of them has a jurisdiction beyond its own limited domain. Such adjudication can only be provided by the practitioners of an intellectual discipline which aspires to complete universality in its subject matter and aims – and that discipline is metaphysics, as traditionally conceived.

The foregoing argument may be looked upon suspiciously as special pleading on the part of self-styled metaphysicians seeking to guarantee themselves an intellectual role. And, to be fair, it would be wrong to advance that argument in a purely dogmatic spirit, as though its conclusion was beyond debating. But, in a way, this point merely serves to strengthen the claims of metaphysics to be an autonomous and indispensable form of rational inquiry: because the point is that absolutely *everything*, including even the status and credentials of metaphysics itself, comes within the purview of the universal discipline which metaphysics claims to be. None of this means that metaphysicians have to be seen as a caste apart from other people, loftily making their pronouncements from intellectual heights above the level of the common crowd. Precisely because metaphysics is a universal intellectual discipline, it is one which no rational being can avoid engaging in at least some of the time. We are all metaphysicians whether we like it or not, and whether we know it or not. But this isn't to say that anyone's opinion on a question of metaphysics is just as good, or as bad, as anyone else's. There is no reason to deny that there can be such a thing as expertise in metaphysical thinking, which takes some pains to acquire. If I had had any doubts about this, I would not have bothered to write this paper!

Of course, the argument that we have just been examining in defence of metaphysics as traditionally conceived – the argument from the indivisibility of truth, or from the unity of the world – may seem vulnerable to attack from those who question this conception of truth and its associated 'universalist' conceptions of reason and rationality. I am thinking of those philosophers, and practitioners of some other intellectual disciplines, who espouse some form of cultural or historical relativism. Such people may deny that truth is single and indivisible, maintaining that what is true for one culture or at one epoch of history may not be true for or at another, and that different cultures and epochs have different and incommensurable conceptions of reason and rationality. But, of course, such a doctrine is itself a metaphysical thesis, in the sense of 'metaphysics' that I have been expounding and trying to defend; for it is nothing less than a claim about the fundamental nature of reality, which could not be substantiated solely by the methods of any special science or intellectual discipline, such as anthropology or history or sociology. To the extent that the practitioners of any such discipline are tempted to espouse such a doctrine, they must acknowledge that what they are advocating is precisely a metaphysical thesis, because it is one which transcends the boundaries of any more limited form of rational inquiry. So, once again, we see that the attempt to undermine or eliminate the metaphysical dimension of our thinking is self-defeating, because the very attempt necessarily constitutes a piece of metaphysical thinking itself.

This shows that the argument from the indivisibility of truth is not absolutely essential to the defence of metaphysics, in the sense that metaphysics would be left completely without justification in its absence – which, once again, should not surprise us, because *everything*, including even the question of whether truth is indivisible, is potentially open to metaphysical inquiry. On the other hand, this isn't to say that the argument from the indivisibility of truth is idle or superfluous; for I think that the doctrine of the indivisibility of truth can survive critical inquiry, whereas the denial of that doctrine cannot. This being so, metaphysics may be said to contain within itself, in the form of this argument, the grounds of its own justification. That is to say, metaphysical reasoning may be used to defend the doctrine of the indivisibility of truth, and that doctrine can in turn be used to argue for the indispensability of metaphysics. There need be nothing viciously circular or question-begging about such a procedure.

Naturalized epistemology and metaphysical knowledge

There are, however, other people besides cultural and historical relativists who seek to undermine the credentials of metaphysics, traditionally conceived as a universal discipline of a non-empirical character, concerned with the fundamental structure of reality. For instance, there are those philosophers who adhere to what is often known as the programme of 'naturalized epistemology'.[4] The thought here is that any kind of knowledge that is attainable by human beings, including anything that might deserve to be called 'metaphysical' knowledge, must be compatible with our status as a kind of natural creature – in fact, a species of animal – that has arisen through wholly natural processes of biological evolution. Moreover, any inquiry into the nature of such knowledge must, it may be alleged, be part of a more general scientific inquiry into the cognitive capacities of creatures of our kind. Thus, epistemology – the theory of knowledge – is properly to be conceived of as being a part of the natural science of human psychology, which must in turn have a biological and ultimately a purely physical foundation. But what scope does such a conception of human knowledge and its sources have for acknowledging the existence of metaphysical knowledge, as traditionally conceived? Very little if any, it may be thought. For how could a naturally evolved life form, with cognitive capacities 'designed' by nature solely to equip it to survive in a hostile environment, attain non-empirical knowledge of the fundamental structure of reality? On this view, the only kind of 'metaphysics' deserving of recognition would be, if there can be such a thing, *naturalized* metaphysics – that is, a metaphysics knowledge of whose truths could plausibly be seen as attainable by and practically advantageous to animals with our particular biological capacities and needs. Any such 'metaphysics', it may be alleged, must be at least continuous with natural science itself, or more likely just a part of it. So, on this view, there is no question that metaphysics is equipped to answer which isn't properly in the domain of some natural science – either the fundamental science, physics, or one of the special sciences, if these are not ultimately reducible to physics.

The trouble with this line of thinking is, once more, that it is liable to undermine itself and in the course of doing so demonstrate yet again the indispensability or ineliminability of metaphysics as traditionally conceived. In the first place, to the extent that a wholly naturalistic and evolutionary conception of human beings seems to threaten the very possibility of metaphysical knowledge, it equally threatens the very possibility of *scientific* knowledge – for it is equally mysterious how a naturally evolved creature should have any capacity to acquire knowledge of such arcane matters as the formation of stars or the structure of DNA. No other animal species with which we are acquainted is or ever has been capable of such scientific knowledge. It is debatable whether the possession of such knowledge is advantageous to our species; indeed, it may well turn out to be the cause of our untimely extinction. More to the point, though, no one has the slightest idea as to how or why early humans acquired this capacity, within the constraints imposed by the theory of evolution by natural selection. Natural science itself cannot presently explain, then, how natural scientific knowledge is possible in creatures like ourselves. So the fact that it cannot explain how metaphysical knowledge, as traditionally conceived, is possible in creatures like ourselves gives us no very good reason to suppose that such knowledge is *not* possible. For if it did, we would equally have good reason to suppose that natural scientific knowledge is not possible in creatures like ourselves – and this would mean that we would no longer have any grounds to believe in the scientific theories to which naturalized epistemology appeals, such as the theory of evolution itself.

Furthermore, it has to be recognized that the very debate that I am now conducting with the advocate of naturalized epistemology is one which itself necessarily rests upon certain metaphysical assumptions – some of which are shared and some of which are disputed. In short, the very doctrine of naturalized epistemology, and the kinds of arguments that are invoked in its support, have a metaphysical dimension to them which is at odds with the central claims of that doctrine – so that the naturalized epistemologist is apparently guilty of a curious failure of self-awareness, casting all human kind in a severely naturalistic mould but not recognizing that this very act betrays a style of thinking on his own part which cannot easily be accommodated by such naturalism.

Kant's question and Kantian metaphysics

We should not allow these defensive moves on the part of metaphysics to lull us into thinking that there is, after all, no need to explain the possibility of metaphysical knowledge. It may well be that this possibility cannot be explained entirely naturalistically, and we may be entitled to conclude from this *not* that there is no such possibility but rather that naturalism is inadequate. But this still leaves us looking for a positive explanation of the possibility. Here we may be reminded that it was Kant who first posed the momentous question, 'How is metaphysics possible?'[5] Kant's answer, however, was inimical to metaphysics as traditionally conceived – that is, conceived as a form of rational inquiry into the fundamental structure of reality. For Kant held that metaphysical claims in fact concern not the fundamental structure of a mind-independent reality, even if such a reality exists, but rather the fundamental structure of rational *thought* about reality. Kant believed that only by construing metaphysical claims as having this concern could our non-empirical knowledge of their truth be explained and certified – the assumption here being that the structure of our own thought is something that is unproblematically accessible to us in a way in which the structure of mind-independent reality is supposedly not.

That assumption may itself be questioned. More fundamentally, however, it may be objected to the Kantian conception of metaphysics that if nothing about the structure of mind-independent reality is accessible to us then, by the same token, nothing about the structure of *our own thought* is accessible to us either – for, in the relevant sense of 'mind-independent', our thought itself is nothing if not part of mind-independent reality. By 'mind-independent reality', here, I mean the sum total of things *whose existence is not dependent upon our thinking of them*. (In this sense, *money*, for instance, is not – or, at least, is not wholly – part of 'mind-independent reality', since money very arguably would not exist if no one *thought* that it did. This is because a system of currency depends upon the confidence of its users that its units can reliably be exchanged for goods. Obviously, though, a *piece* of money, such as a coin or a banknote, could exist without anyone thinking of it or anything else as *being* money: it would just not qualify as *money* in that case, but merely as a piece of metal or paper.) Now, our own thoughts have an existence which is not dependent upon our thinking of them and so constitute part of mind-independent reality in this sense. It is true that our thoughts would not exist if we were not *thinking* them, but that is not to say that we must think *of* them for them to exist. Some metaphysicians have held that the only things that exist are thoughts and their thinkers, that is, the things having those thoughts. This is not, however, a position according to which there is no 'mind-independent reality', in the relevant sense of that expression. (Thoughts are unquestionably 'mind-dependent' only in a very different sense, namely, in the sense that they have to *belong* to minds in order to exist: it by no means follows that no thought can exist without some mind *thinking* that it does – a requirement which would, in any case, appear to give rise to a vicious infinite regress.)

It may be objected to the foregoing argument that it misconstrues the nature of the Kantian view of metaphysical claims. In maintaining that metaphysical claims concern the structure of our thought about reality as opposed to the structure of mind-independent reality itself, it is saying that such claims concern structural features of the *contents* of our thoughts, not any features of the thoughts themselves, conceived as real psychological processes going on in our minds or heads. But how can it coherently be said that structural features of the contents of our thoughts are *not* features of our thoughts themselves? The content of a thought – what it is a thought *about* or *of* – is an *essential* feature of that thought, partly serving to determine the very identity of that thought. A thought of mine that two plus two equals four, or that lemons are bitter, would not be that very thought but for its having that very content. Consequently, it seems that there is no possibility of our circumscribing the supposed subject matter of metaphysics in such a way that it can be held to concern the *contents* of thoughts without having any concern for the nature of thoughts themselves. And, I repeat, thoughts themselves are nothing if not part of mind-independent reality. Moreover, even if such circumscription *were* possible, there would remain the problem that any theory of content inevitably has its own ontological commitments and cannot coherently pretend to have nothing whatever to do with mind-independent reality and its structure.

Perhaps the Kantian will try to counter this latest line of objection in some way. But, ironically enough, any such attempt would undermine the very position that he is trying to defend; for in order to make any such attempt, the Kantian will have to engage in genuine metaphysical argument as traditionally conceived. He will have to deny, for instance, that the content of a thought is an essential feature of that thought; and this is to deny a certain thesis concerning the nature of a certain category of entities – thoughts – conceived as being elements of a mind-independent reality. Once again we see how metaphysics, as traditionally conceived, is inescapable for any rational thinker. The Kantian attempt to avoid metaphysics in this sense by restricting our critical concerns purely to the contents of our thoughts appears doomed to failure. Questions to do with content themselves have, inescapably, a genuinely metaphysical dimension – a dimension which does not have solely to do with the content of thoughts about content.

The reason why Kant sought to redefine the nature of metaphysical claims as being claims about the structure of our thought about reality rather than about the structure of reality itself is that he believed that only in this way could the absolutely certain and non-empirical character of metaphysical knowledge be explained. If metaphysical claims concerned mind-independent reality, he thought, we could not possibly have certain knowledge of their truth – and yet, he considered, we do know some metaphysical truths with absolute certainty. Notice here, first of all, that the very assertion that it would not be *possible* to have certain knowledge of metaphysical truths if metaphysical truths concerned mind-independent reality is itself a *metaphysical* claim, in the traditional sense of 'metaphysics', rather than in Kant's own redefined sense of the term. This in itself shows, once more, the self-defeating nature of Kant's attempted redefinition. Secondly, however, even granting the truth of this metaphysical assertion, why shouldn't we respond to it by saying *not* that metaphysical knowledge as traditionally conceived is impossible (a self-defeating claim itself, inasmuch as it is precisely a metaphysical claim as traditionally conceived), but rather that metaphysical knowledge is almost never *certain* knowledge – that is, that metaphysical knowledge claims can almost never be absolutely invulnerable to falsification or disproof. Why should we imagine that metaphysics affords us a method of rational inquiry which *guarantees* the truth of its conclusions, beyond any possibility of their subsequent reversal in the light of further inquiry? Not even in mathematics do we think that we have such incontrovertible methods of discovery. It is true, of course, that a mathematical 'proof' relinquishes the title of 'proof' once it has been 'proved' to be invalid, so that any genuine 'proof' cannot but be successful. But that is like saying that all knowledge is, by definition, knowledge of what is *true*, and consequently that what we 'know' cannot but be true.

Contingency, possibility, and metaphysical knowledge

Of course, it may be considered that the greater problem about metaphysical knowledge claims, as traditionally conceived, is not so much how they could attain to certainty as how they could be *non-empirical*. Now, in this respect, too, metaphysical knowledge claims are akin to mathematical knowledge claims, which are likewise held to be non-empirical, in the sense that they are not answerable to empirical evidence for their support or confirmation. And then the worry might be this. If metaphysical knowledge claims concern the fundamental structure of mind-independent reality then, if that structure is, at least in some respects, *contingent* rather than *necessary*, it is hard to see how we can have knowledge of it which does not rely upon empirical evidence, for it seems that only such evidence could reveal to us that the world we inhabit has one contingent structure rather than another which it would be equally *possible* for the world to have had. In this respect, metaphysics differs from mathematics, it may be said, where there is no element of contingency since the objects and structures investigated by mathematics are purely abstract. (Of course, it may be urged that the supposedly abstract nature of mathematical objects – numbers, sets, functions, and the like – makes our putative knowledge of them also problematic, but for a quite different reason, namely, because it is hard to understand how our minds, which belong to the concrete world of things in space and time, can grasp relationships between purely abstract objects. However, this is, I suspect, an acute problem only for proponents of 'naturalized' epistemology, who may on that account be strongly attracted to some form of nominalism – or else fictionalism – where mathematics is concerned. Non-naturalistic episte-mologists might be better advised to reject the kind of causal theory of knowledge that seems to generate the supposed problem in the first place.)

This kind of consideration, then, may seem to drive us in the direction of regarding metaphysical knowledge, to the extent that it is possible at all, as being a species of *empirical* knowledge. But then it is not clear, after all, that metaphysics can legitimately claim to be distinct from and in any sense prior to natural science: we seem to be compelled, after all, to accept the view of naturalized epistemology that the only kind of metaphysics available to us is one that is continuous with, or indeed just a part of, empirical scientific inquiry into the nature of the world.

The proper response to this apparent difficulty is, I think, the following. We should concede that when a metaphysician asserts the actual existence of some fundamental feature of reality which he deems to be *contingent* in character, then indeed he should acknowledge that this claim is answerable to empirical evidence, at least in part. But it is important to see that such a claim is not and cannot be answerable *solely* to empirical evidence. For when anyone makes such a claim, it is incumbent upon him to try to establish – although not necessarily with absolute certainty, for reasons given earlier – that the existence of that feature is at least *possible*. The key point here is that empirical data cannot be regarded as bona fide evidence for the actual existence of anything which is not at least a *possible* feature of reality. There could, for example, never be bona fide empirical evidence for the existence of a round square, simply because such a geometrical figure is *impossible*. Similarly, only if time travel into the past is at least *possible* could it be legitimate to treat certain empirical data as bona fide evidence for the *actual occurrence* of an episode of time travel into the past, as opposed to something quite different, such as an elaborate hoax or an unusual coincidence. Someone might certainly be deemed to possess prima facie empirical evidence for the existence of time travel into the past, but for this to qualify as bona fide evidence, some reason must be forthcoming to suppose that the phenomenon in question really *could* exist. Without such a filter on prima facie empirical evidence, the 'hypotheses' that we might seek to 'confirm' empirically would be utterly unconstrained in their potential extravagance and charlatans of all sorts would be free to peddle their wares, from perpetual motion machines to manuals of astrology. However, establishing that the existence of a certain feature of reality is indeed *possible* is not something that can, in general, be achieved solely by any purely empirical means of inquiry. For if the feature in question is possible, it will either be possible *but not actually exist* – in which case no purely empirical means of inquiry can establish its possibility, since the empirical data available to any such inquiry must all be drawn from the actual world, not from any merely possible world in which the feature in question does exist – or else it will be both possible *and* actually exist. Now, if it actually exists, then it must indeed be possible, since it is a basic principle of modal logic that what is actually the case is also possibly the case. But, as we have just observed, prima facie empirical evidence for its actual existence can only count as bona fide evidence on the presumption that the feature in question is indeed genuinely *possible*. Hence, no purely empirical means of inquiry can establish the possibility of that feature by establishing that it *actually* exists, since to do so it would need already to be entitled to regard that feature as being possible. Either way, then, no purely empirical means of inquiry can by itself establish the real possibility of any conjectured feature of reality.

My conclusion is that metaphysics, like mathematics, does have a non-empirical subject matter, to the extent that it is the intellectual discipline whose primary concern it is to chart the *possibilities* of real existence. Metaphysics is primarily concerned to discover what the totality of existence *could* embrace, that is to say, what categories of entities could exist and which of them could coexist. Having charted the possibilities, a question will still remain as to which of many mutually incompatible possibilities for the fundamental structure of reality *actually obtains* – and this question can be answered, if at all, only with the aid of empirical evidence, and even then only tentatively and provisionally. Thus we see how, on this conception of the task of metaphysics, metaphysics can genuinely be concerned with the fundamental structure of reality itself, rather than just with the structure of our *thought* about reality, but at the same time can have a non-empirical character which distinguishes it from natural science.

But still, perhaps, a problem remains. For how, it may be asked, is non-empirical knowledge of what is possible itself possible? How is it possible for creatures like ourselves to chart the realm of possibilities? Of course, this is a curious question, to the extent that it is, itself, a question – addressed to ourselves – about the very realm of possibilities, access to which, by us, is being put in question. Suppose, however, that we were to come up with an argument whose conclusion was that it is *not* possible for us to chart the realm of possibilities. That conclusion would seem to undermine itself, because the conclusion itself concerns the realm of possibilities, maintaining that that realm does not include the possibility of our charting it. We could thus only have reason to believe the conclusion if the conclusion were false: so we can have *no* reason to believe it. Is this just a trick? I don't think so; rather, it is yet another example of the unavoidability of metaphysics. As rational beings, we cannot but consider ourselves capable of knowing at least something about the realm of possibilities. This should not be surprising. Reasoning itself depends upon a grasp of possibilities, because a valid argument is one in which it is not *possible* for the conclusion to be false if the premises are true – and a rational being is a creature which can discern the validity of at least some arguments.

Real possibilities, semantics, and reflection on concepts

Some philosophers maintain that questions of what is possible are, ultimately, just questions about what concepts we deploy or the meanings of our words. For example, it may be said that the only reason why it is not possible for a bachelor to be married is that 'bachelor' *means* 'unmarried man'. If all possibility is grounded in the meaning of words, which is purely conventional in nature, perhaps there is, after all, no 'realm of possibilities' for metaphysics to chart in any ontologically serious sense. Indeed, the task that we have been assigning to the metaphysician might, on this view, more appropriately be assigned to the lexicographer. But, in fact, it doesn't make sense to suppose that all possibility is grounded in the meaning of words, not least because there are possibilities and impossibilities concerning the meanings of words themselves, which cannot without absurdity be taken to be grounded in the meanings of words. In any case, returning to our bachelor example, it is clear that there is in fact a perfectly good sense in which it *is* possible for a bachelor to be married: what is not possible is for a bachelor to be married and still correctly be described as a 'bachelor', given the meaning of this English word. This is an impossibility concerning the meaning of a word. But the sense in which it *is* possible for a bachelor to be married has nothing whatever to do with the meanings of words. Similarly, the sense in which it is possible for a human being to run a mile in four minutes, or the sense in which it is possible for a pint of water to be contained in a two-pint jug, has nothing whatever to do with the meanings of words. These are 'real' possibilities, which are grounded in the natures of things, not in the meanings of the words that we use to describe things.

There may be an innocuous sense in which at least some possibilities have a 'conceptual' basis. Reflection on the 'concepts' of a pint of water and of a two-pint jug suffices to persuade us that it is possible for the latter to contain the former, just as reflection on the 'concept' of an isosceles triangle suffices to persuade us that it is possible to divide it into two equal right-angled triangles. But this isn't to deny that the possibilities in question are grounded in the natures of the things concerned, nor is it to imply that these possibilities are grounded merely in the meanings of the words that we use to describe those things. For an adequate concept of a thing of a certain kind should embody a correct grasp of that thing's nature. Someone cannot, for instance, be in possession of an adequate concept of an isosceles triangle if he conceives of this as a three-sided geometrical figure none of whose sides are the same in length – because an isosceles triangle is not a figure of that nature. No harm is necessarily done, then, in saying that a knowledge of real possibilities may be arrived at by reflection on concepts: properly understood, this needn't be seen as implying that possibilities don't exist independently of our ways of thinking about or 'conceptualizing' the world.

I make these points about meanings and concepts because there are some philosophers who would seek a basis in language, or more precisely in the theory of meaning, for any legitimate claims that they would be prepared to characterize as 'metaphysical'.[6] In many ways, such a view of the status of metaphysical claims is a modern-dress version of Kant's view of metaphysical claims as being concerned with the structure of thought. Indeed, for those philosophers who consider that the structure of thought just is, at bottom, the structure of the language in which thought is expressed, the two views are very close indeed, if not identical. In any case, similar objections may be raised against what we may call the *semantic* conception of metaphysics as may be raised against Kantianism. It is quite possibly true that different languages reflect in their vocabulary and grammatical structures the different metaphysical preconceptions of the speech communities whose languages they are. But even if true, this wouldn't serve to show that metaphysical claims are grounded purely in language. Moreover, it is important to recognize that human beings are not incapable of challenging and rejecting the metaphysical preconceptions of the speech community in which they happen to be born and educated. To be persuaded of this fact, one has only to reflect on the enormous variety of metaphysical systems that have been proposed and defended over the centuries by philosophers belonging to the same or closely related speech communities. So there really is no evidence that metaphysical thinking is invariably or unavoidably subject to a strong degree of linguistic or cultural relativity. However, I have already said enough, earlier, in rebuttal of the relativist critics of metaphysics as traditionally conceived.

At the outset, I mentioned Aristotle, whose view was that metaphysics is the science of being *qua* being, and for that reason conceptually prior to any special science with a more limited subject matter. This view places *ontology* – the study of what categories of entities there are and how they are related to one another – at the heart of metaphysics. Clearly, it is a view which accords well with the conception of metaphysics that I have been defending – the view that metaphysics is concerned with the fundamental structure of reality as a whole. Aristotle does not commit what I have characterized as the Kantian error of supposing that metaphysics concerns the structure of our *thought* about being rather than being itself. It is true, of course, that we can only discourse rationally about the nature of being inasmuch as we are capable of entertaining thoughts about what there is or could be in the world. But this doesn't mean that we must substitute a study of our thought about things for a study of things themselves. Our thoughts do not constitute a veil or curtain interposed between us and the things we are endeavouring to think of, somehow making them inaccessible or inscrutable to us. On the contrary, things are accessible to us precisely because we are able to think of them. The things that we think of do not thereby collapse into the thoughts that we have of them, as idealist philosophers are apt to suppose. In this respect, then, I follow Aristotle's lead rather than Kant's concerning the nature of metaphysics as an intellectual discipline. But, for reasons given earlier, my stance on this issue does not imply that it is inappropriate in metaphysics to attempt to justify certain judgements by means of a process of reflection on concepts. Indeed, it is indicative of the autonomous and irreducible status of metaphysics as an indispensable intellectual discipline that it sustains its own distinctive corpus of fundamental concepts – concepts such as those of *object, event, state of affairs, property, relation, identity, change, persistence, necessity, possibility, causation, space,* and *time.* And it is only if we can achieve a clear understanding of such fundamental metaphysical concepts and their interrelationships that we can hope to deploy them successfully in our attempts to articulate the fundamental structure of reality.

Experience and modal knowledge

I want to conclude by saying what I think is right and what wrong about a certain model for the acquisition of metaphysical knowledge of a modal character that has received some support in recent years. The model draws its inspiration from the famous Barcan–Kripke argument for the necessity of identity.[7] This argument has two premises, both of which are taken to be necessary truths, knowable a priori. The first premise is that everything is necessarily identical with itself – the principle of the necessity of self-identity. The second premise is Leibniz's law – the principle that whatever is true of something is true of anything identical with that thing. And the argument goes like this. Suppose that a certain identity proposition is true: say, the proposition that *a* is identical with *b*, where *a* and *b* are any objects whatever. Then, by the principle of the necessity of self-identity, we can say that *a* is necessarily identical with *a*. From this it follows that it is true of *a* that it is necessarily identical with *a*. But from this and the assumption that *a* is identical with *b* it follows, by Leibniz's law, that it is also true of *b* that it is necessarily identical with *a* – from which it follows that *a* is necessarily identical with *b*. What we seem to have proved, then, is that if it is *true* that *a* is identical with *b*, then it is *necessarily true* that *a* is identical with *b* – and consequently that there cannot be an identity proposition that is merely *contingently* true (true in some possible worlds but not in others).

There are many reasons why the conclusion of this argument is interesting and perhaps even surprising. One is that, if the argument is correct, it shows us that there can be necessary truths that are knowable only a posteriori, that is, not independently of empirical evidence. Take the proposition that Hesperus is identical with Phosphorus, these being the ancient Greek names for the evening star and the morning star respectively. Astronomers now know, of course, that the evening star and the morning star are one and the same heavenly body, namely, the planet Venus. If the Barcan–Kripke argument is correct, it is a necessary truth that Hesperus is identical with Phosphorus; but if so, it is plainly one whose truth was, and had to be, discovered empirically, by means of astronomical observation. The epistemological status of this identity proposition is quite different, thus, from that of the identity proposition that Hesperus is identical with Hesperus, which is an a priori truth of logic. This implication of the Barcan–Kripke argument renders it suspicious in the eyes of some philosophers, especially those who think that necessity cannot reside in the natures of things themselves, independently of the ways in which we conceptualize things or describe them in language. However, I am not at all sympathetic to the latter view of the nature of necessity, as I have made clear already, and so I shall raise no objection to the Barcan–Kripke argument from this direction.[8]

As we have just seen, it is a consequence of the Barcan–Kripke argument that if Hesperus is identical with Phosphorus – if they are in fact one and the same object – then Hesperus and Phosphorus *could not have been* distinct. In the language of possible worlds: if Hesperus and Phosphorus are one and the same object in the actual world, then there is no possible world in which Hesperus and Phosphorus are two distinct objects. Against this claim, it may perhaps be urged that one can perfectly well *imagine* a possible world in which the astronomers discover that Hesperus and Phosphorus are two distinct planets. However, that one can imagine a situation does not necessarily imply that it is genuinely a possible situation. We can perhaps imagine a time-traveller going back to the past and changing the course of history; but it is not genuinely possible to change the course of history, that is, to make it the case that something that has happened has not happened, for this involves a contradiction. Furthermore, when it is urged that one can imagine a possible world in which the astronomers discover that Hesperus and Phosphorus are two distinct planets, it may be questioned whether this really does characterize the content of a possible act of imagination: perhaps all that we can really imagine is a possible world in which there exist two planets *very similar* to Hesperus and Phosphorus, which the astronomers of that world discover to be two distinct planets. So this, too, is not a line of objection that I consider promising.

However, there is a danger that philosophers may think that the Barcan–Kripke argument provides a model for the easy acquisition of metaphysical knowledge of a modal character.[9] The model is this. We first establish, by means of deductive argument from uncontroversial premises that are knowable a priori, the truth of a conditional proposition whose consequent is modal in character and whose antecedent is non-modal in character. The archetype is provided by the conclusion of the Barcan–Kripke argument itself: if *a* is identical with *b*, then *a* is *necessarily* identical with *b*. Then we establish by purely empirical means the truth of the non-modal antecedent of this conditional. Finally, again by means of deductive argument, we infer the truth of the modal consequent of the conditional, thereby acquiring a posteriori knowledge of that modal truth. This model for the acquisition of a posteriori metaphysical knowledge of a modal character holds out the promise of dividing the task of acquiring such knowledge between the a priori science of logic on the one hand and the empirical sciences on the other, thereby denying any distinctive role for metaphysics as an independent intellectual discipline. It will be seen immediately why I consider this model to be a threat to the account of metaphysics and metaphysical knowledge that I have been promoting.

However, the threat can easily be deflected. This can best be seen, perhaps, if we reflect on the bearing that the Barcan–Kripke argument has on one of the perennial problems of metaphysics, the mind–body problem. According to one currently prevalent view, a person is identical with his or her body. But if the Barcan–Kripke argument is correct, one thing that it shows is that the claim that a person is identical with his or her body is in fact an extremely strong claim, because it has implications not only for what is the case in this, the actual world, but also for what is the case in *every* possible world (or, at least, in every possible world in which either the person or his or her body exists). Indeed, for this reason, one may doubt whether *empirical* evidence – which can only make reference to what is the case in this, the actual world, since that is the only world that we can observe – could ever suffice to establish the truth of such an identity claim. This may not be at all congenial to the philosophers who are apt to make such identity claims, because in support of those claims they tend to appeal to scientific evidence of correlations between the psychological states of persons and physiological states of their bodies. It would be much more convenient for these philosophers if they could simply concede that a person *could have* failed to be identical with his or her body, while insisting nonetheless that a person *is* identical with his or her body, as a matter of contingent fact. However, if the thesis of the necessity of identity is correct, such a position is simply not available to these philosophers.

Now, here it may be remarked that, earlier, I raised no such problem for the empirically based claim that Hesperus is identical with Phosphorus, which I represented as having been established by astronomical observation. Yet, if the thesis of the necessity of identity is correct, this identity claim equally has implications for what is the case in every possible world. However, there is a significant difference between the two cases. In the case of Hesperus and Phosphorus, we are already satisfied, quite independently of the identity claim made concerning them, that they are *objects of the same kind*, governed by the same identity conditions. We are satisfied that each of them is a *planet* – a persisting mass of matter which orbits the sun in a certain clearly definable path. It is easy to see how careful astronomical observations could establish that the orbits of Hesperus and Phosphorus coincide, so that they can be predicted to be in the same place at the same time. Given that they are masses of matter and that numerically distinct masses of matter cannot exist in the same place at the same time, it follows that Hesperus and Phosphorus are identical. The reasoning here does clearly appeal to more than merely empirical evidence: it appeals also to certain metaphysical principles, albeit ones which are relatively uncontentious. However, in the case of a person and his or her body, what are fundamentally in contention are the relevant metaphysical principles themselves. If it could be agreed that persons and their bodies are objects of the same kind, with the same identity conditions, it would be no more problematic to appeal to empirical evidence to establish an identity between a particular person and a particular body than it is to do so in the case of Hesperus and Phosphorus. The question would not be whether a particular person was identical with any body at all, but merely *which* particular body a person was identical with. But that is *not* how matters stand with regard to persons and bodies: here the dispute is precisely as to the nature of entities of these kinds and whether, indeed, they are entities of the *same* kind or not. That is why it is facile to suppose that the question of whether or not a person is identical with his or her body could be settled straightforwardly by appeal to empirical evidence, such as evidence of correlations between a person's psychological states and physiological states of that person's body.

What this discussion brings out is, first, that even when the Barcan–Kripke argument is used to support an a posteriori modal knowledge claim of a relatively uncontroversial sort, such as that Hesperus is necessarily identical with Phosphorus, it is an illusion to suppose that the relevant non-modal premise – in this case, that Hesperus is indeed identical with Phosphorus – can be established by purely empirical means, without appeal to any metaphysical principle of a modal character. (In this case, one such modal principle is the principle that numerically distinct masses of matter cannot exist in the same place at the same time.) Secondly, it brings out the fact that if this form of argument were to be appealed to in support of any metaphysical knowledge claim of a more controversial sort, it would leave the real burden of metaphysical argument still to be taken up. The lesson is that we should not be deceived into thinking that this burden can be neatly shared out between logic and empirical science, leaving nothing substantive for metaphysics, as traditionally conceived, to do. All the hard work remains to be done and can be done only by doing metaphysics – and doing it 'directly'. I readily concede that this conclusion still leaves many important questions unanswered, not least regarding the true source of our knowledge of modal truths, given that this cannot reside merely in our grasp of certain a priori logical truths in conjunction with our knowledge of certain empirical truths of a purely non-modal character. My own view is that the true source lies in our grasp of certain *essential* truths, that is, certain truths concerning the *essences* or *natures* of things, as revealed by their 'real definitions'.[10] This requires me to adopt a very different conception of the relationship between essence and modality from the one that has become so widely disseminated as a result of the work of Saul Kripke – one whose intellectual origins lie instead in the works of Aristotle.[11] But that is a topic for another occasion.

Notes

1 The present chapter is also designed to develop further the views first advanced in my *The Possibility of Metaphysics: Substance, Identity, and Time* (Oxford: Clarendon Press, 1998), ch. 1.

2 See J.L. Ackrill, *Aristotle the Philosopher* (Oxford: Oxford University Press, 1981), ch. 9. For an English translation of Aristotle's *Metaphysics*, see W.D. Ross (ed.), *The Works of Aristotle Translated into English*, vol. 8: *Metaphysica*, 2nd edn (Oxford: Clarendon Press, 1928).

3 See further my *The Four-Category Ontology: A Metaphysical Foundation for Natural Science* (Oxford: Clarendon Press, 2006), ch. 11.

4 Much of the inspiration for this programme stems from the work of W.V. Quine; see, especially, 'Epistemology Naturalized', in his *Ontological Relativity and Other Essays* (New York: Columbia University Press, 1969). For discussion, see Hilary Kornblith (ed.), *Naturalizing Epistemology* (Cambridge, MA: MIT Press, 1985).

5 See Immanuel Kant, *Critique of Pure Reason*, trans. Norman Kemp Smith (London: Macmillan, 1929), B22.

6 See, for example, Michael Dummett, *The Logical Basis of Metaphysics* (London: Duckworth, 1991), Introduction.

7 For Kripke's version of the proof, see his 'Identity and Necessity', in Milton K. Munitz (ed.), *Identity and Individuation* (New York: New York University Press, 1971), repr. in Stephen P. Schwartz (ed.), *Naming, Necessity, and Natural Kinds* (Ithaca, NY: Cornell University Press, 1977). See also Saul A. Kripke, *Naming and Necessity* (Oxford: Blackwell, 1980), which first appeared in Donald Davidson and Gilbert Harman (eds), *Semantics of Natural Language* (Dordrecht: D. Reidel, 1972).

8 I do, as it happens, have some doubts about the acceptability of the Barcan–Kripke argument, which may be subtly question-begging; see my 'On the Alleged Necessity of True Identity Statements', *Mind* 91 (1982): 579–84, and also my 'Identity, Vagueness, and Modality', in J.L. Bermúdez (ed.), *Thought, Reference, and Experience: Themes from the Philosophy of Gareth Evans* (Oxford: Clarendon Press, 2005). However, I shall set aside these doubts for present purposes.

9 For examples of this tendency, see Graeme Forbes, *The Metaphysics of Modality* (Oxford: Clarendon Press, 1985), 231, and Christopher Peacocke, *Being Known* (Oxford: Clarendon Press, 1999), 168. See also Frank Jackson, *From Metaphysics to Ethics: A Defence of Conceptual Analysis* (Oxford: Clarendon Press, 1998), ch. 3. I discuss Jackson's position in my review of his *Mind, Method and Conditionals: Selected Essays* (London: Routledge, 1998); see *Mind* 110 (2001): 211–15.

10 For further details, see my 'Two Notions of Being: Entity and Essence', in R. Le Poidevin (ed.), *Being: Developments in Contemporary Metaphysics* (Cambridge: Cambridge University Press, 2008) and my 'What Is the Source of Our Knowledge of Modal Truths?', *Mind*, 121 (2012): 919–50.

11 My sympathies in this regard lie much more with Kit Fine's conception, as presented, for example, in his 'Essence and Modality', in J.E. Tomberlin (ed.), *Philosophical Perspectives*, vol. 8: *Logic and Language* (Atascadero, CA: Ridgeview, 1994).

10 Three dogmas of metaphysical methodology

JESSICA WILSON

> Disputes are multiplied, as if every thing was uncertain; and these disputes are managed with the greatest warmth, as if every thing was certain.
>
> (Hume 1739/1939, *A Treatise of Human Nature*, xiv)

A puzzle about progress in philosophy

In what does philosophical progress consist?

Let us start by distinguishing, by attention to certain extrema, two ways in which progress in a given field might proceed. The first presupposes a single standard paradigm, accepted by most practitioners of the field, where by "paradigm" I have in mind what Kuhn (1962) called a "disciplinary matrix," and what Carnap (1950/1956) called a "linguistic framework." Paradigms, so understood, are not so much theories as frameworks for inquiry – ways of thinking about the subject matter, which include certain theoretical and methodological assumptions effectively treated as axiomatic or constitutive of the investigative approach at issue. Here progress consists mainly in constructing, refining, extending, exploring the consequences of, and testing theories within the constraints of, the preferred paradigm. Revolutions aside, such "vertical" progress, involving development of a single framework for theorizing, is characteristic of the sciences. Such common focus plausibly reflects that scientists are typically concerned to explore what is actually the case, so that their efforts are most efficiently expended within the framework(s) seen by their community as most likely to encode or otherwise model the way things actually are. Hence it is that when a given paradigm is ultimately deemed unworkable, it is replaced by a new paradigm – there is a *shift* from one preferred framework (or one restricted set of such frameworks) to another.

A second, more ecumenical sort of progress consists in the identification and development of new paradigms – new ways of thinking about or engaging with the subject matter at issue. Conservatism aside, this sort of "horizontal" progress, involving the creative construction and development of new frameworks for inquiry, is characteristic of progress in the arts and in pure mathematics. To be sure, individual practitioners in these fields may (at least for a time) primarily operate within a preferred paradigm and make vertical progress therein; but the fruitful identification of new terrain is itself seen as valuable, and importantly, there is no general presupposition that any one paradigm is closer to actuality or otherwise more "correct" for purposes of inquiry into the topic. The visual arts, for example, have seen a huge expansion of means, motive, and execution, and suppositions that new forms of expression would overthrow the old have repeatedly been seen to be unsound: to the extent that there are recognizable "schools" or associated "isms" – realism, cubism, fauvism, abstract expressionism, conceptualism – these are now understood as irreducibly diverse ways of visually exploring life's rich pageant. Pure mathematics has also seen enormous diversification, with areas such as number theory, analysis, group theory, and Boolean algebra being identified and developed in separate streams, notwithstanding the recent ultimate unification of these branches in set- or category-theoretic terms. Diverse focus on multiple paradigms plausibly reflects that both art and mathematics admit of a number of potentially interesting ways of thinking about the general subject matter at issue. These disciplines are in part constituted by such diversity, and indeed, competence and creativity in either field is frequently marked by the ability to identify new and interesting frameworks for inquiry, to be added to the mix.

Does philosophical progress primarily proceed along horizontal or vertical dimensions? The answer is delicate, and, as we'll see, initially puzzling.

Certainly, much significant progress in philosophy involves the horizontal identification and development of new ways of thinking or theorizing about a given phenomenon. Here we might think of Hume's revolutionary reconception of causation as a matter of systematic correlations (as opposed to locally productive powers or forces), or of Lewis's initially astonishing suggestion that modality is grounded in concrete worlds, each as real as our own.

Such horizontal conceptual leaps are not only interesting in their own right, as expanding (in Lewis's case, quite literally!) the space of possibility, but also as giving practitioners in fields other than philosophy new theoretical tools. So, for example, Hume's correlational conception of causation was massively influential in the sciences (see J. Wilson 2006), first in providing a broadly empiricist motivation and basis for the descriptive accounts of natural phenomena advanced by Galileo and Newton, and later in directly inspiring Pearson, the founder of modern statistics. Hume's legacy continues to this day, with the work of Pearson, Wright, and others having contributed, for better or worse, to the prevailing approach to causal inference in the sciences as proceeding via statistical or probabilistic notions, according to which, as Pearl (2000, xiii) put it, "probabilistic relationships constitute the foundations of human knowledge, whereas causality simply provides useful ways of abbreviating and organizing intricate patterns of probabilistic relationships."[1] Other cases in which a philosophical framework is incorporated into some other field of inquiry include the influence of logicians such as Frege and Turing on computational science, of American pragmatists such as Dewey and Peirce on education and public policy, of functionalists such as Putnam and Lewis on artificial intelligence, of ethicists such as Rawls and Nozick on competing notions of the welfare state, and so on, and so on. In identifying new paradigms and bringing them up to speed for the use of philosophers and non-philosophers alike, philosophy is indeed, as Hellie (2011, n.p.) evocatively put it, "the neonatal intensive care unit of theory."

Interestingly, however, these horizontal efforts are not of the same ecumenical character as those in art or mathematics. Rather, philosophers tend to suppose, like scientists, that only *one* of the candidate paradigms treating a given phenomenon is correct. (To be sure, philosophers may offer anti-realist or relativist views of a given phenomenon; but these views do not so much as embrace diversity as subsume it within a single paradigm.) Hume did not just offer his account of causation as a logically or metaphysically possible alternative – he thought that it was the only viable such account; Lewis similarly took the truth of concrete modal realism to be supported by considerations of simplicity and fruitfulness. Indeed, it is common for philosophers to suppose that their favored theories – hence the theoretical presuppositions of the paradigms guiding the construction of these theories – are not just true, but are *necessarily* so.[2]

It is no surprise, then, that much philosophical progress occurs along the vertical dimension, with philosophers often working for the majority of their careers within a single paradigm, refining the framework, extracting its consequences, and testing these for internal coherence and fit with reality, in ways that – modulo the more general purviews of subject matter and methodology in philosophy – are not much different from practitioners of this or that normal science. For example, Hume's various projects were conducted within the strict epistemological constraints of his version of empiricism, requiring that the content and justification of our beliefs be ultimately traceable to experiences of outer or inner sensations, either individually or as combined in one of a few acceptable ways; and one can plausibly see his oeuvre as aimed at establishing that a representative range of important concepts and beliefs could be treated in accord with these foundational presuppositions. Lewis too had a favored framework, as per the introductory remarks to his (1986c) collection: "Many of the papers, here and in Volume I, seem to me in hindsight to fall into place within a prolonged campaign on behalf of the thesis I call 'Humean supervenience' … the doctrine that all there is to the world is a vast mosaic of local matters of particular fact, just one little thing and then another" (ix).

It seems, then, that philosophical progress proceeds along *both* vertical and horizontal dimensions. And this fact poses something of a puzzle. If – as philosophical vertical investigations typically presuppose – not all philosophical paradigms are created equal, then what explains the multiplicity of philosophical paradigms, and continued disagreement about which paradigms are most likely to be true?

Resolving the puzzle

One response to the previous question would be to say that philosophers are wrong to disagree about which paradigms are true or are otherwise best suited for inquiry into a given phenomenon. Philosophy, one might maintain, is not about finding the "right" answer to this or that question; it is about mapping the space of possible answers. Much of Hawthorne's work reflects such an ecumenical view, perhaps also expressed in his remark that "metaphysics is a speculative endeavor where firm opinions are hard to come by (or rather, they ought to be)" (2006, vii). And it seems that such a view is what Hellie (2011) has in mind when conceiving of philosophy as the neo-natal intensive care unit of theory, with the idea being that the job of philosophers isn't to defend a specific paradigm or theory, but rather to cultivate and "bring up to speed" a range of paradigms and associated theories.

While I agree that it is some part of the project of philosophy to neutrally map theoretical space, I don't see why this isn't compatible with its also being some part of the project of philosophy to figure out which paradigms and associated theories are most likely correct. After all, a philosophical paradigm, like a scientific paradigm, typically does aim to get it right about how to think about some or other aspect of reality. Why not suppose that there is a fact of the matter about which paradigm (or limited set of competing paradigms) achieves this aim, as the many philosophers engaging in committed vertical investigations apparently do?

I'll shortly consider one sort of pessimistic answer to this question. First, though, I want to offer what seems to me to be a better explanation of continuing philosophical disagreement; namely, that we are at present very far from the end of philosophical inquiry. It is not just that, for any given phenomenon of interest, we are not yet in full possession of all of the data that might possibly be relevant to our theorizing about that phenomenon – this much is true of the sciences. It is more crucially that, for any given phenomenon of interest, we are not yet in full possession of agreed-upon standards for assessing whether a given philosophical theory about that phenomenon is correct. The problem here is not lack of data; it is lack of agreed-upon methodology.

Note that I say that we are not *yet* in full possession of agreed-upon methodology. Carnap famously suggested that metaphysical claims, in particular, were lacking any agreed-upon methods of confirmation, and so, by his verificationist lights, were meaningless:

> Suppose that one philosopher says: "I believe that there are numbers as real entities." ... His nominalistic opponent replies: "You are wrong: there are no numbers." ... I cannot think of any possible evidence that would be regarded as relevant by both philosophers, and therefore, if actually found, would decide the controversy or at least make one of the opposite theses more probable than the other.
>
> (1950, 254)

Such a pessimistic view might be used to support the claim, above, that philosophers should not be in the business of trying to figure out which philosophical frameworks best match reality, or are otherwise correct. But unlike Carnap, I don't see any reason to think that we might not someday come to principled consensus on what sort of evidence would decide such questions. Indeed, just in the last decades there has been considerable progress in determining what sorts of evidence, and more generally what sorts of methodological considerations, might weigh in favor of or against a given metaphysical or other philosophical hypothesis. As it happens, a verificationist criterion of meaning of the sort endorsed by Carnap has been widely rejected as a necessary condition on the truth of a given theory (philosophical or otherwise).[3] A number of philosophers have raised concerns about whether conceiving alone can provide a suitable basis for a priori deliberation.[4] Much attention has lately focused on identifying the sorts of theoretical desiderata (simplicity, fruitfulness, etc.) that may enter into inference to the best explanation, in elucidating how these desiderata may compete against or support one another, and the extent to which these should be individually weighted.[5] And so on. We are making methodological strides in philosophy, and presumably will continue to do so, notwithstanding that we still have a considerable way to go.

So there is no special mystery about the fact that philosophers work within multiple paradigms (like artists and mathematicians) while maintaining that only one of these paradigms is correct (like scientists): this fact is plausibly explained by the still-rudimentary state of philosophical methodology. There is no need to respond to this acknowledgement either with methodological or metaphysical nihilism, however, for we are slowly but surely making progress in clarifying and achieving consensus about our methodological standards. In addition to exploring the space of theoretical possibility for its own sake (or the sake of practitioners in other disciplines), philosophers can and should aim to figure out which philosophical frameworks come closest to capturing the reality at issue.

That's the good news. The bad news is that, while the lack of consensus about methodological standards is plausibly behind continuing philosophical disagreement, such disagreement at least sometimes reflects insufficient sensitivity to our present epistemic situation. Hence it is that philosophers engaged in vertical investigations within their preferred framework frequently dogmatically take for granted their favored paradigms – that is, their favored theoretical and methodological assumptions – never putting these, as they periodically should, to the test. In the next sections I'll offer three case studies of dogmatism presently operative in metaphysical contexts; along the way we'll see how dogmatism impedes both horizontal and vertical progress, in philosophy and beyond.

Dogma 1: Hume's Dictum

Hume famously argued that there are no necessary causal connections between distinct existences, and more generally claimed:

> There is no object, which implies the existence of any other if we consider these objects in themselves ...
>
> *(Treatise,* bk I)

The contemporary version of Hume's Dictum, further generalized and refined, is along the lines of:

(HD): There are no metaphysically necessary connections between distinct, intrinsically typed entities.[6]

Contemporary philosophers frequently appeal to HD in service of destructive projects – against, e.g., states of affairs (Lewis 1982) or necessitarian accounts of properties and laws (Armstrong 1983; Schaffer 2005). And they frequently appeal to HD in service of constructive projects – in support, e.g., of combinatorial accounts of modality (Armstrong 1989; Lewis 1986b), "lonely world" accounts of intrinsicness (Lewis and Langton 1998), and supervenience-based formulations of physicalism (Van Cleve 1990; Kirk 1996). HD frequently serves as a crucial combinatorial premise, as in e.g., arguments that certain supervenience relations are equivalent (Paull and Sider 1992; Bennett 2004; Moyer 2008). And many take violation of HD by a theory as sufficient reason to reject it, such that efforts are expended to show that certain theories of tropes or truthmakers do *not* so violate the dictum (Cameron 2006, 2008).

HD, then, serves as a foundational assumption and methodological guide in a wide range of metaphysical debates, constitutive of a broadly Humean approach to metaphysical theorizing. But why believe HD – why operate within the paradigm – if you're not Hume?

If you're Hume, HD makes some sense. On Hume's strict, idea-istic version of empiricism, the content and justification of all of our beliefs has ultimately to be grounded in experience – in particular, of sensory qualities or experienceable combinations of such qualities. On this view, for example, one's idea of a billiard ball (or idea of a billiard ball's rolling) would be a compendium of certain of the ball's superficial sensory characteristics. It is indeed plausible that objects and events characterized so superficially do not stand in any necessary connections. But contemporary proponents of HD don't accept Hume's strict empiricist constraints; rather, they are typically happy to allow that we can justifiably believe in the existence of entities lying beyond the reach of experience (e.g. as a matter of inference to the best explanation).

Nor do proponents of HD provide other reasons for believing HD. As MacBride (2005) notes:

> [I]t is a curious fact that the proponents of the contemporary Humean programme—Lewis included—having abandoned the empiricist theory of thought that underwrites Hume's rejection of necessary connections provide precious little by way of motivation for the view.
>
> (127)

But surely some motivation is needed here! For underlying HD is the supposition – plausible for superficial objects of perception but decidedly less so for objects themselves – that *what it is to be* an object (or property, or event) of a given broadly scientific type is completely divorced from anything the object (property, event) does or can do. But again, why believe this? Surely neither common sense nor the sciences give us the faintest reason to believe that, e.g., the property of being negatively charged has some intrinsic character that is only contingently associated with – really, has nothing deep to do with – the fact that negatively charged entities repel each other, such that electrons might have attracted each other, or played leapfrog, or whatever. On the contrary: in everyday thought and action we obviously characterize the objects (features, processes, etc.) of our attention in terms of what these can do with or for us – which characterization is not crudely behavioral, of course, but includes how their qualitative aspects may affect us or other entities, sensorily or otherwise; and the sciences are even more explicitly concerned with characterizing, in the laws that are their ultimate expression of understanding, natural phenomena in terms of broadly causal evolution. We have no clear access, and moreover no clear concern, with whatever non-causal core is, according to the Humean, supposed to underlie the contingently sprinkled causal and other connections.[7] So again: why believe HD?

One of my pet projects is looking for good reasons to believe HD, on the assumption that you aren't Hume. So far, I haven't found any (see J. Wilson 2010a, 2010b, forthcoming-a, and forthcoming-b). But my project isn't complete, and in any case my point here is not that there aren't any good reasons to believe HD. My point is that, though HD is open to question for obvious reasons, it is, as above, nonetheless frequently taken for granted – indeed, very commonly wielded as a decisive methodological sword – in metaphysical contexts.

Relatedly, I am not suggesting here that philosophers shouldn't continue their vertical explorations of the Humean paradigm, as characterized by HD. Maybe we should judge a project by its fruits, independent of our confidence in its seeds. What I am suggesting is that failure to be explicit that one is operating under still-unsettled presuppositions – or worse yet, not recognize that this is the case – impedes philosophical progress along both horizontal and vertical dimensions.

Such dogmatism impedes horizontal philosophical progress, for it perpetuates the false impression that the truth and methodological import of the presupposition is a settled affair, encouraging ignorance of and discouraging exploration of still-live and indeed – for all that has been yet established – potentially more promising alternative paradigms. Such dogmatism also impedes vertical philosophical progress, for part of rigorously developing and testing a paradigm and associated theories is setting these up against worthy rivals. To the extent that horizontal alternatives are underdeveloped or ignored, vertical testing cannot effectively proceed – which in turn may further encourage unwarranted complacency and dogmatism about the paradigm-relative presuppositions at issue.

Consider, by way of illustration, supervenience-based formulations of physicalism, according to which the distinction between an entity's being nothing, rather than something, over and above some physical entities upon which it synchronically depends can be cashed in terms of the distinction between nomological and metaphysical necessitation. This sort of "correlational" criterion of what is effectively a grounding relation is subject to a number of counterexamples, including – to take a personal favorite – one where a supremely consistent Malebranchean God occasions a mental state of a given type upon the occurrence of a physical state of a given type in every possible world. I still remember my surprise – which inspired my investigations into existing support for HD – when this counterexample was dismissed on grounds that it violated HD. This response struck me, and still strikes me, as quite beside the point of the case, which serves perfectly well to indicate that mere correlations, no matter how strong, do not suffice for the holding of a relation sufficiently intimate to serve physicalist purposes. Adherence to HD here served mainly – with years of attention lavished on specifying varieties of supervenience and associated (unsuccessful) versions of physicalism – to distract from more potentially illuminating investigation into what specific metaphysical relations might be up to the task of establishing the requisite nothing-over-and-aboveness (see J. Wilson 2005 for further discussion).

Moreover, lack of attention to alternatives to supervenience among the many philosophers working in the Humean paradigm has had a further unfortunate consequence, namely, that as the cumulative weight of problems with supervenience-based approaches has made inroads with these philosophers, their response has been, not to turn attention to the specific metaphysical relations already on the scene, but rather to introduce a broadly primitive relation or notion of "Grounding" as needed to do the work that supervenience can't do. Hence Schaffer (2009) motivates a primitive notion of Grounding as follows:

> [S]upervenience analyses of grounding all fail (cf. McLaughlin and Bennett 2005: S3.5). ... There have been other attempts to analyze grounding, including those centered around existential dependence counterfactuals ... I know of none that succeed.
>
> (364)

> Grounding should rather be taken as *primitive*, as per the neo-Aristotelian approach (cf. Fine 2001: 1). Grounding is an unanalyzable but needed notion – it is *the primitive structuring conception of metaphysics*.
>
> (364)

But it's wrong to present the main alternative to supervenience or other correlational relations (e.g. those at issue in "existential dependence counterfactuals") as being a broadly primitive "Grounding" relation. Metaphysicians working outside the Humean paradigm have been identifying, cultivating, and testing specific metaphysical alternatives to supervenience (for purposes of characterizing physically acceptable dependence, among other tasks) for decades – including type and token identity, the determinable/determinate relation, the part/whole relation, and the subset relation between powers of the dependent and base entities. It is, I think, some testament to the hegemony and broadly dogmatic endorsement of Humeanism that such non-HD-based accounts are not, post-supervenience, even on the menu of options.

Premature dogmatism in favor of a broadly Humean world view has also impeded scientific progress. Hume's correlation-based account of causation was, after all, offered as a revisionary alternative to one more intuitively based in locally productive causal relations (which Hume took to involve suspect necessary connections); and as above, a correlational (statistics-based or probabilistic) approach to scientific inference has been wholeheartedly embraced in the sciences. But there is increasing suspicion that the Humean assumption that productive causation can be reduced to or dispensed with in favor of statistical or probabilistic correlations is incorrect. Consider the larger context of Pearl's (2000, xiii) remarks:

> Ten years ago ... I was working within the empiricist tradition. ... Today, my view is quite different. I now take causal relationships to be the fundamental building blocks both of physical reality and of human understanding of that reality, and I regard probabilistic relationships as but the surface phenomena of the causal machinery that underlies and propels our understanding of the world. Accordingly, I see no greater impediment to scientific progress than the prevailing practice of focusing all of our mathematical resources on probabilistic and statistical inferences while leaving causal considerations to the mercy of intuition and good judgment.

Whether Pearl is correct that scientific inquiry cannot satisfactorily proceed using statistical or probabilistic inference alone is controversial. I'm inclined to think that he's correct, but again, the deeper point is that it is too early for either philosophers or scientists to be throwing all their metaphysical or methodological eggs into one basket.

Dogma 2: Composition as mereology

A second dogma of metaphysical methodology starts with the embrace of classical mereology. Classical mereology is a particular theory of wholes and parts, according to which (among other presuppositions) it is assumed that any collection of parts "sums" to a whole, and that wholes having the same parts are identical.[8] It's a nicely vertically developed formal theory, useful in a variety of contexts. Embracing classical mereology is fine; what is dogmatic is taking classical mereology to be the only possible way of understanding the relations between parts and wholes — even when, in particular, what is at issue is how a material object is composed by smaller parts. Lewis (1986a) expresses this highly restricted understanding of part/whole relationships in saying:

> What is the *general* notion of composition, of which the mereological form is supposed to be only a special case? I would have thought that mereology already describes composition in full generality.
>
> (39, italics in original)

Under Lewis's influence (one may already be sensing a pattern here – the sociology of philosophy deserves greater attention[9]), the latter claim has taken on the status of dogma. As Koslicki (2008) notes:

> [F]or Lewis, there is no other mereology besides standard mereology. This conception of parts and wholes … proved to be a perfect fit with Lewis's more general ontological outlook [and] gave rise to something akin to a "movement" among contemporary metaphysicians, an approach to many of the classical problems in metaphysics that has proven to be simply irresistible to several generations of philosophers.
>
> (5)

But why believe that there is no other mereology besides classical mereology, such that cases of ordinary composition involving, e.g. tables and chairs, should be understood as conforming to the principles of classical mereology – notably, the principle that objects having the same parts are identical? If you're a nominalist like Quine, who thinks that only particulars exist, you might have some reason to understand material object composition in terms of classical mereology, with mereological "fusion" standing in for more substantive relations among objectual parts. But philosophers endorsing the assumption – including Lewis, who granted the viability of an ontology including tropes or universals, as per his (1983) – are typically not nominalists, but rather accept the irreducible existence of properties in one form or another.

In addition to having no clear motivation, the assumption that material object composition is a matter of classical mereology faces clear prima facie difficulties, which can only be addressed by endorsing one or other counter-intuitive account of material objects. To start, the difficulties. Some of these reflect the broadly axiomatic assumption that a fusion has its parts essentially or necessarily.[10] Intuitively, material objects typically do not have their parts essentially or necessarily; so how can they be fusions? Other difficulties reflect the standard assumption (reflecting, perhaps, the initially nominalist applications of classical mereology) that neither relations nor formal components (imposing constraints on or expressing the holding of certain relations) are among the composing parts. Given this, and given that fusions with the same parts are identical, can a heap of disassembled motorcycle parts be distinct from the motorcycle assembled from these same parts? The obvious concerns here are that both *modal flexibility* and *structure* are crucially relevant to the composition of material objects;[11] yet classical mereology appears to be both modally inflexible and blind to structure.

Here again, dogmatic adherence to a specific thesis and associated theoretical framework has led to heavy vertical focus on developing positions that are less than perfectly natural. So, for example, the seeming persistence of composed material objects through changes in their parts can be accommodated by endorsing a view of such objects as four-dimensional entities that, in being spread out in time as well as space, exist in the manner of events (as per perdurantism); effectively, here objects are understood as diachronic collections of synchronic fusions (that is, of "temporal parts"). With perimeters on the collections appropriately drawn, the strategy also serves to distinguish heaps from structured entities (motorcycle and heap are collections of different temporal parts), and more general modal flexibility can be accommodated by appeal to counterpart theory. But a perdurantist conception of objects is counter-intuitive (as proponents typically admit), unmotivated (Lewis's 1986b argument for perdurantism is notoriously enthymematic), and brings other difficulties in its wake;[12] and similarly for other attempts (e.g. Sider's "stage-theoretic" account) to characterize the persistence and modally flexible nature of composed objects using only the resources of classical mereology. Vertical explorations may be more or less illuminating; but in my view, the valuable time of Lewis, Sider, and many other able philosophers wasn't particularly well spent on this sort of project.

Meanwhile, more plausible ways of understanding material or abstract object composition have gone ignored or underexplored. Here again it's indicative of the degree of assimilation of the dogmatic assumption at issue that the primary alternatives to classical mereological accounts of composition largely retain the mereological approach to material object composition, notwithstanding that they admit "formal" entities (Fine 1999 and Koslicki 2008) or trope-theoretic relations (McDaniel 2001) as parts in addition to the standardly assumed material parts (perhaps with some function-theoretic bells and whistles, as on Fine's account). But why think material composition has anything at all to do with classical mereology? Isn't the intuitively plausible thing to say here that material object composition involves *causation* – in particular, for a start, bonding relations between the material parts?[13]

Again, the point here is simply that the assumption that material composition must be understood in classical mereological terms is both lacking in motivation and clearly open to question. It is yet another distracting dogma of metaphysical methodology.

Dogma 3: Metametaphysics as quantifier semantics

A third dogma of metaphysical – more precisely, metametaphysical – methodology is that the best way to approach metametaphysical issues is by attention to semantics, and more specifically by attention to what quantifier or quantifiers might be at issue in ordinary or philosophical discourse.

So, for example, fourteen of the seventeen papers in the recent *Metametaphysics* anthology (Chalmers *et al.* 2009) take this as an operating assumption.[14] Among variations on the theme, Hirsch (2009) characterizes metaphysical dispute as reflecting disputants' using different (e.g. "nihilist" and "compositionalist") quantifiers, and more generally endorses "quantifier variance" as a metaontological position; Chalmers (2009) characterizes metaphysical indeterminacy as involving a defectively indeterminate quantifier; Hofweber (2009) couples the Carnapian supposition that metaphysical questions asked "internal" to a framework are insubstantial with the methodological supposition that metaphysicians should not meddle with other theories to imply that there is nothing substantive for metaphysicians to do; Thomasson (2009) argues that Carnapian insubstantialism is motivated by a theory of reference taking "frame-level application conditions" to be built into nominal terms; Yablo (2009) argues that since the truth of number-theoretic claims is independent of whether number terms refer, the question of whether numbers exist is objectively indeterminate; Hawthorne (2009) expresses concerns about the semantic presuppositions of Hirsch's translation-based account of verbal disputes; Hale and Wright (2009) reject claims that Fregean abstractionism requires quantifier variance; McDaniel (2009) develops the Heideggerian idea that there are many fundamental ways of being, interpreting this view as involving multiple equally fundamental ontological quantifiers; Sider (2009) argues that ontological discourse involves a single distinguished quantifier, that determinately tracks the natural ontological joints; and so on. More generally, both pessimists and optimists about metaphysics proceed in agreement with Sider's claim that "the central question of metaontology is that of whether there are many equally good quantifier meanings, or whether there is a single best quantifier meaning" (2009, 397).

Why look to language for insight into dispute about or prospects for answering metaphysical questions? Pessimist proponents of the approach typically cite Carnap by way of motivation. To be sure, Carnap expresses his metaphysical nihilism in terms of questions asked "inside" or "outside" linguistic frameworks; as such one might suppose that his nihilism reflected broadly semantic facts. In fact, however, Carnap's appeal to semantics is just so much verificationist window dressing. As above, Carnap's real beef with metaphysics is his supposition that there are no, and moreover could be no, common standards among metaphysicians that could serve to confirm or disconfirm metaphysical claims; it is on these clearly epistemological grounds that he supposes that (unlike frameworks involving numbers, or physical objects) there can be no properly metaphysical linguistic framework. Arguably, then, not even Carnap *really* thought that investigation into metametaphysical questions should proceed by attention to semantics. Moreover, even after the rejection of Carnap's verificationism, his concern about metaphysical methodology remains entirely relevant. So, why suppose that language is the proper route to metametaphysics, even if you are Carnap? Why not cut to the chase and engage directly with the more fundamental epistemological concern?

Nor does Quine's commonly endorsed dictum – ironically, yet another dogma – that "to be is to be the value of a variable" support a semantic or quantificational approach to metametaphysics. To start, as Quine (1951) insists, his dictum "explicates only the *ontological commitments* of a theory and not the *ontological truth* about the world" (12). Only if we were in possession of a nature-revealing language would his dictum be a guide to what there is, as opposed to what a theory says there is. Moreover, Quine supposes that theories typically admit of multiple interpretations – as involving e.g. multiple variables of quantification, or only a single variable whose instances may be predicatively restricted; hence the commitments at issue pertain to a specific interpretation of a theory, not the theory *simpliciter*. Extracting ontological results from Quine's dictum thus requires us to have reason to think that a given theory has a privileged interpretation (aka "regimentation") and reason to think that the theory, so interpreted, is a trustworthy guide to reality. But whether we have these reasons will depend on metaphysical considerations. For example, the ontological status of properties will likely bear on whether the proper interpretation of a theory should include second-order variables of quantification, and general metaphysical considerations will bear on whether predicative claims in a candidate interpretation plausibly track genuine features of reality. Indeed, both observations apply to Quine's favored application of his dictum, which, on nominalist grounds that remain hotly debated, assumed that predicates do not encode properties, metaphysically understood. The upshot is that Quine's criterion provides no motivation for thinking that metaphysics should proceed by attention to semantics in general, or quantification in particular: no metaphysics in, no metaphysics out. But if metaphysics is not a semantic matter, why think metametaphysics is a semantic matter?

The last best motivation, also accepted by pessimists and optimists alike, is that acceptance of a "hands-off" approach to metaphysical theorizing, according to which metaphysicians should leave the truth values of other disciplines' claims alone, is best couched in quantificational terms: for the pessimist, these quantifiers are broadly on a par; for the optimist, there is a privileged ontological quantifier. But again, there is no serious motivation here, for four reasons. First, as per Fine 2009, the hands-off view can be couched in other terms (appealing directly to notions of Reality or fundamentality). Second, optimist characterizations of the hands-off view in quantificational terms are inefficient: what's the point of approaching metaphysical or metametaphysical questions from a quantificational point of view if doing so requires introducing a new form of language? Third, the hands-off view is an unuseful fiction. As above, the historical record makes clear that the posits and presuppositions of metaphysics frequently inform science, math, and logic; and results from all these disciplines inform ordinary language. And there are ways of making sense of this influence (which indeed, goes in both directions) on which metaphysics is neither hegemonic over nor irrelevant to other areas. Suppose (methodological concerns aside) that metaphysical investigation in the limit of inquiry indicates that numbers don't really exist. Why not take this as evidence, not that metaphysics and math have nothing to do with one another, but that mathematical claims are true in virtue of facts – plausibly, cardinality and associated relational facts – which are neutral on the existence of numbers? Fourth, and relatedly, if an area other than metaphysics has clear bearing on metametaphysics, it is epistemology, not semantics. As I argued above, the persistent disagreement associated with metaphysical disputes is plausibly explained by reference to our understanding of methodological standards still being a considerable way from the end of inquiry. This result is more optimistic than Carnap's, but it similarly creates pressure on the philosophical community to consider the status of our methodological standards. Again, why not engage with these most-pressing epistemological issues directly?

I think the semantic approach to metametaphysics is fatally flawed, but here again my point is not so much to argue against the approach as to show that it obviously can be challenged, on any number of fronts, so that its present hegemony is unwarranted. Unwarranted hegemony of a given paradigm impedes horizontal philosophical progress, of course. And in the present case the problem is exacerbated along both horizontal and vertical dimensions, since heavy focus on semantics encourages neglect of the very epistemological issues that might allow us to non-dogmatically choose between frameworks, or determine that there really is nothing to choose, as in Bennett (2009), the only contribution in *Metametaphysics* that directly engages with whether metaphysical methodology is up to the deliberative task. And here again there is an additional problem for vertical progress in the form of "ineffective overachievement," whereby the advanced vertical articulation of the semantic approach is likely not worth the effort. On the contrary, the semantic approach introduces, as a "degenerating problem shift," distracting attention to linguistic distinctions and questions, concerning the individuation, interpretation, and translation of languages; the nature of meaning and its relation to truth and reference; the taxonomy of varieties of verbal dispute; the status of various quantifiers as indeterminate, context-dependent, relativist, multi-sorted;

and so on. Surely there are more natural and more illuminating approaches to the topic.

A remaining puzzle about progress in philosophy

The above case studies indicate that in many contemporary metaphysical investigations — and presumably the same is true in other areas of philosophy — certain dogmatic presuppositions are operative. More generally, we might say that many philosophical investigations are horizontally dogmatic, in failing to be properly sensitive to live concerns with presuppositions of the preferred framework and/or to live motivations for presuppositions of competing frameworks. These case studies also indicate that horizontal dogmatism is clearly problematic in at least three respects: first, in acting to shut down or marginalize alternative frameworks, impeding horizontal progress; second, in encouraging failure of practitioners to test their theories against an appropriate range of rivals, hence impeding vertical progress; third, in encouraging expenditures of effort on behalf of the dogmatic presupposition that are both distracting and misguided.

On the other hand, horizontal dogmatism may not be *all* bad; indeed, in certain respects it may be positively conducive to vertical philosophical progress. On some theories of action, acting requires that you commit to the course of action: I must believe — rightly or wrongly — that I will perform the barrel roll to even have a chance of doing it (see Hellie, forthcoming). Perhaps engaging in rigorous theoretical investigation also requires commitment, or at least the presupposition of commitment, to the assumptions constituting the paradigm at issue. Perhaps it is because they really *believe*, or fully occupy the stance of one who believes, that philosophers, like priests and painters, may be inspired to greater heights of theoretical inspiration. If so, then commitment (real or presupposed) to the assumptions of a given paradigm might be an important — perhaps even a crucial — component of vertical philosophical progress.

Let's assume that this last is correct. It follows that there is a tension between the two dimensions of philosophical progress. On the one hand, it is part of our job description to take a given paradigm and lovingly cultivate it, test it, and apply it. Such effort requires commitment. Why cultivate what you don't care about? On the other hand, we are presently far from the end of philosophical inquiry — in particular, far from any consensus regarding metaphysical, and more generally, philosophical methodology. We are just now starting to get just the faintest bit clear about the complex, multifaceted epistemology of our discipline. Moreover — and here I refer back to Hawthorne and Hellie's understanding of philosophy as mapping theoretical space – there is no doubt quite a bit of theoretical space that we haven't even thought up, much less appropriately assessed. At this rudimentary state of philosophical history, it would be unwise in the extreme to insist that *this* framework, involving *these* methodological assumptions, *must* be correct. Appropriate sensitivity to our present distance from the end of philosophical inquiry requires a *lack* of commitment.

Does this tension indicate that philosophical practice is inconsistent? What ways out might there be? Various philosophical paradigms may be able to help us out here.

One strategy might be to go contextualist or relativist so far as the notion of belief or commitment is concerned (see DeRose 1992). Qua neo-Humean, I am committed to HD; qua philosopher … not so much. Another might be to endorse "fragmentalism" as regards our mental states (see Lewis 1982; Fine 2005; Hellie, forthcoming). We are complex: we contain multitudes. There is no view from nowhere, and there is no one view from somewhere. There are only many views from many potentially shifting (and competing) perspectives. To be sure, the aforementioned tension will also arise about our allegiance to these views. But at least these understandings provide a way of thinking about our practice on which we do not end up being strangely inconsistent.

Alternatively, we can accept that our paradigms and associated theories are still in the neonatal intensive care unit, and acknowledge that, notwithstanding that commitment to a specific theoretical framework might be personally inspiring, philosophy is just at too rudimentary a stage for us to entirely commit ourselves in this way. This much is compatible, of course, with our being inclined, for one reason or another, to think that a certain paradigm or set of paradigms is most worth developing or testing. The suggestion here is that one works hard at what seems to one to be the most promising approach, while keeping at least periodically open to the horizontal possibilities. This seems reasonable to me, though whether we can reach the vertical philosophical heights enabled by a less circumspect attitude remains to be seen.

However the tension between vertical and horizontal progress in philosophy is resolved, one thing seems clear: it is crucial both for philosophical progress and for progress in the many fields in which philosophers have some influence that they explicitly acknowledge that philosophical methodology and theorizing is still at a fairly rudimentary stage of development – so rudimentary that any dogmatic presuppositions are unavoidably premature. For now we should take to heart an updated version of Carnap's (1950) counsel: Let us be cautious in making assertions and critical in examining them, but tolerant in permitting philosophical paradigms.

Notes

1 It might also be – though the pedigree here is less transparent – that Lewis's (1986b) development of concrete modal realism played a role in providing a metaphysical foundation for the increasingly popular "many-worlds" or "multiverse" interpretations of quantum mechanics. Hugh Everett (1957) suggested such an interpretation some decades before Lewis's work, but neither physicists nor anyone else took the idea seriously until relatively recently. Though Everett's worlds branch from a common point and Lewis's are spatially and causally isolated, one might reasonably speculate that Lewis's well-publicized development of the key idea underlying many-worlds interpretations – of there being a "plurality" of worlds, each as real as our own – showed this idea to be not just coherent but in certain respects attractive.

2 How this view is supposed to comport with philosophical ambitions to map the space of theoretical possibility (as to be discussed shortly) is an interesting question, into which I won't enter here.

3 See e.g. Quine 1951 and Boyd 1983.

4 See e.g. M. Wilson 1982 and Melnyk 2008.

5 See Harman 1964; Biggs 2011; Nolan, forthcoming.

6 The restriction to intrinsically typed or characterized entities reflects its typically being granted, even by proponents of HD, that extrinsically or relationally characterized entities might stand in necessary connections (such that e.g. the existence of a planet necessitates the existence of a sun). More precise formulations of HD also need to reflect (among other refinements) the distinction between *de re* and *de dicto* (broadly: particular vs general) applications of HD, and the operative notion of "distinctness" (as e.g. numerical or spatio-temporal), different strengths of which eventuate in different strengths of HD. See J. Wilson 2010b for further discussion.

7 Williams (1953) makes a similar observation about universals: "[A] little observation of a baby or of oneself in a babyish mood will convince the candid and qualified that the object of such absorption is not the abstract universal (the infant does not 'fall from the clouds upon the topmost twig of the tree of Porphyry') … but is in sooth the abstract particular or trope, *this* redness, *this* roundness, and so forth."

8 See Leonard and Goodman 1940; Simons 1987.

9 Collins 1998 is a fine start.

10 Admittedly, classical mereology is not an explicitly modal theory; but insofar as the theory takes fusions having the same parts to be identical, and identities are necessary, the modal supposition follows.

11 Structure is also clearly relevant to the composition of abstract objects: how can the set {a, b} and the set {{a}, {b}} be distinct, given that they share the same objectual members?

12 So, for example, there are concerns about whether a perdurantist view can accommodate genuine change, and concerns about whether a systematic account of change in non-instantaneous properties (e.g. being lazy) of intuitively enduring objects can be given in terms of collections of temporal parts. See Fine (2006) for discussion of yet further difficulties for four-dimensionalism.

13 Simons (2006) argues that composition has little to do with classical mereology, and that we should be investigating causal composition relations instead.

14 See J. Wilson 2011 for more detailed discussion; the material in this section draws heavily on this review.

References

Armstrong, David (1983) *What Is a Law of Nature?* Cambridge: Cambridge University Press.

——(1989) *A Combinatorial Theory of Possibility*, Cambridge: Cambridge University Press.

Bennett, Karen (2004) "Global Supervenience and Dependence," *Philosophy and Phenomenological Research* 68: 510–29.

——(2009) "Composition, Colocation, and Metaontology," in Chalmers *et al.* 2009, 38–76.

Biggs, Stephen (2011) "Abduction and Modality," *Philosophy and Phenomenological Research* 83: 283–326.

Boyd, Richard N. (1983) "On the current status of the issue of scientific realism," *Erkenntnis* 19: 45–90.

Cameron, Ross (2006) "Tropes, Necessary Connections, and Non-transferability," *Dialectica* 60: 99–113.

——(2008) "Truthmakers and Necessary Connections," *Synthese* 161: 27–45.

Carnap, Rudolph (1950) "Empiricism, Semantics, and Ontology," *Revue Internationale de Philosophie* 4: 20–40.

Chalmers, David J. (2009) "Ontological Anti-realism," in Chalmers *et al.* 2009, 77–129.

Chalmers, David, David Manley, and Ryan Wasserman (eds) (2009) *Metametaphysics: New Essays in the Foundations of Ontology*, Oxford: Oxford University Press.

Collins, Randall (1998) *The Sociology of Philosophies: A Global Theory of Intellectual Change*, Cambridge, MA: Harvard University Press.

DeRose, Keith (1992) "Contextualism and Knowledge Attributions," *Philosophy and Phenomenological Research* 52: 913–29.

Everett, Hugh (1957) "'Relative State' Formulation of Quantum Mechanics," *Reviews of Modern Physics* 29: 454–62.

Fine, Kit (1999) "Things and Their Parts," *Midwest Studies in Philosophy* 23: 61–74.

——(2001) "The Question of Realism," *Philosophers' Imprint* 1: 1–30.

——(2005) "Tense and Reality," in *Modality and Tense*, Oxford: Oxford University Press.

——(2006) "In Defense of Three-Dimensionalism," *Journal of Philosophy* 103: 699–714.

——(2009) "The Question of Ontology," in Chalmers *et al.* 2009, 157–77.

Hale, Bob and Crispin Wright (2009) "The Metaontology of Abstraction," in Chalmers *et al.* 2009, 178–212.

Harman, Gilbert (1964) "The Inference to the Best Explanation," *Philosophical Review* 74: 88–95.

Hawthorne, John (2006) *Metaphysical Essays*, New York: Oxford University Press.

——(2009) "Superficialism in Ontology," in Chalmers *et al.* 2009, 213–30.

Hellie, Benj (2011) "The Neonatal Intensive Care Unit of Theory," University of Toronto, <individual.utoronto.ca/benj/nicut-hvd.pdf>.

——(forthcoming) "What We Ought to Do," in Nate Charlow and Fabrizio Cariani (eds), *Essays on Imperatives*, Oxford: Oxford University Press.

Hirsch, Eli (2009) "Ontology and Alternative Languages," in Chalmers *et al.* 2009, 231–59.

Hofweber, Thomas (2009) "Ambitious, Yet Modest, Metaphysics," in Chalmers *et al.* 2009, 260–89.

Hume, David (1739/1939) *A Treatise of Human Nature*, ed. L.S. Selby-Bigge, with text revised and notes by P.H. Nidditch, Oxford: Oxford University Press.

Kirk, Robert (1996) "Strict Implication, Supervenience, and Physicalism," *Australasian Journal of Philosophy* 74: 244–57.

Koslicki, Kathrin (2008) *The Structure of Objects*, Oxford: Oxford University Press.

Kuhn, Thomas (1962) *The Structure of Scientific Revolutions*, Chicago: University of Chicago Press.

Langton, Rae and David Lewis (1998) "Defining 'Intrinsic,'" *Philosophy and Phenomenological Research* 58: 333–45.

Leonard, H. S. and Nelson Goodman (1940) "The Calculus of Individuals and Its Uses," *Journal of Symbolic Logic* 5: 45–55.

Lewis, David (1982) "Logic for Equivocators," *Noûs* 16(3): 431–41.

——(1983) "New Work for a Theory of Universals," *Australasian Journal of Philosophy* 61: 343–77.

——(1986a) "Against Structural Universals," *Australasian Journal of Philosophy* 64: 25–46.

——(1986b) *On the Plurality of Worlds*, London: Blackwell.

——(1986c) *Philosophical Papers*, vol. 2, Oxford: Oxford University Press.

MacBride, Fraser (2005) "Lewis's Animadversions on the Truthmaker Principle," in Helen Beebee and Julian Dodd (eds), *Truthmakers: The Contemporary Debate*, Oxford: Clarendon, 117–40.

McDaniel, Kris (2001) "Tropes and Ordinary Physical Objects," *Philosophical Studies* 104: 269–90.

——(2009) "Ways of Being," in Chalmers *et al.* 2009, 290–319.

McLaughlin, Brian and Karen Bennett (2005) "Supervenience," in Edward N. Zalta (ed.), *Stanford Encyclopedia of Philosophy*.

Melnyk, Andrew (2008) "Conceptual and Linguistic Analysis: A Two-Step Program," *Noûs* 42: 267–91.

Moyer, Mark (2008) "Weak and Global Supervenience Are Strong," *Philosophical Studies* 138: 125–50.

Nolan, Daniel (forthcoming) "Method in Analytic Metaphysics," in H. Cappelen, T.S. Gendler, J. Hawthorne, and D. Sgaravatti (eds), *The Oxford Handbook of Philosophical Methodology*, Oxford: Oxford University Press.

Paull, C.P. and T.R. Sider (1992) "In Defense of Global Supervenience," *Philosophy and Phenomenological Research* 32: 830–45.

Pearl, Judea (2000) *Causality: Models, Reasoning, and Inference*, Cambridge: Cambridge University Press.

Quine, W.V. (1951) "Ontology and Ideology," *Philosophical Studies* 2: 11–15.

Schaffer, Jonathan (2005) "Quiddistic Knowledge," *Philosophical Studies* 123: 1–32.

——(2009) "On What Grounds What," in Chalmers *et al.* 2009, 347–83.

Sider, Theodore (2009) "Ontological Realism," in Chalmers *et al.* 2009, 384–423.

Simons, Peter M. (1987) *Parts: A Study in Ontology*, Oxford: Clarendon.

——(2006) "Real Wholes, Real Parts: Mereology without Algebra," *Journal of Philosophy* 103: 597–613.

Thomasson, Amie (2009) "Answerable and Unanswerable Questions," in Chalmers *et al.* 2009, 444–71.

Van Cleve, James (1990) "Mind-Dust or Magic? Panpsychism versus Emergence," *Philosophical Perspectives* 4: 215–26.

Williams, D.C. (1953) "The Elements of Being," *Review of Metaphysics* 7: 3–18, 171–192; cited from *Principles of Empirical Realism* (Springfield: Charles C. Thomas, 1966), 74–109.

Wilson, Jessica (2005) "Supervenience-Based Formulations of Physicalism," *Noûs* 29: 426–59.

——(2006) "Causality," in Jessica Pfeifer and Sahotra Sarkar (eds), *The Philosophy of Science: An Encyclopedia*, London: Routledge.

——(2010a) "From Constitutional Necessities to Causal Necessities," in Helen Beebee and Nigel Sabbarton-Leary (eds), *The Semantics and Metaphysics of Natural Kinds*, London: Routledge, 192–211.

——(2010b) "What is Hume's Dictum, and Why Believe It?," *Philosophy and Phenomenological Research*, 80: 595–637.

——(2011) "Much Ado about 'Something': Critical Notice of Chalmers, Manley, Wasserman, *Metametaphysics*," *Analysis* 71: 172–188.

——(forthcoming-a) "Hume's Dictum and Metaphysical Modality: Lewis's Combinatorialism," in Barry Loewer and Jonathan Schaffer (eds), *The Blackwell Companion to David Lewis*, Oxford: Blackwell.

——(forthcoming-b) "Hume's Dictum and Natural Modality: Counterfactuals," in Alastair Wilson (ed.), *Asymmetries of Chance and Time*, Oxford: Oxford University Press.

Wilson, Mark (1982) "Predicate Meets Property," *Philosophical Review* 91: 549–89.

Yablo, Stephen (2009) "Must Existence-Questions have Answers?," in Chalmers *et al.* 2009, 507–25.

11 The poverty of conceptual analysis[1]
DAVID PAPINEAU

Many different ideas parade under the banner of philosophical naturalism. One is a thesis about philosophical method. Philosophy investigates reality in the same way as science. Its methods are akin to scientific methods, and the knowledge it yields is akin to scientific knowledge. This 'methodological naturalism' is to be distinguished from 'ontological naturalism', understood as a general view about the contents of reality. Ontological naturalism maintains that reality involves nothing more than the entities studied in the natural sciences and contains no supernatural or transcendent realm. While both ontological and methodological naturalism claim a species of affinity between philosophy and science, the two doctrines are largely independent.

Part of the task in understanding these matters is to bring definition to this pair of naturalist doctrines. A surprisingly wide range of philosophers wish to style themselves as naturalists, and by no means all understand either the methodological or ontological commitments of naturalism in the same way. My focus in this chapter will be on methodological naturalism. I shall aim to refine and defend methodological naturalism as a thesis about philosophical method. The ontological dimension of naturalism will not feature in what follows.

Methodological naturalism asserts that philosophical investigation is like scientific investigation. Clearly more needs to be said before we can subject this claim to serious assessment. Nobody can doubt that the two enterprises are similar in some respects (both aim for precision and truth, say) and different in other respects (philosophers don't use particle accelerators). If methodological naturalism is to have any significant content, it needs to be specified in which respects philosophical and scientific methods are supposed to be alike.

I am going to argue that philosophy is like science in three interesting and non-obvious ways. First, the claims made by philosophy are synthetic, not analytic: philosophical claims, just like scientific claims, are not guaranteed by the structure of the concepts they involve. Second, philosophical knowledge is a posteriori, not a priori: the claims established by philosophers depend on the same kind of empirical support as scientific theories. And finally, to complete the traditional trio, the central questions of philosophy concern actuality rather than necessity: philosophy is primarily aimed at understanding the actual world studied by science, not some further realm of metaphysical modality.

I do not intend these claims in a revisionary spirit. I am not recommending that philosophers start doing something different. Here I diverge from other philosophers in the methodologically naturalist camp who take their position to require a shift in philosophical method—philosophers should get out of their armchairs and become more involved with active scientific research. This is not my view. When I say that philosophical is akin to scientific investigation, I am not urging philosophers to change their ways. I think that most philosophy is just fine as it is, including philosophy that sticks to traditional methods of abstract theorizing, argument, and reflection on possible cases. My aim is to show that philosophy of this kind is already akin to science, not that it needs reforming in order to become so.

In what follows I shall avoid offering any positive characterization of philosophy, and in particular of what makes it different from science. For what it is worth, I do have some views about this. If pressed, I would say that philosophy is characteristically concerned with theoretical tangles. It deals with issues where deep-seated assumptions pull us in opposite directions and it is difficult to see how to resolve the tension. Because of this, the gathering of new empirical data is often (though by no means always) of no help in resolving philosophical problems. The characteristic philosophical predicament is that we have all the data we could want, but still cannot see how to resolve our theoretical problems.

Still, as I said, I am not going to commit myself to any positive characterization of philosophy. My argument does not need one. My intended subject matter is philosophy as it actually is, not a hypothetical philosophy that fits some set of prior specifications. Of course, this sociological dimension means that my claims are, strictly speaking, hostage to the activities of any philosophical eccentrics or extremists who deviate from my account of philosophical practice. But I hope that readers will understand my claims sympathetically in this respect. I don't want to show that everybody who has ever called themselves a 'philosopher' vindicates my claims about the nature of philosophy. It will be quite enough if I can establish my theses for those kinds of philosophy that most of you regard as mainstream.

Before proceeding, I need to qualify my claims in another respect. They do not apply equally straightforwardly to all philosophical subject matters. The areas that fit my claims best are the 'theoretical' branches of philosophy, including metaphysics, philosophy of mind, philosophy of language, and epistemology. Things become more complicated when we are dealing with areas of philosophy that trade in normative claims, or mathematical claims, or logical or modal claims. Part of the difficulty here is that the contents of these claims are themselves matters of philosophical debate, and so any attempt to show that they fit my theses about the nature of philosophy will itself become embroiled in these debates. As it happens, I think that most of the spirit of my theses about the nature of philosophy applies to these claims too, give or take a bit. But to show this would require far more space than I have available here. For present purposes it will be enough if I can show that my theses apply to the more easily interpretable claims of theoretical philosophy.

In what follows, I shall devote most of my attention to my first thesis. The next four sections will be about the synthetic nature of philosophical claims. After that, there are two sections on aposteriority and one on modality.

Inferential concepts

It might seem that my account of philosophy falls at the first hurdle, at least in so far as it is intended as non-revisionary. What about the many philosophers who overtly proclaim themselves to be concerned with the analysis or explication of concepts? A wide and varied range of contemporary philosophers describe their own philosophical practice as in large part concerned with the elaboration of conceptual truths. Does this not immediately belie my first thesis that philosophy as it is currently practised deals with synthetic rather than analytic claims?

I say that these philosophers misdescribe their own practice. They may claim that they are concerned with conceptual truths, but they are wrong. When we look more carefully at what they actually do, we can see that they are in fact concerned with synthetic and not analytic matters. Indeed their claims about their practice are not even supported by everything they *say* they do. I shall show that when these philosophers go on to fill out their account of philosophy, their own characterization of their practice is perfectly consistent with my first thesis.

Anybody who thinks that there are conceptual truths to be uncovered must suppose that the relevant concepts have some kind of structure. They must be constitutively linked to other concepts in such a way as to place constraints on their proper application. The idea is then that this structure can be uncovered by reflection and analysis, perhaps including reflection on what we would say about a range of possible cases.

An initial question to ask about this kind of putative conceptual structure is how it relates to *theories* involving the relevant concepts. By 'theories' I mean sets of claims with synthetic consequences. A simple theory of pain in this sense would be constituted by the two claims that (a) bodily damage typically causes pains, and (b) pains typically cause attempts to avoid further damage. For note that together these two claims have the manifestly synthetic consequence that bodily damage typically causes attempts to avoid further damage. We can take it that everyday thought endorses theories like this about a wide range of philosophically interesting topics, including not only mental kinds like pain, but also such categories as persons, free will, knowledge, names, and so on—after all, this is simply to assume that everyday thought includes various synthetic assumptions about these kinds.

It is widely supposed that there is a close connection between everyday concepts and everyday theories. But there are different views about the nature of this connection. In this section and the next I shall distinguish 'verificationist' from 'descriptivist' accounts of the connection between concepts and theories. As we shall see, neither account lends any support to the thesis that philosophy is centrally concerned with analytic truths.

Let me start with the verificationist account. This assumes that possessing a concept is a matter of being *disposed to use* that concept in a certain way. In particular, it is a matter of applying the concept in response to perceptual experiences and other judgements, and of drawing further inferences in turn from judgements involving the concept.

Given this account of concepts, which concepts a thinker possesses will depend on what theories that thinker *accepts*. This is because accepting a theory affects your dispositions to apply the concepts it involves. For example, if you accept the phlogiston theory of chemistry, then you will hold that burning causes air to become saturated with phlogiston, that dephlogisticated air is easily breathable, and so on. Similarly, if you accept the baby theory of pain offered above, then you will be disposed to hold that those with bodily damage are in pain, and that those who are in pain will engage in avoidance behaviour. From the verificationist perspective, then, your commitment to these theories determines your concepts *phlogiston* and *pain*. Since the theories affect your dispositions to apply the concepts, they determine your concepts themselves.

Now, one issue which arises at this point is *how much* of accepted theory is supposed to make such a constitutive contribution to concepts? Do all accepted assumptions make a difference, or only some distinguished subset—and if the latter, what distinguishes this subset? However, we can bypass these familiar questions here. The points I now want to make are quite orthogonal to this issue. They will apply to any view that takes the acceptance of sets of synthetic claims to affect concepts, however those claims might be identified.

A more basic issue is whether it makes sense to suppose that the mere possession of a concept can require a thinker to embrace synthetic commitments. Some of you may suspect that there must be something amiss with an account of concepts which implies this. However, not all philosophers share this worry. Robert Brandom, for instance, does not. He is insistent that concept possession incurs synthetic commitments. For example, after discussing Michael Dummett's example of the concept Boche, Brandom says that this

> shows how concepts can be criticized on the basis of substantive beliefs. If one does not believe that the inference from German nationality to cruelty is a good one, then one must eschew the concept Boche.
>
> (1994, 126)

Again, a page later, he explains:

> The concept temperature was introduced with certain criteria or circumstances of appropriate application and with certain consequences of application. ... The proper question to ask in evaluating the introduction and evolution of a concept is ... whether the inference embodied ... is one that ought to be endorsed.
>
> (127)

This account of concepts plays an important part in Brandom's understanding of the philosophical enterprise. Brandom takes philosophy to be centrally concerned with the explication of concepts. But for Brandom this is not a merely descriptive enterprise. Since concepts carry synthetic commitments, it is possible to criticize concepts on the grounds that these commitments are unwarranted. Brandom is quite explicit about this:

> I see the point of explicating concepts rather to be opening them up to rational criticism ... Defective concepts distort our thought and constrain us by limiting the propositions and plans we can entertain ... Philosophy, in developing and applying tools for the rational criticism of concepts, seeks to free us from these fetters, by bringing the distorting influences out into the light of conscious day, exposing the commitments implicit in our concepts as vulnerable to rational challenge and debate.
>
> (2001, 77)

The notion that concepts have synthetic implications and are therefore open to criticism is not peculiar to Brandom. It is a commonplace of much discussion of the role of concepts in philosophy.[2] Thus in a recent discussion of philosophical intuitions Alvin Goldman asserts that

A concept that embeds a bad theory is of dubious worth.

(2007, 22)

Again, to take just one further example, in a recent paper on moral concepts we find Richard Joyce arguing that

> Sometimes discoveries lead us to decide that a concept (e.g. phlogiston or witch) is hopeless; sometimes we prefer to revise the concept, extirpate the problematic element, and carry on much as before.

(2006, 142)

I alluded a moment ago to the oddity of a view of concepts on which the mere possession of a concept can incur synthetic commitments. In fact there are further aspects of the verificationist approach that should make us even more suspicious of its account of concepts. For a start, verificationism implies that theoretical change inevitably leads to conceptual change. If you alter your theoretical assumptions involving some concept, perhaps because empirical evidence has shown that these assumptions are mistaken, then you will change your dispositions to apply that concept— and so, according to verificationism, will end up with a new concept. 'Meaning incommensurability' then quickly follows: adherents of different theories must mean different things even when they use the same words, and so cannot communicate with each other in a common language. In the extreme case, this implies that those who reject the ontological commitments of some theory cannot use the language of that theory to convey this. Since I do not accept the phlogiston theory, I cannot mean the same by 'phlogiston' as the theory's adherents, and so cannot communicate my disagreement to them by saying 'There is no phlogiston'.

For my money, these points are enough to discredit the verificationist account of the relation between concepts and theories. Still, I do not need to take a stand on the nature of concepts here. This is because I have no objection to what verificationists like Brandom say about philosophical practice itself, as opposed to their funny way of thinking about concepts. Brandom says that philosophy is concerned with concepts, and then explains that for him this means that philosophy should identify the synthetic assumptions that guide our use of concepts, and criticize these assumptions when necessary. This vision of philosophical practice is entirely in accord with my first thesis that philosophy is concerned with synthetic claims.

When philosophers like Brandom say that they are explicating concepts, an unwary audience might conclude that this means that they are not concerned with synthetic matters. But this conclusion is belied, not only by their philosophical practice, but also by their official explanation of this practice. If the possession of concepts requires commitment to synthetic claims, and explication of these concepts involves the assessment of these claims, then there is no difference between conceptual explication and ordinary synthetic theorizing.

Descriptive concepts

Even if we reject verificationist thinking, there may still be a close connection between concepts and theories. Suppose that we dismiss the notion that concept possession hinges on dispositions to apply concepts. Then our concepts will not depend on which theories we *accept*. But they may still depend on which theories we *understand*.

To see how this might work, suppose that $T(F)$ is some synthetic theory involving the concept F. Then it is open to us to regard the concept F as having its reference fixed via the description 'the $\emptyset$ such that $T(\emptyset)$'. That is, F can be understood as referring to the unique $\emptyset$ that satisfies the assumptions in T, if there is such a thing, and to fail of reference otherwise. In this spirit, we might regard *pain* as referring to the mental state, if there is one such, that is typically caused by damage and gives rise to avoidance behaviour, and *phlogiston* as referring to the substance, if there is one such, that is emitted in combustion and absorbed during chemical reduction; and so on.

On this descriptivist account, there is still a close connection between concepts and theories. But your concepts no longer depend on which theories you *accept*. Which theories you accept will of course affect your dispositions to *apply* concepts. But for non-verificationists this won't make a difference to the concepts themselves. Even though I reject the phlogiston theory, and so apply the concept phlogiston quite differently from the eighteenth-century chemists who endorsed the theory, this doesn't stop me having the same concept as they had. For we can all understand the concept phlogiston as equivalent to the relevant description—the putative substance that is emitted during combustion and absorbed during reduction—independently of our divergent views as to whether this description is satisfied.

In line with this, note that on the descriptivist account of concepts no synthetic commitments are incurred by the mere possession of a concept. Somebody who possesses a concept F defined by some theory T will be committed to the 'Carnap sentence' of the theory—if $(\exists\emptyset)(T(\emptyset))$, then $T(F)$—but this claim will be analytic, not synthetic. For example, if you have the concept phlogiston you will be committed to the relevant analytic claim, that *if* there is a substance emitted during combustion and absorbed during reduction, *then* it is phlogiston. But you needn't thereby be committed to the synthetic commitments of the phlogiston theory itself.

From the perspective of this approach to concepts, the original theory $T(F)$ can be decomposed into the analytic Carnap sentence and the synthetic 'Ramsey sentence' of the theory—$(\exists\emptyset)(T(\emptyset))$. The Ramsey sentence expresses the substantial commitments of the theory—there is an entity which … —while the Carnap sentence expresses the definitional commitment to dubbing that entity 'F'. The original theory framed using the concept F is thus equivalent to the conjunction of the Ramsey and Carnap sentences.

This understanding of the relation between theories and concepts informs an influential contemporary vision of philosophical practice, inspired originally by the work of David Lewis and more recently codified by Frank Jackson (1998). As conceived by Jackson, philosophy proceeds in two stages. The first stage involves the identification and articulation of folk concepts. Here the aim is to figure out how everyday thought conceives of free will, mental states, persons, moral value, and other important philosophical categories. At this stage we will use traditional methods of conceptual analysis and reflection on possible cases. Then, once we have analysed such everyday concepts, we can turn to our most serious theories of the world to investigate what satisfies them. This second stage will involve synthetic claims about the underlying nature of reality—we will look to physics and any other basic sciences to inform us about possible candidates which might realize our everyday concepts. But while this second stage appeals to synthetic knowledge, it depends essentially on the first analytic stage, where the identification of everyday concepts plays an essential role in setting the agenda for further philosophical investigation.

Thus Jackson:

> What then are the interesting philosophical questions that we are seeking to address when we debate the existence of free action and its compatibility with determinism, or about eliminativism concerning intentional psychology? What we are seeking to address is whether free action *according to our ordinary conception*, or something suitably close to our ordinary conception, exists and is compatible with determinism, and whether intentional states *according to our ordinary conception*, or something suitably close to it, will survive what cognitive science reveals about the operations of our brains.
>
> (1998, 31, his italics)

One worry about this programme is whether the relevant concepts really have the requisite descriptive structure. Strong externalists about content will doubt that there are any analytic assumptions involving *free will* say, or *person*, that you must be committed to if you have these concepts, let alone assumptions that will uniquely identify the referents of these concepts (see Williamson 2007, ch. 4).

Another worry, which arises even if we reject strong externalism, relates to the familiar question of *which* everyday assumptions play a definitional role. As before, are all assumptions to be included, or only some distinguished subset—and if the latter, what marks the distinction?

I think that these are serious worries, but I shall not press them here. This is because I think I can show that, *even if* there are analytic truths of just the kind that Jackson supposes, they are of no significance to philosophy.

Jackson says that everyday concepts set the agenda for further metaphysical investigation. It is because everyday thought conceives of free action, and intentional states, and so on, in such-and-such ways that we philosophers are prompted to probe the nature of those things that fit these specifications.

But why think of the matter in this way? Doesn't it make far more sense to suppose that it is the synthetic *theories* implicit in everyday thought that raise the initial philosophical questions, not the mere analytic commitment to concepts? Even after we allow that everyday thought is indeed structured as Jackson supposes, the natural assumption is surely that it is the synthetic Ramsey sentences that matter to philosophy, not the analytic Carnap sentences. What makes philosophers interested in investigating further is the pretheoretical supposition that there *are* entities fitting such-and-such specifications, not just the hypothetical specification that *if* there were such entities, *then* they would count as free actions, or intentional states, or whatever.

The point is most easily brought out by considering cases where current everyday thought endorses the definitional Carnap sentence involving some concept, but not the substantial Ramsey sentence. I think, and so do all of you, that *if* there is a category of women who ride on broomsticks, cast spells, and enter into pacts with the devil, *then* these women are witches. But of course none of us think that there is a real kind of this sort, and so have no inclination at all to conduct metaphysical investigations into its nature. Again, to take a somewhat more serious example, we can all agree, I take it, that if there are entities that are conscious, separable from bodies, and can survive death, then those things are souls. But only those few among us who think that there actually are souls will have any motive to probe their metaphysical nature further.

Concepts themselves set no philosophical agendas. They are ontologically non-committal. The mere possession of concepts carries no implications at all about the contents of reality, and so cannot point the way to further investigations of reality in the way that substantial synthetic claims can.

I am very much in favour of the idea that much philosophy involves subjecting everyday ideas to serious scrutiny. All of us, philosophers included, absorb much of our understanding of the world automatically and uncritically as we grow up. Some of this everyday lore is sound, and some is not. If we are serious about our understanding of the world, we need to examine the assumptions that we acquire from everyday thinking, and see how many of them stand up to serious examination. But none of this is anything to do with concepts. Since concepts on their own are non-committal about reality, they cannot lead us astray. But the synthetic commitments of everyday thought can, and so do need to be properly examined.

When Jackson and others who subscribe to his programme actually address serious metaphysical issues, they of course proceed in just the way I am advocating. That is, they take cases where everyday thinking commits us to substantial assumptions about the contents of reality, and ask whether these assumptions are sustainable. To this extent, I would say that their official account of what they are doing is belied by their actual practice. Officially they say they start with concepts, but in fact they start with theories.

Moreover, even the official account of what they are doing is not always strictly maintained. The difference between concepts and theories is not always respected. So in a number of passages Jackson talks about the initial exploration of folk ideas as a matter of identifying theories rather than concepts.

For example:

> my intuitions reveal my theory of free action ... , your intuitions reveal your theory ... to the extent that our intuitions coincide with those of the folk, they reveal the folk theory.
>
> (1998, 32)

And later we find him saying that

> My intuitions about which possible cases to describe as cases of K-hood ... reveal my theory of K-hood.
>
> (37)

As I have said, I am all in favour of beginning philosophical investigation with everyday theories. But this is not the same as beginning with mere concepts. Theories involve significantly more than concepts, as is shown by the cases of witches and souls, where we have the concepts but not the corresponding theories.

The method of possible cases

My thesis that philosophy deals in synthetic claims might seem to be inconsistent with one salient feature of philosophical practice. Philosophers characteristically test philosophical claims by considering whether counterexamples are in some sense *imaginable*. At first pass, this certainly seems to support the view that philosophical claims are conceptual in nature. Imagination can plausibly show us whether or not certain situations are conceptually possible, but presumably not whether they are actual. Correspondingly, it looks as if imagination can usefully test claims about what is conceptually required, but not about what actually occurs.

For example, consider Gettier's demonstration that knowledge is not true justified belief. Gettier showed us how to construct possible cases in which people have true justified beliefs, but are not knowers (because, roughly speaking, the truth of their belief is accidental relative to their method of justification). Surely this shows that the philosophical claim being tested is that true justified belief *conceptually* requires knowledge. Otherwise how could the mere conceivability of counterexamples disprove it?

Again, consider Kripke's demolition of the descriptive theory of ordinary proper names. Kripke invited us to consider possible cases in which someone (Schmidt, say) satisfies all the descriptions associated with some name ('Gödel') yet is not the bearer of that name (because he is not the causal origin of its use). Here too it looks as if the mere conceivability of a counterexample is enough to discredit the thesis of interest, and thus that this thesis must be conceptual in nature.

One possible naturalist response would be to reject the method of reasoning by possible cases. Since philosophy is concerned with synthetic claims, just like the sciences, it can't possibly make progress just by reflecting on what is conceptually possible. Instead philosophers should get out of their armchairs and engage directly with experimental and observational findings.

This is not my view. I take it to be uncontentious that Gettier's and Kripke's thought experiments led to genuine philosophical advances. More generally, I regard reflection on possible cases as a highly fruitful mode of philosophical investigation. As I said at the beginning, I am not proposing any revisionary account of philosophical practice. From my point of view, the methods that philosophers use are just fine, including the method of reflection on possible cases. So instead of rejecting armchair reflection, I am going to argue that armchair methods evince synthetic rather than purely conceptual intuitions, and so are relevant to the assessment of synthetic claims.

The obvious comparison here is with thought experiments in sciences. Many important advances in science have been prompted by pure reflection on possible cases. Famous examples include Archimedes on buoyancy, Galileo on falling bodies and the relativity of motion, Newton's bucket experiment, Maxwell's demon, and Einstein on quantum non-locality. Cases like these certainly suggest that armchair reflection can be relevant to establishing synthetic claims.

Scientific thought experiments display a range of different structures. Let me focus on one of the simpler cases—Galileo's analysis of falling bodies. According to the Aristotelian orthodoxy of Galileo's time, heavier bodies fall faster than lighter ones. Galileo asks his readers to consider what will happen if a lighter body is tied to a heavier one by a piece of string (Galileo 1638). Since the Aristotelian theory says the lighter body will be inclined to fall more slowly than the heavier, it follows that the lighter should slow the heavier down when joined to it. But by the same coin the compound body consisting of the two tied together is heavier than the two individual bodies, and so should fall faster than both. The Aristotelian theory is thus shown to be inconsistent. Moreover, it looks as if the only consistent account will have the compound body falling at the same speed as the individual components, which implies that speed of fall is independent of weight.

In this kind of case it is clear that the relationship between weight and speed of fall is a synthetic matter. Concepts alone cannot determine the falling speeds of differently weighted bodies. How then can armchair reflection show us what to think? The answer must be that armchair reflection is showing us more than that certain scenarios are conceptually possible. Of course, it can't show that there are any actual cases in which a compound body falls at the same speed as its components. Galileo didn't create a real case of two bodies tied together just by thinking about it. Still, Galileo didn't need an actual case to disprove the Aristotelian theory. If we construe that theory as saying that the faster fall of heavier bodies is *required* by the laws of nature, it will be enough for Galileo to show that a case of a heavier body falling at the same speed as a lighter one is *consistent* with the laws of nature. And that is just what Galileo argues. He asks us to consider a manifestly naturally possible scenario in which two bodies are tied together, and then judges that in such a case the laws of nature will lead the compound body to fall at the same speed as its components.

Obviously the crucial step here is played by Galileo's intuition that a compound body will fall at the same speed as its components. And this is clearly a synthetic intuition, by no means guaranteed by the concepts it involves. That is why it can contradict the synthetic Aristotelian theory.

I want to suggest that philosophical thought experiments have the same structure. Explicit philosophical theories about the requirements for a thinker to know something, or for a thing to bear a name (or for someone to have acted freely, or for one person to be the same as another, ...) are synthetic claims about the relevant categories. Philosophers then assess such synthetic proposals against their intuitions about possible scenarios. Thus Gettier appealed to the intuition that a belief whose truth is accidental relative to its method of justification is not knowledge; Kripke appealed to the intuition that something that is not the causal origin of a name is not its bearer; and so on. On my account, all these intuitions are synthetic claims about the relevant kind of scenario. This is why they have the power to argue against the initial philosophical theories.

From this perspective, there is nothing in the method of reasoning about possible cases to undermine the idea that philosophy is concerned with synthetic claims. It is simply a technique that enables us to counter the synthetic theories proposed by philosophers by the synthetic intuitions elicited by thought experiments.

There is one respect in which this account of thought experiments may be an oversimplification. I have suggested that thought-experimental intuitions express certain general principles, such as that an accidentally true believer isn't a knower, or that the causal origin of a name is its bearer, and so on. However, Timothy Williamson (2007, ch. 6) has pointed out that such general claims are arguably more than the thought experiments committed us to. For example, in order to disprove the tripartite analysis of knowledge, Gettier only needed the particular counterfactual claim that, in the most obvious understanding of his scenario, the relevant thinker would not be a knower. There is no need to suppose that *any* thinker satisfying the explicit specifications of his scenario would fail to know, still less to suppose some still more general principle as that 'all accidentally true believers aren't knowers'. For Williamson, philosophical thought experiments thus appeal only to our ability to reason counterfactually, and do not demand any grasp of general principles.

I am happy to agree that counterfactual reasoning is enough for thought-experimental purposes, and correspondingly that it is by no means mandatory to suppose that general principles lie behind the relevant intuitions. Even so, I would like to continue working on the assumption that thought experiments display general principles. This may be an oversimplification, but I don't think it is too far from the truth. We may not fully understand counterfactual reasoning, but it is clear that it is strongly constrained by general claims about the working of the world. Williamson (2007, chs 5–6) alludes to the role of imagination in counterfactual reasoning. But when I think about what would happen if I had dropped a vase, say, I do not imagine every outcome that is permitted by the concepts involved, such as that the vase floats gently onto the table. Rather I consider just those outcomes that are consistent with some such synthetic general claim as that heavy bodies fall rapidly when unsupported. Perhaps this general claim as just formulated is more precise than anything that governs our counterfactual thinking. Still, it seems clear that our counterfactual thinking must be informed by some such principle. In line with this, I shall continue to assume that the intuitions in philosophical thought experiments are informed by general principles. Attempts to state these principles explicitly may inevitably lead to oversimplification, but I propose to overlook this in the interests of facilitating investigation into their nature. (In what follows I shall use 'intuition' to refer to the general principles informing our counterfactual reasoning, rather than the specific judgements about counterfactual and other situations that issue from them.)

Philosophical intuitions and falsifiability

There is an obvious objection to my proposed analogy between philosophical and scientific thought experiment. Consider Galileo's thought experiment again. The crucial intuition was that tying two bodies together won't make any difference to their speed of fall. Now, it is clear that this conjecture is hostage to further empirical investigation. It may strike us as obvious that Galileo is right, but even so, empirical observation remains the ultimate test of his intuition. Galileo is in effect hazarding a guess— albeit a highly informed guess—as to the synthetic facts, and the final arbiter of this guess will be some real observations. For we can always find some actual bodies that are tied together and see how they fall. Either they will conform to Galileo's intuition or they won't. And both options are clearly left open by the terms in which the issue is posed.

Things seem rather different in philosophy. In the Gettier thought experiment, for example, the analogous intuition was that a belief isn't knowledge if its truth is an accident relative to its method of justification. But there seems no analogous room to check this intuition against real cases, by seeing whether or not actual thinkers with such accidentally true beliefs are knowers. For we already know what we will say about any such cases—namely, that these thinkers are certainly not knowers. The reflection involved in the philosophical thought experiment is by itself enough to tell us what we will judge in any similar real situation, and thus to rule out any possibility of observing someone who is an accidentally true believer yet a knower.

The same seems true of philosophical thought experiments in general. Take the Kripke case. We don't need to find any real cases like the Schmidt–Gödel example in order to check whether the relevant name really does name the person originally baptized with it. For again, we already know what we will say about any real such cases—namely, that the names apply to the one originally baptized, even if that person doesn't satisfy the descriptions. And this again seems to rule out any possibility of observing a name which turns out to refer to the satisfier of associated descriptions rather than the original bearer.

One natural response to this disanalogy between the Galilean and the philosophical thought experiments is to conclude that philosophical intuitions, unlike Galileo's, are not synthetic after all. After all, they do not seem *falsifiable* by observations, the way that Galileo's was. Galileo's intuition committed him to a certain view of the synthetic facts, and as a consequence was clearly open to refutation by observational evidence. In contrast, the Gettierian and Kripkean intuitions do not seem similarly open to observational refutation, and one natural explanation would be that they are analytic. On this diagnosis, when Gettier invokes the intuition that knowledge must be non-accidental, or Kripke the intuition that any name will refer to the causal origin of its use, they aren't appealing to plausible but corrigible synthetic assumptions about the workings of the world, but rather to unfalsifiable analytic truths implicit in the structure of the concepts *knowledge* and *name*.

However, this is not the only way of viewing the matter. For the philosophical intuitions may still be *indirectly* testable in a way that would accord with their having a synthetic status, even if they aren't *observationally* testable in the way that Galileo's intuition was. There may be no independent observational faculty that we can apply to real putative knowers, or real putative name–bearer pairs, in order to directly confirm or discredit the Kripkean and Gettierian intuitions. But this doesn't mean that there is no way of evidentially confirming or discrediting them at all. If that is right, then the differences between the Galilean and philosophical thought experiments wouldn't be that the former rested on a synthetic intuition where the latter rested on analytic intuitions, but simply that in the philosophical cases, by contrast with the Galilean one, there is no other immediate route to judgements about naming and knowing, apart from the kind of inferences applied in the thought-experimental scenarios.

To see how this would work, let us look at the Gettier case more closely. As I am viewing it, when we are presented with a description of a Gettier scenario, we apply some such principle as that: if a belief's truth is an accident relative to its method of justification, then that belief is not knowledge. Now, it could be that the truth of this principle is analytically guaranteed by the structure of the concept *knowledge* and the other concepts involved. But it could equally be that it is a substantial synthetic claim connecting conceptually distinct notions. The fact that we have no way of *directly* judging whether such a belief is knowledge, independently of the principle in question, does not decide the issue either way.

Consider an analogy. Suppose that some sixteenth-century philosophers, aiming to explore contemporary thinking about souls, had asked their colleagues to imagine that some non-human organism had learned a human language, and moreover had turned out to speak intelligently and with moral sensitivity. They then asked their colleagues whether this creature would have a soul. I presume that most of them would have judged that it would.

Now, we could take the view that the implicit assumption displayed here, that a creature who talks intelligently and sensitively must have a soul, was an analytic truth ensured by the structure of the sixteenth-century concept of a *soul*—that is, we could assume that by definition nothing more was required for the immediate satisfaction of this concept than talking intelligently and sensitively.

However, this would be the wrong diagnosis. Far from being so definitionally ensured, the sixteenth-century inference from talking intelligently and sensitively to soul possession was surely a genuinely ampliative inference, underpinned by the substantial synthetic thesis that intelligent and sensitive speech can only stem from a soul. (After all, we nowadays think, using the same concept of a soul, that the sixteenth-century thinkers were *wrong* to suppose that intelligent and sensitive speech requires a soul.)

But note that neither the sixteenth-century philosophers nor we ourselves have any way of *directly* observing whether or not something has a soul, apart from looking for intelligent and sensitive behaviour. In this respect the sixteenth-century thought experiment lines up with Kripke and Gettier rather than Galileo. It is not as if we could directly test the thought-experimental intuition about souls, if only we could get hold of an intelligent and sensitive non-human creature. Rather we already know what anybody who subscribes to this intuition would say about such an actual case.

The moral is that, while a synthetic thesis must indeed be answerable to empirical evidence, this need not require independent direct observational access to the categories it involves. Rather its assessment can be bound up with the evaluation of some larger set of assumptions involving those categories (such as standard assumptions about the nature of souls).

Indeed, put like this, the point should be a familiar one. Many synthetic claims are 'theoretical' in the sense that their answerability to empirical evidence hinges on the way they fit into some larger body of assumptions. My view is that the thought-experimental intuitions about knowledge and names are of just this kind. They may not be directly evidentially assessable, but are rendered indirectly so by the larger theories in which they feature.

Note that a claim's being 'theoretical' in this sense—its evidential assessment depending on its theoretical role—does not automatically imply that the concepts involved must be *defined* by their theoretical role, along some such lines as those discussed in the second and third sections above, 'Inferential Concepts' and 'Descriptive Concepts'. Meaning is only required to shadow evidence if we presuppose some form of verificationism. In truth it is perfectly possible for a concept to have its reference fixed in some direct externalist non-theory-mediated way, and yet for claims involving it to be empirically assessable only in virtue of the way it is embedded in some set of theoretical assumptions.

Still it could be, for all I have argued, that philosophically interesting concepts like *knowledge* and *naming* are indeed theoretically *defined* as well as being theoretically embedded—as I allowed Jackson, for the sake of the argument, in 'Descriptive Concepts', above. And, if this were right, then there would remain a way for my opponents to defend the analytic status of the philosophical intuitions, despite the fact that the concepts involved feature in substantial synthetic theories. They could appeal once more to the distinction between Ramsey and Carnap sentences. That is, they could allow that it is a synthetic ampliative step to move from the conditions specified in the thought experiments to conclusions about knowledge or naming. But they could free the philosophical intuitions associated with these moves from any synthetic commitments by 'Carnapifying' them.

In this way, my opponents could view the Gettier thought experiment as showing that *if* there is a significant mental attitude evidenced by truth, justification, non-accidentality, and so on, *then* it is knowledge, and the Kripke cases as showing us that *if* there is a significant semantic relation between words and the causal origins of their use, *then* it is the name–bearer relation. By adopting this line, my opponents would thus portray the philosophical intuitions as free of any commitment to theories implying the existence of these categories, and only as displaying the adoption of the concepts *knowledge* and *name*.

My response to this ploy is that it portrays the philosophical thought experiments as much less interesting than they actually are. I suppose that we could in principle view the thought experiments as merely revealing the structure of concepts that we happen to possess—as we possess the concept of a soul, say—and not as displaying any synthetic assumptions about the world itself. But this seems an odd way of viewing philosophical thought experiments, by comparison with understanding them as also articulating our positive synthetic dispositions to apply concepts like *knowledge* and *name* in given situations (in a way that we are *not* nowadays disposed to apply the concept of *soul*).

After all, we are now taking it to be agreed that substantial synthetic assumptions involving concepts like *knowledge* and *name* inform the application of these concepts on the basis of information about justification, causal histories, and so on. Given this, it would seem perverse to continue maintaining that the thought-experimental intuitions only manifest our belief in the hypothetical Carnap analyticities, and fail to display our further commitment to the synthetic Ramsey sentences that in fact underpin our active application of the relevant concepts.

A priori provenance, a posteriori justification

Let me now turn to my second thesis that philosophical knowledge is a posteriori, not a priori. It might seem that this will now follow quickly, given my first thesis that philosophical claims are synthetic. How can a synthetic claim possibly be known to be true independently of experience, given that its content alone leaves it open that it might be false? But of course this is too quick. Traditional theists and transcendental idealists both take themselves to have good answers to this question. And even if we reject these particular answers, there may yet be room for other non-experiential accounts of synthetic knowledge.

On this topic, Timothy Williamson (2007, 165–69, 189–90) has argued that philosophical intuitions, though synthetic, should not be counted as a posteriori. His rationale is that experience does not play a normal evidential role in generating them. We can't point to past obser-vations of supporting instances to support such claims as that accidentally true believers are not knowers, or that names refer to their causal origins. Our route to these claims is thus clearly unlike the normal justification of synthetic generalizations by inductive or abductive evidence. (Williamson does not conclude that such philosophical intuitions are a priori: he thinks that the traditional contrast is not useful here, and that philosophical intuitions should be viewed as neither a posteriori nor a priori. But we need not pursue this point, given that I am about to argue, contra Williamson, that philosophical intuitions are definitely a posteriori.)

I am happy to agree with Williamson's view about the *provenance* of philosophical intuitions. They are not products of normal inductions or abductions. Rather they are part of accepted everyday lore. They are part of the great network of assumptions that we acquire involuntarily as we grow up.

Still, the source of philosophical intuitions is one thing, their justification another. Even if philosophical intuitions do not *derive* from experience, it may still be that they can only be *justified* a posteriori. This is my view.

It is scarcely as if everyday lore wears its epistemological credentials on its sleeve. Most of our everyday lore is probably a joint product of biolo-gical bias and local tradition. Our evolved biological nature makes it easy for us to adopt certain ways of thinking, and local cultures then elaborate more detailed stories to fit the biological mould. No doubt the mix is different in different subject areas. I suspect that our everyday assumptions about basic metaphysical, physical, and psychological categories are strongly biologically constrained, while folk ideas about diseases, astronomy, and weather patterns, say, owe much more to cultural contingency.

In any case, whatever the precise mix along these dimensions, there seems no reason to place much epistemological trust in the fabric of everyday lore. It is not hard to think of biologically natural assumptions that are factually mistaken (inanimate objects don't move unless pushed), and the same goes for culturally contingent assumptions (health depends on the balance of the four humours). In general, neither biology nor culture is a particularly reliable source of truth. Biological evolution favours assumptions that have yielded selective advantages in past environments, and these are by no means guaranteed to be accurate. Cultural influences are if anything even less likely to track the truth.

I think that philosophical intuitions are by and large in the same boat as the rest of everyday lore. There is no automatic reason why they should be more epistemologically secure than the assumptions of folk physics or humoural medicine. And indeed it is not difficult to think of once deep-seated philosophical intuitions that we now know to be mistaken. Descartes took it to be obvious that a purely mechanical being cannot reason. Kant assumed that triangles must contain exactly 180°. Until recently it was regarded as philosophically obvious that skilled action is guided by conscious vision. Many philosophers have taken it for granted that an effect cannot be 'greater' than its cause, that every event is determined, that temporal succession cannot be relative, and so on.

The recent findings of 'experimental philosophy' are relevant here. They indicate that many central philosophical intuitions, including those invoked by Gettier and Kripke, are by no means universal, but rather peculiar to certain cultures, social classes, and genders (Knobe and Nichols 2008). At one level, it is not always clear what to make of these findings. Presented as a challenge to 'conceptual analysis', they invite the response that the variability of intuitions only establishes the philosophically insignificant point that different groups of people express different concepts by words like 'knowledge' and 'name'. However, the variability of intuitions has an obvious moral if, as I have argued, philosophical intuitions are substantial claims whose truth is not analytically guaranteed. In that case, the variability of the intuitions is in tension with their reliability. If different people have opposed philosophical intuitions, then it cannot be that intuitions of this kind are always true.

Of course, none of this is to say that all philosophical intuitions *must* be mistaken. Alongside the erroneous ones, many will be perfectly correct. But, even if accurate, philosophical intuitions can only be *justified* after they have been subject to a normal process of a posteriori evaluation.[3] Like the rest of everyday lore, their warranted acceptance requires that they be assessed against the empirical evidence. Philosophical intuitions may have an a priori provenance, in the sense that we find ourselves with them prior to any engagement with empirical evidence, but they do not count as knowledge until they have been properly evaluated against the data of experience.

In saying this, I do not mean to imply that all philosophical claims need to be assessed directly against specific empirical findings from empirical disciplines. A synthetic theory can be vindicated a posteriori even though it has no specific empirical evidence to call its own, on the grounds that it provides a more coherent and natural overall account than the alternatives.

As it happens, I do think that specific empirical findings bear directly on a surprisingly wide range of philosophical issues. These include not just topics from philosophy of science, such as the logic of natural selection or the interpretation of quantum mechanics, but also such central and traditional topics as the nature of causation and the relation between mind and brain. Still, I am happy to allow that there are other central philosophical issues, such as the nature of persisting objects or realism about properties, where the philosophical claims float free of any specific matters investigated by the empirical sciences.[4] In such cases, we will then have no alternative but to evaluate alternative philosophical positions by comparing their 'simplicity', in the sense of their overall coherence and naturalness.

Still, I would say that this kind of inference, to the 'simplest' of underdetermined alternatives consistent with all the empirical evidence, is itself a source of a posteriori knowledge. After all, the exclusion of implausibly complex alternatives in favour of simple ones lies behind all scientific inferences from finite data to general patterns. When we embraced Copernicus rather than Ptolemy, or special relativity rather than the Lorentz–Fitzgerald reworking of classical mechanics, or indeed the claim that all emeralds are green rather than grue, this was not because of any specific empirical findings, but because of the superior coherence and naturalness of the preferred theory. It would be absurd to conclude on this account that Copernicanism, special relativity, and the thesis that emeralds are green are all instances of a priori knowledge.[5]

I am arguing that the intuitions invoked in thought experiments cannot be trusted until they have been subject to proper a posteriori evaluation. Now, some philosophers take the view that intuitions in general are unreliable, but those of philosophers in particular can be trusted. Thus Timothy Williamson (2007, 191) has defended armchair methods against the findings of experimental philosophy, by arguing that a proper philosophical training winnows out mistaken reactions to test cases. And C.S. Jenkins (2008a, 2008b, 2012) holds that when philosophers extract substantial synthetic theses about the world from their 'concepts', this is in itself enough to constitute those theses as a priori knowledge.

I myself am highly doubtful about the general veracity of philosophical intuitions. The historical record is not good—we need consider only the above list of once deep-seated assumptions that were discredited by subsequent history. Still, suppose that we did grant, for the sake of the argument, that the training of philosophers rendered their intuitive judgements better informed than most everyday guesses. There would then be an obvious question about the precise nature of the processes that led to this superior reliability. It couldn't just be magic, or some God-given insight into the nature of things, that made the thoughts of philosophers superior to those of ordinary people, if this were indeed the case. And the natural answer to this question would be that the training of the philosophers had brought their thinking into line with the best theories of the relevant matters, in the above sense of those theories that are best in accord with the empirical evidence and other criteria of scientific theory choice. This answer would then seem to undermine any continued insistence that the intuitive knowledge of philosophers is not a posteriori.

The importance of intuitions

It may seem as if the last section was backtracking on my earlier enthusiasm for armchair philosophy. If philosophical intuitions are not to be trusted until they have been subject to serious a posteriori investigation, then isn't the moral that we philosophers should get out of our armchairs and examine the empirical evidence?

Among philosophers who agree with me that philosophical intuitions are synthetic, we can distinguish two broad positions. There are those who think that philosophical intuitions are little more than manifestations of naive folklore, and should therefore carry little weight in serious philosophical discussion. According to this point of view, philosophers should turn away from intuitions and instead engage with proper empirical theorizing (Kornblith 2002; Knobe and Nichols 2008). On the other side are the philosophers like Timothy Williamson and C.S. Jenkins, who think that philosophical intuitions are by and large reliable, and that the doubts about them raised by experimental philosophers and others are not as worrying as they appear. My line of argument in the last section may seem to place me on the former side and thus against armchair investigation.

However, I think this conclusion is based on a false dichotomy. Just because I am doubtful about the authority of philosophical intuitions, it doesn't mean that I have to reject the method of reasoning about merely possible cases. Armchair thinking can be useful, even if the intuitions involved are unreliable.

Go back to the idea, briefly aired earlier, that philosophy is characteristically concerned with theoretical tangles. We find our thinking pulled in opposing directions and cannot see how to resolve the tension. In such cases thought experiments can bring the principles behind our conflicting judgements to the surface. They make it clear what intuitive general assumptions are governing our thinking and so allow us to subject these assumptions to explicit examination. Nothing in this requires that thought-experimental thinking is generally reliable. When some explicit prior theory conflicts with an intuitive judgement elicited by a thought experiment, this needn't always result in the rejection of the theory. We can also end up rejecting the implicit assumptions behind the thought-experimental intuition.

Just this pattern is displayed by some of the most famous and important thought experiments in science. Consider the 'tower argument' against Copernicanism, which appeals to the intuition that an object dropped from a moving source will be 'left behind' as it falls. Or take the Einsteinian argument against the completeness of the Copenhagen interpretation of quantum mechanics, which appeals to the intuition that space-like separated events cannot be coordinated without a common cause. In cases like these, the assumptions generating the thought experiments eventually came to be recognized as mistaken.

But this certainly did not mean that the thought experiments were worthless. Both the tower and Einstein arguments were hugely important in the history of science. By showing us which of our implicit assumptions conflicted with new theoretical ideas, they led to crucial new advances. Galileo responded to the tower argument with his innovatory formulation of a principle of inertia, and J.S. Bell to the Einstein argument with his derivation of the eponymous inequality whose experimental confirmation ruled out local hidden variable theories.

It is not hard to think of similar philosophical cases. The worth of philosophical thought experiments does not always require that the intuitions they elicit are sound. In some cases, of course, the intuitions will turn out be correct. But in other cases thought experiments can clarify the issues even if the accompanying intuitions point us in the wrong direction.

Consider the classic Lockean set-up where someone's memories are transferred to a new body. We all have an intuition that the person goes with the memories, not the old body, as evidenced by our reactions to the many fictions which trade on just this kind of scenario. But few philosophers of personal identity would nowadays hold that this intuition is decisive in favour of Lockeanism. We need to follow through the implications of the Lockean views and assess the overall resulting theory against its competitors, and in this context the initial intuition is indecisive. But, for all that, it would be hard to deny that Locke's thought experiment has led to advances in our understanding of personal identity.

Again, consider the intuition that conscious properties are ontologically distinct from physical ones, as displayed in our immediate reaction to zombie scenarios. Here too, few would suppose that these intuitions are decisive in refuting physicalism. But at the same time, even physicalists will allow that reflection on zombie cases has helped to clarify what is at issue in the mind–brain debate. (I shall return to this particular example in the next section.)

From the perspective being defended here, the role of thought experiments is essentially to facilitate argument. They help us to lay out the premises supporting the conflicting positions when we find ourselves in a theoretical tangle. But simply to put it like this is in danger of underestimating the importance of thought experiments. Often thought experiments are needed to *unearth* the relevant assumptions in the first place, and not just to articulate them. This is because the intuitions operative in thought experiments are often implicit and unconscious. We don't know that these assumptions are driving our thinking until the thought experiments bring them to the surface.

We might think of this as a matter of our possessing subpersonal 'modules' whose purpose is to issue in particular judgements about philosophically interesting categories like knowledge, names, persons, free will, and so on. Judgements like these are important to us in our daily life, and so it would be natural for us to have unthinking mechanisms which take in information that does not involve these categories and then quickly and efficiently produce verdicts that do. But if this is right, then the general principles driving those modules may well be opaque to us, and only recoverable with the aid of thought-experimental 'probes' that reveal the structure of our implicit inferences.

By way of confirmation of this picture, note how many philosophical intuitions persist even after explicit argument and analysis has convinced us that they are mistaken. It is hard to stop thinking that persons go with their memories, or that the mind is separate from the body, or that temporal succession is absolute, and so on, even for those who have addressed the matter explicitly and concluded that these assumptions are erroneous. This 'persistence of illusions' is just what we would expect if the relevant assumptions are 'encapsulated' in subpersonal mechanisms that we acquired relatively early in our development, and operate automatically at a level below conscious reasoning.

If the function of thought experiments is to unearth hidden assumptions, then there is a sense in which some recent 'experimental philosophy' can be viewed as complementing traditional armchair methods. Earlier I pointed out that some of the findings of experimental philosophy carry the implication that everyday intuitions cannot generally be reliable, given that they vary across culture, class and gender. But in addition to this 'negative' message, there is also room for experimental philosophy to make a *positive* philosophical contribution, even in cases where there is no variation in intuitions across different categories of people.

What I have in mind is the possibility that careful experimental probing might helpfully augment traditional armchair methods as a way of identifying the structure of implicit assumptions that drive everyday judgements about test cases. Sometimes thought experiments may be enough. But in more complicated cases systematic questionnaires and surveys may well be a better way of identifying the implicit cognitive structures behind our everyday philosophical reactions.

Of course, experimental philosophy, even viewed in this positive light, is at most an addition to our philosophical armoury, not a new way of doing philosophy. For once we have sorted out the intuitive principles behind our philosophical judgements, whether by armchair reflection or empirical surveys, we still need to assess their worth. Even if the claim that the folk intuitively think a certain way is supported by hard empirical data, this doesn't make that way of thinking correct. That can only be shown by subjecting that way of thinking itself to proper a posteriori evaluation.

Philosophy and necessity

Can the account of philosophy offered so far accommodate the *modal* dimension of philosophical knowledge? It is sometimes said that the difference between philosophy and science is that philosophy seeks necessary truths where science trades in contingencies. Thus Russell 1914, 110:

> [A philosophical proposition] must not deal specially with things on the surface of the earth, or with the solar system, or with any other portion of space and time. … A philosophical proposition must be applicable to everything that exists or may exist.

This modal view of philosophy might seem to be in tension with my account of philosophy as synthetic and a posteriori. Don't we need a priori analysis to uncover necessary truths?

But of course this line of thought is far too quick. There is no reason why necessities should not be synthetic and a posteriori. Empirical science provides plenty of familiar examples. Water is H_2O. Heat is molecular motion. Stars are made of hot gas. Halley's comet is made of rock and ice. All these claims are necessary, but clearly they are not knowable a priori on some analytic basis.

These claims are necessary because they use rigid terminology to report on facts of identity or constitution. All claims of these kinds are necessary, notwithstanding any synthetic a posteriori status they may have. It is a nice question, worthy of further discussion, why claims like these should count as necessary, while truths about spatio-temporal location, say, do not. But this is not the place to pursue this issue. For present purposes the important point is simply that the necessity of claims of these kinds is perfectly consistent with their synthetic a posteriori status.

The central questions of philosophy are almost entirely concerned with issues of identity and constitution. When we ask about knowledge, names, persons, persisting objects, free will, causation, and so on, we are seeking to understand the nature of these categories. We want to know whether knowledge is the same as true justified belief, whether naming involves descriptive content, whether persisting objects are composed of temporal parts, and so on. Any truths we might establish about such matters will inevitably be necessary rather than contingent, even if they are also a posteriori and synthetic.

The answers to the central questions of philosophy may be necessary, but that is no reason to suppose that philosophy is here concerned with necessity per se rather than actuality. Consider empirical science once more. As I have just observed, many of the claims established by science are necessary. But it would be odd to infer from this that empirical science is aiming to explore some wider modal realm rather than simply to understand the actual world. When science investigates the chemical make-up of water, or the composition of the stars, it is primarily concerned with how things are in this world ('with things on the surface of the earth, or with the solar system, or with any other portion of space and time ...') That these discoveries have implications about the contents of other possible worlds, so to speak, is an inevitable side effect of the content of these claims, but not something that we need regard science as actively seeking.

I say the same about the central areas of philosophy. Our primary philosophical concern is to find out about things in this world. We want to know about such actual categories as knowledge, free will, persons, and so on—kinds that exist and make a difference in this world. Of course, given that answers to our questions will normally take the form of claims about identity and constitution, philosophical knowledge will also place constraints on what is necessary and possible. But there is no reason to regard such modal corollaries as our main aim. We are first seeking to understand this world, and are only derivatively concerned with modal matters. We want to know whether *p*, not whether necessarily *p*. That the former implies the latter does not make the latter our focus of interest, any more than my interest in whether you are forty-seven years old makes me interested in whether your age is a prime number.

Of course, some philosophers are specifically interested in modal questions as such. They are interested in whether necessary truths are necessarily necessary, or in whether modal claims commit us to an ontology of possible worlds, or in the connection between metaphysical and conceptual necessity, or indeed in why facts of identity and constitution but not spatio-temporal location should count as necessary, and so forth. These are certainly substantial philosophical issues worthy of serious discussion.[6] But most central philosophical questions are not of this form. The study of modality is a specialist subject within philosophy, engendered by specific theoretical interests. There is no reason to suppose that an interest in modality infects all of philosophy, even if all philosophical claims have modal implications.

Having said this, it is worth recognizing that it is often heuristically useful to focus on modal implications, even in cases where our real interest is in non-modal matters. Given the immediate modal upshot of claims of identity and constitution, it is sometimes easier to articulate our thinking by starting with the modal consequences rather than their this-worldly counterparts. Take the relation between individual objects and their property instantiations. In the actual world there is a one-to-one correspondence between objects and sets of property instantiations. But is this a matter of identity, as in the 'bundle theory' of objects, or mere association? A good way to clarify our thinking on this issue is to consider the modal question of whether there could be a world in which this blue cup, say, acquired all the properties of that red one, and vice versa. To the extent this strikes us as possible, then we are thinking of objects as distinct from their property instantiations; but if it seems that this is not a real possibility, then we are identifying objects with their property instantiations.

I am not of course here suggesting that such modal intuitions are somehow a privileged route to the truth. Whether we are *right* to think of objects as bundles of properties, say, would remain a substantial further issue, even after modal reflection has made it clear that this is our intuitive view. The role of the modal reflection is merely to clarify the content of our intuitive commitments in cases where thinking about actuality alone leaves them unclear, not to decide the substantial issues. From this perspective, modal thinking is a special case of the kind of thought-experimental reflection described in previous sections. It is a useful way of identifying the implicit assumptions that drive our reasoning. Once these assumptions have been identified, we are then in a position to subject them to serious a posteriori evaluation.

Let me conclude with one further example. Consider the relation between conscious mental properties and brain properties. Let us agree that pairs of these properties go hand in hand in the actual world. Still, is this association due to the identity of the relevant properties, or merely to a correlation between distinct properties?

Well, ask yourself whether there could possibly be a being with all your brain properties but who lacks your conscious properties. If you think that such zombies are possible, then you must be of the view that conscious properties are distinct from brain properties in this world. Conversely, if you think that conscious properties are in actuality one and the same as brain properties, then you won't think that zombies are so much as possible.

Many recent writers look at this thought experiment differently. They think we can start with our *concepts* of consciousness and brain states, proceed to the point that zombies are conceivable, somehow move from this to their possibility, and thence end up with the conclusion that conscious and brain properties are distinct in the actual world (Chalmers 1996; Bealer 2002). I don't think that this works at all (Papineau 2007). The interesting thing about zombies isn't that we can conceive them— after all, we can conceive lots of things that aren't possible—but that they strike us as *possible*. This shows us something rather surprising, namely that at an intuitive level we are all dualists about the mind–brain relation.

Of course, it is one thing to identify this intuition, and another to justify it. As I have argued throughout, philosophical intuitions need a posteriori backing before we can place confidence in them. In this case it seems clear that the a posteriori evidence counts against the intuition (Papineau 2002, appendix). Still, this is not the place to pursue this issue, which is in any case independent of my present point—which is that in most familiar cases the purpose of modal reflection is not to find out about other possible worlds per se, but simply to clarify our pretheoretical assumptions about the actual world.

Notes

1 This is a revised version of my 'The Poverty of Analysis' (2009). Thanks are due to the Aristotelian Society for the rights to reproduce parts of the earlier paper. Apart from a few tweaks, the main changes are in the fifth, sixth, and seventh sections ('Philosophical Intuitions and Falsifiability', 'A Priori Provenance, A Posteriori Justification', and 'The Importance of Intuitions'). I presented versions of the earlier paper in many places, including a seminar on the philosophy of philosophy in London in 2008, and thanks are due to all those who responded on these occasions. I can particularly remember helpful comments from George Bealer, David Chalmers, Keith Hossack, Fraser McBride, Tom Pink, Andrea Sangiovanni, Gabriel Segal, Jonathan Shaffer, Barry Smith, Stephen Stich, Scott Sturgeon, Celia Teixeira, Mark Textor, Lee Walters, Tim Williamson, and Crispin Wright. The changes to the earlier paper were largely occasioned by a remark by

Jonathan Ichikawa at the first conference of the Experimental Philosophy Group UK in Bristol in 2010.

2 C.S. Jenkins (2008a, 2008b, 2012) holds that concept possession carries substantial synthetic commitments about a mind-independent world, but does not infer from this that concepts ought to be subject to active evaluation and possible criticism. I shall comment further on this kind of position in the sixth section, 'A Priori Provenance, A Posteriori Justification', below.

3 This is my attitude to the Gettier and Kripke intuitions. In the last section I argued that these are falsifiable, but I did not argue that they are false—and indeed I doubt that they are. But this is not because I think that these claims have some special a priori warrant, but because I expect them to feature in our best a posteriori theories. Note that it is not to be taken for granted that our best theories will even refer to knowledge and naming, let alone maintain that these categories require non-accidentality and causal origination respectively. We do not yet have good theories about either knowledge or naming. (We aren't even sure why knowledge, as opposed to true belief, is so significant a state; or again how far, or in what way, the name–bearer relation is constituted by speakers' explicit judgements about which words name which things.) My expectation, as I have said, is that when we do have good a posteriori theories of these matters, they will uphold the Gettier and Kripke intuitions. But I do not find it hard to imagine the a posteriori verdict going the other way.

4 But see Maudlin (2007), who brings scientific considerations to bear even on these two topics.

5 On a number of occasions I have heard philosophers say that metaphysics is 'a priori', when all they mean by this is that choices between alternative metaphysical theories hinge on considerations of simplicity—which, as I have just observed, leaves metaphysics in exactly the same boat as science. Still, in addition to the issue of status of the *conclusions* we get from simplicity-preferring inferences, there is a further question of the status of our presumed *metaknowledge* that inferences of this kind are a reliable route to the truth. I myself think that this metaknowledge can be arrived at 'self-supportingly' using a meta-application of the same simplicity-preferring inference, which would make it a posteriori too. Those who think that the relevant metaknowledge is a priori face a nasty choice between holding it to be analytic, which would require an implausibly anti-realist view of truth, or taking it to be synthetic, which would seem to require some unexplained form of insight (see Papineau 1993, ch. 5).

6 This branch of philosophy obviously demands a qualification to the third of my initial theses—philosophers of modality are certainly concerned to understand modality per se, even if other philosophers are not. But it may still satisfy my other two theses by being synthetic and a posteriori; as before, however, we cannot expect to decide these issues in the absence of an agreed view about the nature of modal claims.

References

Bealer, George (2002) 'Modal Epistemology and the Rationalist Renaissance', in Tamar Szabó Gendler and John Hawthorne (eds), *Conceivability and Possibility*, Oxford: Oxford University Press.

Brandom, Robert (1994) *Making It Explicit*, Cambridge, MA: Harvard University Press.

——(2001) 'Reason, Expression, and the Philosophical Enterprise', in C.P. Ragland and Sarah Heidt (eds), *What Is Philosophy?*, New Haven, CT: Yale University Press, 74–95.

Chalmers, David J. (1996) *The Conscious Mind: In Search of a Fundamental Theory*, Oxford: Oxford University Press.

Galilei, Galileo (1638/1974) *Discourses Concerning Two New Sciences*, trans. Stillman Drake, Madison, WI: University of Wisconsin Press.

Goldman, Alvin I. (2007) 'Philosophical Intuitions: Their Target, Their Source, and Their Epistemic Status', *Grazer Philosophische Studien* 74: 1–26.

Jackson, Frank (1998) *From Metaphysics to Ethics: A Defence of Conceptual Analysis*, Oxford: Oxford University Press.

Jenkins, C.S. (2008a) 'A Priori Knowledge: Debates and Developments', *Philosophy Compass* 3: 436–50.

——(2008b) *Grounding Concepts: An Empirical Basis for Arithmetical Knowledge*, Oxford: Oxford University Press.

——(2012) 'A Priori Knowledge: The Conceptual Approach', in A. Cullison (ed.), *The Continuum Companion to Epistemology*, London: Continuum Press.

Joyce, Richard (2006) 'Metaethics and the Empirical Sciences', *Philosophical Explorations* 9: 133–48.

Knobe, Joshua and Shaun Nichols (eds) (2008) *Experimental Philosophy*, New York: Oxford University Press.

Kornblith, Hilary (2002) *Knowledge and Its Place in Nature*, Oxford: Oxford University Press.

Maudlin, Tim (2007) *The Metaphysics within Physics*, New York: Oxford University Press.

Papineau, David (1993) *Philosophical Naturalism*, Oxford: Blackwell.

——(2002) *Thinking about Consciousness*, Oxford: Oxford University Press.

——(2007) 'Kripke's Argument Is Ad Hominem Not Two-Dimensional', *Philosophical Perspectives* 21: 475–94.

——(2009) 'The Poverty of Analysis', *Proceedings of the Aristotelian Society Supplementary Volume* 83: 1–30.

Russell, Bertrand (1914) 'On Scientific Method in Philosophy', repr. in his *Mysticism and Logic*, London: Longmans, 1917.

Williamson, Timothy (2007) *The Philosophy of Philosophy*, Oxford: Oxford University Press.

12 Is there room for armchair theorizing in epistemology?

HILARY KORNBLITH

Quine argued, of course, for the rejection of the very notion of the a priori,[1] and in "Epistemology Naturalized," in 1969, he argued for a general approach to epistemological questions which would be straightforwardly empirical.[2] Precisely what that program might be, however, was very much in dispute, both among those who wished to reject it and those who were eager to sign on. In the 1980s and 1990s, largely under the influence of Alvin Goldman,[3] the possibility of a thoroughly empirical approach to epistemology once again came to the fore, and the question of whether epistemological theorizing might profitably be approached a priori, and what, if anything, the empirical sciences might contribute to epistemology, was much discussed.[4] Those who wished to defend traditional approaches to epistemological questions typically acknowledged the relevance of empirical results to certain questions about knowledge, but then went on to minimize the importance of this fact. Richard Feldman, for example, is typical here. He comments,

> Obviously, empirical work is relevant to "the study of human knowledge." But this shows its relevance to epistemology only if epistemology is as broad as the study of human knowledge. The complete study of human knowledge would, presumably, include historical studies of what people knew when; studies in neuroscience concerning the ways the brain processes information, sociological studies about the ways knowledge is transmitted in societies, and so on. While some philosophers may think that they have something to say from their armchairs about many of these topics, no sensible person could think that all such inquiries can succeed without scientific input. So it is hard to imagine any disagreement with the view that methodological naturalism is true given such a broad interpretation of what counts as epistemology.[5]

As Feldman went on to suggest, however, epistemology need not be understood as nearly so broad an enterprise, and, as Feldman urged, one might not need experimental input to epistemological issues more narrowly – and plausibly – conceived.

Feldman's response here, which was not at all atypical,[6] involves two points which deserve to be separated. First, there is the point about the breadth of epistemology properly speaking. But second, Feldman no longer talks about whether epistemological theorizing is a priori. Instead, he talks about whether epistemology might profitably be pursued from the armchair. This is an important distinction.

Thus, for example, in Timothy Williamson's recent book, *The Philosophy of Philosophy*,[7] Williamson sets out to defend an armchair approach to philosophical questions. As Williamson is eager to point out, however, this does not mean that empirical information is not relevant here. Indeed, Williamson rejects the a priori/a posteriori distinction, although for reasons importantly different from those of Quine.[8] More than this, Williamson is at pains to reject what he calls "philosophical exceptionalism," the view that proper methods in philosophy are different in kind from other sorts of inquiry. Nevertheless, Williamson, like Feldman, wishes to defend the integrity of philosophy as an armchair discipline. When we theorize from the armchair, our empirical beliefs will inevitably and properly play some non-trivial role in the conclusions which we reach. Nevertheless, there is a real difference between armchair theorizing and the straightforwardly empirical work which one sees, for example, in experimental psychology or experimental physics. Williamson, like Feldman, is concerned to defend the legitimacy of armchair methods in philosophy generally, and especially in epistemology. So the issue about the status of epistemological theorizing seems to have changed. Many defenders of traditional methods in epistemology no longer seek to defend these traditional methods as a priori; instead, it is the integrity of theorizing from the armchair which is now seen as the real issue.

One further trend in recent philosophy should be mentioned, by way of introduction. One of the salient alternatives to the armchair method, in recent years, is the newly emerging field of so-called "experimental philosophy." I say "so-called" not because I believe that the label is not apt, let alone in order to somehow cast aspersions on this approach, but rather to indicate that this label is a name and not a description. Experimental philosophy is not merely an approach to philosophical questions which attempts to draw on experimental work of whatever kind. Rather, this approach, championed in work by Stephen Stich, Jonathan Weinberg, Joshua Knobe, Shaun Nichols, and a host of others, seeks to cast light on philosophical issues by way, typically, of questionnaires which probe our folk conceptions of various key philosophical notions.[9] This is, beyond doubt, an experimental approach to philosophical questions, but it is not at all the kind of empirical work which was suggested by Quine or Goldman as forming the basis for a properly scientific epistemology. Much of the recent discussion of armchair methods in philosophy has focused, unlike the earlier periods in which this issue was prominently discussed, on the question of whether the approach of the experimental philosophers is likely to shed light on issues of real philosophical importance.

Let me lay my cards on the table. I will argue here that armchair methods are unlikely to shed real light on central issues in epistemology. Without direct and substantive input from experimental work, I will argue, we are likely to remain ignorant of, or to misunderstand, the very nature of epistemological problems and their likely solution. The source of real enlightenment here, as I see it, is not likely to come from the work of experimental philosophers, but rather from more traditional work in the cognitive sciences, work not directed at our folk conceptions of anything. My complaint about work by experimental philosophers will not, of course, be an objection to the idea that empirical work might shed light on philosophical problems, but rather that much (though not all) of the work that experimental philosophers have done and wish to do is misdirected, indeed, that it is misdirected in much the same way, I believe, that a good deal of armchair theorizing in philosophy is. So I will be arguing in defense of a thoroughly empirically informed approach to epistemology, but one which is fundamentally different from that pursued by the experimental philosophers.

***

While questions about the relevance of psychology to epistemology have been much discussed in the recent literature, they were not a subject of discussion at all among the philosophers of the seventeenth and eighteenth centuries. Descartes, Locke, Hume and Kant, for example, would not likely have understood the question of whether they were engaged in philosophical theorizing or psychological theorizing. The discipline of psychology did not emerge as an independent discipline until the late nineteenth century, but, more than that, the epistemological views of all of these philosophers were clearly influenced by their views about psychology. For them, an epistemology which was not informed by a theory of mind would have been inconceivable.

Of course, the view of the mind which these philosophers had was not informed by experimental results in psychology, since there was no such thing as experimental psychology at the time. Rather, these philosophers all held that introspection and reflection together provided the key to understanding the mind, and thus, even though beliefs arrived at by way of introspection are not a priori justified,[10] the use of introspection is clearly an armchair method of investigation. If we can understand the features of the mind which are needed for a fully informed epistemology entirely from the armchair, then armchair methods may well be all that is needed once one turns more directly to epistemological questions themselves.

These philosophers were right, I believe, to think that an understanding of the way the mind works is a prerequisite for constructing a reasonable epistemology, but they were mistaken, of course, in thinking that we might understand the relevant features of the mind by way of armchair investigation. It is not just that experimental work in psychology has proven necessary to fill in minor gaps in the view which introspection provides us of the mind, or that experimental work is needed to correct some small errors around the edges, so to speak, of an otherwise largely accurate picture provided by armchair methods. Rather, it has turned out that on issue after issue, we cannot even begin to understand how the mind works without extensive experimental work, and the picture of the mind which armchair methods provide us with is fundamentally flawed from beginning to end. Let us consider a number of topics here which will prove to be especially important when we turn from the nature of mind to epistemology.

Descartes held, famously, that introspection provides us with a picture of our current states of mind which is both infallible and complete; in a word, the mind is wholly transparent to itself. Such a view is no longer defended these days, but the extraordinarily vivid picture which introspection provides of our own mental states and processes is an important part of the armchair view of the mind. Consider, for example, the manner in which epistemological problems are often introduced. Chisholm suggests, in a discussion which is in many ways quite typical, that we should engage in Socratic questioning. Introspect, and you will detect a large number of your beliefs. Choose one of these and ask yourself, "Why do I hold this particular belief?" At least in the typical case, you will note that the initial, target belief is one which you hold for various reasons: that is, you hold it on the basis of still other beliefs. And then we may ask about each of these why you hold it. We may continue this process, Chisholm argues, until we arrive at beliefs which provide some sort of appropriate stopping place for inquiry.[11]

Let us leave aside the Chisholmian defense of foundationalism. When we engage in the kind of Socratic questioning which Chisholm encourages, introspection not only provides us with a view of our beliefs, but it provides us with a view of the source of our beliefs. Thus, when I consider some belief A of mine, and I ask myself why it is that I hold it, introspection seems to reveal to me why it is that I currently believe A: I believe it, say, because I believe B and C. Vivid and powerful as this introspective view of the source of our beliefs may be, we may ask how accurate the impressions are which introspection conveys. This is an issue which social psychologists have investigated in some detail.

Much of what introspection seems to reveal, when we engage in this sort of exercise, amounts to little more than confabulation.[12] What appears in introspection to be the direct apprehension of causal relations among our mental states is really, at bottom, the result of a process of rational reconstruction: we are actually engaged in a subconscious process of theorizing about what the source of our beliefs must have been. More than this, this process of reconstruction is, in a wide range of cases, not terribly accurate. A good many of our beliefs are formed in ways which are not at all reasonable, but it seems that in reconstructing what our reasons were, we help ourselves to a crucial minor premise: that whatever it is we believe, we probably came to believe it on the basis of good reasons.[13] It should thus come as no surprise that, when we turn reflective and scrutinize the reasons for which we hold various beliefs, by and large it turns out that we find that our reasons pass muster. What looks, from the point of view of introspection, like a responsible, extra check on our first-order unreflective processes of belief acquisition turns out, in fact, to be little more than an exercise in self-congratulation. But this is not something which we can tell from the armchair. Indeed, there is a powerful illusion which arises precisely from the use of armchair methods of investigation. Unless we get up and out of the armchair, we are likely to misunderstand the sources of our beliefs.

Much of our belief acquisition is unreflective. For example, when I walk into my office, I inevitably come to believe that there is a desk in front of me. I don't stop to reflect about whether such a belief is justified given my evidence. And in this respect, this particular belief of mine is not unusual; most of my beliefs are formed unreflectively. Moreover, this is not some peculiarity of mine; the vast majority of beliefs are formed unreflectively. Nevertheless, we do, at times, stop to reflect and ask ourselves what it is that we ought to believe. When we do so, we have the distinct impression of epistemic agency. Forming beliefs, at least on these reflective occasions, seems to be something that we do rather than something that merely happens to us.[14]

To what extent should this impression of agency be taken at face value? In order to answer this question, we need to get out of the armchair and look to experimental work in social psychology. In general, our judgments about our own agency are not terribly reliable. People who are emotionally healthy tend to have an exaggerated impression of their own efficacy in a great many areas of life.[15] In addition, the idea that there is some deep asymmetry with respect to agency when it comes to the difference between reflective and unreflective belief acquisition is one which does not survive careful scrutiny. While unreflective belief acquisition is, of course, mediated by a host of mental processes which operate at the subpersonal level in ways of which we are typically unaware,[16] the same is quite clearly true of reflective belief acquisition. We are no more aware, through introspection, of the full range of mental processes at work in reflective belief acquisition than we are in the unreflective case. Finally, the fact that our introspective judgments about the source of our beliefs turn out largely to be a matter of after-the-fact rationalization rather than genuinely contemporaneous monitoring shows, at a minimum, that the deliverances of introspection greatly exaggerate the extent to which we play an active role in forming our beliefs when we stop to reflect.[17] An accurate understanding of the extent to which we are genuine agents in reflective belief acquisition cannot be achieved from the armchair.

The workings of some of the most fundamental processes underlying cognition are not only invisible to introspection, but they work in ways which are strikingly different from the armchair view which we have of them. Thus, for example, the operation of memory leaves little by way of introspective trace. When memory is operating most efficiently, we may be aware of forming a memory belief, but nothing more than the belief itself is available to introspection. The armchair view of memory is simply that we initially gain beliefs by other means – for example, by way of perception – and then these beliefs are stored in memory; later, on suitable occasions, they are brought out of storage and made available to introspection. But this very simple picture of the working of memory is entirely inaccurate. The initial process of encoding, the storage process, and the retrieval process all involve a great deal of construction and reconstruction. Genuine human memory is nothing at all like the process of taking a picture and entering it into a file, only to bring it out of the file on subsequent occasions when it might be needed.[18]

Much the same may be said about our responsiveness to testimony. Introspection reveals little if anything about the cognitive processes which go on when a speaker states that p and we, immediately thereafter, come to believe that p. Armchair theorizing about the process has led to a variety of accounts, some of which suggest that very little actually goes on here in the typical case; the transmission of information involves nothing more than "content preservation."[19] On other views,[20] there is a certain amount of screening that goes on to check, for example, for the speaker's sincerity and capacity to know whereof he or she speaks. But the empirical literature on such screening reveals features of the situation which armchair methods could not begin to detect.[21] We do indeed screen testifiers for sincerity on the basis of a variety of observable cues, and there are, as a matter of fact, a number of behavioral cues which are reliable indicators of insincerity; unfortunately, the cues we tend to rely on are not the ones which reliably indicate whether the testifier is genuinely sincere. The psychological and epistemological situations here are highly complex,[22] and they are complex in a way that introspection and armchair methods cannot reveal.

The content and format of our concepts plays an important role in a variety of epistemological issues, but the character of our concepts cannot be settled from the armchair.[23] The classical view of concepts has it that they are represented by a set of necessary and sufficient conditions in much the same format as traditional philosophical analyses. Thus, for example, the concept of a bird might be represented as an animal with a beak, wings, and two feet. Following work by Eleanore Rosch,[24] however, it has been suggested that the format in which concepts are represented might be quite different. Instead of a set of necessary and sufficient conditions in the standard format, a concept might be represented by way of a proto-typical case, together with a set of dimensions of similarity such that any object sufficiently similar to the prototypical case falls under the con-cept.[25] And there are other accounts as well.[26] Indeed, it is not at all clear that our concepts are represented in any single format. Not only may different concepts be represented in different formats; one and the same concept may well be represented in more than one format.[27] However concepts may be represented, it is perfectly clear that we cannot deter-mine the format of their representation by way of introspection. Nothing short of experimental work can be of use in addressing this issue.

Issues about the large-scale structure of the mind have been an impor-tant focus of work in philosophy from the time of Plato to the present day. Here, as elsewhere, armchair theorizing has been replaced by work which is empirically informed. Issues about modularity, and related con-cerns about domain-specific inference, can only be profitably addressed by way of experimental work. At this late date, how things seem from the first-person point of view or how they seem from the armchair are no more relevant to these inquiries than they are for an investigation of the mechanisms involved in digestion.

The same is true about the role of emotion in cognition. Introspection provides us with a vivid impression of our emotional states and their effects. Armchair views about these issues based on this introspective picture may be of interest to cognitive anthropologists or sociologists, but they are simply irrelevant to an inquiry into the actual effects of emotion on cognition. If we want to understand how the mind actually works, our introspective view of things is not only not the last word on these matters; it is no longer seen as even the first word. A proper investigation of these phenomena does not begin with our introspective view of them, or our armchair view, and then proceed to make corrections where needed. The armchair view of these matters is simply irrelevant to a serious inquiry into the workings of the mind.

***

What has any of this to do with epistemology? Understanding how the mind works, it may be granted, cannot be achieved from the armchair. At the same time, epistemology is not a simple investigation of how it is that the mind operates. Even if we grant, then, as of course we must, that psychology cannot profitably be pursued from the armchair, what bearing does this have on the methodology of epistemology?

I will begin to address these questions by way of examples. I will argue that a number of issues central to epistemology cannot profitably be addressed without the kind of direction and constraint which experimental work offers. This will leave open, of course, the question of whether there are other issues within epistemology which might usefully be addressed without the aid of experimental work. I will have something to say about this question as well.

Consider, then, the debate between internalists and externalists in epistemology.[28] Internalists and externalists disagree about the determinants of justification: the features which make a belief justified, internalists insist, must, in some important sense, be internal to the agent; externalists deny this. Thus, for example, access internalists insist that the features of a belief which make it justified must be accessible to introspection or reflection. Some internalists, such as Laurence BonJour, argue that beliefs which are justified in the internalist sense are more likely to be true than beliefs which fail to meet internalist standards.[29] Once one has an internalist account of justification on the table, so to speak, BonJour's requirement makes an empirical claim: that beliefs which meet those standards are more likely to be true than beliefs which don't. Since there is a great deal of empirical research on what happens when we introspect and reflect, this experimental work becomes relevant to examining BonJour's claim. And much as we have an armchair view about what happens when we engage in introspection and reflection, this armchair view, as I've pointed out above, is not at all accurate. So in order to examine whether BonJour's claim is actually true, and not just whether it seems true from the armchair, we need to take a serious look at the empirical research here. The view from the armchair gives us a thoroughly misleading picture.

Now BonJour is, admittedly, an unusual internalist in that he wants to identify the property of being justified with an internally recognizable property, while, at the same time, insisting that beliefs which have this property are likely to be true. Not all internalists want to make this second claim, a claim which amounts to insisting that internally justified beliefs are reliably produced. But the empirical research on the mechanisms involved in introspection and reflection is not, for that reason, entirely irrelevant to the claims of these other internalists. If, as I've argued, the empirical literature shows that the very procedures which internalists view as a kind of check on unselfconscious processes of belief acquisition do not effectively carry out any such check, then the motivation for identifying justification with such internal monitoring is, at a minimum, severely compromised. Internalism gains a specious plausibility from the fact that an armchair view of introspection and reflection generates the illusion that such checking procedures are genuinely effective.

The same is true, of course, of a good deal of the discussion of epistemic responsibility. A variety of claims are made about what it is that an epistemically responsible agent must do in order to make it likely that his or her beliefs be true, but most of the literature on epistemic responsibility is nothing more than armchair theorizing. The empirical literature on the actual effects of the very checking procedures which armchair theorists insist constitute epistemically responsible behavior can be quite salutary.[30] It is, of course, always open to such theorists to insist that they are not identifying epistemically responsible belief acquisition with reliable belief acquisition, and, indeed, that they are not committed to the view that responsibly acquired belief tends to be reliable. All of this is true, but it does not by any means show that the empirical results are irrelevant to the evaluation of claims about epistemic responsibility. At a minimum, the empirical results place a certain pressure on these theorists, for the very procedures which they insist are definitive of responsible epistemic behavior turn out, on empirical examination, to do little more than increase the confidence of already benighted agents. Depending on the details of the particular view about epistemic responsibility, the empirical results need not constitute any kind of conclusive refutation of them, but it would surely be a mistake to view such information as irrelevant to a full evaluation of these claims. The results are deeply surprising, and they are surprising because they contradict our armchair view of these matters. But it was precisely the armchair view which made the claims about epistemic responsibility appear plausible in the first place.

There is a long tradition in epistemology of offering epistemic advice, that is, suggestions about how it is that one ought to go about arriving at one's beliefs if one's goal is to gain true beliefs. Talk of "rules for the direction of the mind" was once common, and, in recent years, epistemologists have discussed at some length the extent to which an account of justified belief should provide some sort of guidance to the concerned epistemic agent. As with the discussion of epistemic responsibility, it is quite clear that the empirical literature on the effects of introspection, reflection, and various inferential strategies is directly relevant here. And, again, precisely because this body of literature has regularly produced surprising results – results which directly contradict the way things seem from the armchair – it is clear that these issues cannot profitably be addressed in ways which are not informed by experimental work.

Many philosophers believe that proper method in epistemology, and in philosophy more generally, is a matter of conceptual analysis, and Ed

Gettier's famous counterexample[31] to the suggestion that knowledge might be identified with justified, true belief is seen as a model of how such conceptual analysis might be carried out. On this view, the target of philosophical analysis is seen as a concept, and armchair methods are seen as the means for eliciting the content of our concepts.[32] So there is a large body of philosophical literature which attempts to provide an account of the content of various philosophically interesting concepts. There is, moreover, a standard format in which these analyses proceed, namely by providing necessary and sufficient conditions of a certain sort. There is also a large body of literature in psychology which investigates the content and format of our concepts, and this literature has produced a body of interesting and surprising results. The format in which our concepts are mentally represented seems to be quite different from the format of traditional philosophical analyses, and the content of our concepts is also quite different from the way it appears from the armchair.[33] How should we regard the relationship between these two investigations? How, if at all, does the experimental investigation of our concepts bear on the armchair inquiry?

Alvin Goldman has argued that the armchair investigation is a kind of proto-scientific version of the experimental work engaged in by psychologists.[34] Goldman argues that, as a matter of fact, armchair methods turn out to be fairly reliable in giving us information about the content of our concepts, although experimental work may certainly provide a needed check on our results, and, on occasion, a source of correction for the armchair view. On this view, armchair methods give us a fairly accurate account of the content of our concepts, but they need to be supplemented by experimental work. Others are less sanguine about the extent to which armchair methods here will approximate the results achieved by careful experimentation,[35] and this has led many experimental philosophers to suggest that the task of conceptual analysis needs to be pursued, not from the armchair, but from the psychological laboratory. But the difference between Goldman and these experimental philosophers is just a matter of degree. They are in full agreement that the target of philosophical analysis and the target of experimental inquiry are one and the same, and they agree, as well, that experimental inquiry is the most reliable means for pursuing this inquiry. In particular, when armchair methods and experimental methods yield different results, it is the experimental methods which are to be trusted.

What is difficult to defend, I believe, is any attempt to insulate the philosophical project of conceptual analysis from the results of the experimental investigations. It is not, after all, just an orthographic accident that both philosophers and psychologists refer to the object of their investigation as a concept. This is surely not a simple case of homonymy, as with "bank" and "bank." Both the object of philosophical investigation and the object of psychological investigation are thought to be implicated in explaining the content of our thoughts, the kinds of inferences we are inclined to make, and our classificatory behavior. Given this extensive overlap in the causal and explanatory endeavors which talk of concepts is meant to engage with, it surely looks for all the world as if the objects of study in these two investigations are identical. At a minimum, if some case can be made out that there are real differences here, it will still be hard to see how the results of the experimental investigation could possibly be irrelevant to an understanding of the object of philosophical analysis. Given, once again, the extent to which the experimental results turn out to be surprising – that is, given that the experimental results are so deeply at odds with the view we have from the armchair – this raises a serious challenge to armchair methods in epistemology.

There is another way in which experimental results bear on the project of conceptual analysis as traditionally conceived. Most epistemologists reject skepticism, and their rejection of skepticism is quite a deep commitment.[36] They offer analyses of justification and of knowledge, and they believe that these accounts serve to explain why it is that we are justified and why it is that we know in various paradigmatic cases. So it is an important part of the defense of their analyses that paradigmatic cases of justification and knowledge turn out to fit these analyses. An account of justification, or an account of knowledge, which has the consequence that we have little if any justified belief or knowledge, is, for that very reason, held to be implausible. But now the psychological facts about belief acquisition and retention are directly relevant to the evaluation of philosophical analyses, even on the most traditional conception of the project of analysis. Most accounts of knowledge, for example, include some sort of basing requirement, and this basing requirement is typically explained in causal or counterfactual terms: one belief cannot be based on another unless the first is caused by the second, or unless one would not have the first were it not for having the second.[37] Our armchair understanding of causal and counterfactual dependencies among beliefs, however, is notoriously deficient. Thus, in order to see whether paradigm cases of knowledge actually meet the conditions laid out in our analyses, we need to leave the armchair and enter the psychological laboratory.[38] The same is true of accounts of justification. In the case of doxastic justification, a basing requirement is as essential a feature as it is in accounts of knowledge. But even accounts of propositional justification must come to terms with their consequences for paradigmatic situations. An account of propositional justification which had the consequence that most people rarely meet its conditions would, for that very reason, be extremely implausible. But whether the conditions are in fact met in real world situations cannot be determined from the armchair.

This point, I believe, has very broad implications. Consider some of the central terms of epistemological discourse: perception, memory, testimony, reasoning. These terms seem to pick out various real-world phenomena, and there is a great deal of psychological work that goes on in figuring out just what these phenomena come to. Side by side with this psychological work, we see philosophers attempting to offer analyses of these fundamental epistemological notions, and these analyses are often presented in isolation from, and, indeed, in ignorance of, the psychological literature. Epistemologists are interested in these topics, however, because they are interested in the nature and scope of human knowledge. A philosophical analysis of these notions which fails to fit with the real-world phenomena is, for that very reason, missing its target. Just as in the case of knowledge and justification, there is a serious problem with any account of perception, memory, testimony, or reasoning which has the consequence that there isn't very much of it going on. The fit, however, between philosophical analyses and real-world phenomena cannot be determined from the armchair. This is not just a worry in principle. Some of these phenomena – particularly memory, as I noted above – turn out to be quite a bit different than they seem from the armchair. Armchair analyses of such phenomena thus run a serious risk of simply failing to capture the very phenomena they seek to analyze. The analogue of skepticism here is eliminationism, the claim that it really turns out that there is no perception, memory, testimony, or reasoning; and eliminationism is about as plausible as skepticism. When the phenomena of cognition turn out to be quite different from what we thought they were – that is, when our armchair view of these phenomena is deeply mistaken – we cannot allow our epistemology to be built around our armchair misconceptions. But just as elsewhere in science, psychology periodically reveals that our armchair view of things is not merely incomplete or mistaken in detail; our armchair view of psychological phenomena is, at times, extremely wide of the mark. It would be a very bad mistake to engage in epistemological theorizing in ways which simply ignore this fact. But this means that we cannot rest content with an epistemology conducted from the armchair.

If this argument is accepted, as I believe it should be, then it counts against seeing our concepts as the target of epistemological analysis.[39] It is not our concept of knowledge, or justification, or reasoning, or memory which is the target of philosophical analysis; it is knowledge, justification, reasoning, memory, and so on themselves. Just as we may mentally represent such things as gold and water in ways which fail to do justice to the substances themselves, we may mentally represent the objects of epistemological investigation in ways which build in substantive misunderstandings. We are interested in certain real phenomena – human knowledge, for example – and there is little point in elucidating, in however great detail, what our personal or folk conceptions of those phenomena are. For this reason, I am no more sympathetic to the work of the experimental philosophers than I am to those who practice conceptual analysis in a more traditional manner. It is true, as the experimental philosophers have argued, that if one wants to get at what our concepts are, then one must proceed experimentally. The traditional methods of conceptual analysis amount to little more than social psychology done badly. But while the experimental philosophers respond to this problem by trying to do the social psychology well, it seems to me that they have addressed the wrong problem here. Doing a better job at getting at our concepts does not constitute progress, in my view, since the proper target of philosophical analysis is simply not our concepts. Our concepts are the vehicles by way of which we represent the target of philosophical analysis, but this is altogether different from taking the concepts themselves to be the object of study.

There are thus a great many central projects in epistemology which would be dramatically affected by experimental results from the cognitive sciences. Our armchair view of psychological phenomena is often deeply mistaken, and these mistakes are then incorporated into our philosophical analyses if we rely on nothing but armchair methods. The subject matter of epistemology is so closely tied to these psychological phenomena, and our armchair view of them is so badly skewed, that our epistemological theories will inevitably suffer if they are insulated from experimental results. But it is not just a handful of, admittedly important, epistemological projects which need to be informed by laboratory work. The very phenomena which epistemologists seek to illuminate are ones which are the object of experimental study, and this experimental work has often led to surprising results. We ignore this work at our peril. When philosophical theories in epistemology are constructed from the armchair, they run a serious risk of being divorced from the very phenomena they seek to illuminate. The only way to assure that we do not build elaborate castles in the air, unconnected to the real world phenomena which motivated our work in the first place, is to base our work on the best available experimental understanding of those phenomena. Any such empirically informed epistemology will inevitably leave the armchair very far behind.

***

Although Timothy Williamson and I agree on a great deal about philosophical method,[40] there is also a good deal about which we disagree. Williamson is far more optimistic about the prospects for philosophy generally, and epistemology in particular, as carried out from the armchair.[41] Now Williamson remarks that, "The legitimacy in principle of experimental philosophy does not make armchair philosophy illegitimate in principle."[42] This is quite right, of course, and no one has argued that it does. My argument here, as elsewhere,[43] is not that armchair methods might, in principle, lead to errors and omissions, but rather that, in actual practice, armchair methods have regularly led to very substantial errors in epistemology. The features of cognition which are most directly relevant to epistemology are ones which we badly misunderstand when we remain in the armchair. It is for this reason that I worry about formal models designed to square with our armchair view of matters. It is not that I think there is something wrong with developing formal models – very far from it. As Williamson rightly points out,[44] formal modeling and experimental methods need not be seen as rivals; in the ordinary practice of science, they are, quite typically, mutually beneficial. Experimental input provides useful data to inform our formal models; formal modeling provides useful information about where best to test our available theories. What I object to, then, is not formal modeling per se, but rather formal models in epistemology which do not have the benefit of this substantive interaction with experimental data. When the input to our formal models comes from the armchair rather than the laboratory, and when the output of our formal models is not used to inform experimental tests but, instead, merely to prompt more interactions with the view from the armchair, the resulting epistemological theories are likely to be badly mistaken. Even when this method does not result in errors, it is a method in which we should not place our confidence. Formal modeling uninformed and unchecked by experimental results makes for bad epistemology.

No one could reasonably object to the use of armchair methods as a component of philosophical methodology. After all, we do need, at times, to step back from the data which have been collected, and the theories we have constructed on that basis, and think about their implications. From the armchair, we can construct various formal models and examine their consequences. But to acknowledge this is to say no more than that philosophy, like any intellectual activity, involves thinking things through. What is at issue between those who are optimistic about the prospects of armchair methodology in philosophy and those who are more pessimistic is not whether stopping to think can be a good idea. It is, instead, a question of what we need to bring to the armchair to think about. Those who favor a thoroughgoing armchair methodology believe that no special experimental input is really necessary for at least a good deal of philosophical theorizing. Those of us who are more pessimistic about this sort of methodology believe that experimental data are needed to keep us in touch with the phenomena we seek to understand.

***

There is one more motivation for adopting armchair methods in epistemology which I want to discuss. Many philosophers have the conviction that the most fundamental questions of epistemology are, at bottom, questions that must be asked from the first-person point of view, and, to the extent that they are convinced of this, they will see armchair methods as essential to the pursuit of fundamental epistemological questions. Thus, for example, Richard Foley argues that a particularly fundamental question for epistemology is, "What am I to believe?" and although he acknowledges that there is a way to answer such a question from a third-person perspective, by, for example, engaging in psychological research about the reliability of one's own processes of belief acquisition, such an investigation would not approach this question in the way that treats it as the fundamental epistemological question he has in mind. The approach he favors, one which respects the fundamental nature of the question, is as follows.

> I am to make up my mind by marshaling my intellectual resources in a way that conforms to my own deepest standards. If I conduct my inquiries in such a way that I would not be critical of the resulting beliefs even if I were to be deeply reflective, then these beliefs are rational for me in an important sense, an egoistic sense. ... The basic idea is that if I am to be egoistically rational, I must not have internal reasons for retraction, ones whose force I myself would acknowledge were I to be sufficiently reflective.[45]

So armchair reflection plays an essential role in addressing a fundamental epistemological issue, and any attempt to answer a question which sounds like Foley's, by third-person means, simply fails to get at the issue about which he is concerned.

Laurence BonJour says something quite similar. Although he allows that there may be a perfectly legitimate externalist notion of justification, and of knowledge – and that accounts of these notions would make no special appeal to the first-person perspective or to armchair reflection – nevertheless, there is also a legitimate internalist notion of justification, and a notion of knowledge which requires such justification. Such a notion requires that "what is appealed to for justification must be *internal to the individual's first-person cognitive perspective*."[46] Moreover, BonJour insists, these two notions of justification, and of knowledge, are not on a par.

> I want to insist that there is a clear way in which an internalist approach, in addition to being intellectually legitimate on its own, has a fundamental kind of priority for epistemology as a whole.[47]

So for both Foley and BonJour, there are fundamental questions about what we ourselves should believe, and the most fundamental way to pursue such questions must itself be from the first-person perspective. This will inevitably involve reflecting on our beliefs, and their sources, and the relationship among them. In order to answer the fundamental questions of epistemology, armchair reflection will need to play a leading role.

Debates about which questions in a discipline are really the most fundamental can often seem terribly unproductive, with members of each side of the debate doing little more than insisting that it is their preferred approach which really gets to the bottom of things. But that is not the case here. There are arguments for the priority of the first-person perspective, and if these arguments are successful, then justification and knowledge will inevitably involve a heavy dose of armchair reflection. Let us look at how these arguments play out.

While some internalist epistemologists characterize internalism by way of a metaphysical distinction – e.g. that the justificatory status of a person's beliefs depends exclusively on states of the person which are, in some suitable sense, internal (in the way that, say, mental states are)[48] – BonJour rightly rejects this way of thinking about internalism. While it is certainly true that for Descartes, as clear a case of an internalist epistemologist as one might try to find, the justificatory status of a person's belief did have to supervene on features of that person's mental state, this is only because Descartes held a view which made this metaphysical distinction – the distinction between things internal to the mind and those external to it – correspond to an important epistemological distinction: namely, the distinction between those things which are known directly and with certainty, as opposed to those things which are known only indirectly and fallibly. For those who reject the claim that the metaphysical distinction between mental and non-mental items tracks this epistemological divide – as everyone now must – it must therefore be acknowledged that the metaphysical distinction does not capture, and is not even extensionally equivalent to, any epistemological distinction at all. There are some mental states, such as the early states of perceptual and linguistic processing – to which our epistemological access is extraordinarily indirect.[49] We have far better cognitive access to many states of the so-called external world than we do to some of the states of our own psychology. And, finally, even mental states to which we seem to have some sort of direct access of a sort which would license claims about certainty turn out, on further examination, not to answer to that description. When internalists talk about things internal to us, they need to have an epistemological notion in mind rather than a metaphysical one.

What is this epistemological notion of the internal, a notion which will illuminate the fundamental nature of the question both Foley and BonJour wish to address? BonJour, I believe, is especially helpful here.

> A person's conscious mental states play the role that they standardly do in internalist conceptions of justification, I would suggest, *not* simply because

they are internal to him or her in the sense merely of being his or her individual states, but rather because it is arguable that some (but not all) of the properties of such states, mainly their specific content and the attitude toward that content that they reflect, are things to which the person has a first-person access that is direct and unproblematic, that is, that does not depend on other claims that would themselves have to be justified in some more indirect way.[50]

BonJour thus rightly gives an epistemological characterization of the features which make an internal state internal: it must be a state to which one has "first-person access that is direct and unproblematic." Internalism is thus defined in terms which assure the importance of reflection, for first-person access here just is the sort of access that armchair reflection affords.

Why should we think, however, that armchair reflection affords access which is unproblematic? It is clear enough that, when we reflect, the access which reflection affords us to various features of our mental life certainly *seems* unproblematic from the first-person perspective. What reason do we have, however, for taking such appearances at face value?

Notice, first of all, the context in which BonJour speaks of our access to certain features of our mental life[51] as unproblematic. BonJour comes to talk about unproblematic access in the context of raising the problem of radical skepticism.[52] The same is true of Foley; his question about what one is to believe is presented, unsurprisingly, as a distinctively Cartesian question, one which serves to make vivid the problem of skepticism. And Sosa too, in recent work, sees an important connection between the importance of reflective knowledge and the traditional project of responding to the skeptic.[53] So how is it that our access to certain features of our mental life is supposed to be unproblematic in the context of responding to radical skepticism?

There is no denying that one can raise a skeptical challenge to knowledge of the physical world by granting, for the sake of argument, that we have perfect access to (at least some features of) our mental states. We can raise skeptical challenges of all sorts, by granting, for the sake of argument, that certain sorts of knowledge are unproblematic. Thus, for example, we might grant, for the sake of argument, that we have unproblematic knowledge of the behavior of others, and then ask, in the light of this knowledge, how knowledge of their mental states is possible. Or we might grant, again, for the sake of argument, that knowledge of the observable features of the world is unproblematic, and then ask how knowledge of unobservables is possible. We can raise all sorts of skeptical challenges in this way. When we do so, however, the knowledge that we take as unproblematic is not, automatically, unproblematic *tout court*. At least without additional argument, to say that a certain body of knowledge is unproblematic for the purposes of raising a skeptical problem is simply to allow that, within a certain dialectical situation, we are not going to raise challenges to that sort of knowledge. But this shows nothing at all about the epistemic status of the knowledge which we agree not to challenge. What BonJour, and Foley, and Sosa need to show, if they are to secure the importance of the first-person perspective, and the importance of armchair reflection which goes with it, is that our first-person access to relevant features of our mental life is unproblematic in a far more substantive way.

But this is just what they cannot do. One can raise skeptical worries about features of one's mental life just as easily as one can raise worries about our knowledge of the physical world. Descartes prepared the ground for skepticism about the physical world by, initially, pointing out that we do in fact make mistakes about various features of the external world. This is enough to show that there is not only in principle, but, at times, in practice as well, a gap between how the world actually is and how we represent it in our beliefs. This is all that is needed to generate the skeptical worry: What reason is there to believe that the world is anything like the way we represent it to be?

But the very same strategy will generate a skeptical worry about our access to our mental states. As we have already seen, there is not only in principle, but, at times, in practice as well, a gap between how our mental life actually is and how it is presented to us when we engage in armchair reflection. Considerations of cases involving self-deception show that we may, at times, be mistaken about what it is that we believe, so here too, there is, not only in theory, but in practice as well, a non-trivial gap between appearance and reality. And it is the possibility of such a gap which raises the skeptical worry: What reason is there to believe that our mental life is anything like the way it appears to us when we reflect on it?

I am not, in any way, a radical skeptic. These considerations are not meant to provide support for radical skepticism. What they do show, however, is the sense in which the beliefs about our mental life which are generated from the first-person perspective – that is, the beliefs which result from armchair reflection – are not unproblematic in any way that matters to epistemology.[54]

The idea that the first-person point of view presents some sort of neutral and unproblematic starting point for epistemological inquiry is, to my mind, a product of two not unrelated facts. First, there is an important historical tradition in epistemology, a tradition of which Descartes is the pre-eminent representative, according to which the way the mind is presented to us in reflection genuinely is unproblematic: it is unproblematic because it is absolutely certain and utterly resistant to any sort of skeptical doubt whatsoever. Second, there is the psychological fact that when we do reflect on our own mental states, we are presented with a view of our mental life which we tend to find utterly compelling. Neither of these facts, however, should convince us that the access to our mental life which reflection provides and which is represented in our first-person perspective on our mental lives genuinely is unproblematic. Descartes's views about the powers of reflection are, for very good reason, no longer accepted, and without them, the claim that reflection provides an unproblematic view of our mental life is wholly undermined. The psychological fact about the compelling nature of the first-person perspective is itself put in proper perspective by the surprising experimental results which we have surveyed. Viewed in this light, there is nothing epistemically unproblematic about the first-person perspective or the epistemological projects which flow from treating it as if it were.

I have argued that it would be a mistake to pursue epistemological theorizing entirely from the armchair. Let me end, however, on a conciliatory note. Philosophy is a cooperative enterprise. Just as there is a division of labor in physics, with some physicists actively engaged in laboratory work, and others, more theoretically inclined, engaged in armchair theorizing, there is obviously room for such a division of labor in philosophy, even on my view. This is not to say that any old armchair theorizing, however, is likely to be constructive. The physicists who engage in armchair theorizing do not do so in splendid ignorance of the work of their experimental colleagues. Armchair physics carried on in ignorance of experimental results would be entirely worthless. When we talk about the actual phenomenon of armchair theorizing in physics, then, what we have in mind is not work that is wholly independent of experimental results. Instead, talk of theorizing from the armchair in physics amounts to a simple acknowledgement of the diverse interests and talents of those who contribute to physical theorizing, together with a recognition that progress in physics is not typically attributable to individuals acting in perfect isolation, but is instead the product of a community of investigators. The same is true, in my view, of epistemology. Individual theorists may pursue their work in constructive ways from the armchair, so long as they are part of a community which keeps them in touch with real epistemological phenomena by way of experimental work. We misunderstand the role of armchair theorizing, in my view, if we think that it is possible to make progress in epistemology without experimental work playing this important role.[55]

Notes

1 See especially, "Truth by Convention" (originally published in 1935) and "Carnap and Logical Truth" (originally published in 1954), both reprinted in Quine's *The Ways of Paradox and Other Essays*, revised and enlarged edition (Cambridge, MA: Harvard University Press, 1976); and "Two Dogmas of Empiricism" (originally published in 1951), reprinted in Quine's *From a Logical Point of View* (New York: Harper Torchbooks, 1961).

2 In *Ontological Relativity and Other Essays* (New York: Columbia University Press, 1969), 69–90.

3 See especially "Epistemics: The Regulative Theory of Cognition," *Journal of Philosophy* 75 (1978): 509–23; the papers collected in his *Liaisons: Philosophy Meets the Cognitive and Social Sciences* (Cambridge, MA: MIT Press, 1992); and *Epistemology and Cognition* (Cambridge, MA: Harvard University Press, 1986).

4 See also the papers collected in Hilary Kornblith (ed.), *Naturalizing Epistemology* (Cambridge, MA: MIT Press, 1985; 2nd edn, 1994). My own approach to these issues is presented and defended in *Inductive Inference and Its Natural Ground* (Cambridge, MA: MIT Press, 1993), and *Knowledge and Its Place in Nature* (Oxford: Oxford University Press, 2002).

5 "Methodological Naturalism in Epistemology," in John Greco and Ernest Sosa (eds), *The Blackwell Guide to Epistemology* (Malden, MA: Blackwell, 1999), 171.

6 For similar sorts of remarks about the importance of externalism, and the way in which empirical information is thereby brought to center stage in epistemology, see Laurence BonJour, "The Indispensability of Internalism," *Philosophical Topics* 29 (2001): 47–65.

7 Timothy Williamson, *The Philosophy of Philosophy* (Malden, MA: Blackwell, 2007).

8 See *Philosophy of Philosophy*, chs 3 and 4.

9 See, for example, Jonathan Weinberg, Shaun Nichols, and Stephen Stich, "Normativity and Epistemic Intuitions," *Philosophical Topics* 29(2001): 429–60; Peter A. French and Howard K. Wettstein (eds), *Midwest Studies in Philosophy*, vol. 31: *Philosophy and the Empirical* (Oxford: Wiley-Blackwell, 2007); Joshua Knobe and Shaun Nichols (eds), *Experimental Philosophy* (Oxford: Oxford University Press, 2008).

10 At least in the typical case. There is some real disagreement about whether certain judgments arrived at by way of introspection are a priori justified. For a particularly useful discussion of this issue, see Philip Kitcher, "A Priori Knowledge," *Philosophical Review* 89 (1980): 3–23.

11 To my mind, Chisholm's best presentation of this way of thinking about epistemological questions is to be found in the second edition of his *Theory of Knowledge* (Upper Saddle River, NJ: Prentice-Hall, 1977), ch. 2.

12 See especially Richard Nisbett and Timothy Wilson, "Telling More Than We Can Know: Verbal Reports on Mental Processes," *Psychological Review* 84 (1977): 231–59; Richard Nisbett and Lee Ross, *Human Inference: Strategies and Shortcomings of Social Judgment* (Upper Saddle River, NJ: Prentice-Hall, 1980), ch. 9; Timothy Wilson, *Strangers to Ourselves: Discovering the Adaptive Unconscious* (Cambridge, MA: Harvard University Press, 2002).

13 I have argued for this at some length in chapter 4 of *Knowledge and Its Place in Nature*.

14 A number of authors have attached a great deal of significance to this fact. See, for example, Christine Korsgaard, *Source of Normativity* (Cambridge: Cambridge University Press, 1996), ch. 3; Richard Moran, *Authority and Estrangement: An Essay on Self-Knowledge* (Princeton, NJ: Princeton University Press, 2001).

15 See, for example, Shelley Taylor and Jonathan Brown, "Illusion and Well-Being: A Social Psychological Perspective on Mental Health," *Psychological Bulletin* 103 (1988): 193–210, and Shelley Taylor, *Positive Illusions: Creative Self-Deception and the Healthy Mind* (New York: Basic Books, 1989).

16 Ernest Sosa makes this point in an attempt to support the idea that "reflection aids agency." See Sosa, "Replies," in John Greco (ed.), *Ernest Sosa and His Critics* (Malden, MA: Blackwell, 2004), 292.

17 I have discussed these issues in greater detail in "The Myth of Epistemic Agency," manuscript.

18 David Christensen and I have discussed this in "Testimony, Memory and the Limits of the A Priori," *Philosophical Studies* 86 (1997): 1–20. For an extremely useful review of the psychological literature, as well as a discussion of its philosophical implications, see K. Michaelian, "Generative Memory," manuscript.

19 The phrase comes from Tyler Burge, "Content Preservation," *Philosophical Review* 102 (1993): 457–88. I should make clear that it is not Burge's view that, in the typical case, little more goes on beyond content preservation.

20 See, for example, Elisabeth Fricker, "Against Gullibility," in B.K. Matilal and A. Chakrabarti (eds), *Knowing from Words* (Dordrecht: Kluwer, 1994), 125–61. For a sampling of the (now very large)

epistemological literature on testimony, see J. Lackey and E. Sosa (eds), *The Epistemology of Testimony* (Oxford: Oxford University Press, 2006). As is typical of this body of literature, the papers in this last anthology do not engage with the relevant empirical literature.

21 Here I rely on K. Michaelian, "In Defence of Gullibility: The Epistemology of Testimony and the Psychology of Deception Detection," *Synthese* 176, no. 3 (2010): 399–427. I have also benefited from reading a manuscript on this topic by Joseph Shieber.

22 Again, see the papers cited in n. 21, above by Michaelian and Shieber.

23 For a discussion of these issues, see Alvin Goldman, "Philosophical Intuitions: Their Target, Their Source, and Their Epistemic Status," *Grazer Philosophische Studien* 74 (2007): 1–26; and Hilary Kornblith, "Naturalism and Intuitions," *Grazer Philosophische Studien* 74 (2007): 27–49.

24 "Principles of Categorization," in Eleanore Rosch and B.B. Lloyd (eds), *Cognition and Categorization* (Hillsdale, NJ: Laurence Erlbaum Associates), 27–48.

25 It is, of course, a mistake to say that this kind of format for the representation of concepts does not provide necessary and sufficient conditions for falling under the concept. Any account of what concepts are will inevitably provide necessary and sufficient conditions. What is at issue is whether those necessary and sufficient conditions are presented in the kind of format characteristic of traditional philosophical analyses.

26 For a useful collection of papers on these issues, see Eric Margolis and Stephen Laurence, (eds), *Concepts: Core Readings* (Cambridge, MA: MIT Press, 1999). For a very helpful discussion of the literature, see Gregory Murphy, *The Big Book of Concepts* (Cambridge, MA: MIT Press, 2002).

27 See Joachim Horvath, "Conceptual Analysis and Naturalized Epistemology," manuscript; and Daniel Weiskopf, "Atomism, Pluralism and Conceptual Content," *Philosophy and Phenomenological Research* 79 (2009): 131–63.

28 For a collection of some of the central papers on this issue, see Hilary Kornblith (ed.), *Epistemology: Internalism and Externalism* (Malden, MA: Blackwell, 2001).

29 *The Structure of Empirical Knowledge* (Cambridge, MA: Harvard University Press, 1985), 8.

30 I first addressed this issue in "Introspection and Misdirection," *Australasian Journal of Philosophy* 67 (1989): 410–22. In addition to chapter four of my *Knowledge and Its Place in Nature*, see also Michael Bishop, "In Praise of Epistemic Irresponsibility: How Lazy and Ignorant Can You Be?" *Synthese*, 122 (2000): 179–208, and Michael Bishop and J.D. Trout, *Epistemology and the Psychology of Human Judgment* (Oxford: Oxford University Press, 2005).

31 "Is Knowledge Justified True Belief?," *Analysis* 23 (1963): 121–23.

32 For a defense of this approach, see, for example, Frank Jackson, *From Metaphysics to Ethics: A Defence of Conceptual Analysis* (Oxford: Oxford University Press, 1998).

33 See work cited in n. 26, above.

34 "Philosophical Intuitions."

35 I present reasons for doubting that Goldman is right in "Naturalism and Intuitions."

36 My remarks here apply equally to contextualists. Thus, although contextualists will want to allow that skepticism is true in high-standards contexts, they will also want to insist that skepticism is false in everyday contexts. The kinds of concerns I address here would raise worries about everyday contexts.

37 See, for example, Richard Feldman and Earl Conee's discussion of well-foundedness in their paper, "Evidentialism," in their *Evidentialism: Essays in Epistemology* (Oxford: Oxford University Press, 2004), 83–107, especially 92–93.

38 I don't mean to suggest that philosophers need to carry out experiments themselves. In most cases, philosophers simply lack the relevant training to carry out experiments properly, and one does no better to engage in philosophical theorizing by way of amateurish experimentation than by way of armchair theorizing. What is needed, however, and what I mean to be claiming here, is that philosophical theorizing must be informed by experimental work, whether done by (appropriately trained) philosophers or by psychologists.

39 I have presented this argument at length in *Knowledge and Its Place in Nature*. Timothy Williamson defends this view as well, in a somewhat different way, in *Philosophy of Philosophy*. Williamson and I disagree about the upshot of this thesis for the use of armchair methods in philosophy.

40 See my "Timothy Williamson's *The Philosophy of Philosophy*," *Analysis* 69 (2009): 109–16; and Williamson's "Replies to Kornblith, Jackson and Moore," *Analysis* 69 (2009): 125–35.

41 Thus, Williamson remarks, "I expect armchair methods to play legitimately a more dominant role in future philosophy than [Kornblith] expects them to – of course, such difference in emphasis can result in widening differences in practice." "Replies to Kornblith, Jackson and Moore," 126.

42 Ibid., 126.

43 In "The Role of Intuition in Philosophical Inquiry," in M. DePaul and W. Ramsey (eds), *Rethinking Intuition* (Lanham, MD: Rowman & Littlefield, 1998), 129–41; in *Knowledge and Its Place in Nature*; in "Appeals to Intuition and the Ambitions of Epistemology," in Stephen Hetherington (ed.), *Epistemology Futures* (Oxford: Oxford University Press, 2006), 10–25; in "Naturalism and Intuitions"; and in "Timothy Williamson's *The Philosophy of Philosophy*."

44 "Replies to Kornblith, Jackson and Moore," 128.

45 "What Am I to Believe?," in Steven Wagner and Richard Warner (eds), *Naturalism: A Critical Appraisal* (Notre Dame, IN: University of Notre Dame Press, 1993), 148.

46 "Indispensability of Internalism," 54.

47 Ibid., 62.

48 This is the way that Conee and Feldman characterize internalism. See *Evidentialism: Essays in Epistemology* (Oxford: Oxford University Press, 2004), 56: "The justificatory status of a person's doxastic attitudes strongly supervenes on the person's occurrent and dispositional mental states, events, and conditions."

49 This is going to be so on any way that one tries to make sense of the direct/indirect distinction. I do not mean to be endorsing any particular way of making out such a distinction, or, indeed, even the claim that we can make good sense of it.

50 "Indispensability of Internalism," 54.

51 And various extramental items as well. BonJour rightly points out that, on standard internalist accounts, we have such unproblematic access by way of reflection to at least some a priori knowable truths. "Indispensability of Internalism," 55. I will focus in the text, however, on our access to relevant features of our mental lives. If internalists cannot secure this, then internalism is committed to an extremely broad skepticism, and, indeed, the coherence of the entire position is threatened. More than this, there is every reason to believe that the kind of argument I make against unproblematic access to mental items can easily be generalized to cover the cases in which BonJour believes we have unproblematic access to a priori knowable truths. I have discussed these problems about the a priori in "The Impurity of Reason," *Pacific Philosophical Quarterly* 81 (2000): 67–89. It would take us too far afield from the issues under discussion here to pursue these questions about the a priori.

52 "Indispensability of Internalism," 53.

53 "Replies," 292.

54 BonJour seems to come quite close to acknowledging this. At one point he remarks that,

> Certainly it would be a very unusual brand of scepticism which would challenge whether my belief that B is justified by raising the issue of whether I do in fact accept B, the normal sceptical claim being precisely that certain beliefs which are in fact held are nonetheless unjustified.
>
> (*The Structure of Empirical Knowledge*, 81)

But claims about which skeptical challenges are common in the history of philosophy, or which are unusual, tell us nothing about which kinds of claims are unproblematic *tout court*. And it is this sense of what is unproblematic, rather than the dialectical sense, which is epistemologically relevant.

55 I am indebted to Timothy Williamson for conversations on this topic on a number of occasions. In addition, I have presented versions of this paper at Fortaleza, Brazil; the University of St Andrews; and the University of Cincinnati. I am grateful to audiences on all of these occasions for helpful comments and criticisms. Thanks too to Matthew Haug for helpful suggestions.

13 Methods in analytic epistemology
KIRK LUDWIG

In this chapter, I defend the program of conceptual analysis, broadly construed, and the method of thought experiments in epistemology, as a first-person enterprise, that is, as one which draws on the investigator's own competence in the relevant concepts. I do not suggest that epistemology is limited to conceptual analysis, that it does not have important a posteriori elements, that it should not draw on empirical work wherever relevant (and non-question-begging), or that it is not a communal enterprise. Although discussion in the space available will necessarily be brief, and many points must be elided altogether, I aim to sketch salient features of the landscape, clarify issues, set aside some confusions, and outline responses to some recent challenges.

In the next section, "What Are Concepts?," I sketch a traditional account of concepts and conceptual truths. In the section following, "What Is Conceptual Analysis?," I review a broad conception of analysis as encompassing not just reduction but also articulation of conceptual connections. In "How Could Conceptual Analysis Tell Us Anything about the World?," I address the charge that in studying epistemic concepts we turn away from our proper target of study, the actual phenomena of knowledge, justification, and so on. In "What Is the Role of Thought Experiments?," I give a brief overview of the method of thought experiments. Then in "What Are the Lessons of Experimental Philosophy?," I address objections to thought experiments that have their source in "experimental philosophy." Finally, in my concluding section, "Is 'Knowledge' a Natural Kind Term?," I address the charge that pursuing conceptual analysis in epistemology is misplaced because "knowledge," "justification," "evidence" and so on, are natural kind terms, and hence that we must engage in empirical research to discover their real essences.

What are concepts?

Concepts, in the sense we are concerned with, are common (general) elements in different thought contents. For example, the thoughts that chess is a strategic game and that chess is a popular game are distinct but share the concepts of chess and of games. The concepts in a thought content, and how they are combined in it, determine its truth conditions, which in turn individuate it.[1] Concepts in turn are individuated by the systematic contributions they make to the truth conditions of thought contents. Concepts fall in different categories. There are monadic, binary, triadic, etc., concepts expressed with one-place, two-place, three-place predicates, etc. But there are also logical concepts such as that of negation, conjunction, disjunction, universal and existential quantification, and so on. I will call the conditions for the correct deployment of concepts their application conditions. If a noun or adjective "*F*" expresses a concept, we specify it as the concept of *F*, and we say that something falls under the concept of *F* iff it has the property of being *F*.

A conceptual truth is true in virtue of its contained concepts and their mode of combination. It is a conceptual truth that the arithmetic mean of a range of numbers lies within it, as it is a conceptual truth that the arithmetic mean is always greater than or equal to the geometric mean. Similarly it is a conceptual truth that if something is completely transparent, then it is not colored, that for any rigid bodies *a*, *b*, *c*, if *a* is longer than *b* and *b* is longer than *c*, then *a* is longer than *c*, that no one knows that the moon is larger than the earth if it is not true, that no person is identical to two distinct people, and so on. These are conceptual truths in the sense that we can explain why they are true by adverting to facts about the application conditions of the contained concepts and their mode of combination.

The link between something's being a conceptual truth and our being in a position to come to know it can be expressed in three connected theses.

- *Possession*. To think that *p*, one must possess the concepts involved in it.
- *Competence*. To possess a concept *C*, one must be competent in its deployment, in the sense of being in a position to deploy it correctly in thought, on the basis of its application conditions, in response to conditions as one takes them actually to be or in response hypothetically to conditions so specified.
- *Recognition*. A judgment or thought that *p* which is an expression solely of one's competence in deploying the concepts involved in light of their mode of combination counts as knowing (or being justified in believing) that *p* on the basis of their application conditions.

To have a concept is to have a competence expressed in thinking rightly in response to conditions that are relevant to the truth conditions that individuate the thought. Having thoughts is linked to competences connected to their components and their structure and implies the possibility of knowledge on that basis.[2]

Possession has been challenged on the ground that when a speaker uses a sentence intending to use it as others in his community do, we are licensed (at least sometimes) in attributing to him an attitude whose content is given by the sentence, even if the speaker doesn't fully understand all the words in it (Burge 1979). This would allow (us to say) that someone had a thought though he failed to possess all the concepts in it. Whether this is right or not, clearly we could engage in such a practice. The possession condition then should be understood to exclude attitudes whose attribution rests on such a practice—which could not exist in the first place if there were no thoughts attributed independently of it.

Competence is a weak condition: it says only that one is in a position to deploy concepts one possesses correctly in thought.[3] It does not say that one invariably does, or that it is easy to see the right thing to think in response to conditions that are relevant.[4] Nor does it say that deploying a concept correctly in thought is always a matter of recognizing features of objects. One's possession of the concepts of disjunction and negation will be expressed in part, e.g., in how one responds to accepting that p when one believes that q or not-p. Even for non-logical concepts application might not be based on accepting a set of propositions, but involve rather certain experiences, e.g., thinking something red given how it looks, or application on the basis of similarity to a prototype, etc., given other beliefs.[5]

Suppose that it is a conceptual truth that anything that is red is colored. If one judges on the basis of the concepts involved that anything red is colored, one thereby knows that anything red is colored. A judgment one reaches on the basis solely of competence in the deployment of the concepts involved in it is not based on facts about experience, the deliverances of introspection, or memory. Hence, on one plausible way of understanding the claim, the knowledge one has is a priori.

What is conceptual analysis?

Conceptual analysis in philosophy subsumes two projects, one narrower and one broader, though critics often seem to focus only on the first of these. There is, on the one hand, the project of providing informative necessary and sufficient conditions for the application of a concept, i.e., reductive analysis. On the other hand, there is the project of tracing constitutive connections between concepts, propositions, and experience, and ordering families of concepts, so far as that is possible, in terms of relative priority, i.e., conceptual elucidation (Strawson 1992, ch. 2; McGinn 2012, ch. 7). A concept or family of concepts is prior to another just in case one can have it without having the other but not vice versa.

Conceptual analysis is sometimes dismissed on the grounds that few concepts of philosophical interest admit of informative analyses. But the interest of getting a clear view of the conceptual structure of the world is hardly exhausted by an interest in reductive analysis. It was never in the cards that we would get informative necessary and sufficient conditions for every concept of philosophical interest. On pain of an infinite regress, we must find some concepts that we can't analyze in terms of other more basic concepts. And the concepts that structure most deeply how we think about the world are just those that we should not think capable of reductive analysis. Here we turn to elucidation.

Nor should conceptual analysis be rejected with conceptual atomism, the analog of foundationalism for concepts, which holds that all concepts can be reduced to a set of basic concepts. An example is a version of empiricism that holds that all simple ideas (blurring the distinction between sensation, experience, and concept) derive from sensory experience and that complex ideas are built up out of them. This is not a definition of conceptual analysis but a substantive hypothesis about the global structure of our concepts, and the way that our concepts hang together may not conform to the model. A sense of the possibilities is suggested by Davidson's program in the theory of meaning (see the discussion in Davidson (2001, 137)), on which the idea is that a family of interlocking concepts (of meaning, truth, belief, desire, intention, agency, rationality, etc.) may be illuminated by tracing constitutive connections with a distinct family of concepts used to describe canonical evidence for a theory involving members of the first family, without one-by-one reduction of concepts, or even a holistic reduction of a theory to a set of statements about evidence for it.[6]

How could conceptual analysis tell us anything about the world?

Why think that conceptual analysis tells us anything about the world? The view that it does not has been forcefully stated by Hilary Kornblith:

> On my view, the subject matter of ethics is the right and the good, not our concepts of them. The subject matter of philosophy of mind is the mind itself, not our concept of it. And the subject matter of epistemology is knowledge itself, not our concept of knowledge.

(2002, 2)

> By bringing in talk of concepts … in an epistemological investigation, we
> only succeed in changing the subject: instead of talking about knowledge,
> we end up talking about our concept of knowledge.
>
> (2002, 9–10)

Analysis of the *concept* of knowledge is fine as far as it goes, but if we are
really interested in *knowledge*, shouldn't we put the concept aside and look
at the phenomenon itself?

This is a false dilemma. Conceptual analyses (for "predicative" concepts)
are standardly presented in a biconditional of the form [C] in which
"*F*(…)" expresses the concept of interest (I focus on reductive analysis,
but the point extends to elucidations).

> [C]   For any $x, y, z, \ldots F(x, y, z, \ldots)$ iff …

An instance of [C] counts as a reductive analysis provided that (a)
expressions used on the right-hand side express concepts that are more
basic than the concept being analyzed and (b) [C] expresses a conceptual
truth. [C] is a material mode statement. It does not mention any
concepts, or any words, and in particular it does not mention the concept
of which it gives an analysis. For illustration, take an instance (Klein
1971):

> [K]   For any x, for any p, x knows p iff (i) p is true, (ii) x believes p,
> (iii) p is evident to x, and (iv) there is no proposition q such that if q
> became evident to x, then p would no longer be evident to x.

This is not about the *concept* of knowledge: it is about *knowledge* itself. If it
is true, then it says something about the conditions under which someone
has knowledge.

Then is it not a conceptual analysis after all? Knobe and Burra raise
exactly this objection (2006, 332): "The problem with such an account is
that it seems to say nothing about people's *concepts*. (It would tell us, not
about people's concepts, but about the actual properties in the world that
these concepts pick out.)" This rests on a misunderstanding. [C] is a
material mode statement. When it is put forward as a conceptual analysis,
it is claimed to meet conditions (a) and (b). This is a claim about the
statement, and if it is correct, the statement express a conceptual truth,
and the right-hand side both *expresses* the application conditions of the
concept of knowledge and *states* what it is for someone to have knowledge. If [K] meets the conditions, we can use it to give a formal mode
statement about the application conditions of the concept of knowledge
in [KC].

[KC]   For any x, for any p, the concept of knowledge is true of the pair $<x, p>$ iff (i) p is true, (ii) x believes p, (iii) p is evident to x, and (iv) there is no proposition q such that if q became evident to x, then p would no longer be evident to x.

For this to be a conceptual analysis, it also has to meet conditions (a) and (b). From it one can infer [K]. As it is a mistake to think that [K], because it is about knowledge, cannot be used to express a conceptual analysis, so it is a mistake to think that [KC], because it is about the concept of knowledge, does not give us information about what knowledge is.[7] As Quine put it in the parallel case of giving the truth conditions of sentences: "The truth predicate is a reminder that, despite a technical ascent to talk of sentences, our eye is on the world" (1986, 9).

What are the sources of the curious view that conceptual analysis does not tell us anything about what our concepts are of? I think there are a number of things that have exerted an influence, sometimes perhaps in conjunction with one another.

One may simply be the failure to recognize that in specifying the application conditions of a concept of C one thereby gives information that suffices to produce a material mode statement about necessary and sufficient conditions for being C.

A second may be the conflation of the psychological study of concepts with a concern for understanding concepts in their role in fixing the contents, and, hence, truth conditions, of thoughts. The former psychological project – whether it concerns how concepts are realized, or contingent laws involving them – gives no insight into how concepts fix the truth conditions of thoughts, and so would not be thought to be relevant to the natures of the things which the concepts pick out. The thought that psychologists are studying the very concepts for which we seek analyses may also encourage the thought that analysis should be an empirical enterprise.[8] But this is confused twice over. First in thinking that psychologists are in the business of analysis and second in thinking their techniques are relevant to it.[9]

A third source is the conflation of the concept of F with a mini-theory about Fs, a folk theory of sorts, which may not accurately characterize Fs, and might in fact be radically mistaken.[10] If one thinks this, then one will not think that an analysis of the concept of F *ipso facto* gives you knowledge of Fs. But this is a category mistake. The theory would itself have to involve beliefs that include the concept because that is what fixes its subject. Thus, any beliefs one has about Fs presuppose possession of the concept. One's possession of the concept therefore could not be explained by one's having the theory. What it is to possess a concept is to have the ability to apply it correctly in accordance with a rule. The mistake of the mini-theory of concept possession is to confuse a competence in the deployment of a concept with having beliefs involving it.

A fourth source of confusion stretches back to Kant in one form, the idea that analytic truths do not provide ampliative knowledge. A purer form is found in the *Tractatus Logico-Philosophicus* (Wittgenstein 1961), namely, the idea that analytic truths are non-factual. If all conceptual truths are expressed with analytic sentences, we get the conclusion that conceptual truths are non-factual. The doctrine's origins in the *Tractatus* are tied to Wittgenstein's picture theory of representation and truth-functional theory of propositions. Wittgenstein held that atomic propositions represented atomic states of affairs. Atomic propositions were independent of one another. We represent how the world is by atomic propositions and truth functions out of them. A proposition has a sense to the extent to which it locates us in logical space. The logical apparatus of truth-functional logic aids in sketching positions in logical space, but the mechanism allows for limiting cases in which the truth values of the sentences constructed out of the connectives are insensitive to those of the contained atomic sentences, and so always true (tautologous) or false (contradictory). These do not locate one in logical space, have no sense, and hence are devoid of factual content. Identifying analytic truths with tautologies entails analytic truths are non-factual. This idea was adopted by the logical positivists, and associated with analytic truths by Quine in his criticism of the analytic/synthetic distinction (Quine 1953). But the framework in the *Tractatus* that made sense of it was not adopted along with the doctrine, and no substitute has been offered, though the view itself has continued to exert an influence. This is an example *par excellence* of the persistence of a theoretical dogma after its support has been removed.

A fifth source is the view that concepts correlate with semantic competence, which should be construed on the model of competence in the use of natural kind terms like "gold" or "oak," which point us to real essences rather than providing us with a way of directly apprehending them. Though not all terms are natural kind terms, I agree that competence with natural kind terms does not put one in a position to give their essence. Nor, however, does it suffice to grasp the concept of the kind (in the sense of "concept" we've discussed), because that is fixed by the kind property it attributes (if any). As competence with the term doesn't fix the kind property, it doesn't fix the concept of the kind either. So this doesn't bear on the present issue. I take up the question whether epistemic terms are natural kind terms in the concluding section ("Is 'Knowledge' a Natural Kind Term?").

What is the role of thought experiments?

Conceptual analysis requires us not just to make judgments on the basis of conceptual competences but to reflect on how those judgments express their structure. We exercise conceptual competence *inter alia* when we make judgments on the basis of our beliefs and perceptual representations of the world and when we form and act on intentions in pursuing goals in the light of what we want most to get. Most of the judgments we make are not conceptual truths, however, because they are the products of antecedent beliefs about contingent features of the world and present experience. We could make a start on identifying necessary or sufficient application conditions for concepts by considering what features are invariably present when we deploy them, or reflecting on patterns of inference. But since we are interested in the patterns induced by competencies, it is more expedient to draw on those competencies directly by asking when it is correct to judge one or another thing, in the sense of its following from the description of the conditions—e.g. whether someone who infers justifiably from a justified but false belief something which is true thereby knows it.[11] It may help to describe a scenario involving hypothetical individuals as placeholders for things with relevant features and then to ask whether it is correct to make certain judgments about them. In this case, we engage in a thought experiment.

Though the scenarios involve hypothetical individuals, the import is general. An example will illustrate. In arguing that neighborhood reliabilism (NR) allows illegitimate bootstrapping, Jonathan Vogel describes the following thought experiment (2000, 353–56): Roxanne, who drives a car with a reliable gas gauge, believes what it reports, but she doesn't know that the gas gauge is reliable. However, she often notes how much gas is in the tank and what the gauge reads. The perceptual process by which she comes to believe what the gauge reads is reliable, as is the process by which she comes to believe how much gas is in the tank. She infers on such occasions that the gauge reads N and the tank is N. As deduction is a reliable process, her beliefs on these occasions are reliably produced. Roxanne concludes by induction (again a reliable process) that the gas gauge is always accurate, and then concludes that the gauge is reliable. Question: Does Roxanne know in virtue of the process she follows in coming to believe that the gauge is reliable that the gauge is reliable? Vogel says:

> I assume that bootstrapping is illegitimate. Roxanne cannot establish
> that the gas gauge is reliable by the peculiar reasoning I have just described.

The challenge to NR is that it may go wrong here. On the face of things, it does improperly ratify bootstrapping as a way of gaining knowledge.

(2000, 354)

Here the scenario functions as a schematic description of a type of case, and it is the type of case that we are to reason about. Hence, the question could be recast in terms of a universally quantified conditional, "Is it the case that for any x, if x ... , then x knows that the gas gauge is reliable?" where the intention is that one should answer on the basis of whether the antecedent states a condition conceptually sufficient for the consequent.[12] Thus, thought experiments draw on our ability to tell whether one proposition follows from another.

A creature can have concepts without the concept of a concept. But conceptual analysis requires the concept of a concept, and in particular the concept of conceptual entailment (what follows from what). Since having these concepts puts us in a position to deploy them correctly, this is both necessary and sufficient for the possibility of conceptual analysis.[13]

Thought experiments have played, and continue to play, a significant role in epistemological theorizing. Usually thought experiments do not establish outright an analysis, but rather provide starting points and test cases. We begin with observations that on the face of it express conceptual truths, such as that knowing p requires believing p and p being true. This being insufficient, we may propose that knowledge is e.g., justified true belief. Typically with concepts situated in a family of concepts related in diverse ways with others, it is not immediately obvious that the conditions proposed are correct. It need be no more obvious than it is obvious right off the bat that there is no greatest prime number. We can then test the proposal against judgments in cases where we have filled in details that may be thought to be relevant to whether the conditions are sufficient. The process has the familiar pattern of observation, hypothesis, prediction, and test, with the role of observation played by judgments with respect to scenarios in thought experiments, that is, judgments about entailment relations.

Thus, while the judgments we make, if properly based, are expressions of our competence, and are thus a priori, the analysis is often based on a form of inference to the best explanation. We may be able, once the proposal is formulated, to see directly that it is correct. In many cases, however, confidence that we have a correct analysis rests on the claim that we have surveyed representative cases and not overlooked anything important. In these cases, the justification we have is in part a posteriori (see Henderson and Horgan 2001). In this respect, though, philosophy seems no worse off than mathematics. Confidence that Peano's axioms axiomatize the natural numbers rests in part on their entailing classical results.

Problems in conducting thought experiments arise from at least three sources:

Problems of design. A well-designed thought experiment has (a) a clearly characterized target proposition, (b) a clear, unambiguously described scenario, which constitutes a test case, and which is complete in the respects relevant to the test, and (c) a clear, unambiguous test question relevant to the target proposition (see Ludwig 2007, §2, for an example that fails these conditions).

Problems of execution. The subject should have a clear understanding of (a) the purpose of the thought experiment, (b) the scenario, (c) the questions, and (d) the possible responses, including the response that insufficient information is given or that a presupposition of the thought experiment is not met, and (e) the answer to the question understood literally should be based solely on conceptual competence.

Problems of presupposition. A thought experiment, perforce couched in language, presupposes that the words used express concepts, and that competence in their use involves grasp of the concepts they express. This presupposition fails for natural kind terms (see the concluding section, "Is 'Knowledge' a Natural Kind Term?") and for words that are semantically defective, as in the case of vagueness and the semantic paradoxes (Ludwig and Ray 2002).

We can check judgments by how they fit with other cases, with judgments by others (who are good "observers"), by fit with well-developed accounts in surrounding areas, and by various theoretical considerations. Withdrawing a judgment, we seek to explain the mistake and re-evaluate the case so as to see it in a different light. This is a form of the method of reflective equilibrium.

Reflective equilibrium is criticized sometimes for providing only internal justification (Stich 1988), and so being subject to the objection that there can be conflicting but equally coherent sets of judgments. But the suggestion is not that coherence makes for justification. The assumption underlying the method of reflective equilibrium in conceptual analysis is that most of the judgments we make under optimal conditions will be correct. We employ similar methods to correct mistakes about memory: on the assumption that we remember mostly accurately, we test cases by how well they cohere with the rest and with general knowledge; where our own resources give out we can appeal to others. Why accept the assumption in the case of thought experiments? First, to think about a subject matter requires being competent in the deployment of the relevant concepts. This guarantees that we are in a position to make correct judgments about scenarios in thought experiments. Second, while it is consistent with this that in practice we typically fail to express our competences, there is (a) no special reason to think that this is so and (b) the supposition that we get it wrong generally throws all inquiry into doubt, since it undermines confidence that we can assess evidence for any hypothesis, including the skeptical one.

I turn to two objections to the traditional use of thought experiments in epistemology. The first objection challenges the reliability of relying on one's own conceptual competence. Here I distinguish two charges. The more radical is that "intuitions" are relative to such things as cultural or socio-economic background, and that in consequence "it is wrong for philosophers to assume a priori the universal validity of their own ... intuitions" (Machery *et al.* 2004, B8). The less radical is that given individual fallibility, a more reliable method of tracking correct responses is to take up the survey methods of the social sciences. The second objection is that most of the terms of interest in epistemology are natural kind terms, so that thought experiments at best reveal e.g., the stereotype of knowledge and not its essence.

What are the lessons of experimental philosophy?

I cannot discuss in detail the now large literature surrounding experimental philosophy. But I wish to urge two points. First, surveys of undergraduate responses to thought experiments go very little way toward calling into question philosophical practice. Second, coming to a view from one's own perspective is ultimately necessary to assess such surveys and also essential to the aim of philosophy.

I begin with the charge that "cognitive diversity" across cultures or socio-economic groups undermines the probative value of thought experiments. Among the many papers in the genre I will focus for illustration on one that has attained the status of a classic in the field, "Epistemic Intuitions and Normativity" by Weinberg *et al.* (2001).[14]

Weinberg *et al.* characterize an epistemic intuition as "a spontaneous judgment about the epistemic properties of some specific case—a judgment for which the person making the judgment may be able to offer no plausible justification" (2001, 19). They then adduce evidence to show that "epistemic intuition" so characterized varies, for example, across cultural groups. The evidence consists in survey data of undergraduates responding to probes involving thought experiments that have appeared in the philosophical literature such as Gettier cases, Dretske's zebra case (1970, 1015–16), and Lehrer's Trutemp case (2000, 187). In the case of some probes, there were differences in majority responses across Westerners,

East Asians, and students from the Indian subcontinent. For example, in the case of a probe about a "Gettier case" involving Bob's thinking Jill owns a Buick and so an American car, though she recently replaced it with a Pontiac, students were asked whether Bob really knows or only believes Jill drives an American car. Seventy-four percent of Westerners said Bob only believes Jill drives an American car, whereas 57 percent of East Asians and 61 percent of the students from the Indian subcontinent said Bob really knows that she does. Thus, it looks as if "epistemic intuitions" and therefore concepts of knowledge must differ across cultures.

An initial mistake here confuses the issues. "Epistemic intuition" is given a stipulative definition as a spontaneous judgment about epistemic properties for which the person making it may be able to offer no plausible justification. But the method of thought experiments calls on us to respond on the basis solely of our understanding of the scenario and the question asked about it. Given this, and that concepts individuate the thoughts they are involved in, it is clear that there could be no relativity of the target response to cultural background or anything else, and no sense in which the concept of knowledge could differ across cultures. The most that relativity of response to cultural background or other factors could show (assuming shared concepts) is that there are errors traceable to something connected with those differences. This need not involve errors in the application of concepts, for it may involve errors in understanding the task, or differences in how unarticulated details are filled in, affected by different background assumptions, or ways of taking a question or statement. In the probe involving Bob and Jill, for example, if one assumes that most Americans who own an American car buy American cars generally, one might think Bob knows this also and so is justified in believing that Jill drives an American car independently of being justified in believing that she is now driving a Buick.[15]

But so what? So what if the varied responses of undergraduates to these questions can't all be taken to be judgments based on conceptual competence in response to the scenario, task, and questions, properly understood? Isn't the problem now that this just shows that *none of us* are very good at saying when one thing follows from another?

How could it show this? We know, after all, the correct answer in Gettier cases (properly described). The results show students, even a majority in some cases, can make mistakes, but we knew that. Does every mistake on a homework assignment in logic shake the foundations of the subject? No, not even if every student makes the same mistake. Analysis is a cognitive skill. It can be inculcated. It draws on basic shared competencies. But that doesn't entail everyone is equally good at it, or good at it right off the bat. Students are often not very good at recognizing deductive validity, or in solving math problems, or elementary probabilistic reasoning. But many get better at it. They don't acquire new concepts, but get better at exercising them systematically, and beyond the usual range of cases they confront, and at a host of other related cognitive skills.[16]

What would show trouble? It can't be a general skepticism about our ability to recognize when one thing follows from another. That undermines all inquiry, including inquiry aimed at casting doubt on our abilities. Doubts about thought experiments in philosophy have to focus on something specific to them. But there is no special reason to think that we cannot identify entailment relations when we put a query about an entailment in the form of a thought experiment.[17] While as in any investigation there are methodological problems, we have also developed sophisticated tools for dealing with them (work on logical form and conversational pragmatics for example). Thought experiments should be approached with those tools in hand, and placed in the context of other thought experiments as well as theoretical considerations, both from within the field and from other fields. (For a case study, see the discussion of trying in Ludwig 2007, 145–46; see also Cullen 2010, for discussion of pitfalls in conducting surveys involving thought experiments.)

I turn now from these general skeptical concerns to the thought that, perhaps precisely because of the problem of identifying probative responses, we should move away from a first-person methodology to a third-person methodology.

It would be a mistake to dismiss how most people respond to surveys as completely irrelevant. One might even be encouraged by reflection on the Condorcet jury theorem to think that with enough participants, the probability that the majority is right becomes greater than that any individual is right. But as already noted, we can't take it for granted either. The Condorcet jury theorem assumes that everyone in the relevant class has a positive bias toward truth on the matter in hand and makes independent judgments (Dietrich and List 2004). The prevalence of the gambler's fallacy, as well as the mistakes students make on surveys about Gettier cases, shows this does not always obtain. We cannot assume most people are good at drawing relevant distinctions, or have the facility for the type of thinking involved. We cannot assume that most people are armed against the various pitfalls in conducting thought experiments. And for untutored or untrained subjects, we can't assume task understanding, even when we think we have explained the task clearly.

Ultimately, to assess whether the majority response on a survey is correct, we need to have an independent view of the matter. We need to have insight ourselves into the correct answer. That is how we detect the fallacy in the gambler's fallacy. Furthermore, this independent view of the right response is exactly the kind of understanding that we seek in philosophy. Just as our interest in mathematics would not be served by knowing merely that a certain theorem was true because a majority of mathematicians endorsed it, so our interests in philosophy would not be served merely by knowing that a certain claim is true because most people endorse it. We want to see why it is true, to understand it ourselves. This is the most fundamental reason why surveys cannot replace the first-person approach to conceptual analysis.[18]

Is "knowledge" a natural kind term?

The general question facing us is whether the family of epistemic terms such as "knowledge," "truth," "evidence," "justification," "warrant," and the like, are all natural kind terms like "gold," "air," "water," "tiger," "gene," etc., discovery of whose real essences requires empirical investigation, or whether they are like "number," "circle," "cylinder," "necessity," and "logical consequence," whose essence is revealed in reflecting on our grasp of the application conditions of the concepts they express. It is beyond the scope of this chapter to take up the question with respect to all epistemic terms. I will restrict attention to "knowledge," which may be the best case for the hypothesis.

What are natural kind terms?

Let's take "gold" as our example. If (1) is true, then (1N) is true, but (1) is also, it seems, an empirical discovery. Thus, it seems to be both necessary and a posteriori.

(1)   Gold is an element with atomic number 79.

(1N)   Necessarily, gold is an element with atomic number 79.

How do the characteristic features of natural kind terms give rise to the view that (1), if true, expresses a necessary a posteriori truth?

We should distinguish natural kinds from natural kind terms. A natural kind we may take to be a stable explanatory kind relative to some range of phenomena. A natural kind term like "gold" is embedded in a practice which treats its purpose as that of "picking out" a natural kind, but not by way of our having been given the relevant property. The practice doesn't directly give us the kind but rather (a) involves a basis for the application of the term to objects or phenomena, (b) an explanatory relation the kind is to bear to the basis of application in at least most of the objects we apply it to, and (c) thereby a mode of identifying the kind the term is to pick out, as, roughly, the kind, if any, which provides the best explanation of the relevant sort for the basis of its application in most actual cases (the kind property), and, possibly, (d) a default option for what the term picks out if there is no kind which explains the basis of its application in most actual cases (the default property). Competence in the use of the term, in the sense of counting socially as having mastered the practice, amounts to learning, along with its grammatical category, its role as picking out a natural kind, the basis of application, and the explanatory relation it is to bear to (most of) the instances picked out on its basis of application, and the default option. For "gold," the basis of application includes being (in typical circumstances of application) a malleable incorruptible yellow metal that dissolves in aqua regia. The intended explanatory relevance relation is something on the order of constitutive explanation, and for a kind to bear this relation to the basis of application of the term "gold" is for it to explain in virtue of the structure of the items to which the term is applied those features of it which constitute its basis of application. (Details won't matter so much as the form of the account.)

"Gold" is a mass noun like "snow" or "flesh" or "garbage." In logical form, mass nouns contribute predicates (Koslicki 1999). Thus, I represent (1) as having the form: For all x such that x is gold, x is an element with atomic number 79. The predicate "is gold" then is used to attribute a property to an object. But the property it is intended to attribute is not given by the basis of application, but rather is the relevant kind property, if any, and otherwise the default property. Suppose that the relevant kind property for the term "gold" is being an element with atomic number 79. Then: the truth conditions for "For all x such that x is gold, x is an element with atomic number 79" are given by "For all x such that x is an element with atomic number 79, x is an element with atomic number 79," and that is necessarily true. However, it is clear that empirical inquiry is required in order to identify the relevant kind. It therefore appears that "Gold is an element with atomic number 79" expresses a necessary, a posteriori truth.

What proposition is expressed by "Gold is an element with atomic number 79"? If we mean what determines the truth conditions for (1), "gold" contributes, not anything having to do with its basis, but instead the property it attributes. If that is being an element with atomic number 79, then the proposition is that anything that is an element with atomic number 79 is an element with atomic number 79. That proposition is a conceptual truth—indeed, it is true in virtue of its structure alone. A proposition is a priori if someone who grasps it is in a position to judge it correctly. By this standard, the proposition expressed by (1) is an a priori conceptual truth. And as the property attributed by "gold" is fixed by what kind explains its basis of application, so is the concept expressed by it, in the sense of "concept" on which concepts are individuated by their contributions to the truth conditions of thought contents. (1) then turns out not to be a counterexample to only a priori truths being necessary. It expresses a logical and hence conceptual truth. The necessity involved in (1N) is old and familiar, not new and exotic.

Of course something here requires empirical investigation: what we didn't know is that the stuff to which we apply "gold" properly on its basis of application is for the most part something the fundamental constituent property of which is being an element with atomic number 79. That is, we didn't know prior to investigation what property "gold" attributes (or what concept, in the relevant sense, it expresses). And this is the same as saying that what required empirical work was discovery of what proposition "Gold is an element with atomic number 79" expresses.

This is no help, however, with the methodological challenge to epistemology. For it is clear that given the way "gold" is introduced, we cannot discover what (what we call) gold is without empirical investigation. Therefore, to the extent to which a domain of discourse that attracts philosophical interest traffics in natural kind terms, to that extent also traditional methods that presuppose grasp of the thoughts expressed by sentences in the domain of discourse are inapplicable. I turn now to the question whether "knowledge" in particular is a natural kind term.

Is "knowledge" a natural kind term?

One might be tempted to argue that "knowledge" is a natural kind term because knowledge is a natural kind: "There is a robust phenomenon of human knowledge and a presupposition of the field of epistemology is that cases of knowledge have a good deal of theoretical unity to them; they are not merely some gerrymandered kind, united by nothing more than our willingness to regard them as a kind" (Kornblith 2002, 10). From this we might pass to the thought that since "[u]nderstanding what that theoretical unity is is the object of our study ... it is to be found by careful examination of the phenomenon, that is, something outside of us, not our concept of the phenomenon, something inside us. In short, ... the investigation of knowledge, and philosophical investigation generally [should be pursued] on the model of investigations of natural kinds" (11). The suggestion that we should not examine our concept of knowledge but the phenomenon itself suggests that the claim that "the investigation of knowledge" should be pursued "on the model of investigations of natural kinds" is to be construed as the claim that we should treat it as on the model of the investigation into the natures of things we picked out with natural kind terms. Thus, it is natural to take the intent here to be expressible in the following argument (even if not Kornblith's intent, this will clear the ground).

(1)   For any kind *K* expressible using a term *T*, if kind *K* is a natural kind, then term *T* is a natural kind term.

(2)   Knowledge is a natural kind.

(3)   Knowledge is expressible using "knowledge."

(4)   Therefore, "knowledge" is a natural kind term.

But the argument is unsound because the first premise is false. "Gold" is a natural kind term, and gold is a natural kind, namely, the element with atomic number 79. However, "element with atomic number 79," which picks out the same natural kind, is not a natural kind term. Thus, it doesn't follow from knowledge being a natural kind that "knowledge" is a natural kind term. And it doesn't follow from something's being a natural kind that we don't possess the concept of it in the sense that puts us in a position to specify what its essential nature is (to the extent possible) by analysis.[19]

We might at this point entertain other indirect arguments. But the claim that "knowledge" is a natural kind term is a claim about its use in the language. So let us instead ask directly how to test whether a term is a natural kind term.

A good test is provided by the kind of thought experiment Putnam used to bring out what's special about our practice with respect to terms like "water" and "gold" in the first place (1975). A hallmark of a natural kind term is that what property it attributes is fixed by what explanatory kind if any actually explains the features that constitute its basis of application in the samples to which we apply it. Fixing the practice, if the underlying kind that explains the features had been different, then the property attributed, and the propositions expressed by sentences containing it, would have been different. And if there were no underlying kind that explained the basis of its application, then either it would track a default property if provision is made for it, or not attribute any property at all, and so no sentence containing the term in a use position would express a proposition. We can then test the hypothesis by considering a circumstance in which a community of individuals associates with "knowledge" the same linguistic practices as we do, but where there are salient differences in the states they pick out which suffice for us to judge them not to constitute knowledge, though those states explain the basis for their application of "knowledge" to them. We then ask whether when they call those states "knowledge" they are speaking truly, as the hypothesis predicts.

Consider a possible circumstance in which we have doppelgängers who are bodies in vats (BIVs) in the style, say, of the 1999 film *The Matrix* by the Wachowski brothers. A supercomputer tracks outputs and regulates inputs to their brains (or bodies if you like), and generates coordinated experiences so as to take into account outputs from brains in determining, relative to the plan of the fictitious world they are presented with, inputs to other BIVs. For example, when it seems to my doppelgänger that another is speaking or moving, that is because the other's motor cortex is firing in a way that would be appropriate for that, and that in turn, through the mechanism of the supercomputer, generates inputs of the sort that generate in my doppelgänger experiences of the requisite sort for a body moving in the appropriate ways. The BIVs are therefore partly causally responsible for the co-evolution of their experiences. Their dispositions with respect to language use are to be exactly the same as ours, as is, modulo references to the self and time, the course of their experiences. They can, in a fairly straightforward sense, carry on "conversations" about "what goes on around them" (we can even imagine they move their lips and utter sounds, though otherwise immobile in their vats). I stipulate that we know that the actual world is not like this. The point is not to raise any skeptical worry about our own knowledge, but to test a linguistic hypothesis. *We* will judge (correctly) that *they* would not know very much at all, since most of their beliefs are false.[20] The question to focus on, however, is whether, for example, when my BIV doppelgänger says or thinks "Jones knows a lot about Volkswagens" he is (a) speaking the truth, (b) speaking falsely, or (c) not expressing a proposition at all. The hypothesis that "knowledge" is a natural kind term would seem to predict either (a) or (c).[21]

The states (in themselves and others) that most of their uses of "knowledge" would track would be states that are reliably connected, not with what they are about, but with features of the supercomputer that realize its model of the illusory world which their experiences represent to them (and perhaps certain other features corresponding to internalist constraints on knowledge—throw in whatever else seems relevant). For convenience, let us sum up these features pertaining to the proposition that p as the illusion that p. Now we can ask: when my BIV doppelgänger says "Jones knows a lot about Volkswagens" does he speak truly in his language? Is the proposition expressed by his sentence expressed in our language by "Jones is in a belief state that is caused by a process that reliably produces belief that p in circumstances in which Jones is presented with the illusion that p, and ... "? Alternatively, does he express no proposition at all?

On the face of it, neither of these suggestions has any plausibility. Were it us in that situation, and we were to wake up, as it were, and find we could leave the vats, and learned of what had happened, and were instructed in what our use of "knowledge" had actually tracked, what would we think or say? Would we say (in the language that we would in those circumstances speak): "We no longer have any knowledge but we used to"? Would we say: we were speaking neither truly nor falsely when we claimed such things as "Many people know where they live"? Or would we say: "We did not previously have any knowledge but thankfully we now do"? If we would say the latter, even given that we believe that "knowledge" formerly tracked states that were reliably produced by illusions, then we would be expressing allegiance to a practice that is incompatible with treating "knowledge" as a natural kind term. It is very clear that we would in fact say the latter, and it is very clear that this is exactly what our BIV doppelgängers (who have our linguistic dispositions) would say. But this is not what the hypothesis that "knowledge" is a natural kind term predicts.

I will leave it as an exercise to the reader to construct further test cases, but the preliminary result is that whether or not knowledge is a natural kind, "knowledge" is not a natural kind term. I dare say this is not much of a surprise. It was not to be expected that epistemic concepts, which must form the framework for our thinking about the rational investigation of any subject matter, should themselves be outsourced to the world that we are investigating.

Notes

1 I have in mind truth conditions in the sense in which we say that "*p*" in "*s* is true iff *p*" gives the truth conditions of *s* iff "*p*" translates *s*.

2 This is intended to capture the core of a traditional view that in one form goes back at least to Frege. See Peacocke 1992 for one presentation of the general form of the idea, and Chalmers and Jackson 2001 for another.

3 Most of Williamson's arguments against epistemic conceptions of analyticity in 2007, ch. 4, aim to show that grasp of conceptual truths is insufficient for assent or disposition to assent. I don't know that anyone ever maintained otherwise. He considers only one proposal for an epistemic approach in the last pages of the chapter, and gives a schematic and unconvincing argument against it, but in any case it is not the proposal advanced here.

4 Goldman suggests competence views may be alright in theory but little help in practice (2010, 135), but the truth is that we have made a lot of progress in conceptual clarification in non-ideal conditions.

5 Contrary to what is sometimes suggested (Stich 1988; Ramsey 1998), there is nothing in so-called prototype concepts per se incompatible with the tradition in analysis. Goldman makes this point (2007, 23).

6 I elide discussion of what must be an integral part of the overall project when we confront the fact that our access to the structures of thoughts relies on the analysis of the structure of the sentences we use to express them, namely, that a first step is analysis of the logical form of the domains of discourse we are interested in.

7 See Ludwig 2007, 131; McGinn 2012, ch. 5. Semantic descent is not a recent discovery.

8 Kornblith writes, for example: "If concepts are psychologically real, and also ... there is a well established tradition in experimental psychology that studies them, then what room is left for the armchair methods of philosophers, methods designed to illuminate the very same target?" (2007, 30).

9 Except when it takes the form of statistical studies of patterns of application of concepts to things in the context of subjects seeking to say what is true. This takes us in the direction of experimental philosophy, which I discuss below ("What Are the Lessons of Experimental Philosophy?").

10 Both Ramsey (1998) and Cummins (1998) seem to make this mistake. I detect this thought in Kornblith (2007, 37) as well.

11 This answers the paradox of analysis. Grasp of concepts is *competence in correct deployment*. An analysis is a proposition we come to know *on the basis of exercising competence in the concepts deployed* in it. See McGinn 2012, ch. 4, and Strawson 1992, 5–13, for essentially the same account; a similar line can be found in Fumerton 1983, and earlier in Myers 1971.

12 I have avoided the word "intuition." While I have a position (Ludwig 2010), given the dust raised by extensive debate about the word, it seems best avoided in favor of an independent characterization of what we are interested in. See Nagel 2007 for a historical review. Recently, Herman Cappelen has argued through case studies that philosophers do not rely on intuitions, including in this judgments based on conceptual competence (Cappelen 2012). In my view, Cappelen is looking too hard for metaphilosophical remarks in philosophers' texts. Though Vogel in the passage quoted doesn't talk about intuitions or conceptual analysis, the fact is the article is part of an ongoing discussion understood to be concerned with the analysis of (the concept of) knowledge.

13 Perhaps this itself has an air of illegitimate bootstrapping, for this reasoning is itself presented as resting on our understanding of the contained concepts, and there seems to be no higher court of appeal (Cummins 1998). But this is true of every fundamental source of justified belief (Goldman 2007, 5).

14 In the same vein see Nichols *et al.* 2003; Alexander and Weinberg 2007; Swain *et al.* 2008. See Ludwig 2010 for further discussion of the 2001 paper.

15 I draw attention to this (rather obvious) point in my 2010; Sosa (2008) made the point earlier.

16 One response is that it is an empirical matter whether philosophers theorize better with the aid of thought experiments than undergraduates (Weinberg *et al.* 2010). Yes, but survey results give us no reason to think otherwise. See Williamson 2011. In any case, resolution of the challenge presupposes we can come to a correct view. But who are we going ask about this? In this connection, see the next note. For a response that draws on empirical work, see Nagel 2012.

17 Weinberg (2007) argues, not that there is special reason to doubt the reliability of the method of thought experiments, but rather that it is defective because not open to independent error correction. For a response, see Grundmann 2010.

18 On a different view, experimental philosophy aims merely "to provide an account of the factors that influence applications of a concept, and in particular, the internal psychological processes that underlie such applications" (Knobe and Nichols 2008, 5). On this view, experimental philosophy doesn't aim to engage in or undermine conceptual analysis, but to help identify pitfalls in conducting thought experiments. It is hard to see any objection to or in this.

19 Goldman has suggested that it is incompatible with philosophical practice that knowledge is a natural kind (2007, 8; 2005). But the practice doesn't rule it out. A natural kind we pick out by a natural kind term doesn't cease to be one when we discover the kind property—but when we do, we grasp its concept. The standard practice seems incompatible with "knowledge" being a natural kind term, which is evidence against the claim. But I will suggest we can test the hypothesis more directly below.

20 I don't think that a form of externalism about thought content that undermines the description of the scenario is correct. But, in any case, the hypothesis should predict a result even relative to the hypothesis that externalism about thought content is false.

21 Perhaps one could appeal to a default property, but it is a mystery what it could be.

References

Alexander, Joshua and Jonathan Weinberg (2007) "Analytic Epistemology and Experimental Philosophy," *Philosophy Compass* 2: 56–80.

Burge, Tyler (1979) "Individualism and the Mental," *Midwest Studies in Philosophy* 4: 73–121.

Cappelen, Herman (2012) *Philosophy without Intuitions*, Oxford: Oxford University Press.

Chalmers, David and Frank Jackson (2001) "Conceptual Analysis and Reductive Explanation," *Philosophical Review* 110(3): 315–60.

Cullen, Simon (2010) "Survey-Driven Romanticism," *Review of Philosophy and Psychology* 1(2): 275–96.

Cummins, Robert (1998) "Reflection on Reflective Equilibrium," in M. DePaul and W. Ramsey (eds), *Rethinking Intuition: The Psychology of Intuition and Its Role in Philosophical Inquiry*, New York: Rowman & Littlefield.

Davidson, Donald (2001) "Radical Interpretation," in *Inquiries into Truth and Interpretation*, New York: Clarendon Press. Original edition, 1973.

Dietrich, Franz and Christian List (2004) "A Model of Jury Decisions Where All Jurors Have the Same Evidence," *Synthese* 142: 175–202.

Dretske, Fred (1970) "Epistemic Operators," *Journal of Philosophy* 67(24): 1007–23.

Fumerton, Richard A. (1983) "The Paradox of Analysis," *Philosophy and Phenomenological Research* 43(4): 477–97.

Goldman, Alan (2005) "Kornblith's Naturalistic Epistemology," *Philosophy and Phenomenological Research* 71: 403–10.

——(2007) "Philosophical Intuitions," *Grazer Philosophische Studien* 74: 1–26.

——(2010) "Philosophical Naturalism and Intuitional Methodology," *Proceedings of the American Philosophical Association* 84(2): 115–50.

Grundmann, Thomas (2010) "Some Hope for Intuitions: A Reply to Weinberg," *Philosophical Psychology* 23(4): 481–509.

Henderson, David and Terry Horgan (2001) "The A Priori Isn't All It Is Cracked Up to Be, But It Is Something," *Philosophical Topics* 29: 219–50.

Klein, Peter (1971) "A Proposed Definition of Propositional Knowledge," *Journal of Philosophy* 66(16): 471–82.

Knobe, Joshua and Aruda Burra (2006) "Experimental Philosophy and Folk Concepts: Methodological Considerations," *Journal of Cognition and Culture* 6 (1–2): 331–42.

Knobe, Joshua Michael and Shaun Nichols (2008) *Experimental Philosophy*, Oxford: Oxford University Press.

Kornblith, Hilary (2002) *Knowledge and Its Place in Nature*, Oxford: Clarendon Press.

——(2007) "Naturalism and Intuitions," *Grazer Philosophische Studien* 74: 27–49.

Koslicki, Kathrin (1999) "The Semantics of Mass-Predicates," *Noûs* 33: 46–91.

Lehrer, Keith (2000) *Theory of Knowledge*, 2nd edn, Dimensions of Philosophy, Boulder, CO: Westview Press.

Ludwig, Kirk (2007) "The Epistemology of Thought Experiments: First Person versus Third Person Approaches," *Midwest Studies in Philosophy* 31: 128–59.

——(2010) "Intuitions and Relativity," *Philosophical Psychology* 23(4): 427–45.

Ludwig, Kirk and Greg Ray (2002) "Vagueness and the Sorites Paradox," *Philosophical Perspectives* 36(16): 419–46.

Machery, E., R. Mallon, S. Nichols and S. Stich (2004) "Semantics, Cross-cultural Style," *Cognition* 92: B1–B12.

McGinn, Colin (2012) *Truth by Analysis: Games, Names and Philosophy*, Oxford: Oxford University Press.

Myers, C. Mason (1971) "Moore's Paradox of Analysis," *Metaphilosophy* 2(4): 295–308.

Nagel, Jennifer (2007) "Epistemic Intuitions," *Philosophy Compass* 2(6): 792–819.

——(2012) "Intuitions and Experiments: A Defence of the Case Method in Epistemology," *Philosophy and Phenomenological Research* 85(3): 495–527.

Nichols, Shaun, Stephen Stich and Jonathan M. Weinberg (2003) "Meta-Skepticism: Meditations in Ethno-epistemology," in S. Luper (ed.), *The Skeptics: Contemporary Essays*, Aldershot: Ashgate.

Peacocke, Christopher (1992) *A Study of Concepts*, Cambridge, MA: MIT Press.

Putnam, Hilary (1975) "The Meaning of 'Meaning,'" in *Mind, Language and Reality: Philosophical Papers*, Cambridge: Cambridge University Press.

Quine, W.V. (1986) *Philosophy of Logic*, 2nd edn, Cambridge, MA: Harvard University Press.

——(1953) "Two Dogmas of Empiricism," in *From a Logical Point of View*, Cambridge, MA: Harvard University Press.

Ramsey, William (1998) "Prototypes and Conceptual Analysis," in M. DePaul and W. Ramsey (eds), *Rethinking Intuition: The Psychology of Intuition and Its Role in Philosophical Inquiry*, New York: Rowman & Littlefield.

Sosa, Ernest (2008) "A Defense of the Use of Intuitions in Philosophy," in M. Bishop and D. Murphy (eds), *Stich and His Critics*, Oxford: Blackwell.

Stich, S. (1988) "Reflective Equilibrium, Analytic Epistemology and the Problem of Cognitive Diversity," *Synthese* 74(3): 391–413.

Strawson, Peter (1992) *Analysis and Metaphysics: An Introduction to Philosophy*, New York: Oxford University Press.

Swain, Stacy, Joshua Alexander and Jonathan Weinberg (2008) "The Instability of Philosophical Intuitions: Running Hot and Cold on Truetemp," *Philosophy and Phenomenological Research* 76: 138–55.

Vogel, Jonathan (2000) "Reliabilism Leveled," *Journal of Philosophy* 97(11): 602–23.

Weinberg, Jonathan (2007) "How to Challenge Intuitions Empirically without Risking Skepticism," *Midwest Studies in Philosophy* 31: 318–43.

Weinberg, Jonathan, Chad Gonnerman, Cameron Buckner and Joshua Alexander (2010) "Are Philosophers Expert Intuiters?," *Philosophical Psychology* 23(3): 331–55.

Weinberg, Jonathan, Shaun Nichols and Stephen Stich (2001) "Normativity and Epistemic Intuitions," *Philosophical Topics* 29: 429–60.

Williamson, Timothy (2007) *The Philosophy of Philosophy*, Malden, MA: Blackwell.
——(2011) "Philosophical Expertise and the Burden of Proof," *Metaphilosophy* 42(3): 215–29.
Wittgenstein, Ludwig (1961) *Tractatus Logico-Philosophicus*, ed. D.F. Pears and B.F. McGuinness, London: Routledge & Kegan Paul. Original edn, 1921.

Part III

METHODS IN PHILOSOPHY
OF LANGUAGE AND PHILOSOPHY
OF MIND

14 The possibility of a naturalistic Cartesianism regarding intuitions and introspection

GEORGES REY

No doubt, intuitions deserve respect, ... [but] informants, oneself included, can be quite awful at saying what it is that drives their intuitions. ... It is always up for grabs what an intuition is an intuition of.

(Fodor 1998, 86, quoted in Bach 2002, 32)

1 Introduction

There has been much discussion recently about philosophical methodology and, specifically, about the status of so-called "intuitions" to which philosophers and linguists sometimes appeal on behalf of various claims. So-called "Cartesians" claim intuitions and introspection provide special, peculiarly reliable, often empirically incorrigible evidence for linguistic theories and for philosophically significant views such as the "Cogito," theses about the nature of much mentality, or analyses of important concepts of e.g. substance, causality, consciousness, knowledge, freedom and truth. Anti-Cartesians reject all such special epistemic claims.

Anything is, of course, evidence of whatever best explains it. Complaints of "heartburn" can be evidence of an upset stomach, American Indian rabbit pots evidence of a supernova, and patterns of white noise evidence of the big bang.[1] Similarly, people's intuitive reactions could be due to explicit teaching, male domination, bits of philosophy or linguistics in the air, underlying conceptual and linguistic competencies, and maybe even to special insights into the nature of the respective domain. Everything depends upon what best explains them.

The only reason the question has seemed to involve more than this commonplace is that many traditional philosophers have pressed certain *sorts* of explanations of many intuitions and introspections. In this chapter, I want to consider some of these sorts, and argue that many Cartesians, as well as some of their opponents, underestimate the difficulty of the explanatory project. I don't intend to argue here that any of the traditional explanations on one side or the other are actually *mistaken*. To the contrary, I want to argue that we have reason to think that some versions of some of them may well be correct. But I also want to insist that we are not remotely in a position to *insist* that they are. What bothers me about the traditional views is not their falsity, but what strikes me as their "superficialism" about the mind, according to which the important distinctions about the mind are available at either its introspective or ordinary behavioral surface.[2] I want to urge that particularly the processes responsible even for privileged intuitions may be as hidden and only indirectly accessible as the processes posited in most any other serious science. Ironically enough, it's only by avoiding this superficialism that I think we can hope to legitimize surface Cartesian appeals.

I should emphasize, however, that the Cartesianism whose possibility I will be defending is a good deal more modest than its traditional adherents have had in mind. I make no claim for intuitions and introspections being indubitable or serving as the foundation of knowledge. Unlike Descartes, I think it's at least a conceptual possibility that we have *no attitudes at all*, and that it's a serious scientific possibility that there are no such things as the "consciousness" or "qualia" that people standardly take themselves to introspect (see Rey 1997, chs 3, 11). All I'm defending here is the serious possibility of some special intuitive knowledge of material in *some* specific domains, and *some* introspective knowledge of *some* propositional attitude states.

The relevant literature on the topic is of course vast, and I can't possibly do it justice in this short space. What I'll do is focus on some specific discussions: Laurence BonJour and George Bealer as representatives of Cartesianism, and Michael Devitt and Peter Carruthers as representatives of their opponents. I trust the moral of the discussion can be extended to other authors to whom I apologize for not including.

2 Traditional Cartesianism

Putting aside its historical roots in Descartes, what I regard as superficialism appears recently in Laurence BonJour's (1998) defense of "pure reason."[3] He regards a priori knowledge of a necessary truth as based upon

> an act of *rational insight* or *rational intuition* ... [that] is seemingly (a) direct or immediate, non-discursive, and yet also (b) intellectual or reason-governed ... [It] depends upon nothing beyond an understanding of the propositional content itself ... [It is] *rationally self-evident*.
>
> (102)

One might well wonder wherein such a "direct" intuitive grasp of the necessity of a proposition could possibly consist. Here BonJour supplements his remarks with an account of a person's grasp of meaning:

> The key claim of such a view would be that it is a necessary, quasi-logical fact that a thought instantiating a complex universal involving the universal triangularity in the appropriate way (about which much more would obviously need to be said) is about triangular things. In this way, the content of the thought would be non-contingently captured by the character of the mental act, and could accordingly be accessible to the thinker ...
>
> (184)

Of course, the "appropriate way" that a thought "instantiates a universal" is obviously different from the way an *object* enjoying the universal does: after all, thoughts about triangularity aren't themselves triangular. Here BonJour invokes a distinction from Aquinas between *esse intentionale* and *esse naturale*, whereby e.g.,

> the form triangularity informs my mind in a special way that is different from the way in which it informs triangular things.
>
> (183)

These different ways actually give rise to "distinct, though presumably intimately related universals" (183). BonJour does acknowledge the need of "some more articulate account ... of the two universals and the relation between them" (184), but confesses that, despite "the venerable history of this kind of view" (185), this is "something that is not found in Aquinas – or, so far as I know, anywhere in that tradition" (184).[4]

However these "intimately related universals" are supposed to work, BonJour hopes to explain the (supposed) *a priori* incompatibility of e.g. being red and green, by appeal to them:

> Given [my] understanding of the ingredients of the proposition, I am able to see or grasp in a seemingly direct and unmediated way that the claim in question cannot fail to be true – that the natures of redness and greenness are such as to preclude their being jointly realized. It is this direct insight into the necessity of the claim in question that seems, at least prima facie, to justify my accepting it as true.
>
> (101)

The only point I want to make about BonJour's proposal at this point is not that it is particularly mistaken (though I suspect it is), but only that it involves extravagant speculations remote from any serious psychology, based almost entirely on the superficial appearances of thought and reason. One can readily agree that it certainly *seems* to many of us that we are "directly acquainted" with red and green themselves and their incompatibility. The question is whether there's any good explanatory reason to take this seeming seriously. Outside of philosophical insistence, I know of none. No current program of research in psychology begins to posit the phenomena BonJour is proposing. To the contrary, psychologists routinely deny that there are in fact any objective color properties into which they or anyone can have any special insight (see e.g. Palmer 1999, 97).

Somewhat less extravagantly, George Bealer (1998, 207–8) defends intuition as

> a *sui generis*, irreducible, natural (i.e. non-Cambridge-like) propositional attitude that occurs episodically. … Intuition is an "intellectual seeming," [just as] perception is a sensory seeming (an appearing).

As such, they have the following important role to play:

> Philosophical investigation and argument approximate the following idealization: canvassing intuitions, subjecting those intuitions to dialectical critique, constructing theories that systematize the surviving intuitions, and so on until equilibrium is approached. This procedure resembles the procedure of seeking "reflective equilibrium" but differs from it crucially. In the latter procedure, an equilibrium among beliefs – including empirical beliefs – is sought. In the present procedure, an equilibrium among intuitions is sought.
>
> (205–6)

Now, again, Bealer may well be right that there are such intuitions, and that something interesting might be gained from systematizing them. We certainly have strong *prima facie* evidence that this is true in the case of logic and mathematics, which do appear to be peculiarly self-contained. But the case of intuitions in *philosophy* more generally is notoriously fraught: scientists have drawn attention to empirical assumptions about e.g. space, time, causation and perception, that have been claimed to be *a priori*, but have turned out to be empirically refutable, and sometimes refuted, which led Quine (1953) to raise serious skeptical doubts about the entire category. In view of this manifest instability, it's hard to see how Bealer would be entitled to press his claims until he's done some serious psychology that might establish there's a faculty here to be trusted. And, short of knowing pretty much the whole of psychology, it's hard to see how to establish that it's *sui generis*, "irreducible" (whatever that means these days), and "natural (non-Cambridge-like)," since so many things in psychology, e.g. color perception, phonology, very many "folk" concepts, are strikingly *un*natural, "Cambridge"-(or *grue-*)like, and completely arbitrary from the point of view of any other science. The important task here ought not to be to "systematize" possibly mistaken intuitions in order to achieve an equilibrium among them (one doesn't, after all, go out of one's way to *systematize* perceptual intuitions), but, again, to go beyond the superficial appearance of "rational intuitions" and *explain* them in a way that gives us reason to trust them, or discard ones that are unreliable (I'll return to Bealer's proffered explanation in Section 3.3).

It is worth comparing Bealer's posit of a faculty of rational intuition with an analogous posit of the philosopher and fellow armchair psychologist, Alvin Plantinga. Plantinga (2000) claims on behalf of his theological views that human beings are endowed with a special faculty, a *"sensus divinitatus,"* by means of which belief in God

> is triggered or occasioned by a wide variety of circumstances, including ... the marvelous, impressive beauty of the night sky; the timeless crash and roar of the surf that resonates deep within us; the majestic grandeur of the mountains ... , [and] awareness of guilt.
>
> (174–75)

However, aside from references to John Calvin, Plantinga provides no serious evidence for such an astonishing postulation, much less for its reliability about the relevant domain.[5]

A more extreme case that ought to at least give Plantinga and the traditional rationalist pause is that of the brilliant mathematician, John Nash, who was asked (while he was in his schizophrenic phase in a mental hospital), "How could you, a mathematician devoted to reason and logical proof ... how could you believe that extraterrestrials are sending you messages?" He replied:

> Because the ideas about supernatural beings came to me the same way that my mathematical ideas did. So I took them seriously.
>
> (Nasar 1998, 11, based on interview with George Mackey)

Again, my point in drawing attention to these claims is not to show that they are mistaken. For the purposes of this chapter, all of them might be true: there might be special extraterrestrial communication, a *sensus divinitatas*, and a *sui generis* rational intuition (in due course, I'll defend the serious possibility of this last). My concern here is only with the *empirically psychological nature of these claims*, and the lack of serious evidence adduced by Nash, Plantinga, BonJour or Bealer on behalf of them.

What sort of evidence would be germane?

2.1 Empirical worries about intuitions

Why are we justified in not taking Nash's claims seriously? Obviously, because in this case we *do* know enough about psychology and the natural world to know that knowledge of extraterrestrials is not obtainable in this way. There are better explanations of his ideas about them than that they are true. Here the psychology is not too hard. It is only slightly harder in the case of Plantinga's speculations (which, however, I won't pursue here[6]), and a lot harder in the case of Bealer's.

Indeed, the psychology of reasoning, reflection and introspection involves a now rapidly expanding empirical literature to which I only briefly refer.[7] Nisbett and Wilson (1977) adduced considerable experimental evidence that people are a lot less reliable about their own mental processes than they suppose, often taking themselves to be introspecting what can be demonstrated to be simply popular, folk theories of psychology, and efforts to "rationalize" their actions. Carruthers (2011) cites evidence of surprising confabulations that pass as introspections of even occurrent states (I'll discuss his view in §3.2 below). And, most famously, Kahneman and Tversky and others have demonstrated experimentally people's persistent susceptibility to various "cognitive illusions," e.g. disregard of base rates and "framing" inconsistencies, some of which may be irresolvable even on sustained reflection.[8]

Bealer dismisses all such empirical results, complaining that they "have not attempted to study intuitions in the relevant sense," not isolating

> intellectual (vs sensory) seemings that present themselves as necessary; distinct from "physical intuitions," thought experiments, beliefs, guesses, hunches, judgments, common sense, and memory ... and so forth. ... Clearly, it will be a delicate matter to design experiments that successfully test for such criteria.
> (1998, 213)

Now, it is probably true that neither Kahneman and Tversky nor any other psychologists have yet tested for all the issues Bealer reasonably raises about his target concern. But, then, neither has he. If it is such a delicate matter (as indeed it would be) to design experiments to control for these confounds, then that should be all the more reason to do more careful experimentation – not *none*, as Bealer recommends, in claiming the issue can be settled *a priori*!

2.2 Traditional motivations

Why is Bealer so confident about his view in advance of any experiments, especially in view of the disturbing results of many of the experiments already performed? Why in particular is he so confident that the thesis that intuitions have the indicated strong modal tie to the truth is a philosophical (conceptual) thesis not open to empirical confirmation or refutation[?] The defense of it is philosophical, ultimately resting on intuitions.

(Bealer: 1998, 202)

There seem to be two main philosophical worries driving Cartesians to such extreme views. One is that, without some special faculty of intuition, they fear modal truths would be unknowable. Kant famously claimed that "experience can only teach us about what does happen; only *a priori* reason can tell us about what must happen" (1787/1929, A1/B5). Along similar lines, Bealer writes, for example, that a denial of the *a priori*, like Quine's,

> fails to explain the status of our *modal* intuitions – arguably the most important class of intuitions for philosophy. Given Quinean arguments, no truly acceptable empirical theory would contain modals at all.
>
> (213; also 217)

Bealer is, of course, right that Quine was happy to dispense with modality. However, many of us who think Quine was onto something right about epistemology, don't think that his was the last word about his three *bêtes noires*: mind, meaning and modality. Indeed, it's perfectly reasonable to argue, on general Quinean epistemic grounds, that any adequate empirical theory of the world may well require all three. Given the failure of Quine and Skinner's behaviorism, psychology may well need mind and meaning, which in turn may require determinate intentionality; and all of science may require various forms of properties, intensionality, metaphysical probabilities, counterfactuals and modality.[9] Precisely the character of the modalities needed by science is, of course, not at all clear – it is by no means obvious that (*pace* Bealer 1998, 201) modality is any sort of unified phenomenon. But it would certainly appear to be a piece of ongoing empirical science to delineate precisely what's needed.[10]

Another motivation is a "foundationalist" one: without basic intuitions, knowledge would be impossible. Bealer regards intuitions, along with perception, as one of the "basic sources of evidence" (217–18), a view seconded by Gary Gutting:

> As I see it, despite their admittedly questionable status, intuitions still have a fundamental place in philosophy – indeed, in any effort to understand ourselves and our world. They represent *the inevitable starting point of any intellectual inquiry.*
>
> (1998, 8, emphasis mine)

However, for all the inadequacies of Quine's account of mind, meaning and modality, he seems to me to have been right about at least the provisional "starting point" for philosophy: until further notice, there's no "inevitable starting point," either in intuitions or (as Quine once quipped) in Ohio. We start in the middle of our Neurathian rafts, with an immense store of variously well and poorly articulated claims about ordinary objects, time, space, causality, material objects, number, minds, etc., any of which we might repair or replace while remaining afloat (although, of course, not all at once).

3 Quineanism

Most Quineans would probably leave it at that, and would agree with Michael Devitt (1996, 2) when he writes, in the spirit of Quine:

> there is only one way of knowing, the empirical way that is the basis of science (whatever way that may be).

Devitt takes this to be piece with his rejection of *a priori* knowledge, since he takes this only way of knowing to be Quine's global confirmation holism:

> with the recognition of the holistic nature of confirmation, we lack a strong motivation for thinking that mathematics and logic are immune from empirical revision.

Not surprisingly, he rejects any special role for the kind of intuitions to which BonJour and Bealer are appealing:

> We have no need to see philosophical intuitions as *a priori*. We can see them as being members of a general class of empirical intuitions.
>
> (Devitt 2011, 13)

Devitt rejects the *a priori* not because of his confidence in Quine's holistic account of knowledge, but chiefly because he finds the notion obscure:

> the whole idea of the *a priori* is too obscure for it to feature in a good explanation of our knowledge of anything. If this is right, we have a nice abduction: the best explanation of all knowledge is an empirical one.
>
> (21)

Against this charge of obscurity, I have elsewhere (Rey 1993, 1998) described the serious possibility that our logical competence is partly the result of an axiom-free, Gentzen-style natural deduction system that is wired into our brain. Intuitive judgments produced as a causal result of this competence would count as *a priori* knowledge since they would not be based on any experiential premises, but merely on applications of rules that are perspicuous to their user, absolutely reliable (producing truths in any world the person could possibly experience or inhabit), and, arguably, the constitutive basis of their competence with the contained operators.[11] This not being a paper on that topic, there is no need to rehearse that defense in full here. But I do want to press a certain methodological twist of that defense that will play a role in my analogous defense of Cartesianism.

The twist is this: although, as I've said, we do well at this point in history to *start* doing epistemology as pure Quinean holists, there is, *on those very grounds*, no guarantee that we will *end up* in that position: it can't, after all, be *a priori* that there's no *a priori*! Indeed, if epistemology is just a "chapter of natural science," then no one is in a position to say in advance whether or not a Quinean epistemology itself is in fact part of the right psychology for human beings, neither BonJour nor Bealer on behalf of their Cartesianism, nor Quine nor Devitt on behalf of their rejection of it. As Devitt (2011) acknowledges, Quine's proposal about evidence "can undermine itself" (63).[12]

This fact should, I think, be particularly vivid in view of what at least linguists and psychologists, but also, increasingly, many philosophers have come to appreciate to be the enormous difficulty of epistemology, and how much further we are from a satisfactory account of it than traditional philosophers have supposed.[13] Given that Devitt (1998, 49) agrees with this point, one wonders why he presumes we are nevertheless remotely in a position to make any sweeping claims about "the only way of knowing."[14] There's no question Quine did a great service to the field by raising the interesting *possibility* that confirmation in science, logic and mathematics are a piece of a seamless, holistic web. However, as Quine (1986, 493) himself acknowledged, this mere interesting possibility is hardly a serious *theory* of how people manage to know *anything*. *Pace* Devitt, I don't see yet any reason to suppose it is genuinely true of human beings, for whom logic and mathematics, strikingly unlike the "empirical" sciences, seem *never* to have been revised in view of empirical considerations – indeed, unlike most other claims "central" to our web, it seems well nigh impossible even seriously to *conceive* their being so.[15]

So Devitt is in no position to reject the empirical possibility of *a priori* knowledge. Indeed, discovering that our brains were structured as I have imagined would *begin* to be an empirical vindication of the kind of faculty of "rational intuition" Bealer is after. By analogy with that fact, I want to turn now to Devitt's similar rejection of the reliance of linguists on intuitive verdicts as a "voice of competence" (VoC), and then to Carruthers' analogous rejection of introspection.[16] Attention to these domains will display ways in which there may be routes to knowledge other than by Quinean holism.

3.1 Devitt on linguistic intuitions

In several articles and a book, Michael Devitt rejects a VoC view, proposing instead:

> The competent speaker has a ready access to a great deal of linguistic data just as the competent typist has to a great deal of typing data ... As a result she is likely to be able to judge in a fairly immediate and unreflective way that a token *is* grammatical, *is* ambiguous, *does* have to co-refer with a certain noun phrase, and so on. Such intuitive opinions are empirical central-processor responses to linguistic phenomena. They have no special authority: although the speaker's competence gives her ready access to data it does not give her Cartesian access to truths about the data.
>
> (2006, 109)

As in the case of his rejection of the a priori, Devitt's chief argument against a Cartesian, VoC view is what he takes to be its obscurity: not only is there no evidence for a "standard Cartesian view," according to which intuitions are *deduced from explicit representations of the rules* (2006, 96), he doesn't think anyone has provided a "nonstandard Cartesian explanation" according to which intuitions would be the manifestation of "implicit" representations (or rules the language faculty obeys without representing them):

> Can we find what I called a "nonstandard Cartesian explanation" of the evidential role of intuitions ... ? I know of no such explanation and I don't think that any one will be forthcoming.
>
> (2006, 117)

Now, it's true that linguists haven't always been forthcoming or clear about just what sort of mechanism they presume underlies and ratifies native speaker intuitions.[17] However, there's a perfectly straightforward version of the non-standard Cartesian proposal that seems to me at least implicit in several proposals that have been made. This is that linguistic intuitions have the same status as standard reports of perceptual experience in vision experiments. Insofar as they are to be taken as evidence of linguistic and perceptual processing, both linguistic intuitions and perceptual reports are presumed to be fairly directly caused by representations that are the output of, respectively, a language faculty and a visual module – just as logical intuitions might, per above, be the causal consequence of a logical competence. In the case of language, the faculty produces structural descriptions (SDs) of various syntactic objects (phrases, sentences), and the intuitions are reliable insofar as those descriptions play a crucial role in the production of the intuitions. They are evidence for the rules obeyed by the faculty insofar as those rules are the best explanation of, *inter alia*, the SDs.[18]

For example, it's because

(1) John seems to Bill to want to help himself

is produced by the language faculty with something like the SD below, that a speaker would spontaneously have the "intuition" that "himself" refers to John, not Bill (which, without the description, might seem the "closer" antecedent)[19] – just as the visual system seems to produce alternative SDs, with differently labeled nodes, of a standard Necker cube diagram (see Pylyshyn 2003, quoted below). Both systems issue in

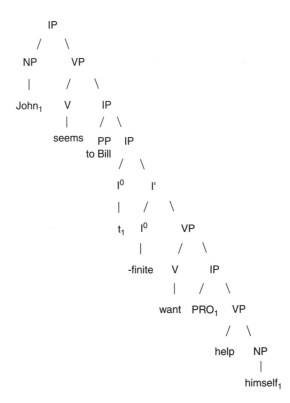

perceptual intuitions of ambiguity, structural relations (what's "part of" and/or "subordinated" to what) and even anomaly (ungrammatical strings and "impossible," Escheresque figures). To hazard a more graphic guess as to the process: the SDs in both cases are activated by mechanisms of conscious attention which respond to the descriptions with whatever overt vocabulary is available, e.g. "No, himself can't be John, but has to be Bill"; "The lower face seems to be in the foreground. Ah! No, wait! It can also be a cube facing upwards with that face in the back!" Again, the brief of the present paper is not to argue that either of these proposals is *correct* (although the evidence for both seems pretty impressive), but that, *pace* Devitt, it's a perfectly scientifically respectable model of a VoC, just as it is of the outputs of a vision module, and, per above, of a special (arguably *a priori*) access an agent may have to logical truths.

Devitt doesn't think the analogy to vision helps a VoC:

> Consider the visual module. *Its task is to deliver information to the central processor of what is seen*, information that is indeed the immediate and main basis for judging what is seen; ... "That grass is brown," "That person is angry," "This is an echidna but that isn't" and "a pig's jawbone" are examples of such judgments. ... The language module['s] ... task of comprehension is ... to deliver information to the central processor of what is said, information that is the ... basis for judging what is said, for judging "the message," ... [T]hey are not intuitions about the syntactic and semantic properties of expressions.
>
> (2006, 112, emphasis mine)

I'm not sure precisely what Devitt has in mind in allocating "tasks" to vision and language perception, but, putting aside the truism that vision and language certainly help with these tasks, surely neither the vision theorist nor the linguist need *confine* the levels of representation deployed by those systems to merely those tasks; nor are they committed to the *output* of these systems being confined to ordinary reports about the external world. Indeed, all the evidence suggests that speech perception involves not only understanding the *message* conveyed, but a highly modularized perception of *linguistic features of the speech vehicles* themselves (see Fodor *et al.* 1974, 296–301; 1983, 50–56, 86–93).

Precisely what the output is of perceptual modules is, not surprisingly, an issue of subtle empirical detail, not likely to be settled by speculations about their teleology,[20] nor by ordinary reflection and introspection.[21] The presumption of modularity theorists is that the output is fairly "shallow," not requiring access to categories stored in central memory. Thus, in passages just a page before the passage on this topic that Devitt (2006, 112) himself quotes, Fodor (1983, 93) insists that the visual module "should not categorize visual stimuli in such terms as proton trace." And, more recently, Pylyshyn (2003) writes:

> The perceptual classes induced by early vision ... do not, for example, correspond to meaningful categories in terms of which objects are identified when we talk about "perceiving as," e.g., perceiving something as a face or as Mary's face, and so on. To a first approximation, the classes provided by the visual system are shape classes, expressible in something like *the vocabulary of geometry*.
>
> (134, emphasis mine)

Thus, the outputs of vision ("what is seen"?) are unlikely to be the centrally informed "This is an echidna" or "That's a pig's jawbone." Similarly, in the same discussion of modularity that Devitt cites, Fodor (1983, 51ff.) adduces considerable evidence regarding e.g. categorical perception, for the very claim Devitt is denying, namely that the language module "deliver[s] representations which specify, for example, morphemic constituency, syntactic structure and logical form" (Fodor 1983, 93).[22] We *hear* the utterances of a language we know in terms of these properties, and the intuitive judgments about sentences that interest linguists are those that reflect (i.e. are caused by) how we hear them (cf. Smith 2006, 949–55).

Devitt thinks all of this is implausible. But he needs to engage with the empirical (not to mention phenomenological!) evidence in much more detail if he is to reject it.[23]

3.2 Carruthers on introspection

Like Devitt, Peter Carruthers (2011) also targets what he regards as Cartesian views:

> Descartes (1641 [in the *Meditations*]) famously believed that we have *infallible* knowledge of our own [occurrent] thought and thought processes. Few today would endorse such a strong claim. But almost all hold that knowledge of our thoughts is somehow *privileged* (arrived at in a special way that isn't available to others) and especially *certain* and *authoritative* (incapable of being challenged by others).
>
> (xii)

He proposes instead his "Interpretative Sensory-Access" (ISA) theory, according to which self-knowledge of most forms of thought doesn't differ in kind from knowledge of the thoughts of other people (xii).

More specifically, Carruthers claims that concurrent self-ascription of attitudes is based only upon sensory, behavioral and contextual (SBC) data, and not on any other data to which people might have special introspective access.[24] For Carruthers, like Devitt, what seem to be special reports are merely the result of one's general cognitive capacities (especially one's "theory of mind").

As in the case of Devitt's view, I think Carruthers' view also suffers from not considering sufficiently seriously a naturalistic version of Cartesianism. As an alternative to his view, I have elsewhere[25] proposed what I call a "Tags" view, according to which people introspect many of their attitudes by virtue of the causal efficacy of tags affixed to some of the representations that are the output of some of their mental processes, much as standard computers mark the output of different programs run on them (e.g. ".doc" for MS-Word documents, ".jpg" for photos), and as the proprioceptive system does when it seems to produce "efferent copies" by which one knows that one's limbs have moved (see Gallistel 1980, 170–75). The proposal is of course a cousin to the one in the previous section about the causal efficacy of SDs. When one consciously attends to one's states, the tagged representations are activated and causally responsible for whatever self-ascriptions the person is able to formulate in her natural language. Many self-ascriptions, say, of concurrent doubt, grief, resentment, can be especially reliable insofar as they are the consequence of complex constellations of such tagged representations.

Again, I don't want to pretend here to *settle* whether Carruthers' ISA or my Tags view is right. As in the case of linguistic intuitions, I am only concerned to show how a modest Cartesian reliance on introspection is a viable scientific possibility, one involving difficult empirical questions that would need to be researched to decide the issue. I'll mention two: inattentional blindness and explanations of actual reliability. But, first, an important clarification:

ISA involves *two* claims that need to be distinguished: (i) that introspection is *interpretative*, and (ii) that the only data available for self-ascription is SBC data. However, attributions of *any* property to *anything* can of course be (unconsciously) inferential, *or* they can involve quick sensory pattern matching, with no serious "inference" or effort at "explanation" at all: attributions of fear to *anyone* might sometimes involve a quick match between a sensory display and a stored prototype, whether it be SBC data (and/or tags) in one's own case, or only BC data in the case of others. Moreover, the Tags view can allow that *sometimes* self-attributions might be inferential, as when someone concludes she has selfish motives because everyone does; and it can allow that many cases might well be mixes of inference and pattern-matching. *Pace* Carruthers (2011, 325ff.), the issue between ISA and the Tags view is not about "dual *methods*," but only whether there is special "dual" *data*.

Turning to empirical issues:

Inattentional blindness and competence vs performance

People's attention can easily be affected by their background beliefs, expectations and interests, as in recent studies of "inattentional blindness," where people attending to one stimulus can fail to notice another (Mack and Rock 1998). The Tags view could easily explain the confabulations that Carruthers cites – e.g. split-brain cases, cognitive dissonance, and source confusion (see 2011, 39–43, 162–65, 356–65) – as just such cases of people failing to attend to their inner Tags, because of their interests, desires, expectations or distraction by other data.

The possibility of inattentional blindness points to a general methodological problem in Carruthers' discussion: performance errors alone aren't sufficient for refuting a competence claim. Errors in self-ascription are no better evidence of lack of introspective competence than the inattentional blindness cases are of an actual defect in vision. What would show a lack of competence is failure across the board, especially when interfering factors, like inattention, are controlled for.

Are there introspective failures across the board? People certainly *appear* ordinarily to know whether they are concurrently e.g. fearing, expecting, doubting, hoping, judging, supposing, etc., far better than they know these facts about anyone else. How reliable are they in fact? I know of no studies; but I also know of no serious doubts. This is at least partly because we have a good deal of indirect evidence of this reliability: people often seem to be able to remember what attitudes they have had at least shortly after they have had them, and usually act consonantly with them. There are, of course, the familiar cases of repression, self-deception, the grip of bad theories, and confounding episodic memory with rational reconstruction. But this is hardly evidence of failure *across the whole attitudinal board*. In any case, all that concerns me here is how to explain whatever general reliability people do in fact display, which would need to be carefully delineated by further research.

Objectivist explanations of reliability

A reasonable strategy for Carruthers to explain what reliability we display is simply to point out, along lines analogous to Devitt's appeal to common observations about language, that we, well, spend a lot of time with ourselves.[26] The question is whether the SBC data gained in this way would be sufficient. One way to bring out the difficulty is to consider relatively contextless cases in which behavioral and contextual data are minimal, say, someone daydreaming, lying insomniac in bed or sitting quietly in a nondescript room, eyes closed, for twenty minutes – what we might call "meditative cases." ISA is committed to our self-knowledge in such cases being based on *sensations and knowledge of one's history alone*, and so should predict that people are *less* reliable in such cases than in wide-open-eyed, contextualized ones, since they would be basing their inferences on significantly less data, certainly less than they use in third-person cases. And, of course, *perhaps* people *are* less reliable in these cases. But, again, taking subsequent behaviors and memories of such episodes at face value – say, paying a bill you recall from such an episode having felt suddenly guilty for neglecting – there is so far no reason to suppose they are.

Carruthers (2011) briefly discusses meditative cases, and supposes that "there are numerous other sensory-involving cues that are available in such circumstances … [e.g.], visual imagery, inner speech, affective feelings, motor imagery, and more besides" (58). But he merely claims that "these *might well* be sufficient to ground attributions of thoughts to oneself" (158, emphasis mine). What needs to be shown, however, is that they *generally* and *reliably* would be. By way of comparison, consider the case of open-eyed vision. Vision theorists face the non-trivial problem of explaining how a three-dimensional representation of a scene can be based reliably upon merely retinal stimulations, a problem partly solved by Shimon Ullman's theorem showing how structure can be inferred from motion, and ultimately three-dimensional forms from retinal intensity gradients (see Palmer 1999). Is there the slightest reason to think there would be any remotely analogous principles in the case of self-ascription on the basis (in meditative cases) of sensory data and background beliefs alone?

If people are even approximately as reliable in their self-ascriptions as they seem to be, it's hard to see how this could be explained by their relying only on SBC data. The Tags view provides at least a more plausible account, even if, as in confabulation cases, the tags might sometimes be ignored. Just which tags there are, and how and when they are used and preserved, would, of course, need much further research, as would ascertaining the degree to which people are in fact reliable, and about which sorts of states. Again, I am not trying here to establish the truth of the Tags view, only its scientific plausibility and thereby the serious possibility of a modest Cartesianism whereby people do have *some* special introspective access to *some* of their attitudes.

3.3 Conceptual introspection and analysis

A last point about semantic self-ascription, an issue on which Devitt's and Carruthers' views converge. Devitt's view that intuitions are the result of general theorizing is, of course, not confined to issues about grammaticality, but includes intuitions about any linguistic matters, including semantic and conceptual ones, and Carruthers takes a similar view of the introspections of the *content* of an attitude self-ascribed.

The semantics of attitude attributions generally is, of course, a vast industry, which I won't begin to summarize here. I only want to press two points: (i) again, the methodological difficulties of a satisfactory theoretical account in the near future, but (ii) the nevertheless not hopeless strategy of a contextual "redeployment" account that would naturally supplement a Tags proposal.

Regarding the first issue, even Bealer (1998) notes that

> traditional rationalists (and also moderate empiricists who, like Hume, accepted intuition as a basic source of evidence) did not successfully explain why intuition is a basic source of evidence.
>
> (221)

He proceeds to provide what he apparently regards as a satisfactory theory of concept possession, arguing that his claims about rational intuition are supported by it:

> Modal reliabilism provided a natural explanation in these gaps left by the traditional theories. The explanation is in terms of the indicated modal tie between these sources and the truth. But why should there be such a tie to the truth? ... The theory of concept possession promises to fill in this gap.
>
> (221)

In an extended discussion, he lays out his general strategy in terms of "determinate concept possession" (in contrast to less determinate, often mere "nominal" ascription, as in the case of children). He suggests that

> determinate concept possession might be explicated (at least in part) in terms of the metaphysical possibility of relevant truth-tracking intuitions (in appropriately good cognitive conditions and with appropriately rich conceptual repertoires).
>
> (225)

There is not space to go through here all the details of Bealer's theory. However, a general problem can be raised for it, as for any extant theory of the topic, namely that we simply don't know enough about how the mind works to be confident about what a concept *is*, much less about how we deploy one. What insures that the "truth-tracking intuitions" in even the best cognitive conditions and the richest conceptual repertoires don't depend on all manner of background empirical assumptions about the nature of the world and the context in which the intuitive verdict is being elicited?[27] Indeed, Bealer needs experimentally to control for precisely all the confounds we noted he himself mentioned in his rejection of experimental work on reasoning!

In any case, one of the morals of much of the history of science and philosophy is that such confounding was precisely the case for many of what Bealer regards as

> the central concepts of philosophy to be possessed determinately – substance, mind, intelligence, consciousness, sensation, perception, knowledge, wisdom, truth, identity, infinity, divinity, time, explanation, causation, freedom, purpose, goodness, duty, the virtues, love, life, happiness, and so forth.
>
> (222)

Now, *perhaps* the concepts of [identity] and [infinity] can be isolated as part of logic and mathematics, which, as we've allowed, do certainly *seem* to enjoy a certain autonomy and authority. But all the others have been subject to pressures and revision in the light of empirical theory, from Einstein on time, to Marr, Fodor and Pylyshyn on perception, to Jackendoff, Block, Carruthers and Prinz on consciousness – and from practically everyone on such notoriously difficult, popular concepts as [wisdom], [goodness], [duty], [happiness] and [love]! In any case, everything depends here upon the details of just how the faculty of concept deployment works. Not only would we have to sort out the confounds Bealer himself acknowledged, but we should have to settle the myriad issues about e.g. polysemy, impli-*ca*-ture, impli-*ci*-ture, analyticities and just the oddities of ordinary "language games" that have been increasingly challenging linguists in the last sixty or so years.[28] Although, again, intuitions undoubtedly provide evidence relevant to theories about these issues, as things stand they can hardly be relied upon to deliver *a priori* insights in the fashion Bealer suggests. As Kent Bach (2002, 24) nicely put it:

> To "preserve intuitions" in our theorizing about what is said would be like relying on the intuitions of unsophisticated moviegoers about the effects of editing on a film. Although people's cinematic experience is dramatically affected by such factors as cuts and camera angles, there is no reason to suppose that their intuitions are reliable about what produces what effects.

(He goes on to quote the line from Fodor that serves as the epigraph of this chapter.) Thus, before we tackle the hard philosophical cases Bealer has in mind, we need a good empirical theory of the etiology of intuitions in the relatively innocuous ones.[29]

None of this is meant to imply that we couldn't have *some* introspective or "intuitive" knowledge of the content of our occurrent attitude states. In the first place, as many have noted,[30] deploying [σ] in an attitude ascription, ⌜A[σ]⌝, may just be a *re-deployment* of that very content, [σ], as it occurs in *having* the attitude itself. Thus, I might know that *I want water* just by deploying the same representation deployed in the want itself ("Water!") And I can do so even if "water" doesn't mean for me what it might mean for someone like myself in a radically different environment. Or, to take my favorite semantic puzzle: I can think *I'm annoyed that the sky is grey and not as blue as it was earlier*, redeploying the words following "that," even though I may be very hard put to say exactly what the truth conditions of "The sky is grey but was blue earlier" might be (what is *the thing* that is grey, but was blue?). Relatively direct, introspective knowledge of the content of our own intentions may be relatively easy, even if it is not very substantive.

But it could be substantive. Morphemes doubtless activate specific files, some of which might include representations of semantic constraints for the deployment of the morpheme, and such representations, like the SDs of syntax, might also be sometimes causally responsible for people's judgments about when the morpheme would be properly applied. If so, then this would go some way towards vindicating some of traditional philosophical reflection, analysis, and, again, perhaps claims to *a priori* knowledge.[31] But, of course, while the claims themselves might be vindicated in this way, it doesn't follow, indeed, it doesn't seem likely, that claims *that* the claims are so vindicated can themselves be so vindicated. There's no reason to think that representations of the processes by which representations may be specially causally efficacious are themselves specially causally efficacious. The relevant epistemic operators, "knows specially that *p*," don't iterate any more than "knows that *p*" does by itself.

4 Conclusion

Perhaps, per Quine and Devitt, there *is* just one way of knowing, and that's *only* the massive global, holistic empirical confirmation of a sort that seems to them to be exemplified in empirical sciences, and it's only this that gives rise to people's intuitions. Similarly, per Carruthers, introspection may involve only the kinds of processes and data for attitude ascription that we employ for others. My point here has not been to decide those issues, but only to point out that modest, naturalistic Cartesian alternatives are still entirely live theoretical options. These options, however, can't be taken for granted or defended quite as easily and non-empirically as traditional Cartesians like BonJour and Bealer have supposed.

What is the proper methodology in philosophy? Well, it certainly should include much of what it's always done – examining and reflecting on introspections and intuitions, but, now, not with any eye merely to *systematizing* them, but rather to *explaining* them. And this is a task that can't be carried out in the splendid *a priori* isolation sought by traditional Cartesians. As the above discussions should indicate, it is of a piece with the explanations that emerge only from naturalistic accounts of mind and language generally. Navel-gazing is fine, so long as you're trying to explain what you see.[32]

Notes

1 The nice example of the rabbit pots is discussed in Antony 2003. Much of the present paper is a development of the same, essentially Quinean point about evidence that Antony presses there against different targets, e.g. Soames 1984, than those treated here.

2 See my 1993, 1995, 1997 and 2002b for discussion of the view as it is explicitly defended in Wittgenstein, Quine, Davidson, Dennett and their followers. Versions of it, of course, are presupposed also in Locke, Hume and Kant, and are part of the "methodological dualism" that Chomsky frequently deplores.

3 I discuss BonJour's views at greater length in my 2001, from which these two paragraphs have been taken. BonJour (2001) claims in reply that his view of rational insight doesn't depend entirely on the view of shared properties; however, it's enough for present purposes that at least some of the crucial cases do, as he seems to insist at p. 675.

4 Despite efforts to distance himself from this commitment in his replies to me and other commentators, BonJour (2001) nevertheless writes "the idea of rational insight requires only that we do sometimes have the sort of access to the contents of our thought just indicated, that we can actually think about and have in mind such things as properties and relations" (675; see also 683).

5 Failure to distinguish claims in a domain from claims about knowledge of that domain persists in Thomas Nagel's (2012) recent discussion of Plantinga; see Rey (2012b) for discussion.

6 See my 2002a for further discussion.

7 See the rich discussions of the topic in Adler and Rips 2008.

8 Consider Kahneman's (2011, 368–70) disturbing discussion of what appear to be irresolvably contradictory attitudes towards risk and tax policy.

9 At least some modalities might be justified in a fashion closely analogous to Quine's own justification of belief in enduring material objects. Just as enduring objects may simplify our understanding of the play of phenomenal experience (see his 1953, 17), so might modality round out our under-standing of the conditionals needed in science, most of which would not automatically be true just because their antecedents were false. With regard to metaphysical probabilities and properties, one need only look to the standard accounts of quantum physics, and the probabilities associated with such fundamental *properties* of the universe as mass, spin and electric charge, to wonder at Quine's confidence that science could dispense with them.

10 For an example that's of special concern to traditional philosophy of mind: it's by no means clear, given present science, that ghosts, angels or "zombies" are *genuinely metaphysically possible*, no matter how vividly many people may claim to be able to "conceive" them. Bealer's (1998, 215–16) dismissal of the kind of contingent reliablism I'm suggesting here seems to me similarly based on mere conceivabilities, e.g. of telepathy and "nomological guessing," that need to be shown to be genuine metaphysical possibilities; or, if they are genuine *nomological* possibilities, then why they don't count as a kind of perception and knowledge after all (don't those *idiots savants* who can weirdly compute large primes have an unusual kind of knowledge?).

11 For the record: Devitt (1998) rejects this possibility, claiming that, since a person's competence of this sort might be a matter of luck, the verdicts to which such a system gives rise couldn't count as (justified) knowledge (51–56). But this doesn't follow. It is wholly possible that the

human ability to have knowledge of *anything* may well be a result of evolutionary "luck." In any case, an inference can be fully justified without including premises *that* the inference is justified, much less the justification of *that* fact. Lewis Carroll's (1895) tortoise is fully justified in drawing a logical inference without need of premises that he is so justified, or metalogical justifications that he is.

Note that I've added "or inhabit" here to rule out the accidentally believed *a posteriori* necessities, such as "Water is H_2O," that also worry Devitt. For further replies to him, see my 1998, which appeared in the same place as his critique.

12 Actually, all I intend to undermine here is Devitt's (and Quine's 1953, 41) unwarranted insistence that holism is the "only" way of knowing, not the suggestion that confirmation can be holistic, which I wouldn't be surprised it can be (should it ever be specified in sufficient detail to assess). Without the "only," holistic confirmation is entirely compatible with more local sorts, and therefore with *a priori* knowledge – it would just turn out that one of the constraints on acceptable confirmations is that, e.g. logic and math always be preserved, which, come to think of it, seems to accord extremely well with actual scientific practice!

13 Consider the difficulties of a theory of abduction, the "frame problem," setting Bayesian priors, the Goodman and Hempel paradoxes of confirmation, the Quinean worries about translation, the Chomskian questions of language acquisition, or just the problems to be discussed in Sections 3.2 and 3.3 below, of how someone even knows what she is thinking! It's all *a lot* harder than Hume seemed to think when he aspired to be the Newton of the mind.

14 Devitt thinks that, despite our epistemic ignorance, the "empirical way" starts with "an intuitively clear ... idea ... [that] a belief is justified if it is formed and/or sustained by ... experiences ... that are appropriately sensitive to the putative [content of the belief]" (2011, 22). However, as he notes in his (1998, 55), it is difficult to make sense of how logic is sensitive in this way, since (even the experiences appropriate to) illogical worlds are not options with which one might sensitively covary. The "intuitively clear idea" is notoriously obscure for *precisely* the cases at issue of logic and mathematics!

15 Note that, as Devitt (2011) emphasizes, revising our *theory* of our logic is not the same as revising the actual logic we use.

16 The present paper of course doesn't need the claim that logical intuitions are *a priori*. It would be enough that thoughts produced as a causal consequence of this implemented natural deduction system would be a "voice of *logical* competence," whether or not the competence provided *a priori* knowledge.

17 The problem is particularly exacerbated by the denial by Chomsky and others that talk of "representations" in a Chomskian theory of linguistic competence should be taken to involve intentionality, see Chomsky (2000, 45–47, 105, 159–60; 2003). I shall assume in this discussion that such a view is mistaken; see Rey (2003) for extended discussion.

18 At least intimations of this view can be found in Chomsky (1965, 8–9; 2000, 125); Fodor *et al.* (1974) and Fodor (1983), and it is explicitly defended recently in Collins (2007, 421); Fitzgerald (2010, §3), and Rey (2006, 563–68), from this last of which I have drawn some of the present discussion. The analogy with perception is also discussed in Textor (2009).

19 I am indebted to Dan Blair for the particularly nice example, involving a speaker's sensitivity to the interesting effects of a "seems" context on cross-indexing.

20 In correspondence, Devitt has claimed that he meant nothing teleological in speaking of the "tasks" of the visual or language systems, but merely to describe "just what the systems do." But systems do many things, and Devitt needs *something* to rule out the linguist's proposal that they deliver structural descriptions of the syntactic and semantic properties of utterances.

21 To take an issue close to Devitt's insistence on linguistic intuitions being mere central processor speculations, consider the difficulty of disconfounding *central* from *module-internal* top–down processing in the case of the phoneme restoration effect (Fodor 1983, 65), and in trying to characterize the output of the visual system generally (Pylyshyn 2003, 73–76).

22 Still further, more recent evidence of the rich causal roles of SDs is reviewed in Pereplyotchik 2011.

23 Note that a common suggestion about the output of vision is that it *does* consist of Marr's 2–1/2D sketch (see Jackendoff 1987; Pylyshyn 2003, 136; Prinz 2012)! Devitt may have been misled in this case by Fodor's (1983, 94) passing comment that the visual system does not deliver "Marr's 'primal,' '2.5 D,' and '3 D' sketch," for which, unlike the case of language perception, Fodor offers no real evidence – indeed, the comment seems belied by his discussion of the 3D sketch at 1983, 137 n. 34.

24 In his 2011, he adds data regarding affect (ch. 5) and briefly considers my Tags model (156–78), his rejection of which he bases largely on a presumption that "working memory" is confined to "sensory data" into which conceptual contents are somehow "bound" (57–58, 72–78, 166–78). Since these (to my mind, highly problematic) emendations aren't crucial here, I leave them for another place (see Rey 2011, 2012a, forthcoming).

25 In my 2011, 2012a and forthcoming, from which much in this section is drawn.

26 He also appeals to the way that some attitudes can be "self-fulfilling" (2011, 94–95), as when one feels committed to a decision one thinks one has made. But it's hard to see how this would apply to any but a minority of cases. Many self-ascriptions, e.g. of wonderings or imaginings, seem committally quite neutral, and others, e.g. of fears, anxieties, forbidden desires, are of states one often wishes to get over!

27 As Devitt (2011) also rightly notes, "What needs to be emphasized is that nothing in the experience of having an intuition supports the view *that it is a priori*, or, indeed, supports *any* view of what justifies the intuition. In particular, it does not show that the insight is not justified in a holistic empirical way. This theoretical issue is way beyond anything in the phenomenology" (27).

28 For discussions of the issues, see e.g. Bach and Harnish 1979, Bach 2002, Fodor 1998, Recanati 2004 and Pietroski 2010.

29 And notice how little attention is paid by philosophers to the contextual pragmatics of eliciting people's intuitions or verdicts about thought experiments, a problem that plagues not only traditional classroom philosophy, but even the "experimental philosophy" movement, which relies on questionnaires, in utter disregard of the complexities of polling. Moreover, as Bach (pers. commun.) has emphasized to me, it's one thing to regard intuitions as reliable, quite another to say exactly what they're reliable *about*. Maybe classroom intuitions are reliable – but only about what people *think* are the interests of the philosophers who question them!

30 See Davidson 1987, Burge 1988 and Peacocke 1996, §§3–4; 2008.

31 As well, perhaps, as claims about "semantic and cognitive phenomenology": the special causal roles of certain representations, whether of syntax, semantics or one's own propositional attitudes, may provide better candidates for capturing phenomenology than the more usual "qualia." There may be more to "what it's like" than mere sensation.

32 I think of the central idea of this paper as being implicit in Jerry Fodor's MIT seminar in 1972 on what became his 1975, but I'm grateful to Michael Devitt for forcing me over the years to make it explicit, even if, for some odd reason, he's still not persuaded of it.

References

Adler, J. and L. Rips (2008) *Reasoning: Studies of Human Inference and Its Foundations*, Cambridge: Cambridge University Press.

Antony, L. (2003) "Rabbit-Pots and Supernovas: The Relevance of Psychological Evidence to Linguistic Theory," in Alex Barber (ed.), *The Epistemology of Language*, Oxford: Oxford University Press.

Bach, K. (2002) "Seeming Semantic Intuitions," in J. Keim Campbell, M. O'Rourke and D. Shier (eds), *Meaning and Truth*, New York: Seven Bridges Press, 21–33.

Bach, K. and M. Harnish (1979) *Linguistic Communication and Speech Acts*, Cambridge, MA: MIT Press.

Bealer, G. (1998) "Intuition and the Autonomy of Philosophy," in DePaul and Ramsey 1998, 201–40.

BonJour, L. (1998) *In Defense of Pure Reason*, Cambridge: Cambridge University Press.

——(2001) "Replies," *Philosophy and Phenomenological Research* 63(3): 673–98.

Bruner, J. and L. Postman (1949) "On the Perception of Incongruity: A Paradigm," *Journal of Personality* 18: 206–23.

Burge, T. (1988) "Individualism and Self-Knowledge," *Journal of Philosophy* 85: 649–63.

Carroll, L. (1895) "What the Tortoise Said to Achilles," *Mind* 4: 278–80.

Carruthers, P. (2011) *The Opacity of Mind: An Integrative Theory of Self-Knowledge*, Oxford: Oxford University Press.

Chomsky, N. (1965) *Aspects of the Theory of Syntax*, Cambridge: MIT Press.

——(2000) *New Horizons in the Study of Language*, Cambridge: Cambridge University Press.

——(2003) "Reply to Rey," in L. Antony and N. Hornstein (eds), *Chomsky and His Critics*, Oxford: Blackwell, 274–87.

Collins, J. (2007) Review of *Ignorance of Language*, by Michael Devitt, *Mind* 116: 416–23.

Davidson, D. (1987) "Knowing One's Own Mind," in *Proceedings and Addresses of the American Philosophical Association* 61: 441–58.

DePaul, Michael and William Ramsey (1998) (eds), *Rethinking Intuition*, New York: Rowman & Littlefield.

Devitt, M. (1996) *Coming to Our Senses*, Cambridge: Cambridge University Press.

——(1998) "Naturalism and the A Priori," in *A Priori Knowledge*, special issue of *Philosophical Studies: An International Journal for Philosophy in the Analytic Tradition* 92(1/2): 45–65.

——(2006) *Ignorance of Language*, Oxford: Oxford University Press.

——(2011) "No Place for the A Priori," in M. Schaffer and M. Veber (eds), *What Place for the A Priori?*, Chicago: Open Court, 9–32.

Fitzgerald, G. (2010) "Linguistic Intuitions," *British Journal for the Philosophy of Science* 61: 123–60.

Fodor, J. (1975) *The Language of Thought*, New York: Crowell.

——(1983) *The Modularity of Mind*, Cambridge, MA: MIT Press.

——(1998) *Concepts: Where Cognitive Science Went Wrong*, Oxford: Oxford University Press.

Fodor, J., T. Bever and M. Garrett (1974) *The Psychology of Language*, New York: McGraw Hill.

Gallistel, C. (1980) *The Organization of Action: A New Synthesis*, Hillsdale, NJ: Erlbaum Associates.

Gutting, G. (1998) "'Rethinking Intuition': A Historical and Metaphilosophical Introduction," in DePaul and Ramsey 1998, 3–16.

Jackendoff, Ray S. (1987) *Consciousness and the Computational Mind*, Cambridge, MA: MIT Press.

Kahneman, D. (2011) *Thinking, Fast and Slow*, New York: Farrar, Straus & Giroux.

Kant, I. (1787/1929) *Critique of Pure Reason*, trans. N.K. Smith, New York: Macmillan.

Mack, A. and I. Rock (1998) *Inattentional Blindness*, Cambridge, MA: MIT Press.

Nagel, T. (2012) Replies to letters to editor, *New York Review of Books,* 59(17, 19), 8 November, 6 December.

Nasar, S. (1998) *A Brilliant Mind: The Life of Brilliant Mathematician and Nobel Laureate, John Nash*, New York: Touchstone.

Nisbett, R. and T. Wilson (1977) "Telling More Than We Can Know: Verbal Reports on Mental Processes," *Psychological Review* 84(3): 231–59.

Palmer, S. (1999) *Vision Science: Protons to Phenomenology*, Cambridge, MA: MIT Press.

Peacocke, C. (2008) "Mental Action and Self-Awareness (II): Epistemology," in L. O'Brien and M. Soteriou (eds), *Mental Action*, Oxford University Press.

——(1996) "Entitlement, Self-Knowledge and Conceptual Redeployment," *Proceedings of the Aristotelian Society*, n.s., 96: 117–58.

Pereplyotchik, D. (2011) "Psychological and Computational Models of Language Comprehension: In Defense of the Psychological Reality of Syntax," *Croatian Journal of Philosophy* 11(31): 31–72.

Pietroski, P. (2010) "Concepts, Meanings, and Truth: First Nature, Second Nature and Hard Work," *Mind & Language* 25: 247–78.

Plantinga, A. (2000) *Warranted Christian Belief*, Oxford: Oxford University Press.

Prinz, J. (2012) *The Conscious Brain*, Oxford: Oxford University Press.

Pylyshyn, Z. (2003) *Seeing and Visualizing: It's Not What You Think*, Cambridge, MA: MIT Press.

Quine, W. (1953) *From a Logical Point of View*, New York: Harper & Row.

——(1986) "Reply to Henryk Skolimowski," in *The Philosophy of W.V. Quine*, expanded edn, ed. L. Hahn and P. Schilpp, LaSalle, IL: Open Court, 492–93.

Recanati, F. (2004) *Literal Meaning*, Cambridge: Cambridge University Press.

Rey, G. (1993) "The Unavailability of What We Mean: A Reply to Quine, Fodor and LePore," in J. Fodor and E. LePore (ed.), *Holism: A Consumer Update*, Grazer Philosophische Studien 46, Amsterdam: Rodopi, 61–101.

——(1995) "Dennett's Unrealistic Psychology," *Philosophical Topics* 22(1–2): 259–89.

——(1997) *Contemporary Philosophy of Mind*, Oxford: Blackwell.

——(1998) "A Naturalistic *A Priori*," *Philosophical Studies* 92: 25–43.

——(2001) "Digging Deeper for the *A Priori*," commentary on *In Defense of Pure Reason*, by Laurence BonJour, *Philosophy and Phenomenological Research* 63(3): 649–56.

——(2002a) "Meta-atheism," in D. Kolak and R. Martin (eds), *Wisdom without Answers: A Brief Introduction to Philosophy*, Belmont, CA: Wadsmorth, 335–54.

——(2002b) "Physicalism and Psychology: A Plea for a Substantive Philosophy of Mind," in Carl Gillett and Barry Loewer (eds), *Physicalism and Its Discontents*, Cambridge: Cambridge University Press, 99–128.

——(2003) "Representational Content and a Chomskyan Linguistics," Alex Barber (ed.), *Epistemology of Language*, Oxford: Oxford University Press, 140–86.

——(2006) "Conventions, Intuitions and Linguistic Inexistents: A Reply to Devitt," *Croatian Journal of Philosophy* 6(18): 549–70.

——(2011) "Introspection, Inattentional Blindness and an Insufficient Inferential Base," *On the Human*, National Humanities Center website, <http://onthehuman.org/>. Commentary (followed by a reply to the author's reply) on Peter Carruthers, "Knowledge of Our Own Thoughts Is Just as Interpretive as Knowledge of the Thoughts of Others" (same website).

——(2012a) "Postscript to 'We Aren't All Self-Blind,'" <http://sites.google.com/site/georgesrey>.

——(2012b) Letters to editor in reply to Nagel (2012), *New York Review of Books*, 8 November, 6 December.

——(forthcoming) "We Aren't All Self-Blind: A Defense of a Modest Introspectionism," *Mind & Language*. Available at <http://sites.google.com/site/georgesrey>.

Smith, B. (2006) "What I Know When I Know a Language," in E. Lepore and B. Smith (eds), *The Oxford Handbook of the Philosophy of Language*, Oxford: Oxford University Press, 941–82.

Soames, S. (1984) "Linguistics and Psychology," *Linguistics and Philosophy* 7: 155–79.

Sosa, E. (1998) "Minimal Intuition," in DePaul and Ramsey 1998, 257–69.

Textor, M. (2009) "Devitt on the Epistemic Authority of Linguistic Intuitions," *Erkenntnis* 71: 395–405.

15 Linguistic intuitions are not "the voice of competence"
MICHAEL DEVITT

1 Introduction

How should we go about finding the truth about a language? The received answer in linguistics gives a very large role to the intuitive linguistic judgments of competent speakers about grammaticality/acceptability,[1] ambiguity, coreference, and the like. Thus, Noam Chomsky claims that "linguistics ... is characterized by attention to certain kinds of evidence ... largely, the judgments of native speakers" (1986, 36). Carson Schütze remarks:

> Throughout much of the history of linguistics, judgments of the grammaticality/acceptability of sentences (and other linguistic intuitions) have been the major source of evidence in constructing grammars.
>
> (1996, xi)

Liliane Haegeman, in a popular textbook, goes even further, saying that "all the linguist has to go by ... is the native speaker's intuitions" (1994, 8).[2] This raises a question: *Why* should we think that these intuitive judgments are good evidence for a syntactic theory of the speaker's language, good evidence for its grammar? What could be their source that would make them reliable?[3]

(a) In a discussion of linguistic intuitions in *Ignorance of Language* (2006a, ch. 7; see also 2006b), I took the received Chomskian answer to be that these intuitions are "the voice of competence" (VoC). This is the view that linguistic competence, all on its own,

> provides information about the linguistic facts. ... So these judgments are not arrived at by the sort of empirical investigation that judgments about the world usually require. Rather, a speaker has a privileged access to facts about the language, facts captured by the intuitions, simply in virtue of being competent ...
>
> (Devitt 2006a, 96)

Competence not only plays the dominant role in *linguistic usage*, it also provides informational content to *metalinguistic intuitions*.[4] Those intuitions are indeed, "noise" aside, the voice of competence. That is why they are reliable.

(b) I argued that VoC was wrong (2006a,100–119). Instead, I urged that intuitive judgments about language, like intuitive judgments in general, "are empirical theory-laden central-processor responses to phenomena, differing from many other such responses only in being fairly immediate and unreflective, based on little if any conscious reasoning" (2006a, 103). Although a speaker's competence in a language obviously gives her ready access to the *data* of that language, the data that the intuitions *are about*, it does not give her ready access to the *truth* about the data; the competence does not provide the *informational content* of the intuition. In this respect my view is sharply different from VoC. And it is sharply different in another respect: it is *modest*, making do with cognitive states and processes we were already committed to. So, following Mark Textor (2009), let us call it "the Modest Explanation" (ME).[5]

Both (a) and (b) have been criticized. My main aim in this paper is to defend (a) and (b) from these criticisms. But first we should consider the methodological significance of this debate about linguistic intuitions.

2 Methodological significance for linguistics

It needs to be noted, first, that claims like those by Chomsky and Haegeman are exaggerations in two respects. (i) These claims are clearly intended to be statements about the evidential role of the intuitive judgments of *ordinary* native speakers, *folk* intuitions. Yet, as a matter of historical fact, linguists have relied much more on their own intuitions than on those of the folk. This has often been noted and has become the subject of much concern in recent years (Schütze 1996; Gordon and Hendrick 1997; Sorace and Keller 2005; Featherston 2007; Myers 2009). (ii) Furthermore, even though the debate about linguistic methodology is dominated by attention to the role of intuitions – far too much so, in my view (2006a, 98–100) – the role of usage as a source of evidence is often acknowledged.[6] Thus evidence is found in the corpus, elicited production, reaction time studies, eye tracking, and electromagnetic brain potentials.[7]

So grammar construction is not solely reliant on native speakers' intuitions for evidence. But the degree to which it should be so reliant clearly depends on whether VoC or (something like) ME is right. Thus, if VoC is right and competence really does produce these intuitions, then of course the intuitions should be the pre-eminent source of evidence for grammars: "noise" aside, they must be true. On the other hand, if VoC is not right and hence, presumably, (something like) ME is right, then *intuitions should surely lose that pre-eminence: other evidence should come to the fore*. Indeed, the extent to which the folk are reliable about their language at all becomes an open question. At least that reliability needs to be thoroughly tested against other evidence.

We should note further that if VoC is right, the frequent criticism of the common practice of relying for evidence largely on the intuitions of linguists rather than folk is appropriate. VoC gives no reason to prefer the intuitions of native-speaking linguists to those of native-speaking folk. Indeed, we should prefer those of the folk because those of the linguists may be prone to a sort of noise that lessens their credibility: theoretical bias. In contrast, ME *supports* the common, but criticized, practice. For, according to ME, intuitions are like ordinary "observation judgments" in being "theory-laden." The antipositivist revolution in the philosophy of science, led by Thomas Kuhn and Paul Feyerabend, drew our attention to the way in which even the most straightforward judgments arising from observational experiences may depend on a background. We would not make the judgments if we did not hold certain beliefs or theories, some involving the concepts deployed in the judgments. We would not make the judgments if we did not have certain predispositions, some innate but many acquired in training, to respond selectively to experiences.[8] In light of this, when we do use intuitions as evidence, we should prefer those of the linguists to those of the folk because linguists have the better background theory and training; they are more expert (Devitt 2006a, 111, 115).[9]

3 Methodological significance for the philosophy of language

Just as linguists take native speaker's intuitions to be the main source of evidence for syntactic theories, philosophers of language take them to be so for semantic theories, for example, for theories of reference.[10] And philosophers, like linguists, have typically relied on their own intuitions rather than the folk's.[11] However, there is a significant difference between the disciplines. Whereas linguists typically give some role to evidence other than these intuitions, philosophers seem not to: they do not acknowledge other evidence and their practice seems to involve only appeals to intuitions.[12]

This practice of relying on intuitions, just like the similar practice of linguists, raises a question: Why suppose that these intuitive judgments about the semantic properties of linguistic expressions are good evidence for a semantic theory? What could be their source that would make them reliable? Philosophers seem to think that these intuitions are a priori, as Michael McKinsey points out (1987, 1). But appeals to the a priori are always dubious, in my view, and are particularly so about semantic properties (1994, 1996, 1998, 2011a). Might philosophers have a more respectable justification for their practice? Stephen Stich has an interesting suggestion: philosophers might be implicitly extending the linguists' VoC to semantics, in particular, to the theory of reference (1996, 40). Philosophers may think that a speaker's underlying competence provides her not only with syntactic intuitions but also with semantic ones.

ME is a rival to this VoC view of semantic intuitions just as it is to the VoC view of syntactic intuitions. And, the significance of this rivalry for the philosophy of language is analogous to that for linguistics. In particular, if VoC is not right and (something like) ME is, then, insofar as we use intuitions as evidence, we should prefer those of the more expert philosophers to those of the folk.[13] *Much more importantly, we should be looking for other evidence for semantic theories.* And we should be using that other evidence to assess the reliability of intuitions.

This raises an interesting question: *What* other evidence? As noted, philosophers, unlike linguists, do not acknowledge any other evidence. I argue that they are very wrong not to. There is in fact lots of other evidence, and philosophers should take ideas from linguists in trying to find it. In particular, philosophers should seek evidence in *usage*. They should seek direct evidence in linguistic reality itself rather than simply relying on the indirect evidence of intuitions about that reality (Devitt 2011b, 2011c).

A major source of such evidence is the corpus, the linguistic sounds and inscriptions that the folk have produced and are producing as they go about their lives. I illustrate what a rich source of evidence the corpus could be for the theory of reference with a vignette to be found, ironically, in an experiment aiming to test folk intuitions about reference in Kripke's famous Gödel case (Machery *et al.* 2004). I point out that the experimenters' own uses of "Gödel" in the vignette, are inconsistent with what (standard) description theories would predict (2011c, 27–28).

There are well-known difficulties in using the corpus as evidence. Fortunately, linguists have shown that we don't have to rely on the corpus: we can *induce* usage from competent speakers in experimental situations using the technique of "elicited production." Experimental situations "are designed to be uniquely felicitous for production of the target structure" (Thornton 1995, 140). I proposed an easier way of eliciting production: rather than *creating* situations in which we see what people say or under- stand, we can *describe* such situations and see what they say or understand about them (2006a, 99). I recently argued that this method can be a ready source of evidence for theories of reference and is the way forward in experimental semantics (2011b, 430–32; 2011c, 29–30). Wesley Buckwalter and I have begun conducting experiments of this sort (2011).

In sum, whether VoC or (something like) ME is correct is of great methodological significance for the study of language by both linguists and philosophers.

I turn now to my two main issues: (a) Do Chomskian linguists actually hold VoC? (b) Is VoC really false?

4 Is VoC the received view in Chomskian linguistics?

4.1 *Background*

I confidently attributed VoC to Chomskian linguistics at the beginning of *Ignorance* (2006a, 4) and later supported that attribution with five quotes and four further citations (96). I shall discuss the five quotes in a moment (Section 4.2), but I want to start the case for the attribution with an expanded version of the first of those quotes. This striking passage from Chomsky has always seemed to me to be as clear a statement of VoC as one could want:

> it seems reasonably clear, both in principle and in many specific cases, how unconscious knowledge issues in conscious knowledge … a person has unconscious knowledge of the principles of binding theory, and from these and others discussed, it follows by computations similar to straight deduction that in [*I wonder who the men expected to see them*] the pronoun *them* may be referentially dependent on *the men* whereas in [*The men expected to see them*] it may not … That this is so is conscious knowledge.
>
> (1986, 270)

I had made the attribution of VoC years earlier (Devitt and Sterelny 1989, 521) without hearing complaint. Stephen Stich has been making it for decades (see e.g. 1996, 40). The VoC view of linguistic intuitions is the explicit inspiration for the "theory-theory" explanation of folk psychological judgments (as I noted, 2006a, 204 n.). It never occurred to me that the attribution of VoC would be controversial. Yet it has turned out to be. It has been controverted by three knowledgeable philosophers: John Collins (2008a, 17–19), Gareth Fitzgerald (2010), and Peter Ludlow (2011, 69–71). I have responded to Fitzgerald already (2010b, 845–47). In brief, despite resisting the attribution, Fitzgerald's description of the "orthodox" Chomskian view is in fact VoC! And I would argue much the same about Collins. Ludlow's discussion of the attribution is by far the most thorough to date and I shall respond to it here.

But first let me draw attention to others who seem to go along with the attribution. (i) Barry Smith, in a critical response to *Ignorance*, states what amounts to VoC: "Unconscious, information-bearing states of the language faculty give rise to conscious knowledge that is immediately reflected in the speaker's intuitive linguistic judgements" (Smith 2006, 443; and see 451, 454). (ii) Similarly, Mark Textor, in talking of intuitions being "derived from mentally represented or tacitly known grammatical principles" like "a theorem [being] derived from already established truths" (2009, 396). (iii) We shall see in Section 6 that Georges Rey embraces the attribution. (iv) Both Jaakko Hintikka (1999) and Timothy Williamson (2007) attribute VoC to the linguists in the course of critical looks at the use of intuitions in philosophy.[14]

Here is a powerful reason for thinking that Chomskian linguists do hold VoC: *How else* can we explain the great evidential weight that linguists attach to intuitive judgments, particularly to the judgments of ordinary folk? The only explanation seems to be that linguists think that folk, simply in virtue of being native speakers of a language, have a privileged access to the truth about that language.

It would be nice, of course, to have some recent statements of VoC by linguists themselves. These are hard to find. The best I have come up with is talk of "the 'true' acceptability response generated by the cognitive system of language" (Sprouse and Almeida, forthcoming). Indeed, so far as I can see, linguists hardly ever discuss the source of intuitions *at all*, presumably feeling that they have better things to do, like constructing grammars. Linguists mostly seem to just *presuppose* VoC without even stating it explicitly. There seems to be little if any attention to the key epistemological question: *Why* are these meta-linguistic intuitions good evidence in grammar construction? This is surprising given the importance attached to the intuitions as evidence. It is particularly surprising given the already-mentioned concern about relying on the intuitions of linguists rather than those of the folk (Schütze 1996). This concern is exemplified, for example, in the following recent papers: Sorace and Keller 2005, Featherston 2007, and Myers 2009. Yet none of the papers raise the key epistemological question about these intuitions.

VoC is not often stated. More interestingly, to my knowledge, it has never been stated in the sort of detail that could make it a real theory of the source of intuitions. Furthermore, again to my knowledge, no argument has ever been given for it (until Rey's, considered in Section 6).

What are we to make of this lack of interest in articulating, let alone arguing for, VoC? I think it may stem from the received Chomskian "psychological conception" according to which the grammar for a language is about a cognitive system in the language faculty of its speakers.

It follows from this conception that the rules (and principles) of the true grammar are embodied in a speaker's mind. A lot of work would still have to be done to get from this to an adequately detailed VoC: *How* do the embodied rules yield a speaker's metalinguistic intuitions? Still, it may be tempting to think that the embodied rules *must* be responsible for her intuitions, even *sans* details. Tempting or not, VoC does still need the details. Aside from that, this route to VoC faces a serious problem, in my view: the psychological conception is false. I have argued against it and in favor of a "linguistic conception" according to which, a grammar is about a non-psychological realm of linguistic expressions, physical entities forming a symbolic or representational system (2003; 2006a, ch. 2; Devitt and Sterelny 1989).[15] It is then an open question whether competence in a language is constituted by the embodied rules of the language.

4.2 Ludlow

In his recent book, *The Philosophy of Generative Linguistics* (2011), Ludlow claims to reject VoC: "I want to stress (in partial agreement with Devitt) that such a view of linguistic intuition is mistaken" (69). But he is very dubious, at least, of my attribution of VoC to linguists. He lists (70) the five quotes that I gave in support of the attribution (2006a, 96) – but without the four further citations I also offered – and discusses each of the quotes. He writes as if this discussion shows that the quotes do not in fact support my attribution of VoC. I have been alarmed to discover people who find Ludlow's discussion convincing. Yet, with one exception, his discussion does not undermine my evidence at all. Indeed, it looks as if Ludlow does not really understand VoC. This may be because he never attends to my actual definition (Section 1 above) but rather responds negatively to my (somewhat playful) *name* for the doctrine – "the voice of competence" – and my (somewhat provocative) *name* for the special sort of access to linguistic facts claimed by the doctrine – "Cartesian access" (Ludlow 2011, 70).

(1) I shall start (though Ludlow does not) with my first Chomsky quote:

> it seems reasonably clear, both in principle and in many specific cases, how unconscious knowledge issues in conscious knowledge ... it follows by computations similar to straight deduction.
>
> (1986, 270)

This quote is a shortened version of the "striking passage" that I have just claimed to be as clear a statement of VoC as one could want (Section 4.1). Ludlow responds:

> The first Chomsky quote goes to the question of conscious knowledge, but I would take this to be knowledge of linguistic facts or phenomena (what I earlier called "S-facts") – not knowledge of the rules which give rise to the linguistic phenomena. This is entirely consistent with the picture I am advocating.
>
> (2011, 68)

What Ludlow means by "S-facts" are "surface facts … like this: 'Who did you hear the story that Bill hit' is not acceptable" (52). So judgments of these S-facts simply are the intuitive judgments that VoC is about. So Ludlow is in fact construing Chomsky as endorsing VoC! On Ludlow's construal, the intuitive judgment – conscious knowledge of an S-fact – "follows by computations similar to straight deduction" from the unconscious knowledge of the linguistic rules and principles. So why does Ludlow resist the attribution of VoC to Chomsky? The reference to "knowledge of the rules" is revealing. It looks as if Ludlow takes VoC to require speakers to have conscious knowledge of the rules (see also 66, 69). But this would be a preposterous thing to suppose and is a bad misunderstanding of VoC. As I point out, the explanation of intuitions offered by VoC "does not suppose that the speaker has Cartesian access to the linguistic rules, just to the linguistic facts captured by the intuitions" (2006a, 96 n.). According to VoC, the speaker has access to *the results* of a derivation from underlying rules not to the rules themselves.

(2) Among the five quotes, the one that Ludlow discusses first is:

> Our ability to make linguistic judgments clearly follows from our knowing the languages that we know.
>
> (Larson and Segal 1995, 10)

Ludlow has this to say:

> is there anyone who could possibly disagree with this quote? Surely the linguistic judgments that I make follow from my knowing the language that I know. If, for example, I knew Japanese I would have different judgments.
>
> (2011, 70)

I disagree with the Larson and Segal quote! And I do so because "follows from" implies VoC: it implies that Ludlow's judgments are *deduced from* his knowledge of English; see the Chomsky quote above. And this is why VoC is mistaken. We should all accept, of course, that knowledge of English provides ample *data* for linguistic judgments about that language and not some other language like Japanese. But the data for judgments are not judgments (Section 1). So, once again, we have Ludlow endorsing a statement of VoC that he does not recognize as such. It really does look as if he misunderstands VoC.

(3) Ludlow next considers my second Chomsky quote. Ludlow gives good reason for thinking that the quote does not support my attribution of VoC.[16] It is the one exception I mentioned.

(4) Now consider this quote from Jerry Fodor:

> We can use intuitions to confirm grammars because grammars are internally represented and actually contribute to the etiology of the speaker/hearer's intuitive judgments.
>
> (1981, 200–1)

Again we seem to have a quote that clearly expresses VoC. But not to Ludlow:

> Likewise, when Fodor says that grammars contribute to the etiology of the judgments, I take this to mean that they contribute in this way: they give rise to the facts, and those facts are the objects of our linguistic judgments.
>
> (2011, 70)

This construal is obviously wrong. First, for someone like Fodor who believes in an internally represented grammar, it would be too obvious to be worth saying that it gives rise to the linguistic facts. Second, and more important, giving rise to those facts would not even appear to explain what Fodor claims to be explaining: why "we can use intuitions to confirm grammars." It would not explain *why intuitions about those linguistic facts are likely to be true* and hence *why they are evidence for* grammars. Fodor clearly thinks that the explanation of this evidential role is that the internally represented grammar *gives rise to those intuitions*. If we simply take Fodor to mean what he says we have a commitment to VoC.

(5) Finally, consider this quote:

> [A speaker's judgments about the grammatical properties of sentences are the result of] a tacit deduction from tacitly known principles.
>
> (Graves *et al.* 1973, 325)

Ludlow has a truly remarkable response to this:

> The passage from Graves et al. is completely misrepresented by Devitt's editorial addition. Graves et al. are not discussing linguistic *judgments*, but rather tacit knowledge of linguistic phenomena – of what I have called explanatory facts.
>
> (2011, 70)

First, Ludlow provides no evidence for this charge of complete misrepresentation: he simply makes a pronouncement. Second, the charge is quite false, as even the most cursory look at Graves *et al.* would show. Ludlow's claim that Graves *et al.* are discussing "tacit knowledge of … explanatory facts" is doubly wrong: (a), the knowledge discussed is explicit not tacit; and (b), it is not of Ludlow's "explanatory" facts.

I'll start with (b). Ludlow contrasts "explanatory" facts with the above-mentioned "surface" facts. "Explanatory" facts "incorporate information about the explanations for … surface linguistic facts – for example this: 'Who did you hear the story that Bill hit' is unacceptable *because it violates subjacency*" (2011, 52, emphasis added). Contrary to what Ludlow claims, in the passage I quote Graves *et al.* are quite obviously discussing knowledge of "surface" not "explanatory" facts. Indeed, only a few lines before, Graves *et al.* give six examples of the knowledge that concerns them. All are of "surface" facts. Here is one:

> English speakers know that …
>   (4) John overestimated himself
> … [is a] well-formed, grammatical sentence.
>
> (Graves *et al.* 1973, 325)

So much for (b). Turn now to (a). Graves *et al.* describe how the field linguist can deduce his judgments of "the grammatical properties and relations of novel sentences" from explicitly formulated principles (324). Their idea then is that this "paradigm of explanation should be transferred" to ordinary speakers:

> The untutored speaker has the same information, in *explicitly* knowing that certain sentences have certain grammatical properties. But we can assume that the speaker, unlike the linguist, does not explicitly know the principles from which it follows that these sentences have these grammatical properties. Why not then extend the paradigm of explanation to the speaker, by assuming that the speaker performs the same deduction as the linguist, only tacitly, and thus that the principles in the deduction are tacitly known?
>
> (325, emphasis added)

So, Graves *et al.* are indeed proposing that a speaker's *explicit* knowledge of Ludlow's *surface* facts is deduced from tacitly known principles. They are proposing VoC, just as I said. Indeed, this is the most detailed presentation of VoC that I know of. (The difference between "explicit knowledge" and "judgment" is of no significance here, of course. Graves *et al.* also talk of judgments in this context (324, 327–28), as is appropriate.) So, my "editorial addition" is in order and the misrepresentation is all Ludlow's.

Ludlow's persistent and extraordinary misrepresentations of the evidence leaves untouched my recent claim that evidence shows, "overwhelmingly," that the orthodox Chomskian view of metalinguistic intuitions is VoC.

Indeed, if Chomskians did not hold VoC, they would have no view of the source of linguistic intuitions (Devitt 2010b, 847).

One is left wondering what Ludlow's view of linguistic intuitions really is. His endorsement of the first Chomsky quote and the Larson and Segal quote suggests that he subscribes to VoC. Yet he resists the obvious VoC interpretation of both the Fodor quote and the Graves *et al.* quote, which suggests that he doesn't subscribe. Further investigation adds to the mystery. A few pages later he claims that "linguistic judgments are no different than judgments of experts with regard to a theoretical apparatus in the lab," for example, chemical judgments (2011, 76). This is just the sort of comparison I make in urging ME (2006a, 103–11) and seems quite at odds with VoC. Yet a later discussion of a "hypothetical character" that he cutely names "Michael" suggests adherence to VoC. "Michael has a grammar as part of his cognitive architecture" but "is deeply confused" (2011, 92). The center of Michael's alleged confusion seems to be that he does not believe that his acceptability judgments are the products of this cognitive grammar. In other words, Ludlow seems to think that to deny VoC is to be confused. All in all, I doubt that a clear and coherent view of the source of intuitive linguistic judgments can be found in Ludlow's book. Certainly there is no argument for VoC.

5 Summary of the case against VoC

So, what is wrong with VoC? Why should ME be preferred? Before answering we should distinguish two possible versions of VoC.

What I call the "standard" version of VoC, implied by most of the quotes, is based on the "representational thesis" that linguistic rules (and principles) are *represented* in the language faculty. Speakers are then thought to derive their intuitive judgments from these representations by a causal and rational process like a deduction. Despite the evidence that this is the right way to understand VoC, it is not certain that linguists really do see intuitions as having their source in *represented* rules. And that representational thesis is rejected by many Chomskian philosophers of linguistics (e.g. Smith 2006; Collins 2006, 2007, 2008a; Pietroski 2008; Slezak 2009). So, perhaps what I call the "nonstandard" version of VoC is the right interpretation: the intuitions are provided somehow by embodied but *unrepresented* rules (2006a, 96–98).

I offer several objections that count against both versions. Very briefly, these are as follows. (i) If competence really spoke to us, why would it not use its own language and why would it say so little (100–103)? (ii) There would be a disanalogy between the intuitions provided by the language faculty and by perceptual modules (114). (iii) There would be problems arising from the differences between the intuitions of the folk and the linguists (115). (iv) If rules in the language faculty provided the linguistic intuitions they would surely also govern language use and yet there is empirical evidence that they don't do both (115–16). Aside from these objections in common, there are further, more important, objections to each version in particular.

The first further objection to the standard version is the already-noted point that we need details to turn this sketch into a theory. Graves *et al.* have provided the most details in extending the explanation of the field linguist to the untutored speaker. This is an ingenious idea but how does the explanation really work? The intuition that a linguistic expression has certain properties is in the central processor. How can representations of principles in a faculty of the mind that is inaccessible to the central processor be brought to bear on a representation of that expression to "deduce" that intuition in the central processor? But my main objection to the standard version is its extreme *im*modesty. This immodesty lies in its commitment to the representational thesis (116–17). A major conclusion of *Ignorance* is that there is no significant evidence that linguistic rules *are* represented in the minds of speakers and, given what else we know, it is implausible to suppose that they are (2006a, 272).

The further objection to the "nonstandard" version is simple and apparently overwhelming: we do not have *any idea* how embodied but unrepresented rules might provide linguistic intuitions (2006a, 118).[17] Not only do we lack the details needed for a plausible explanation but attention to other similar systems gives good reason to suppose that the linguistic system does not provide these intuitions and so we *could never* have the details. The explanation would require a relatively direct cognitive path from the embodied rules of the language to beliefs about expressions of that language, a path that does not go via central-processor reflection on the data. What could that path be? Consider some other examples. It is very likely that rules that are embodied but not represented govern our swimming, bicycle riding, catching, typing, and thinking. Yet there does not seem to be any direct path from these rules to relevant beliefs. Why suppose that there is such a path for linguistic beliefs? Why suppose that we can have privileged access to linguistic facts when we cannot to facts about these other activities? We do not have the beginnings of a positive answer to these questions and it seems unlikely that the future will bring answers.

Since writing *Ignorance*, I have become aware of a body of developmental literature that provides persuasive empirical evidence against VoC.[18] The evidence suggests that the ability to speak a language and the ability to have intuitions about the language are quite distinct, the former being acquired in early childhood, the latter, in middle childhood as part of a *general* cognitive development. Schütze ends a critical discussion of much of this evidence with the observation that "it is hard to dispute the general conclusion that metalinguistic behavior is not a direct reflection of linguistic competence" (1996, 97). It looks as if VoC is false.

6 Rey's defense of VoC

Georges Rey, like Chomsky and Haegeman (Section 1), gives a great deal of evidential weight to linguistic intuitions: they "provide not only excellent evidence, but, by and large, the only serious evidence we have" (Rey 2006b, 563). Only VoC could underlie this extreme – and, I argue (2006a, 98–100), quite false – view and so it is no surprise that Rey subscribes to VoC. But, unlike anyone else I know of, Rey has taken up the challenge of arguing for it (2006b and this volume).[19] The version of VoC that he proposes is a "nonstandard" one.

Rey thinks, contrary to what I have just claimed, that there is "a perfectly scientifically respectable model" of how embodied but unrepresented rules might provide linguistic intuitions (this volume, p. 254). His proposal stems from the view that language processing generates "structural descriptions" (SDs), metalinguistic representations of the syntactic and semantic properties of the expressions being processed. These processes are not, of course, in the central processor: they might be described as "subpersonal," "subdoxastic," or "non-conscious." Let us just say, in a theory-neutral way, that these processes are in a "non-central language system." Rey's suggestion is that *the central processor has access to these SDs*. On the basis of the information they provide, the central processor forms the speaker's intuitive judgments.

I will give Rey's presentation of his view in a moment. But first some preliminaries.

6.1 Preliminaries

The view that language processing generates SDs is widespread and so it is surely reasonable for Rey to adopt it. Nonetheless, I think the view is dubious. I argue that the speedy automatic language processes are fairly brute-causal associationist ones that do not operate on SDs (2006a, 220–43). If that is right, there are no SDs in the language system for the central processor to access. My brute-causal view is explicitly "tentative" but I claim that it is better supported by current evidence than the widespread one. However, my earlier criticism of VoC rested nothing on that tentative view and I shall rest nothing on it here. I will go along with the widespread view for the sake of argument.

In filling out his proposal, Rey makes much of what he, along with many others, sees as an analogy between intuitions about language and intuitions about vision. Rey emphasizes something that I am happy to accept: that vision *processing* is analogous to language *processing*. And I accept that *certain* vision intuitions are analogous to *certain* language ones: intuitions about *what is seen* are analogous to intuitions about *what is said*. Just as the non-central vision system provides the central processor with "the immediate and main basis for judging what is seen" so too does the non-central language system provide the central processor with "the immediate and main basis for judging what is said."[20] But intuitions about what is said are not the metalinguistic intuitions that concern VoC; they are not intuitions about grammaticality/acceptability, ambiguity, coreference, and the like. The vision analogy does nothing to support the view that the latter intuitions are provided by the language system, hence nothing to support VoC (Devitt 2006a, 112–13; 2010b, 850–52, 854).

In response, Rey claims that my discussion of the vision analogy

> seriously misconstrues the projects of both the vision theorist and the Chomskyan linguist. ... neither the vision theorist nor the linguist confine the levels of representation deployed by those systems to merely [the tasks of delivering information to the central processor about what is seen or said]; nor are they committed to the *output* of these systems being couched as reports about the external world. Precisely what the output is of perceptual modules is, not surprisingly, an issue of subtle empirical detail, ... it remains a vexing methodological problem with regard to both language and vision how to disconfound central from module-internal top–down processing, ... The presumption of modularity theorists is that the output is fairly "shallow," ...
>
> (2006b, 563–64)

Rey's first point reflects a misunderstanding. My discussion does not confine the level of representations deployed by those systems at all. Indeed, I clearly accept that the operations of these systems may involve all sorts of representations (2006a, 114). My claim is simply about what representations those systems *deliver to the central processor*.

Rey's second point is more interesting. I do talk of the outputs of the vision and language "module." This was a mistake. My argument that the vision analogy gives no support to VoC does not need such commitments to the architecture of the vision and language systems. In particular, the argument needs no commitment about the place of Fodorian modules within these systems, nor about how "shallow" the outputs of any such modules are, nor about any "top–down" processing the systems may engage in. The nature and workings of these systems are indeed "subtle empirical" matters. And our study of them is, as Fodor says, "in its infancy" (1998, 129). So it is wise to remain as non-committal as possible about them. Fodor's own discussion of them in his classic, *The Modularity of Mind* (1983), is explicitly tentative and speculative. Thus, in considering the outputs of his modules he is pulled two ways. On the one hand, his requirement that a module be "encapsulated" makes him think that its outputs are "shallow" (73–91). If they are shallow, I insist, they must be subject to further non-central processing to arrive at something suitable for delivery to the central processor (on which more below). On the other hand, Fodor's criterion of "phenomenological accessibility" for outputs – "the visual processor ... makes the deliverances of perception available as the premises of *conscious* decisions and inferences" (136 n. 31) – pulls him away from shallowness (94–97, 136–37, nn.). My argument against VoC should have no commitment on such speculative matters. Its only commitment concerns what these systems *make available to the central processor*, a "*bottom–up*" process. Whatever the outputs of one part of the non-central vision system to another part – say "early vision" to "higher-level vision" – what information does the system as a whole ultimately pass on to the central part of the mind that makes intuitive judgments?[21] My argument assumes that the system provides a version of the scene that is the immediate and main basis for the conscious judging of what is seen, *and nothing else*. Now I take it that the only part of this that Rey could think a "subtle empirical" issue is "and nothing else." Yet, so far as I can see, his discussion of vision, on which more below, provides no reason for thinking that the vision system does deliver anything else, in particular, no reason for thinking that it delivers *a description of the worldly vehicle* of the information, which would be an analogue of an SD. So I hold fast to my view that the vision analogy does not support VoC.

6.2 Rey's proposal

In presenting his proposed VoC, Rey allows "that linguists haven't always been forthcoming or clear about just what sort of mechanism they presume underlies and ratifies native speaker intuitions" (this volume, p. 252). This is too generous, given that linguists have said *almost nothing* about these mechanisms. And I think Rey may be too modest in thinking that his proposal is "at least implicit in several proposals that have been made" (ibid.).[22] Here is his proposal:

> linguistic intuitions ... are presumed to be fairly directly caused by representations that are the output of ... a language faculty ... the faculty produces structural descriptions (SDs) of various syntactic objects (phrases, sentences),

and the intuitions are reliable insofar as those descriptions play a crucial role in the production of the intuitions. ... For example, it's because

(1) John seems to Bill to want to help himself.

is produced by the language faculty with something like the SD below, that a speaker would spontaneously have the "intuition" that "himself" refers to John, not Bill. ... the SDs ... are activated by mechanisms of conscious attention which respond to the descriptions with whatever overt vocabulary is available, e.g. "No, himself can't be John, but has to be Bill" ...

(this volume, pp. 253–54)

There are two serious objections to this proposal. (I) *Why* should we suppose that the language system, in processing (1), makes this SD of (1) available to the central processor? (II) Even if it did, how would the SD's information "fairly directly cause" the intuitions that are the concern of VoC? I shall consider these in turn. In so doing, I will adopt "the language-of-thought hypothesis." This is not essential to the argument but it is very convenient for its presentation.

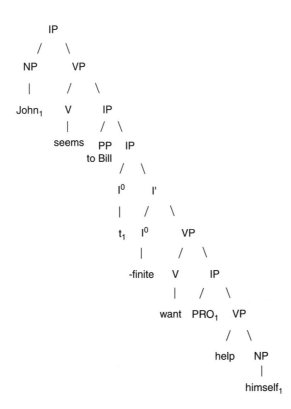

6.3 Serious objection (1)

I assume that for a hearer to understand (1) is for her to come to have a mental representation of the message that *John seems to Bill to want to help himself* in the appropriate part of her central processor. She comes to have something that is a rough translation of (1). With this in mind, we can distinguish two possible versions of Rey's proposal.

According to an *"online" version*, the language system's contribution to the process of understanding *is* the deliverance to the hearer's central processor of the above SD of (1); it delivers something that *describes* (1). The central processor uses this SD to come up with the required rough translation of (1), but it *can also* use it to form intuitions about (1), for example the intuition that "himself" corefers with "John." In contrast, according to an *"offline" version*, the language system contributes to understanding by itself delivering the rough translation of (1). So, on this version, the system delivers a representation of a worldly situation involving Bill and John whereas on the online version it delivers a representation of a representation of that situation.[23] Nonetheless, the central processor can access the SD offline and use it to form intuitions. So accessing the SD would be something *additional to* understanding, not essential to it.

Each version of Rey's proposal is a very substantial one about the workings of the mind. Each needs evidence. I shall now try to demonstrate the prima facie implausibility of each. If this is right the evidential burden of the proposal is very great.

Consider the online version. I am going along with the widespread view that SDs play a rich causal role in the non-central language system. But playing that role in the process of understanding (1) does not entail, of course, that the system's final step is the deliverance of an SD of (1) to the central processor. Because of the causal role of SDs, language processing takes account of the syntactic and semantic information that SDs provide. As a result of what the system then delivers to the central processor, the mental representation involved in the hearer's final understanding of the utterance will have something like those syntactic and semantic properties and be a rough translation of (1). But this is not to say that it has those properties *because the system delivers an SD that describes those properties*. And it is highly implausible that it has those properties because of that.

The central processor is the home of a person's thoughts (propositional attitudes), including linguistic intuitions, that she can normally express in language. In the central processor she can move from one thought to another in practical and theoretical reasoning. Anything that is delivered to the central processor is, as Fodor says, "available to the cognitive processes that eventuate in the voluntary determination of overt behavior" (1983, 56), "available as the premises of *conscious* decisions and inferences"

(136 n. 31). *So if the SD of (1) is delivered to the central processor it must be available as a premise in an inference that leads to the final understanding of (1), an inference that takes the hearer from a description of (1) to a rough translation of (1).* Here are three problems with this. (A) Phenomenology: ordinary hearers understanding (1) have no conscious awareness of its SD or of any inference from the SD to a translation of (1). (B) Given that it takes a few classes in syntax even to understand an SD, it is hard to see how ordinary hearers could use it as a premise even if they had access to it. (C) The speed of language processing is, as Fodor emphasizes, "mind-boggling": "the recovery of semantic content from a spoken sentence" is "very close to achieving the theoretical limit" (1983, 61). Given, as Fodor also notes, "the relative slowness of paradigmatic central processes" (63), it is unlikely that such a significant part of understanding as moving from SD to translation is a central process

Consider now the offline version. According to this version, the deliverance of SDs to the central processor is not an essential part of understanding yet; nonetheless, these SDs can be made available offline and used to form meta-linguistic intuitions. This version is spared problem (C): we seem to arrive at intuitions at a speed suitable for a central process. But the version still has a problem like (A): as we form our intuitions, it does not seem to us that Rey's "conscious attention" yields access to an SD like the one displayed. And the version has problem (B) arising from the difficulty in understanding an SD.

Finally, there is another problem for both versions. (D) Suppose that an SD of (1) *was* made available to the central processor and the hearer based her intuitive linguistic judgments on the rich information it contained. How come then that she does not have the intuition that, say, in (1) "John" c-commands "himself"? If her competence speaks to her in this way, "how come it says so little" (Devitt 2006a, 101)? Presumably, this reticence would have to be explained as follows. Online version: although the hearer accesses a full SD in understanding, she can use only part of its information in forming an intuition. Offline version: the hearer can access only part of the SD offline. What are we to make of these apparently arbitrary restrictions?

These problems are not decisive against Rey's proposal, of course, but they do put a heavy evidential burden on the proposal. Rey directs us to Fodor for the evidence:

> Indeed, all the evidence suggests that speech perception involves not only understanding the *message* conveyed, but a highly modularized perception of *linguistic features of the speech vehicles* themselves.
>
> (Fodor, cited in Rey, this volume, p. 254)

Now I think that there is some truth in this claim. And I have no quarrel with much in the cited passages. Those passages contain lots of evidence and speculation about the nature of perceptual systems, particularly Fodor's modular "input systems," and about how much they contribute to what is ultimately perceived. But their evidential focus is not on what Rey needs to support VoC. He needs powerful evidence of one of the following: that these systems make their perceptual contributions by delivering online to a perceiver descriptions of the vehicles of these perceptual messages; or, that these descriptions in these systems can be accessed offline by perceivers. I don't find any evidence of *that*.

As Rey notes (p. 255), Fodor holds that the language module "deliver[s] representations which specify, for example, morphemic constituency, syntactic structure and logical form" (Fodor 1983, 93). This seems to be the online idea that an SD is delivered to the central processor in language processing. (i) But we need evidence that the language module has an SD-output that *specifies* those properties rather than an output that *has* those properties. Why would the final result of the module's analysis be a metalinguistic representation of (1) rather than a representation with similar properties to (1)? (ii) And if the module did output an SD, we would need evidence that the SD is delivered to the central processor rather than to some other part of the non-central language system. And the evidence would need to be powerful enough to overshadow problems (A) to (D). Given those problems, we should look rather for some other part of the non-central system to handle the transition from the module's SD-output to the rough translation of (1) that must feature in final understanding.

One wonders, of course, how *any* part of the language system might handle this transition from the metalinguistic level to the linguistic level. But it is a consequence of assuming that SDs play a causal role at all that this transition has to be made somewhere. (A) to (D) make it seem very implausible that the transition is in the central processor. So we should look for the transition being made elsewhere, if not in a Fodorian module, then in some other part of the language system.[24]

Elsewhere, Fodor is receptive to the idea of metalinguistic intuitions arising from offline access to SDs (1998, 127–41). But, once again, *no evidence is cited* that we have this access (beyond that we have intuitions allegedly based on those SDs).

Finally, I hasten to add that I am not resisting the familiar Fodorian claim that "you can't help hearing an utterance of a sentence (in a language you know) as an utterance of a sentence" (1983, 52–53). Indeed, I emphasize that language processing is typically "automatic" (2006a, 209). And Rey has me wrong in supposing that I find remarks like the following "implausible": "speech perception involves … a highly modularized perception of *linguistic features of the speech vehicles* themselves"; "we *hear* the utterances of a language we know in terms of [morphemic constituency, syntactic structure, and logical form]" (this volume, pp. 254, 255). In understanding (1), we hear it as having those linguistic features and not others *in that*, as a result of all the processing in the language system, we come up with a representation that *has* those features and not others; for example, it *has* a feature that takes "himself" to corefer with "John" not "Bill." What I do find very implausible is that, in hearing (1) in this way, the central processor *thereby* has the informational basis for the intuitive judgment that "himself" corefers with "John." We have been given no reason to believe that. Hearing an utterance in a certain way is one thing, judging that it has certain properties, another.

In sum, despite Rey's bold claim about "all the evidence," what he cites provides *no evidence at all* of what is needed: no evidence that the non-central language system provides SDs to the central processor. Still, we might sometime get some evidence. Is that *possibility* enough to sustain Rey's claim that he has proposed "a perfectly scientifically respectable model of a VoC" (p. 254)? I think not, given the second serious objection to Rey's proposal.

6.4 Serious objection (II)

Suppose that the language system did deliver a partial SD to the central processor, how would the SD's information "fairly directly cause" the intuitions that are the concern of VoC? Rey's example is of an intuition about coreference. That was a wise choice. Deriving that intuition from the SD of (1) requires some grasp of theoretical syntax but still it would arguably be fairly direct.

But what about the most commonly used intuitions, those of grammaticality/acceptability? Consider the processing of an ungrammatical string. There would be two relevant possibilities: (i) the language system provides an SD of the string to the central processor; or, (ii), it does not (it "crashes").[25] If (i), then that SD would *not* directly cause intuitions of grammaticality. For, that SD does not come with a sign saying "ungrammatical." To judge that the SD is of an ungrammatical string, the subject would have to apply her theoretical knowledge of the language to the SD. That's ME not VoC. If (ii), then *information* provided by SDs would have nothing to do with a subject's grammaticality intuitions. Rather, *the presence or absence* of the SD would be the *data* for the central processor's response. So, not VoC again. Indeed, what does talk of SDs add to the explanation? We might as well say that the intuitions arise from the subject's central processor reflection on the data of trying to understand the string. In sum, either way, competence would be providing the *data for* an intuitive judgment not the *content of* that judgment. That's ME.

Now consider ambiguity intuitions. Once again the information provided by SDs is irrelevant and VoC fails. The intuition will be a central-processor judgment based on noting that the expression has *two* (or more) SDs. And talk of SDs again seems redundant: we might just as well say that the judgment is based on noting that the expression has two (or more) meanings. ME again.[26]

In sum, even if the language system did provide SDs to the central processor, those SDs would mostly not provide the informational content of speakers' intuitions. So Rey has not provided a respectable model of VoC.

7 Conclusion

I have previously attributed to Chomskians the VoC view that a native speaker's linguistic competence provides the informational content of her metalinguistic intuitions. A main aim of this chapter has been to defend this attribution from Ludlow's criticisms. I have argued that these criticisms fail. The evidence that the orthodox Chomskian view of metalinguistic intuitions is VoC is overwhelming.

In previous criticisms of VoC I have claimed that we do not have any idea how embodied but unrepresented rules might provide linguistic intuitions. Rey has proposed a version of VoC to show that I am wrong. My second main aim has been to argue that his proposal fails to show this.

Instead of VoC I have urged ME, the view that linguistic intuitions are ordinary empirical theory-laden central-processor responses to linguistic phenomena. If this is right, it has serious methodological consequences. First, the evidential focus in linguistics should move away from the indirect evidence provided by intuitions to the more direct evidence provided by usage. Second, insofar as the evidence of intuitions is sought, there will seldom be good reason for preferring those of folk over those of experts about language. Finally, what goes for linguistics goes for the philosophy of language. But here the needed change is more drastic because philosophers do not seem even to acknowledge the evidence available from usage. Finally, the focus on usage should yield a place for experimental work in, for example, the theory of reference.[27]

Notes

1 Linguists tend recently to make much of the distinction between intuitions about grammaticality and acceptability. I argue that ordinary acceptability intuitions are evidence only insofar as they are grammaticality intuitions (2010b, 839–44); see Gross and Culbertson 2011 for a response.

2 Despite the received view, John Collins (in the guise of "Ling") talks dismissingly of "the absurd idea that we are after speaker/hearers' explicit propositional judgments on the linguistic status of strings" (2006, 480). For discussion, see Devitt 2010b, 838–39.

3 Mark Textor (2009) hankers after non-judgmental "linguistic seemings" as evidence; see also Gareth Fitzgerald 2010, 138; Barry Smith, this volume. I argue (2010a) that there are no such seemings.

4 Some discussions of VoC are vitiated by a failure to keep these potential roles of competence sharply distinct; see particularly Fitzgerald 2010, discussed in my 2010b; also Collins 2006, 480; 2008a, 31; Textor 2009. It is trivial that competence (along with some other factors) is causally responsible for linguistic usage. But that is not what VoC is about. It is about competence as a source of metalinguistic intuitions.

5 My account of linguistic intuitions in *Ignorance* is misleading in two respects (and contains a minor misstatement); see my 2010a, 254–55 for clarification.

6 It is acknowledged by Haegeman (1994, 10), despite her earlier claim about "all the linguist has to go by." And it is acknowledged by Andrew Radford (1988, 24) after an extensive discussion of the evidential role of intuitions.

7 See Krifka 2012 for a helpful summary of the evidence that linguists use.

8 So "theory" in "theory-laden" has to be construed *very* broadly to cover not just theories proper but also these dispositions. For more on this theory-ladenness, see Devitt 2011c, 19.

9 For an exchange on this issue, see Culbertson and Gross 2009; Devitt 2010b; Gross and Culbertson 2011.

10 For evidence of this, see Devitt 2012, 554–55.

11 This practice has been challenged by "experimental philosophers"; see Machery et al. 2004.

12 I say "seems" because I think that, in fact, some evidence comes from observations of usage (2011c, 25; 2012, 563).

13 This supports "the Expertise Defense" of traditional philosophical methodology against the findings of Machery et al. 2004; see Devitt 2011c, 14–26.

14 Maynes and Gross (forthcoming) contains a subtle discussion of the position of linguists on intuitions.

15 This rejection has received a deal of criticism (some of it very harsh): Antony 2008; Collins 2007, 2008a, 2008b; Dwyer and Pietroski 1996; Laurence 2003; Longworth 2009; Matthews 2006; Pietroski 2008; Rattan 2006; Rey 2006a, 2008; Slezak 2009; Smith 2006, this volume; Devitt 2006c, 2008a, 2008b, 2008c, and 2009 are recent responses to some of these criticisms.

16 Ludlow has considered my attribution of VoC before in a review of *Ignorance*. He there discusses, along much the same lines as in his book, this second Chomsky quote and the Larson and Segal quote. He does not discuss the other three more telling quotes. Nonetheless, he declares that *none* of my quotes "speak to the point in question" (2009, 400). This blatantly false pronouncement is all he offers in support of one of his three sweeping criticisms of my book: "Devitt is not particularly charitable in his interpretation of what linguists have to say about the nature of their enterprise" (399). It is remarkable that Ludlow should make this criticism in a review that is about as uncharitable as it gets – plain nasty really. For comments on the review, see my "Responding to a Hatchet Job" at my homepage at the Graduate Center, City University of New York, <http://devitt.commons.gc.cuny.edu/>.

17 "[N]ot much is known about the mechanisms implicated specifically in the formation of linguistic intuitions" (Maynes and Gross, forthcoming).

18 See particularly, Hakes 1980; Ryan and Ledger 1984; Bialystok and Ryan 1985; Bialystok 1986.

19 Robert Matthews (under review) is about to take up the challenge. Rey is also, so far as I know, the only person to mount a thorough defense of another common view in linguistics: anti-realism about linguistic entities (2006a, 2006b, 2008). According to this curious view, the sounds, inscriptions, etc., of a language do not really have the phonological, syntactic and semantic properties that we naturally suppose them to have. I have responded to Rey's argument (2006a, 184–92; 2006c, 597–604; 2008a, 221–29). My "linguistic conception" of grammars, mentioned in Section 4.1, presupposes linguistic realism.

20 Rey (2006, 563–66; this volume, p. 253) is strangely bothered by my saying that it is the "task" of these systems to provide such information. Yet this is surely a harmless way of identifying what these systems do – their "functions" – *that makes us posit them in the first place*. It is quite compatible, of course, with these systems doing many other things as well. (For another example of such harmless talk, see Fodor on the "tasks" and "function" of the language parser; 1998, 131.)

21 So Rey's point about the "shallow" outputs of early vision is not pertinent (2006a, 564; repeated in this volume).

22 He sees "intimations" of his view in Chomsky and Fodor. Furthermore, he claims that the view "is explicitly defended recently in Collins (2007, 421 [and] Fitzgerald (2010, §3)" (p. 263 n. 18). There is nothing close to such a defense in either of the places cited: Collins does not even mention SDs; and Fitzgerald, rather than providing the details that a plausible VoC needs, tries to make us feel better about their absence, as I point out (2010b, 849–52).

23 A common use/mention sloppiness in linguistics may make it easy to overlook this distinction: it is often unclear whether a discussion concerns SDs of expressions or the expressions themselves, as I note (2006a, 69–71). At one point Chomsky even claims the SDs *are* expressions of the language (1993, 1).

24 I speculate that the transition "would have to be some brute-causal process" and see this as a reason for supposing, contrary to the widespread view, that the automatic process of language understanding *as a whole* is brute-causal, with no role for SDs and hence no need for the transition (2006a, 224).

25 Maynes and Gross propose (ii) as a possible defense of VoC (forthcoming).

26 We should say much the same about the "ambiguity" of the Necker cube (Rey, this volume, p. 254).

27 I am indebted to Steven Gross for comments on a draft. I am indebted to Georges Rey not only for such comments but especially for very many fruitful discussions of the issue.

References

Antony, Louise (2008) "Meta-linguistics: Methodology and Ontology in Devitt's *Ignorance of Language*," *Australasian Journal of Philosophy* 86: 643–56.

Barber, Alex (ed.) (2003) *Epistemology of Language*, Oxford: Oxford University Press.

Bialystok, Ellen (1986) "Factors in the Growth of Linguistic Awareness," *Child Development* 57: 498–510.

Bialystok, Ellen and Ellen Bouchard Ryan (1985) "A Metacognitive Framework for the Development of First and Second Language Skills," in D.L. Forrest-Pressley, G.E. MacKinnon, and T.G. Waller (eds), *Metacognition, Cognition, and Human Performance*, New York: Academic Press, 207–52.

Buckwalter, Wesley and Michael Devitt (2011) "Testing Theories of Reference: Usage vs Intuitions," invited presentation, Metro Experimental Research Group, City University of New York Graduate Center, 11 February 2011.

Chomsky, Noam (1986) *Knowledge of Language: Its Nature, Origin, and Use*, New York: Praeger.

——(1993) "A Minimalist Program for Linguistic Theory," in Kenneth Hale and Samuel Jay Keyser (eds), *The View from Building 20: Essays in Honor of Sylvain Bromberger*, Cambridge, MA: MIT Press, 1–52.

Collins, John (2006) "Between a Rock and a Hard Place: A Dialogue on the Philosophy and Methodology of Generative Linguistics," *Croatian Journal of Philosophy* 6: 469–503.

——(2007) Review of *Ignorance of Language*, by Michael Devitt, *Mind* 116: 416–23.

——(2008a) "Knowledge of Language Redux," *Croatian Journal of Philosophy* 8: 3–43.

——(2008b) "A Note on Conventions and Unvoiced Syntax," *Croatian Journal of Philosophy* 8: 241–47.

Culbertson, Jennifer and Steven Gross (2009) "Are Linguists Better Subjects?," *British Journal for the Philosophy of Science* 60: 721–36.

Devitt, Michael (1994) "The Methodology of Naturalistic Semantics," *Journal of Philosophy* 91: 545–72.

——(1996) *Coming to Our Senses: A Naturalistic Program for Semantic Localism*, Cambridge: Cambridge University Press.

——(1998) "Naturalism and the A Priori," *Philosophical Studies* 92: 45–65. Reprinted in Devitt 2010c.

——(2003) "Linguistics Is Not Psychology," in Barber 2003, 107–39.

——(2006a) *Ignorance of Language*, Oxford: Clarendon Press.

——(2006b) "Intuitions in Linguistics," *British Journal for the Philosophy of Science* 57: 481–513.

——(2006c) "Defending *Ignorance of Language*: Responses to the Dubrovnik Papers," *Croatian Journal of Philosophy* 6: 571–606.

——(2008a) "Explanation and Reality in Linguistics," *Croatian Journal of Philosophy* 8: 203–31

——(2008b) "A Response to Collins' Note on Conventions and Unvoiced Syntax," *Croatian Journal of Philosophy* 8: 249–55.

——(2008c) "Methodology in the Philosophy of Linguistics," *Australasian Journal of Philosophy* 86: 671–84.

——(2009) "Psychological Conception, Psychological Reality: A Response to Longworth and Slezak," *Croatian Journal of Philosophy* 9: 35–44.

——(2010a) "What 'Intuitions' Are Linguistic Evidence?" *Erkenntnis* 73: 251–64.

——(2010b) "Linguistic Intuitions Revisited," *British Journal for the Philosophy of Science* 61: 833–65.

——(2010c) *Putting Metaphysics First: Essays on Metaphysics and Epistemology*, Oxford: Oxford University Press.

——(2011a) "No Place for the A Priori," in *What Place for the A Priori?*, Michael J. Shaffer and Michael L. Veber (eds), Chicago: Open Court, 9–32. Reprinted in Devitt 2010c.

——(2011b) "Experimental Semantics," *Philosophy and Phenomenological Research* 82: 418–35.

——(2011c) "Whither Experimental Semantics?," *Theoria* 27: 5–36.

——(2012) "The Role of Intuitions," in Gillian Russell and Delia Graff Fara (eds), *Routledge Companion to the Philosophy of Language*, New York: Routledge, 554–65.

Devitt, Michael and Kim Sterelny (1989) "Linguistics: What's Wrong with 'the Right View,'" in James E. Tomberlin (ed.), *Philosophical Perspectives*, vol. 3: *Philosophy of Mind and Action Theory, 1989*, Atascadero: Ridgeview, 497–531.

Dwyer, Susan and Paul Pietroski (1996) "Believing in Language," *Philosophy of Science* 63: 338–73.

Featherston, S. (2007) "Data in Generative Grammar: The Stick and the Carrot," *Theoretical Linguistics* 33: 269–318.

Fitzgerald, Gareth (2010) "Linguistic Intuitions," *British Journal for the Philosophy of Science* 61: 123–60.

Fodor, Jerry A. (1981) "Introduction: Some Notes on What Linguistics Is Talking About," in Ned Block (ed.), *Readings in Philosophy of Psychology*, vol. 2, Cambridge, MA: Harvard University Press, 197–207.

——(1983) *The Modularity of Mind: An Essay on Faculty Psychology*, Cambridge, MA: MIT Press.

——(1998) *In Critical Condition: Philosophical Essays on Cognitive Science and the Philosophy of Mind*, Cambridge, MA: MIT Press.

Fodor, Jerry A., T.G. Bever, and M.F. Garrett (1974) *The Psychology of Language: An Introduction to Psycholinguistics and Generative Grammar*, New York: McGraw-Hill.

Gordon, P.C. and R. Hendrick (1997) "Intuitive Knowledge of Linguistic Co-reference," *Cognition* 62: 325–70.

Graves, Christina, J.J. Katz, Y. Nishiyama, Scott Soames, R. Stecker, and P. Tovey (1973) "Tacit Knowledge," *Journal of Philosophy* 70: 318–30.

Gross, Steven and Jennifer Culbertson (2011) "Revisited Linguistic Intuitions," *British Journal for the Philosophy of Science* 62: 639–56.

Haegeman, Liliane (1994) *Introduction to Government and Binding Theory*, 2nd edn, Oxford: Blackwell Publishers; 1st edn 1991.

Hakes, David T. (1980) *The Development of Metalinguistic Abilities in Children*, Berlin: Springer.

Hintikka, J. (1999) "The Emperor's New Intuitions," *Journal of Philosophy* 96: 127–47.

Krifka, Manfred (2012) "Varieties of Semantic Evidence," in Claudia Maienborn, Paul Portner, and Klaus von Heusinger (eds), *Handbook of Semantics*, Berlin: Mouton de Gruyter.

Larson, Richard and Gabriel Segal (1995) *Knowledge of Meaning: An Introduction to Semantic Theory*, Cambridge, MA: MIT Press.

Laurence, Stephen (2003) "Is Linguistics a Branch of Psychology?," in Barber 2003, 69–106.

Longworth, Guy (2009) "Ignorance of Linguistics," *Croatian Journal of Philosophy* 9: 21–34.

Ludlow, Peter (2009) Review of *Ignorance of Language*, by Michael Devitt, *Philosophical Review* 118(3): 393–402.

——(2011) *The Philosophy of Generative Linguistics*, Oxford: Oxford University Press.

McKinsey, Michael (1987) "Apriorism in the Philosophy of Language," *Philosophical Studies* 52: 1–32.

Machery, Edouard, Ron Mallon, Shaun Nichols, and Stephen P. Stich (2004) "Semantics, Cross-Cultural Style," *Cognition* 92: B1–B12.

Matthews, Robert J. (2006) "Could Competent Speakers Really Be Ignorant of Their Language?" *Croatian Journal of Philosophy* 6: 457–67.

——(under review) "Linguistic Intuition: An Exercise of Linguistic Competence."

Maynes, Jeffrey and Steven Gross (forthcoming) "Linguistic Intuitions," *Philosophy Compass*.

Myers, J. (2009) "Syntactic Judgment Experiments," *Language and Linguistics Compass* 3: 406–23.

Pietroski, Paul (2008) "Think of the Children," *Australasian Journal of Philosophy* 86: 657–69.

Radford, Andrew (1988) *Transformational Grammar: A First Course*, Cambridge: Cambridge University Press.

Rattan, Gurpreet (2006) "The Knowledge in Language," *Croatian Journal of Philosophy* 6: 505–21.

Rey, Georges (2006a) "The Intentional Inexistence of Language – But Not Cars," in R. Stainton (ed.), *Contemporary Debates in Cognitive Science*, Oxford: Blackwell Publishers, 237–55.

——(2006b) "Conventions, Intuitions and Linguistic Inexistents: A Reply to Devitt," *Croatian Journal of Philosophy* 6: 549–69.

——(2008) "In Defense of Folieism: Replies to Critics," *Croatian Journal of Philosophy* 8: 177–202.

Ryan, Ellen Bouchard and George W. Ledger (1984) "Learning to Attend to Sentence Structure: Links Between Metalinguistic Development and Reading," in John Downing and Renate Valtin (eds), *Language Awareness and Learning to Read*, New York: Springer, 149–71.

Schütze, Carson T. (1996) *The Empirical Base of Linguistics: Grammaticality Judgments and Linguistic Methodology*, Chicago: University of Chicago Press.

Slezak, Peter (2009) "Linguistic Explanation and 'Psychological Reality,'" *Croatian Journal of Philosophy* 9: 3–20.

Smith, Barry C. (2006) "Why We Still Need Knowledge of Language," *Croatian Journal of Philosophy* 6: 431–56.

Sorace, Antonella and Frank Keller (2005) "Gradience in Linguistic Data," *Lingua* 115: 1497–1524.

Sprouse, Jon and Diogo Almeida (forthcoming) "The Role of Experimental Syntax in an Integrated Cognitive Science of Language," in Kleanthes Grohmann and Cedric Boeckx (eds), *The Cambridge Handbook of Biolinguistics*, Cambridge: Cambridge University Press.

Stich, Stephen P. (1996) *Deconstructing the Mind*, New York: Oxford University Press.

Textor, M. (2009) "Devitt on the Epistemic Authority of Linguistic Intuitions," *Erkenntnis* 71: 395–405.

Thornton, Rosalind (1995) "Referentiality and *Wh*-Movement in Child English: Juvenile *D-Link*uency," *Language Acquisition* 4: 139–75.

Williamson, T. (2007) *The Philosophy of Philosophy*, Oxford: Blackwell.

16 Philosophical and empirical approaches to language

BARRY C. SMITH

It is barely conceivable that anyone should set out to study the mind or language without trying to find out what the science of those subjects has to say about them. This is not because science answers all the legitimate questions: many philosophical issues may remain when all the empirical findings are in. But one would expect that an adequate philosophical explanation of linguistic or mental phenomena ought, at least, to be compatible with what the best-attested science has to say about those phenomena. So it is surprising, to say the least, that some philosophers regard themselves as entitled to turn their backs on relevant branches of science be they linguistics, psychology or neuroscience.

There may be a variety of reasons for distancing oneself from the science. First, there are often ill-informed attempts to criticize a science as confused or muddled, not by assessing it in its own terms, but by taking a particular claim from, say, psychology or neuroscience, and reading it, uncharitably, as though terms like 'representation', 'calculate' or 'decide' functioned in the way they do in ordinary talk, and finding it wanting. This pointless exercise could equally well be carried out, with suitable adjustments, on philosophical claims involving terms used in a specialized way. We needn't spend any more time on this strategy.

Second, there is the idea that the subject matter in question, when focusing on mind or language, must be exactly as common sense, and reflections on it, take it to be, and that the attempt to replace these conceptions with more scientifically tractable notions will simply count as changing the subject. These accusations are widespread in certain parts of philosophy, but the justification for making them is not always so clear. Also, this stance assumes that our folk conceptions of language or mind are in good shape to begin with.

Finally, we have the view that the very nature of mental and meaningful phenomena renders them incapable of scientific explanation, which is why philosophical thinking about them will be immune to scientific challenge. We might think here of Donald Davidson who set out a view of the mental as constituted and exhausted by the application of the intentional concepts used to make sense of one another's behaviour in rational terms. The application of these concepts is normatively governed by a priori principles of interpretation, such as the principles of rationality and charity. And according to Davidson, the norms of rationality have no echo in the physical realm.[1] Rather, they constitute another level of description of otherwise physical things. To accept this position of distance from the sciences one has to subscribe to Davidson's thesis that an event is mental only *as described:* a far cry from our ordinary ways of thinking about the mind, and for that reason resisted by many.

In contrast to each of these stances, there are philosophers who take it as a requirement for the study of a given topic that they should be informed about the science of that subject, and not merely when they are engaged in the philosophy of a special science, like biology, psychology or linguistics. Philosophers who draw on scientific findings to shape their philosophical theories often see themselves as contributing to a larger, interdisciplinary project of providing a fully comprehensive account of a given subject, and they see philosophy as playing a fundamental role alongside other disciplines in arriving at a comprehensive account. No single discipline can hope to explain something as complex as, say, the human mind and its attributes. Many disciplines are needed for such an interdisciplinary project, and philosophers will contribute, alongside psychologists, neuroscientists, biologists and anthropologists, so long as each of them start from a strong disciplinary base. In this way, there is no blurring of the boundaries between disciplines, no dilution of philosophy: there are just different methodological approaches to a common subject matter.

Genuinely interdisciplinary work is thus very different from what has come to be called 'experimental philosophy'. Here, philosophers focus on other philosophers' use of intuitions to guide their theorizing, or to decide between competing accounts of notions like knowledge or reference.[2] Experimental philosophers attempt – not always with the greatest methodological sophistication (though some are better than others) – to conduct 'experiments' in which they gather intuitions from different demographic groups in response to certain thought experimental situations, and attempt to show that philosophers' intuitions cannot be trusted as a good guide to what it is correct to think about the cases, so such intuitions cannot serve the intended purpose of guiding philosophical theory choice.

The point of such results is not always clear. Where it serves as a corrective to the over-reliance, by certain philosophers, on intuitions in arriving at their conclusions, it performs a service. But the achievement is limited and the programme will eventually exhaust its mission. On the other hand, if intuitions do matter, and different groups have conflicting intuitions, what should we say then? Another problem is that in soliciting rival intuitions, the so-called 'experimental philosophers', have often over-stated the role that intuition plays in generating philosophical knowledge, or in settling philosophical claims.[3] Claims to truth in philosophy depend on many things besides intuitions.

More importantly, there is little value in untrained philosophers attempting to carry out 'experiments' by themselves, as opposed to taking part in experimental work with colleagues in the sciences who know about experimental design, know how to control for intervening factors and can analyse data. Learning these skills, or at least learning what is going on, can be useful. But we do not need to train a new generation of amateur scientists; nor do our colleagues in the sciences want that. Where they recognize the need for cross-disciplinary collaboration they want philosophers who can contribute a distinct kind of competence that they themselves don't have but which is complementary to theirs and needed for the common project.[4] And if philosophers need empirical input they do best to turn to practising scientists, and in that way ensure that their philosophical thinking is compatible with the currently best-attested science of the topic. Interdisciplinary work is hard and to do it one has to start from a strong disciplinary base. Good fences make good neighbours.

The philosophy of language

So how should we proceed when studying language? It is natural to expect the starting point in the philosophy of language to be an inquiry into the scope and nature of linguistic phenomena. What precisely *is* the nature of the linguistic phenomena under study? This is a fundamental question for the philosophy of language, and yet one that is seldom asked.[5] Why is that? It may be that philosophers overlook such founda-tional questions because people's dealings with language are so common-place: a familiar part of their everyday lives. But so are episodes in consciousness and there is no similar temptation to suppose that we know the nature of these phenomena. Perhaps language is thought to be easier to identify because linguistic phenomena, unlike mental phenomena, are audible or visible. Focusing on these items would allow us to move directly to the genuinely philosophical questions about their meaning. For example, Michael Dummett tells us:

> The philosopher ... is, very properly, perplexed by the notion of meaning. He quite rightly regards it as an extraordinary thing, demanding explanation, that words – noises that issue from our mouths or marks we make on paper – should *have* meanings.
>
> (Dummett 1991, 14)

Equating words with audible noises and visible marks, Dummett is able to take these bits of language to be unproblematically available to us. However, it would be a mistake to equate *language* with writing, or *words* with written marks. We have to be taught writing, and when we learn it, we are already language users. Besides, a large proportion of language users never learn to write, and even if they did, individuation is no easier. Does each instance of the marks 'marks', on the screen, or on paper, count as the same word? Should we treat 'marks' and 'mark' as the same word? And since a word can be spoken, written or signed, words are not easily identified with sounds, or with any items in any of the media in which they were articulated.

Those who think of words as sounds have to remember that 'luck' and 'look' sound the same in some Manchester accents in English, just as 'caught' and 'cot' do in most Scottish accents. The sounds system of a language, from which words can be constructed, concerns phonemes, which stand at one remove from the acoustical variations of their articulation across speakers, or within speakers across contexts. There is no precise way to correlate phonemes in a given language with the acoustical signals found in speech. For Japanese speaker-hearers, but not for Westerners, /l/ and /r/ count as the same phoneme, as do /b/ and /v/ for some Spanish speaker-hearers. And the fact that for every speaker-hearer a variety of acoustic patterns count as the articulation of the same phoneme, lends credence to the idea that phonemes are not constituted by sounds but perceived in them as a matter of what the mind of the speaker-hearer brings to bear on those sounds: what is read-in rather than read-off. This is why the phonemes that make up the word 'hand' are identified in articulations of the word 'handbag' despite its phonetic realizations being more like /hambag/. Hearing phonemes in speech sounds is a bit like seeing three-dimensional objects in two dimensional drawings: a matter of the mind going beyond the environmental inputs. As sounds, speech sounds are special. We respond to them differently and we may even be equipped to do so from birth.[6] So how accurate is it to speak of 'linguistic items' as being audible?

Supposedly 'audible' linguistic items are only perceived as occurring when sounds are heard *as* meaningful speech, and we need to remember that not everyone hears them this way. If you listen to an utterly foreign language you won't hear it as a sequence of discrete items with clear word boundaries. What you will hear is a continuous sound signal. The spaces between words don't exist in the sound stream but they do obtain in the mind of the listener. So what enables us to hear certain sounds as meaningful speech? Knowledge of language is necessary, and hearing given acoustic signals as particular speech sounds is a matter of tokens falling under types specified by the phonological component of that knowledge.

How each sound token is typed depends on the particular settings of the internal phonological system. It is these setting that determine the phonemes of the language. Phonemes build morphemes, and morphemes build words. Something many philosophers appear to forget when they go on to answer questions about meaning.[7]

The structure of language

Philosophers begin with questions like: How do words and sentences get their meanings? Can we explain their meanings in terms of the content of thoughts and concepts? Is word meaning individual or social? What is it for words to refer to objects? Does non-linguistic context play an essential role in fixing the meaning or reference of the words we utter? All these questions presuppose the unproblematic occurrence of words and sentences as the bearers of these properties, as if bits of language were just as readily accessible to us as tables and chairs. But what is the real nature of these entities and why do so many philosophers of language fail to ask or answer such questions? Dummett is emphatic:

> The central task of the philosopher of language is to explain what *meaning* is, that is, what makes a language *language*.
>
> (1978, 216)

But why think that what makes language *language* is just meaning? Part of the reason is that:

> All that *physically* occurs when two people converse is that they alternately make certain noises.
>
> (Ibid., italics mine)

And yet:

> they are exchanging thoughts, asking questions, giving information, raising objections, etc.
>
> (Ibid.)

It is these facts that stand in need of explanation and meaning is needed to supply that explanation. But is meaning alone sufficient for the task? Even if we could pick out words from the sound stream, and could explain what it was for them to have the meanings they do, how would we account for the extraordinary power each speaker has to express indefinitely many thoughts? As Frege tells us:

It is remarkable what language can achieve. With a few sounds and combinations of sounds it is capable of expressing a huge number of thoughts, and in particular, thoughts which have not hitherto been grasped or expressed by any man. How can it achieve so much? By virtue of the fact that thoughts have parts out of which they are built up. And these parts, these building blocks, correspond to groups of sounds, out of which the sentence expressing the thought is built up, so that the construction of the sentence out of parts of a sentence corresponds to the construction of a thought out of parts of a thought. And we may take a thought to be the sense of a sentence, so we may call a part of a thought the sense of that part of the sentence which corresponds to it.

('Logic in Mathematics', in Frege 1979, 225)

The power to say indefinitely many things, express indefinitely many thoughts, is due to the arrangement and rearrangements of parts of language into whole sentences, where the meaning of the whole depends on the meaning of the parts. But what is the nature of the parts, and how exactly do the meanings of the wholes depend on the meanings of parts? Frege tells us these parts 'correspond to groups of sounds'. But this is inadequate to the data. The very same group of sounds can express more than one thought:

(1) Lee loves his mother and so does John.

Read in one way, (1) can be saying that Lee and John love their own mothers; read in another, it can be saying that both Lee and John love Lee's mother. Syntactically ambiguous strings can realize different relations between the parts, and these relations amount to different sentence structures. A sentence is not just a list of words that make up a shopping list: butter, eggs, cheese, coffee. Instead, it articulates grammatical dependencies between the parts. But what are the dependent parts in (1)? Not all of them appear in the sound stream. To capture the different relations at play, we need to fill out the phonetically null, elided part of the sentence:

(1′) Lee$_i$ loves his mother and so does John$_j$ [VP love his$_{i/j}$ mother]

But now we can see the reference of the hidden pronoun 'his', construed as shared with that of 'John' or 'Lee', fixes the meaning of the string or group of sounds:

(1″) Lee$_1$ loves his mother and so does John$_2$ [love his$_1$ mother]

(1‴) Lee$_1$ loves his mother and so does John$_2$ [love his$_2$ mother]

Such referential connections do not occur in the group of sounds themselves but in the minds of the speaker-hearers. In fact, as we find out from the briefest acquaintance with linguistics:

> the crucial properties of sentences are not revealed by thinking of them as they are outwardly presented to us, namely as strings of signs [or sounds] but rather by their unobservable grammatical structure ... What it is for something to be a sentence for a person is for it to be a grammatical structure that is apprehended and applied to a certain perceptible objects [sounds or signs].
>
> (Higginbotham 1991, 555–56)

Such grammatical structures are remote from surface form and they are certainly not fully apprehended in consciousness. So instead of treating words and sentences as utterances of sounds, Noam Chomsky treats languages as internal to the minds of speakers:

> language has no objective existence apart from its mental representation.
>
> (Chomsky 1972, 169, n.)

As a result:

> linguistic theory is mentalistic, since it is concerned with discovering a mental reality underlying actual behaviour.
>
> (Chomsky 1965, 4)

It is not the sounds and signs people produce that constitute the subject matter of generative linguistics, but the *linguistic forms* people impose on those sounds and signs as a result of their internal states. It is only creatures like us, with the linguistic capacities we have, that can assign signs and sounds the linguistic meaning and structure on which their significance for us depends. On this empirically motivated conception of language, which Chomsky calls I-language (where 'I' stands for internal, intensional and idiolectical), the focus of linguistic inquiry shifts from the actual and potential behaviour of speakers (what Dummett takes to be all that physically occurs) to the internal organization of individual speakers' minds. The study of language is part of the study of mind, and so linguistics— the science of language—is treated as a branch of cognitive psychology. According to Chomsky, any account of language must be an account of a speaker's knowledge of language:

> The person who has acquired knowledge of a language has internalized a system of rules that relate sound and meaning in a particular way. The

linguist constructing a grammar of a language is in effect proposing a hypothesis concerning this internalized system.

(Chomsky 2006, 26)

The I-language theorist takes linguistic phenomena to be cognitive phenomena, due in large part to the specialized component of the mind that enables human infants to acquire and develop a language with an elaborate syntactic structure, without need for explicit training. Dummett was wrong to limit himself to what *physically* occurs – what outwardly appears – when speakers communicate, and to contrast that only with intentional talk of making statements, asking questions, issuing commands. Why think there are just these two levels of description? Davidson is explicit about such a two-level picture, and he argues for it. But many philosophers simply assume it implicitly, neglecting an intermediate level of cognitive organization in the speaker below the level of conscious-ness in a subpersonal language system. It is here that word-like items are represented along with the hierarchical (not linear) syntactic relations between them.

The failure to recognize this cognitive level is probably due to a publicity assumption: namely, that all the features of a language must be outwardly and publicly displayed. Why is this? W.V. Quine tells us that:

Language is a social art which we all acquire on the evidence solely of other people's overt behaviour under publicly recognizable circumstances.

(1969, 26)

This astonishing statement radically underplays what the child, who acquires language, brings to bear on the publicly observable evidence. Without a certain internal organization, nothing happens when animals are exposed to such evidence, as we see in the case of dogs and chimps. Also, sadly, when that internal cognitive organization is impaired, it is no longer possible to recognize the same publicly available evidence as language. So why does Quine make this hopeless assumption? He tells us that:

In psychology one may or may not be a behaviourist, but in linguistics one has no choice. ... We depend strictly on overt behaviour in observable circumstances. ... There is nothing in linguistic meaning beyond what is to be gleaned from overt behaviour in observable circumstances.

(Quine 1990, 37–38)

But the view expressed here is wholly mistaken about language acquisition. The child learning a language and the field linguist are not in the same predicament, facing the same task and subject to the same evidential constraints. The linguist, unlike the child, is not trying to acquire the language by observation of the data, but trying, rather, to explain how the child could have acquired her language on the basis of the evidence *she* was exposed to. The linguist attempts to explain this on the basis of specific hypotheses about the information the child is innately endowed with that would enable her to map a particular course of linguistic experience on to an ability to assign complex syntactic structures to the sounds she produces and responds to: structures that go well beyond the observable, audible data.

> The problem, then, is to determine the innate endowment that serves to bridge the gap between experience and knowledge attained.
>
> (Chomsky 1986, 38)

The shadow of Quine hangs heavily over the philosophy of language, as does Wittgenstein's doctrine that nothing is hidden, which inspires Quine's view of the publicity of meaning. The idea that all is available to view on the surface of our practices supports what Chomsky calls an E-language, a 'construct understood independently of the properties of the mind/brain' (1986, 20). The drive towards such a conception is often a desire to steer clear of an epistemologically hopeless Cartesian picture of the mind as hidden from view. For example, Dummett tells us that an expression's meaning cannot

> contain anything which is not manifest in the use made of it, lying solely in the mind of the individual who apprehends that meaning.
>
> (1978, 216)

If the meanings people attach to their words were items residing solely in the minds of individuals, there would be no knowing for sure what anyone meant by their utterances. Working out what others mean would be, as John McDowell insists,

> a mere matter of guesswork as to how things are in a private sphere concealed behind their behaviour.
>
> (1981, 225)

Such a story is phenomenologically off-key, as McDowell would put it, running counter to our everyday experience of effortlessly understanding one another. It also puts at risk the possibility of interlocutors ever addressing the same subject matter. For this reason, McDowell and many others conclude that the significance of others' utterances in a language must, in general, lie open to view, in publicly available facts about linguistic behaviour in its circumstances.

(McDowell 1981, 314)

The general conclusion from this line of thought is that

when we want to understand meaning and communication we should not turn inward, towards mental states, but outward, to what is publicly observable.

(Føllesdal 1990, 98)

And Davidson tells us that:

The semantic features of language are public features. What no-one can, in the nature of the case, figure out from the totality of the relevant evidence cannot be part of meaning.

(1984, 235)

It is remarkable that what makes these observations seem so compelling, at least in the case of McDowell, is the phenomenological datum of the immediate upshot of linguistic understanding, the very datum of fast, mandatory response with shallow output which Jerry Fodor uses to support his claim that speech perception must be the result of unconscious and automatic modular processes: the work of an input module.

You can't help hearing an utterance of a sentence (in a language you know) as an utterance of a sentence ... You can't hear speech as noise *even if you would prefer to.*

(Fodor 1983, 52–53)

Thus:

'I couldn't help hearing what you said' is one of those clichés which, often enough, expresses a literal truth; and it is what is *said* that one can't help hearing, not just what is *uttered.*

(55, emphasis in original)

For Fodor: 'understanding an utterance involves establishing its analysis at several different levels of representation: phonetic, phonological, lexical, syntactic, and so forth' (64). This is the work of fast, dedicated, and mandatory cognitive processes that perform inference-like computations on their domain-specific representations. There is no guesswork, no figuring out by us, or wondering whether we know what the speaker is saying. We are simply presented with what a speaker is saying, or what our language systems take her to be saying. The outer phenomena stand in need of inner processes.

Chomsky talks of the cognitive states of the internal language faculty as the speaker's knowledge of language, and insists that the theory of language is really a theory of a speaker's knowledge of language. It's easy to be mistaken by what he calls 'knowledge of language'. It is not a set of rules but a finite cognitive function or mechanism which assigns linguistic properties to certain sounds, enabling the speaker to recognize them as words and sentences.[8] Far from being mere noises or marks, nothing counts as a word until it carries its full freight of semantic, syntactic and phonological properties.

Of course, it is no mean feat to connect the workings of the internal language faculty and the conscious phenomenology of speech perception.[9] The language faculty does not operate in isolation, but operates in concert with other cognitive systems to gives rise to a way things seem to the subject in conscious speech perception. So what does the subject perceive? Here, we are helped by an insight of James Higginbotham:

> In language, how you represent things is how they are.
>
> (1991, 556)

This is clearly true at the level of language faculty: the particular configuration of your language faculty, or I-language, and what it assigns to sounds and signs is how things are in your language: i.e. the language the I-language specifies. However, hearing things a certain way linguistically, is the result of the workings of your language faculty and other cognitive systems. And when all goes well, how things seem to *you* linguistically is how they are according to your language faculty. In good cases, the experience of hearing sounds as meaningful speech will be the upshot of a reliable connection between the linguistic properties the I-language assigns to the sounds subpersonally and what at the personal level you hear in those sounds. The subpersonal goings on will give shape and character to conscious perceptions of speech.[10]

In these cases, speakers count as having knowledge of language. Notice the contrast here between my view of knowledge of language as a conscious, personal-level state of the speaker, and Chomsky's view of knowledge of language as an internal and subpersonal state of the speaker. Knowledge of language goes missing in Chomsky's account. There is no object of knowledge independent of the states of the mind/brain for the speaker-hearer's linguistic competence, for the speaker to be right or wrong about. The facts about a language are fixed by the psychological states of the speaker that constitute his or her competence. So in what sense can we talk about those states as providing the speaker-hearer with *knowledge* of the facts of his or her language, when those states are not answerable to the linguistic facts but determine them? I call this the missing object of knowledge objection. (See Smith 2008a, 2008b.) Chomsky is happy to give up talk of competence giving us knowledge *of* anything. My strategy by contrast, can accommodate genuine knowledge of language while maintaining the internalist conception of language as cognitive phenomena by saying under what conditions the subject knows the facts determined at the subpersonal level by the language faculty

Internal and external conceptions of language

Despite the huge advances generative grammar has brought about in our theoretical understanding of language, and the cognitive revolution it inspired, many philosophers despite disavowing behaviourism still labour under the old Quinean influences. Michael Devitt is one such. We see vestigial traces of the Quine- and Wittgenstein-inspired publicity thesis in the following recommendation to philosophers of language:

> philosophers should seek evidence in *usage*. They should seek direct evidence in linguistic reality itself rather than simply relying on the indirect evidence of intuitions about that reality.
>
> (Devitt, this volume, p. 271)

Notice the talk of direct evidence. It is as though the items of interest were just lying around, or as McDowell says, 'open to view on the surface of practice'.

We can see further signs of Devitt's way of thinking when he says:

> Although a speaker's competence in a language obviously gives her ready access to the *data* of that language, the data that the intuitions *are about*, it does not give her ready access to the *truth* about the data.
>
> (Devitt, this volume, p. 269)

How does he try to substantiate his talk of direct evidence of linguistic reality as being out there? In his book, *Ignorance of Language*, Devitt tells us that linguistic entities, or symbols of the sort linguists study, are, 'parts of the spatio-temporal physical world' (2009, 24). Linguistic expressions are physical entities, tokens of sound that partake in a representational system. (See ibid., 8.) As we have just seen, there are no good reasons to think this. The talk of 'physical sentence tokens' is barely coherent: physical sound tokens – acoustic signals – can be *typed* by different syntactic structures, and the same syntactic structure – or type – could be assigned to a variety of sounds made by different speakers, or the same speaker on different occasions, let alone to written marks, or instances of sign language. It is what these realizations have in common that linguists are studying. It simply makes no sense to suppose linguists are studying physical tokens rather than linguistic types. Devitt attempts to dodge this inconvenient truth by retreating to 'as if' talk:

> It is often convenient to talk of the objects posited by these theories as if they were types not tokens, as if they were abstract Platonic objects [or better, mental represented structures], but this need be nothing more than a manner of speaking.

(2009, 26)

Perhaps we can make sense of what Devitt has in mind by taking acoustic signals to be physical tokenings of the syntactically structured sentence types that linguists actually study. But physical sound tokens instantiate sound types. What is it to token a syntactic structure? Just how are the particular acoustic tokens *typed*? What makes them count as 'physical *syntactically structured* tokens', or what makes them physical sound types that have syntactic properties? This story has to be got straight since the role of syntax is crucial in giving an account of language, especially in delivering the kind of account of meaning that philosophers of language see it as their task to provide. Syntax plays a pivotal role in the compositional semantic theories that philosophers of language appeal to in order to explain our capacity to produce and comprehend indefinitely many sentences. As Gareth Evans puts it:

> If (but only if) speakers of a language can understand certain sentences they have not previously encountered, as a result of acquaintance with their parts, the semanticist must state how the meaning of these sentences is a function of the meanings of those parts.

(Evans 1985, 26)

It is by providing a systematic account of how the semantic properties of complex properties depend on the semantic properties of their parts that a compositional theory aims to explain how speakers and hearers are able to understand one another's utterances. The relation between form and meaning, so vital to compositionality's task of connecting parts and wholes, is cemented by syntax. For example, the grammatical dependency relations between elements in syntactic strings contribute to semantics by constraining their interpretations: e.g:

(2) John$_1$ shaved him$_2$

(3) John$_1$ shaved himself$_1$

(4) John's$_1$ mother likes him$_{1/2}$

(5) Mary$_1$ expected to feed herself$_1$

(6) I wonder who$_1$ Mary$_2$ expected to feed herself$_1$.

These are facts about referential dependence (or disjointness) of one item on another, as indicated by the indices – not facts of coreference, as Devitt puts it.[11] (Items may corefer whether or not they are dependent for their reference on one another.) These dependencies, indicated by the indices, show which interpretations we can and cannot give to these sentences, and these constraints on semantic interpretation depends on purely structural configurations (on whether some items c-command others[12]). They are syntactic constraints on sentence meaning.

Often there are moved or displaced elements in a string, and the sentence structure is richer than the string that gets pronounced or inscribed:

(7) John seems to be happy

(7′) John$_1$ seems [t$_1$ to be happy].

The noun phrase (actually, determiner phrase) 'John' is not the subject of 'seems' but is semantically interpreted as if it was in the position occupied by the trace t$_1$ from which it was moved. Similarly:

(8) John seems to Bill to want to leave

(8′) John$_1$ seems to Bill [t$_1$ to want PRO$_1$ to leave].

Here, we have the subject of 'seems', namely John construed semantically as the subject of the empty category PRO, which serves as the subject of 'leave'. We have a similar structure but with binding of an anaphoric element in (9):

(9) John seems to Bill to doubt himself

(9′) John$_1$ seems to Bill t$_1$ to doubt himself$_1$.

Notice, some syntactic movements of elements in the linguistic form of the sentence make no difference to the semantic content of the sentence; e.g. quantifier floating:

(10) All the children were in the garden

(11) The children were all in the garden.

Sometimes word order can affect the likelihood of our adopting one reading or another although both are available. For example with scope readings:

(12) Everyone in the class speaks two languages.

Either everyone has their two languages is the natural reading, but the same string can read as meaning there are two languages and everyone speaks them, depending on whether the quantifier 'everyone in the class' takes wider scope over 'two languages' or vice versa. Normally the fronted expression is read as taking the widest scope. However, consider

(13) A person from every city complained about it.

Here, 'a person' takes narrow scope and 'every city' takes wide scope over it. All such facts have to be studied when arriving at a theory of meaning and use, and for this we need a theory of linguistic competence and performance. These facts have to be uncovered by checking with speakers' intuitions about acceptability, the possibility of (non-obvious) scopal readings pointing to underlying structure and dependency relations.

What does Devitt take syntax to be? He tells us that 'physical sentence tokens' are 'governed by a system of rules' (2006, 26):

> Something counts as a particular sentence, has its particular syntactic structure, *in virtue of* the particular structure rules that govern it.
>
> (Ibid., 24, italics mine)

Standing in certain functional relations a physical token must be part of a representation system governed by structure rules:

> In virtue of what does a sentence have its syntactic structure, whether explicit or not? What makes it the case that a particular token ... has the structure it has, perhaps the structure revealed by [generative grammar]? This question does not seek a *description* of the structure that the sentence has – a description that linguists have been so successful at providing – but rather an *explanation* of its having that structure. Since this structure along with the sentence's word meanings determines the sentence's meaning, this explanation is part of an explanation of the sentence's meaning. It is part of an explanation of in virtue of what the sentence has whatever meaning it has.
>
> (Ibid., 155)

The question is a good one and the requirements of an answer are correctly laid out. Devitt hopes to appeal to sentence meaning, and ultimately to the meaning of sentences in Mentalese to help explain why a string has the structure it has. But sentence meaning depends systematically on form and so the meaning comprehended depends systematically on the syntactic structure of the string speakers give to it. So in virtue of what does a string of sounds or marks have the structure the linguist describes? Devitt acknowledges that:

> A triumph of generative grammar has been to make us appreciate how much of the syntax is not explicit, 'how unrevealing surface structure may be as to underlying deep structure'; 'surface similarities may hide underlying distinctions of a fundamental nature' (Chomsky 1965, 24).
>
> (Ibid., 154)

So how does Devitt propose to get at the fundamental level of syntactic structure? He offers us the following tentative suggestion. The syntax of public-language sentences follows from, or, is the same or similar to, the syntax of mental sentences. The 'sketch of an explanation of the syntactic properties of public-language sentences' (Devitt 2006, 156) proceeds as follows. Thought is prior to language, in a Gricean way, with the content of thought explaining speaker meaning, and speaker meaning explaining conventional linguistic meaning. There is the speaker meaning of a sentence on the occasion of its utterance, determined by the speaker meaning of words and what Devitt calls 'speaker syntax'. The speaker meaning of expressions derives from the meaning of words in the mental sentence it expresses, while:

> The 'speaker syntax' of a sentence on an occasion of utterance is determined by the structure of the underlying mental sentence that the utterance expresses on that occasion and by the way in which the utterance was produced from the mental sentence.
>
> (Ibid.)

Before we ask how a mental sentence produces the speaker syntax of a sentence on the occasion of its utterance, we need to know:

> In virtue of what does a mental sentence have its syntax?
>
> (Ibid.)

Devitt suggests it will have to do with the syntax's role in determining the mental sentence's meaning as shown in:

> ... the structure's role in determining a sentence's possible inferential interactions with other sentences.
>
> (Ibid.)

He goes on to give a toy example of the sort philosophers of a certain stripe seem wedded to, telling us no more than that <Regan is wrinkled> will be similar to <Thatcher is tough>, and <All politicians are rich> will be similar to <All police are corrupt>. This somewhat underdeveloped suggestion links syntactic structure tightly to the semantic relations between sentences, but there are many empirical reasons for doubting any such convenient mesh between syntax and semantics. John Collins, for example sets out in forensic detail the problems with so many philosophers of language's presumption that:

> the structures provided by syntactic theory mesh with or support our conception of content/linguistic meaning as grounded in our first-person understanding of our communicative speech acts.
>
> (Collins 2007, 505)

Collins argues that there is no such tight fit. He documents the way results of generative grammar show that:

> *syntactic structure provides both too much and too little to serve as the structural partner for content*, at least as that notion is generally understood in philosophy.
>
> (Ibid.)[13]

Undaunted by the empirical evidence, Devitt entertains the idea the regular use of linguistic sentences with the same speaker syntax will conventionally fix the syntactic properties of public-language sentences; and the speaker syntax of a sentence will be the same or similar to that of the mental sentence it expresses. Devitt has conceded that:

> the syntactic properties of public-language sentences are not explicit.
>
> (2006, 157)

And yet they will, he supposes – for no empirical reason whatsoever – have the same or a similar syntax to the mental state. But why shouldn't an SOV structure of a mental sentence produce a linguistic sentence of SVO form? Devitt tells us no more than:

> It seems rather unlikely to me that the production would make these sorts of changes.
>
> (Ibid.)

At any rate, linguistic sentences will have the same implicit syntactic properties as mental sentences. Thus, a public-language sentence in the passive voice may have the implicit syntax of the active voice if the mental sentence it expresses is in the active form. But what determines mental syntax? The rules of thought, according to Devitt. In this sense, at least:

> a language is largely psychologically real in a speaker in that its rules are similar to the structure rules of her thought.
>
> (Ibid.)

And as long as we stick to implicit properties:

> The speaker syntax of [the] public-language sentence would be the same as that of the mental sentence.
>
> (Ibid.)

Why should we accept any of this speculation when what is needed is a realistic and well-worked out example to convince us that a full account could be given? We are not told in any detail what the syntax of mental sentences is like. If it is the same as the linguistic speaker syntax why introduce two levels? If it is different and it dictates the implicit properties of speaker's syntax, then we need an account, or need to know what will determine an account of, mental syntax. Hints about semantic inferential connections hardly begin to address the task of explaining syntax. So should we pursue the philosophy of language by relying on mere mental sketches without any worked out details of the sort Devitt offers, or on empirically informed and detailed characterizations of the syntax–semantics interface, along the lines provided (and contested) by the likes of Collins (2007), King (2007) and Stanley (2000)? The choice is clear.

In the face of scientific advances in linguistics, we have to relinquish our intuitive ways of thinking about languages, just as we have done in other arenas of common sense. The sun does not literally sink behind the hill. Linguistic structure rules do not apply to physical sound properties: they apply to elements in a structure, elements that carry information about grammatical roles and categories including phonetically null elements in the syntax. It is these elements that are said to be represented in the minds of speakers.

Another strong counter-influence that props up the idea of languages as 'out there', is the common-sense intuition (not a linguistic intuition in the technical sense) which holds sway with many philosophers, that speakers succeed in communicating by taking advantage of an existing language in which words and sentences have meaning. It is what *sentences mean* in the language that can explain what *speakers mean* in uttering them. This anti-Gricean thought runs counter to what Devitt suggests but it drives towards the same outward focus on language use.

However, the common-sense view needs to say what it is for there to be a language with meaningful expressions that speakers can make use of, and what it is for there to be an indefinite range of sentences that belong to that language. Here, interest in language and meaning must be addressed independently of speakers' meaning something if the former is to help us explain the latter. The public language must be characterized first and then we must say something about what it takes for, or what counts as, people successfully using that language. But where do we get the resources to characterize language in this way? What is the metaphysics and epistemology of language on this picture? It would have to be a Platonic account of languages as abstract objects, which relies on defining infinitely many sets of expression–meaning pairs and providing an account of the Actual Language Relation that connects speakers and their languages.[14] There is good reason to believe no such account can be given without reference to the internal cognitive organization of speaker-hearers.[15] By contrast, the idea of the public language 'out there', according to Devitt, will be a conventional representational system: a reflection of (a product of?) rules of thought encoded in a language of thought. Unfortunately, we are given not a single example of how we get from rules of thought – whatever form and content they have – to physical entities standing in functional relations to one another that determine a representational system with a particular syntax. Without even one detailed specification of how a given syntactic structure emerges and is assigned to a particular physical sound token, via its mental sentence equivalent, let alone an account of *all* the syntactic structures of the language, it is impossible to assess this merely programmatic suggestion.

It is also highly ironic to hear Devitt complain that his opponents in the generative tradition have given no account of how the syntactic structures posited by generative grammar are mentally represented or how the grammar that licences them is encoded, when he has given not a single worked out example of how the rules of thought, conventions and functional relations he talks of produce something public with a syntactic structure. Moreover, there are plenty of signs of why Devitt is unable conceive of generative grammarians or their philosopher co-workers coming up with any story about the mental representation of linguistic syntax. For instance, he misunderstands talk of: 'structural descriptions' (SDs) as

> metalinguistic representations of the syntactic and semantic properties of the expressions being processed. These processes are not, of course, in the central processor: they might be described as 'subpersonal', 'subdoxastic', or 'non-conscious'.

(Devitt, this volume, p. 280)

But of course they are not metalinguistic at all. The SDs theorists talk of are ways of specifying the structure that is mentally represented, not an account of the way this structure is represented in the speaker's language faculty.

One gains some insight into the struggle Devitt takes himself to be engaged in, and the frustration he feels with his critics, in their clinging to the methodology of generative grammar, when one sees things as he does and distinguishes between intuitions on the one hand as mere opinions, and the linguistic reality they are about on the other. But the distinction in Devitt's hands is based on a confusion. The linguistic intuitions the theorist tries to tap are not beliefs of some sort about an externally existing reality: they are – when all goes well cognitively – a presentation to the subject's consciousness (or seemings) of the linguistic reality constituted by the underlying states of the language faculty that, in part, gives rise to them. Linguistic intuitions are immediate responses to offline presentations of putative speech samples. Our response to them, and what we can subsequently say about that response when prompted, is a source of data about the underlying structure of the language faculty: a partial account of the mind.

Devitt tells us intuitions are better when the theorist produces them:

> when we do use intuitions as evidence, we should prefer those of the linguists to those of the folk because they have the better background theory and training; they are more expert.
>
> (2006: 111, 115)

But this is very wide of the mark. It assumes, falsely, that there is one language we all use. But the theorist may be studying a speaker's language not all of whose properties are properties of his language. His own intuitions are entirely beside the point.

Let us be clear. Intuitions are data for a theory; they are not the subject matter of linguistic theory. They help us get at linguistic reality, which is a cognitive reality. (The best treatment of this point is to be found in Ludlow 2011).

Of course, things do not always goes well so our linguistic intuitions are not just the voice of competence, as Devitt rather tendentiously puts it.[16] We are likely to hear (14) as perfectly intelligible:

(14) Many more people have been to Paris than I have.[17]

Though, on further reflection the sentence strikes us (another intuition) as gibberish. Similarly, we can fail to see the legitimate use of (15) at first.

(15) Sailors sailors sailors fight fight fight.[18]

When we add further elements we can recognize (15) to mean what (16) does.

(16) Sailors who sailors that sailors fight, fight, also fight.

That my language faculty does not always deliver the right result, or even every result it could, is due to the influence of other factors in performance than competence. For example, the parser that actually does the processing in accordance with the grammar can help us to recognize a structure under some conditions but not others. If you are asked is (17) ambiguous, at first you may say, no.

(17) Time flies like an arrow.

But if we read it again after parsing (18) the other reading pops out.

(18) Fruit flies like a banana.

In all these cases, we need a story about why what my initial linguistic intuitions deliver is at odds with what the language faculty dictates; a processing story that is about why performance and competence come apart. Performance is the upshot of several cognitive systems and we have to factor out the contribution made by our linguistic competence. Devitt tells us that:

> It is trivial that competence (along with some other factors) is causally responsible for linguistic usage.
>
> (2006, 7)

But it is a far from trivial matter to factor it out. To do so we need philosophers, linguists and psychologists. The task for the I-language theorist is an interdisciplinary one.

The E-language theorist needs to say what it is for there to be a language with indefinitely meaningful expressions, and go on to explain what it is for speakers to make use of them. An account of language and meaning must be provided independently of speakers' *meaning something* if the former notions really can help to explain the latter. The language must be characterized first and then we must say something about what counts as *using* it. The biggest worry for the E-language theorist, is how to motivate an account of the syntactic structure of sentences and their recombinable parts – needed to explain the potential for a discrete infinity of sentences – without making any mention of speakers' psychology. It is not clear where the resources for this task will come from, and so far there is not a lot to go on.

Notes

1 Davidson 1980, 231.
2 See, for example, Machery *et al.* 2004.
3 See Herman Cappelen's useful corrective to this way of viewing philosophy, in his 2012.
4 It is tempting to endorse Jerry Fodor's quip about 'Experimental Philosophy' being like Christian Science. It's neither.
5 The topic has been more widely covered in the philosophy of linguistics. See Collins 2005, 2008a, 2008b; Devitt 2006, 2008; Laurence 2003; Ludlow 2006, 2009, 2011; Matthews 2006, manuscript; Pietroski 2009, 2011; Smith 2006, 2008a, 2008b.
6 See Dehaene-Lambertz *et al.* 2005.
7 A useful corrective to this neglect of phonology in the identification of words is S. Bromberger and M. Halle's 1992, and Rey 2006. See also Smith 2009.
8 The best account of what Chomsky means by a faculty of language is John Collins' 'Faculty Disputes' (2004).
9 For some attempts to cast light on these relations see Smith 2006, 2008a, 2008b, 2009.
10 Versions of this story appear in Smith 1992, 1998, and 2008a and 2008b. A similar approach can be found in Textor's 2009.
11 For example: 'linguistics gives a very large role to the intuitive linguistic judgments of competent speakers about grammaticality/acceptability, ambiguity, coreference, and the like' (Devitt, this volume, p. 268); 'What I do find very implausible is that, in hearing (1) in this way, the central processor *thereby* has the informational basis for the intuitive judgment that "himself" corefers with "John"' (p. 287); 'Rey's example is of an intuition about coreference' (ibid.).
12 In terms of tree geometry, an expression α c-commands an expression β when, α does not dominate β, β does not dominate α, and the first branching node dominating α dominates β. Anaphors like himself/herself must be bound but pronouns like him/her must be free. An item binds another when it c-commands it. For more on c-command and binding see Chomsky 1995.
13 I leave readers to grind though the plethora of examples in Collins' paper for themselves.
14 See Schiffer 1993.
15 See Smith 2008b, 961–65.
16 For a substantive response to Devitt's voice-of-competence attributions, see Matthews, manuscript.
17 I owe the use of this wonderful example to Paul Pietroski.
18 I owe the use of this beautiful example to John Collins.

References

Bromberger, S. and M. Halle (1992) 'The Ontology of Phenomenology', in S. Bromberger, *On What We Know We Don't Know: Explanation, Theory, Linguistics, and How Questions Shape Them*, Chicago: University of Chicago Press; republished in D. Prawitz, B. Skyrms and D. Westerstahl (eds), *Logic, Methodology and Philosophy of Science* (Dordrecht: Elsevier Science, 1994), pp. 725–43.

Cappelen, H. (2012) *Philosophy without Intuitions*, Oxford: Oxford University Press.

Chomsky, N. (1965) *Aspects of the Theory of Syntax*, Cambridge, MA: MIT Press.

——(1972) *Language and Mind*, New York: Harcourt Brace Jovanovich; repr. by Cambridge University Press in 2006.

——(1986) *Knowledge of Language*, New York: Praeger.

——(1995) *The Minimalist Program*, Cambridge, MA: MIT Press.

——(2006) *Language and Mind*, Cambridge: Cambridge University Press.

Collins, J. (2004) 'Faculty Disputes', *Mind & Language* 19: 503–33.

——(2007) 'Syntax, More or Less', *Mind* 116(464): 805–50.

——(2008a) *Chomsky: A Guide for the Perplexed*, London: Continuum.

——(2008b) 'Knowledge of Language Redux', in *Croatian Journal of Philosophy* 8: 3–43.

Davidson, D. (1980) *Essays on Actions and Events*, Oxford: Oxford University Press.

——(1984) *Essays on Truth and Interpretation*, Oxford: Oxford University Press.

Dehaene-Lambertz, G., C. Pallier, W. Serniiclaes, L. Sprenger-Charolles, A. Jobert and S. Dehaene (2005) 'Neural Correlates of Switching from Auditory to Speech Perception', *NeuroImage* 24: 21–33.

Devitt, M. (2006) *Ignorance of Language*, Oxford: Oxford University Press.

——(2008) 'Methodology in the Philosophy of Linguistics', *Australasian Journal of Philosophy* 86: 671–84.

Dummett, M. (1978/1991) 'What Do I Know When I Know a Language?', repr. in *Frege and Other Philosophers*, Oxford: Oxford University Press.

——(1991) *Frege: Philosophy of Mathematics*, London: Duckworth.

Evans, G. (1985) *Collected Papers*, Oxford: Oxford University Press.

Fodor, J. (1983) *The Modularity of Mind*, Cambridge, MA: MIT Press.

Føllesdal, D. (1990) 'Indeterminacy and Mental States', in R. Barrett and R. Gibson (eds), *Perspectives on Quine*, Oxford: Blackwell.

Frege, G. (1979) *Posthumous Writings*, trans. P. Long and R. White, ed. H. Hermes, F. Kambartel, and F. Kaulbach, Oxford: Basil Blackwell.

Higginbotham, J. (1991) 'Remarks on the Metaphysics of Linguistics', in *Linguistics and Philosophy* 14(5): 555–66.

King, J. (2007) *The Nature and Structure of Content*, Oxford: Oxford University Press.

Laurence, S. (2003) 'Is Linguistics a Branch of Psychology?', in A. Barber (ed.), *The Epistemology of Language*, Oxford: Oxford University Press, 69–106.

Ludlow, P. (2006) 'The Myth of Human Languages', in *Croatian Journal of Philosophy* 6(3): 385–400.

——(2009) Review of *Ignorance of Language*, by M. Devitt, *Philosophical Review* 118(3): 393–402.

——(2011) *The Philosophy of Generative Linguistics*, Oxford: Oxford University Press.

McDowell, J. (1981) 'Anti-realism and the Epistemology of Language', repr. in his *Meaning, Knowledge, Reality*, Cambridge, MA: Harvard University Press.

Machery, Edouard, Ron Mallon, Shaun Nichols, and Stephen P. Stich (2004) 'Semantics, Cross-Cultural Style', *Cognition* 92(3): B1–B12.

Matthews, R. (2006) 'Could Competent Speakers Really Be Ignorant of Their Language?' *Croatian Journal of Philosophy* 6: 457–67.

——(manuscript) 'Linguistic Intuitions: An Exercise of Linguistic Competence'.

Pietroski, P. (2009) 'Think of the Children', in *Australasian Journal of Philosophy* 86: 657–69.

——, with S. Crain (2011) 'The Language Faculty', in E. Margolis, S. Laurence and S. Stich (eds), *The Handbook for Philosophy of Cognitive Science*, Oxford: Oxford University Press.

Quine, W.V. (1969) *Ontological Relativity and Other Essays*, Cambridge, MA: Harvard University Press.

——(1960) *Word and Object*, Cambridge, MA: MIT Press.

——(1990) *Pursuit of Truth*, Cambridge, MA: Harvard University Press.

Rey, G. (2006) 'Conventions, Intuitions and Linguistic Inexistents: A Reply to Devitt', *Croatian Journal of Philosophy* 6: 549–69.

Schiffer, S. (1993) 'Actual-Language Relations', *Philosophical Perspectives* 7: 231–58.

Smith, B. (1992) 'Understanding Language' in *Proceedings of the Aristotelian Society* 92: 109–41.

——(1998) 'On Knowing One's Own Language', in C. Wright, B. Smith and C. Macdonald (eds), *Knowing Our Own Minds*, Oxford: Oxford University Press.

——(2006) 'Why We Still Need Knowledge of Language', *Croatian Journal of Philosophy* 6: 431–56.

——(2008a) 'What Remains of Our Knowledge of Language? Reply to Collins' in *Croatian Journal of Philosophy* 8(22): 557–75.

——(2008b) 'What I Know When I Know a Language', in E. Lepore and B. Smith (eds), *The Oxford Handbook of Philosophy of Language*, Oxford: Oxford University Press.

——(2009) 'Speech Sounds and the Direct Meeting of Minds', in M. Nudds and C. O'Callaghan (eds), *New Essays on Sound and Perception*, Oxford: Oxford University Press.

Stanley, J. (2000) 'Context and Logical Form', *Linguistics and Philosophy* 23(4): 391–434.

Textor, M. (2009) 'Devitt on the Epistemic Authority of Linguistic Intuitions', *Erkenntnis* 71: 395–40.

17 The first-person perspective and its relation to natural science

LYNNE RUDDER BAKER

Naturalism, as I shall construe it here, is the philosophical method that takes the natural sciences to authorize ontological and epistemological claims.[1] The natural sciences are "objective" in that they regard reality from, as Thomas Nagel put it, "the view from nowhere." Whatever a first-person perspective is, it decidedly is not a view from nowhere.

So right off the bat, we have an apparent tension between the first-person perspective and the non-perspectival natural sciences. Dennett explicitly says that "all science is constructed from that [the third-person] perspective" (Dennett 1991, 71). I'll join Dennett in saying that science is "third-personal," although the real contrast is not between first- and third-person perspectives, but between a world with irreducible first-personal perspectives and a world without perspectives at all. Many naturalists, including Dennett, are unworried about the apparent tension between the first-person perspective and the non-perspectival natural sciences inasmuch as they think that the first-person perspective can be either eliminated or reduced to third-personal terms.

I hope to show that such philosophers are mistaken: the first-person perspective is neither eliminable nor reducible to non-first-personal elements. Although I have a detailed account of a two-stage first-person perspective elsewhere (Baker 2013), here I intend to focus on a single datum and argue that it cannot be treated adequately by the natural sciences. The datum can neither be eliminated nor cast in non-first-personal terms; it seems invisible from the perspective of cognitive science.

Here is my plan: First, I formulate the datum. Second, I consider a couple of ways that naturalists try either to render the datum in non-first-personal terms or to eliminate it. Third, I give an argument that the datum cannot be treated adequately by natural science. Fourth, I look at some empirical literature from cognitive science and show that cognitive science does not even recognize the datum, much less treat it adequately from a scientific point of view. Finally, I make some (perhaps idiosyncratic) remarks about method in philosophy.

The datum

The robust first-person perspective, which I discuss in detail in Baker (2013), is not just the ability to refer to oneself; it is the ability to refer to oneself *as* oneself, in the first person. What is of interest is a distinction that we draw frequently:

(D) There is a distinction between conceiving of oneself as oneself in the first person and conceiving of someone who is in fact oneself (perhaps unbeknownst to the thinker).

The distinction (D) issues in two kinds of belief about oneself, one tied to a first-person conception of oneself and the other not. Here is an example of the distinction close to home. Suppose that Mitt Romney did not realize that a certain *New York Times* columnist (Maureen Dowd) referred to him as Mittens. Suppose that one of the *Times'* columns is accompanied by a photograph of Romney from the back. Suppose that Romney reads all about Mittens, sees the photo and comes to believe that Mittens is the man in the photo. Although Romney himself is the man in the photo, he does not come to believe that *he (himself)* is Mittens. He would express his belief by saying, "Mittens is the man in the photo," not by saying, "I am the man in the photo." But Romney refers to himself by "Mittens" just as surely as he refers to himself by "I"; so the difference between his saying "Mittens is the man in the photo" and "I am the man in the photo" is not a difference in reference. The difference is that the latter, but not the former, manifests a capacity to conceive of himself as himself.

The same point can be made in terms of *de re* belief: Romney believes of Mittens/himself that he (Mittens) is the man in the photo, but Romney does not believe of Mittens/himself that he (himself) is the man in the photo—even though Mittens is himself. So, distinction (D) is right there in ordinary phenomena and deserves to be taken as a datum.

The distinction (D) depends on the capacity to conceive of oneself as oneself in the first-person. I call this capacity a "robust first-person perspective."[2] It is a capacity that is *directly* manifested in thoughts and sentences like, "I am glad that I am a philosopher," or "I believe that I am a fair-minded person." The first occurrence of "I" in these sentences is a simple first-person reference; the second occurrence of "I" self-attributes a first-person reference. To put it another way: the first occurrence of "I" in these sentences refers to me in the first-person as thinker or speaker; the second occurrence refers to me in the first-person as part of the object of my thought. I'll use an "*" to signal this latter ability.[3] I'll say "I am glad that I* am a philosopher" and "Romney believes that he* is not the man in the photo" to mark direct manifestation of a robust first-person perspective. So, any sentence with a "*" (pronounced "star") in it makes a commitment to a robust first-person perspective.

A robust first-person perspective is *indirectly* manifested in thoughts or sentences like, "I am LB"—thoughts or sentences that presuppose that the speaker has the capacity to conceive of herself as herself in the first person. People with a robust first-person perspective indirectly manifest it whenever they are thinking about what they* are saying or doing.

The problem posed by distinction (D) for the natural sciences is this: Distinction (D) seems not to be formulable in wholly third-personal terms nor can it be eliminated altogether. Since the natural sciences cannot countenance anything that is irreducibly first-personal, any genuine phenomenon that entails distinction (D) seems to elude the net of the natural sciences.

Since to have the capacity to conceive of oneself as oneself* is to have a robust first-person perspective, distinction (D) cannot be made without commitment to a robust first-person perspective. It is the robust first-person perspective that I shall focus on as not falling within the purview of the natural sciences. The natural sciences do not tell us, I shall argue, how to make the distinction (D) in non-first-personal terms, nor do they eliminate the distinction altogether. I'll call distinction (D) "the datum."

Will the first-person perspective be adequately treated by science?

If naturalism, as I am construing it, is correct, then the natural sciences must be able to provide a complete description of reality. The natural sciences, as I mentioned at the outset, are formulated in entirely third-personal terms. So, if naturalism is correct, then any first-person phenomena must ultimately be treated from a non-first-personal point of view. It would not be enough for natural science to find third-personal causes of first-person phenomena. A complete description of reality must render the first-person phenomena themselves in scientifically acceptable terms. *If naturalism is correct, then a complete description of reality will mention nothing first-personal.*

So, a naturalistic treatment of the first-person perspective will either eliminate the datum altogether (as, for example, Dennett tries to do; Dennett 1991; Huebner and Dennett 2009), or reduce it to something entirely impersonal (as, for example, Perry tries to do; Perry 2002). In Baker 2013, I discuss (and find wanting) these attempts to naturalize the first-person perspective either by reduction (Perry and Lewis) or by elimination (Dennett and Metzinger). Due to lack of space here, I'll not try to summarize these long and complicated arguments. Instead, I'll go straight to my own argument that all such attempts will fail.

Against naturalizing the first-person perspective

Now I shall present a positive argument that the robust first-person perspective will not be reduced or eliminated.[4]

Call the concept of oneself as oneself* a "self-concept" or an "I*-concept". I*-sentences express propositions that contain I*-concepts—concepts by means of which we conceive of ourselves as ourselves*. First, I argue from I*-concepts to I*-properties. If I*-concepts are not empty, then they express I*-properties—the property of conceiving of oneself as oneself*. Since necessarily, one has an I*-concept if and only if one has the capacity to conceive of oneself as oneself*, the only way that an I*-concept could fail to express a property would be for such a capacity to fail to exist. However, such a capacity is manifested in all aspects of life—from marriage vows to volunteering for a suicide mission. Since the capacity to conceive of oneself as oneself* in the first-person undoubtedly exists, the concept of that capacity—unlike, say, the concept *phlogiston*—expresses a property.[5] To have an I*-concept is to have that capacity and to exemplify the property of conceiving of oneself as oneself*. So, there is a property of conceiving of oneself as oneself* in the first-person. So, I*-concepts express I*-properties. Say that:

> (R) An I*-property is reducible if and only if it is entailed by non-first-person properties recognized by a natural science.

> (E) An I*-property is eliminable if and only if a complete ontology does not entail that there is such a property.

I'll start with the irreducibility and ineliminability of I*-sentences, characterized as follows:

> An I*-sentence S is *reducible* if and only if S is replaceable *salva veritate* by non-first-person sentences recognized by a natural science, where non-first-person sentences are sentences expressing propositions that neither entail nor presuppose a first-person reference.

> An I*-sentence S is *eliminable* if and only if whatever purposes S serves could be served equally well by a sentence or sentences lacking any first-person constituent (e.g. "I," "me," "my," "mine," "he*," "she*") and recognized by a natural science.

The argument proceeds as follows:

(1) I*-sentences are neither reducible nor eliminable.
(2) If I*-sentences are neither reducible nor eliminable, then neither are I*-properties.

(3) If I*-properties are neither reducible nor eliminable, then the robust first-person perspective cannot be adequately treated by natural science.
∴ (4) The robust first-person perspective cannot be adequately treated by natural science.

The first premise is supported by a thought experiment. Consider an I*-sentence and what I call its "corresponding non-first-personal sentence":

(i) I believe that I* am wealthy (assertively uttered by Jones).
(ii) I believe that Jones is wealthy (assertively uttered by Jones).

There are circumstances in which (i) is true and (ii) is false, and circumstances in which (i) is false and (ii) is true. Consider this fantasy (adapted from Baker 1981, 159):[6]

> Jones is a multimillionaire hedge-fund manager, who has a belief that he expresses by saying at *t*, "I believe that I* am wealthy." One unhappy day, Jones is abducted, bopped on the head and left on the side of the road in Vermont. When he recovers, he cannot remember his prior life. Eking out a living as a farmhand in Vermont, he regularly reads in the newspaper and on the Internet of Jones, the missing millionaire. He thus comes to believe at *t'* that Jones is wealthy and he expresses his belief at *t'* by "I believe that Jones is wealthy"; not realizing that he* is Jones, he dissents at *t'* from "I believe that I* am wealthy." In these circumstances at *t'*, (ii) is true and (i) is false.[7]
>
> Now suppose that farmhand Jones wins the state lottery; so Jones comes to believe at *t''* that he* is wealthy; at about the same time (at *t''*), he reads that, due to mismanagement, Jones's hedge fund has collapsed, and that Jones is a pauper. So he comes to disbelieve at *t''* that Jones is wealthy. In these later circumstances, (i) is true and (ii) is false: At *t''*, (i) expresses a true proposition and (ii) does not; so, (i) is not reducible to (ii).
>
> Therefore, (i) cannot be replaced *salva veritate* by (ii). So, I*-sentences like (i) are irreducible to their non-I* counterparts, like (ii)—counterparts that express propositions lacking first-person constituents. (This bears out the earlier claim that I*-sentences are not instances of "*x* believes that *x* is F".) Since (ii) is the most plausible non-first-person candidate for the reduction of (i), we can conclude that (i) is not reducible simpliciter.

The above story about Jones also shows that I*-sentences are not eliminable. One of the main purposes that I*-sentences and thoughts expressed by them serve is to rationally guide action. Rationally guiding action is a vital human purpose. When Jones came to believe that Jones was wealthy, but not that he* was wealthy, he took work as a farmhand. If Jones had continued to believe that he* was wealthy, he would have gone back to his opulent life. The purpose of guiding action cannot be achieved without beliefs expressed by I*-sentences. No propositional attitude lacking a self-concept could move Jones to resume his former black-tie-and-champagne life. Certainly, his belief that Jones (who was in fact himself) was wealthy was impotent to restore Jones to his former station. So, I*-sentences are neither reducible nor eliminable.

The second premise moves from I*-concepts to I*-properties. I'll divide the defense of the second premise into two parts: (a) If I*-sentences are irreducible, so are I*-properties. I*-sentences express I*-propositions that contain I*-concepts, and—as I just argued—I*-concepts express I*-properties. (I am using "express I*-properties" here as short for "express propositions that contain I*-concepts that express I*-properties.") So, I*-properties expressed by irreducible I*-sentences must also be irreducible, for this reason: If I*-properties were reducible, then they would be entailed by non-first-person properties. In that case, the I*-sentences that express the I*-properties would be replaceable *salva veritate* by non-first-person sentences. But we have just seen that the I*-sentences are not replaceable *salva veritate* by non-first-person sentences. Therefore, if I*-sentences are not reducible, then I*-properties are not reducible.

(b) If I*-sentences are ineliminable, then so are I*-properties. I*-sentences express I*-propositions that contain I*-concepts; we just saw that I*-concepts are not eliminable; no propositional attitude lacking an I*-concept could move Jones to resume his well-heeled life. Since I*-concepts are not eliminable, neither are the properties that I*-concepts express: I*-properties.[8]

The third premise—if I*-properties are neither reducible nor eliminable, then the robust first-person perspective cannot be adequately treated by natural science—simply follows from the fact that the natural sciences recognize no first-person properties. So, the natural sciences treat the robust first-person perspective adequately only if a natural science either reduces it to non-first-personal elements or eliminates it altogether.

So, since the three premises are true, and the argument is valid, we can conclude that the robust first-person perspective cannot be adequately treated by the natural sciences.

Does cognitive science step in on behalf of naturalism?

I anticipate an objection that would go like this: "Cognitive science is a natural science in the broad sense, and there are a myriad of experiments on what is called 'the first-person perspective.' The thrust of the experiments is to call into question the reliability of the first-person perspective and thus to diminish its significance.[9] So, rather than saying that the first-person perspective impugns naturalism, the cognitive-science objector concludes, we should say that naturalism (by means of empirical studies) impugns the first-person perspective."

In the first place, this objection from cognitive science, I believe, misses the point of my argument. The cognitive-science objector unsurprisingly is concerned with cognition, but cognition is only a small part of my concern. I'm concerned with the fact that we (many of us) have a capacity for inwardness. We can think about our own desires and resentments—states that we may try (perhaps successfully) to conceal from other people. My concern is not with the accuracy of our own assessments of our desires and resentments. (For all we know, we may be deceiving ourselves.) My concern is how we can have inner lives in the first place. Distinction (D) is part of the answer: We can have inner lives only because we can conceive of ourselves in the first person ("from the inside," as it were) and can distinguish the way that we can think about ourselves in the first person from the way that we can think about entities (ourselves and other things) as just further objects in the world. Regardless of how reliable or unreliable first-person perspectives are for acquiring beliefs about ourselves, we make distinction (D) and thus have first-person perspectives.

Now I want to argue that particular cognitive-science theories lack the resources to recognize distinction (D) at all, much less to reduce distinction (D) to non-personal terms.

(I) Some philosophers and cognitive scientists (e.g. Jerry Fodor 1987) hold that to have a belief or desire is to "token" a mental representation in a special language of thought. Call this "representationalism." Perhaps a cognitive scientist would say that when Romney is thinking of himself as Mittens, he tokens one mental representation, but when he is thinking of himself as himself* in the first person, he tokens a different mental representation. He doesn't realize that these mental representations refer to the same individual (himself), until his wife informs him that he (himself) is Mittens.

But the difference between exercising one's capacity to conceive of oneself as oneself* and merely conceiving of oneself as something or other is not a matter of which mental representation is tokened. According to representationalism, the subject does not even realize that he* is tokening a mental representation, much less does he have any opinions about what it refers to. When his wife tells Romney that he* is Mittens, Romney learns something about himself—the person—not just something merely about mental representations.

If conceiving of oneself as oneself* were simply the tokening of a special mental representation that is causally connected to certain other mental representations, then our mental lives would be flat. The only difference between Mach's thinking, on seeing himself in the mirror, "That guy is unkempt," and his coming to think, "I am unkempt" would be which mental representation he tokened. This would put his disgust that he* was unkempt exactly on a par with his disgust that the man who he took to be someone else was unkempt.[10] This does no justice to the importance in our lives of I*-thoughts, nor to their moral significance. So, appeal to mental representations seems inadequate to reduce distinction (D).

Relatedly, self-monitoring is inadequate to accommodate the datum. To make distinction (D), a self-monitoring system would have to recognize in the first person that it was monitoring itself*. However, a self-monitor cannot distinguish between monitoring (the thing that is) itself and monitoring itself as itself*. An object x can monitor x without realizing that it is itself* that it is monitoring.

(II) Many cognitive scientists have a "dual-process" conception of cognitive processing. They distinguish what they call "System 1" and "System 2." System 1 operates "automatically and quickly, with little or no effort and no sense of voluntary control." System 2 "allocates attention to the effortful mental activities that demand it, including complex computations. The operations of System 2 are often associated with the subjective experience of agency, choice and concentration" (Kahneman 2011, 20–21). System 1 seems to coincide with what I call "the rudimentary first-person perspective": "The capabilities of System 1 include innate skills that we share with other animals. We are born prepared to perceive the world around us, recognize objects, orient attention, avoid losses and fear spiders" (Kahneman 2011, 21–22). By contrast with System 1, Kahneman says (21), "When we think of ourselves, we identify with System 2, the conscious, reasoning self that has beliefs, makes choices, and decides what to think about and what to do."

Without a doubt, System 2 is a capacity more similar to the robust first-person perspective than is System 1. However, System 2 does not have conceptual space for the distinction between thinking of oneself as oneself* and thinking of someone who happens to be oneself. Consider some of the diverse examples that Kahneman gives of the operations of System 2: Some seem to require or presuppose a robust first-person perspective ("Tell someone your phone number"); others do not ("Look for a woman with white hair"), and still others are ambiguous with respect to the robust first-person perspective ("Monitor the appropriateness of your behavior in a social situation" is ambiguous between monitoring the behavior of yourself as yourself* from the first person or the behavior of someone who is in fact yourself, via a surveillance camera). The examples have in common only that they "require attention and are disrupted when attention is drawn away" (Kahneman 2011, 22). Requiring attention is not going to distinguish between cases in which you are manifesting a robust first-person perspective and cases in which you are not.[11]

So, although the dual-process conception of System 1 and System 2 may make an important distinction about mechanisms, it does not underwrite the crucial distinction between conceiving of oneself as oneself* in the first-person and conceiving of someone who happens to be oneself; hence, the dual-process view does not have room for the robust first-person perspective.

(III) Metacognition fares no better. Metacognition is a trivial shift of mind-reading—i.e. a trivial shift from third-personal attribution of mental states to others on the basis of their behavior to attributions of mental states to ourselves: Metacognition is "merely the result of turning our mindreading capacities on ourselves" (Carruthers 2009, 123). This is ambiguous between my turning my mind-reading capacities on someone who is in fact myself and turning them on myself conceived of as myself* in the first person.

So, there seems to be a dilemma: Presumedly, mind-reading does not require an I*-concept. If metacognition does not require an I* concept (if metacognition really is the trivial shift from mind-reading that it is billed as being), then it leaves out the robust first-person perspective altogether and cannot recognize distinction (D). On the other hand, if metacognition does require an I*-concept, then it is no trivial shift, but covert introduction of a robust first-person perspective without reducing it to non-first-personal terms. In neither case, can metacognition, understood as mind-reading turned on ourselves, make the distinction (D) without presupposing an irreducible robust first-person perspective. Metacognition either fails to make distinction (D) or it does not reduce or eliminate the first-person perspective.

(IV) Cognitive scientists are concerned with introspection and its epistemic warrant or lack of it. For example, Carruthers (2010) argues that we do not have introspective access to our decisions and (non-perceptual) judgments; our attributions of decisions and judgments to ourselves depend on self-interpretation, just as our attributions of decisions and judgments to others depend on interpretation of their behavior. The only difference is that we have a much greater evidential base in our own case. However, whether we know our decisions and judgments by introspection or by self-interpretation is irrelevant to my argument about the first-person perspective. Self-interpretation raises the same basic issue about the first person as introspection.

What is self-interpretation? Cognitive science seems not to distinguish between an interpretation of somebody who happens to be yourself, and interpretation of yourself from the first person. But this, again, is the crucial distinction (D). Suppose that a cognitive scientist is studying the results of an Implicit Association Test of an anonymous subject, and judges that the subject is biased. Unbeknownst to the cognitive scientist, he (himself) is that subject. His judgment is indeed about himself, but not about himself in the relevant (first-personal) sense. (The scientist may recommend therapy for the subject, but balk at the idea of therapy for himself.) This plausible example shows the need to recognize distinction (D).

If self-interpretation is to have to do with what we want from self-knowledge, it had better be interpretation of oneself conceived of *as* oneself, from the first person, and not just interpretation of someone who happens to be oneself. So, the robust first-person perspective is presupposed as much by self-interpretation as by introspection (Cartesian or not).[12]

As I said, the cognitive scientist's interest in the first-person perspective is not to consider it within the strictures of science (i.e. not per se in eliminating or reducing it), but in ascertaining its reliability as a cognitive faculty. No matter how unreliable cognitive scientists deem the first-person perspective, they have not begun to show how non-first-personal science can accommodate it.

(V) However, perhaps Carruthers' views may be brought to bear against distinction (D) altogether. In an important new book, *The Opacity of Mind*, Carruthers (2011) argues that "there is a single mental faculty underlying our attributions of propositional attitudes, whether to ourselves or to others" (Carruthers 2011, 1). In that case, given the inference from an underlying mechanism to the single mental faculty that it supports, "self-knowledge" and "other-knowledge" are on a par.[13] This view clearly has no ability even to recognize distinction (D), which implies a distinction between two kinds of knowledge and belief about ourselves. Suppose then that we follow Carruthers and reject the datum.[14]

Which half of distinction (D) do we reject? (Since "self-knowledge" implies truth, I'll switch the locution to "self-belief.") On Carruthers' theory, there is nothing distinctive about self-belief except that it happens to be about ourselves—that our access to our own current discursive mental states is "no different in principle from our access to the mental states of other people, at least insofar as both are equally grounded in sensory input [as he thinks they are]" (Carruthers 2011, 1).

This passage strongly suggests that Carruthers' theory would retain the notion of self-belief as belief about someone who is in fact ourselves, and reject the notion of self-belief as belief about ourselves as ourselves*. If this is right, then to follow Carruthers, we should reject the robust first-person perspective and with it our ability to conceive of ourselves in the first-person, without aid of a name, description or other third-person referring device.

This point seems to leave the door open for an instance of "one philosopher's modus ponens is another's modus tollens": If there is a robust first-person perspective, then there is a distinction between thinking of oneself as oneself* in the first person and thinking of someone who happens to be oneself. I go the "modus ponens" route: we have robust first-person perspectives, and hence can make the distinction. Cognitive scientists may go the "modus tollens" route: we can't make the distinction, and hence do not have robust first-person perspectives (as I have characterized them).

However, there are good reasons to recognize distinction (D). Here are two empirical reasons: (i) The fact that we need distinction (D) to make sense of what people do and say is good empirical evidence that there is such a distinction. (Remember poor Jones.) (ii) Distinction (D) makes a difference in behavior. Contrast: "I believe that I* destroyed Jack's property" vs "I believe that Suspect 2 destroyed Jack's property," where the speaker is in fact Suspect 2. If the former is true, then the speaker may take steps to make restitution to Jack; but if the latter is true (and the former is false), then the speaker will not take steps to make restitution to Jack. Since the beliefs lead to a difference in ensuing action, and the only difference between them is that the former directly manifests a robust first-person perspective, distinction (D) makes a difference in what happens.

Moreover, there is a theoretical reason not to reject distinction (D): Distinction (D) and the robust first-person perspective unify all our self-directed attitudes—being glad that I* ... , anticipating that I* ... , being embarrassed that I* ... , regretting that I* ... and all the rest. Carruthers' theory, which concerns only epistemic states like knowing and believing, leaves us with an un-unified motley of attitudes. In the interest of theoretical unity, we should prefer the robust first-person perspective to a view that provides no natural way to unify all of our self-directed attitudes.

So, rather than denying a robust first-person perspective, I suggest taking Carruthers' theory to cast doubt on the notion—which I believe is his own—that "differences at the personal level are only possible if realized in subpersonal differences" (Carruthers 2011, 23–24). The problem with a subpersonal level—with any level of mechanisms and processes—is that it leaves out actual phenomena at the personal level, the level of distinction (D) and the robust first-person perspective.

To sum up: On the one hand, as we have just seen, cognitive science cannot reject distinction (D) and the robust first-person perspective without theoretical and empirical impairment. On the other hand, cognitive science cannot recognize distinction (D), without acknowledging the robust first-person perspective. The arguments have shown that the robust first-person perspective can be neither reduced to nor eliminated by the natural sciences. Hence, no wholly non-personal theory—including cognitive-science theories—can accommodate the datum, distinction (D). In that case, the natural sciences are unable to accommodate all of reality, and naturalism (as I am construing it) is false.

Methodological consequences

If correct, my argument that the sciences fail to recognize part of reality has consequences for methods in philosophy. In particular, distinctive methods of science like experimentation do not suffice for philosophy. But if natural sciences don't supply the methods to exhaustively describe reality, then, what else is there? The obvious answer is "armchair philosophy." Armchair philosophy, as I construe it, is what you do by thinking, reading, talking, arguing, and analyzing, often using I*-thoughts. Just because armchair philosophers do not conduct experiments does not imply that their activities are extra-empirical.[15]

Some philosophers consider armchair philosophy to be a priori, but the idea of the "a priori" is traditionally bound up with the idea of being "independent of experience." And armchair philosophy characterized by the above activities is anything but independent of experience. From the armchair, we have access to all the knowledge that follows from our conceptual and linguistic competence, all our expertise, and—with the aid of the Internet—much of extant knowledge. No doubt scientists use these methods too, but scientists, unlike armchair philosophers, also depend on being able to replicate experiments with increasingly more subjects.[16]

In my opinion, we should not slavishly follow some single method in philosophy. For philosophers, I would advocate *bricolage*—using whatever materials are at hand. Philosophers may avail themselves of close-to-home thought experiments; they may also draw on knowledge of history, literature, science, and mathematics.

Speaking personally, my advice is to let your goal be your guide. My aim is to make sense of the shared world that we all live in and interact with. The methods I use are those suitable to that aim. For example, when philosophical reasoning leads to rejection of something without which we cannot make sense of the world—e.g. when philosophical reasoning leads to the conclusion that nobody has an interior life—I repudiate the conclusion, as I just did in the preceding section. When philosophers hit a brick wall, and find that they cannot climb over it, cannot go around it or knock it down, they do well to retrace the steps that led to the impasse and reject one or more of them.

Let me illustrate my "bricolage" approach with a brief discussion of introspection. First, I heartily reject a Cartesian view of introspection: we do not have infallible access to our own mental states, and anyone with a robust first-person perspective has many beliefs about her environment and other people. (I have argued this at length in Baker 2011.) However, one can reject Cartesian infallibility without wholesale distrust of introspective judgments. Carruthers' view that takes our beliefs about our current mental states to be subject to "frequent confabulation" undetectable by the thinker (Carruthers 2011, 6) seems unduly pessimistic.

Global distrust of introspection is self-defeating: the more emphasis on the unreliability of what you think that you* are thinking, the more unreliable is your view of unreliability; the more emphasis there is on confabulation, the more likely it is that one's own view is itself infected with confabulation. (Much of the empirical evidence for confabulation of decisions, intentions, and judgments depends on experimenters' trickery or hypnosis.[17]) If you cannot trust what you take to be your own thoughts or discern which deliverances are trustworthy, it is difficult to see how you could have a coherent view of reality (my goal).

So, while rejecting a Cartesian notion of introspection, I do not place introspection generally under suspicion.[18] I endorse a broader view of introspection, a view according to which your beliefs about yourself* have many sources and are variably reliable, depending partly on the content of the belief introspected. As I see it, introspection falls into a more general category of beliefs-without-discernible-evidence—a category that includes not only my believing that I* am thinking about what to eat at lunch, but also my believing that a certain word is appropriate in a certain context, or that certain colors look good together, or that certain remarks are rude, or that what I* did was wrong. The first of these beliefs is about my own mental state, and is known by introspection; but the other beliefs-without-discernible-evidence are not about my mental states, but about words, colors, remarks, and deeds. Beliefs about my own mental states (known by introspection) are generally no more defective than the other beliefs-without-discernible-evidence.

Moreover, showing that some of our beliefs-without-discernible-evidence are false does not show that we do not have those beliefs. I know by introspection that I am thinking about what to eat for lunch, and I also know by introspection that my belief that I am thinking about what to eat at lunch is true. On the other hand, although I know by introspection that I believe that I* am a fair-minded person, I do not know by introspection that my belief that I am a fair-minded person is true. Indeed, it may well be false.

Others—intimate friends, therapists—are in a better position to know whether I am self-deceived than I am. (But I do not believe that cognitive-science experiments will tell me that I am self-deceived—any more than epidemiology will tell me whether I have cancer.) The cognitive-science objector is surely right that we do not know our own mental states as well as we suppose. However, with respect to our mundane beliefs without emotional charge, we do seem to have a privileged epistemological status: I have more confidence in my belief that I am thinking about an issue in philosophy than I would in any empirical claim that what I was really thinking about was not philosophy, but kinesiology.[19] (And I would have even less confidence in an inference from a statistical study of what people are thinking under various circumstances to what I am thinking.)

However—and without the help of empirical studies—I realize that in certain cases I should be leery of my own judgment. For example, recently there was a controversy about two versions of Leonardo's *The Virgin of the Rocks*. The *London Review of Books* and the *New York Review of Books* had articles that came to diametrically opposed conclusions. I had no antecedent opinion on the matter, but I judged the *LRB* article to be the more convincing. It occurred to me that the *LRB* article, which I read first, had biased my reading of the *NYR* article. So, I suspended judgment until I have more information. My own (first-personal) self-assessment, whose reliability is questioned by cognitive science, sufficed. Empirical work may have a bearing on certain areas—e.g. gender bias—but does not generally trump the carefully considered judgment of experts with long records of being astute judges.

The natural sciences tell us a lot about the nature of reality, but if I am right, they don't tell us everything. They don't tell us that reality is personal, and this is the question at issue: Is the world, with us in it, ineliminably personal or not? Those who take natural science to be their methodological guide say no; I say yes.

Let me conclude with a methodological query: Our ability to conceive of ourselves as ourselves* is a personal-level capacity. Why does it resist being reduced to or replaced by subpersonal phenomena? If I am right about the robust first-person perspective, then we have an answer to this methodological question: the personal level of reality—the level on which we live and love—is neither eliminable nor reducible to subpersonal levels that supply the mechanisms that make it possible for us to live and love.

Notes

1 The label "naturalism" subsumes numerous views. So-called "liberal naturalists" do not restrict their philosophical resources to the deliverances of natural science. McDowell says that Sellars suggests that it is a kind of naturalistic fallacy to equate "the logical space of natural-scientific understanding" with "the logical space of nature" (McDowell 2004, 95). Plantinga takes ontological naturalism to be the claim that "there is no such person as God or anything at all like God;

there is no supernatural realm at all" (2011, 169). My concern here is only with the claim that natural science is the exclusive arbiter of knowledge and reality.

2 More precisely, a robust first-person perspective is the second stage of a first-person perspective, the first stage of which I call a "rudimentary first-person perspective." Language users, who have self-concepts, have a robust first-person perspective, and human infants and higher animals have only a rudimentary first-person perspective. The robust first-person perspective develops along with the ability to use language; neither is ontologically prior to the other. I have a whole theory of the first-person perspective (Baker 2013), but the datum at issue does not depend on the theory.

3 Hector-Neri Castañeda introduced "he*" to attribute a first-person reference to someone else, e.g. "The editor believes that he* is wise," which is not true unless the editor would express his belief in the first person, by "I am wise." Gareth B. Matthews extended the "he*" from sentences with a third-person subject to "I*" for sentences with a first-person subject. Castañeda studied phenomena expressed by sentences like "The editor believes that he* is *F*" (Castañeda 1967, 1966). Gareth B. Matthews extended the discussion to phenomena expressed by "I think that I* am *F*" (Matthews 1992).

4 Some of this and the following section are a reworking of some arguments in chapters 3 and 5 of Baker 2013.

5 The I*-property is an essentially dispositional property. For further details about dispositional properties, see Baker 2013.

6 Although some philosophers may reject thought experiments as inherently unreliable, they have been used fruitfully for centuries in both science (e.g. Galileo) and philosophy (e.g. Kripke). I agree with the skeptics about thought experiments presenting bizarre cases that are wholly implausible, but I take thought experiments that remain within familiar territory to be useful tools in philosophy.

7 For possible-worlds advocates (like Stalnaker 2008): A possible world in which Jones loses his I*-belief is a different possible world—different things happen—from a possible world in which Jones retains his I*-belief. One set of worlds is compatible with Jones's beliefs at *t*, and a different set of worlds is compatible with Jones's beliefs at *t'*. At *t'*, Jones had the non-I* counterpart of his I*-belief that he* was wealthy without his first-person belief; as a result, he did what he never would have done before he was abducted: he found work as a farmhand.

8 Note that (E) together with the ineliminability of I*-properties does not entail that there are no I*-properties. It entails only that either the (putatively complete) ontology is incomplete, or there are no I*-properties.

9 For example, "reflection on the manner in which our beliefs are formed may ... lead to entirely erroneous beliefs about the source of our first-order states" (Kornblith 2012, 139).

10 Moreover, this example (like others) raises the question of how many boxes—belief box, hope box, disgust box, and so on—we will need.

11 Non-linguistic entities that lack a robust first-person perspective are able to pay attention when, say, they are tracking their prey.

12 I'll later consider the possibility that Carruthers would reject distinction (D) and deny that there is a robust first-person perspective.

13 Although I do not have space to argue for it here, I think that such inferences from internal mechanism to person-level phenomena are fallacious. In the last chapter of Baker 2013, I sketch an alternative account that avoids such inferences.

14 Alternatively, Carruthers may accept distinction (D), but on pain of admitting an ineliminable and irreducible first-person element into his view. The general tenor of his view suggests that he would reject the datum.

15 In Baker 2007, I argued that there are three grades of empirical involvement: ordinary-empirical, experimental-empirical, and theoretical-empirical. The armchair philosopher is very engaged with the ordinary-empirical, and may be somewhat engaged with the two higher grades of empirical involvement.

16 I am taking the experimental method to be paradigmatic of science. Although there is no clear line between science and non-science, there is no doubt that science is altogether third-personal and that the first-person perspective is not.

17 It is noteworthy that in many of the empirical studies that impugn introspection, the subjects are not typical believers like you and me. They are commissurotomy patients (Carruthers 2009,

2010), subjects who confabulate following hypnosis (Carruthers 2010), subjects given a forced choice or duped—as in studies of position effect (Nisbett and Ross 1980, 207)—or primed (Frankish and Evans 2009, 14). They are in obviously non-optimal (even non-normal) epistemic situations. Moreover, the studies are statistical, and hence inapplicable to a particular individual.

18 I'm not sure that Carruthers does either. Carruthers only claims that there are "numerous instances" when our self-attributions of propositional attitudes are false, "made on the basis of misleading behavioral or other sensory evidence (just as happens when we attribute attitudes to other people)."

19 Like van Inwagen in a different context, I believe that I am justified in this view, but I don't know how (van Inwagen 1999).

References

Baker, Lynne Rudder (1981) "Why Computers Can't Act," *American Philosophical Quarterly* 18: 157–63.

——(2007) *The Metaphysics of Everyday Life: An Essay in Practical Realism*, Cambridge: Cambridge University Press.

——(2011) "How to Have Self-Directed Attitudes," in Anita Konzelmann Ziv, Keith Lehrer, and Hans Bernard Schmid (eds), *Self-Evaluation: Affective and Social Grounds of Intentionality*, Dordrecht: Springer, 33–43.

——(2013) *Naturalism and the First-Person Perspective*, New York: Oxford University Press.

Carruthers, Peter (2009) "How We Know Our Own Minds: The Relationship between Mindreading and Metacognition," *Behavioral and Brain Sciences* 32: 121–82.

——(2010) "Introspection: Divided and Partly Eliminated," *Philosophy and Phenomenological Research* 80: 76–111.

——(2011) *The Opacity of Mind: An Integrative Theory of Self-Knowledge*, Oxford: Oxford University Press.

Castañeda, Hector-Neri (1966) "'He': A Study in the Logic of Self-Consciousness," *Ratio* 8: 130–57.

——(1967) "Indicators and Quasi-indicators," *American Philosophical Quarterly* 4: 85–100.

Dennett, Daniel C. (1991) *Consciousness Explained*, Boston: Little, Brown & Co.

Fodor, Jerry A. (1987) *Psychosemantics: The Problem of Meaning in the Philosophy of Mind*, Cambridge, MA: MIT Press.

Frankish, Keith and Jonathan St.B.T. Evans (2009) "The Duality of Mind: An Historical Perspective," in Keith Frankish and Jonathan St.B.T. Evans (eds), *In Two Minds: Dual Processes and Beyond*, Oxford: Oxford University Press, 1–29.

Huebner, Bryce and Daniel C. Dennett (2009) "Banishing 'I' and 'We' from Accounts of Metacognition," *Behavioral and Brain Sciences* 32: 148–49.

Kahneman, Daniel (2011) *Thinking, Fast and Slow*, New York: Farrar, Straus & Giroux.

Kornblith, Hilary (2012) *On Reflection*, Oxford: Oxford University Press.

Matthews, Gareth B. (1992) *Thought's Ego in Augustine and Descartes*, Ithaca, NY: Cornell University Press.

McDowell, John (2004) "Naturalism in the Philosophy of Mind," in Mario De Caro and David Macarthur (eds), *Naturalism in Question*, Cambridge, MA: Harvard University Press, 91–105.

Nisbett, Richard and Lee Ross (1980) "The Lay Scientist Self-Examined," in *Inductive Inference: Strategies and Shortcomings of Social Judgment*, Englewood Cliffs, NJ: Prentice-Hall, 195–227.

Perry, John (2002) *Identity, Personal Identity, and the Self*, Indianapolis: Hackett.

Plantinga, Alvin (2011) *Where the Conflict Really Lies: Science, Religion, and Naturalism*, New York: Oxford University Press.

Stalnaker, Robert C. (2008) *Our Knowledge of the Internal World*, Oxford: Oxford University Press.

van Inwagen, Peter (1999) "It Is Wrong, Everywhere, Always, and for Anyone, to Believe Anything upon Insufficient Evidence," in Eleonore Stump and Michael Murray (eds), *Philosophy of Religion: The Big Questions*, Malden, MA: Blackwell, 273–84.

18 Phenomenological methods in philosophy of mind

DAVID WOODRUFF SMITH

Phenomenology in philosophy of mind

If consciousness is the hard problem for scientific philosophy of mind, methodology is the hard problem for phenomenology, which is precisely the study of forms of consciousness ("phenomena").

The philosophy of mind is of course the philosophical *theory* of mind, and this line of theory is as old as the hills of ancient India and ancient Greece including Asia Minor. As the twentieth century led into the twenty-first, however, the philosophy of mind has been an increasing locus of activity in the broad tradition of analytic philosophy, as the tradition moved from logic and language to mind. Within this movement the theory of mind has advanced from behaviorism to materialism and on to functionalism and computational models, and onward into neurobiology. In this rich tradition *consciousness* has turned out to be the "hard problem" in the theory of mind, as David Chalmers so memorably christened the issue. In recent years several models of consciousness per se have emerged, mostly within a naturalistic model of mind as a bio-neuro-computational process in the human brain, occurring in the wider natural environment.

Within this recent philosophy of consciousness, several models have been developed as to just what makes a mental state or activity *conscious*. Some form of higher-order monitoring of brain–mind has been seen as what differentiates conscious from unconscious mental life. In one vivid image (imagine a revealing fMRI scan), one part of the brain is monitoring activity in another part of that same brain. For example, as a neural process of vision or emotion develops, involving massively interactive processes throughout the neural system, the relevant activity involved in vision or emotion is monitored or registered in an appropriate part of the brain, say, in portions of the cortex or thalamus. Today scientists speak comfortably of the neural correlates of consciousness, recognizing that a conscious mental activity carries *intrinsically subjective* characters, often called the *phenomenal* character of the activity. For some years it was convenient to say that specifically *mental* features of mind–brain processes – that is, *subjective* properties of consciousness – are "supervenient" on specifically *physical* features of brain process. 'Tis better simply to say that mental features of mind and specifically subjective characters of consciousness are *dependent* ontologically on neurobiological properties of the human or animal organism. (My take on the role of ontological dependence is apparent in Smith 2007, wherein phenomenology is set in relation to ontology as well as logic and epistemology, with dependence playing critical roles along the way.)

Okay, but what precisely is the *form* of these subjective characters? And, of present concern, how should – how can – we study these subjective or phenomenal characters of consciousness?

Phenomenology is by definition the answer. In a direct formulation, appropriate to current philosophy of mind, we may simply say:

Phenomenology is the study of consciousness – namely, various forms of conscious experience – as experienced from the first-person perspective.

The issues of phenomenology proper arrived rather late on the scene in twentieth-century analytic philosophy of mind, which had focused on the mind–brain problem. Already by 1900, however, classical phenomenologists were busy at work on the *subjective* side of conscious mental life – well before cognitive neuroscience arrived. Interestingly, we are now seeing a confluence of phenomenology with naturalistic philosophy of mind, even a variety called "neurophenomenology." (See: Petitot *et al.* 1999, *Naturalizing Phenomenology*, and Smith and Thomasson 2005, *Phenomenology and Philosophy of Mind*; see also Thompson 2007, *Mind in Life*.)

Let us recall the origins of the discipline of phenomenology and its methods.

The term "phenomenology" was coined in the seventeenth century. However, the philosophical discipline now called phenomenology was envisioned by Franz Brentano and subsequently elaborated in detail by Edmund Husserl. Husserl defined phenomenology simply as "the science of the essence of consciousness" (Husserl 1913/1983, *Ideas* I, §34). By science is meant a well-defined discipline, with a subject matter and a methodology. By essence is meant the types and properties of something, here of properties of acts of consciousness. And by consciousness is meant, well, all the forms of conscious activity, including perception, thought, emotion, volition, and indeed embodied conscious volitional action. However, for Husserl, the essence of consciousness lies not in the brain activity subserving consciousness, but in the *experienced* properties of conscious mental activity, including sensations of green, sensory perceptions of trees, thoughts about things around one, and so on. Specifically, Husserl held, the generic essences of nature, consciousness, and culture are quite different. Each of these three "regions" of essence is differentiated by distinctive properties: objects in nature, by spatio-temporal features, and more; acts in consciousness, by intentionality, phenomenal character, and more; interactions in culture, by intersubjective or communal activity, and more. This is to say that, already in Husserl's day, and indeed from Descartes to Hume to Kant and onward, properties of consciousness were carefully appraised in their own right. (Husserl's conception of phenomenology is explored, within a reconstruction of his holistic system of philosophy, in Smith 2007, *Husserl*.)

Husserl was writing on the heels of Brentano in *Psychology from an Empirical Standpoint* (1874), a text that helped to launch psychology as a proper empirical science. For Brentano, the new science of psychology was to divide into "descriptive" psychology, and "genetic" psychology. Descriptive psychology, subsequently called "phenomenology," is to study the types and properties of mental phenomena, whereas genetic psychology is to study their causal origins and effects. Descartes already wrote in the first person about his own thoughts and sensations and passions. William James offered 1,300 pages of analysis of consciousness in *The Principles of Psychology* (1890). On the heels of Brentano's *Psychology from an Empirical Standpoint*, and also of James's *Psychology*, Husserl set about rethinking the foundations of the philosophy of consciousness in what he conceived as the new discipline of phenomenology. Husserl's result was 1,000 pages of his *Logical Investigations* (1900–1, rev. 1913, 1920). (Consider also the studies of time-consciousness in Husserl 1893–1917/1991, which resonate with James's theory of consciousness.) Interestingly, Husserl insisted that phenomenology be distinguished from empirical psychology: in a word, phenomenology studies the *logic* of the phenomena of consciousness, as opposed to the happenstance of what flows through our minds as a matter of empirical fact. Subsequently, in *Ideas* I (1913), Husserl emphasized the "transcendental" approach to phenomenology. These themes of the logical and the transcendental invite rethinking in today's era of the scientific theory of consciousness. (Consider here the structure of embodied consciousness analyzed in Husserl 1912/1989.)

For Husserl, consciousness is to be studied by a special methodology called "epoché" (a term borrowed from the ancient skeptics). We are to "bracket" the question of the existence of the world around us, suspending judgment about what we seem to see and touch and think about in the world. Thereby we are to focus on the contents of our own consciousness. We are to approach consciousness thus from the *first-person* perspective, the perspective of "I" as subject of consciousness. Yet, according to Husserl, this phenomenological approach is supposed to differ sharply from the "introspection" practiced in the early days of empirical or experimental psychology, historically in the work of Wilhelm Wundt and Edward Titchener in the late nineteenth century.

Before turning to the methods of phenomenology in philosophy of mind today, we must note a twist in terminology. In the idiom of Brentano and Husserl, "phenomenology" is the name of a discipline, namely, the study of structures of conscious experience, in perception, judgment, etc. In recent years, in the tradition of philosophy of mind, the term "phenomenology" has often been used to name, not the discipline of studying consciousness, but the *phenomenal* properties of a conscious mental state. In that usage the "phenomenology" of my current visual experience is the character of "what it is like" for me to experience this state of consciousness. For one schooled in the writings of Brentano, Husserl, and others, this latter usage takes a little getting used to. By analogy, physics is the discipline that studies, for example, the gravitational force between the Earth and the Moon. We might say, then, that the "physics" of the Moon's pull on the Earth causes the rising of the tide along the Pacific Coast. For my purposes, I'll speak of the discipline, phenomenology, and I'll speak of the *phenomenal character* – or sometimes the *phenomenological character* – of a conscious experience. So the discipline of phenomenology studies inter alia the phenomenal or phenomenological characters – if you will, the "phenomenology" – of different types of experience.

Now let us move on to address the methodology appropriate to the discipline of phenomenology, which I take to be a proper part of the philosophy of mind.

Consciousness from first-person and other-person perspectives

Interestingly, the subject matter and the methodology of a discipline are intertwined. We cannot say how to study something without saying what it is we are thereby studying; and we cannot in practice go about studying something without saying how we are to study it. However, this intertwining is particularly tight in the study of consciousness.

The scientific method is part of our contemporary *Lebenswelt*. We make observations about a given type of phenomenon, such as the gravitational attraction between massed bodies. We proceed to formulate a theory about this phenomenon. Then we make further observations to confirm the theory. And this methodology unfolds in a pattern repeatable by anyone competent in the discipline. Of course, the theory often involves mathematical formulations, as in Newton's theory of gravity. But notice something we take for granted. The *object* of study is observable and characterized from a particular perspective on the object, the perspective of the observing *subject*. Anyone can observe the object falling from the leaning tower of Pisa, in the Galilean experiment. Each observer observes the falling object from her own first-person perspective, and that perspective type can be inhabited by anyone else repeating the observation. This perspective is not only the observer's *spatial* perspective on the falling object. This perspective is also the *subjective* perspective of the observer, i.e. qua perceiving subject, actually seeing the object from the spatial perspective defined by the subject's eyes, line of sight, etc. A sightless subject inhabiting the spatial relation to the falling object cannot *observe* the falling, and so cannot participate in the methodology. And, indeed, the same holds for each scientist working with the developing *theory*. That is, in formulating and extending the theory, any competent scientist can grasp the propositions put forth in the theory, say, Newton's law of gravitational attraction, and that means from the scientist's subjective perspective as thinking subject, say, actually thinking through Newton's law. Again, the object of study is there in the world, existing independently of any scientist's observing and theorizing. Of course, and this is what we take for granted, the scientists are experiencing perceptions and thoughts about the falling object, but their subjective perspectives on the object are not part of the object of study!

Consciousness, however, is in a very different boat.

If we are dealing with the neural substrate of a conscious visual state, any competent neuroscientist can observe and theorize about the pattern of neural firings that subserve that form of visual experience. Here are the scientists themselves at work in the lab. Yet only the *subject* of the visual state can *experience* that state, that is, from the first-person point of view, the perspective of the subject "I," say, where (as the experiment runs) "I see that bouncing yellow tennis ball." The *theory* about such states is itself proposed and developed in a pattern of conscious activities enacted by the many scientists involved in the study of these conscious states. But the scientists' activities of consciousness are not the object, but the means, of study. How does the *subjective, phenomenal, first-person* character of that type of experience figure in the *theory* of that type of experience? Here is where phenomenology mixes with theory of consciousness. In the practice of neuroscience the scientist's consciousness remains completely in the background, no part of the object of study; in the practice of phenomenology, however, the object of study is precisely the type of consciousness experienced, either actually or potentially, by the practicing phenomenologist. Here is a critical feature of methodology unique to the discipline of phenomenology, a feature that has vexed the discipline since its inception. Husserl, in his last writing, stressed the role of consciousness in scientific theorizing, noting how scientists' own consciousness informs their theory of the object of study, and how this interaction complicates the methodology of phenomenological reflection. (See Husserl's critique of the "crisis" of the sciences, and its implications for phenomenology, in Husserl 1935–38/ 1970. A contemporary volume pursues issues of the *Crisis* in the context of philosophy of science today; see Hyder and Rheinberger 2010.)

Professor Mary Rouge, neuroscientist, can read an fMRI scan of her own brain as she experiences her own visual experience of seeing magenta red. She can observe the scan and form a judgment about which exact subsystems of neurons are at work in subserving her own visual experience. Yet the phenomenal character of her seeing this magenta red is not yet specified in her neuroscience work. That character remains to be *experienced* as she consciously sees the magenta red of the rose before her. An alien neuroscientist might well observe and theorize about Professor Rouge's type of visual experience, assaying the neural processing in her visual system. But the alien scientist – of a different biological species than us – may be so constituted that it cannot *experience* that same type of consciousness. Such thought experiments make an important point about the subject matter of phenomenology: a *conscious experience* is something I experience, even as I may go on to reflect on it and develop a theory about it. (Pardon the pun on "subject.")

As John Searle (2004, 85) has put it, appearance and reality *coincide* in the case of consciousness. But, I add, *only* in the case of consciousness: that is the point of separating the two roles of consciousness above, i.e. as the object of study and as a part of the conscious activities involved in the studying.

In consequence, Searle rightly emphasizes (78–79), consciousness has a *first-person ontology*. That is, the first-personal or subjective character of a conscious mental state is not only part of its "appearance" in one's consciousness, but also part of the "reality" of one's consciousness. That is, the subjective or phenomenal character of an experience – in current parlance, its "phenomenology" – is part of the *being* of a conscious experience, without which it would not be conscious.

Accordingly, in phenomenology we approach consciousness from the first-person perspective (methodology), and that consciousness itself is a first-personal structure (ontology). This dual role of first-personal or phenomenal character is key to the peculiarity of methodology for the discipline of phenomenology. Consciousness is both the avenue of knowledge formation in the discipline of phenomenology, central to method, and the object of study in the discipline.

To address the *methods* of studying first-person experience in the discipline of phenomenology, we need to assay and to distinguish a variety of forms of *awareness* of conscious experience itself. We need to survey the lay of the land in phenomenology, as we address the methodology of surveying the *phenomenal character* of various forms of experience.

Transparency

A good many philosophers of mind have come to hold that consciousness is "transparent" in the sense that one is conscious of some object in the environment but not of one's consciousness per se. The thesis of *transparency*, when formulated in the first person, proclaims that:

> Whenever I am conscious, I am conscious *of* something, but I am not conscious of my *experience* itself.

Often the thesis is supported by a claim of introspection: if you will introspect carefully, you will notice that you are never conscious of your experience itself, which is "transparent" or (in G.E. Moore's suggestive idiom) "diaphanous." Our immediate concern now is not introspection, but the transparency claimed, by whatever introspection may or may not deliver. (Dretske 1995 involves an extended study of the transparency of consciousness, especially in perception, with an eye to the flow of information from the environment.)

The paradigm offered in support of transparency is typically a simple visual experience. When I see a red tomato, I am visually conscious of the red tomato and not of my seeing it. Thus, it is claimed, when in introspection I observe my consciousness in seeing the tomato, I do not find anything but the thing I am conscious of, i.e. the visually presented red tomato. Often the exampled object of vision is simply the red itself: thus, in seeing (something) red, I am conscious of the red, period, not of my-seeing-red. Of course, we are now on the slippery slope between the primary quality called red and the secondary quality called red, between the quality in the tomato and the "qualia" in the experience. So I prefer the less slippery case of seeing not simply red, but the red tomato. Well, then, where Hume claimed that I can never observe "my self," as I can only observe (my) experiences ("perceptions"), now the transparency theorist claims that I can never observe my *experiences*, as I can only observe what I am conscious of. Officially, then, the transparency model is supposed to wholly acknowledge consciousness-of-X but deny any form of self-consciousness, or *consciousness of* consciousness-of-X.

The transparency thesis has some plausibility in cases of absorbed perception: say, where a van Gogh is absorbed in the exact shade of yellow he is seeking to capture on the canvas, or where a surgeon is intently focused on the area of flesh in which he is inserting the scalpel, or where the long-distance driver is intent on the curve in the road ahead. We do not want to say the subject is in such cases really or particularly *conscious* of her *experience* of seeing that ochre yellow, or that line on the patient's chest, or that unexpectedly sharp curve in the road. Fine, but such cases are really rather exceptional. Far more typical are experiences in which I am attending primarily to one thing but peripherally aware of something else. I see the red Porsche ahead of me in traffic, I notice the shade of red, and I am aware of the black Maserati overtaking me – *and* I am aware of my *hearing* the Maserati engine, my fleeting *anxiety* as the Maserati cuts closely in front of me, and my *letting up* on my accelerator. I am conscious of many things, my *attention* distributed variously over those things, and – commonly enough – among those things of which I am aware are various *experiences* I am currently living through. If I am an experienced *plein-air* painter, I may well be conscious of both the ochre yellow on that house in this light *and* my visual experience thereof. Or if I am an experienced athlete, I may well be conscious of both *what* I am doing, in hitting a high-kicking serve to my opponent's backhand, *and* how my serving action *feels* in kinesthesia.

As we delve into the phenomenology of more complex experiences, then, the transparency thesis loses its grip. And then we need to consider what sorts of awareness of my experience I may have when my consciousness is *not* wholly exhausted in what I am seeing or hearing or thinking or doing. In the Gestalt model of perception, I typically see an object against a background. To this point, Husserl sometimes seemed to hold that when, say, I see a bird flying by, I have a background awareness not only of the trees in the periphery of my visual field, but also of my visual experience. That is, I am focally aware of the bird I see, but peripherally aware of my seeing the bird – especially if I have to squint into the sun to see the bird. (Lay 2010 explores this peripheral model of self-consciousness as part of time-consciousness. Peripheral and inner awareness are distinguished in Ford and Smith 2006. See Smith 2011 on related distinctions among forms of more or less "transparent" consciousness.)

Allowing that we may be aware of our own experience in various ways, beyond transparency, our concern here will be to home in on forms of experience at work in phenomenological reflection – in the practice of the discipline of phenomenology.

Inner awareness

What makes a conscious mental state or activity *conscious*? The traditional answer – contra transparency – is that every consciousness is *eo ipso* a self-consciousness. That is, in a conscious mental act the subject is *aware* of the act's transpiring, and that awareness is what makes the act conscious. What is the form of that awareness – which we may call *inner awareness*?

Brentano held that every mental act is essentially conscious and therewith directed toward something-or-other and also directed secondarily toward itself. This secondary consciousness Brentano called "inner consciousness," and he distinguished this form of consciousness from "inner observation." Somehow, inner consciousness is built into the mental act itself, rendering it conscious. Inner observation, by contrast, consists in a separate mental act directed toward the first. Okay, then, what is the form of inner awareness if it is not a second higher-order observation?

As consciousness re-entered philosophy of mind by the late 1980s, several models of awareness emerged. This awareness-of-experience might consist in a higher-order perception, where the mind/brain monitors itself somewhat as the mind/brain observes external events in vision, hearing, etc. Or, weakening the perception flavor, this awareness might consist in a higher-order thought, where the mind observes that a given mental act is occurring, and this higher-order monitoring renders the act conscious. Or, still better (by my lights), this awareness-of-experience might consist in a form of reflexive self-representation, where the mental act includes a proper part that represents itself to itself, rendering the act conscious. Here let me pick up the debate with this model of self-representation. On this line of analysis, the *subjective* or *phenomenal* character of a conscious mental act or state is defined by its reflexive self-representation – a "same-order" form of self-monitoring. (Kriegel 2009 details a particular account of this self-representational subjective character; Kriegel and Williford 2006 addresses the self-representational approach vis-à-vis models of higher-order monitoring.)

Now, a kindred approach to inner awareness is that I've called the "modal" model of inner awareness. On this model, a conscious experience has a multifaceted character that defines inner awareness. In the formulation I've used we articulate the phenomenological structure of a simple experience as follows:

Phenomenally in this very experience I now here see that bouncing yellow ball.

Here we distinguish several characters (as underscored): phenomenality (how the experience appears in consciousness), reflexivity (as reflexively self-aware), egocentricity (as experienced or enacted by me), location (as centered in my lived space–time), and so on. On this model, a conscious experience characteristically includes, as a dependent part of its phenomenological structure, a form of inner awareness articulated as "phenomenally in this very experience I ... ." (This modal model is developed in Smith 1986, 1989, 2004, 2005, 2011.)

Initially, I assumed the traditional principle that an appropriate form of inner awareness is essential to any conscious experience, an awareness defining the character that makes it conscious: if you will, the subjective character "consciously." Subsequently, I sought to widen the range of consciousness, allowing for more elementary forms of consciousness. Thus, we may allow that an experience may be conscious yet lack inner awareness, whether a form of transparent consciousness, or highly absorbed consciousness (being wholly attendant to one thing), or a state of distracted consciousness (being not at all focused). Or we may allow lower levels of consciousness in creatures lacking the power of reflexive awareness-of-experience (perhaps a squirrel or a pelican lacks such awareness, whereas a dolphin or bonobo is surmised to have some level of self-awareness).

Inner awareness, I believe, is the *ground* of a distinct form of experience – phenomenological reflection proper – in which we grasp the phenomenological character or structure of a given type of conscious experience. That is our target as we move toward a methodology for the discipline of phenomenology. (See Thomasson 2005, also Smith 2005, on the way in which phenomenological reflection may be grounded in our immediate experience of consciousness.)

Introspection

The term "introspection" is comfortably used for any form of awareness or contemplation or reflection directed inwardly at our experience. But, soon enough, varied ways of focusing on experience begin to stand out as importantly different – we've just been contrasting inner awareness with inner observation. In the early days of empirical psychology, in the labs of Wundt and Titchener, introspection was considered a very particular act of observing one's experience as it happens, starting with observing one's sensations. The methodology of introspective psychology was sternly rejected in the era of twentieth-century behaviorism, and the reliability of introspection is again under scrutiny today, as philosophers of mind once again talk of introspection. Notably, experiments where one is asked to report on what was just going through one's consciousness are assessed, and the results seem of mixed merit. (See Schwitzgebel 2011.)

As noted, Brentano had already distinguished inner *observation* – of which introspection à la Wundt or Titchener is surely a particular variety – from inner *consciousness*. And in today's discussion, for the self-representational approach, as for the "modal" model, *inner awareness* is to be an integral part of an experience, a component of the experience that cannot occur separately (that is, where such awareness occurs, even if it does not inhere in every conscious experience). How does a subsequent act of introspection relate to the experience observed in this introspection? Well, this form of introspection is an empirical fact: that is why psychologists – or "experimental" philosophers – may run experiments to gather results on what people report they have just experienced. We are talking about a first-person perspective, where "I" live through an experience and then, when prompted, I attempt to recount what I was just feeling (a pain in my foot), or seeing (that pelican diving), or thinking, or wishing. Here the experience and its observation are empirical facts in the subject's stream of consciousness.

Now, when Husserl laid out the proposed foundations for the new discipline of phenomenology, he explicitly rejected "psychologism." That meant that the merely contingent observations reported about a particular individual's experiences were part of an empirical study of experiences that happen to occur in nature, albeit unfolding in the first-person perspective. Our empirical claims about our experiences – recounted within the structure of the psychologists' experiment – are subject to the usual methods of empirical science. But Husserl sought something different as the new "science" of phenomenology. The title of the work in which he laid the groundwork for this discipline was: *Logical Investigations* (Husserl 1900–1). Phenomenology was to be something other than "psychology," an empirical discipline: phenomenology was to be, if you like, a *logic* of consciousness. (The interdependence between logic and phenomenology, within Husserl's holistic philosophy, are detailed in Smith 2007. See Mohanty 2008 on the historical development of Husserl's conception of logic, intentionality, and the foundations of phenomenology.)

It has been notoriously difficult to figure out just what methodology is at work in phenomenology. What can we say *today* about the methods of analysis of experience appropriate to a distinctive discipline of phenomenology? If phenomenology is not to proceed by simple "introspection," then how else?

Consider how we have been pursuing our issues just above.

The thesis of transparency of consciousness has been pressed on the basis of claims of "introspection." We have resisted the thesis above. How? By theoretical *reflection* on features of experience known through immediate experience, that is, in virtue of inner awareness. We have not proceeded as if by putting up a phenomenological periscope and looking around in the mind, each peering into our own inner Cartesian theater, if that is what "introspection" is supposed to be like. Indeed, *what is it like* to perform a piece of phenomenological analysis? Not by simply peering about in the privacy of one's mind, but by *reflecting* on what a given form of experience is like, a form of experience familiar to us all, familiar from living through that form of experience, living through such an experience *with inner awareness* thereof.

Phenomenological reflection on lived experience

We have all experienced a variety of forms of consciousness in sensory perception, thinking, wishing, daydreaming, willingly acting, and so on.

Each form of experience has its characteristic phenomenal character, experienced through immediate "inner" awareness (whatever the structure of that awareness may be, and however ubiquitous it may or may not be). On the basis of our familiarity with these *forms* of lived experience, we can step back and *reflect* on what their structure would be. We proceed to develop an *analysis* of the structure of experiences familiar to us already. Here is a less daunting sense of method than the experience of withdrawing from the world and entering our private streams of consciousness, "introspecting" on what we find there, and so on. And, roughly enough, this is the method of analysis in the discipline of phenomenology.

Such phenomenological analysis of forms of experience is comparable to logical analysis of forms of language. We experience speaking and hearing and understanding in our own well-mastered language. In constructing a piece of logical theory about a part of everyday English, we step back and reflect on forms and uses of nouns, adjectives, verbs, adverbs, sentences, conjunctions, etc. From Aristotle to Frege, we find theoretical proposals about *logical forms* in a given language. We develop more comprehensive theories about how logical forms of expression interact and how they *mean*: how they bring to expression forms of thought or experience, how expressions are correlated with ideal meanings or "senses" (*Sinne* per Frege and Husserl), how they represent things in the world, how the truth conditions of a sentence are to be formulated (à la Tarski). The more Platonistic concepts of sense are parts of a *theory* of language that we are debating as we practice logical analysis of our *familiar* language. Now, phenomenological analysis can be seen as proceeding in a similar way. When Brentano, Husserl, and others, sought to define phenomenology as a discipline, logic was linked with the intentionality of thought. In philosophy of mind today, I submit, philosophers are engaged in a theoretical reflection on the subjective or phenomenal characters of conscious experience as we know these characters in our own experience – much as we know our own language.

The current debate about "cognitive phenomenology" offers a case in point.

The "conservative" view says that introspection shows that only *sensory* experience has a "phenomenology," a phenomenal character of what it is like. The "liberal" view says, rather, that introspection shows that *every conscious experience* has a distinctive phenomenology, a phenomenal character of what it is like, say, to see, to hear, to think, to wish, and so on. Introspection is supposed to put us in touch with the phenomenal character of the given type of experience. We immediately experience and so observe that form of consciousness. As I prefer, we have an *inner awareness* of the experience, a direct *acquaintance* with the experience as we live through it (per Smith 1989). And that awareness includes an immediate awareness of the particular phenomenal character of the given experience. Now, if we each experience a variety of phenomenal characters, how can philosophers of mind – the conservatives and the liberals – differ so markedly on cognitive phenomenology? How can the theorists' feelings about what consciousness "feels" like be so deeply felt? Well, the debate consists precisely in *theoretical reflection* on the phenomenal characters purportedly experienced first-hand in the first-person perspective. Theoretical reflection proceeds by argumentation as in any scientific dispute. The object of study here is phenomenal character, a subjective property of experience. But the method of study does not end with inner awareness, or with a more detached form of introspection. Rather, as the debate shows, the theorists sift and assess observations of experience, concepts of phenomenality, principles about phenomenal characters in experience, and so on, arguing therewith for the best overall *theory* about phenomenal character itself. (See Bayne and Montague 2011 for a rich display of the debate about cognitive phenomenology.)

Similarly, we find the same sort of theoretical reflection at work in the writings of Brentano, Husserl, Heidegger, Merleau-Ponty, and others – even as they debated specific methods such as Husserlian "bracketing." Broadly speaking, then, phenomenological reflection is a form of theoretical reflection, where we reflect on structures of conscious experience, forms of consciousness we each typically live through. Our reflections on these forms of consciousness take place, however, as we step back out of our ordinary experiences and take a different, theoretical perspective on them.

Importantly, as "we" phenomenologists analyze the first-person structure in which "I" see or think or wish or will such-and-such, we must practice *empathy* with the position of the subject of the form of experience under phenomenological analysis. We scientists must place ourselves each as if in the ostensible subject's role in that form of consciousness. And the structure of empathy itself reflects the structure of *inner awareness*. Thereby we grasp the phenomenal character of the form of experience we are studying. (Smith 1989 develops an account of empathy in relation to inner awareness.)

Phenomenological bracketing revisited

Arguably, we all know roughly how to understand a given form of experience. Still, there may be particular techniques that bring us to a heightened awareness of our own experience just *as* we experience it, an awareness from which we enter into theoretical reflection on that lived form of experience. Of course, Husserl's intense concern for method was precisely to characterize such a technique. The technique he stressed – famously and infamously – was that of epoché, or bracketing. How might we view this technique in the context of philosophy of mind today?

Husserl proposed to turn our attention to our own consciousness by "bracketing" the question of the existence of the world around us. (Husserl 1913/1983, *Ideas* I, §§27ff.) This image suggests a practice of the ancient skeptics, whereby we turn away from the world we seem to know and approach the world as mere "appearance." Indeed, the Greek term *"phenomena"* just meant appearances, ostensibly the subject matter of "phenomenology," literally the study of "phenomena." And the skeptics' term "epoché," which Husserl adapted for his technique of bracketing, just meant abstaining from judging the existence of the world we thought we knew. Accordingly, the familiar parody of the method of epoché may seem to leave phenomenology focused on our *sensory* appearances, as opposed to real objects in the world around us. Indeed, as noted, one strain in contemporary philosophy of mind takes the discipline of phenomenology to be by definition limited to the phenomenal character – the "phenomenology" – of sensory experience, i.e. sensation shorn of conceptual content. However, Husserl proposed epoché as a technique for appreciating a much wider range of "appearances" of things in the world *as* experienced in our consciousness. In Husserl's hands the methodology leads into his detailed theory of intentionality. (Mohanty 2011 includes a comprehensive study of Husserl's methodology in his evolving conception of "transcendental" phenomenology. Compare the articles on method in Luft and Overgaard 2012. In Smith 2007 I offer a reconstruction of Husserl's famous method of bracketing; in that understanding, outlined since the 1960s by Dagfinn Føllesdal in his courses at Stanford University, the *method* is elucidated largely in terms of the *theory* of intentionality. In Smith 2013, ch. 9, I revisit the method in a contemporary perspective.)

Whatever else we are to say about epoché, or bracketing, the technique executes a shift in attitude or perspective. In a typical form of experience, I see that bird swooping into my yard: my attitude is one of being directed visually toward the bird. Then, practicing epoché, I bracket the question of the existence of what I see, and thereby enter a new attitude: my attitude now is one of being directed toward what I see *just as it is given* in my visual experience – regardless of whether the bird exists and is, as presented, a neighborhood raven. The method of bracketing is thus a technique for shifting my attention (in the case at hand) away from the object of my visual consciousness and toward the character of my visual experience itself. My first observation, in phenomenological reflection, is that my visual experience is a consciousness as if *of* that bird – as we say, the experience is intentional.

Approaching this methodology with an eye to recent philosophy of mind, Amie Thomasson (2005) has argued that phenomenological "reduction," or epoché, effects a *cognitive transformation* in our experience. The practice of bracketing will "enable us to shift from world-oriented experience to a reflective knowledge of our own mental states" (127). In the first person: I shift from my experience in (say) seeing that raven swooping into the tree, to my attitude wherein I can now *reflect* on my visual experience itself. Thus, in reflection, I find that my experience is intentional, a visual consciousness as of that swooping raven. In this way the practice of phenomenology leads into self-knowledge. Apropos our discussion above, we note, Thomasson argues that the transparency thesis then gives way to a more nuanced view of consciousness.

What is perplexing about the method of bracketing, I now think, is that epoché actually involves *two levels of experience* in the practice of phenomenological reflection. First, epoché leads me to *experience* my own consciousness in a new way. In the everyday attitude, I have a visual experience of the raven; but in the reflective attitude, practicing epoché, I live through the experience with a heightened awareness of my consciousness itself. We may say, indeed, that this newly experienced perspective is precisely *what it is like* to practice phenomenological reflection at the first level – that is, in the immediacy of the attitude of epoché. But then, in a second level of experience, we proceed into a *theoretical* analysis of the structure of intentionality and beyond. This further activity of analysis arguably leads us into the ontology of intentionality, and into the "logic" of consciousness, the *theory* of how consciousness *represents* something like a raven in the surrounding world.

In the first stage of reflection, I experience a visual presentation of "that black raven swooping into the tree." The object of my consciousness *as so presented* is what I now experience reflectively. Husserl called this entity the "noema" of the experience (borrowing the Greek word for what is known). What sort of thing is that, the raven-*as*-perceived? Entering the second stage of reflection, we find rather different theoretical proposals put forth. On one account, the object-as-perceived is a *phenomenal* entity. On another account, the object-as-perceived is an ideal *logical* entity: like a concept or proposition, only for perception, well, a percept, typically a fusion of sensory and conceptual content. Husserl, like his contemporary Frege, called this entity a "sense" (*Sinn*). The debate about what sort of thing the noema is continues today. We need not go into those issues here, for the point at hand is that we have moved beyond the immediate *experience* of bracketed consciousness into the *theory* of what sort of entity we now experience in reflection. (Issues about the object-as-intended, the noema, and ideal sense are detailed in Smith 2007, ch. 6, reflecting a long history of Husserl interpretations. In Smith 2013, ch. 9, I distinguish between a "phenomenal" and a "logical" aspect of the noema; thus the two stages of phenomenological reflection here distinguished.)

The conditions of the possibility of experience bear the neo-Kantian label as "transcendental" structures of consciousness, and Husserl's method of bracketing is sometimes called "transcendental reduction," i.e. leading from the *object* perceived back into the structure of the *visual experience* as *of* that object. We start "transcendental" reflection on the experience by characterizing its *phenomenal* character. We then proceed further in "transcendental" reflection on its *logical* character: on the work of ideal logical meanings, or "sense," through which the object is perceived or "intended" in a certain way, with a particular "mode of presentation." This further level of reflection enters the realm of logic, where we study the semantic or intentional properties of appropriate types of sense. Here, then, are two levels of "transcendental" phenomenological reflection on a given form of experience. First comes the account of phenomenal character as experienced, proceeding through the practice of "transcendental" analysis in the modified attitude of epoché. Second comes the account of the idealized meaning at work in the lived form of experience, proceeding through the practice of "transcendental" analysis in the theoretical attitude of logic. If you will, the "transcendental" phenomenological structure of an experience is precisely its phenomenal-logical structure, without which the experience could not be a consciousness as *of* its object.

If we focus on the epistemological conditions of the possibility of experience, in the wake of Hume and Kant, we will address the *phenomenal* aspect of consciousness. If we focus on the logical conditions of the possibility of experience, in the wake of Husserl and Frege, we will address the *semantic* aspect of consciousness, i.e. how the content or noema of an experience directs consciousness toward an appropriate object in the world. What I am proposing today is that we rethink the "transcendental" methodology of phenomenology so that, in phenomenological reflection, we distinguish and integrate the phenomenal and the logical or semantic aspects of a given type of experience.

Varied methods of phenomenological analysis

We have sought to articulate certain methods by which phenomenological analysis may proceed in the context of contemporary philosophy of mind. The transparency thesis served to set the scene. Notice now how the technique of epoché begins with the object of consciousness and pulls back into the consciousness of the object – as if consciousness is experienced as transparent and must be brought into view by this technique. We turned then to the analysis of inner awareness, which is the ground of subsequent retention (short term) and recollection (longer term) of that experience. Our familiarity with our own experience, in the first-person perspective, is the residue of having lived through and retained or recollected such experience. Introspection proceeds in some manner by observing one's experience. But in what way? We turned to the practice of phenomenological reflection as, if you will, a highly structured form of introspection – or, better, a practice of logical/theoretical reflection beyond empirical "introspection." Bracketing, we proposed, is a technique for shifting attention toward one's own experience. And that technique opens the door to full-blooded reflection on a given form of experience. Here is one style of methodology for the discipline of phenomenology.

References

Bayne, Tim and Michelle Montague (eds) (2011) *Cognitive Phenomenology*, Oxford: Oxford University Press.

Dretske, Fred (1995) *Naturalizing the Mind*, Cambridge, MA: MIT Press.

Ford, Jason and David Woodruff Smith (2006) "Consciousness, Self, and Attention," in Uriah Kriegel and Kenneth Williford (eds), *Self-Representational Approaches to Consciousness*, Cambridge, MA: MIT Press, 353–77.

Husserl, Edmund (1893–1917/1991) *On the Phenomenology of the Consciousness of Internal Time (1893–1917)*, trans. John Barnett Brough, Dordrecht: Kluwer. (Now New York: Springer.)

——(1900–1/2001) *Logical Investigations*, vols 1 and 2, trans. J.N. Findlay, ed. and revised by Dermot Moran, London and New York: Routledge. German original, 1st edn, 1900–1; 2nd edn, 1913, 1920; English translation, 1st edn, 1970.

——(1912/1989) *Ideas pertaining to a Pure Phenomenology and to a Phenomenological Philosophy, Second Book: Studies in the Phenomenology of Constitution*, trans. Richard Rojcewicz and André Schuwer, Dordrecht: Kluwer. Original manuscript dating from 1912, posthumously published in German in 1952. Called *Ideas* II.

——(1913/1983) *Ideas pertaining to a Pure Phenomenology and a Phenomenological Philosophy, First Book: General Introduction to Pure Phenomenology*, trans. Fred Kersten, Dordrecht: Kluwer. German original 1913. Called *Ideas* I.

——(1935–38/1970) *The Crisis of European Sciences and Transcendental Phenomenology: An Introduction to Phenomenological Philosophy*, trans. David Carr, Evanston, IL: Northwestern University Press. Original German manuscripts written 1935–38. German edition first published 1954.

Hyder, David and Hans-Jörg Rheinberger (eds) (2010) *Science and the Life-World: Essays on Husserl's Crisis of European Sciences*, Stanford, CA: Stanford University Press.

Kriegel, Uriah (2009) *Subjective Consciousness: A Self-Representational Theory*, Oxford: Oxford University Press.

Kriegel, Uriah and Kenneth Williford (eds) (2006) *Self-Representational Approaches to Consciousness*, Cambridge, MA: MIT Press.

Lay, Christopher (2010) *"Time to Account for Consciousness,"* PhD diss., University of California, Irvine.

Luft, Sebastian and Søren Overgaard (eds) (2012) *The Routledge Companion to Phenomenology*, London: Routledge.

Mohanty, J.N. (2008) *The Philosophy of Edmund Husserl: A Historical Development*, New Haven, CT: Yale University Press.

——(2011) *Edmund Husserl's Freiburg Years: 1916–1938*, New Haven, CT: Yale University Press.

Petitot, Jean, Francisco J. Varela, Bernard Pachoud, and Jean-Michel Roy (eds) (1999) *Naturalizing Phenomenology: Issues in Contemporary Phenomenology and Cognitive Science*, Stanford, CA: Stanford University Press.

Schwitzgebel, Eric (2011) *Perplexities of Consciousness*. Cambridge, MA: MIT Press.

Searle, John R. (2004) *Mind: A Brief Introduction*, Oxford: Oxford University Press.

Smith, David Woodruff (1986) "The Structure of (Self-) Consciousness," *Topoi* 5 (2): 149–56.

——(1989) *The Circle of Acquaintance: Perception, Consciousness, and Empathy*, Dordrecht: Kluwer.

——(2004) "Return to Consciousness," in *Mind World: Essays in Phenomenology and Ontology*, Cambridge: Cambridge University Press, 2004, 76–121.

——(2005) "Consciousness with Reflexive Content," in Smith and Thomasson 2005, 93–114.

——(2007) *Husserl*, 1st edn, London: Routledge.

——(2011) "The Phenomenology of Consciously Thinking," in Bayne and Montague 2011, 345–72.

——(2013) *Husserl*, 2nd edn, London: Routledge.

Smith, David Woodruff and Amie L. Thomasson (eds) (2005) *Phenomenology and Philosophy of Mind*, Oxford: Oxford University Press.

Thomasson, Amie L. (2005) "First-Person Knowledge in Phenomenology," in Smith and Thomasson 2005, 115–39.

Thompson, Evan (2007) *Mind in Life: Biology, Phenomenology, and the Sciences of Mind*, Cambridge, MA: Harvard University Press.

19 Some Husserlian reflections on the contents of experience

MATTHEW RATCLIFFE

This chapter explores the potential for fruitful interaction between philosophy of mind and work in the phenomenological tradition of philosophy. I focus on the theme of what it is that we experience, my aim being to show how phenomenology can contribute to current debates about the nature and scope of 'phenomenal content', with particular emphasis on 'cognitive phenomenology'. 'Content' is generally understood as a matter of 'representation'. As Crane (2011, 86) remarks, it involves an 'object' being 'represented under an aspect'. However, experiential content need not be tied so closely to representation – one could refer in a less committal way to how something 'appears' to us or is 'presented' in experience, and that is how I use the term here. Even then, content need not be exhaustive of experience. There may be an attitudinal phenomenology too, an experience of perceiving, imagining or remembering that accompanies what is perceived, imagined or remembered. It has also been argued that certain so-called 'qualia', such as bare experiences of colour, are wholly distinct from intentionality.[1] Hence there is considerable disagreement over what the 'content of experience' includes and whether or not there is more to experience than content. Recent years have seen growing interest in the more specific question of whether we have a 'cognitive' as well as a 'sensory' phenomenology and, if so, what it consists of. Although many different positions have emerged, most are premised on the assumptions that perceptual experience is largely a matter of something called 'phenomenal content' and that we have a good enough grasp of what that consists of to be able to address (a) how far it extends and (b) whether or not there is a distinct kind of non-sensory content.

How else could we think about sensory and cognitive experience? In what follows, I draw on the phenomenological tradition, with an emphasis on some of Husserl's later, more 'existential' writings, in order to question conceptions of experience that shape debates over phenomenal content. I suggest that, if Husserl is broadly right, these debates are hampered from the outset by an inadequate grasp of perceptual experience. I draw two central claims from Husserl. First of all, perceptual content incorporates a sense of the possible. If this is accepted, it gives us the means to provide detailed and precise descriptions of both sensory and cognitive experiences, taking us beyond vague appeals to 'what-it-is-likeness' and complaints of ineffability that are commonplace in philosophy of mind. The second claim I extract from Husserl is that phenomenological methods reveal an aspect of experience that discussions of phenomenal content are mostly oblivious to. Experience incorporates something that might be described as a 'sense of being situated in a shared world' (hereafter 'world-experience'). This operates as a phenomenological framework within which experiences and thoughts, of the kinds that can be construed in terms of attitudes and contents, arise. If Husserl is right, accounts of phenomenal content that overlook it end up offering descriptions of experience that are impoverished and misleading.

Philosophers of mind might worry that phenomenological talk of 'world-experience' is too obscure to inform their work. However, I suggest that it can be clarified and elaborated by building on Husserl's account of possibility. There is a further complication though, which is that the differences between accounts of experience offered by phenomenologists and current philosophers of mind are not to be construed solely in terms of disagreements over an already established, shared subject matter. According to Husserl, among others, a methodological reorientation is needed in order to recognize the sense of belonging to a world that permeates all experience and thought. What I will call a 'phenomenological stance', which can be achieved to varying degrees and in different ways, is thus needed in order to comprehend one's subject matter in the first place. I will conclude by defending the view that experience incorporates something along the lines of what Husserl and other phenomenologists attempt to describe. To do so, I turn to phenomenological psychopathology and show how reflection on forms of anomalous experience that occur in psychiatric illness can help nurture the perspectival shift that lies at the heart of phenomenological method, while at the same time supporting and refining phenomenological claims. Thus a phenomenological stance and an appreciation of its subject matter gradually crystallize together.

The cognitive phenomenology debate

The cognitive phenomenology debate concerns the nature and scope of so called 'phenomenal content'.[2] It addresses two principal questions. First of all, how cognitively rich are the contents of sensory experience? As Siegel (2010, 3) asks with regard to visual perception:

Do you just visually experience arrays of colored shapes, variously illuminated, and sometimes moving? Or does visual experience involve more complex features, such as personal identity, causation, and kinds of objects, such as bicycles, keys, and cars?

The question can be asked with more specific reference to cognitive phenomenology: does the phenomenal content of perception in one or more modalities incorporate conceptual, propositional or other ingredients that are properly regarded as 'cognitive'? The second question is whether non-sensory cognitive states and processes have phenomenal content too, the focus being on 'thinking'. Strawson (e.g. 1994, 2004, 2011) answers with an emphatic 'yes', and suggests that the existence of a 'cognitive phenomenology' should be obvious to anyone on the basis of brief reflection. For instance, the experience of reading and understanding a sentence is quite different from that of reading the same sentence without understanding. Strawson accounts for this in terms of an 'understanding-experience' that is present in only one case.[3] If this much is conceded, there are several more specific issues to consider. It is debatable what the experience of thought is attributable to: does one have it due to concept application, propositional attitude adoption or something else? It is also unclear how discriminating the relevant phenomenology is: does a kind of attitude, such as consciously believing something, have a distinctive kind of phenomenology or does the phenomenology vary from one instance to the next? If the latter, do phenomenological differences track differences in content? And, if phenomenology is partly ascribable to content, is it tied to types of content, such as 'The Eiffel Tower is in Paris', or are phenomenal differences more fine-grained, with each token intentional state having its own unique phenomenal content?

Setting aside the specifics, it might at least seem uncontroversial that thought has *some kind of* phenomenal content, regardless of whether or not it differs from sensory content, but even that much can be challenged. For example, one could appeal to Block's (1995) distinction between 'access consciousness' and 'phenomenal consciousness', to argue that we have conscious access to our thoughts without phenomenal content (although Block himself indicates that thoughts can be phenomenally conscious). However, most participants in the cognitive phenomenology debate agree that some kind of phenomenal content is associated with conscious thinking. Disagreements concern (a) whether that content is causally or constitutively related to thought and (b) whether it differs from sensory phenomenology. Whereas philosophers including Strawson (2011) and Smith (2011) maintain that thought incorporates non-sensory experiential content, others, such as Prinz (2011) and Tye and Wright (2011), insist that alleged experiences of thinking are exhausted by their sensory accompaniments; thought only seems to have phenomenal content because of a contingent causal connection with sensory experience.[4]

At this point, I worry that the debate grinds to a halt. Once an opponent of cognitive phenomenology has distinguished constitution from causation, she can reject *any* alleged example of thought's phenomenal content by attributing it to associated sensory experiences, such as those involved in inner speech or visual imagination. The same move is equally effective against the claim that perception incorporates cognitive experience. For example, Carruthers and Veillet (2011) reject the claim that the phenomenal content of perception is partly conceptual, by maintaining that concepts merely *cause* phenomenal changes by altering patterns of sensory attention. The kinds of example used to defend versions of the cognitive phenomenology thesis are thus rendered ambiguous. For instance, Bayne (2011, 16) appeals to the experience of associative agnosia in order to argue that category perception is integral to experience, concluding that 'high-level content can directly inform the phenomenal character of perception'. However, a more conservative view can be retained by insisting that any 'high-level' content – conceptual or otherwise – causally influences rather than constitutes phenomenal content. It is far from clear how to arbitrate between 'causation' and 'constitution' accounts of cognitive experience. Appeals to introspection will not suffice; although introspection may give us some access to the nature of experience, it surely does not incorporate reliable categorization of an experience as 'sensory' or 'non-sensory'. Furthermore, it is doubtful that an 'introspected phenomenal feel' of any kind could clearly distinguish constitutive from causal relationships. More generally, the problem is that it is difficult to arbitrate between conflicting accounts of experiential content unless one has a grasp on the phenomenon that is, to some extent, independent of those accounts. Unfortunately, it often seems that there is little more to go on than vague, suggestive talk of 'what-it-is-likeness', some inherited from Nagel (1974) and some from elsewhere.[5] Although this might suffice to establish a shared *referent*, to at least identify what it is that we want to explore further, it is certainly not an adequate *description* of the phenomenon. By analogy, pointing at the North Star and saying 'you know – that shiny thing up there and other things that are like it … that's what we're talking about' establishes a topic but without any understanding of it. So appeals along the lines of 'imagine having an experience of type x as opposed to type y – can't you see the phenomenal difference; isn't it obvious?' will inevitably fail to move an opponent. With so little articulate grasp of one's subject matter, it is not clear how to weigh up competing intuitions over what is and is not an instance of it.

To avoid a stalemate, I propose that we step back to re-examine the presuppositions of the debate. In what follows, I will sketch an alternative to entrenched conceptions of phenomenal content, extracted from some of Husserl's later work. Many Husserlian themes are of potential interest to current philosophy of mind and, in what follows, I will concentrate on one of them: 'world-experience'.[6] Although I focus on Husserl, I should add that much the same broad conception of world-experience characterizes the phenomenological tradition more generally, despite differing terminologies and disagreements over more specific claims. Phenomenologists seek to convey something that is neither an attitude nor the content of an attitude, but instead a sense of belonging to the world that all content-bearing attitudes presuppose.

The experiential world

In order to appreciate the existence and nature of world-experience, phenomenologists stress the need for a shift in perspective. For Husserl, this is achieved through performance of an 'epoché', a suspension or bracketing of what is habitually taken for granted. This facilitates the 'phenomenological reduction', a kind of stance or standpoint through which aspects of experience that are more usually overlooked are explicitly reflected on and studied. The epoché is sometimes explained through the analogy of putting a sentence in parentheses. I can endorse the sentence 'there is a cat on the chair' or, alternatively, bracket it and study its structure without committing to its truth or falsehood. Husserl proposes that we do something similar with our experiences. Right now, I see a cup in front of me, and I take it as given that the cup is actually there. However, I can bracket my acceptance of the cup's existence and instead treat my experience of the cup's being there as a phenomenological achievement to be studied. In the process, I do not reject my more usual acceptance that the cup is there in front of me, in a world of which I am also a part. Instead, I preserve the sense of conviction that is part of the experience but detach myself from it so as to study its structure.

Now, in bracketing an experience of a cup, I do not bracket my experiences and thoughts more generally. My habitual acceptance of the world's existence is retained, along with a sense of my residing in it. In order to study world-experience, Husserl proposes something more radical: a complete epoché, a total suspension of the 'natural attitude' of believing in the existence of the world and all that it contains. Once this is achieved, the sense of belonging to a world that is ordinarily presupposed as a backdrop to experience and thought is revealed as a phenomenological achievement. This opens the door to the phenomenological reduction, a sustained attitudinal shift through which the structure of experience as a whole is subjected to scrutiny. To quote Husserl, the world 'goes on appearing, as it appeared before' but without 'the natural believing in existence involved in experiencing the world – though that believing too is still there and grasped by my noticing regard'. The epoché thus involves a 'modification' of standpoint, an 'inhibiting' or 'putting out of play' of the natural attitude (1960, 19–20). The phenomenological stance that arises through this is therefore quite different from introspection, where the latter is construed as reflection on subjective as opposed to objective aspects of experience. What the phenomenologist attends to, among other things, is the experience of being part of a world *within which* one occupies a contingent and partial perspective. In focusing attention 'inwards' or 'outwards', one has already accepted world-experience as a backdrop against which some things are experienced as internal and others external.

To appreciate how world-experience is phenomenologically distinctive, it is important to make clear that a 'belief' in the world's existence is quite different from perceptions and beliefs of the kind 'I perceive that there is a cup in front of me' or 'I believe that the Eiffel Tower is in Paris'. They can be expressed in much the same terms, but 'the world exists and I am part of it' is not a very general belief content (which might or might not also feature in perceptual experience). A belief in the world's existence is not really a 'belief' at all. What Husserl seeks to neutralize and make explicit is an all-pervasive practical orientation that is seldom an object of experience or thought. This orientation amounts to a sense of both the world's existence and one's participation in the world. When we perceive, believe, remember, imagine or anticipate something, when we adopt any kind of intentional state, we already 'find ourselves in the world' in this way:

> What is thematic is whatever one is directed towards. Waking life is always a directedness toward this or that, being directed toward it as means, as relevant or irrelevant, toward the interesting or the indifferent, toward the private or public, toward what is daily required or intrusively new. All this lies within the world-horizon; but special motives are required when one who is gripped in this world-life reorients himself and somehow comes to make the world itself thematic, to take up a lasting interest in it.
>
> (Husserl 1970b, 281)

One might worry that the epoché, construed as a complete neutralization of all habitual commitments regarding the existence of the world and its contents, is psychologically impossible. Hence the 'phenomenological reduction' that it facilitates is equally unachievable. However, complete neutralization of 'belief' or total suspension of the 'natural attitude' is not a necessary prerequisite for what I take as central to the phenomenological reduction. The reduction can be thought of in a less puritanical way, as something messy and incomplete that still yields at least some insight into the existence and nature of an experiential structure that would otherwise be overlooked. When a permissive conception is adopted, we can see that much the same 'attitudinal shift', what we might call a 'phenomenological stance', is at work in the phenomenological tradition more generally. For example, Merleau-Ponty describes his project as returning to a 'world which precedes knowledge', to a kind of experience that is 'not even an act, a deliberate taking up of a position' but 'the background from which all acts stand out', something that is 'presupposed by them'. He adds that, despite the disagreements between Husserl and Heidegger, what Heidegger in *Being and Time* calls 'Being-in-the-world' is exactly what one gains reflective access to by performing the phenomenological reduction (Merleau-Ponty 1962, ix–xiii).[7] If Husserl, Heidegger and Merleau-Ponty are right to claim that experience and thought are embedded in some kind of pre-attitudinal orientation, it follows that something is missing from approaches in the philosophy of mind that take our experiences, perceptual or otherwise, to be comprised entirely of contents or contents plus attitudes (and perhaps plus non-intentional 'qualia' too).

A closely related theme in phenomenology is that the world I find myself in is a s*hared* world, where I experience myself as occupying one perspective among others. Again, this is so pervasive and deep-rooted that it is easy to overlook when reflecting on the nature of experience. It is nicely illustrated by Sartre's description of his participation in a laboratory experiment (although I am not using the example quite as he intended):

> Why indeed should we use the term 'subjectivity' for the ensemble of luminous or heavy or odorous objects such as they appeared to me *in this laboratory at Paris on a day in February,* etc. And if despite all we are to consider this ensemble as subjective, then why should we recognize objectivity in the system of objects which were revealed to the experimenter, this same day in February? ... I shall give the name subjectivity to the objectivity which I have not chosen.
>
> (1989, 312)

In contrasting the subject's perspective with that of the experimenter and questioning a certain conception of objectivity, Sartre's example also illustrates how world-experience incorporates a non-contrastive element; it is 'we' who experience the various objects differently *'in this laboratory at Paris on a day in February'*. One's experience is not comprised solely of what can be explicitly contrasted with the experiences of others. There is a residual sense of dwelling from the outset in a shared world, in the context of which contrasts between one's own experiences and those of others are made. When one's own experience or that of another person is taken to consist exclusively of what can be tied to a single subjective perspective and contrasted with what is tied to another, the experiential sense of belonging to a common world is ignored.[8] The point is nicely made by R.D. Laing (1969, 22):

> *the* world – the world around me, the world in which I live, *my* world – is, in the very texture of its mode of being-for-me, not exclusively my world, but your world also, it is around you and him as well, it is a shared world, *one* world, *the* world.

Hence what I draw from the phenomenological tradition is the general view that experience incorporates something that is neither content nor attitude, something that can only be recognized and investigated if we somehow and to some degree suspend habitual acceptance of the world as an already established realm within which experiences and thoughts occur. This suggests a problem for the cognitive phenomenology debate: if that debate is premised on a partial characterization of sensory experience, which treats attitudes and contents in abstraction from world-experience, then the various accounts of sensory and cognitive phenomenology that it generates are likely to be unreliable. However, phenomenologists' talk of 'world' does not translate easily into the vocabulary of contemporary philosophy of mind. Indeed, it is arguable that phenomenological claims about world-experience are vague, metaphorical and perhaps even gesture at nothing. One might respond that phenomenologists' talk of world-experience is no less clear or precise than appeals to qualia, what-it-is-likeness, phenomenal content and the like. So why dismiss it if one is prepared to tolerate all that? But there is a better way to proceed than competing over who is the least vague, and that is to describe the relevant phenomenological achievement in a way that is clear and detailed, rather than suggestive. In the remainder of the chapter, I will outline how Husserl's work – with a bit of interpretation and elaboration – supplies us with the resources to do that.

The phenomenology of possibility

To develop a clearer conception of world-experience, I will start by returning to the topic of phenomenal content and cognitive experience, in order to extract from Husserl a partial account of experiential content. I will then adapt this account and apply it to the 'world' within which our various experiential 'contents' arise. One might think that 'phenomenal consciousness', cognitive or otherwise, cannot be further described, that 'seeing red is just – well – like seeing red, and the experience of thinking about *Macbeth* is – you know – like thinking about *Macbeth*, which is different from thinking about *War and Peace* or running through a string of nonsense sentences'. However, phenomenologists offer detailed descriptions of the structure of perception and thought, and central to Husserl's approach is the claim that we experience possibilities. I will suggest that, if this is right, we have a means of offering clear, detailed descriptions of a structure that is common to perception and thought. His account begins with the observation that, when you see an object, what you perceive is a three-dimensional entity of a certain kind, rather than a two-dimensional appearance that is then inferred to be the partial presentation of a type of object. So there is a seemingly paradoxical phenomenon to account for: we experience *the object* even though only part of it is perceptually accessible. An object, as Husserl (2001, 35) says, is 'naturally and simply there for us as an existing reality as we live naively in perception'. In order to accommodate this, he proposes that perceptual experience includes not only what is actually perceived but also a sense of what *could* be perceived and how. For instance, a cup, as seen from one angle, offers up the possibility of its being seen from other angles. Husserl suggests that the experience of being presented with a complete entity, of one or another kind, is constituted by the structured interplay between actuality and possibility. Experienced possibilities involving an entity comprise an organized system, which he calls its 'horizon':

> Everywhere, apprehension includes in itself, by the mediation of a 'sense', empty horizons of 'possible perceptions'; thus I can, at any given time, enter into a system of possible and, if I follow them up, actual, perceptual nexuses.
>
> (Husserl 1989, 42)

Husserl and Merleau-Ponty both claim that the horizon-structure of perception is inextricable from bodily experience. The body is not just an object of experience; it is also that through which we experience the world, a '*medium of all perception*' or '*organ of perception*' (Husserl 1989, 61). To be more specific, certain kinds of experienced bodily disposition also manifest themselves as potentialities that are integral to the experienced world. Perception is thus 'animated by *perceptive tendencies*' (Husserl 1973, 84).[9] However, claims about the horizon-structure of perception can be endorsed without also endorsing claims about how exactly the body contributes to that structure, and my concern here is with the former.

Husserl's account of horizons can be elaborated and fine-tuned in a number of ways, so as to yield an elaborate and fairly clear description of how possibilities feature in 'phenomenal content'. To start with, the phenomenology of possibility is intermodal; a cup as perceived visually not only incorporates visual possibilities but possibilities for other senses too, such as that of touching the handle or tasting the contents. Thus, what we experience through one sense incorporates possibilities for other senses (Husserl 1989, 75). This theme is more prominent in the writings of Merleau-Ponty, who describes how possibilities and actualities for different senses jointly comprise a unified experiential content:

> The sensory 'properties' of a thing together constitute one and the same thing, just as my gaze, my touch and all my other senses are together the powers of one and the same body integrated into one and the same action. ... any object presented to one sense calls upon itself the concordant operation of all the others.
>
> (1962, 317–18)[10]

Another detail addressed by Husserl is that perceived possibilities vary in their determinacy: a perceived object might incorporate the possibility 'turn me around to see another side that has shape x and colour y' or, alternatively, just 'turn me around to reveal some kind of shape and colour'. He also claims that the horizon-structure of perception is inter-subjective: entities are experienced as accessible to others. This, Husserl proposes, is inextricable from an appreciation of their residing in a realm that is not wholly dependent on one's own perspective.[11] Something he does not make sufficiently clear is whether or not perceived possibilities relate exclusively to *perceptual access*. I doubt, however, that he would endorse such a restrictive view. He writes in several places of 'enticing' possibilities for perception that draw us in with an 'affective force', soli-citing us to act in ways that actualize them (e.g. 2001, 83–91). If that much is accepted, then it is surely just as plausible to maintain that we experience enticing possibilities for goal-directed activity too. Indeed, this is suggested by various passages where Husserl observes that we do not first of all perceive neutral, detached, value-free entities and then impose various kinds of significance on them. Perceptual experience incorporates an appreciation of the practical significance of things: 'This surrounding world is comprised not of mere things but of use-Objects (clothes, uten-sils, guns, tools), works of art, literary products, instruments for religious and judicial activities' (Husserl 1989, 191). It can be added that entities are experienced as significant, as 'mattering', in a range of different ways and that they also 'draw us in' to differing degrees. Something might be experienced as threatening, potentially useful, immediately enticing, required in the context of a project, of specific relevance to oneself or of relevance to others, and so on. It could be argued that they acquire these properties through the application of concepts. However, phenomenologists such as Heidegger, Merleau-Ponty and Sartre (and Husserl too) indicate that, in many instances, the significance and 'affective pull' of a thing are not registered through a conceptual or more specifically propositional appreciation that is integral to a perception or imposed on the product of perception. Although we can always describe the perceived significance of a thing in propositional terms, that significance is often comprised principally of the possibilities that it is imbued with. To see something as threatening, one need not apply the concept 'threat', and one need not entertain a propositional attitude with the content 'x is threatening'. The thing *appears* threatening; it embodies a kind of significant possibility; the threat is *there*. Here is an example from Sartre, for whom the perceived world is experienced as a system of salient possibilities that reflect one's capacities, concerns and projects:

> The possible appears to us as a property of beings. After glancing at the sky I state, 'It is possible that it may rain.' I do not understand the possible here as meaning 'without contradiction with the present state of the sky.' The possibility belongs to the sky as threat; it represents a surpassing on the part of these clouds, which I perceive, toward rain.
>
> (1989, 97)[12]

One might object that the notion of 'perceiving possibilities' is rather mysterious. However, we could say exactly the same about 'perceiving actualities'. How is it that my current experience of a coffee cup incorporates an appreciation of its being 'there', 'real', 'part of the world in which I reside'? Husserl's answer is that this depends on the experience's inclusion of certain kinds of possibility. Possibilities are not isolated perceptual contents; one does not see a possibility in the way that one sees a cup. Rather, possibilities contribute to perceptual contents. For instance, without a sense of something's being potentially accessible to others in various ways, the appreciation of its having an existence independent of one's own perspective on it would be eroded or absent. So we do not first experience something as 'there' and then experience its possibilities. What is actually presented and what is presented as possible together comprise the sense of something's being 'there' that is integral to many experiential contents.[13]

Husserl's approach bears at least some resemblance to certain accounts of experiential content that are already on the table. For instance, it complements – to a degree – enactivist theories like that of Noë (2004), which similarly emphasize perception of possibility and the perceptual role of action tendencies.[14] Hence, one might argue, it is susceptible to some of the same objections. For instance, Prinz (2011, 180) advocates a more conservative account of phenomenal content by maintaining that 'visual experience' comes first and is only later united with action tendencies to generate a 'total experience', with the implication that visual perceptual content can be extricated from possibility. However, that kind of move can be undermined by further emphasizing the dynamism of Husserl's approach. For Husserl, many experienced possibilities take the form of *anticipated* events, including the effects of one's own actions. Anticipation shapes all our experiences and thoughts. Anticipated possibilities can present themselves as certain (as is often the case in the context of habitual activity), as uncertain to varying degrees or as doubtful. As an example of experienced doubt, Husserl reflects on coming to recognize something in a shop window as a mannequin, an experience that can involve conflicting expectations:

> the visual appearance, the spatial form imbued with color, was until now provided with a halo of anticipatory intentions which gave the sense 'human body' and, in general, 'man'; now there is superposed on it the sense 'clothed mannequin'.
>
> (1973, 92)

He adds that anticipated occurrences also have differing degrees of salience. Some, such as that of a falling glass smashing on the floor, not only come with a sense of certainty but also with a particular allure (2001, 91). To further elaborate on the account, I suggest that what is anticipated can have various different kinds of significance. An event is not only experienced as likely, unlikely or certain, distant or imminent, and to some degree salient. Experienced anticipation can also take the form of curiosity, fascination, excitement, impatience, dread or unease. All of our experiences are shaped by an ongoing interplay between anticipation and its fulfilment or lack thereof. Whether and how something is expected influences how it is experienced when it does occur. Thus a pure, primary visual experience cannot be extracted; visual experiences are shaped from the outset by a framework of anticipation that is already in place when they arise. Perception and thought incorporate a sense of temporal coherence, habitual anticipation, confidence, certainty, uncertainty, doubt, and so on. When you listen to a language that you do not understand, the inability to anticipate what is coming next shapes what one currently experiences, and distinguishes it from experience of a familiar language. In the latter case, there is already a variably determinate sense of what is about to occur, as illustrated by the fact that some things present themselves as anomalous, surprising. Is the experience of possibility principally perceptual or non-perceptual? The answer is surely 'neither'; perception and thought have equal claim on it. So this aspect of cognitive phenomenology is neither an instance of sensory phenomenology nor something wholly different from sensory phenomenology; it is something that belongs equally to sensory and cognitive experience. Many – but not all – of the same kinds of possibility feature in both: styles of anticipation, kinds of significance, degrees of determinacy, and so on.

What we have here is an account of at least *some* aspects of experiential content. If Husserl is right, both perception and thought incorporate a dynamic interplay of anticipation and fulfilment, involving a structured system of various different *kinds* of possibility. And I think there is some plausibility to this. It is doubtful that the phenomenology of perception and thought can be extricated from experiences of anticipation and fulfilment. And it is equally doubtful that the dance of anticipation and fulfilment can be recast in terms of conceptual understanding. It can be described in that way, of course, but it would be implausible to insist that the experience always takes that form. When I put one foot in front of another, my experience neither incorporates nor is associated with the proposition 'my foot will be met by flat, solid ground'. Even so, as my foot sinks into a muddy puddle and I lose balance, I am surprised; things have not unfolded as expected.

The approach I have sketched is – of course – contentious, but it does offer the potential to generate clear and elaborate descriptions of experience (especially if further refined to include a more detailed account of the kinds of possibility that experience incorporates and how they interrelate). It thus paves the way for analyses of phenomenal differences between perceptions and thoughts that differ markedly from cursory claims about perceptions or thoughts having different phenomenal feels. The story does not end here though. As I understand Husserl, possibilities not only comprise a phenomenology that is common to perception and thought; they are also implicated in something that perception and thought presuppose. Husserl describes certainty as the 'primal mode' of anticipation (1973, 100). For experience to have any kind of structure, the dance of anticipation and fulfilment needs to occur, for the most part, in a reliable way. It is only against the backdrop of a system of certainties that uncertainty or doubt over something specific can occur. Hence we return to his conception of world-experience as a kind of habitual dwelling, a structured system of practical certainties in the context of which intentional states and their contents arise:

> It belongs to what is taken for granted, prior to all scientific thoughts and all philosophical questioning, that the world is – always is in advance – and that every correction of an opinion, whether an experiential or other opinion, presupposes the already existing world, namely, as a horizon of what in the given case is indubitably valid as existing, and presupposes within

this horizon something familiar and doubtlessly certain with which that which is perhaps cancelled out as invalid came into conflict.

(Husserl 1970a, 110)

World-experience, for Husserl, is a condition of intelligibility for the various ways of encountering things *within* a world, determining the kinds of experience that are accessible to us. Much the same conception is adopted by Merleau-Ponty, who describes the presupposed world as an overarching 'style of all possible styles', which permeates all perception and thought, constituting an all-pervasive experience of rootedness in a structured, shared world (1962, 327–30). One might object that describing the world as a 'style' is no more helpful than gesturing at a mysterious aspect of experience that perception and thought presuppose. However, the general point that they both seek to convey can, I think, be clarified and elaborated by adapting Husserl's account of how possibilities contribute to experiential content.

Disturbances of world

What Merleau-Ponty refers to as an all-encompassing 'style' of experience and thought is, I suggest, a sense of the possible. World-experience can be construed in terms of receptiveness to the various different kinds of possibility that feature in our experiences, an openness to possibility that not only manifests itself in particular perceptions and thoughts but also has a phenomenology in its own right. Let us return to the experience of a cup. It incorporates numerous token possibilities, such as that of seeing the cup from another angle, of touching it, of its being seen by other people, and so on. And we can only experience it as having these possibilities if we are able to experience possibilities of the relevant *types*. World-experience consists (at least in part) of a sense of the types of possibility that are on offer. If we did not have experiential access to the various types of possibility, we would not be able to adopt intentional states of the kinds that we do. We inhabit a world where things have the potential to appear as 'there', as 'real but not present', as 'remembered', as 'anticipated', as 'imagined', and so forth. A grasp of these intentional state types as distinct from each other is inextricable from a sense of the various kinds of possibility. For instance, if the world were without any sense of things being perceptually or practically available to others, the distinction between something's being 'there' or more generally 'real' and its being 'imagined' would be eroded, in so far as the relevant sense of 'real' incorporates an appreciation of the distinction between what is publicly accessible and what depends on the perspective of a particular individual. The same general point applies to other kinds of possibility, such as tangibility. If we could not experience anything as available to the touch or as practically manipulable, our sense of what it is for something to be 'there', and thus our distinction between 'there' and 'not there', would be somehow altered, diminished. Hence at least some types of experienced possibility contribute to what we might call a 'sense of reality'. By this, I mean a sense of what it is for something to be 'there', 'real' or otherwise. For Husserl, the sense of reality is inextricable from the sense of belonging to a world. World-experience is thus what we might call 'pre-intentional'; it determines the kinds of intentional states that are intelligible possibilities for us. That this pre-intentional sense of immersion in a world is itself integral to experience, rather than amounting to a non-phenomenological *capacity* to have various different kinds of experience, becomes more readily apparent once it is emphasized that many kinds of possibility take the form of anticipation. Anticipation often does have a phenomenological structure, and world-experience involves a general 'style' of anticipation that shapes perception and thought.

The concern might be raised that all of this amounts to an elaborate – and still not very clear – story, for which evidence is lacking. So, one might be inclined to simply dismiss it on the basis that 'it's not like that for me'. However, there is, I suggest, much potential support for the view. That support comes from numerous first-person testimonies, all of which can be plausibly interpreted in terms of an 'experienced modal space' and would otherwise remain mysterious. Of course, first-person accounts of experience can be interpreted in order to fit any number of different views. Even so, the sheer quantity, variety and consistency of reports is sufficient to convince me that (a) perception and thought occur against the backdrop of a pre-intentional sense of belonging to a shared world, and (b) this 'world-experience' can be analysed in terms of access to types of possibility. An especially rich – although by no means the only – source of testimony is the experience of psychiatric illness. Thus, in the remainder of this chapter, I turn specifically to phenomenological psychopathology.[15] Many people with psychiatric illness diagnoses describe, sometimes in exquisite detail, something that is a change, not just in perception or thought content, but in an overarching sense of belonging to a shared world. For example, first-person accounts of depression often emphasize how the 'world' within which one is situated has somehow changed, in a way that is elusive, profound, pervasive and not ascribable to any number of experience or thought contents:

> Most of all I was terribly alone, lost, in a harsh and far-away place, a horrible terrain reserved for me alone. There was nowhere to go, nothing to see, no panorama. Though this landscape surrounded me, vast and amorphous, I couldn't escape the awful confines of my leaden body and downcast eye.
>
> (Shaw 1997, 40)

Such experiences can be understood in terms of the kinds of possibility offered by the world. Depression involves loss of the sense that anything could be significantly different from the present in a positive way. There is not merely an absence of something from experience but also an *experienced absence*, perhaps because the person still anticipates experiencing certain kinds of possibility even though she cannot, resulting in an overall feeling of unfulfilled anticipation. Interpreting first-person accounts in such terms often takes little effort. Many of them explicitly describe the experience of losing certain kinds of possibility, in ways that affect not only perception but other kinds of intentional state too, including memory, belief and imagination. Consider the following responses to a questionnaire study on the experience of depression:

> 'It is impossible to feel that things will ever be different (even though I know I have been depressed before and come out of it). This feeling means I don't care about anything. I feel like nothing is worth anything.'

> 'The world holds no possibilities for me when I'm depressed. Every avenue I consider exploring seems shut off.'

> 'When I'm not depressed, other possibilities exist. Maybe I won't fail, maybe life isn't completely pointless, maybe they do care about me, maybe I do have some good qualities. When depressed, these possibilities simply do not exist.'[16]

A diminished appreciation that things could be significantly different from the present (in a good way, at least) amounts to a sense of one's predicament as oddly timeless. With such possibilities gone from perception, imagination, memory and thought, the person cannot contemplate the possibility of ever recovering from depression, of inhabiting a world that could differ in a significant way: 'There was and could be no other life than the bleak shadowland I now inhabited' (Shaw 1997, 25).[17] While the person might remember – in a propositional way – *that* she was once not depressed, she cannot recall what it was to experience things that way. Consequently, such propositions – even when endorsed – are experienced by her as curiously hollow.

An alternative interpretation is that a substantial number of perceptual contents are affected, thus affecting a substantial number of thought contents, or vice versa, and that there is therefore no need to appeal to the additional dimension of 'world-experience'. But many first-person accounts are quite clearly directed at something pervasive and deep-rooted, which cannot be accommodated in terms of however many intentional states and their contents. Consider the following quotations, offered by patients with psychiatric diagnoses:

It became impossible to reach anything. Like, how do I get up and walk to that chair if the essential thing that we mean by chair, something that lets us sit down and rest or upholds us as we read a book, something that shares our life in that way, has lost the quality of being able to do that? [...] You know that you have lost life itself. You've lost a habitable earth. You've lost the invitation to live that the universe extends to us at every moment. You've lost something that people don't even know is. That's why it's so hard to explain.

(From an interview quoted by Hornstein 2009, 213)

It's almost like I am there but I can't touch anything or I can't connect. Everything requires massive effort and I'm not really able to do anything. Like if I notice something needs cleaning or moving, it's like it's out of reach, or the act of doing that thing isn't in my world at that time [...] like I can see so much detail but I cannot be a part of it. I suppose feeling disconnected is the best way to describe it.

(Patient quoted by Horne and Csipke 2009, 663)

Both authors convey an alteration in the sense of belonging to a world, which implicates the experience of possibility. In the first case, the world is bereft of practical familiarity, functionality and tangibility. In the latter, salient practical possibilities are still experienced, but they present themselves as impossible to actualize. Various other kinds of experience can be interpreted in the same general way. Consider experiences of schizophrenia, which differ – in various ways and to differing degrees – from the kinds of experience typical of depression. In several works, Louis Sass has developed a detailed account of the phenomenology of schizophrenia, according to which there is an all-enveloping transformation of the experience of self and world. The sense of being habitually, practically rooted in a shared world is lost. Alongside this, there is an involuntary over-attentiveness to one's body, experiences and thoughts, which become strangely object-like and alien. Implicated in all of this is what we might describe as a disruption of ordinarily taken-for-granted styles of anticipation, amounting to an erosion of habitual certainty and belonging:

[There is] a loss of the usual common-sense orientation to reality, that is, of the unquestioned sense of obviousness and of the unproblematic background quality that normally enables a person to take for granted so many aspects and dimensions of the social and practical world.

(Sass 2003, 159)

The person no longer feels grounded in the world. There is an 'existential reorientation' that shapes all her experiences and thoughts (Parnas and

Sass 2001). According to Sass, it is only once this is acknowledged that the various positive symptoms, such as hallucinations and delusions, can be understood phenomenologically. They are not merely anomalous perception and/or belief contents, given that the sense of reality has itself been transformed and the modalities of intentional state, such as 'belief', 'perception' and 'imagination', have been altered along with it. Nothing is experienced as 'real' in quite the way it was before; the sense of conviction attaching to belief is different. An approach like this can be used to make sense of symptoms such as 'thought insertion', where the sufferer experiences certain thoughts as generated by someone else. Having acknowledged that the phenomenology of thought is partly attributable to styles of anticipation, we can appreciate how a thought might be experienced as *alien*, as arising from somewhere else. Husserl maintains that thought – like experience more generally – has a temporal structure. Experience of the present is inextricable from and partly constituted by past-oriented 'retentions' and future-oriented 'protentions'. Unlike a memory, the 'retention' is part of one's current experience, but it is experienced *as* 'having just passed', whereas the protention is a variably determinate sense of what is coming next. As already discussed, the present is imbued with possibilities of various kinds, which are anticipated in different ways.[18] Thought is akin to a melody, in that we might not know exactly what is coming next but we do have a sufficient sense of it to feel surprised by anomalies, like a note that is out of tune. Even the most passive of thoughts, the tune in the back of one's head, the seemingly unbidden impulse to insult a friend or make a hurtful comment that conflicts with one's value system, arguably involve at least some degree of anticipation, some sense of what is coming. However, drawing on Husserl's account of time-consciousness, Gallagher (2005) proposes that thought insertion in schizophrenia involves disruption of protention, with the result that the thought is experienced as unanticipated, utterly alien: 'Thought generation, like any experience, is normally protentional. Without protention, thought continues, but it appears already made, not generated by me, appearing suddenly, already formulated as it enters into retention' (2005, 195). This is something that a person would be more susceptible to when afflicted by a more enveloping loss of habitual familiarity, an alteration of world-experience where all thoughts are – to a slightly lesser degree – alien, object-like, detached. Hence it is consistent with Sass's approach.

Another feature of anomalous experience in schizophrenia that can be plausibly interpreted in terms of experienced possibility is the so-called 'delusional mood' or 'delusional atmosphere' that often precedes onset of full-blown psychosis. As famously described by Karl Jaspers:

Patients feel uncanny and that there is something suspicious afoot. Everything gets a new meaning. The environment is somehow different – not to a gross degree – perception is unaltered in itself but there is some change which envelops everything with a subtle, pervasive and strangely uncertain light. A living-room which formerly was felt as neutral or friendly now becomes dominated by some indefinable atmosphere. Something seems in the air which the patient cannot account for, a distrustful, uncomfortable, uncanny tension invades him.

(1963, 98)

There is something paradoxical about this description: everything is strangely different but perception is also 'unaltered'; everything remains what it was and where it was, with all its features intact. However, the experience makes sense once we think of it as an alteration in the style of perception, in the kinds of possibility that the perceived world incorporates. Exactly what that change consists of is debatable. Indeed, it may vary considerably from one instance to the next (Ratcliffe, forthcoming). However, it is at least apparent from Jaspers' description that an all-enveloping sense of inchoate threat or menace plays a role. Everything is somehow uncertain, untrustworthy; the habitual certainty that usually orients us is replaced by a kind of doubt, altering the quality of all perception and thought.

The same approach can also be applied to 'depersonalization', an experience that often occurs (perhaps in different forms) in depression and schizophrenia but is arguably also a syndrome in its own right. First-person accounts relate an experience of everything as somehow strange or lacking, along with a feeling of being oddly cut off from the world:

Self-reports emphasise the strange and disturbing quality of the depersonalization experience: some patients report feeling 'like a robot', 'different from everyone else' and 'separate from myself' … Others describe feeling 'half-asleep' or 'as if my head is full of cotton wool', with associated difficulties in concentration. External reality may also be strangely altered: it may appear somehow artificial – as if 'painted, not natural', or 'two-dimensional' or 'as if everyone is acting out a role on stage, and I'm just a spectator'.

(Medford *et al.* 2005, 93)

Depersonalization encompasses experience of thought too: 'thinking just *felt* different, as if coming from somewhere else' (Simeon and Abugel 2006, 26). Again, this is something that cannot be conveyed by invoking specific sensory or cognitive 'phenomenal contents'. The point applies to many other profound and sometimes disturbing forms of experience. For instance, depersonalization is frequently associated with trauma, and first-person accounts of trauma likewise emphasize something that cannot be adequately conveyed in terms of however many intentional states and their contents, something that shapes all experience. For example, Améry (1999, 40) describes how his world was irrevocably 'shattered' by torture, something that led to enduring loss of the 'habitual trust' in which all his experiences and thoughts were once embedded:

> Whoever has succumbed to torture can no longer feel at home in the world. The shame of destruction cannot be erased. Trust in the world, which already collapsed in part at the first blow, but in the end, under torture, fully, will not be regained.

Many victims of traumatic experiences describe a similarly profound experience of loss, an enduring destruction of one's 'world' or an irrevocable loss of comfortable, confident belonging.[19]

Thus, an ordinarily presupposed aspect of experience can be made salient through reflection on those occasions when it is altered radically. Although I have focused on psychiatric illness here, one could scrutinize a range of other circumstances to similar effect. Reflection on certain first-person experiences also has a role to play – consider the kinds of experience sometimes associated with illness, jet lag, hangovers, grief or other circumstances, where everything seems somehow strange or not quite right, in ways that are hard to describe in terms of specific experiential contents. As one pursues such reflections, the world that is ordinarily presupposed by experience and thought gradually comes to light as a fragile, contingent and elusive phenomenological achievement. Hence, by increasingly engaging with a certain subject matter, one can nurture a 'phenomenological stance', construed permissively as an acknowledgement of world-experience and a commitment to study it.

In certain respects, the method that I have tentatively sketched in this section (which is just one of many different ways in which phenomenology might be pursued) resembles what Siegel (2010, 15) and others call the 'method of phenomenal contrast', which has been used to defend various claims about the nature of phenomenal content. It involves an invitation to consider two experiences, acknowledge a difference between them and then concede that this difference is most plausibly attributed to one factor rather than another. There are differences though. The contrastive method that I advocate also seeks to 'awaken' the attitude through which one comes to appreciate one's subject matter. In addition, reflection on forms of anomalous experience can feed into the development of a phenomenological account, rather than just arbitrating between different accounts of content – the structure of experience is further brought to light by exploring its variations.

Conclusion

In this chapter, I turned to the phenomenological tradition in order to cast light on the nature of 'phenomenal content'. Drawing principally on Husserl, I sought to articulate an aspect of experience that is presupposed by intentional states and their contents, a possibility space that is not attributable to any one perceptual modality or to non-perceptual 'cognition'. I suggested that experiences of thinking should not be contrasted with sensory experiences or wholly attributed to sensory experiences, as the phenomenology of possibility is common to both and neither has a stronger claim on it than the other. I also sided with phenomenologists in maintaining that phenomenal contents and attitudes presuppose a framework of world-experience, and I suggested that this be analysed in terms of a possibility space. Where does this leave us? If the view I have extracted from Husserl and others is broadly right then, although there are complementary themes to be found in current debates about phenomenal content, there is also something missing from those debates. Experience is much richer than often assumed, in ways that cannot be adequately understood unless one nurtures a sort of perspectival shift and adopts a broadly 'phenomenological stance'. Engagement by philosophers of mind with a phenomenological approach has the potential to enrich discussion in a range of ways. As I have shown, the kinds of experience that a phenomenological approach can cast light on and at the same time invoke as support include experiences of torture, depersonalization, depression, grief, illness and many others. In contrast, philosophers of mind have concentrated on examples such as the redness of red, the smell of a rose, the feeling of an itch or the experience of hearing a sentence that one does not understand. The 'what-it-is-likeness' of such experiences is dutifully remarked on, after which there is often a struggle to say much more about what 'phenomenal consciousness' consists of. So one might raise the concern that the subject matter of much of philosophy of mind is overly restrictive, often rather trivial and also – if the experiential 'world' has indeed been forgotten – confused. But this is not to imply that a phenomenological account of possibility can offer us a detailed analysis of everything that philosophers of mind have addressed under the heading 'phenomenal content'. For example, there are the so-called 'qualia' that have been fetishized in recent years (which might or might not end up being absorbed by a comprehensive account of intentionality). It might be able to, but – then again – it may well turn out that the phenomenologists are preoccupied with different aspects of experience. Even so, the point remains that phenomenology is open to a richer subject matter, which it approaches in a distinctive way, so as to yield detailed descriptions of experience (which are surely preferable to gesturing at some phenomenon and asking people to go along with one set of intuitions rather than another). So philosophy of mind may well have something to learn from it.[20] What I am advocating here is not a one-way exchange, though. It is similarly worth exploring how the technical resources of philosophy of mind, and of analytic philosophy more generally, might be brought to bear in order to distinguish, clarify and further refine various phenomenological claims.[21]

Notes

1 A more liberal conception of 'content', which would accommodate attitudes and non-intentional 'qualia' too, is adopted by Strawson (2011, 291) who takes it to include '*absolutely everything that is experienced in the having of the experience*, everything that is experientially registered in any way'.

2 For convenience, I will focus mostly on contributions to a recent edited volume, *Cognitive Phenomenology* (Bayne and Montague 2011b). This excellent collection includes almost the full range of views at play in current philosophy of mind, and so what I say here applies equally to discussion of cognitive phenomenology and phenomenal content more generally.

3 Strawson coined the term "understanding-experience" in his 1994 book *Mental Reality*.

4 Both positions could be read as positive responses to the question of whether or not there is cognitive experience, although the term 'cognitive phenomenology' is more often reserved for the latter (e.g. Bayne and Montague 2011a, 12).

5 See Bayne and Montague 2011a, 8–9 for a discussion of how this term is used. See Siewert 2011 for an attempt to clean it up.

6 For discussion of other ways in which Husserlian phenomenology can inform work on experiential content, see, for example, Smith 2011.

7 For example, Heidegger writes that 'the world itself is not an entity within-the-world; and yet it is so determinative for such entities that only in so far as "there is" a world can they be encountered and show themselves, in their Being, as entities which have been discovered' (1962, 102). This conveys much the same broad conception of world that we find in Husserl and Merleau-Ponty – something that is seldom an explicit object of experience or thought; something that we are already practically, unreflectively immersed in when we experience, think and act.

8 This relates to what Husserl (1970a, 178) calls the 'paradox' of subjectivity: the sense of 'being a subject for the world and at the same time being an object in the world', which presents us with the problem of reconciling experience of oneself as a contingent entity in the world with acknowledgement of that same world as a phenomenological achievement attributable to oneself. See Carr 1999 for a good discussion.

9 It has been argued that such claims are complemented by recent work in empirical science. For example, Gallagher (2005) draws on a range of empirical sources to defend the view that a 'body schema' is a 'structural feature of the phenomenal field of consciousness' (2). In other words, the phenomenology of the body is not exhausted by its appearing as the content of some attitude; it also plays a role in shaping experiential content: 'In its *prenoetic* roles the body functions to make perception possible and to constrain intentional consciousness in various ways' (138–39). Like Husserl, Gallagher suggests that this role includes a contribution to our experience of the possibilities that the perceived environment offers (141).

10 There are parallels here with some recent work in philosophy of mind on perceptual content and multimodality. For instance, O'Callaghan (2007, 2011) emphasizes the intermodal structure of perceptual experience and argues that perception through one sense incorporates an appreciation of what else *could* be perceived through that and other senses: 'You hear a sound as the sound of something that could be seen or brought into view, and that has visible features' (2011, 157).

11 See Gallagher 2008 for a discussion of Husserl, perception, possibility and intersubjectivity.

12 It is debatable how the experience of possibility relates to a conceptual/propositional appreciation of the possible. The proposition 'it is likely to rain' can be endorsed and also recognized as relevant to one's concerns without one's seeing the possibility there in the clouds, and vice versa. However, that the two can be distinguished does not imply independence. Although I do not address the phenomenology of concepts in this chapter, I do not want to rule out the view that certain aspects of experience are attributable to concept application. I also acknowledge that the relationship between concept application and experience of possibility is likely to be a very close one.

13 Few participants in the cognitive phenomenology debate address this sense of an entity's being 'there', which at least seems to be part of perceptual experience. An exception is Montague (2011), who offers an account according to which perception incorporates a kind of 'object positing'. Unlike Husserl, she construes it as a 'bare demonstrative *thought*', whereby a particular entity is posited (135).

14 There are also some similarities with J.J. Gibson's well-known account of perceptual systems. But there is also a substantial difference between the two approaches – Gibson's is explicitly non-phenomenological. As he puts it, he is concerned with 'detecting information', not 'having sensations' (1968, 2).

15 There is a long tradition of interaction between phenomenology (Husserlian or otherwise) and psychopathology. Influential figures in the field include Jaspers, Minkowski, Binswanger, Blankenberg, van den Berg, Laing and others. See Ratcliffe and Broome 2012 for further discussion.

16 These are representative responses to an Internet questionnaire study, which I conducted in collaboration with colleagues, along with the mental health charity SANE, in 2011. Most participants had current or recent diagnoses of 'major depression'.

17 See Ratcliffe 2012, in prep., for a more detailed discussion of these and other aspects of the phenomenology of depression.

18 See Gallagher and Zahavi 2008, ch. 4, for a good introduction to Husserl on time-consciousness.

19 See also Bernstein 2011 for an account of trauma as loss of habitual trust in the world.

20 The phenomenological approach has potential practical applications too, in psychiatry for instance. Understanding what a delusion or hallucination consists of surely demands a characterization of the relevant experience that is not wildly inaccurate (even though phenomenological description alone will not add up to a comprehensive explanation). If someone's complaints of hearing voices or experiencing inserted thoughts are treated as symptoms that arise in the context of a more pervasive change in the modal shape of experience, the resultant phenomenological analysis will be quite different from the sort of account that arises when they are treated as isolated perceptual and/or cognitive contents. The former approach may well apply to many cases. For example, Merleau-Ponty (1962, 334) remarks that 'the fact that patients so often say that someone is talking to them by telephone or radio, is to be taken precisely as expressing that the morbid world is artificial, and that it lacks something needed to become a "reality"'. If something like this is right, then seemingly isolated phenomena, such as auditory hallucinations, emerge against the backdrop of an altered sense of reality. A case along such lines can also be made for at least some allegedly 'monothematic', 'circumscribed' delusions (Ratcliffe 2008, chs 5 and 6).

21 The research reported in this chapter was supported by a Wellcome Trust Strategic Award (WT098455MA).

References

Améry, J. (1999) *At the Mind's Limits: Contemplations by a Survivor on Auschwitz and Its Realities*, trans. S. Rosenfeld and S.P. Rosenfeld, London: Granta Books.

Bayne, T. (2011) 'Perception and the Reach of Phenomenal Content', in K. Hawley and F. Macpherson (eds), *The Admissible Contents of Experience*, Chichester: Wiley-Blackwell, 16–35.

Bayne, T. and M. Montague (2011a) 'Cognitive Phenomenology: An Introduction', in Bayne and Montague 2011b, 1–34.

——(eds) (2011b) *Cognitive Phenomenology*, Oxford: Oxford University Press.

Bernstein, J.M. (2011) 'Trust: On the Real But Almost Always Unnoticed, Ever-Changing Foundation of Ethical Life', *Metaphilosophy* 42: 395–416.

Block, N. (1995) 'On a Confusion about a Function of Consciousness', *Behavioral and Brain Sciences* 18: 227–47.

Carr, D. (1999) *The Paradox of Subjectivity: Self in the Transcendental Tradition*, Oxford: Oxford University Press.

Carruthers, P. and B. Veillet (2011) 'The Case against Cognitive Phenomenology', in Bayne and Montague 2011b, 35–56.

Crane, T. (2011) 'Is Perception a Propositional Attitude?', in K. Hawley and F. Macpherson (eds), *The Admissible Contents of Experience*, Chichester: Wiley-Blackwell, 83–100.

Gallagher, S. (2005) *How the Body Shapes the Mind*, Oxford: Clarendon Press.

——(2008) 'Intersubjectivity in Perception', *Continental Philosophy Review* 41: 163–78.

Gallagher, S. and D. Zahavi (2008) *The Phenomenological Mind*, London: Routledge.

Gibson, J.J. (1968) *The Senses Considered as Perceptual Systems*, London: George Allen & Unwin.

Heidegger, M. (1962) *Being and Time*, trans. J. Macquarrie and E. Robinson, Oxford: Blackwell.

Horne, O. and E. Csipke (2009) 'From Feeling Too Little and Too Much, to Feeling More and Less? A Non-paradoxical Theory of the Functions of Self-Harm', *Qualitative Health Research* 19: 655–67.

Hornstein, G.A. (2009) *Agnes's Jacket: A Psychologist's Search for the Meanings of Madness*, New York: Rodale.

Husserl, E. (1960) *Cartesian Meditations: An Introduction to Phenomenology*, trans. D. Cairns, The Hague: Martinus Nijhoff.

——(1970a) *The Crisis of European Sciences and Transcendental Phenomenology*, trans. D. Carr, Evanston, IL: Northwestern University Press.

——(1970b) 'The Vienna Lecture', in his *The Crisis of European Sciences and Transcendental Phenomenology*, trans. D. Carr, Evanston, IL: Northwestern University Press, 269–99.

——(1973) *Experience and Judgment*, trans. J.S. Churchill and K. Ameriks, London: Routledge.

——(1989) *Ideas Pertaining to a Pure Phenomenology and to a Phenomenological Philosophy: Second Book*, trans. R. Rojcewicz and A. Schuwer, Dordrecht: Kluwer.

——(2001) *Analyses concerning Passive and Active Synthesis: Lectures on Transcendental Logic*, trans. A.J. Steinbock, Dordrecht: Kluwer.

Jaspers, K. (1963) *General Psychopathology*, trans. J. Hoenig and M.W. Hamilton, Manchester: Manchester University Press. Translated from the German 7th edn (1959).

Laing, R.D. (1969) *Self and Others*, 2nd edn, London: Tavistock Publications.

Medford, N., M. Sierra, D. Baker and A.S. David (2005) 'Understanding and Treating Depersonalisation Disorder', *Advances in Psychiatric Treatment* 11: 92–100.

Merleau-Ponty, M. (1962) *Phenomenology of Perception*, trans. C. Smith, London: Routledge.

Montague, M. (2011) 'The Phenomenology of Particularity', in Bayne and Montague 2011b, 121–40.

Nagel, T. (1974) 'What Is It Like to Be a Bat?', *Philosophical Review* 83: 435–50.

Noë, A. (2004) *Action in Perception*, Cambridge MA: MIT Press.

O'Callaghan, C. (2007) *Sounds: A Philosophical Theory*, Oxford: Oxford University Press.

——(2011) 'Lessons from beyond Vision (Sounds and Audition)', *Philosophical Studies* 153: 143–60.

Parnas, J. and L.A. Sass (2001) 'Self, Solipsism and Schizophrenic Delusions', *Philosophy, Psychiatry, & Psychology* 8: 101–20.

Prinz, J.J. (2011) 'The Sensory Basis of Cognitive Phenomenology', in Bayne and Montague 2011b, 174–96.

Ratcliffe, M. (2008) *Feelings of Being: Phenomenology, Psychiatry and the Sense of Reality*, Oxford: Oxford University Press.

——(2012) 'Varieties of Temporal Experience in Depression', *Journal of Medicine and Philosophy* 37: 114–38.

——(forthcoming) 'Delusional Atmosphere and the Sense of Unreality', in G. Stanghellini and T. Fuchs (eds), *One Century of Karl Jaspers' General Psychopathology*, Oxford: Oxford University Press.

——(in prep.) *The Modalities of Melancholy: A Phenomenological Study of Depression*, Oxford: Oxford University Press.

Ratcliffe, M. and M. Broome (2012) 'Existential Phenomenology, Psychiatric Illness and the Death of Possibilities', in S. Crowell (ed.), *The Cambridge Companion to Existentialism*, Cambridge: Cambridge University Press, 361–82.

Sartre, J.P. (1989) *Being and Nothingness*, trans. H.E. Barnes, London: Routledge.

Sass, L.A. (2003) '"Negative Symptoms", Schizophrenia, and the Self', *International Journal of Psychology and Psychological Therapy* 3: 153–80.

Shaw, F. (1997) *Out of Me: The Story of a Postnatal Breakdown*, London: Penguin.

Siegel, S. (2010) *The Contents of Visual Experience*, Oxford: Oxford University Press.

Siewert, C. (2011) 'Phenomenal Thought', in Bayne and Montague 2011b, 236–67.

Simeon, D. and J. Abugel (2006) *Feeling Unreal: Depersonalization Disorder and the Loss of the Self*, Oxford: Oxford University Press.

Smith, D. Woodruff (2011) 'The Phenomenology of Consciously Thinking', in Bayne and Montague 2011b, 345–72.

Strawson, G. (1994) *Mental Reality*, Cambridge MA: MIT Press.

——(2004) 'Real Intentionality', *Phenomenology and the Cognitive Sciences* 3: 287–313.

——(2011) 'Cognitive Phenomenology: Real Life', in Bayne and Montague 2011b, 285–325.

Tye, M. and B. Wright (2011) 'Is There a Phenomenology of Thought?', in Bayne and Montague 2011b, 326–44.

Part IV

METHODS IN ETHICS AND AESTHETICS

20 Intuitions and experimental philosophy: comfortable bedfellows

NEIL LEVY

The philosophical landscape has been transformed over the past several decades by what might be called the *empirical turn*. This turn comes in two flavors (Prinz 2008). The older flavor develops philosophical accounts (of the nature of mind, consciousness, free will or what have you) which are deeply informed by empirical data. The newer flavor – experimental philosophy (x-phi) – itself produces the empirical data which it then puts to philosophical purposes. In their wake, these developments have brought great controversy, in particular concerning whether philosophy should abandon its traditional methods in favor of a more scientific approach.

In this paper, I shall focus on one aspect of this debate, the controversy over the role of intuitions (and, closely related, of thought experiments – intuition pumps, as Dennett (1984) called them) in philosophy. X-phi has apparently discovered that the intuitions of "the folk" – non-philosophers – often diverge from those of philosophers. These findings have led to charges of parochialism from experimental philosophers: rather than inquiring into the nature of (our concepts of) knowledge or free will, they argue, we are simply investigating the idiosyncratic conceptions of a particular cultural and socio-economic group (perhaps just WEIRD people – those who are Western, Educated, Industrialized, Rich and Democratic; Henrich *et al.* 2010). Together with other worries (concerning, for instance, the fact that intuitions may be influenced by apparently irrelevant factors, like the order in which cases are presented), this fact suggests that we have little reason to think that our intuitions track the features of genuine interest, and therefore undermines their warrant.

I shall argue that though the worry is a serious one, it does not undermine the value of the appeal to intuitions. Rather, the empirical turn helps to inform us *how* intuitions should be utilized. Though the appeal to intuitions can be vindicated, philosophy must change to accommodate x-phi concerns. It must become more scientific: in structure, as well as in content. The use of intuitions is not incompatible with taking the relevant science very seriously. On the contrary, taking science very seriously will help us to vindicate the appeal to intuitions.

Before turning to setting out the nature of the challenge to intuition-mongering from x-phi, a word on how I shall use the word "intuition." As I understand it, an intuition is an intellectual seeming (Bealer 1998); to intuit that *p* is for one to have the relatively forceful impression that *p* seems to be the case. Intuitions, in this sense, are generated by what some psychologists call System 1 processes: fast, automatic, perhaps encapsulated processes triggered by relevant stimuli. An intuition is *not* a personal-level judgment: I may intuit that *p* but judge that ~*p*. System 2 processes may override System 1 output. Typically, however, subjects endorse the contents of their intuitions. However, though this is what *I* mean by "intuition," I will often be forced to use the word in a more inclusive way. The x-phi challenge to intuition-mongering turns on data from studies of how naive subjects, and (to a lesser extent) philosophers, classify various cases. Most of these studies do not allow us to distinguish between subjects who simply endorse the content of their intuitions (narrowly construed) and those who form considered judgments at variance with their intuitions. Since we cannot distinguish between these groups of subjects (though we can be confident that both were represented), in what follows I often use the word "intuition" in a broader sense, to represent subjects' judgments however generated. Nevertheless, the defense offered of the use of intuitions in philosophy is of the use of narrow-construal intuitions as data by philosophers, self-consciously aware that the way things seem to them may not be the way they are.

The nature of the challenge from x-phi

Philosophers often have recourse to their intuitions in developing their theories. Typically, though not invariably, these intuitions are generated by the contemplation of cases, actual or imaginary. It has become standard practice for intuitions to be taken to be defeasible evidence.[1] Consider the generation of counterexamples to an account that claims to give an analysis of some philosophically interesting concept, *C*. If it is possible to generate a case which either is, intuitively, an instance of *C* but which does not satisfy the conditions set down in the analysis, or in which the conditions set down in the analysis are satisfied but the case is not, intuitively, an instance of *C*, then it is standardly thought that the analysis has a problem. Roughly, the stronger the intuition the case generates, the bigger the problem for the analysis. Intuition-mongers hold that proponents of the analysis owe us a compelling case for setting contrary intuitions aside; failing that, they must modify the analysis.

There are two, closely related, challenges from x-phi to the use of intuitions. One focuses on the mechanisms that produce particular intuitions, the other focuses on the fact that there is diversity in the intuitions generated by cases. Following Ichikawa (forthcoming) I shall call these challenges the *defeater critique* and the *arbitrariness critique*. The defeater critique rejects a particular use of an intuition on the grounds that it is generated by a process that is faulty. For instance, Tamara Horowitz (1998) argues that intuitions about the relative moral significance of harming versus not aiding are generated by the same processes that generate inconsistent intuitions in losses versus forgone gains cases; since a process that generates inconsistent intuitions in response to irrelevant features of a case – whether it is framed as a loss or a forgone gain – cannot be tracking features that are genuinely morally significant, we ought to reject the intuitions in question.

In this chapter, I shall have little controversial to say about the defeater critique. I take it as obvious that the fact that an intuition is generated by a process that does not track the features of interest is a reason to discount the intuition. Indeed, I have advanced defeater-based arguments myself, arguing that the intuitions that are systematized by the doctrine of double effect are generated by the same – irrational – process that generates intuitions about intentionality in Knobe effect cases (Levy 2011). My main focus will be on the arbitrariness critique.

The arbitrariness critique turns on the finding that intuitions differ systematically across groups of people. The confident intuitions of philosophers are apparently not shared by subjects in different cultures, perhaps not even by naive subjects in the Western countries that produce most analytic philosophers. The fact of intuition diversity raises the suspicion that the intuitions reported by philosophers are either the product of special training or perhaps reflect the views of the members of a particular social class. In either case, there is little reason to think that these intuitions give us any insight into the nature of the concepts or the features of the world which they are supposed to illuminate. It is the arbitrariness critique that more or less launched x-phi, in the form of an influential article by Weinberg *et al.* (2001). They found that though Western and higher socio-economic status subjects shared the common philosophical intuition that agents in Gettier cases do not *know* what they believe, East Asian and subcontinental subjects, and lower socio-economic status subjects, thought that agents in the cases *do* know what they believe.

The arbitrariness critique demands a response. Why privilege the intuitions of WEIRD people, or (even more narrowly) of those WEIRD people who become professional philosophers, over those of non-Western people, or other social groups? The fact of diversity in intuitions all by itself shows that a once popular defense of the use of intuitions fails. According to this argument, philosophy can proceed from the armchair because anyone who is a competent speaker of their native language has mastery of the relevant concepts, and therefore can consult their linguistic intuitions in order to analyze them. The fact of diversity in intuitions apparently shows either that this is false, or that there are an enormous variety of idiolects. In either case, we urgently require an answer to the arbitrariness critique: why is it not arbitrary to investigate $knowledge_{WEIRD}$ (say), and not $knowledge_{East\ Asian?}$ In the absence of an answer to this challenge, it seems that we have no reason to take ourselves to be analyzing *knowledge* itself, rather than a merely local and parochial concept (Stich 1990).

The arbitrariness critique forces us to confront an issue that lurks behind these debates: why should we believe that our intuitions give us insight into the nature of concepts, or, more pointedly, of the referents of concepts, at all? Our intuitions may not be good guides to the nature of reality. Our intuitions about physical forces and their effects, for instance, seem to be predictably unreliable. Naive subjects assume, falsely, that an object that is travelling through a curved tube will continue to follow a curved trajectory when it leaves the tube (McCloskey *et al.* 1980). If we constructed physical theory by systematizing our intuitions, we would end up with a false theory. If this is true for physics, however, it seems it is likely to be true for metaphysics as well. The resulting metaphysics will tell us more about the idiosyncratic properties of our minds than about the nature of reality (Cummins 1998).

Responding to the arbitrariness critique

My response to the arbitrariness critique will come in two main parts. First, I shall argue that the uses of intuitions as data can survive the challenge from the diversity of intuitions. Second, though, I shall argue that fully responding to the challenge from diversity requires that we reconfigure philosophical practice in a way that is sensitive to the x-phi critique but which does not abandon the use of intuitions.

The uses of intuitions

The arbitrariness critique targets the use of intuitions as data for theories. An intuition is a datum, in this sense, when it is *independent* evidence for or against a philosophical claim. The critique is not taken by its advocates to count against many other uses of intuitions and intuition pumps: to illustrate arguments, for instance, or as heuristics. In this section, I shall argue that the boundary between these kinds of uses of intuitions is not sharp. Some of the intuitions that play an illustrative or heuristic role also pull sufficient weight in theory construction to count as genuine data. More significantly, I shall suggest that some intuitions satisfy the more demanding independence condition: they do not merely illustrate a claim but are genuinely independent evidence for that claim.

The weakest way in which intuitions may function as evidence is by drawing our attention to features of cases we might otherwise have overlooked. A striking thought experiment might not merely illustrate an argument, but also point to features of cases that ought to be important for theory. Intuitions often function like this; it ought not to be any part of the x-phi critique to impugn this fact (the fact that some subjects think that the agents in Gettier cases know what they believe is no reason to deny that these cases drew attention to the role of chance in belief formation). However, a full vindication of the use of intuitions requires something stronger: showing that they are not redundant evidence. If the only role of Gettier cases was drawing our attention to the role of chance in belief formation, the intuitions they generate would seem redundant — at least once their lesson was absorbed. Some defenses of the use of intuitions seem to concede their redundancy, and therefore do not count as full vindications. Consider Ichikawa's (2011) defense of Kripke's use of thought experiments in advancing his case for a causal theory of reference, against the apparent discovery by Machery *et al.* (2004) that the intuitions he expects his cases to generate are not universally shared. Ichikawa argues that Kripke's thought experiments illustrate his claims, rather than provide evidence for them. If it is true that Kripke's cases *merely* illustrate his argument, we may be justified in ignoring dissent from the intuitions they generate, but that is only because the intuitions do not play the role of independent evidence for his argument. Similarly, Ichikawa's argument that intuitions generated by esoteric cases might be corroborated by both theoretical considerations and more mundane cases risks leaving these intuitions redundant.

However, demonstrating that an intuition is independent evidence threatens to make the arbitrariness critique more powerful. If the only reason we have to believe a claim is that it is intuitive — if it is unsupported by theoretical considerations — the intuition should be regarded with suspicion. Hence the more independent it is, the more suspect it seems to be. Vindicating intuitions as evidence requires some degree of independence, but too much independence renders the intuition suspect. Intuitions that pull their weight in theory construction will sit somewhere on the continuum between full independence and full (and immediate) redundancy; those at either extreme fail to pull weight. There are various points along this continuum at which intuitions count as evidence. It is worth looking at examples to see how intuitions at different points along this continuum can pull their weight.

X-phi has recently extended the, by now, quite rich set of studies on intuitions concerning free will (see Sommers 2010 for review) to the study of Frankfurt-style cases (FSCs). FSCs were originally introduced into the debate concerning free will to show that the principle of alternative possibilities (which appears itself to be highly intuitive) is false (Frankfurt 1969). According to the principle, an agent is morally responsible for an action only if she could have done otherwise than perform that action. In an FSC, agents apparently cannot do otherwise and yet seem to be morally responsible. FSCs feature a *counterfactual intervener*, a person with the power to cause the agent to perform the act for which they are apparently morally responsible. Most philosophers who have considered the cases apparently have the intuition that agents in FSCs are morally responsible despite lacking alternative possibilities, and therefore conclude that the principle of alternative possibilities is false. The introduction of FSCs into the free will debate reconfigured it significantly. By apparently showing that alternative possibilities were not necessary for freedom, these cases undermined a major plank in incompatibilist arguments.

The use of FSCs in the free will debate looks like just the kind of intuition-mongering that is the target of the arbitrariness critique. It seems that insofar as we are reliant upon intuitions as evidence for the nature of free will, we had better check that these intuitions are widely shared, or give an argument why the intuitions of an unrepresentative subset of individuals should be given more weight than those of the folk. Miller and Feltz (2011) recently tested whether the folk agree with the majority of philosophers in holding that agents are morally responsible in FSCs. Though their evidence is a little hard to interpret – because an unexpectedly high proportion of subjects apparently thought that there was some sense in which the agents who featured in Miller and Feltz's cases had alternative possibilities – it appears that the folk tend to agree with most philosophers in holding that a lack of alternative possibilities does not rule out moral responsibility. To that extent, it seems that FSCs are not subject to the arbitrariness critique. Nevertheless, it is worthwhile to consider the question whether we would rationally have been required to abandon the intuitions FSCs pumped had it turned out that the folk had divergent intuitions.[2]

Suppose then the folk, or some subset of them, had the intuition that agents in FSCs were not morally responsible. By itself that would not show that the appeal to these cases was mistaken. Examining the features of FSCs has led philosophers, beginning with Frankfurt (1969) himself, to conclude (roughly) that a lack of alternative possibilities cannot make a difference when their absence has nothing to do with the explanation of how the agent actually acted. Nothing in (supposed) folk rejection of the intuitions the cases are supposed to pump would alter the fact they draw our attention to different ways in which access to alternatives could be lost, and thereby force us to ask whether (and how) the *mere* absence of alternative possibilities could matter for moral responsibility.

As a matter of fact, I think that this question can be answered affirmatively: a mere counterfactual intervener can make a difference to agents' capacities and therefore to their moral responsibility (Levy 2008). I was led to this conclusion via *another* thought experiment, concerning a counterfactual intervener whose mere presence, I suggested, entails that an agent possesses a capacity they would otherwise have lacked. Fighting thought experiment with thought experiment, I sought to show that the intuitions generated by FSCs are unreliable. However, I do not take my argument to show that the entire detour via thought experiments was wasted time. Rather, I think the debate had the salutary effect of focusing us on the features underlying the agential capacities exercised in morally responsible action. To that extent, the detour via thought experiments was necessary: it focused us in a direction in which we might not otherwise have looked, and prompted us to develop new accounts of such capacities and the role they play.

Obviously, though, showing that intuitions played this kind of role in debates over moral responsibility does not fully vindicate their use. A full vindication depends on showing that they *continue* to pull their weight in theory construction. It is worth noting that the demand for continuing non-redundancy sets the bar higher for intuitions than it is for much scientific data. As more comprehensive scientific theories are developed, theories that systematize and explain innumerable observations, individual observations are often rendered redundant. The theory might lose nothing in either its explanatory power or its ability to persuade us were any single observation to be discovered to be spurious, which is sufficient to show that the observation is redundant (though were many such observations rendered spurious, the theory might be falsified; the body of observations, each of which is redundant by itself, is not redundant). In any case, I shall suggest, some intuitions pass this more demanding test.

Even after the relevant arguments have been constructed, it may be necessary for appreciation of the force of an argument that a consideration of cases generates the appropriate intuitions.[3] Consider my claim that because agential abilities can supervene on properties external to agents, the mere presence of a counterfactual intervener can result in the agent losing or gaining an ability. The construction of cases illustrating this argument might well bring some people who would otherwise find the argument unconvincing to accept it, and I see no reason to think they would be irrational in being moved by the intuition combined with the argument, even when they were not moved by the argument alone. Intuitions may be necessary not merely for the construction of arguments but also for the ongoing appreciation of the rational force of the arguments.[4]

Intuitions may play the heuristic role of focusing us on features of cases that matter. Even after they have refocused our attention, moreover, the appeal to them may be necessary for our continued appreciation of why these features matter. To that extent, their use is vindicated. Vindication of intuitions should not be confused with vindication of "armchair" philosophy, however: our intuitions are not the only ones that matter, and there may be defeaters of our intuitions that cannot be grasped without looking to the sciences. We need to leave the armchair (sometimes), but that does not entail rejecting the appeal to intuitions.[5]

Reconfiguring philosophy

I take the remarks above to constitute a defense of the use of intuitions in philosophy. They are not, however, intended as a defense of intuition-mongering *rather than* x-phi. On the contrary, the responsible use of intuitions requires attention to the data from x-phi.

Evidence of diversity is valuable because it forces us to seek explanations not just for our own intuitions but also those of others. Just as the generation of intuitions in response to cases advances philosophical debates by focusing us on the features that cause the intuitions, so the discovery of a divergence in intuitions helps us to identify further features that require investigation. Sometimes we may be able to identify these features and dismiss the intuitions they cause. There is good evidence, for instance, that various "thinking dispositions," indexed especially by what psychologists call "need for cognition," predict the extent to which subjects consider alternative hypotheses in thinking tasks, while so-called "fluid intelligence," roughly the ability to think abstractly, predicts the ability to sustain offline simulations and therefore to think through hypothetical scenarios (Evans 2008). Fluid intelligence is a component of what is measured by extant IQ tests; thinking dispositions are not measured by IQ tests and are moderately dissociable from intelligence (Stanovich 2010). Some thinking dispositions may also predict the extent to which subjects replace the facts stipulated to hold in thought experiments with more realistic assumptions – an instance of the so-called focal bias (Stanovich 2010). The extent of this tendency cannot be assessed using standard paradigms in x-phi, though Greene *et al.* (2009) and Haidt *et al.* (1993) both produced evidence that subjects with this tendency were more likely to endorse their (narrow-sense) intuitions. Since some thinking dispositions and lower fluid intelligence predict, respectively, the failure to process the thought experiment as stipulated and the failure to sustain processing in depth, we seem to have a prima facie reason to test for these factors and control for them; these factors are reasons to discount the intuitions of those subject to them.

Suppose, though – as seems to me likely – that controlling for these factors would still leave us with an interesting diversity in intuitions, responding to which is incumbent on us. Sometimes we know what factors generate diverse intuitions. Order effects influence both moral (Zamzow and Nichol 2009) and epistemic (Swain, Alexander, and Weinberg 2008) intuitions. The effect seems to be explained by the desire for consistency: when a difficult case is presented subsequent to an easier case that seems relevantly similar, the probability rises that subjects will give the same judgment in the difficult case as in the easier. In a similar vein, intuitions are subject to framing effects. Petrinovich and O'Neill (1996) found that subjects' judgments differ depending on whether cases were presented as involving people dying or people being saved, even though only the language used to describe the cases differed across scenarios. What should we make of these findings?

We should respond in the way Dennett has long recommended: when confronted with a thought experiment, twiddle all the knobs (Dennett 2003, 2007).[6] The discovery that intuitions can be influenced by order effects or by framing provides guidance as to which knobs it may be important to turn. Effects like these are closely related to focal biases, and the appropriate response to them is to engage in offline simulation of hypotheticals (the kind of activity that is associated with need for cognition). As Kahneman (2003) has noted with regard to framing, inconsistency of responses arises in these kinds of cases because the subject passively accepts the formulation given; active reframing – knob twiddling – can cause the effect to dissipate.[7]

There is a significant remaining worry, however. Mightn't our intuitions be contaminated, such that twiddling the knobs does not shake them, even if they arose as a result of arbitrary features (the order in which we encountered cases, for instance)? There is evidence that responses that were initially effortful may become "compiled" such that they are produced effortlessly and without conscious reasoning (Stanovich 2010). Thus, the fact that my intuitions *now* are resistant to order effects (for example) does not entail that they were not initially the product of the order in which I considered cases.

This is a real possibility, even a likelihood. We can defang the worry by emphasizing the extent to which knowledge production, at its best, is a distributed activity. We need to refocus our attention, from the individual with her (possibly contaminated) intuitions and toward the community of enquirers. This is a cross-generational community, and twiddling the knobs may alert us as to how the next generation of philosophers should be trained. Though *our* intuitions may be "contaminated" by order effects now crystallized, *theirs* need not: we can introduce thought experiments more carefully and with greater attention to relevant variation, as well as greater humility when they respond differently to us (we should highlight the factors that may help to explain diversity in intuitions, in order to alert our students to the fact that failing to share our intuitions is not an indication of lack of philosophical talent, or what have you). So doing might encourage a diversity of intuitions in philosophy, which may prove productive: because philosophers with intuitions differing from those of the WEIRD may identify features of concepts that would otherwise be overlooked and thereby aid in developing better accounts of these concepts.

Further, the fact that knowledge production is distributed entails that there may be an important role even for contaminated intuitions. The transmission of philosophical errors may be bad for individuals, especially those who are unlucky enough to be inculcated into more than their share of unreliable intuitions. But because knowledge production is distributed, the misfortunes of individuals may be fortunate for the enterprise as a whole. As Kitcher (1993) has argued, a diversity of views is conducive to progress in science, even when some of those views are false. Having different background assumptions or holding different theories encourages individuals and teams to explore different hypotheses. Moreover, there is overwhelming evidence that people are far better at assessing arguments they are motivated to reject than they are arguments they are disposed to accept (Lord *et al.* 1979; Ditto and Lopez 1992). As a consequence, a diversity of views ensures that hypotheses are subjected to more thorough scrutiny than they would otherwise receive. Able defenders of false theories are motivated to subject the correct views to searching criticism, thus hastening their development and ensuring that their strengths are properly brought out. Able defenders of false theories may produce evidence that the correct theory does not seem capable of explaining; in attempting to explain, or explain away, the evidence, the correct theory is strengthened. Dennett (1995) for instance has stressed how the constant attacks on Darwinian and neo-Darwinian views from opponents motivated more by religion than by a concern for scientific truth has strengthened the Darwinian synthesis. Group deliberation is often better than individual deliberation because it ensures that more information is brought to the table; even false information can raise deliberation quality (Surowiecki 2004, 184); similarly, a diversity of scientific views, including false views, may be truth conducive. As Zamzow and Nichols (2009) have argued, we should expect many of these benefits of diversity in science to transfer over to intuition-mongering philosophy.

These benefits can be garnered, however, only if the debate is properly structured and open to all players: if there are, as alleged (by e.g. Buckwalter and Stich, forthcoming) gender differences and cultural differences in intuitions, and these differences cannot be explained away, it is important that there be far greater gender and cultural diversity in philosophy than is currently the case.[8,9] Further, debates must be structured so that all relevant players can have their voices heard (a condition which, it is fair to say, contemporary philosophy does not adequately satisfy).

Reaping the benefits of diversity may also require a restructuring of philosophy at an institutional level. Science reaps the benefits of diversity because it is appropriately structured.[10] We might model this structure by thinking of the scientific enterprise as consisting in competing teams of researchers competing for peer-reviewed rewards, where these rewards consist of publications and grants. The system of peer review is central to the reaping of the benefits of diversity: it ensures that claims are scrutinized by rival researchers as well as those sympathetic to the claims made. Moreover, having journals and grants open to rival perspectives ensures that competition is not arbitrarily limited. The available evidence suggests that this system is reasonably good at weeding out false claims relatively quickly, at least in medicine (Prasad *et al.* 2011). Of course philosophy has a system of peer review too. Jackson (2011) notes that this system serves as a kind of informal poll: in sending a paper to a journal we are conducting a kind of poll of the editor and the referees: do they share the intuitions we have generated? Can they be brought to share these intuitions by the arguments we have presented? If the paper is published, the subject pool is widened: now it is the whole profession, or at least those who specialize in the area, whose responses we test. There are reasons to think, however, that this system is not functioning anywhere nearly as well in philosophy as it does in science: the very fact that contradictory intuitions seem to be dramatically unreported prior to the emergence of x-phi is testimony to this fact. It may be that this is the product of a biased subject pool, due to a lack of diversity in philosophy; on the other hand, it may be due to problems in institutional design (perhaps use of too small a pool of referees, or excessive deference to authority, or the channeling of those with different intuitions into other areas of the profession). Of course, these explanations are not mutually exclusive. It is often argued that we need to improve refereeing standards and increase diversity in philosophy for reasons of justice; there are also epistemic reasons to bring about these changes.

Why think that our intuitions track the truth?

Rising to the challenge from diversity in intuitions requires that we show that intuitions are more likely than not to track the truth in the relevant domain. But intuitions may stem from a variety of sources, and some of these sources might be expected to produce dispositions that do not track truths. The intuitions that it proved useful to have in the environment of evolutionary adaptiveness are not necessarily the intuitions that it would be good to have when one does epistemology or ethics. What reason do we have to think that our actual intuitions are truth-tracking?

Given that knowledge production is a distributed enterprise, we need not demand too much of our intuitions for them to be truth-conducive. As the Condorcet jury theorem shows, individual deliberators need only to be more likely to be right than wrong for their contribution to truth-seeking to be positive. The right question is therefore whether we have good reason to believe that our intuitions are more likely to be right than wrong. There is no general answer to this question, I suggest. With regard to some areas of enquiry, untutored intuitions seem highly suspect. Intuitions about the mind are often highly unreliable: not only are the workings of the mind not transparent to us, but we may in fact be evolved to have systematically false intuitions about it (Carruthers 2011). The mechanisms of mind exist independently of our beliefs about them; these beliefs do not affect their structure and may often be inaccurate. For other targets of philosophical investigation, our beliefs partially *constitute* the domain. On the naturalistic metaethics I favor, for instance, moral facts are partially constituted by the responses, including the linguistic responses, of suitably placed observers. This entails that the extent to which our intuitions (with a stress on *our*) can go systematically wrong is constrained.

There are further reasons to think that our intuitions in the moral domain are likely to be truth-conducive, reasons which generalize to other areas of enquiry. If our moral terms refer to the set of properties that *causally regulate* our use of these terms (Boyd 1988) then – at least under certain conditions – we shall become progressively better at picking out the correct properties. If our moral theories are even roughly in the right ballpark, we should expect observation and experiment (with new social policies and arrangements, for instance) to enable us to produce better theories and better observations, promoting a virtuous circle. Boyd believes that the conditions for this kind of progressive honing in on truths prevail in morality, as they have prevailed in science since the seventeenth century. With regard to morality, unlike science, we probably *began* with our notions being guided by the relevant properties. It is a necessary condition of our successfully living in groups that we be able to recognize and regulate our behavior by the good, however imperfectly grasped. On the response-dependent theory I favor, too, our initial moral intuitions will track the relevant properties sufficiently well for the virtuous circle to get going.[11] If it is the case that we have been under constant pressure to adjust our semantics to track the properties that actually pertain in some domain, then – at very least to the extent to which our intuitions are linguistically mediated, either directly or as a result of our tending to automatize the responses reflected in our semantics – we ought to expect our intuitions to become progressively better at tracking these properties.

To what extent Boyd's account can be extended to other areas of human enquiry is an open, and very significantly empirical, question. There are reasons to believe that in some areas our intuitions are likely to be better than chance at tracking the truth;[12] in others, the picture is likely to be less rosy. We cannot tell from the armchair alone which is which; once again, doing armchair philosophy well requires that we do not do armchair philosophy only.

Conclusion

Intuition-mongering is not incompatible with x-phi. Rather, intuition-mongering can benefit from x-phi. The results generated by x-phi should help us to focus on features of cases that we might otherwise have overlooked; the features generating the intuitions in dissenters (ironically, in playing this role the empirical data serves one of the purposes which thought experiments are routinely called upon to play). They also challenge us to explain the diversity. In doing so, we might identify factors that distort intuitions – I have suggested a few in the course of this chapter – but there is no a priori guarantee that the distortions will be found only in the intuitions of the dissenters, and not in *our* intuitions. X-phi should not be a movement that is resisted by more traditional philosophers; rather, they have every reason to welcome it.

However, properly responding to the x-phi challenge requires that philosophy be reconfigured, at least somewhat. Philosophy must become more scientific: not only insofar as it is called upon to be more responsive to empirical evidence, but also in its structure. We need to take seriously the fact that knowledge production is a distributed enterprise, and that requires that we open up debate to all qualified participants and remove barriers to the acquisition of qualifications. It also requires that the institutions central to knowledge production and assessment, such as the journals, are properly structured so that knowledge may emerge from – not despite – the diversity of views brought to the table. Rising to these challenges is both an epistemic and a moral obligation.[13]

Notes

1 See Hintikka 1999 for a sketch of some of the history of the practice.

2 It is not entirely clear how relevant *actual* conflict between the intuitions of the folk and those of philosophers is supposed by experimental philosophers to be to the arbitrariness critique: some remarks by some of them suggest that *possible* disagreement should be sufficient to shake our confidence in the intuition method. Weinberg et al. (2001), for instance, present us with a thought experiment in which epistemic intuitions differ across groups of people, and claim that the mere conceivability of such a scenario is "bad news" for advocates of intuition-driven philosophy. In any case, the question is worth considering even if we think that only actual disagreement matters, because the data can only be informative if different data would have supported a different conclusion.

3 It is for this reason that I do not follow Kahane (2013) in thinking that scientific data on intuitions will make armchair intuition-mongering redundant. Kahane thinks that if intuitions are reliable as a source of evidence, we should expect controlled experiments on intuitions to be a better source of data than armchair theorizing. But because fully appreciating the force of arguments sometimes requires generation of the appropriate intuitions, I do not expect science to render armchair intuition-mongering redundant.

4 Max Deutsch (2010) argues that the question whether a counterexample is successful is independent of the question whether it generates an appropriate intuition. Clearly the two are dissociable: our theoretical commitments may require us to accept that a counterexample is successful despite its failure to generate an appropriate intuition in us; moreover, on most views intuitions are at best defeasible evidence for claims, so the fact that a counterexample succeeds in generating an appropriate intuition is not sufficient for the counterexample to be successful, all things considered. But it does not follow that intuitions are dispensable. Deutsch argues, rightly in my view, that counterexamples succeed *only when* they can be backed up with what he calls "grounds," arguments that the features they identify play an appropriate defeating role. My claim is that the intuitiveness of a counterexample is often epistemically necessary for the identification of such grounds *and* that sometimes intuitiveness is necessary for an appreciation of these grounds. It may be that a counterexample generates the appropriate intuition only *after* we have considered relevant grounds; nevertheless, the intuition may be necessary for appreciation of these grounds.

5 The vindication of intuitions will not always vindicate *our* intuitions over *theirs*, whoever *they* may be. Consider the results reported by Vaesen and Peterson (under review). They found that philosophically trained subjects whose native language is English were more likely than subjects whose native language was Dutch, German or Swedish to attribute knowledge to the people featuring in vignettes. One possible explanation is that the native English speakers were misled by the surface grammar of English. The vignettes asked subjects whether a person said to know that *p* has knowledge that *p*. It is linguistically infelicitous in English to say that "X knows that *p* but does not have knowledge that *p*"; however, in the other languages no such infelicity arises. Since the states or propositions that these languages identify with the word we would translate as "knowledge" appears to be the "gold standard" (Jackson 2011) state that, I suggest, we ought to identify with knowledge, this is a case in which our intuitions may be wrong.

6 Dennett credits the advice to Douglas Hofstadter.

7 If I understand Hintikka (1999), the twiddle all the knobs strategy helps to defuse his criticism of intuitions. Hintikka's target is the use of specific case intuitions. He holds that attempting to generalize from such cases is not truth-conducive, because particular cases do not give us guidance to "the factors affecting our judgment about the situation envisaged in it" (137). The evidence from x-phi, together with the strategy recommended here, will help to uncover these factors.

8 How might we explain away gender and cultural diversity in intuitions? Nagel (2012) has one suggestion: the experiments alleged to demonstrate cultural diversity might be flawed because they drew on a subset of East Asian subjects who are less motivated to engage with philosophical thought experiments. She argues that the response pattern in Weinberg et al. (2001) is consistent with subjects' responding randomly, which reflects their lack of engagement (a function of the fact that East Asians in higher education in the United States are relatively unlikely to be enrolled in

humanities subjects). Here are two more debunking explanations of diversity in intuitions. The subjects in the experiment reported by Zamzow and Nichols (2009) differed in their responses, depending on whether someone who might be sacrificed in a thought experiment was of the same or a different gender to themselves: we can explain away this difference as a result of identification, which seems to be motivated by a myside bias. The differences reported in Haidt *et al.* (1993) correlated with socio-economic class and education: both are moderately reliable proxies for possession of the fluid intelligence and "mindware" (i.e. knowledge of relevant scientific facts, probability theory and so on) needed to sustain offline simulation of scenarios and to experience conflict between an intuition (narrow sense) and a normative response, respectively (Stanovich 2010).

9 Some evidence of the lack of diversity in philosophy, compared to other disciplines: philosophy PhDs are awarded to proportionately fewer women than PhDs in almost any other area, including mathematics. See Kieran Healy's analysis of the survey of earned PhDs in the United States in 2009, "Philosophy in Disciplinary Perspective: Percentage of US PhDs Awarded to Women in 2009," <http://kieranhealy.org/files/misc/phil-all-disciplines.pdf>.

10 It seems likely, for the kind of reasons highlighted by Kuhn, that the structure of science must also constrain diversity so that debate is focused and a sufficient number of background assumptions are shared (thanks to Steve Clarke for pointing this out to me).

11 It should be noted that it is controversial whether a response-dependent theory can be squared with moral realism of the sort promoted by Boyd. I believe it can, but I set the issue aside here. It is also worth noting that Boyd's view is widely rejected today, in the wake of a series of papers by Horgan and Timmons (e.g. 1992a, 1992b). I reply to their argument in Levy 2011.

12 See Nagel 2012 for an independent account of why epistemic intuitions are likely to be reliable.

13 This chapter has benefited greatly from comments from Matthew Haug. Work on it was supported by a grant from the Australian Research Council.

References

Bealer, G. (1998) "Intuition and the Autonomy of Philosophy," in M.R. DePaul and W. Ramsey (eds), *Rethinking Intuition: The Psychology of Intuition and Its Role in Philosophical Inquiry*, Lanham, MD: Rowman & Littlefield, 201–39.

Boyd, R. (1988) "How to Be a Moral Realist," in G. Sayre-McCord (ed.), *Essays on Moral Realism*, Ithaca, NY: Cornell University Press, 181–228.

Buckwalter, W. and S. Stich (forthcoming) "Gender and Philosophical Intuition," in J. Knobe and S. Nichols (eds), *Experimental Philosophy*, vol. 2, Oxford: Oxford University Press.

Carruthers, P. (2011) *The Opacity of Mind*, Oxford: Oxford University Press.

Cummins, R. (1998) "Reflections on Reflective Equilibrium," in M.R. DePaul and W. Ramsey (eds), *Rethinking Intuition: The Psychology of Intuition and Its Role in Philosophical Inquiry*, Lanham, MD: Rowman & Littlefield, 113–27.

Dennett, D. (1984) *Elbow Room: The Varieties of Free Will Worth Wanting*, Cambridge, MA: MIT Press.

——(1995) *Darwin's Dangerous Idea: Evolution and the Meanings of Life*, New York: Simon & Schuster.

——(2003) *Freedom Evolves*, London: Allen Lane.

——(2007) "What RoboMary Knows," in T. Alter and S. Walter (eds), *Phenomenal Concepts and Phenomenal Knowledge: New Essays on Consciousness and Physicalism*, Oxford: Oxford University Press, 15–31.

Deutsch, M. (2010) "Intuitions, Counter-examples, and Experimental Philosophy," *Review of Philosophy and Psychology* 1: 447–60.

Ditto, P.H. and D.F. Lopez (1992) "Motivated Skepticism: Use of Differential Decision Criteria for Preferred and Nonpreferred Conclusions," *Journal of Personality and Social Psychology* 63: 568–84.

Evans, J.St.B.T. (2008) "Dual-Processing Accounts of Reasoning, Judgment, and Social Cognition," *Annual Review of Psychology* 59: 255–78.

Frankfurt, H. (1969) "Alternate Possibilities and Moral Responsibility," *Journal of Philosophy* 66: 823–39.

Greene, J.D., F.A Cushman, L.E. Stewart, K. Lowenberg, L.E. Nystrom and J.D. Cohen (2009) "Pushing Moral Buttons: The Interaction between Personal Force and Intention in Moral Judgment," *Cognition* 111: 364–71.

Haidt, J., S.H. Koller and M.G. Dias (1993) "Affect, Culture, and Morality, or Is It Wrong to Eat Your Dog?," *Journal of Personality and Social Psychology* 65: 613–28.

Henrich, J., S.J. Heine and A. Norenzayan (2010) "The Weirdest People in the World?," *Behavioral and Brain Sciences* 33: 61–135.

Hintikka, J. (1999) "The Emperor's New Intuitions," *Journal of Philosophy* 96: 127–47.

Horgan, T. and M. Timmons (1992a) "Troubles on Moral Twin Earth: Moral Queerness Revived," *Synthese* 92: 221–60.

——(1992b) "Troubles for New Wave Moral Semantics: The Open Question Argument Revived," *Philosophical Papers* 21: 153–75.

Horowitz, T. (1998) "Philosophical Intuitions and Psychological Theory," *Ethics* 108: 367–85.

Ichikawa, J. (2011) "Experimentalist Pressure against Traditional Methodology," *Philosophical Psychology* 25: 743–65.

——(forthcoming) "Who Needs Intuitions? Two Experimentalist Critiques," in T. Booth and D. Rowbottom (eds), *Intuitions*, Oxford: Oxford University Press.

Jackson, F. (2011) "On Gettier Holdouts," *Mind & Language* 26: 468–81.

Kahane, G. (2013) "The Armchair and the Trolley: An Argument for Experimental Ethics," *Philosophical Studies* 162(2): 421–45.

Kahneman, D. (2003) "A Perspective on Judgment and Choice: Mapping Bounded Rationality," *American Psychologist* 58: 697–720.

Kitcher, P. (1993) *The Advancement of Science*, New York: Oxford University Press.

Levy, N. (2008) "Counterfactual Intervention and Agents' Capacities," *Journal of Philosophy* 105: 223–39.

——(2011) "Neuroethics: A New Way of Doing Ethics," *American Journal of Bioethics* (*AJOB-Neuroscience*) 2: 3–9.

——(2011) "Moore on Twin Earth," *Erkenntnis* 75: 137–46.

Lord, C.G., L. Ross and M.R. Lepper (1979) "Biased Assimilation and Attitude Polarization: The Effects of Prior Theories on Subsequently Considered Evidence," *Journal of Personality and Social Psychology* 37: 2098–109.

Machery, E., R. Mallon, S. Nichols and S.P. Stich (2004) "Semantics, Cross-cultural Style," *Cognition* 92: 1–12.

McCloskey, M., A. Caramazza and B. Green (1980) "Curvilinear Motion in Absence of External Forces: Naive Beliefs about the Motion of Objects," *Science* 210 (4474): 1114–39.

Miller, J. and A. Feltz (2011) "Frankfurt and the Folk: An Empirical Investigation," *Consciousness and Cognition* 20: 401–14.

Nagel, J. (2012) "Intuitions and Experiments," *Philosophy and Phenomenological Research* 85(3): 495–527.

Petrinovich, L. and P. O'Neill (1996) "Influence of Wording and Framing Effects on Moral Intuitions," *Ethology and Sociobiology* 17: 145–71.

Prasad, V., V. Gall and A. Cifu (2011) "The Frequency of Medical Reversal," *Archives of Internal Medicine* 171: 1675–76.

Prinz, J. (2008) "Empirical Philosophy and Experimental Philosophy," in J. Knobe and S. Nichols (eds), *Experimental Philosophy*, Oxford: Oxford University Press, 189–208.

Sommers, T. (2010) "Experimental Philosophy and Free Will," *Philosophy Compass* 5: 199–212.

Stanovich, K. (2010) *Rationality and the Reflective Mind*, Oxford: Oxford University Press.

Stich, S. (1990) *The Fragmentation of Reason*, Cambridge, MA: MIT Press.

Surowiecki, J. (2004) *The Wisdom of Crowds*, New York: Doubleday.

Swain, S., J. Alexander and J. Weinberg (2008) "The Instability of Philosophical Intuitions: Running Hot and Cold on Truetemp," *Philosophy and Phenomenological Research* 76: 138–55.

Vaesen, K. and Peterson, M. (under review) *The Reliability of Armchair Intuitions*.

Weinberg, J., S. Nichols and S. Stich (2001) "Normativity and Epistemic Intuitions," *Philosophical Topics* 29: 429–60.

Zamzow, J.L. and S. Nichols (2009) "Variations in Ethical Intuitions," *Philosophical Issues* 19: 368–88.

21 Beyond the experience machine: how to build a theory of well-being[1]

VALERIE TIBERIUS

Well-being, as I intend it, is prudential value in the most general sense. A person who has well-being is living a life that is going well for her; she has achieved her own good. People with different ethical theories will find well-being important for different reasons – consequentialists take it to be the good that ought to be promoted, deontologists take it to be the target of duties of beneficence, and some virtue ethicists take it to be the organizing principle of ethics – but no one denies that it is important in some way or other. It would be a good thing, then, to know what well-being is. Unfortunately, though, there has been disagreement about the nature of well-being since philosophers have roamed the earth, and those disagreements have not changed much.

Sometimes intractable disagreements about normative concepts indicate that the concept cannot be adequately captured by a theory that aims to bring all the relevant phenomena under a single unifying principle. But sometimes intractable disagreements persist because we don't really know what we're looking for, so we have no good way to assess competing alternatives. In this paper I will suppose this is the right hypothesis about "well-being": the problem is that we lack a sound methodology for defining and assessing our theories. If this hypothesis is correct, we should be able to make progress if we have better methodological guidance and I will try to provide some in this chapter.

It isn't quite fair to say that contemporary philosophers working on well-being do not have a methodology. We do tend to proceed by attempting to find reflective equilibrium among our intuitions about cases and various possible unifying principles (such as hedonism or eudaemonism). But I don't think that the way reflective equilibrium is implemented in the contemporary literature on well-being is helping us. The plan for the chapter, then, is first to explain what's wrong with the current state of affairs in which philosophers tend to rely heavily on intuitions about cases. Second, I'll define what I think are the criteria of success for theories of well-being. My aim is not to replace reflective equilibrium, but to argue that principled criteria should play a larger role in it. The result is a version of wide reflective equilibrium that shapes the equilibrium in response to theoretical needs.[2] Finally, to show how these criteria work in practice, I will show how they can be used to argue for a particular theory of well-being, the value fulfillment theory (VFT).

Intuitions and descriptive adequacy

Theories of well-being are often classified into subjective and objective theories. Subjective theories, according to one of the most frequently cited books on philosophical theories of well-being, make it depend on "some (actual or hypothetical) attitude on the part of the welfare subject" (Sumner 1996, 38). Objective theories deny this dependence and hold that a favorable subjective attitude toward something is not a necessary condition of that thing's being good for the subject. Preference satisfaction theories (e.g. Brandt 1979; Harsanyi 1982) are paradigm examples of subjective theories: they make well-being dependent on a person's preferences. Objective list theories (e.g. Arneson 1999; Finnis 1980) are paradigm examples of objective theories: according to such theories, it is the objective value of the items on the list that makes them valuable for a person, not the person's approval or satisfaction.

How can we decide between these two families of well-being theories? In an influential discussion at the beginning of his book, Sumner (1996) tells us that theories of welfare should be normatively and descriptively adequate. By the former he means that a good theory of well-being will make sense of the role of well-being in moral theory. By the latter he means that a good theory of well-being will accommodate as many as possible of our ordinary judgments about well-being.

The idea that a theory of well-being should accommodate our ordinary judgments or intuitions about well-being is implicit in much of the literature, and was so even before Sumner articulated "descriptive adequacy" as a formal criterion of success. An immediate problem with this idea is that, intuitively, both subjective and objective theories have something going for them. It is good for us to get what we want and like what we get, but it also seems good for us to get good things. Perhaps because of this, much of the literature on well-being consists in intuition-pumping on one side or the other, and the debate, as I'll now illustrate, seems to have stalled.

If one has heard anything about the well-being literature in philosophy, one has probably heard of Robert Nozick's (1974) now infamous "experience machine" objection to hedonism. In this thought experiment, Nozick asks us to consider whether we would hook ourselves up to a machine that would, under the control of "super-duper neurophysiologists," guarantee us a more pleasant life than we would have without the machine. Nozick argues that many of us would refuse to hook up to the machine because we care about other things than pleasure and this has been taken to be a devastating objection to hedonism. Of course, hedonists have many replies (Crisp 2006; Feldman 2004). The important point for our purposes is that this high-tech intuition pump has had a profound influence on the debate in philosophy. As Roger Crisp (2008) laments "Certainly the current trend of quickly dismissing hedonism on the basis of a quick run-through of the experience machine objection is not methodologically sound". Crisp's point is that hedonism tends to be dismissed out of hand on the basis of this one intuition pump without any acknowledgement that hedonists like Crisp have actually heard of the example and have had something to say about it. Little attempt is made by critics to consider the resources and advantages of hedonism as a comprehensive theory. This may not be methodologically sound, but it has indeed been the trend.

Many who favor theories that define well-being in terms of mental states have moved on from hedonism to preference satisfaction or life satisfaction views according to which a necessary condition for something's being good for me is that I desire it or like it when I get it. Such subjective theories have a certain immediate intuitive appeal. It seems obvious that wanting or liking what you get is crucially important to whether it's good *for you*, as opposed to morally or aesthetically good. Opera may be objectively valuable, but it doesn't seem to make me better off if I find it excruciatingly boring. The prima facie intuitive case for subjectivism has provoked intuition pumps from those who favor objective theories.

One of the most popular of these intuition pumps has to do with children. As Richard Kraut (1979, 187) argues, when we think about what we want for our children, it seems obvious that we do not want them simply to get what they want or to be satisfied with whatever they get. Rather, there are things such as friendship and the development of skills that are good for people and we hope that our kids will achieve these things in life. This kind of thought experiment provides a prime example of how the current state of play in the well-being literature is stalled. Kraut takes the thought experiment to favor an objective, Aristotelian theory. But Fred Feldman (2004, 135–36, 158) introduces a version of the same thought experiment (which he calls "the crib test") as part of an overall argument for hedonism. Others who defend versions of subjective theories of well-being have tried to accommodate these and other objectivist intuitions without changing their view (Sumner 1996; Tiberius and Plakias 2010).

Thought experiments like the experience machine are not pointless. They do bring us to sharpen our views about what matters and what is at stake in choosing between different theories. Furthermore, it is difficult to deny that capturing intuitions is important.[3] After all, a theory of well-being (of all things) that did not speak to any of our pretheoretic notions of what it is to live well would seem to have a serious strike against it. Granting this, the problem now is that there are different types of theory that have some claim to descriptive adequacy. How to decide between them?

Criteria of success

I think Sumner is right that normative and descriptive adequacy are the two basic criteria for evaluating the relative merits of theories of well-being. If you think about it, what else would we ask for from a theory of something of value that must play a role in real-world decision-making? But, I have come to think that his construal of these criteria leaves out some important desirable features. Here are the criteria I think we ought to apply when we are developing and assessing theories of well-being:

Normative adequacy

A good theory:

- explains the role of well-being in moral theory (this is what Sumner means by normative adequacy), and
- explains how claims about well-being are reason-giving. (I'll call this the criterion of reasons explanation).

Empirical adequacy

A good theory:

- is descriptively adequate (it captures enough of our ordinary judgments about well-being),
- is empirically tractable (explains how well-being can be measured and studied empirically), and
- helps us to interpret empirical research on well-being for our practical purposes.

In this chapter, my main focus will be on the criterion of reasons explanation, because I think normative adequacy in this sense is the feature of a good theory to which the least attention has been paid and, further, because I think it is the criterion the application of which can make the most difference. Nevertheless, I should say something in defense of the criteria I have added to "empirical adequacy."

It is hard not to notice that well-being is a big topic in the social sciences these days. Psychologists and economists are studying well-being, happiness, and pleasure, proposing national indicators for the happiness of the population, and coming up with theories of their own.[4] One might think that social science is social science, philosophy is philosophy, and that there's no reason our philosophical theories of well-being should have anything to do with their studies and measures. But I think this view is misguided.[5] The philosophical interest in well-being is, ultimately, practical. As I mentioned at the outset, well-being is of interest to ethicists because it occupies a profoundly important role in theories of what we ought to do. If social scientists are proposing policy based on their findings about well-being, then philosophers should be interested and concerned. For this reason, it would be a good thing if our theories engaged with the social science literature in some way or other. Moreover, anyone who thinks that well-being ought to be promoted has an interest in ensuring that well-being according to their philosophical theory is something that can be measured and increased, because if it can't be (and on the plausible assumption that ought implies can), then we can't be required to increase the amount of it for anyone.[6]

Finally, philosophical theories of well-being often make empirical assumptions. Frequently this is because philosophical theories make a distinction between what is intrinsically good for a person and what is good for a person because it is instrumental to one of these intrinsic goods. These claims about instrumental goods are, typically, causal: they are claims about what tends to bring about pleasure or satisfaction. John Stuart Mill's claim that selfishness is a chief cause of unhappiness, for example, is an empirical claim about our psychology. Mill thought that focus on oneself caused unhappiness because selfish interests and the pleasures we get in satisfying them dwindle as we get older and approach our own death, whereas those who are engaged with the "collective interests of mankind, retain as lively an interest in life on the eve of death as in the vigor of youth and health" (1861/1979, 13). There is now research that supports Mill's claim: altruism does indeed produce overall life satisfaction for people (Piliavin 2002). Philosophical theories that track the science of well-being in some way or other have the advantage that they can use this science to evaluate their empirical assumptions.

I will say more about empirical adequacy in the next section, when I apply these criteria to a particular theory. For now I want to turn to the criterion of reasons explanation.

Well-being is supposed to be something we have good reason to pursue or promote; it is worth choosing for ourselves and others. A good theory of well-being, therefore, must explain why we should care about it and why we do have normative reasons to promote our own well-being. I take it that what needs to be explained by an account of normative reasons is how they can motivate and justify our actions at the same time.[7] In other words, normative reasons do motivate us under the right conditions (insofar as we are rational, according to Smith 1995), but they also provide standards for the evaluation of our actions which we can meet or fail to meet. That prudential reasons (or, we could say, "well-being reasons") are normative in this sense is often ignored. This may be because of a tendency to make two assumptions: first, that well-being is a psychological state that everyone desires and, second, that our desires provide normative reasons. On this view, well-being reasons are perfectly good instrumental reasons: we want well-being and so we ought to do what our theory of well-being says will bring it about. But this way of seeing things assumes a certain way of thinking about prudential reasons: they are all instrumental to satisfying our desires. Since one of the very things that is at issue between different theories of well-being is whether or not satisfying our desires is what is good for us, more needs to be said here. How its recommendations are normative is something that needs to be explained by a theory of well-being.

In the literature on normative reasons, a distinction is made between reasons existence externalism and internalism (from now on just "externalism" and "internalism").[8] Internalism, in its most basic form, is the view that normative reasons necessarily have *some* relationship to motivation. Externalism denies this relationship.

The first point I want to make is that objective theories of well-being imply externalism about prudential reasons.[9] Here we can distinguish objective list theories from eudaemonist theories. According to an objective list theory, roughly, well-being is made up of certain objective goods such as friendship, knowledge, and achievement; a person is doing well insofar as she attains these things (Arneson 1989; Finnis 1980). According to standard eudaemonist theories,[10] roughly, well-being consists in fulfilling your nature as a human being; a person is doing well insofar as she is successful at being the kind of thing she is (Foot 2001; Kraut 2007), or insofar as she has perfected the kind of thing she is (Hurka 1993). There are important differences between these theories, of course, and much more would need to be said if we were evaluating them individually. But the point here is just that, for all of them, the explanation for the *value* of well-being and hence the explanation for the prudential reasons entailed by this value refer to something beyond the subject. Objective list theories posit objective values that provide the ground for claims about prudential reasons; eudaemonist theories ground these claims, ultimately, in the value of human nature. To put the point in the terms made famous by Korsgaard (1996), the "source of normativity" for well-being, according to objective theories, is not our attitudes.

The second point I want to make is that externalism about *prudential* reasons in particular is not plausible and that insofar as objective theories of well-being do entail externalism, this is a reason to reject them. On the face of it, externalism about practical reasons has a strike against it because reasons are thought to be at least capable of figuring into the explanation of actions. If a person can have a reason to do something without any possible motive, it is difficult to see how this connection to action can be maintained. Externalism is still thought to be a compelling position, however, because of the costs of internalism when it comes to *moral* reasons. In short, internalism, when paired with other plausible assumptions about the contingency of desire, forces us to reject the claim that moral reasons are absolute (that is, that we have the moral reasons we have independently of the motivations we happen to have).[11] Externalism about *prudential* reasons lacks this rationale: it does not fly in the face of our concept of a prudential reason to think that such reasons are not absolute. Further, externalism about prudential reasons does fly in the face of a different aspect of the concept of well-being, namely, that there is an intimate relationship between well-being and the subject whose well-being it is.

This argument is not conclusive, of course. The objectivist about well-being could claim that her account of prudential reasons is internalist, despite initial appearances, or she could provide an argument for thinking that externalism about prudential reasons is the best view after all. My point here is about methodology: once we notice that it is incumbent on theories of well-being to provide explanations for the normative status of prudential reasons, we can evaluate these theories on the quality of these explanations.

Though the argument against objective theories isn't conclusive, for the sake of exploring the methodological concerns, I'm going to take it as a prima facie reason to favor subjective theories of one kind or another. Let's turn to these and ask, once again, whether their accounts of prudential reasons weigh in favor of one view or another.

Among subjective theories we can distinguish unidealized and idealized versions. Unidealized subjective theories take our well-being to consist in the satisfaction of our actual desires or the attainment of our actual goals (Heathwood 2007; Keller 2004). These theories are most naturally paired with an internalist theory of prudential reasons according to which our desires or goals provide normative reasons by themselves. For example, an actual desire satisfaction theory can easily explain the normativity of well-being reasons by appeal to the claim that the desires that constitute well-being themselves provide normative reasons for action.

We could also take attitudinal hedonism (which defines pleasure as a mental state toward which one has a pro-attitude; Feldman 2004) to imply this view about normative reasons, depending on the nature of the pro-attitude.[12]

While such a view about normative reasons has a ready explanation for how reasons motivate us, it is not so clear why such reasons justify our actions. One reason to think that our actual desires do not necessarily provide normative reasons is that these desires may be misinformed or irrational. The point is compelling even when it comes to prudential reasons. Consider that when we deliberate about how to live our lives, one of the things we consider is which of our desires give us reasons to do things and which do not. For example, someone deliberating about whether to have children might very well wonder whether her desire to have someone to visit her in the home when she's old is really a desire that has any authority in this context even if it is a desire that has some motivational force. Again, this argument is not conclusive, but insofar as actual desire theories of well-being presuppose actual desire theories of normative prudential reasons, we have some reason to look elsewhere.

Idealized subjective theories might do better. According to these theories well-being is understood in terms of the subjective attitudes you would have under certain ideal conditions. For example, according to informed desire theories, what is good for you is getting what you would want if you were fully informed about your options or (as the view has come to be developed) what your fully informed self would want your actual self to want (Railton 1986; see also Brandt 1979; Griffin 1986). According to authentic happiness theory, what is good for you is to be authentically satisfied with the overall conditions of your life, where "authentic" means informed and autonomous (Sumner 1996).

Ultimately, idealized subjective theories still locate the source of normativity in our subjective attitudes, but the relevant subjective attitudes – the ones that succeed in generating normative reasons – are corrected in accordance with an appropriate standard. For example, full information theories of well-being might say that it is the inherent normativity of desire that makes well-being as informed desire satisfaction normative and that the reason for insisting that desires must be informed has to do with making sure the desire is really for the option as it is and not "for the option as it is falsely imagined to be" (Sobel 2009, 345). The standard here is a kind of accuracy: only desires that are truly for their objects count as normative. For example, in Railton's (1986) well-known case, dehydrated Lonnie wants to drink milk, which is actually bad for him because he is dehydrated. If Lonnie *knew* he were dehydrated he would want to drink clear fluids, which would help ameliorate his condition. The standard for evaluating desires is the standard of information.

Other theories propose other standards. According to Sumner's (1996) idealized life satisfaction theory of well-being the standard is not just informedness, but authenticity, which includes informedness and autonomy. On his view, a person who is satisfied with her meager life because she is so woefully oppressed that she believes she deserves no better, isn't necessarily achieving well-being. What matters is her life satisfaction insofar as this satisfaction is informed and autonomous.

Now, unidealized subjective theories do provide a standard for evaluating actions, namely the standard of the satisfaction of our actual preferences or the achievement of our actual life satisfaction. But prudential reasons also seem to govern our desires or satisfactions themselves. When we deliberate about what would be good for us we not only ask what we should do but also what our goals should be, what we should want. If this is right, by proposing a further standard that our motivations must meet in order to provide normative reasons, idealized subjective theories of well-being have an advantage.

I now want to turn to consider a particular subjective theory of well-being in some detail as a case study to see how it fares with respect to the criteria of success outlined at the beginning of this section. Hopefully, this discussion will also help to clarify the explanation of normative reasons I've just outlined.

The value fulfillment theory of well-being

According to VFT, we live well to the degree to which we fulfill or realize our appropriate values.[13] What are values? Values (in the sense relevant to well-being) are the ends we take to be normative for us: we endorse or avow them as things that it makes sense to care about, pursue, or promote.[14] I mean to be very inclusive about what counts; values can include activities, relationships, goals, aims, ideals, principles, and so on. There are several distinctive features of the values that are relevant to well-being. The first thing to notice is that to value something is to care about it in a particular way, and to care about something is, at least in part, to have some positive affective orientation toward it.[15] Other things equal, we are *motivated* to pursue or promote the values to which we are committed and we are disposed to react emotionally when these values are helped or threatened. For example, if I value being a teacher I will be motivated to help my students learn, to feel proud when I receive good teaching evaluations and disappointed when my students sleep during class. Typically, valuing involves patterns of disposition to act and to feel. Values are the central objects of these coordinated patterns.[16]

But there is more to a value commitment than affective orientation. If value commitments were simple motivational or affective states, they could not have the function that they seem to have in our lives. If our value commitments are going to serve as the basis for deliberation and planning and for assessments of how well our lives are going, they must include more than good feelings. Not every pro-attitude plays an important role in planning and in the assessment of our lives. Some of our motives are ones we wish we did not have, and would be better off without, and some are just too trivial to be considered in planning. Value commitments have two other features that allow them to play the role that they do in our lives: stability and justification.

If our values were not relatively stable they would not help us in constructing plans to achieve the many rewards that can only come from sustained commitment. But too much stability, or stability for the wrong reasons, isn't desirable either. Values that do not adapt to changing circumstances can become difficult to fulfill for a variety of reasons. For example, if our emotional connection wanes, we won't be motivated to fulfill these values anymore. (Though a certain affective orientation is part of what it is to value something, valuing is a complex pattern of attitudes, and so some emotional dispositions could be dampened or depressed without its being sensible to say that the person no longer has the value at all anymore.) Or if our life changes in such a way that the stubborn old values conflict with new ones, fulfillment will become challenging.

Notice here that our most basic values are unlikely to change much; normal people are likely always to value health, close relationships, and meaningful work. But how these values are instantiated and prioritized in particular can and should change in response to changes in our environment or in our interests and concerns. To elaborate, consider that not only are values made up of patterns of affect, they also exist in patterns. That is, we have values of varying degrees of generality and of various descriptions, and values are related to each other in various ways. I value my career, being a philosopher, being a teacher, helping my students, and helping my students understand Hume. Some of these values are variations on a theme, others are more specific and are valued as a part of, or as a means to, something else. This means that values can be appropriate or inappropriate in virtue of the other values with which they coexist. We need some stability even in our very specific values (like a particular career goal) insofar as such values require some long-term commitment. But specific instantiations of general values need to change with us (fulfilling the same particular career goal over and over would likely be boring).

We need relatively stable values, then, but we do not want them to be stubborn or static (at least not at a certain level of specification). To play the role they need to play, values must be relatively stable patterns of pro-attitudes that we take to be appropriate in the circumstances and that we are willing to change when reasons to change present themselves. I think of this in terms of a second-order endorsement of the pattern of pro-attitudes that constitute what it is to value something. This attitude of endorsement could be one of taking there to be reasons for valuing what one values, but it could also be understood minimally as the attitude that there are no decisive reasons deriving from our other commitments against pursuing it.[17]

I said that according to VFT, what's good for a person is the fulfillment of her *appropriate* values. We can now see what counts as appropriateness. The nature of values and their role in deliberation, planning and assessment gives us a standard by which to assess them. We can assess patterns of values for the degree to which they can be endorsed and pursued together, over the course of a lifetime, in the light of environmental and personal changes. To achieve well-being is to fulfill or realize the values that meet this standard. For many of us, the patterns of values that we actually have require some modest revision in order to meet this standard. But the fact that the values that are relevant to well-being are the person's own values does impose some limit on sensible revisions. A set of values that has a high degree of stability and coherence but which I have *no* emotional connection to and no inclination to endorse cannot be *my* set of values and, therefore, cannot define my well-being.

VFT and the criteria of success

We are now in a position to consider how VFT fares with respect to the criteria for successful theories of well-being with which I began. One thing that VFT has in its favor is a very plausible account of the intimate relationship between well-being and its subject, which Sumner takes to be the main fact about well-being judgments that a descriptively adequate theory will capture. Values are especially related to subjects, unlike mere desires: people identify themselves in terms of their values and values are, by definition, of particular importance to people from their own point of view. Values have special relevance to well-being, then, insofar as well-being is a value that has a special relationship to the subject.[18] Values also have an advantage over hedonism and preference satisfaction theories in accommodating intuitions about the special significance of components of well-being. Trivial pleasures and the satisfaction of fleeting preferences do not seem, intuitively, to count toward a person's well-being. VFT explains why this is so: values are significant goals that we take to structure our planning and deliberation. Small pleasures and satisfactions may contribute to the fulfillment of the value of happiness for a person, but when the overall fulfillment of values is the measure, these trivial experiences do not count as components of well-being in and of themselves.

What about its explanation of the normativity of prudential reasons? Here too I think VFT has an advantage, as I will explain. According to VFT, your life goes well for you insofar as you achieve your appropriate values (values that are relatively stable and can be mutually endorsed and fulfilled over a life time in the face of changes). So, VFT identifies well-being with value commitments that are, in a certain way, idealized; as I've said, appropriate values for a person are likely to be ones that require minimal revision, but even if there are some people whose actual values meet the standard perfectly, the ideal is still there to provide the possibility of error required by normativity.

As I discussed above, an account of prudential reasons must explain both how these reasons justify a person's actions and how they can motivate people to act. When we understand the justificatory aspect of prudential reasons in terms of an ideal that provides a standard for justification (as VFT does), we introduce the possibility of tension between these two features of prudential reasons. The farther away the ideal is from the actual person, the less likely it will be to motivate her. For example, if the ideal or appropriate set of values for a person is one that does away entirely with one of her core values, say because it is completely incompatible with something else she values more, she may herself be unmotivated to take steps to change in the direction of the ideal. This might seem like a cost of the view, but I believe it is in fact an advantage for the following reason. Consider that the cases in which major revisions are required to make a person's values appropriate are cases in which the person's actual values are quite inappropriate, that is, very difficult to pursue together, highly unstable, or very ill-suited to the rest of the person's psychological profile. In such cases, VFT's account of prudential reasons implies that there are prudential reasons that would justify making major changes, but that these reasons will only have weak motivational pull on the people in question. But notice that this is just how things are. Think of a person who values both her marriage to an abusive husband and the welfare of her children. We can see that an ideal set of values for this woman would involve a major change in her pattern of values and it seems clear that she has reasons to make this change. The reason she has to stop valuing her marriage is one that will have some motivational force for her, given the other things she values, but the motivational force of the reason will be dampened by her (unfortunate, from our point of view) attitudes toward her marriage. The justificatory force of her prudential reasons comes from the ideal set of values, which does not track her motivations perfectly. Nevertheless, prudential reasons can typically figure into the explanation of actions, according to VFT, because in normal cases they are tied to some of our actual values and, hence, to some of our actual motivations for action.

The justificatory force of prudential reasons comes from the ideal standard, while their motivational force varies with the distance between the actual person and the ideal. These two features of prudential reasons will never be completely divorced, however, because a person's values have to be *her* values for their fulfillment to count toward her well-being; that is, whatever revisions need to be made to a person's values to make them appropriate, these revisions can't be so radical as to render the person a different person. This seems like a very reasonable thing to say about prudential reasons. Moreover, it allows room for deliberating about well-being by deliberating about the ends or values it would be best for us to have.

The standard of modest revision employed by VFT will give rise to worries about precisely how much a person's values must be improved to count as appropriate. In principle, appropriateness is defined by the set of available lives that have the most value fulfillment for a person, but in practice we will have to appeal to context to determine how much revision it is appropriate to imagine in assessing a person's well-being. First, if a person is assessing her own well-being, greater revision is permitted because the person herself is the one who can undertake to revise her values. External assessments of well-being should rely on more modest, predictable revisions when the point of the third-person assessment is to take some action on behalf of, or for the sake of, the well-being of the subject. Second, the temporal extension of the assessment matters. If a person wants to know what she can do right now to improve her life, modest revision will be very modest indeed, since what the person needs is a reason to do something that she can act on now. If, on the other hand, she is thinking about the long term, it will make sense to think of more significant revisions to her value system, because modest changes now will bring about larger changes over time. In other words, as we expand the time frame that we are considering in our assessment of how someone is doing, the standard will change. In my view, this kind of context sensitivity is an attractive feature of VFT. People fare well to varying degrees in various respects, and a theory of well-being ought to allow for the kind of complexity that we find in our evaluations of how people's lives are going.

Nevertheless, the above admission of context relativity in assessment might raise some worries about the empirical adequacy of VFT. Is well-being something that can be measured empirically according to VFT? If a person's appropriate values comprise an ideal, then we cannot measure whether people have succeeded by this standard. The fact that the ideal is a moving target seems to make matters worse. But I don't think there is a big problem here. When we measure well-being we are taking an external point of view on people's well-being, which makes modest revision appropriate. We can measure very close approximations of a modestly revised set of values by thinking about which are the values most people already have that would be likely to survive minimal reflection and new experiences. In other words, we can measure how people are succeeding by the standards of the most basic and stable values that people have. Indeed, many of the ingredients of well-being according to VFT are things that psychologists already measure. This is because many of the things that psychologists measure – life satisfaction, pleasure, positive affect, lack of stress, and so on – are things that we value and that are very likely to be appropriate values. Life satisfaction might be particularly good evidence of how people are doing by the standard of VFT, because life satisfaction is, at least in part, an endorsement of how life is going which has been shown to track important domains of value in people's lives (Schimmack and Oishi 2005).

Further, VFT provides a rationale for measuring a plurality of items and for measuring objective items such as physical health as components of well-being. This is an advantage on the assumption that these different research programs are all measuring something important – an assumption bolstered by the longevity and fruitfulness of the research programs. VFT also provides a way to think about conflict between different ingredients of well-being, because it provides an ideal of mutual endorsement and fulfillment over the long term. This ideal gives us a standard for assessing trade-offs between different values. For example, given that a certain level of health is a prerequisite to pursuing most of the other things people value, and given that health tends to decline over a lifetime, health (for most people) deserves a kind of priority in an ideal set of values.

Finally, whether VFT can explain the role of well-being in moral theory seems to me to depend on its success against the other criteria. For any theory that holds that well-being is one of the objects of moral action, well-being must be something we both can and should promote. It must be something we can measure at least to find out whether we have had any effect on it and it must be something that gives us reasons for action. Granted, a story needs to be told about how prudential reasons are related to moral reasons, but this is a story for moral theory to tell. Different moral theories have different explanations of this relationship, some of which impose further demands on the theory of well-being. For welfarists who think that well-being ought to be maximized, well-being must be, not only something we can measure, but also something we can meaningfully compare across people. While VFT does not make such comparisons easy, it does not make them impossible. Moreover, the fact that VFT has the means for determining which values get priority does give the theory a way to address problems of commensurating a plurality of values.

Conclusion

I began with the observation that too much arguing about well-being focuses on cases and whether a particular theory can accommodate different cases. I then proposed a set of criteria for a theory of well-being and argued that VFT does a good job of meeting these criteria. A full defense of this theory would require a much more detailed treatment and a thorough comparison to other views. My hope for this chapter, though, is that I have shown the advantage of making clear the theoretical desiderata at the outset of inquiry. There is no theory of well-being that a clever philosopher couldn't counter-example and any theory worth its salt will have something to say in response. Sometimes the right strategy is to modify the theory, sometimes it is to bite the bullet, and sometimes it is to point out that the counter-intuitive implication is not really an implication of the view correctly interpreted. If I'm right about this, trading in counterexamples without an eye to what the theory is supposed to achieve is not the best way to proceed. We need to make sure that our efforts to find reflective equilibrium are attuned to the real concerns that motivate our theorizing about well-being and the constraints on a good theory that arise from these concerns. This is not to say we do not need to think about cases. It is certainly a strike against a theory if it cannot accommodate ordinary convictions about who is faring well and who is faring badly. But at this point, the best versions of the available theories are very similar on this score. Hence the recommendation to turn our attention to other criteria. Once we have a theory that serves the purposes we need it to serve, then I believe we must think about cases in order to fine-tune and to assess how the theory can help us in answering questions about how to make human lives better, which is, after all, the most important purpose that theories of well-being have.

Notes

1 For helpful discussion and comments I would like to thank Michael Bishop, Alicia Hall, Matthew Haug, Dan Haybron, Peter Railton, David Sobel, and J.D. Walker.
2 For a related discussion of wide reflective equilibrium as the methodology for theorizing about wisdom see Tiberius and Swartwood 2011.
3 Perhaps inspired by this methodology, experimental philosophers have entered the fray, using survey techniques to determine empirically people's intuitions about such cases. See De Brigard 2010, Haybron 2008, and Phillips *et al.* 2011.
4 See for example Diener and Seligman 2004.
5 I believe even Fred Feldman 2010, who is quite critical of research in positive psychology for what he sees as the researchers' conceptual confusion, would accept the criteria of empirical adequacy that I have described.
6 Being able to affect well-being and being able to measure well-being are two different things, but it seems to me that we should at least hope that the changes we make to well-being are measurable.

7 Here I draw on discussions of normativity from Christine Korsgaard 1996 and Michael Smith 1994.

8 Williams 1979 is the canonical source. A very good introduction to the topic is Finlay and Schroeder 2008.

9 Haybron (2008, 156–57) characterizes Aristotelian theories as embracing "externalism" in a sense that is parallel, though he isn't talking about reasons existence externalism per se.

10 Here I have in mind theories inspired by Aristotle. For an alternative kind of eudaemonism that takes individual (rather than species) nature to be the key to well-being see Haybron 2008.

11 See Finlay and Schroeder 2008 for a detailed discussion of this argument.

12 Heathwood (2006 and 2007) argues that hedonists ought to characterize this pro-attitude as a desire and, hence, that simple desire satisfaction and attitudinal hedonism are really the same view.

13 For a somewhat different version of a value-based theory of well-being see Raibley 2010.

14 For a more thorough discussion see Tiberius 2008. Values as I intend them are similar to what psychologists would call "life goals": "specific motivational objectives by which a person directs his life over time" (Schmuck and Sheldon 2001, 5).

15 For an illuminating discussion of caring see Jaworska 2007. I agree with Jaworska that caring does not have to involve reflectiveness (one of the main theses she defends in this article), but I do not take caring and valuing to be quite the same thing, as will become clear.

16 If we take "desire" in the broadest sense, where a desire is any pro-attitude, then valuing is a species of desiring and the value fulfillment theory of well-being is a species of a desire theory. It's not clear that this is a helpful way of thinking about "desire," though it is true that VFT shares some of the advantages of desire theories in virtue of its similarity to them.

17 It is worth noting that values are not the same thing as value *judgments*. What we value is determined in large part by our patterns of affect, which usually track our intellectual judgments about what is valuable, but may not always do so. Insofar as values play the role in planning, deliberation and assessment that they do according to VFT, we are committed to their appropriateness, but this does not mean that valuing is primarily a matter of judging or believing. Further, "taking your values to be appropriate" is not the same as "judging your values to be correct." The former involves less cognitive effort, and the two attitudes imply different standards. Valuing is also different from caring, which does not include the same cognitive appraisal. Again, see Jaworska 2007. Jaworska does think that caring includes "finding important," but this attitude is different from what I mean by taking to be appropriate in that it does not invoke particular standards even implicitly.

18 See Jaworska 2007 on the connection between caring and the self.

References

Arneson, R.J. (1989) "Equality and Equal Opportunity for Welfare," *Philosophical Studies* 56: 77–93.

——(1999) "Human Flourishing Versus Desire Satisfaction," *Social Philosophy and Policy* 16: 113–42.

Brandt, R. (1979) *A Theory of the Good and the Right*, Oxford: Clarendon Press.

Crisp, R. (2006) *Reasons and the Good*, Oxford: Clarendon Press.

——(2008) "Well-Being," in Edward N. Zalta (ed.), *Stanford Encyclopedia of Philosophy*, Winter edn, <http://plato.stanford.edu/entries/well-being/> (accessed 20 May 2011).

De Brigard, F. (2010) "If You Like It, Does It Matter If It's Real?," *Philosophical Psychology* 23: 43–57.

Diener, E. and M. Seligman (2004) "Beyond Money: Toward an Economy of Well-Being," *Psychological Science in the Public Interest.* 5: 1–31.

Feldman, F. (2004) *Pleasure and the Good Life: Concerning the Nature, Varieties, and Plausibility of Hedonism*, Oxford: Clarendon Press.

——(2010) *What Is This Thing Called Happiness?*, Oxford: Oxford University Press.

Finlay, S. and M. Schroeder (2008) "Reasons for Action: Internal vs External," in Edward N. Zalta (ed.), *The Stanford Encyclopedia of Philosophy*, Fall edn, <http://plato.stanford.edu/archives/fall2008/entries/reasons-internal-external/>.

Finnis, J. (1980) *Natural Law and Natural Rights*, Oxford: Clarendon Press.

Foot, P. (2001) *Natural Goodness*, Oxford: Clarendon Press.

Griffin, J. (1986) *Well-Being: Its Meaning, Measurement and Moral Importance*, Oxford: Clarendon Press.

Harsanyi, J. (1982) "Morality and the Theory of Rational Behaviour," in A. Sen and B. Williams (eds), *Utilitarianism and Beyond*, Cambridge: Cambridge University Press, 39–62.

Haybron, D. (2008) *The Pursuit of Unhappiness: The Elusive Psychology of Well-Being*, Oxford: Oxford University Press.

Heathwood, C. (2006) "Desire Satisfaction and Hedonism," *Philosophical Studies* 128(3): 539–63.

——(2007) "The Reduction of Sensory Pleasure to Desire," *Philosophical Studies* 133: 23–44.

Hurka, T. (1993) *Perfectionism*, New York: Oxford University Press.

Jaworska, A. (2007) "Caring and Internality," *Philosophy and Phenomenological Research* 74(3): 529–68.

Keller, S. (2004) "Welfare and the Achievement of Goals," *Philosophical Studies* 121: 27–41.

Korsgaard, C. (1996) *The Sources of Normativity*, Cambridge: Cambridge University Press.

Kraut, R. (1979) "Two Conceptions of Happiness," *Philosophical Review* 88(2): 167–97.

——(2007) *What Is Good and Why: The Ethics of Well-Being*, Cambridge, MA: Harvard University Press.

Mill, John Stuart (1861/1979) *Utilitarianism*, ed. George Sher, Indianapolis, IN: Hackett.

Nozick, R. (1974) *Anarchy, State, and Utopia*, New York: Basic Books

Phillips, J., L. Misenheimer and J. Knobe (2011) "The Ordinary Concept of Happiness (and Others Like It)," *Emotion Review* 3(3): 320–22.

Piliavin, J.A. (2002) "Doing Well by Doing Good: Benefits for the Benefactor," in C.L.M. Keyes and J. Haidt (eds), *Flourishing: Positive Psychology and the Life Well-Lived*, Washington, DC: American Psychological Association, 227–48.

Raibley, J. (2010) "Well-Being and the Priority of Values," *Social Theory and Practice* 36(4): 593–620.

Railton, P. (1986) "Moral Realism," *Philosophical Review* 95(2): 163–207.

Schimmack, U. and S. Oishi (2005) "The Influence of Chronically Accessible versus Temporarily Accessible Sources of Life Satisfaction Judgments," *Journal of Personality and Social Psychology* 89: 395–406.

Schmuck, P.E. and K.M. Sheldon (2001) *Life Goals and Well-Being: Towards a Positive Psychology of Human Striving*, Göttingen: Hogrefe & Huber Publishers.

Smith, M. (1994) *The Moral Problem*, Oxford: Blackwell.

——(1995) "Internal Reasons," *Philosophy and Phenomenological Research* 55: 109–31.

Sobel, D. (2009) "Subjectivism and Idealization," *Ethics* 119: 336–52.

Sumner, L.W. (1996) *Welfare and Happiness in Ethics*, New York: Oxford University Press.

Tiberius, V. (2008) *The Reflective Life: Living Wisely with Our Limits*, Oxford: Oxford University Press.

Tiberius, V. and A. Plakias (2010) "Well-Being," in J. Doris and the Moral Psychology Research Group (eds), *The Moral Psychology Handbook*, Oxford: Oxford University Press, 401–31.

Tiberius, V. and J. Swartwood (2011) "Wisdom Revisited: A Case Study in Normative Theorizing," *Philosophical Explorations* 14(3): 277–95.

Williams, B. (1979/1981) "Internal and External Reasons," repr. in *Moral Luck*, Cambridge: Cambridge University Press, 101–13.

22 Ethics makes strange bedfellows: intuitions and quasi-realism

MATT BEDKE

You know the story. You have a few intuitions. You propose a few theories that fit them. It's a living. Of course, things are more complicated than this. We are sensitive to counterexamples raised by others and wish to accommodate or explain away an ever-wider base of intuitive starting points. A great deal of the action occurs in rational reflection that can alter what is intuitive, and in theorizing that overturns formerly justified beliefs and moves us to new justified beliefs. Details aside, this method in ethics and elsewhere—of first relying on intuitions to form justified beliefs, and subsequently using best-fit (or reflective equilibrium) theorizing on all justified beliefs to move to other justified beliefs—has received a lot of critical attention lately. But it is not a bad method. It is a good method caught in a bad relationship. For its presumptive meta-ethical companion, realism, would have us believe that intuitions support beliefs about real, stance-independent facts of the matter. That strikes many as dubious. After sorting through some relevant concerns in this vicinity, I argue that the solution is not to reject intuitional methods but to embrace quasi-realism.

In the next section, I will spend some time describing and defending intuitional methods. The main move there is to notice that there are two roles intuitions might play in an intuitional method. In one role they provide a causal basis for forming beliefs about their contents, as when the intuition that P is the causal basis on which one believes that P. In another role *beliefs about* intuitions provide a causal basis for forming other beliefs, as when the belief that one has the intuition that P is the (perhaps partial) causal basis on which one believes that Q. Moral epistemologists should focus their attention on the first role, for it has the better claim to justify beliefs in propositions with ethical content. In the second role, intuitions have far less epistemic significance for first-order inquiry. We typically do not base ethical beliefs on beliefs about our intuitions or what is intuitive, and even if we did it would be hard to establish the move as justification-conferring. When we focus on that first role, one key ingredient to intuitional methods—that some beliefs are intuitively justified—is easier to defend. The following section also clarifies how intuitions and intuitional justification relate to a priori justification, non-inferential justification, and conceptual analysis, and it briefly considers alternatives to intuitional methods.

In the third section, "Lingering Reservations," I try to put my finger on a lingering concern: that ethical intuitions are not a good way of discovering ethical facts. After it has been made clear that ethical disagreement is not where the action is, the fourth section, "From Disagreement to Coincidence and Error Theory," goes on to argue that metaethical realism is the culprit. Instead of looking for other ways to make up our minds about ethical matters, we should give up the idea that the inquiry uncovers facts about some stance-independent subject matter. Perhaps surprisingly, some arguments designed to induce skepticism in the method do more to undermine a realist understanding of the discourse. The lessons here can be generalized beyond ethics to any domain of normative theorizing that relies on intuitions and is susceptible to a quasi-realist (expressivist) understanding of the discourse, including epistemology, though I just focus on the ethical case in what follows.

Two roles for intuitions

In first-order ethical inquiry one is trying to make up one's mind about ethical matters. It is not uncommon to see ethicists proceed by directing their attention to cases and principles in order to elicit intuitions with substantive ethical content. So, for example, one directs attention to some trolley case, has an intuition that P, for some ethical proposition P, and causally bases the belief that P on that intuition. After a sufficient number of these intuitively based beliefs come along one has enough material to do best-fit theorizing on the content of those beliefs. The outcome is some overarching theory like hedonic act utilitarianism, Rossian deontology, eudaemonistic virtue ethics, etc., or some less ambitious principle, like the doctrine of double effect, the doing–allowing distinction, the transitivity of value, etc., or even some sort of anti-principle position along the lines of particularism. (Best-fit theorizing is messy and difficult, and there are good questions about which theoretical virtues are included in the process, or how much to weigh each one. So it would be no surprise were the process to fail to yield widespread consensus.)

In parallel, ethicists usually *take note* that they have intuitions. That is, not only do they have intuitions and causally base beliefs on them, but they also form beliefs about their intuitions. I think these beliefs about one's mental states are typically based on it seeming (introspectively) that one has those mental states (see Bealer 1998, 205). Ethicists might also be curious about what intuitions others have, and there the beliefs are typically

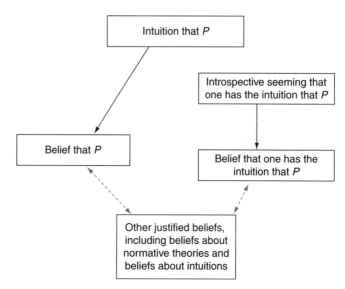

Figure 22.1 Two roles of intuition in ethical theory. Black solid arrows represent causal basing
relations among the contents of our beliefs; dotted double arrows represent best-fit
(or reflective equilibrium) relations.

based on testimony. Like the contents of beliefs about ethical matters, the
contents of beliefs about our intuitions can also enter into best-fit theorizing.
Importantly, however, the conclusions supported by beliefs about intuitions
typically have little bearing on first-order ethical questions.

I diagram these two roles in Figure 22.1. Black solid arrows represent
causal basing relations (leaving it open for the moment whether this is a
justifying relation), and dotted double-arrowed lines represent best-fit
(or reflective equilibrium) relations among the contents of our beliefs
(again leaving it open whether this relation justifies, though I think we
can assume it does if the inputs are justified).

Given these two roles, we should be cautious about claims concerning
intuitions and whether they justify. Consider Jonathan Weinberg, Shaun
Nichols and Stephen Stich, who claim that intuitional methods "must take
epistemic intuitions as data or input" (Weinberg *et al.* 2008, 19). Joel Pust
says something similar: "Most philosophers take the fact that they have
the intuition that S does not know that p in this [Gettier] case to show that S
does not know that p" (2000, 5). And Timothy Williamson speaks of
skeptics who have a "psychological" standard of evidence according to which
"our ultimate evidence consists of the psychological truths that we have
intuitions with [certain] contents, whether true or false" (2004, 119).

These statements (especially the last two) are problematic insofar as
they suggest that moves from beliefs about our having intuitions to

beliefs in their contents are the sorts of moves that putatively generate intuitively justified beliefs. The fact that one has an intuition that P is not like the fact that a tree has *n* rings. In the latter case, the (justified) belief that a tree has *n* rings can support a move to the belief that the tree is *n* years old (with some background assumptions). In the former case, it would be difficult to defend the thought that the (justified) belief that one has an intuition that P can support a move to the belief that P—unusual background assumptions would have to be in place.

In any event, that is not the normal procedure. We should not saddle intuitional methodologies with the view that psychological facts about having intuitions justify beliefs in the contents of those intuitions. More plausible is this: When the belief that P is causally based on the intuition that P (in the right way—no funny causal chains), that is a justifying move. And if one thereby justifiably believes that P, P is part of one's evidential base, to be used in best-fit theorizing with everything else one justifiably believes. This is where the debate should be located.

It is tricky to keep this clear given that ethicists will often provide commentary on their mental moves as they go, commentary that refers to intuitions and intuitive propositions. When theorizing in ethics one might naturally say "Intuitively, P" and then proceed to believe that P and take P as evidence for other things. Or when doing ethical episte- mology one might say, "In having the intuition that P one has a reason to believe that P," or more simply "Intuitions are evidence." These com- ments are fine if they are taken as a commentary on how a belief that P came (or can come) to be justified, i.e. by being based on an intuition. Problems arise when they are taken to express a justifying inference from the *belief* that one has the intuition that P to belief in P. Again, intuitional methods should not champion any such movement of the mind.

This might sound familiar. When using experience, we typically base beliefs on experiential states themselves, not on beliefs about those experiential states. And many epistemologists focus on that former kind of move as the one that yields justified beliefs about the contents of experience (see e.g. Chisholm 1982, 18; Pollock and Cruz 1999, 195; Feldman 2003, 77; Pryor 2000, 519). Those who defend intuitional methods make similar moves. Still, it is important to emphasize the point because it is not sufficiently appreciated. Consider the following comments from Peter Singer.

> A scientific theory seeks to explain the existence of data that are about a world "out there" that we are trying to explain. ... A normative ethical theory, however, is not trying to explain our common moral intuitions. It might reject all of them, and still be superior to other normative theories that better matched our moral judgments. For a normative moral theory is

not an attempt to answer the question "Why do we think as we do about moral questions?" ... A normative morally theory is an attempt to answer the question "What ought we to do?"

(2005, 345)

Singer is right to think that first-order ethics is not trying to explain why some propositions strike us as intuitive. That is a psychological project. But he is wrong to suppose that this is what intuitional justification is meant to look like. Consider the footbridge trolley case, where pushing a large man from a footbridge onto some trolley tracks will result in his death but spare the lives of five others down the track by stopping a runaway trolley (Thomson 1985). It is not as though we wonder why we have the intuition that it is impermissible, and posit the action's impermissibility as the best explanation for why we have that intuition. And we do not otherwise infer beliefs about impermissibility from beliefs about our intuitions, at least not in the normal cases. Instead, we move from the intuition that it is impermissible to push the large man in the footbridge case to the belief that it is impermissible, not as a best explanation or some such, but just in the way we move from experiential seemings to beliefs about their contents. This second sort of move does address the question "What ought we to do?" And it is dubious that a first-order normative ethics that rejects all intuitions in this role could be superior to one that does not.

We might notice that, in the case of experiential seemings, when I ask the partly psychological question of why it seems, say, that I have hands, the best explanation involves the external world impinging on my perceptual capacities, an explanation I come by after first relying on experiential seemings. This seems to buttress the deliverances of the seemings themselves. (Though perhaps it only supports a second-order, external-world interpretation of the discourse, as opposed to an idealist one; the first-order thought that one has hands might get no additional support.) Perhaps, by contrast, the explanation for why I have the ethical intuitions I have does not similarly appeal to stance-independent ethical facts. This might be a relevant disanalogy, along the lines of the one pressed by Gilbert Harman (1977, ch. 1). But it should not make us rethink the method as such, or the impermissibility of certain actions. It should make us wonder whether the method is one by which we discover stance-independent facts. More on this as we proceed.

Intuitive justification *and* intuitive *justification*

I have tried to locate the move that is meant to result in an intuitively justified belief. I use "justification" to talk about *procedural justification*, or how one ought to go about making up one's mind about what to believe, given the information available to one's cognitive system (Pollock and Cruz 1999, 14). And the justification is always defeasible. Of course, one can assess a cognitive, belief-forming system based on how successful it is at producing true beliefs. And one might focus on knowledge attributions. But procedural justification is an assessment less sensitive to considerations that one's cognitive system cannot take note of as it goes about forming and revising beliefs.

I use the term "intuition" to pick out a kind of initial reaction one has to classical hypothetical cases and principles. I have already mentioned trolley cases. Similarly, one might have an initial reaction when considering whether one has less reason to save the life of someone who is far away than one who is nearby, *ceteris paribus* (Singer 1972, 231). When considering whether your good is more important from the point of view of the universe than the good of any other (Sidgwick 1907, 382), or whether one has a prima facie duty to keep promises (Ross 1930, 21), again one might have initial reactions. An intuition is an initial reaction like these whereby some proposition seems true (see also Bealer 2000, 3; Huemer 2005, ch. 5).[1] To say that a proposition is intuitive is to say that it is the object of an initial reaction like these. If one never has initial reactions like these, one does not have intuitions of the sort I'm talking about. I am not sure how best to make up one's mind in ethical matters when no ethical proposition seems true, so I'll pretend that we all have some intuitions that concern ethical matters.

I can say a bit more about what these initial reactions are, or at least what they are not. They are not beliefs. It can seem, for example, impermissible to push the man in the footbridge case even though one believes doing so is permissible. Intuitions are not hunches, guesses, blind impulses, vague sentiments, preferences for action, conclusions from rapid half-conscious processing, or current opinions to which familiarity has given an illusory air of self-evidence. Basically, what Sidgwick said (1907, 211–12). Last, intuitions are distinct from other states that are appropriately called seemings, such as the way things look in experience, and the way things are presented by memory or introspection.

Though I have been mainly describing how intuitional methods should be understood, I also want to endorse the method. In particular, I want to say that intuitively based beliefs are prima facie justified. To make the case, assume that we try to do without intuitions and simply begin with our ethical *beliefs*, or what we already *know* in ethics, and go from there (doxastic or knowledge conservatism, respectively). This might be good advice for beings without non-doxastic seeming states. But if you start with a perfectly coherent set of beliefs or knowledge base, and yet some of what you believe *seems false*, or conflicting propositions *seem true*, this is not a good situation. Your justification is worse than it would be had you no seeming states, or had you seeming states that accorded with what you already believe or know. Recall two of Singer's cases: in one, *A* could save a drowning child before him at little cost; in another, *B* could at little cost save a child halfway around the world from dying of starvation. Imagine that John believes that mere spatial proximity is morally relevant, and this coheres with everything else he believes. Further, we might imagine that John *knows* that spatial proximity is relevant (though maybe he does not know that he knows). However, at some point someone presents him with these cases, and it now *seems* to John that mere spatial proximity is morally *ir*relevant. Does this alter his epistemic situation insofar as he is trying to make up his mind about what to believe? I think so. The seeming here counts against the belief. In terms of how to proceed, John has some reason to abandon or attenuate the belief. For those with seeming states, some reliance on them in making up one's mind is entirely justified. Ignoring them is unjustified without saying more.

The analogue in the case of perception is a situation where John believes that Ed's shirt is red. That coheres with all John's other beliefs and John even knows it. Ed then walks through the door and, lo, his shirt looks blue. How to proceed? Again, adjustment based on the seeming is justified. To ignore it unjustified (see Pollock and Cruz 1999, 84–88).

But what if we lack some way of calibrating our intuitions, or a way of showing they are reliable prior to relying on them (Cummins 1998, 117)? If this demand were pressed against all seeming-based justification it would be impossible to fulfill while avoiding skepticism (Sosa 1998). I suppose one could privilege some seeming states so they do not need to be calibrated before we justifiably rely on them, but I have seen no argument for such preferential treatment, and I myself do not discriminate against seemings with ethical content.

It also helps to consider three kinds of cases before making this demand of any kind of seeming state. In the first, one only has a single sensory modality, say, vision, with no way of checking any information received from that modality against information received from another. In a second, we can imagine that some domains of inquiry are inaccessible to all but one modality, e.g. color might be uniquely discoverable with vision, and so we might well be in a reliability or calibration conundrum with respect to those domains of inquiry. Third and last, we can imagine an artificial being with a single modality. In any of these cases, would the persons (or beings) be unjustified in relying on how things seem via the relevant modality? Surely not. And they can proceed as best they can by doing a bit of intramodal calibration and by ensuring that they do not have justification for believing that their seemings are largely incorrect. If a single window casts light into a room you might lament the absence of more windows. But it would be foolish to draw the blinds on the one window you have.

A priori? A faculty? Inferential?

Intuitive justification is often associated with a priori justification. The initial justification conferred by intuitions, however, is justification one has regardless of whether it is a priori or not. Justified beliefs about whether some of our knowledge counts as a priori come well downstream of relying on intuitions and other seeming states. It is not as though we first have some idea of what a priori reasoning or justification is, and which seeming states and justifying basing relations fit the mold, before we justifiably base beliefs on seeming states. That said, it could well turn out that some intuitions are manifestations of conceptual competence, which would give us reason to distinguish those beliefs based on competence-based intuitions and those that are not, and this amounts to a legitimate a priori–a posteriori distinction. I have argued elsewhere (Bedke 2008) that ethical intuitions are not the conceptual-competence-based variety. But regardless of whether some reliance on seeming states counts as a priori or a posteriori, the amount of justification conferred by such reliance has not thereby been shown to suffer. A lot more needs to be said to make that case. Some think we can make the case if we can show that intuitional methods cannot get beyond conceptual analysis—that it cannot peer into the subject matter those concepts are putatively about— but if I am right ethical intuitions are not caught in that dragnet. The best theory of what is going on in ethics does not ground it in conceptual analysis.

Intuitional epistemologies are also associated with a commitment to a quasi-perceptual faculty of Intuition. The present view assumes no such faculty.

Last, intuitive justification is also associated with non-inferential justification. I do not know why it matters whether a given psychological move counts as an inference or not, so I won't speak in those terms. The main point, as far as I can see, is the one stressed above regarding the two roles intuitions can play. When a belief that P is prima facie justified in virtue of being based on an intuition that P the belief that P is not based on the belief *that one has the intuition that P*. Though the basing relationship between intuition and belief is not aptly characterized as inference to the best explanation, I do not know what else hangs on whether it is an inference or not. The main claim is that the move is justification-conferring.

Alternatives?

It has been noted that there are no serious alternatives for how to proceed in ethics other than best-fit theorizing (or reflective equilibrium) on what seems to be the case (Parfit 2011, 544; Scanlon 2002, 149). But some ethicists want something else. Peter Singer says this: "I want to make a more general objection to any method of doing ethics that judges a normative theory either entirely, or in part, by the extent to which it matches our moral intuitions" (Singer 2005, 346). As suggested above, Singer has not focused on the role of intuitions most relevant to first-order theorizing. In any event, he does not use a method that is intuition-free. Instead, he relies on his intuition that different ways of harming—via methods available in our past (pushing) and via methods not available in our past (flipping a switch)—are morally irrelevant, along with a bit of evolutionary theory and empirical psychology to the effect that deontology-friendly intuitions are overly sensitive to up-close-and-personal ways of harming others that were available in our evolutionary past. The intuitive justification of deontology-friendly intuitions thereby undermined, Singer goes on to rely on intuitions about death being bad in support of some version of consequentialism. Whether or not his arguments are sound, this is clearly no alternative to the standard methodology described above.

When criticizing Derek Parfit's *On What Matters*, Allen Wood seems to endorse another radical departure from the method. He says he favors a method whereby one starts with a "fundamental principle" that is the "articulation of a basic value," whose ground is independent of moral intuitions (2011, 59). What remains unclear is how one justifiably comes to believe in a fundamental principle or basic value without relying on what intuitively seems (in my sense) to be a fundamental principle or basic value. The real difference between him and Parfit is whether to use a top–down or bottom–up approach when relying on intuitions. Parfit primarily starts with particulars and cases and moves by some best-fit inferences to general principles, while Wood prefers to start with principles and then move down to apply them to cases and particulars. Intuitions play a role either way.

In another criticism of Parfit, Philip Kitcher is dubious of the appeal to "puzzle cases" (those cases that elicit intuitions), and suggests instead that we learn to "regulate our own conduct" through "Naturalism," and that we look "as carefully and as comprehensively as we can, at the details of ethical practice and ethical change" (2012). In other work he makes use of anthropology and evolutionary theory to comment on the function of certain prototypically moral behaviors and how they have changed, and he rejects what he calls metaethical realism in favor of what he calls pragmatic naturalism, but when it comes to adopting his own normative stance it is not clear how he avoids relying on what seems right to him (2011). Even if he succeeds in ignoring what seems right, that does not sound like a justifiable way to proceed.

Lingering reservations

So far I have only hinted at anything metaethical that goes beyond moral epistemology. I have not said that what we discover using these methods are stance-independent facts of the matter, for example. This is where legitimate problems arise. There seems to be a default presumption that intuitive methods are aimed at discovering such real facts, encouraged by the observation that this metaethical position is the historical traveling companion with intuitive epistemologies in ethics. This default in place, many are dubious that relying on intuitions is part of a justified way of discovering such facts. In the rest of this chapter I explore these and related concerns. I'll first discuss the significance of disagreement and then turn to the more pressing concern about how intuitions are meant to access or track the facts.

First, disagreement. In this section I will not be focusing on disagreement as a problem for ethical realism as such, but rather disagreement as something that should undermine our justification that we have latched onto fact. It is hard to assess the extent to which intuitions are shared among individuals who consider the relevant cases and principles, but I imagine that at least the clarity and strength of intuitions do vary, and so the ethical beliefs that individuals arrive at after best-fit theorizing are bound to vary as well. Supposing there is disagreement in intuition and belief, Walter Sinnott-Armstrong suggests that this supports the thought that intuitions are generally unreliable. Further, he thinks this makes our epistemic situation akin to random reliance on the reading of one thermometer in a box of one hundred thermometers, some portion of which are known to be unreliable (Sinnott-Armstrong 2007, 201). In sum, disagreement can undermine our confidence that we have latched onto fact.

I think this exaggerates the significance of disagreement. The thermometer analogy is apt only if we can justifiably think of our own intuitions as randomly selected from a pool of intuitions, some portion of which are unreliable. To see why this is not justified, consider the analogous case for experiential seemings. Suppose you are presented with a card whose contents look like those of Figure 22.2. I am guessing that it looks to you that b is the same length as x. Insofar as your belief is based on this seeming it is (procedurally) justified. Now imagine that several other people *report* that a or c is the same length as x, or that that is the way things look to them.[2]

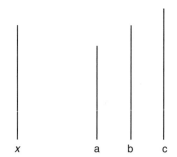

Figure 22.2 Perceptual seemings and line lengths.

What is the justified response on your part? Should you treat your experiential seeming as randomly selected from a set of seemings, some portion of which are unreliable? No. The way things *look to you* plays a different epistemic role than *reports* about the way things look *to others*. These are different pieces of evidence and carry different epistemic weights. Perhaps you would take another look at the lines, or measure things out, but even if you could not do so you would be justified if you continued to believe that b is the same length as *x*. So here we have a clear case where an experiential seeming state is meant to reveal some stance-independent fact of the matter, and where apparent disagreement does not epistemically obligate you to treat how things seem to you as randomly selected from a pool of how things seem to people generally (though some reduction in confidence levels might be called for).

So it goes with those seeming states that are ethical intuitions. As seeming states, they play an epistemic role in supporting the propositions that seem to be the case. If others disagree, and report this to you, you are not epistemically obligated to treat your intuition in the way you treat their testimony. Information about disagreement might be relevant, but it is not nearly as relevant as which ethical propositions seem to be the case. Anyone who would make an exception for ethical intuitions in this regard has some explaining to do.

What if we take others to be epistemic peers—people with the same evidence and as likely to get things right as we are on the relevant question? If this is our attitude prior to the disagreement, the disagreement itself can call into question the belief that others are epistemic peers (see Audi 2008, 490; Enoch 2010, 979–81). This seems to be the right response to the case of the line lengths in the figure, and it might well be the right response in the face of disagreement over what ethical propositions seem true. If we think others are epistemic peers *after* the disagreement comes to light, and so after taking into account the evidence of how things look, this is a conclusion based in part on how things seem to us, presumably the result of antecedent, justified skepticism about the veridicality of our seemings, or antecedent, justified beliefs that others are more likely to get things right on the target question. Either way, the disagreement itself does not provide a case for skepticism. None of this calls into question the methodology of relying on how things seem and treating them differently than reports about how things seem to others, even in cases where the inquiry is clearly about a stance-independent matter of fact. Certainly, treating your seemings as selected at random from a bin of how things seem to people generally is not epistemically compelled.

The above relates to the role of experimental philosophy in first-order ethical theorizing. We should welcome information about what people's intuitions are, and what can influence them. But if the above is right, the relevance of reports of intuitions will not be as probative as one's first-person intuitions, at least when it comes to answering ethical questions. Moreover, the most straightforward information we get from most surveys in experimental philosophy directed at ethics is how people (on average) use some ethical term *T*—they apply it, or are inclined to apply it (on average) to one case, but they withhold it, or are inclined to withhold it (on average) to another case, etc. This is information about language use. Suppose we can additionally draw conclusions about intuitions (or the average intuition, or the average degree of having an intuition). Still, *that someone has intuition* I, or *that* n *number of people have intuition* I, is not the same kind of evidence as *having intuition* I *yourself*, or *having intuition* J (whose content is inconsistent with *I*). Whether it is observational or intuitional, we do not want to neglect the first-personal evidence of how things seem. And we do not want to whitewash these things as mere reports from someone about having an observation or an intuition.

From disagreement to coincidence and error theory

Disagreement can still attenuate one's justification even if it does not wholly defeat that justification or give cause to abandon intuitional methods. Perhaps, however, pervasive, fundamental disagreement can make you more skeptical that you have latched on to the facts.

I think a form of disagreement along these lines passes through any epistemic difficulty and lands on a different target: the hypothesis that ethical or normative judgments are about some reducible facts, facts that can comfortably be located in the natural world. The first thought here is that there is fundamental disagreement over normative matters between people who fully grasp the relevant normative concepts, where there is no way to resolve such disagreements by supplying the parties with information about the natural ways of the world. If so, it is hard to explain how their disagreement is really about such natural facts. The second thought is that, even if there is no fundamental disagreement in fact, it is possible for two agents to fully grasp normative concepts, fully grasp all the truths of the natural world, and yet still disagree about normative matters. This is excellent evidence that the disagreements are not about natural facts after all. Even in light of all the natural facts, ethical language can be used to weigh in on which facts matter and which do not, and people can disagree about this without violating the meanings of ethical terms. I cannot pursue this thought further here (see my 2012), but I do think this is the right place to press disagreement concerns.

In any event, intuitional methods are typically paired with non-naturalist metaphysics, so I want to focus our epistemic and methodological concerns here. Recall a potentially troubling disanalogy between intuitions and other seemings. With other seemings, e.g. experiential seemings, after justifiably relying on them to begin inquiry we have come across a backstory that explains why our experiential and perceptual states would by-and-large successfully represent a world of external facts, whatever they turn out to be. As Allan Gibbard puts things, we have come across, or can hope to come across, a "deep vindication" of vision and other capacities (2003, 254). This is not so with intuitional seemings insofar as they are about non-natural facts of the matter. It is hard to see how they could eventually deliver a backstory that explains how they would by-and-large successfully represent non-natural facts, whatever those facts turn out to be.

I think the way to press this worry is to say that adequate alignment between intuition and belief on the one side, and fact on the other, would be cosmically coincidental (Bedke 2009, forthcoming). In brief, the worry is that whatever the ethical facts turn out to be it would be highly coincidental if the natural, causal order just happened to cause in us intuitions and beliefs that line up (often enough) with those extra-natural, non-causal, facts and properties they purport to be about. Even if we initially, justifiably rely on our intuitions to form beliefs about the ethical and normative facts, we realize that the intuitions and beliefs would be oblivious to the facts in the following way: were the ethical facts otherwise, we would have the very same beliefs and intuitions, and for the same reasons.

While this argument might appear to take aim at intuitive justification in ethics and other normative areas, it only takes aim at this method as a way of discovering stance-independent (non-natural) facts. That meta-ethical position is entirely negotiable. And I think our natural reaction to the skeptical concerns actually does more to undermine the non-natural purport than the intuitional methods.

What I want to suggest is that the first-order ethical views—that it is wrong to torture children for fun, that intending harm is worse than merely foreseeing harm, that one's good is no more important than the good of any other, or what have you—do not change, and are not disposed to change, in the face of skeptical arguments like those above. Nor do people stop relying on what seems to be true. It is not as though the deontologist who comes to embrace the coincidence worry ceases to think it impermissible to push the large man off the footbridge. And it is not as though the utilitarian who comes to embrace the coincidence worry ceases to think that we should maximize intrinsic value. In these cases and others it is hard to believe that the first-order views are disposed to disappear or alter.

This is significant. When a *type* of judgment lacks this disposition—that is, when it is not disposed to disappear in the face of what one acknowledges to be good grounds for being skeptical that one has justifiably latched on to the relevant facts—this is excellent evidence that that type of judgment is not belief about the dubious domain of facts after all. For judgments of this sort do not have the epistemic profile we expect of beliefs about such facts. They do not exhibit an evidence and defeater sensitivity that is typical of belief. Normally, when you initially believe that P, where this belief purports to be about some fact, but subsequently acknowledge good grounds for being skeptical about your belief in that fact, you drop the belief (or are disposed to do so). Ethical beliefs are not sensitive in this way to admittedly good grounds for being skeptical of the thought that one's intuitions coincide with non-natural facts. The clearest explanation for why this is so is that the ethical beliefs, and the intuitions in support of them, are not about non-natural facts after all. If we thought they were, we had a mistaken metaethical belief.

It is important to home in on the evidence insensitivity of ethical beliefs as a type. Single beliefs can fail to be evidence sensitive for a variety of local reasons and still count as beliefs. It is harder to maintain that a type of judgment can be evidence insensitive across the board and still count as belief. This is so regardless of one's theory of belief. The weak evidence-sensitivity claim should operate as a condition of adequacy for any such theory.

So the dispositional tendency of normative judgments in the face of skeptical concerns suggests that they are not beliefs about non-natural facts. This rebuts the assumption that gives skeptical worries bite. Far from undermining the method of relying on intuitions to make up one's mind, the worries reveal that this is not a process of discovery of non-natural fact.

The debates among error theorists help to strengthen the point. Convinced error theorists have various reactions. Some unabashedly continue to moralize (Mackie 1977; Pigden 2007, 445). Of those who fall silent on what they think, or what they are disposed to think, in first-order ethics, some recommend that we continue to moralize (Olson 2011), some recommend revision in the discourse to avoid error (Joyce 2001; Nolan *et al.* 2005), and some recommend abolition of the discourse (Garner 2007). These *recommendations* indicate that prior moral beliefs have not *naturally* disappeared for any of these figures. This makes moral error theories very different than error theories in other domains, like those concerning dodo birds, witches, and phlogiston, where we do not hear of recommendations about what to think after receiving decisive evidence that there are no such things. We are naturally disposed to drop the beliefs.

If I am right, first-order moral judgments based on intuition are not disposed to disappear in light of what one takes to be conclusive evidence that there are no (non-natural) moral properties or facts. Again, this is good evidence that the beliefs are not about those facts after all. I do not think this leaves big puzzles for how to interpret what error theorists say. If they say there are no moral properties, we can take them to mean that there are no *non-natural* moral properties. This is entirely consistent with maintaining judgments that certain acts are wrong, and others right. If the error theorist explicitly says that no act is wrong and no act is right, we can take them to mean that no acts instantiate the non-natural property of being wrong or the non-natural property of being right, which again is consistent with the thought that some acts are wrong and others right so long as this second thought does not feature a belief-like attitude about a non-natural property, as I have argued it does not. The tension in any of this dissipates once we realize that error theorists are expressing their views in light of the mistaken metabelief that their moral judgments are beliefs about non-natural properties. They are making what appear to be first-order views about the moral statuses of things when actually they are blending first- and second-order thoughts, making the fused claim that *nothing has a non-natural property of being wrong* in language easily interpreted as the first-order view that *nothing is wrong*.

So we should give up the thought that views in first-order ethics—the very ones supported by intuition—are about stance-independent facts. Disagreement helps to rule out naturalism; and the dispositions of our beliefs in the face of certain defeaters that would apply, were our beliefs about non-natural fact, help to rule out non-naturalism. The intuitional method is unfazed as the best way to make up our minds about ethical matters. It is just a way of making up our minds about what to be for and what to be against, if I may put things that way. The intuitional method in ethics should be remarried to quasi-realism about the discourse.

If we go down this road, we have to ask ourselves whether it makes sense for attitudes that are not about stance-independent facts to enter into *epistemic* support relations. There are two options here. On the one hand, quasi-realists could maintain that the first-order judgments are sufficiently belief-like to enter epistemic relations, even though their content does not concern facts and properties "out there." On the other hand, quasi-realists could maintain that the first-order judgments are not sufficiently belief-like to enter epistemic relations. Even so, ethical judgments would still be subject to a kind of appraisal that is structurally similar to the procedural-justification-type appraisal I have been speaking about. We would still be evaluating moves from what seems to be the case to beliefs as part of an activity of making up one's mind about normative matters. And one can be more or less justified in how one proceeds. Whether this is an appraisal of a kind with the epistemic appraisal of standard beliefs with descriptive content is not all that important.

Conclusion

I've tried to defend intuitional methods in ethics. Understanding the dual role of intuitions—as bases for ethical beliefs, and as contents of beliefs about our psychology—helps to clear the air. Even so, there are understandable, lingering worries about relying on intuitions to discover facts of the matter. Ironically, skeptical worries that lead some to doubt the method offer redemption just as they threaten the rapture. Skeptical challenges do more to show that the discourse is quasi-realist than they undermine relying on intuitions. Divorcing intuitional methods from realism is the key.

There is no reason to drag conceptual analysis into the fight. Some theories of some intuitions might support the idea that they are manifestations of conceptual competence, and so probing our intuitions is a way of delineating the contours of our concepts. There might be a problem in that, but ethical intuitions are not partners in crime. There is little reason to think our ethical questions can be answered through conceptual analysis, and no clear connection between ethical intuitions and conceptual competence. The quasi-realist metatheory would suggest that we are just trying to make up our minds about what to be for and what to be against in ethics, relying in the first instance on what seems worthy of approbation and disapprobation, and helped along by considering how others have struggled to make up their minds. This seems to me like a responsible way to proceed. I endorse it.

These moves on behalf of intuitional methods are perhaps uniquely available to areas of normative theory (though perhaps also available to probability and modal theory). Quasi-realist moves are attractive here, but not for most other areas. Take debates about mereology. Firstly, it is not so clear that mereological beliefs are recalcitrant in the minds of those convinced that relying on intuitions is no way to discover the target facts of the matter. Thoughts about unrestricted composition are not as steadfast as thoughts about the impermissibility of harming children. Even if the mereological judgments were recalcitrant, quasi-realist treatment of part–whole talk is not very plausible. Unlike normative discourse about oughts, shoulds, values and reasons, it is less disputable that talk of parts, wholes and composition *purports* to represent or describe stance-independent acts about parts and wholes. So the salvation on offer for intuitional methods in ethics is not generally available to just any intuitional methodology.

Notes

1 I am tempted to drop the term "intuition" altogether, in favor of "ethical propositions that seem true." The former term evokes a sense of magical insight for some, and a knee-jerk negative reaction for others. It is harder to disparage the same thing under the guise of what seems true.

2 For a relevant experiment, see Asch (1951). There, participants in the experiment gave the right answer if they could write it down non-publicly. But if participants had to report their answer publicly, they conformed with the group of confederates giving the wrong answer. This suggests that participants retained the belief supported by how things looked to them in the face of disagreement. For a clip go to "Asch Conformity Experiment," YouTube, 22 December 2007, <http://www.youtube.com/watch?v=TYIh4MkcfJA>.

References

Asch, S.E. (1951) "Effects of Group Pressure upon the Modification and Distortion of Judgment," in H. Guetzkow (ed.), *Groups, Leadership and Men*, Pittsburgh, PA: Carnegie Press, 177–90.

Audi, R. (2008) "Intuition, Inference, and Rational Disagreement in Ethics," *Ethical Theory and Moral Practice* 11(5): 475–92.

Bealer, G. (1998) "Intuition and the Autonomy of Philosophy," in M. Depaul and W. Ramsey (eds), *Rethinking Intuition: The Psychology of Intuition and Its Role In Philosophical Inquiry*, Lanham, MD: Rowman & Littlefield, 201–39.

——(2000) "A Theory of the A Priori," *Pacific Philosophical Quarterly* 81: 1–30.

Bedke, M.S. (2008) "Ethical Intuitions: What They Are, What They Are Not, and How They Justify," *American Philosophical Quarterly* 45(3): 253–70.

——(2009) "Intuitive Non-naturalism Meets Cosmic Coincidence," *Pacific Philosophical Quarterly* 90(2): 188–209.

——(2012) "Against Normative Naturalism," *Australasian Journal of Philosophy* 90: 111–29.

——(forthcoming) "No Coincidence?," *Oxford Studies in Metaethics*.

Chisholm, R. (1982) *The Foundations of Knowing*, Minneapolis, MN: University of Minnesota Press.

Cummins, R. (1998) "Reflections on Reflective Equilibrium," in M. DePaul and W. Ramsey (eds), *Rethinking Intuition: The Psychology of Intuition and Its Role In Philosophical Inquiry*, Lanham, MD: Rowman & Littlefield, 113–28.

Enoch, D. (2010) "Not Just a Truthometer: Taking Oneself Seriously (but Not Too Seriously) in Cases of Peer Disagreement," *Mind* 119(476): 953–97.

Feldman, R. (2003) *Epistemology*, Englewood Cliffs, NJ: Prentice-Hall.

Garner, R. (2007) "Abolishing Morality," *Ethical Theory and Moral Practice* 10(5): 499–513.

Gibbard, A. (2003) *Thinking How to Live*, Cambridge, MA: Harvard University Press.

Harman, G. (1977) *The Nature of Morality: An Introduction to Ethics*, New York: Oxford University Press.

Huemer, M. (2005) *Ethical Intuitionism*, Basingstoke: Palgrave Macmillan.

Joyce, R. (2001) *The Myth of Morality*, New York: Cambridge University Press.

Kitcher, P. (2011) *The Ethical Project*, Cambridge, MA: Harvard University Press.

——(2012) "The Lure of the Peak," *New Republic*, 11 January, <http://www.tnr.com/article/books/magazine/99529/on-what-matters-derek-parfit> (accessed 17 April 2012).

Mackie, J.L. (1977) *Ethics: Inventing Right and Wrong*, Harmondsworth: Penguin.

Nolan, D., G. Restali and C. West (2005) "Moral Fictionalism versus the Rest," *Australasian Journal of Philosophy* 83(3): 307–30.

Olson, J. (2011) "Getting Real about Moral Fictionalism," in R. Shafer-Landau (ed.), *Oxford Studies in Metaethics*, vol. 6, Oxford: Oxford University Press, 181–204.

Parfit, D. (2011) *On What Matters*, Oxford: Oxford University Press.

Pigden, C.R. (2007) "Nihilism, Nietzsche and the Doppelganger Problem," *Ethical Theory and Moral Practice* 10(5): 441–56.

Pollock, J.L. and J. Cruz (1999) *Contemporary Theories of Knowledge (Studies in Epistemology and Cognitive Theory)*, 2nd edn, Lanham, MD: Rowman & Littlefield.

Pryor, James (2000) "The Skeptic and the Dogmatist," *Noûs* 34(4): 517–49.

Pust, J. (2000) *Intuitions as Evidence*, New York: Routledge/Garland.

Ross, W.D. (1930) *The Right and the Good*, Oxford: Clarendon Press.

Scanlon, T.M. (2002) "Rawls on Justification," in S. Freeman (ed.), *The Cambridge Companion to Rawls*, New York: Cambridge University Press, 139–67.

Sidgwick, H. (1907) *The Methods of Ethics*, vol. 7, Indianapolis, IN: Hackett.

Singer, P. (1972) "Famine, Affluence, and Morality," *Philosophy and Public Affairs* 1(3): 229–43.

——(2005) "Ethics and Intuitions," *Journal of Ethics* 9(3–4): 331–52.

Sinnott-Armstrong, W. (2007) *Moral Skepticism*, New York: Oxford University Press.

Sosa, E. (1998) "Minimal Intuition," in M. Depaul and W. Ramsey (eds), *Rethinking Intuition: The Psychology of Intuition and Its Role In Philosophical Inquiry*, Lanham, MD: Rowman & Littlefield, 257–70.

Thomson, J.J. (1985) "The Trolley Problem," *Yale Law Journal* 94(6): 1395–1415.

Weinberg, J., S. Nichols and S. Stich (2008) "Normativity and Epistemic Intuitions," in J. Knobe and S. Nichols (eds), *Experimental Philosophy*, New York: Oxford University Press, 17–36.

Williamson, T. (2004) "Philosophical 'Intuitions' and Scepticism about Judgement," *Dialectica* 58: 109–53.

Wood, A. (2011) "Humanity as an End in Itself: Comments on Derek Parfit," in Derek Parfit, *On What Matters*, vol. 2, Oxford: Oxford University Press.

23 On getting out of the armchair to do aesthetics[1]

GREGORY CURRIE

One hundred years ago the reputation of aesthetics stood high in the world of ideas. The idealists of the nineteenth century had placed the philosophy of art at or near the centre of the philosophical enterprise, and there was a thriving industry in psychological work relating to appreciation of art and nature, well received in at least some philosophical quarters.[2] By the 1950s things were rather different. Anglo-American aesthetics was by then conducted largely from the armchair; in so far as there was an empirical study of the arts it was left to the culturally oriented approach of the art historians, while the philosophers thought of themselves as conceptual analysts or ordinary language therapists, licensed by some obscure authority to draw heavily on their own intuitions about cases, and on introspection of their own aesthetic responses and ruminations. And by this time aesthetics had lost its central place in philosophy; philosophers of language, mind and metaphysics never found anything to interest them in aesthetic writing of this period. Psychologists did not know it existed.

Thus might someone deeply unsympathetic to the analytical project in aesthetics dismiss some recent history. While it is not without truth, there is a good deal it leaves out, notably the contributions of philosophers in the broadly analytical tradition who have illuminated such topics as aesthetic judgements and reasons, the nature of pictorial perception, the relation between fiction and imagination. By the standards set by fifty years of work from Sibley, Wollheim and (still in production) Walton, the work of Vischer, Lipps and others on our empathic relations to architecture looks, for all its cross-disciplinary ambition, hopelessly confused. Those years in the armchair did aesthetics a great deal of good.

There is, currently, a good deal of pressure in philosophy to look further, to see in some detail the scientific results which may be relevant to your field; and in aesthetics we can look to the branches of psychology, to linguistics and to economic and sociological studies of the art market for enlightenment. I believe there is much to be learned from these disciplines but that none of it will be worth much unless we retain a commitment to the clarity that philosophical reflection of a traditional kind can bring. Part of what I want to do here is to defend this traditional philosophical method in aesthetics through focus on a particular case. But this is not the whole story. Later I will look at a question which arises frequently in aesthetics where traditional methods, unsupported by serious empirical inquiry, are likely to be very misleading.

Aesthetic intuitions

The careful work of Sibley on the relations between aesthetic and non-aesthetic properties drew attention to the idea that, in some sense it is not easy to specify precisely, aesthetic properties are possessed in virtue of the possession of other properties.[3] One way to think about this is to point out that two objects which have the same non-aesthetic properties—they look or sound the same, for example—could not differ in that one is beautiful and the other not. Speaking more generally, Moore had said that 'two things cannot differ in quality without differing in intrinsic nature'.[4] Philosophers now refer to such ideas as supervenience theses, and Moore's emphasis on 'intrinsic nature' points to a distinction within the class of such theses which we shall immediately notice.

Pressure was brought to bear on this idea of aesthetic supervenience by Walton and others, who imagined cases where two objects have the same intrinsic non-aesthetic properties—the same specification of colours at all points on its surface—yet differ aesthetically, because they differ relationally.[5] They may, as in Walton's example, differ in that they belong to distinct artistic categories, which means that they ought to be compared with a different category of other works. Or they may be works produced at different times, in different milieus and by different artists: differences which are said by the opponents of what we might call 'narrow' supervenience, to matter aesthetically. Thus the debate here followed a dialectic familiar from debates over dependence relations in a range of philosophical areas, of which morals is one already mentioned. Another is the philosophy of mind, where various arguments have pushed us towards the view that a person's mental states are not determined solely by their internal physical state, so that two people 'molecule for molecule indiscernible within the boundaries of their skins' need not be in the same mental state. Rather, mental sameness is guaranteed only when it is stipulated that they are placed in indistinguishable environments as well. This is supervenience, but of a broad kind.

What justifies the shift from narrow to broad supervenience in aesthetics? A tempting answer is intuition, a faculty under much suspicion in philosophy.[6] The narrow supervenience claim says that it is not possible for two pictures to have the same colours in the same places, and to differ aesthetically. But we can present imaginary examples of indistinguishable pairs of pictures concerning which readers—some readers at least—have the intuition that they are aesthetically different. That is what Walton did in his seminal 'Categories of Art'. The generally positive response to the essay, along with a notable absence of replies challenging the claim that the imagined case is a counterexample to narrow supervenience, gives us reason to think that Walton's own intuition about this case is widely shared, at least among philosophers.

'Imaginary cases ...' , 'appeals to intuition ...' Phrases like these will be setting off alarm bells in the heads of many. One worry is that we have little idea how widely these intuitive judgements are shared, and studies in other areas suggest that they may not be shared very widely. It turns out that the intuitions shared, apparently, by most analytic philosophers to the effect that Gettier cases are not cases of knowledge and hence that knowledge is not justified true belief, are not shared (statistically speaking) by East Asian subjects.[7] Similar indications of widespread disagreement have been claimed for intuitions about reference.[8] If intuitions are a reliable guide to how things are in the world, there ought to be (very) widespread, non-collusive agreement in intuition, just as there seems to be in perceptual judgement.

A more general argument contrasts intuition unfavourably with perception; both are fallible sources of knowledge but perception allows for the independent assessment of its own results.[9] We can tell, by and large, in what situations perception will be likely to give the wrong results, for perception itself informs us when the light is poor or when there is an obscuring mist. The different senses, though they are now thought to be somewhat more closely connected than was previously assumed, do provide a degree of cross-checking on each other's deliverances. And the sciences of perception tell us how perceptual systems work and why they are generally reliable; they also pinpoint surprising areas of unreliability, as with change blindness. None of the reliability of our perceptual systems, it is said, applies to intuition.

How much of this ought to concern us in relation to the specific case I mentioned above: the debate over aesthetic supervenience? Should we urgently construct surveys to see how widely the Walton intuition is shared? Should we give up on intuition and try to find some other way to make progress on this question? I suggest we do neither of these things.

The first thing to say is that, while Walton is offering us an imaginary case, nothing much hangs on its being imaginary. Let's remind ourselves of the relevant details. Walton imagines a case where we discover a genre of artworks we will call *guernicas*; they share the surface pattern of the familiar Picasso picture, but differ in the extent of modelling, so that some *guernicas* are hilly or mountainous surfaces, while others are subtly undulating. A minimal *guernica* is flat, and therefore looks exactly like Picasso's *Guernica* (that is, it is just as flat as *Guernica* is, which is of course not quite flat). Call this minimal *guernica Guernica**. Walton's claim is that *Guernica* and *Guernica** have the same intrinsic perceptual features—you could substitute the one for the other and no one could tell that you had done so by looking—but they differ aesthetically.

This is, as I say, an imaginary case. But suppose we actually had discovered this strange genre, and had the two pictures before us. We then set the two side by side, explain to subjects their distinct art-historical profiles, and ask them whether there are aesthetic differences between them. Surely, if we had taken as our subjects all the people who read Walton's article and found themselves sharing his intuition about the possible case, we would find that they came to the same conclusion in the real-life case as well. For what differences between the imaginary and the real-life cases would generate a difference of outcome? There are of course differences between the cases. In the imaginary case (the one Walton actually presented to us) we don't see two pictures—in fact we don't even see one: the case relies on our having a general memory of the sort of picture *Guernica* is. But this doesn't seem to matter: whatever sense of the appearance of the one picture it relies on, that will do for the other picture as well. After all, they are supposed to be visually the same.

The other difference between the cases is that in the one Walton gave us, we have to imagine, of the second picture, that it has a certain art-historical profile, whereas if we had been shown a real live work in the genre of *guernicas* we would, presumably, have believed that it had this art-historical profile. So the difference here is that in the one case we are making a judgement informed by what we imagine, and in the other case a judgement informed by what we believe. And the worrying thought is that there might be subtle or not-so-subtle differences between those judgements as a consequence.

At this point we might turn to empirical data for some indications: when we make judgements informed by what we imagine, do they tend to be different from the judgements we make which are informed by comparable beliefs? I do not know of any studies which address this issue directly. There are studies which show, or purport to show, that when we are asked to imagine what we would do in a situation, the answers we give are in conflict with what we actually do. This has been argued for such cases as the Langer effect, where subjects seek higher compensation for loss of a good if they chose it than if they were given it, or the position effect, where, when asked to choose between items, we show a marked preference for those displayed in a certain position. These effects make no appearance when people merely imagine being in these choice situations, and so their imaginings are not a good guide to what they would actually do.[10] It has also been argued that, when asked to predict, via imagination, how emotionally affected we will be by a future outcome, we are often quite badly wrong.[11] But these are not cases which compare imagination-based judgements with belief-based ones. They are cases where in imagining a certain situation we fail to take into account some feature of the situation to which we will in fact be sensitive—e.g. the position of the items in the display. If we compare prediction via imagination versus prediction via belief, symmetry is restored. For the naive subject— the one who knows nothing about the position effect—would make exactly the same erroneous prediction if they *believed* that a certain object was at top right in the array; you actually have to see the array for the position effect to work.[12] And non-naive subjects, who do know about the position effect, are likely to be correct in their prediction that they would be more likely to choose the item at top right, whether they believed it to be in that position, or whether they imagined it to be there, for they are able to include a new premise into their reasoning: 'An object at top right is likely to be preferred'.

In the absence of evidence strictly relevant to the cases we are considering, I am attracted by the following *principle of equivalence in judgement*:

> Normally, a judgement we make about a case which we imagine has features $F_1, \ldots F_n$, where these are the only features we take into account in making the judgement, will be the same as the judgement we make when we believe the case has features $F_1, \ldots F_n$, where these are the only features we take into account in making the judgement.

Something like this is presumably what underwrites the thought that imagining plays an important role in mind-reading, for the central idea here is that I may approximate your thinking by reasoning from premises you believe and I don't—instead I adopt them imaginatively.[13] If the principle was not roughly right such simulative mind-reading would be very unreliable.

Given all this, I am moderately confident that there is nothing worrying about the *Guernica* case that arises because it is an imaginary rather than a real example. So, if there is a worry about reliance on intuition in this case, the worry would apply equally well if the case had been real. So if there is a worry at all, it would still hold if Walton had discovered a genre of *guernicas* and had presented us with two visually indistinguishable works, one a painting and the other a *guernica*. How would such a concern play out in practice?

One way would be if subjects turned out to have conflicting intuitions about the case. Suppose we found a population of people resolutely unwilling to agree that there is an aesthetic difference between the two works. I say 'resolutely' because of course it is important that we consider only reflective judgements here; we are not interested in cases like the feminist bank teller of Kahneman and Tversky, where subjects respond very quickly with a judgement which defies probability theory but who, presumably, will eventually see that they have made an error, or cases where people make spontaneous mistakes on the Wason card-turning experiment but can eventually see that they were wrong.[14] Walton's case was not built on the assumption that people would *spontaneously* judge the two works to be aesthetically different, and in fact much of the article can be seen as providing the necessary background for informed reflection on the case. Of course the background provided tends to favour the outcome Walton wanted, but philosophical audiences are not known for their docile willingness to see things in just the way that the author of an article they are reading is seeing them. If there were resolute opponents of Walton's intuition out there in the philosophical community we would have heard from them.

Still, it could well be that there are populations of resolute opponents, people untouched by analytical philosophy but willing to say there is no aesthetic difference between the cases. How should we respond to that outcome? One issue will be the status of these groups with respect to the relevant expertise. When we are trying to decide whether the bird in the garden is a willow warbler or a chiffchaff (species which look very similar) we look to the judgements of experienced birdwatchers, because we have reason to think that they are more likely to get it right than the rest of us are. It is surely the same with aesthetic judgement, which is recognized to develop through instruction and experience. And we shall presumably say that the community of philosophers of the arts stand reasonably high in terms of the relevant expertise, so it will not be easy—though it need not be impossible—to find a population of subjects of equal or greater authority who have a different view. At any rate, we cannot simply reject Walton's argument on the grounds that some group or other happen not to express the intuition to which that argument appeals.

But suppose that we find a population of subjects who approximate the conditions required to count as ideal judges (they possess the right knowledge, training and attentiveness, are not related to the artist, etc.) who simply disagree with us about these cases: they resolutely insist that *Guernica* and *Guernica** do not differ aesthetically. One might say that in aesthetics we value fine distinctions, so we should favour the group which *does* claim to find a difference between the cases; not finding a difference raises the suspicion that you are less than ideally sensitive. But this cannot carry much weight, for we can easily imagine a group of people who make spurious distinctions between works, claiming that one of the works is aesthetically better because it sold for more money. It is possible to fail to be an ideal judge because you are *inappropriately* discriminating.

If we don't find a good reason to discount the opinion of the dissenting group, how should we respond to the disagreement? One way is to say that the two groups have distinct concepts of the aesthetic; if true, this would provide a simple and theoretically uninteresting resolution to the difficulty, though it is interesting to speculate on how we might induct members of the two groups into the ways of the other's concepts, aiming to see whether they judged, using that concept, as those others do. I will not pursue that option any further.

Another response would be to say that members of the two groups share the relevant concept and simply come to different judgements about the cases. After all, judgement in aesthetics is not supposed to be a mechanical matter, and Hume allowed that the different humours of 'particular men', as well as the manners and opinions of their various cultures, may produce differences between even ideal judges.[15] Would that show that the intuition to which Walton appeals has no force in philosophical argument? Not if we help ourselves to a quite reasonable pluralism about aesthetic value. There are good and bad valuings of art-works, but not all the good ones need be the same. If it really is the case that we have two communities, both good—and equally good—classes of judges as measured by the sorts of standards to which Hume appealed, neither subject to any internal inconsistency in patterns of judgement and neither susceptible to counter-arguments from positions they ought, given their other commitments, to respect, then we ought to say that we have two good, equally good, yet distinct ways of judging works of art. But then the sensibility in judgement that favours Walton's conclusion is not undermined by the existence of this other community with anti-Waltonian intuitions. Walton's case would then be made in at least this sense: people have tended to suppose that aesthetic judgement *cannot* legitimately discriminate between works with the same visual appearance (or, in music, with the same sonic appearance—the same arguments apply in that case). But Walton's imagined cases give us very good reason to deny this, and to say that there is at least nothing wrong with discriminating more finely than this.

It is worth noting also that this case, and cases like it in aesthetics, is different from some others where intuitions play a role in philosophical argument, and this difference protects the use of intuitions in aesthetics from a certain sceptical line of thought. Thus people have asked why we should take intuition to be a guide to what the real world is like. But in the present case, talk of intuition here could just as easily be replaced by talk of judgement, or sensitivity to cases. What we are doing when we agree with Walton about the relations between *Guernica* and *Guernica** does not draw on some capacity different from what operates when we look at pictures and judge them to be of a certain quality—or so my earlier argument about the relation between Walton's imaginary case and a real-life version we might have had suggests. We are simply making the judgement that these two works (one imagined) have distinct aesthetic qualities. And in aesthetics, aesthetic judgement—the kind of reflective judgement for which we can give reasons—has a peculiar status, or so many of us believe. We don't have to think that the judgements of so-called 'ideal judges' are constitutive of aesthetic value; we may think that ideal judges are simply the best indicators we could possibly have of what is aesthetically valuable. But if we did not take the judgements of those who are the least biased, the best prepared, the most sensitive and attentive among us as very strong indications of where aesthetic value lies, it is difficult to see what we could say about aesthetic value that would be worth anything at all. If you think that aesthetics is worth doing, you will surely take an informed, reflective and diligent judgement to the effect that these two works differ aesthetically very seriously indeed. And you would need very strong counter-arguments to justify rejecting that judgement.

Art and knowledge

So far I have argued in favour of the use of traditional armchair methods in aesthetics; I believe that what I have said in relation to Walton's argument applies to a great many theses in aesthetics. But the problems with which aestheticians deal are very various, and not all of them ought to be approached in the same way. I want to suggest in the latter part of this chapter that quite a lot of thinking about the philosophy of art has gone badly wrong because it has been insensitive to serious empirical inquiry. I am thinking here of issues in the philosophy of the narrative arts.

A question which arises quite generally for the arts is the relation between the aesthetic or artistic value that a work has and its capacity to inform, elevate or otherwise improve those who experience it. One view on this subject is that there is no such connection and the so-called cognitive values in art, where they exist, have no influence on a work's value as a work of art.[16] This view is now much less popular than it was during, say, the heyday of the New Criticism, and what follows speaks to those who believe that cognitive values are or can be aesthetic values, or at least that cognitive values can legitimately impact on our assessment of a work's aesthetic values.

There are two quite separate strands of research going on into the role that literature plays in educating, civilizing and—more broadly and more neutrally—changing people.[17] One is philosophical. Its claims are often remarkably strong and positive, as with the case argued by Martha Nussbaum in *Love's Knowledge,* where theses about the educative value of literature are interwoven with arguments to the effect that literature is itself a form of moral philosophy.[18] Philosophers particularly emphasize literature's insight into moral psychology, stressing the extent to which it is well adapted to represent moral problems as arising for concretely situated individuals subject to complex psychological forces.[19] Indeed, some philosophers simply assume that, when it comes to evidence for claims about human psychology, fictional examples will do as well as real ones; Wollheim, for example, illustrates theses in moral psychology by appealing to incidents from Proust and Tolstoy.[20]

While views of this kind take many forms, they are united by an optimism about the idea that works of fiction, especially those of high quality, have an important capacity to educate. Views of this kind I will call 'literary optimism'.

The other strand is of much more recent origin and involves the carrying out of systematic experiments to determine the effects of reading or watching works of fiction, not always or even usually ones of artistic quality and in a variety of media, most often written literature, film and television.[21] These two projects go on in almost total disregard of each other, pursuing entirely different methods and drawing, by and large, different conclusions. On the face of it, this is an odd situation. One might regard it as worrying in the way that it would be worrying if philosophers were still speculating in the manner of the Presocratics about the nature of the universe, oblivious of the progress, and perhaps even the existence, of experimental physics.

Also noteworthy, and a little worrying, is the remarkable asymmetry in the attitudes of philosophers to evidence, when it comes to thinking about the effects of literature. There is of course a debate going on about the negative effects of narrative fiction—particularly in film and television—in relation to violent and antisocial behaviour. To the extent that philosophers have noticed this debate and chosen to discuss it, they have been careful to examine the empirical evidence in some detail, considering, for example, complex arguments about the extent to which human beings are prone to semi-automatic forms of imitation in their behaviour.[22] But philosophers who want to argue for the positive, educative and civilizing effects of literature never seem to take any interest in the empirical literature.

One might defend the philosophers of art here by saying that these two projects—the philosophical and the psychological—attempt to answer different questions, in which case their different methods and conclusions may be no cause for concern. In what way are they different? The philosophical, and in some versions the literary, project is a normative one, concerned with how the best narrative art might educate us, if we are maximally prepared by dint of knowledge, attention and all other necessary things, to meet its challenge. The psychological project, on the other hand, is concerned with the sorts of mass phenomena we measure in terms of means and standard deviations, relating to the normal, uncommitted and not especially well-prepared audiences that make up the vast bulk of the consumers of fictional narratives.

Let's begin by agreeing that questions about the educative or civilizing powers of some phenomenon are not to be answered merely by examining its actual effects in a range of cases counted as normal. Nail polish dissolves in water, but one would not know this unless one examined their interaction at unusually high temperatures. We tend to say that nail polish is not soluble in water because the temperature necessary for dissolution makes it an extremely impractical means of removing polish from nails attached to the body, and we have an excellent alternative in the form of acetate. Similarly, literature's (supposed) disposition to educate might be visible, or easily visible, only in unusual circumstances, as when we have very well-prepared or intelligent subjects. And people who say that literature has this power in special circumstances may see a significant disanalogy with the case of nail polish. While the circumstances in which literature's educative powers are shown to best advantage may be unusual, they are not impractical in the way that using very hot water to dissolve nail polish is; they are simply circumstances that not everyone is currently able to be in. So it's fine (not conversationally misleading) to say that literature educates, and not fine (without substantial qualification) to say that water dissolves nail polish. But nonetheless, the claim that literature has this capacity, however restrictively understood, is surely an empirical one. It is not intellectually respectable to hold that the educative effects of literature are knowable a priori, even when those effects are said to manifest themselves only in special conditions.

Advocates of the a priori philosophical approach might admit all this, and point out that, since the available studies do not address the relevant special conditions, they are entitled to ignore them. Two considerations suggest that this would not be a good line of defence. It may be true that, by and large, the experiments we have so far do not target the conditions philosophers consider most conducive to literary education—those involving highly sensitive and well-prepared subjects and highly valued literary works—but if true this is knowable only by taking an interest in the experimental work being done. More importantly, there are dangers in fashioning a thesis which, you claim, holds only in special, and difficult to test, circumstances. At least very often, a psychological effect occurs across a range of circumstances and for a very broad class of subjects, though it may be intense, and hence easy to observe, only in some circumstances and for some subjects. Indeed, advocates of the educative function of literature do usually say that these supposed beneficial effects are available not only to the few lucky enough to possess unusual levels of preparedness, attention, etc. They are often keen to stress the role of literary works of varying qualities and difficulty in moving people (often young people) towards those conditions of preparedness and attention from which they can benefit from the most demanding of such works. While hoping for better experiments, sensitive to more subtle effects and involving a more complex set of circumstantial variables, one ought to be interested in the evidence (or lack of evidence) for the effects of literature in circumstances your theory rates as less than ideal.

A philosopher might be tempted at this point by the nuclear option, insisting that their claims about the value of literature are analogous to claims about what is right or valid. The widespread occurrence of bad behaviour and of fallacious reasoning does not refute any moral principle or logical law. Why should it be different when it comes to the value of literature? There are people who will argue the relevance of empirical inquiry for both the moral and logical case, but let's grant that logical laws are laws of valid inference and not laws of thought, and that at least some moral principles are requirements on the behaviour of any rational being and independent of how that rationality is embodied in a particular, contingent psychology. No comparable defence can be mounted concerning the a priori status of claims about the educative value of narrative art. These are essentially claims about the effects of literature on human beings in certain circumstances. They are claims that ascribe dispositional properties to objects of a certain kind—works of narrative art. The appropriate analogy here is not with the laws of logic but with the claim that thinking logically makes you a more effective agent, not with moral principles, but with the effect of belief in certain moral principles on character or personality. Those are all empirical claims and their truth values are not obvious to casual observation, though we have often treated them as if they were.

This does leave some empirical slack in the system. The claim that work W has a positive educative value is perfectly consistent with the claim that no one's encounter with W ever has realized or ever will realize that value. And one may be in a position to believe that many actual works of literary art have entirely unrealized educative dispositions, just as we may believe that many bottles of acid never dissolve anything. But to be in that position with respect to narratives requires that one rationally believe that things of the kind to which W belongs—works of narrative art—tend to have certain effects. And one can rationally believe that, only by having evidence that some things of that kind have manifested that disposition in specific circumstances about which we know a good deal.

In a sense these arguments are unnecessary, because the philosophical advocates of literature manifestly do not see themselves as arguing a purely dispositional case, devoid of claims about the actualization of dispositions. Such general arguments as they have for the educative power of literature are always bolstered with concrete examples of works which, it is claimed, do have educative dispositions which the advocates go some way towards describing, pointing to specific textual features and their interpretations which are supposed to make manifest—though they rarely make explicit—those educative dispositions. Nonetheless, these are all empirical claims with no self-validating power. They are claims which need to be tested.

Why is it that the philosophical advocates of literary optimism never think to test it? I have no very confident answer to this question. Perhaps it is because they see their activity as comparable to (and perhaps of a piece with) the activity of the art critic whose job it is—on one conception anyway—to indicate to the audience what is valuable in the work. The critic sees what is valuable, and is able to identify the features of the work responsible for the various values it exemplifies, and her job is then to help others to see those features in the same way; critical communication is achieved when the audience does see those features in those ways. That, at any rate seems to be more or less the method of writers such as Nussbaum, who aim to get us to see an artistic narrative as having certain features which are the bases of the educative capacities to which she rather vaguely points. But the analogy is in fact a poor one. The project of pointing out what is aesthetically valuable in a picture is not at all like the project of identifying the features of a work which are responsible for its supposed power to educate. To show that acids are disposed to dissolve metals it is not enough to point to the features of acids which, on your theory, produce the dissolution—their being proton donors for example. One must show that acids do in fact dissolve metals. Until then, all you have is an untested theory. Similarly, one can show that works of art are educative only by showing that people are educated by them.

But is it not sufficient, from the point of view of the optimist's project, merely to say what the educative potential of the work is—to say, in other words, what the work itself is able to convey, though perhaps in an inexplicit form? We show that works contain truths by saying what those truths are, and we need do no more than that. Two thoughts show that this is not an appropriate response. The first reminds us that it is rare for a philosophical advocate of literary optimism to say that the educative value of a work of literature is given by a set of propositions it is apt to convey; more often the work is said to embody a way of seeing things which is not reducible to propositions, or its power is said to consist in its being a source of the kind of experience which enhances our empathic capacities, enlarges our vision, trains our emotions to be more responsive and responsible—or something else which is not purely propositional in nature. Such claims as these are certainly empirical, and cannot be known in advance of seeing what sorts of behavioural changes exposure to the narrative in question leads to. Detecting those behavioural changes is no doubt very hard; perhaps we currently lack methods which would detect them. But that cannot be a reason for supposing that the claims in question can be treated as knowable a priori. Nor can we depend on the philosopher's capacity for introspection; we have learned—largely, it must be said, through work in experimental psychology—to be wary of claims that it is obvious that someone has acquired skills of empathy, and what we know about the fallibility of self-knowledge and the failures of introspection should make us particularly sceptical of the strategy of arguing for any particular effect of literary experience on the basis of one's own case.[23]

The second thought is that, even to the extent that the educative value of a literary work is propositional (as to some extent it may be), merely stating those propositions will not demonstrate that educative value. One has to show that they are true. A child who comes to believe that 2 + 2 = 5 has surely not learned anything, though she has acquired a new instance of propositional belief.

Perhaps one does not always have to show that the propositions are true. After all, education occurs when a person goes from being in a worse epistemic state to being in a better one, and there are many ways a person can do that which fall short of the acquisition of propositional knowledge. One might go from believing a claim which is far from the truth to believing a claim which is close to the truth—one goes from thinking it was five o'clock to thinking it is six o'clock, when in reality it is 6.01. Or one might supplement one's stock of beliefs with a new false but approximately true one that is, as relevance theorists say, highly relevant. But none of this helps the optimist who wishes for a quiet life in the armchair. She has to show that the propositions in question are close to the truth, or highly relevant, or meet whatever other criterion of doxastic improvement is thought appropriate. These are all projects which can be carried out only by producing evidence in their favour.

Perhaps the propositions in questions are ones we generally agree are true, and the point of communicating them by means of the narrative is that we remind the reader of their significance; literature is often said to educate us by repackaging, reconceptualizing or merely making vivid what in some sense we already know. Or perhaps the educative value of these propositions is not a function of their truth, or their closeness to truth, or their relevance, but of some other feature; perhaps believing certain wildly false propositions makes us better citizens. Perhaps the propositions in question should be understood as expressive of preferences or attitudes or perspectives in ways which make inquiry into their truth values impossible or inappropriate. But in all these cases, the claim that these propositions are educative is, once again, an empirical claim, however this educative value is understood.

There is reason enough here to conclude that claims about the educative value of literature ought to take account of, and ought ideally to cohere with, the best work in experimental psychology, though it needs also to be said that psychologists may learn from philosophers about the sorts of effects of literature it would be most interesting to look for and about the circumstances in which they are most likely to be found. But there is another way in which the optimist (or anyone interested from a philosophical point of view in the effects of literature) should learn from psychological work. For psychologists interested in the cognitive, emotional and other effects of literature do not have any special bias towards showing that these effects are beneficial or rationally defensible. Work in this area has often suggested quite the opposite, with studies of the ways in which people are led, without having much or any awareness of the process or even of its result, to form beliefs—or at least to express themselves in ways which suggest belief— prompted, but not evidentially supported, by the fictional narratives they encounter.[24] And turning from theoretical to practical knowledge, there are the well-evidenced claims I mentioned earlier about the worrying effects of media violence on behaviour.[25] Philosophers ought to have a lively awareness of the possibility that artistic narratives have bad effects as well as good ones, just as drug companies should investigate and advertise the negative as well as the positive effects of their products. This can be done only with the help of serious, carefully controlled empirical inquiry.

Notes

1 Work on this chapter was supported by a research grant from the Arts and Humanities Research Council. A version of the paper was given at a conference in honour of Kendall Walton, at the University of Michigan, Ann Arbor, October 2012. I am grateful to Stacie Friend, Dan Jacobsen, Ken Walton, David Hills and others for their comments at the conference, to Anna Ichino, Matthew Kieran, Aaron Meskin, Margaret Moore and Jon Robson for extensive discussion of these issues, and to Matthew Haug for comments on an earlier draft.

2 For an anthology of writing from this period see H. Mallgrave and E. Ikonomou (eds), *Empathy, Form and Space* (Los Angeles: Getty Centre for the History of Art and the Humanities, 1994). See also my 'Empathy for Objects', in Amy Coplan and Peter Goldie (eds), *Empathy: Philosophical and Psychological Perspectives* (Oxford: Oxford University Press, 2011).

3 See especially Essays 2 and 3 in J. Benson, B. Redfern and J.R. Cox (eds), *Approach to Aesthetics* (Oxford: Oxford University Press, 2001).

4 G.E. Moore, *Philosophical Studies* (London: Routledge, 1922), 263.

5 See Kendall Walton, 'Categories of Art', *Philosophical Review* 79 (1970): 334–67; Jerold Levinson, 'What a Musical Work Is', *Journal of Philosophy* 77 (1980): 5–28; Gregory Currie, *An Ontology of Art* (London: Macmillan, 1989), ch. 2.

6 I'm indebted in what follows to the discussion in Frank Jackson, 'On Gettier Holdouts', *Mind & Language* 26 (2011): 468–81.

7 See J. Weinberg, S. Nichols and S. Stich, 'Normativity and Epistemic Intuitions', *Philosophical Topics* 29 (2001): 429–60.

8 See E. Machery, R. Mallon, S. Nichols and S. Stich, 'Semantics, Cross-cultural Style', *Cognition* 92 (2004): B1–B12.

9 See Jonathan M. Weinberg, 'How to Challenge Intuitions Empirically without Risking Skepticism', *Midwest Studies in Philosophy* 31 (2007): 318–43.

10 See E. Langer, 'The Illusion of Control', *Journal of Personality and Social Psychology* 32 (1975), 311–28; S. Nichols, S. Stich, A. Leslie and D. Klein, 'Varieties of Off-line Simulation', in P. Carruthers and P. Smith (eds), *Theories of Theories of Mind* (Cambridge: Cambridge University Press, 1996), 39–74. But see also A. Kühberger, Josef Perner, M. Schulte and R. Leingruber, 'Choice or No Choice: Is the Langer Effect Evidence against Simulation?', *Mind & Language* 10 (1995): 423–36.

11 See e.g. Timothy D. Wilson and Daniel T. Gilbert, 'Affective Forecasting', *Advances in Experimental Social Psychology* 35 (2003): 345–411.

12 It is important to see that, in this example, it is propositional imagining that is in question. Other factors would come into play if we were considering a situation in which you imagine seeing the array.

13 Jane Heal calls this 'co-cognition'; it is fundamental to most versions of the simulation theory of mind-reading. See Essays 1 to 6 in her *Mind, Reason and Imagination* (Cambridge: Cambridge University Press, 2003).

14 See A. Tversky and D. Kahneman, 'Extensional versus Intuitive Reasoning: The Conjunction Fallacy in Probability Judgments', *Psychological Review* 90 (1983): 293–315; P.C. Wason and Diana Shapiro, 'Natural and Contrived Experience in a Reasoning Problem', *Quarterly Journal of Experimental Psychology* 23 (1971): 63–71.

15 David Hume, 'Of the Standard of Taste', in *Essays Moral, Political and Literary* (Indianapolis, IN: Liberty Fund).

16 For a version of this view see Peter Lamarque and Stein Haugom Olsen, *Truth, Fiction, and Literature: A Philosophical Perspective* (Oxford: Oxford University Press, 1994).

17 From here on, 'education' will be my label for any positive benefit claimed for engagement with fiction.

18 See Martha C. Nussbaum, *Love's Knowledge* (Oxford: Oxford University Press, 1994). Her position is close to that of Lionel Trilling, *The Liberal Imagination* (New York, Viking Press, 1950); see also Peter Kivy, 'The Laboratory of Fictional Truth', in his *Philosophies of Arts: An Essay in Differences* (Cambridge: Cambridge University Press, 1997).

19 Nussbaum again; see also Berys Gaut, *Art, Emotion and Ethics* (Oxford: Oxford University Press, 2007); Noël Carroll, 'Art, Narrative and Moral Understanding', in his *Beyond Aesthetics* (Cambridge: Cambridge University Press, 2001); Jenefer Robinson, *Deeper than Reason* (Oxford: Oxford University Press, 2005), ch. 6. While Lamarque and Olsen, *Truth, Fiction, and Literature*, claim that psychological or moral truthfulness in literature is irrelevant to its value as literature, they do not dispute the claim that literature contains substantial amounts of this sort of truthfulness.

20 Richard Wollheim, *The Thread of Life* (Cambridge, MA: Harvard University Press, 1984), 82–83, 170.

21 See e.g. R.J. Gerrig, *Experiencing Narrative Worlds: On the Psychological Activities of Reading* (New Haven, CT: Yale University Press, 1993); M.C. Green and T.C. Brock, 'The Role of Transportation in the Persuasiveness of Public Narratives', *Journal of Personality and Social Psychology* 79 (2000): 701–21; J. Hakemulder, *The Moral Laboratory: Experiments Examining the Effects of Reading Literature on Social Perception and Moral Self-Concept* (Philadelphia: John Benjamins, 2000). In work currently in preparation, Anna Ichino and I argue that a good deal of this psychological literature suffers from an impoverished sense of the explanatory options (Anna Ichino and Greg Currie, 'Rational (and Irrational) Beliefs from Fiction').

22 See e.g. Susan L. Hurley, 'Bypassing Conscious Control: Media Violence, Unconscious Imitation, and Freedom of Speech', in S. Pockett, W. Banks and S. Gallagher (eds), *Does Consciousness Cause Behavior?* (Cambridge, MA: MIT Press, 2006).

23 On the fallibility of self-knowledge see the psychological literature reviewed in Peter Carruthers, 'Introspection: Divided and Partly Eliminated', *Philosophy and Phenomenological Research* 80 (2010): 76–111.

24 See Green and Brock, op. cit.

25 See Hurley, op. cit.

Index